T0340046

ASSESSMENT, MEASUREMENT, AND PREDICTION FOR PERSONNEL DECISIONS

ASSESSMENT, MEASUREMENT, AND PREDICTION FOR PERSONNEL DECISIONS

Second edition

Robert M. Guion
Bowling Green State University

LONDON AND NEW YORK

First published 1997 by Lawrence Erlbaum Associates Inc.

2 Park Square, Milton Park, Abingdon, Oxfordshire OX14 4RN
52 Vanderbilt Avenue, New York, NY 10017

Routledge is an imprint of the Taylor & Francis Group, an informa business

First issued in paperback 2019

Typeset by Graphicraft Limited, Hong Kong
Cover design by Andrew Ward

Library of Congress Cataloging-in-Publication Data
Guion, Robert M.
  Assessment, measurement, and prediction for personnel decisions /
Robert M. Guion. — 2nd ed.
    p. cm.
  Includes bibliographical references and index.
  ISBN 978-0-80586-023-8 (hbk. : alk. paper)   1. Personnel management–Decision making.   2. Prediction of occupational success.   3. Employees–Rating of.
4. Employment tests.   I. Title.
  HF5549.G794 2011
  658.3'125–dc22

                                                                    2010023619

ISBN: 978-0-8058-6023-8 (hbk)
ISBN: 978-0-367-86436-1 (pbk)

Dedicated to the memory of Chuck Lawshe,
my mentor throughout my career, and of Frank Landy,
my first doctoral student, colleague, and a delightfully
disputatious mentor since his student days

CONTENTS

ABOUT THE AUTHOR

Robert Guion, Distinguished University Professor Emeritus in the Department of Psychology, Bowling Green State University, has been at Bowling Green since 1952, when he initiated its program in industrial psychology (now known as industrial and organizational psychology). He received his Ph.D. in industrial psychology from Purdue University in 1952. Over the years he has served visiting professorships at the University of California, Berkeley, and the University of New Mexico. He was also a resident consultant to the Department of Personnel Services of the State of Hawaii and a visiting research psychologist with the Educational Testing Service.

Prior publications include over 80 articles in professional journals; invited chapters on psychometrics, personnel selection, and related topics in edited books and handbooks; and books (*Personnel Testing,* 1965; *Essentials of Personnel Assessment and Selection* with Scott Highhouse, 2006). He was appointed Editor of the *Journal of Applied Psychology* (1983–1988). As an independent consultant, he has conducted personnel research and monitored test development and validation research for a variety of organizations in the public and private sectors, including appointment as Special Master for the US District Court of Southern New York in *Underwood v. NY Office of Court Administration.* His clients have included both large and small organizations, and his practice has included serving as expert witness in EEO litigation.

Honors include being elected President of SIOP (the Society for Industrial and Organizational Psychology and Division 14 of the American Psychological Association) and of the APA Division 5 (Evaluation and Measurement). He was twice awarded the SIOP James McKeen Cattell award for excellence in research design, and he also received SIOP's Distinguished Contributions Award and its Distinguished Service Award. From the Division on Evaluation, Measurement, and Statistics he received a lifetime contribution award. The Association for Psychological Science named him James McKeen Cattell Fellow for Distinguished Contributions to Psychological Science. He received a similar life honor, the Stephen E. Bemis Award, from the International Personnel Management Association Assessment Council. He was more recently named Scientific Honoree of the Foundation for the Advancement of Behavioral and Brain Scientists.

He retired officially from Bowling Green State University in 1985 and actually in 1990. He pretty much dropped out of the field entirely for a few years; the travel and meetings associated with research and consulting were pretty much precluded because a continuing medical problem in the extended family required him to be always on call. Between calls, there was time to fill, and he did. In season, he was excessive in developing gardens in his hostile, shady yard. He continued an old interest in wood working. He took up glass blowing—and now has retired from that because, as he says, "two or three pounds of molten glass on the end of a five-foot pipe is awfully heavy for an octogenarian." (He has not totally left the glass field; he is now doing fusing but not yet at the art-show level.) He takes pride in being the second of four generations of family candy makers. His mother worked until World War II shortages as chocolate dipper and candy maker, his wife gave classes in candy making (for which he helped) for many years, their five children all make candy each year, and the adult grandchildren are doing it, too. Not all of his activities depart totally from the field of I-O psychology; he has been an active volunteer with the local hospital-based Wheeled Meals program. For Wheeled Meals, he has developed detailed job descriptions for key volunteer positions, has served in three of those positions including a term as chairman of the whole program (and informal, volunteer consultant to the Manager of Nutrition and Dietary Programs which provides the meals for the drivers with wheels). He has done no rocking on his front porch in retirement.

PREFACE

This is my third book on the topic of using assessments in the selection of employees. The first, published in 1965, was (looking back) pretty much limited to what is now called classical test theory and descriptions of tests and inventories developed in that tradition and mostly available from test publishers. The second effort, the 1998 edition of the present book, abandoned the test descriptions and offered in their place descriptions of what I called "modern test theory" as extensions of or replacements for traditional or "classical" psychometric theory and practice. It also was strongly influenced by my experiences in various phases of the aftermath of the passage of the Civil Rights Act of 1964—at least of its Title VII dealing with discriminatory employment matters. It included my personal recollection of participation in drafting regulatory documents and interpretations of major court decisions. The third effort—this one—continues to include developments in psychometric theories unimagined in 1965. Discussions of these developments may represent more mature and less wide-eyed points of view (it's high time I got more mature, in view of the time span covered by these books). Between these two editions, another one (shorter and somewhat simplified for undergraduate audiences) was instigated by Scott Highhouse as an abridgement of the 1998 edition. In joining him in that effort, I learned a great deal about the growing literature during the distractions in the early years of my retirement. And what Scott quietly taught me instigated the return to updating what I have called "the BIG book." Here it is.

I have written this one with three different audiences in mind. One consists of students. After all, this *is* a textbook. It is a book, and it is filled with text, so it is a textbook—and textbooks are for students. The students I have in mind are primarily graduate students in industrial and organizational (I-O) psychology. Others might be graduate students in human resource management. I would be happy if some undergraduate students found it useful for independent study of some sections. I expect that students in any of these categories, whether in classes or independent study, would have their reading enriched by the knowledge and experience of their classroom teachers or supervising professors.

Another audience is smaller but very important to me. It consists of people educated in other fields or specialties but who now, by choice or by circumstances, are relatively new I-O psychologists with specialties in organizational staffing. I have kept these people in mind throughout the time I've been writing for this edition. I have become increasingly aware that this small group is becoming larger. These are bright, well-educated people, and many of them can take the field of personnel assessment in new and broader directions simply by adding psychometrics and decision making to their existing knowledge and experience. I hope this book will help them acquire the factual and theoretical information they need.

This second kind of audience is not an entirely new creation. When I entered graduate school in the 1940s, most of the leaders of the field had received their degrees in other disciplines or specialties. Many focus-changing people that I have worked with in more recent times have also achieved leadership status. I have worked with postdoctoral students from biopsychology and the brain sciences, social psychology, and clinical psychology. I have worked with many eminent scholars in educational psychometrics who have become equally eminent in personnel assessment. I have known and worked with others who, without benefit of postdoctoral study, are picking up the finer points of the field as they work. Although they have surely had at least one graduate-level course in statistics, it is more likely to have stressed various approaches to significance testing than to individual predictions. That's true of stat courses in most universities, I think. Moreover, they (as well as too many I-O grad students) are not likely to have had serious instruction in psychometrics. That topic is disappearing from far too many graduate psychology programs. I believe that anyone involved in personnel research needs to develop genuine expertise in psychometrics, but this book will offer an introduction to measurement theories and provide guides through references to other sources for more advanced information. For example, I give only the early, relatively simple models of item response theory, but I also provide references for those who take assessment seriously and want to know more about advanced methods such as methods for test items beyond those with dichotomous responses. What some in this audience currently know about statistics or psychometrics may be the not-yet-forgotten remnants of prior knowledge, the result of hearsay, or just plain superficial.

The third audience consists of colleagues in the field of employee selection and, more inclusively, organizational staffing. I have been dissatisfied with our unquestioning acceptance of ancient professional habits and the self-limitations that fence in our work, keeping us from enjoying roaming in a free range. Only recently have I felt able to express my dissatisfactions comfortably and reasonably coherently and to point more positively to more satisfying directions. I fervently hope that my development in the course of writing this edition will encourage some new trends to broader, more systematic approaches to our tasks. The trends have already begun. Many books and articles have appeared in the past decade rejecting or ignoring old habits and limitations to our thinking, and simultaneously encouraging broader and more system-related research and practice. I hope that this third audience—and the others, too—will form a parade moving toward broader, more systems-oriented approaches to research and practice.

GOALS OF THE TWO EDITIONS

This edition and the earlier one are alike in trying to give readers a sense of the breadth and complexity of assessment-based personnel decision making. It obviously requires more than giving and scoring tests, but the required background may be less obvious. This edition, like the first one, offers an appropriate blend of the traditional and the new in assessment and selection. One of my favorite classes as an undergraduate was the history of ideas. I learned that *traditional* does not necessarily mean obsolete. Traditional practices can coexist with new ones if they serve valuable purposes well. Further, change in ideas or procedures does not occur everywhere simultaneously. Where it does not occur, or occurs only through slow evolution, traditional tried-and-true practices can trump the new but still relatively untried replacements. Most of the replacements are not as truly new as their proponents suggest; they are often extensions or modifications or improvements of older thought.

I somehow forgot these truisms by the time I joined others in graduate school, circa 1950 ± 2 years. We convinced ourselves that work published before the Second World War was rarely worth our attention. The parallel myth in 2010, accepted by many graduate students (and too many of their professors) is that most things published in a year not starting with a 2 have limited value. I've regained my appreciation of the history of ideas, having learned that I missed a great deal by not reading some old works long before I actually did. The result is a lot of classic or at least influential references, often in preference to more recent ones. I hope that some readers will look for these old books, reports, and articles—even if they are not online—and gain a sense of the history of their work.

The two editions, therefore, share a historical approach to present practice and problems. Through the years much has been learned, collectively, and the way things were done early on has generally been improved—not by sudden or startling innovations, but incrementally, by one small improvement, and sometimes a major one. Many of the problems that we have collectively experienced over the years have come about by forgetting some of the earlier principles in the necessary rush to get things done. I hope that the historical approach, and the return to early basics, will help overcome some of these problems and suggest new and continuing sorts of improvements in thought and in practice.

The chapter on forming predictive hypothesis was central to everything in the first edition. It continues to be so in this one. A carefully formed predictive hypothesis is infinitely more likely to be useful than the vague rationalizations offered by some of the people I have met in various organizations ("we've always used this test" or "they use this one at the company down the road and say that they like it").

In both editions, at the risk of seeming excessively elementary and old-fashioned, I have concentrated mainly on the basics of the statistical and psychometric procedures described. I have intended to concentrate on basic ideas, often by describing early and even pre-computer examples. These can help those for whom the procedures really are new. More importantly, they can help those with good statistical backgrounds by reminding them of basic but long-forgotten principles.

NEW OR DIFFERENT IN THIS EDITION

Even parts of the book that repeat things from the earlier edition have been carefully edited for clarification; I hope it is more readable in spite of the technical load it sometimes carries. Some editing emphasizes potentially important developments that were in the earlier edition but not as forcefully presented as they should have been. Some of this criticizes actions or ideas that have become mere conventions or, worse, not done or thought about at all. Some of them are positive changes in directions I think the fields of assessment and assessment-based decisions should take; in this edition, because I'm not likely to try again, I am now frankly pushing these ideas and choices more bluntly, less diplomatically, and much less tentatively. Frank Landy once described my writing as the work of a common scold, and I've decided to accept the role and to revel in it. I do hope, however, that some of these ideas will be seen as positive changes for practice and for research objectives.

Editing has resulted in a slight, but I think useful, change in the organization of the book. Chapters in the earlier edition were intended to stand alone—to be read independently. That is helpful to those who are more likely to use the book as a reference, but it gives false impressions; for example, that measurement theory is somehow independent of decision making. I've tried, therefore, to achieve some continuity—to let each new chapter build somewhat on the content of the chapters before it. It has not been highly successful: the topics are too interconnected, and different chapter orders could easily be justified. However, the "chapter notes" at the end of each chapter may help identify a transition from the chapter they conclude to the next one. Even the last chapter, which summarizes much, does so as it contemplates sending the reader on to the real work of organizational staffing.

I have long been convinced that it is vitally important for people applying scientific ideas to practical affairs to function jointly as scientist and practitioner. I've held that conviction since before the term *scientist–practitioner model* was invented, and trashing that belief is not in my plans. In this edition I have tried to keep the joint science-and-practice focus in every chapter. Despite devoting much space to the need for theoretical foundations and scientifically honed procedures, I hope the *applied* emphasis of this book will not be hidden. Two personal beliefs have governed my writing. The first was well expressed when my delightful colleague, Pat Smith, told a student bemoaning the immediate applicability of his research topic compared to the paucity of relevant theory: "It's all right to be useful." The second is that those who assess, and those who decide, should understand the assessment process and its meaning—and the limits of permissible interpretations.

This edition more emphatically urges going beyond the bivariate research and thought in which employee assessment has been mired for about a century, and moving toward more serious and pervasive multivariate thinking. One example is a change in the treatment of path analysis. The earlier edition mentioned it only as a causal model; this one goes further to treat it as a possible technique for the simultaneous evaluation of systematic procedures, i.e., multivariate validation. Not incidentally, this edition avoids the word *validation* more than was true in the earlier one. Now, with the stronger emphasis on multivariate hypotheses, the words *validity* and *validation* seem too restrictive and too much the remnant of olden days! I prefer to use the more generic term, *evaluation.* Multivariate thinking is not simply a matter of hypothesizing multiple predictors; it is a matter of taking seriously the multiplicity of organizational problems and goals and of the multiplicity of things that happen in an organization, including aspects of the overall staffing process, to facilitate or mess up the achievement of those goals. Multilevel analysis is not yet as fully developed for organizational staffing as I would wish (and think will happen), but that is no excuse for ignoring the interrelationships of things that happen within an organization that affect or are affected by a full range of staffing practices.

This edition moves gradually away from the earlier emphasis on unidimensional traits to the use of more complex constructs in theory and practice. For example, multidimensional competencies, both as criteria to be predicted and as characteristics assessed for predictive purposes, are said now to be instruments for more useful decision making, not simply as surrogates for thinking about traits. In part, this is a personal change, but it also reflects the more serious and careful delimiting of constructs of competence at work.

This edition strongly and frequently urges reconsideration of Dunnette's model of assessment-based decisions; I call it the "if–then" model. This is another approach to multivariate thinking as well as one of several approaches to individualizing some assessment practices. If a candidate for something brings along a specified sort of background (for example, from personal or work experiences, or high levels of a measurable trait), then one set of assessments should be used. If not, then a different set is appropriate. This is one part of a broader urge to move toward more individualism that I hope gets a good bit of attention—toward more idiographic and domain-referenced assessment than the established tradition of nomothetic research and norm-referenced assessment. It is a call to consider (but not to adopt prematurely) the notion that assessments, instead of being the same for all candidates for a job or position, might appropriately be different for candidates who are clearly different in some respects from the average or anticipated candidates. This is not idle imagination; it had better be done now in finding alternative assessment for use with disabled candidates. Beyond that, however, is the conviction that we should pay more attention to our assertion that our work is based on the psychology of individual differences. That is, we should consider people as individual candidates, not as points on the regression equation in use. This is not a plea for poetic sentimentality or data-free, intuitive subjectivity; I happen to agree with Scott Highhouse.[1] It *is* a plea for new research to study exceptions to normative rules, to find alternative models that take individuality into consideration, and to collect data to solve some pressing practical problems of the fact that people are not all alike. Besides, is there anything more subjective than the assumption for convenience that, were it not for error, everyone would be precisely average? But that unexpressed assumption underlies regression-based selection.

A new chapter in this edition, Chapter 10, describes some current challenges to traditional thinking about assessment and assessment-based decisions. One challenge—not a new one— is to make better use of the ever-present computers in our lives and go beyond current computer-based and computer adaptive testing. An important testing challenge, now being worked on in psychometric research, is to make a new equivalent form of a test for every examinee. In online testing, the challenge to standardization calls for technological changes as well as psychometric advances. The chapter also discusses multilevel analysis, globaliza-tion, and the prediction of individual growth patterns as challenging situations and targets of personnel decision research. Recognizing that growth patterns are not always linear, I have emphasized the need to consider the possibility of nonlinear relationships; that emphasis seems ubiquitous in this edition. In fact, it recurs enough that one reviewer of a draft of the manuscript complained about it. That pleased me. It meant that the emphasis is now strong enough to be noticed. Of course, much of the literature of the intervening decade also urges the abandonment of the automatic use of the linear assumption, and that too is pleasing and is reported.

In the earlier edition I had a fantasy section about a total organization system for selecting, training, transferring, promoting, and making various other personnel decisions. It was some-what tongue-in-cheek. This time, I present it more seriously. I have included in it some deliberate daydreaming about directions that might be taken when ways that are now new have become traditional. It seems to me that in the not-very-distant future, selection for a specified job or kind of work will no longer be feasible, that the practice will be superseded by staffing decisions based on comprehensive systems, and so-called "test validation" and validity coefficients will necessarily be replaced by evaluations of the systems as entities. Or maybe I just hope so. Whether prophecy or fantasy, I hope these relatively short digressions— they appear here and there as well as in the fantasy section—will plant seeds of thought for at least some readers.

Phrases such as "I think . . . ," "I suspect . . . ," or "I hope . . ." are not the words of science, but they appear frequently in this book. They reflect some of the recent activity of one writer who has been fascinated by much of the literature appearing in the past decade, who wishes it had appeared much sooner, and hopes very much that it will produce positive changes in assessment practices and the making of personnel staffing decisions. They do not, however, reflect established theory and practice. A few years ago, my wife gave me a small plaque that hangs on the wall over my scales; it is good advice, in personnel assessment as much as in weight watching. It says "Don't believe everything you think." I will rephrase it

---

[1] Highhouse, S. (2008). Stubborn reliance on intuition and subjectivity in employee selection. *Industrial and Organizational Psychology*, *1*, 333–342.

for readers of this book: Don't believe everything *I* think, but do consider it and give it your own best thinking. Maybe, between us, some of it will turn into real progress.

ACKNOWLEDGMENTS

There is no way I can identify all of the people who have helped make this book what it is, or tried to make it what it could have been. Foremost among them, however, is one easily and quickly identified: Emily, my wife. She has put up (usually cheerfully) with my virtual absence when I have disappeared into my basement office to be with my computer and books. Her cheerfulness and encouragement have been helpful to me personally, but beyond that, she has been an active and invaluable help in checking references at various stages of book development. For all of this, over such an extended time, I thank her most of all.

Jason Kain helped me with the onerous task of tracking down permissions to use copyrighted material. Dev Delal has been indispensable in preparing the figures in these chapters and helping me with persistent but changing computer problems. Some of those whose ideas strengthened (or replaced) mine have been correspondents, mostly by e-mail, and many of them have been acknowledged in appropriately placed footnotes. More of them have been authors of books, chapters, and articles that have made me rethink a lot of firmly held ideas; for the most part—but not always—their influence has been acknowledged in citations to their specific works. Anonymous reviewers were extremely helpful and influential, including one who wasn't really anonymous because I knew his style of criticism very well, and because he had made the same criticisms to me in personal correspondence.

That reviewer was Frank Landy, whom I also asked to review the chapters, one by one, as they were written. He had done so for the first edition, and changes I had made at his suggestion (or insistence) certainly improved the book as a whole. He was serving the same function for me on this one (and was also doing so for the publishers) until his illness and his request to be released from the chore. I wish he could have stayed long enough for the book to come out so we could continue to argue about Chapter 10 (he didn't like it, but others did, including me, so I kept it). More seriously, it has often been said that professors learn from their students. Frank had been mine. Then, and over the years since, he taught me a great deal by his skill at asking penetrating questions. He is sorely missed, and greatly appreciated.

I

FOUNDATIONS FOR PERSONNEL DECISIONS

The four chapters in this first part of the book describe the context within which assessment-based personnel decisions are made. Chapter 1 introduces varieties of personnel decisions but identifies staffing decisions as a prototype for other kinds of personnel decisions; staffing decisions include, among others, selection, transfer, assignment to special training, promotion, or termination decisions. When done best, the decisions are based not on intuition or habit, but on assessments of performance, other contributions to organizational goals, or predictions of such things. We emphasize the ideal of data-based decisions. Chapter 2 describes procedures for analysis of jobs and organizational needs to follow in setting goals to be achieved through assessment and prediction. Chapter 3 describes hypothesis formation in thinking through the ways those goals might be achieved by specifying the variables (i.e., constructs) to be predicted or to be used as predictors. The notion of testing predictive hypotheses is central to the book as a whole and is often returned to. Finally, Chapter 4 presents the legal context for personnel decisions in the United States—and recognizes but offers no details on similar contexts elsewhere—the requirements and constraints that govern what organizations can and cannot do in making assessment-based decisions about people.

1

Membership Decisions in Organizations

Organizations consist of members. Their members; the tools, equipment, and supplies available to them; their goals and purposes; their research activity; the community services they offer; their influence beyond the organization—such things create environments, social and physical and ideational, for their members and also for customers or vendors. Members are important; "workers should be viewed as long-term assets, not short-term costs" (Gowing, Kraft, & Quick, 1998, p. 261).

Organizations change. They grow or decay; they merge with others or divest themselves of functions and find new ones. Members die, retire, or change jobs and may (or may not) be replaced, and member roles change as organizations do. Organizations also face and react to external change. Some buggy-makers, facing the future, started making automobiles. In the automotive industry, skilled craftsmen made cars; product quality depended on their individual skills. Then mechanical equipment made assembly lines possible, and relatively unskilled workers could do what craftsmen had done—and with precision permitting interchangeable parts. Now much of automotive assembly is automated, and robots do things people used to do; fewer workers are needed, and many who are left are highly trained in new electronic crafts. Member roles and required qualifications changed as work environments changed from social to mechanical to electronic.

Change occurs spasmodically and in pockets—like "scattered showers" in a weather forecast. At any given moment, some people, and the organizations within which they work, do things in a totally new way; others stick to tradition. Sticking to tradition is partly perseveration (perhaps resistance to change), but it also happens because the stimulus for change doesn't occur everywhere at once. Besides, to recall collegiate French, *plus ça change, plus c'est la même chose*—the more things change, the more they stay the same. Despite Frank Landy's urging that I follow his trend to find every *job* in this book and replace it with *work*, I find daily use still bemoans the loss of jobs in times of recession/depression, meaning work that gets paid. And, like Ilgen and Pulakos (1999), I believe that employee performance remains paramount to the health of both the employing organization and its members.

Not everyone joins an organization. People in some occupations—professionals, people in trades or crafts, farmers, or consultants among them—may form their own small organizations or work independently. Some of them must be certified individually to the public, to customers, or perhaps to potential employers that they are competent in what they do. Nevertheless, nearly everyone in a modern society works in some form of organization.

Organizations function through their members. Recruiting and hiring new members are chronologically the first steps in bringing in new people. Hiring new people is the end state of a *selection process* and is only one of several kinds of personnel decisions. The selection process—choosing among applicants those will be hired—is a prototype for the processes leading to many other kinds of decisions. I use *selection* as a generic term for deciding who among a field of candidates shall have a specific opportunity. Every hire (at whatever level), every promotion or transfer, every acceptance for special training, implies an agreement that employer and employee will work together for mutual benefit, often called a *psychological contract*, rarely formalized, often unrecognized until it is broken. The term acknowledges that the employer (employing organization) expects to gain something by offering the opportunity for a position in it. The selection process should make clear what the employer expects (e.g., through realistic job previews) and also what may be offered in return (related to pay, hours, working conditions, and more). In return, the person offers something (skills, special knowledge, dependably showing up and working well). The person also has expectations, such as a reasonable degree of permanence or opportunity for advancement.

New members (or old members in new roles) are chosen for fairly specific organizational roles—fairly specific sets of functions, duties, and organizational responsibilities—in the belief that choosing them will benefit the organization. "Fairly specific" is the right term. Some may be chosen to do very well-defined tasks, others to do whatever is needed in a loosely defined area. A role may be quite specific if the new member is simply taking the job of someone who has left. It is less specific if the newcomer offers relief to someone in an overloaded role or does things not assigned to anyone else—or if organizational policy is to give lots of latitude. Work roles may change over time, starting with specified activities but shedding or adding functions and purposes along the way.

Personnel decisions are based, if organizational leaders are not too whimsical and impulsive, on some sort of assessment of the person and prediction (explicit or implicit) of future behavior. It is always hoped that the decisions are wise. Consequences of wise decisions can range from the mere absence of problems to genuinely excellent outcomes promoting organizational purposes, such as substantial increases in mean performance levels and productivity. Consequences of unwise decisions can range from inconvenience to disaster.

The best personnel decisions are based on information permitting at least an implicit prediction that the person chosen will be satisfactory, perhaps better than others, in the anticipated role. The prediction is based on known or assumed attributes (traits) of the candidate.

ANTECEDENTS OF PERSONNEL DECISIONS

Once one or more applicants have been identified, selection decisions follow a typical chain of events: (a) identification of relevant traits, (b) assessment of candidates in terms of those traits, (c) prediction of probable performance or other outcomes of a decision to hire, and (d) the decision to hire or to reject (or, with more promising candidates than positions to fill, the decision to hire one in preference to others). The chain is often longer, but these seem generally minimal.

One illustrative employment process for choosing new members is shown in Figure 1.1. It has two chains. One of them, condensed to three big steps, is the support chain providing data and logic in support of the other. The actual decision chain is presented in more detail. The support chain, a personnel research chain, begins by gathering information about the work to be done in the job at hand, the needs and goals of the organization, and the development of ideas about what should be predicted and what traits are likely to predict it (predictive hypotheses), and the various processes conducted in seeking evaluative

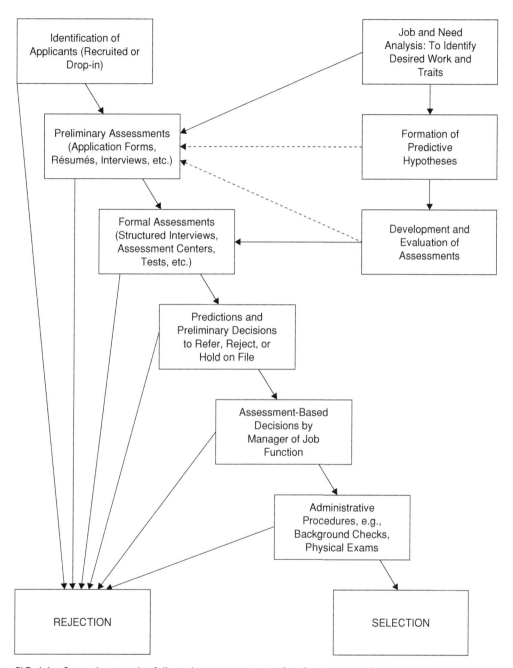

FIG. 1.1   Steps that may be followed in an organization's selection procedure.

evidence to support the hypothesis chosen. The decision chain begins by identifying job candidates, those who have responded to recruiting efforts or have submitted applications. Sometimes a person may not be considered a candidate, even if applying, if not meeting certain basic qualifications such as being old enough to drive a vehicle legally or having required diplomas or other credentials. Each candidate's relevant traits (those defined by predictive hypotheses) are assessed, informally or by formal, structured assessment procedures. From the assessments, predictions and decisions are made. The "selection" might be hiring a new employee, promoting one already on hand, deciding who will get special training or transfer, etc.

Recruiting

Recruiting is intended to attract people to an organization and its work opportunities; selection picks for employment the most qualified people among those who are attracted and become applicants. To recruit good applicants, organizations advertise openings, sometimes using classified ads or internet sites. They may place institutional ads in magazines or electronic media to enhance an organizational image. They may offer incentives to current employees to recruit friends. They send people to interview potential candidates, as in campus recruiting, and they do more image-enhancement in home-base interviews. Job previews, preferably realistic, are considered an integral part of the process. Recruiting is competitive, competing with other organizations "to identify, attract, and hire the most qualified people. Recruitment is a business, and it is big business" (Cascio, 2003, p. 201).

Recruitment is not a one-sided organizational activity. Candidates are not passive. New entrants into the labor market find the recruiting efforts of various employers and even make special efforts to be recruited (including pounding pavements). People who have been employed also seek jobs, whether because of losing jobs, intent to reenter the workforce after a hiatus, or desire to change jobs or to find a different career (Kanfer, Wanberg, & Kantrowitz, 2001). The job seeker must read ads, watch the TV bits, or check internet sites and form evaluative perceptions of advertised jobs and of advertising organizations. At the end of the process, as shown in Figure 1.2, the employer decides to offer employment

	Candidate's Perception of the Organization	
	Positive	Negative
Organization's Perception of the Candidate — **Positive**	Job offer made by organization and accepted by candidate	Job offer made by organization and rejected by candidate
Organization's Perception of the Candidate — **Negative**	Job offer not made by organization but would have been accepted by candidate	Job offer not made by organization and would not have been accepted by candidate

FIG. 1.2 Candidate and organization perceptions: Outcomes of good and poor matching. From Catano, V. M., Cronshaw, S. F., Wiesner, W. H., Hackett, R. D., & Methot, L. L. (1997). *Recruitment and selection in Canada.* © 1997 Nelson Education Ltd. Reproduced by permission.

(or not), and the candidate decides to take it (or not); that is, the candidate self-selects. "Self-selection occurs when individuals choose whether to apply for a job, to continue in a selection process or pursue other opportunities, or to accept or decline offers" (Ryan, Sacco, McFarland & Kriska, 2000, p. 163). Declining or opting out of the process at some point is known as "selecting-out." If the employer makes an offer and the applicant accepts, their mutual expectations constitute an implicit psychological contract. When an organization offers a candidate a job, and when an applying candidate accepts the offer, both decisions seem to imply intent to stay together for a long time. ASA theory (Schneider, 1987; Schneider, Goldstein, & Smith, 1995) points out that this may not be the case. An applicant who is *attracted* to the organization and *selected* as a new member of it may find, in time, that the organization is no longer so attractive; perhaps the organization finds that new employee has not fulfilled the employee part of the implicit contract. In either case, *attrition* may result when the applicant leaves or is terminated.

Applicant Reactions

Attraction to an organization or job depends partly on information and partly on perceptions of, and subjective inferences about, organizational characteristics (Lievens & Highhouse, 2003). On the basis of information, inferences, and perceptions, people decide for themselves whether they will be available to be selected. One important influence is a recruit's expectation of justice; expectations are formed before things actually happen, and it behooves organizations to try to create positive expectations and to avoid unintentional influences that may be negative (Bell, Wiechmann, & Ryan, 2006).

Ryan et al. (2000) followed candidates for police work through a multiple-hurdle process; demographic diversity was a major objective of the process. Early drop-outs from the process were those with a more negative view of the organization and less commitment to police work than those who stayed through the process or dropped out later. Many of those passing the first hurdle also concluded that either staying in their current job or seeking another alternative was preferable. Self-selection may be useful to an organization, if as in this example it helps avoid hiring uncommitted people, but it can be undesirable if it means losing a highly qualified applicant to a competitor. That, of course, might be good for the person if the choice leads to more money, less commuting, a more congenial culture, or some other personally desirable outcome (Harris & Brannick, 1999).

Recruiting research, whether concerned about reactions of applicants or about performance of those hired, tends to be focused at the individual level, a factor in what Saks (2005, title) called "the *im*practicality of recruitment research" (emphasis in original). It is the research he deemed impractical, not recruiting *per se*. Personnel research methods have been largely limited to organizational actions and their consequences at the individual level; only recently have serious research designs begun to take account of the multiple layers of actions and results at and above the individual as multilevel research designs have been developed (see Klein & Kozlowski, 2000).

Recruiting is not a "personnel decision" about an individual applicant. It is not like other decisions grouped under the umbrella of *selection*, but it has an impact on such decisions. Recruiting cannot be separated from selection procedures; it is part of the selection procedure because it influences the applicant population and the usefulness of other aspects of the selection process (Schmitt & Chan, 1998). For example, if recruitment seeks innovative people, it is silly to assess recruits for ability to follow directions (Higgs, Papper, & Carr, 2000).

TABLE 1.1
Comparison of Selected External Recruitment Methods

Methods	Advantages	Disadvantages
Newspaper Ads	Quick, flexible Specific market	Expensive Short lifespan for ads
Periodicals/Journals	Targets specific groups or skills	Long lead time for ad Expensive
Radio & TV	Mass audience Targets specific groups Image advertising	Very expensive Short ad duration Provide little information
Direct Mail	Targets specific groups and skills Can provide much information	Expensive and inefficient Requires mailing list Often not read
Special Events	Useful for filling multiple jobs Relatively inexpensive Targets job pool	Shares job pool with competition Information overload/stress
Walk-Ins	Inexpensive	Random process Inefficient
Private Employment Agency	Person–job fit	Expensive
Recruiting at Schools	Known talent pool Pre-trained applicants	Time-consuming Very expensive
Internet	Inexpensive Mass audience Specific audience	Random process Unknown audience

Adapted from CATANO/CRONSHAW, *Recruitment and Selection in Canada, 1E.* © 1997 Nelson Education Ltd. Reproduced by permission.

Technology in Recruiting

The variety of recruiting devices has ranged from want-ads to open-house dog-and-pony shows. Catano, Cronshaw, Wiesner, Hackett, and Methot (1997) described in detail several kinds of recruiting activity, including such internal techniques as job postings, replacement charts, or nominations and external activities such as direct mail ads, employment agencies, or job fairs. Table 1.1 gives advantages and disadvantages of a few of these.

Recruiting over the years has always used available technology. First was advertising in print, later on radio, still later on TV, and even later on the web. Direct contact with candidates was not only face to face but by telegram or telephone (including conference calls and, more recently, video conferencing). Movies were developed for recruiting; later versions used tape recordings and now DVDs.

The internet and subsequent electronic advances have substantially changed recruiting practice. Organizations can list specific job openings and organizational information on their websites, and these may be visited by current employees desiring to change job assignments or by outsiders. Some websites provide multiple job lists from a variety of organizations, locations, and work fields. People can do daily searches for jobs and compile personal lists of attractive opportunities. Résumés can be posted to be read by many potential employers;

e-mail can be used to submit résumés and instant messaging can be used for interviews. Bartram (2000) reported astonishing statistics on the extent and growth of internet use by the end of the last century, and it has continued to grow through the first decade of this one.

Some caution seems appropriate. Enthusiasm for web-based recruiting and selection procedures often seems to have outrun data, driven instead by hype and the *Zeitgeist* (Sitzmann, Kraiger, Stewart, & Wisher, 2006). This is not to say that they are ineffective, but their effectiveness is often unknown or not considered. These methods are useful if they result in better performance, provide defensible assessments, and are cost-effective, but it is not enough to accept them because they are "cool." It is not enough to want to encourage the march of progress, nor to make facile predictions about the future of technology. Too many enthusiasts predict, for example, that the internet "will replace paper as the default medium before very long" (e.g., Bartram, 2000, p. 261). Futuristic predictions often go awry. Experts in a 1968 issue of *McCall's* predicted, among other things, that by the year 2001 the only power plants being built would be nuclear; another prediction from a knowledgeable scientist was that by 2001, "scientists will commute to the moon, where colonies will be in existence" (McCall's Assembles, 1968). The point, of course, is that predictions of how wondrous things will be in the future need to be accompanied by research on the degree to which things develop at various, potentially different, steps along the way.

Caution is advisable, but not unvarnished skepticism. Caution wants data, not opinion. For example, Sitzmann et al. (2006) compared the effectiveness of web-based and classroom instruction. The two methods were about the same for knowledge of procedures, but web-based instruction was more effective for knowledge about facts and understanding of task requirements. That is the sort of information that is helpful.

Assessment and Decision Making

Qualifications are identified by studying the job, its requirements, and the needs of the organization (Chapter 2). Scientific selection requires identifying and testing predictive hypotheses about qualifying characteristics candidates bring with them and their benefit to the organization (Chapter 3). Qualifications, as assessed, must be evaluated by methods that meet professional standards (Chapters 5 through 8), including legal and ethical standards (Chapters 4 and 9). Preliminary assessments often seek only disqualifying information (that's why the line in Figure 1.1 from evaluation to preliminary assessment is dotted). Candidates who are at least minimally qualified may then be assessed more formally (Chapters 11–15). Hiring decisions may be made by personnel or human resources specialists; in many organizations, however, the manager or supervisor who has requested a new hire may make the final decision. Both preliminary and final decisions are based on the statistical or judgmental predictions made possible by the assessments (Chapters 7, 9, and 12). "Final" decisions may not be final; further steps may result in rejecting an otherwise desirable candidate. Certain diseases may preclude employment in a restaurant, or a background check might unearth a felony conviction that makes hiring the candidate as a law enforcement agent illegal in most jurisdictions.

Assessments should be relevant and competently done. Characteristics important for one organization, or for one role, may not be highly valued or appropriate for another. Wisdom in selection decisions requires knowing the truly important traits for an anticipated role and not being distracted by irrelevant ones. Competence in assessing relevant characteristics may be no more than a matter of looking at a driver's license and noting whether it is current, but most qualifying characteristics are more abstract and more difficult to assess. If qualifications include special skill in getting along with others, that skill *might* be assessed in an interview, or from personal history information, but special efforts are needed to be sure that these procedures actually assess that skill, not something else, and that the assessments are really related to some subsequent behavior on the job requiring social interaction. Many qualifications can be assessed by standardized tests or inventories (Chapter 11), but many other assessment methods, such as special exercises, are also used and are described in Chapters 13–15.

A POINT OF VIEW

Wisdom in making personnel decisions is elusive. There are different points of view about what is wise, desirable, and valued. I want to be explicit about mine.

Organizations exist when people join forces voluntarily to reach a common goal; they earn their existence by producing goods or services valued in at least a segment of the larger society. In an ideal society, organizations prosper according to their contribution to society (Eels & Walton, 1961), and individual members contribute by functioning well in their assigned roles. The interests of the consumers of the goods or services are compromised, no less than the personal interests of those in the organization, when a person who can function very well loses an opportunity given to one less qualified. If such selection errors are common, the organization may fail—with resulting human and economic waste.

When there are more applicants than openings, some basis for choosing among them is necessary. Choices could be random, or quasi-random like "first come, first chosen." Choice might be based on social values, giving preference to veterans, women, or minorities. It might be based on nepotism,[1] prejudice, or a similar-to-me bias. Or it can be, and I think should be, based on a supported predictive hypothesis that serves to define candidate merit.

I believe the principal basis for personnel decisions should be merit. Some people hold a more egalitarian point of view. A few consider profit-oriented concepts of merit inimical to the interests of a broader society. Some people dismiss the idea of selection on the basis of predicted merit, believing that situations influence performance more than the personal traits people bring to the job. Such views reject the basic idea of meritocracy. I do not.

Accepting the principle of merit as the basis for awarding opportunity requires methods for establishing relative merit. Some who accept meritocracy in principle reject typical psychometric assessment as its instrument (Tenopyr, 1994), but I prefer standardized psychometric methods. More often than with most alternatives, these methods give evenhanded assessments of all candidates for specific jobs or work roles, similar results from one time or situation to another, and demonstrable relevance to performance.

It is wasteful to deny qualified people employment for invalid reasons, including whims known only as "company policy." Wasting human resources is at least as inexcusable as wasting physical resources; Paterson (1957), echoed by Dunnette and Borman (1979, p. 481), called for the "conservation of human talent" (Dunnette & Borman, 1979). An organization has a responsibility to itself, to the society that supports it, and to the people who seek membership in it to be sure that it conserves and optimizes human talent.

Other points of view exist. Herriot (1993) suggested that two subcultures coexist in the psychology of assessment, each with differing assumptions. One he called the *psychometric subculture*, one that assumes general stability in jobs and organizations, the predictability of human performance from human attributes, and selection by organizations for their own

---

[1] The dearth of relevant research led Jones et al. (2008, p. 20) to call condemnation of all nepotism "premature."

purposes. In contrast, he suggested and preferred a *social subculture* that assumes that change occurs constantly, that people and their self-perceptions are crucially important, that performance is a process of social interaction, and that selection is a mutually negotiated act. If these patterns are mutually exclusive (I think they are not), this book must be recognized as reflecting the psychometric subculture. However, I reject the notion that psychometrics is necessarily static, ignoring change, especially in choosing what to predict (Chapter 3).

It seems to me that the joining of the two subcultures happens when both recognize and promote, in Rucci's words (2008, p. 17), "the dignity of human beings in organizations." Rucci went to say that human dignity is enhanced when there is a clear link between their work (and I would add the assessed qualifications to do the work) and the attainment of organizational goals. He also considered it enhanced when personal accountability is expected and where civility characterizes the work environment. What good does it do to hire highly qualified people, able to perform magnificently, only to have them leave the organization because they can't stand the overbearing boss? The social subculture is concerned not only with self-perceptions but with perceptions in the broader culture of the organization and of the people and policies it incorporates. In my point of view, organizations must be concerned with the perceptions of individual candidates and employees about the importance of justice and general fairness in the organization.

Rucci (2008) also sees the advancement of the science of human behavior as central to the enhancement of human dignity in the organization, and so do I. I think research on the processes leading to personnel decisions must be varied in scope, design, and intent. The ultimate objective of such research must, I think, focus on predictions of the real-time, real-world organizational consequences of those decisions. These include candidate-oriented consequences such as the organization's reputation for fair processes in employment, organizationally oriented consequences such as product quality or adaptability to changed conditions, or society-oriented consequences such as safety or equality of opportunity. We should not lose sight of the far-reaching practical consequences of what we do.

APPROACHES TO MEMBERSHIP DECISIONS

Different organizations may use different selection processes. The main features of the process—recruiting, assessment, and decision—are common, but differences can be substantial.

Civil service organizations are governed by the political jurisdictions they serve. By statute, the heart of most civil service procedures is merit-based selection—with *merit* defined by scores on a sometimes mandated examination developed expressly to identify relative "merit" for a given job or job classification. Examinations may be written tests, work samples, or "assembled" (documents collected and evaluated). An examination date is announced, recruiting begins, and the examination is developed. In a large jurisdiction, many thousands of candidates may be tested at the same time and using the same test. An eligibility list is organized by test scores, the highest scorers at the top of the list. People will be hired from that list during a period of perhaps two years or more as openings occur, using the process known as *top-down selection*. Until an eligibility list is "closed" and a new examination scheduled, hiring for the position continues from the top of the remaining members of the list.

Top-down selection is often talked about, but it usually seems a fiction in actual employment settings. In private organizations, decisions at management levels may be governed by a *satisficing* approach, maybe accepting the first candidate who satisfies basic requirements set (often idiosyncratically) by the decision maker. At lower levels, with massive hiring programs, the "top" fluctuates from day to day; the best candidate this week may not seem as promising (on the basis of the exam scores) as some who were rejected last week. Since the beginning of civil service programs in the United States, a narrow kind of *banding* (see Chapter 9) has been used in a so-called "rule of 3" (or some other number). The rule permits referral of the top three candidates to a decision-maker who chooses one of them. More recently, banding (with much broader bands) has been common in civil service jurisdictions.

Procedures in private business tend to be more like Figure 1.1. Applicants present themselves at any time and may be assessed immediately; employers do not wait for an exam date occurring only once every year or two. Applicants often specify the kind of position they seek and are rarely considered for other roles. Preliminary assessment may be based on interviews or résumés or application forms—or handshakes. More formal assessment might include written tests, performance tests, structured and scored interviews, assessment centers, biographical data, or others. A decision might be to file the application in a list of potentially desirable applicants for future consideration. It might be to reject. It might be to send the applicant to the supervisor who will make a final decision, keeping policy or legal constraints in mind (Chapter 4).

Military organizations are different; new recruits were traditionally sent to training centers in groups, and later placed in military jobs. The procedure was often intended to accept candidates in terms of general qualifications; a candidate may be rejected for physical, mental, or social problems, or failure to meet minimum test scores, but top-down selection was and is uncommon. Those selected (or not rejected) are given basic training and then assessed for subsequent assignment. The emphasis is less on selection than on placement; that is, finding a job assignment that is good both for the organization and for the recruit. In some respects, modern military staffing is somewhat more like that in private business. People seeking military careers may designate military jobs or job categories that interest them and, if qualified, be sent to the appropriate training centers, but the traditional placement-centered approach describes well an alternative approach not commonly considered in discussions of staffing methods.

The descriptions of these three patterns are abbreviated so much they seem like caricatures, but they do identify substantially different processes: (a) the eligibility list process in which an ordered list of potential employees is developed and is virtually the sole source of employees for an extended period of time, (b) the continuous consideration process, in which matches of position openings and applicants are made more or less serendipitously according to the timing of the opening and application, and (c) the placement process in which candidates are first declared acceptable for the organization and only later are placed in specific military jobs. Any of these patterns may be used in any kind of organization—not just the stereotypical ones—if they fit the purposes at hand.

THE ROLE OF RESEARCH IN PERSONNEL DECISIONS

Personnel research evaluates assessment procedures used in making personnel decisions; traditionally, research-based evaluation is called *validation*. It is such a basic process that this book emphasizes validity and other forms of evaluation more than specific assessment procedures.

Consider Gideon, who faced an embarrassment of riches: he had far too many candidates for his reduced army. On God's advice, he used a two-stage personnel testing procedure. Using a single-item preliminary screening test ("Do you want to go home?"), he cut 22,000 candidates down to 10,000. The remaining candidates were then put through an assessment center exercise—drinking from a stream, preferably by lapping the water like a dog instead of using a cupped hand—and 300 were chosen. Gideon did not ask if these procedures were valid, for they were given by God. Unfortunately, many modern test users behave as if they too had God-given tests and did not need to evaluate them. However, tests and predictions are fallible—and their use needs to be questioned. Such questioning has led to fairly standard research procedures for evaluating (validating) selection procedures.

Personnel selection, and personnel research, traditionally rest on some basic assumptions, some of them articulated long ago by Freyd (1923):

1. People have characteristic traits, including various abilities and skills, knowledge, attitudes, values, and personality traits, among others.
2. Abilities and other traits are at least somewhat stable. It is *not* assumed that abilities, skills, and other traits are permanently fixed—by heredity or early life experiences or later learning—nor is it assumed that all traits are equally stable. It *is* assumed, however, that abilities and other traits are reasonably stable for most adults, stable enough that the trait level of a candidate will not fade away when the candidate becomes an employee.
3. People differ. In particular, they differ in levels of work-relevant traits. That fact is the basis for decisions; those with higher (or perhaps optimal) levels of relevant traits are expected to perform better, other things being equal, than those with lower (or less than optimal) levels.
4. Relative differences in ability remain pretty much the same even after training or experience. People with higher levels of a required ability before exposure to a job will be the better performers on that job after training, whether formal or informal. If a specified ability is required for effective job performance, that ability may be enhanced by experience on the job, but the relative rank orders of people in a group will not often be substantially changed. (I'm not sure that this traditional assumption is merited; more on that in Chapter 10.)
5. Different jobs and selection purposes require different traits. Although testing research in the First World War had resulted in a rank order listing of occupations based on mean intelligence test scores (Yoakum & Yerkes, 1920, pp. 196–200), it is generally assumed that different occupations call for different *patterns* or *combinations* of traits and that effective selection requires matching the traits required for effective job performance to those characterizing the candidate.
6. Relevant traits can be measured, some more easily than others. Cognitive abilities have been measured successfully. Measures of psychomotor abilities have not been used as extensively, but the record is generally pretty favorable. The measurement of attitudes and personality traits (e.g., sense of responsibility, achievement motivation) has been under-researched, but it has a growing record of usefulness in employee selection. The level of research on the definition and measurement of such traits has yet to match that for cognitive abilities.
7. Jobs and job requirements are somewhat stable. (This is a traditional assumption, but it has been blown out of the water in the early years of the twenty-first century. The fact of change and the speed with which it occurs has, in the eyes of some observers, all but made personnel research impossible. My view is different. Job changes change the nature of research hypotheses, and complicate research, but they render the research more urgent than research on traditionally stable jobs. We'll return to this problem more—much more—in several later chapters.)

Steps in Personnel Research

A standard, traditional personnel research paradigm has been used for nearly a century for the empirical evaluation of tests and their use. Even traditions are not static, but the tradition outlined here is basic to various expansions and alternatives. It will be useful for a reader to recognize from the outset that, although we speak of personnel research in the evaluation of predictors and predictions, the results of the research do not necessarily inform or influence actual decisions. Indeed, very little research has been done, and very little is known, about actual decision making compared to the extensive body of selection and assessment research (Wilk & Cappelli, 2003). Keeping this discrepancy in mind may lead to different research avenues.

Tippins, Papinchock, and Solberg (2010) identified four basic decisions that organizational leaders and their researchers must make (jointly) in starting a selection system: deciding (a) what should be measured, (b) how it should it be measured, (c) how validity evidence should be collected, and (d) how to use the resulting scores. Each of these pertains in part to actions taken in developing the system and in part to matters of policy.

What Should Be Measured?

Analyze Jobs and Organizational Needs

Before deciding what to assess, analyses of the job and of the needs and values of the organization are needed. Some analysis procedures are casual; some are complex and systematic. Job analysis traditionally concentrates on one job (or job family) at a time where the need and opportunity for improvement seems greatest. Job and organizational need analyses should consider whether relatively poor performance on a job is a selection problem or is better approached by other means. A better approach in a specific case might be to redesign the job or its immediate work environment, or to change people already on the job through training or improved management. A selection procedure cannot solve a problem that springs primarily from inadequate equipment or inept management. When selection is deemed the appropriate intervention, it must begin with an analysis of the work to be done and of organizational needs as a basis for subsequent decisions.

Choose a Criterion

The criterion in personnel research is that which is to be predicted. It might be overall job performance, or some aspect of performance, or some valued behavior associated with the assigned job role.[2] A criterion varies from time to time or from person to person; it is variable, so it can be measured. It might be a carefully defined aspect of trainability, production quality or quantity, or earnings—or a dichotomy such as staying or leaving the job. Criterion choice is a matter of organizational values and organizational needs. Some organizational needs and values may be general, extending beyond performance on

---

[2] It is unfortunate that such an ambiguous word has become the standard term to designate the behavior to be predicted. In court cases, for example, the term *criterion* is often used by lawyers and judges to refer to the basis for selecting people, such as a cutting score on a test. Such a difference in the denotative meaning of the word has caused much confusion between attorneys and their expert witnesses and in other settings as well.

specific jobs. For example, if an organization wants to maintain tight production schedules, then punctuality, regular attendance, and workforce stability may be the most important criterion concepts for nearly all production jobs. If the organization faces rapid change, adaptability to change may be valued above other criteria. Criterion choice is partly a management decision, but it is a decision to be based on data assembled in job and need analyses.

Form Predictive Hypotheses

Hypothesis development is, or should be, an active process, not to be skipped or done casually. Given what is known about the criterion concept, what candidate attributes or situational characteristics will predict the criterion? Criterion performance may be influenced by characteristics of situations. The influence may be directly predictive, but some variables, personal or situational, may *mediate* or *moderate* predictions; these terms are explained in Chapter 8. The simplest and most traditional hypotheses hold only that worker characteristics will predict the criterion. Some hypotheses require consideration of more than one trait to predict performance in all of its complexity. Different parts of complex performance may require different criteria, not necessarily related (Guion, 1961). For each criterion, selecting a predictor means forming a hypothesis to be tested by research. Historically, employment psychology has been closely tied to psychological testing, so the predictors most commonly chosen have been those successfully measured by psychological tests and inventories, but I argue in Chapter 3 that selection hypotheses should consider a broader array of traits. Most employers seem to consider traits such as dependability, motivation level, work values, and other relatively amorphous constructs to be very important. They may be hard to measure, but a list of potential predictors should not, at least initially, be limited because of anticipated measurement problems.

Organizational variables may be considered in developing the list of predictors. Vicino and Bass (1978) showed that the degree of challenge on an early job was an important determiner of managerial success. Such organizational variables can predict important criteria, sometimes in combination or interaction with applicant traits.

How Should Criteria and Predictors Be Measured?

Select Methods of Measurement

Forming a predictive hypothesis is an act of theorizing. To evaluate it, the criterion and predictor concepts (which we will later call *constructs*) have to be defined in terms of procedures that might allow them to be measured. *Validation* (evaluation of the hypothesis) is not limited to any particular assessment method, but tests and questionnaires are used more often than other procedures—for several reasons. The predictive value of tests has been demonstrated more persuasively and more frequently than for competing approaches to assessment. Further, testing is easily standardized, enabling a fairer assessment than is possible where the method of assessment varies from one person to another. Test use is not, however, free from problems. One serious problem is the tendency to assess candidates on traits for which tests are available rather than for traits not easily assessed (Lawshe, 1959). Whatever the assessment procedure, its selection should be done by people who have wide and thorough understanding of *psychometrics* (the theory and methods by which psychological variables are measured) and of available and appropriate measurement procedures.

How to Validate the Hypothesis

Design the Research

Research design requires careful planning. It tries to assure that results from a research sample generalize to job applicants, the population of interest. Should a predictive hypothesis be tested in a sample of job applicants or a sample of people already on the job? An inappropriate sample may limit generalizability. Incumbents and applicants may differ in motivation to do well on a test, in means and variances of the measured predictors, or in other relevant ways. Employees, as research subjects, may fail to match applicant populations because of rapid changes in workforce demographics (Offerman & Gowing, 1993). Entry-level positions are often filled by students emerging from school; there may not be enough of them. Older workers—not only retirees but people who are unemployed or underemployed—may increasingly define applicant populations for these jobs. Moreover, the traditional applicant pool is increasingly augmented by less traditional applicants: older workers, minorities, and immigrants. Demographic variables so far have shown little effect on the validities of assessments, but research attention on them should continue as applicants (and variables associated with groups of them) become more diverse. In many organizations, demographic diversity has become a goal in itself. If recent immigrants have created a highly diverse candidate pool, research based on those hired at an earlier time from a less diverse population may be misleading; implications of selecting from currently underused sources of job candidates in the search for diversity should be carefully monitored to assure generalizability.

All too often, assessment procedures used in research differ enough from those actually used in operation that research results may not apply. Examples include rigorous timing of tests in the research but careless timing in practice, using continuous score distributions for research but cut scores in practice, or giving rigorously standard instructions in research but more conversational instructions when the assessment methods are used for decisions. Research design should anticipate the way the predictor will be used, and good management should make sure that operational use of predictors is consistent with the evaluative research.

Collect Data

Predictors must be administered with both standardization and tact. The first of these is technical; the second is both technical and civil. Tactless, uncaring treatment undermines motivation to do well and introduces an extraneous and uncontrolled variable into the research. Beyond that, it is simply uncivil to fail to appreciate the apprehension people have when being assessed, and an examiner who appreciates these feelings will approach the research task more humanely than one who does not (see several chapters in Schuler, Farr, & Smith, 1993). If nothing more, civility is good public relations, in research and in operational use.

Since the early days of testing, standardization has been accepted as a *sine qua non* of good practice; it has been virtually unquestioned throughout most of the history of personnel selection research. Everyone who is tested is given the same set of items, identically worded. If there are established time limits, they are rigidly adhered to whenever the test is given; instructions are verbatim, the same for everyone; if the test is printed, type size and style and paper quality always remain the same. This is similar to experimental control of variables not a part of the hypothesis; it is also an assurance of procedural fairness.

Nevertheless, the concept of standardization is due for reappraisal. Advances in psychometrics suggest that the ideals of standardization may be better realized by individually tailoring sets of items to each applicant, and administration by computer may call for varying *de facto* time limits by controlling response times for individual items.

Evaluate Results

Freyd (1923) referred to "evaluating" measurement; the specific evaluation by correlating predictor and criterion measures became known as *validation*, a term later expanded to include a variety of procedures and purposes. If the correlation is high, the predictor is said to be a good one (i.e., a "valid" one), and if it is low, the predictor is said to be poor. High and low are relative terms, often evaluated more against experience than against specified coefficients. Despite the vagueness, empirical evaluation of predictors has traditionally been deemed essential. Failure to do it may be deemed "outright charlatanism" (Thorndike, 1949, p. 119).

The relation of predictor measures to criterion measures defines an established, traditional view of validation in personnel assessment. There is, however, an even older tradition—primarily in assessment for counseling and in educational measurement—defining validation as finding out how well the predictor (in this case, usually a test) "measures what it purports to measure" (Sutherland, 1996, p. 490). A new tradition is developing that defines validity as an accumulation of evidence supporting (or failing to support) an intended inference from assessment results (see American Educational Research Association (AERA), American Psychological Association (APA), & National Council on Measurement in Education (NCME), 1999; Putka & Sackett, 2010; Society for Industrial and Organizational Psychology, 2003). These are profoundly important differences in the concept of validity, discussed in Chapter 5. A test that purports to measure spelling ability may be considered valid in the counseling tradition if it does so very well, but it is not likely to be a valid predictor, for personnel use, of how well mechanics repair faulty brakes. We must distinguish between (a) the validity with which a trait or attribute is measured and (b) the validity with which the measured trait predicts something else—between validity of measurement (*psychometric* or *descriptive validity*) and validity as the job-relatedness of a predictor (*relational* or *criterion-related validity*). Various forms of empirical investigation are available for either concept of validity (Landy, 1986). The newer idea of an evolving concept of validity offers a wide variety of standards of good practice in evaluating validation research results, but the concept begins with a clear definition of the intended inference from, or interpretations of, assessment scores.

Varieties of Research Designs

Traditionally, personnel tests were evaluated by variants of two basic design choices: studying people already on the job, the *present employee* method, versus the *follow-up* method of research, in which actual job applicants are tested and criterion data are collected later for those hired (Lawshe & Balma, 1966; Tiffin, 1942 and later editions). The follow-up method, especially an idealized version of it, is widely, although not universally, considered the better design, in part because it assesses real candidates from the applicant population.

In the idealized follow-up design, the research tests are given to all applicants but not scored until criterion data are available for those who are hired. Hiring decisions are made as if the new tests were not available at all, using existing methods—application forms, interviews, references, tests, hunches, or whatever—whether previously validated or not. The ideal is that neither decisions nor subsequent criteria are affected by knowledge of the test scores so that the range of test scores is about the same as that of applicants in general. When criterion data are collected for those actually hired, the tests are scored, and the scores are compared to criterion data. This procedure was rare even in the early days of employment testing, and I've seen only a few examples of it in my entire professional life. However, the ideal provides a standard against which other designs can be discussed. Traditionally, the only alternative was the present employee method where employees are taken off the job, tested, and scores correlated with existing or concurrently obtained criterion measures. It is a faster method, and practical considerations often favor it.

Unfortunately, these terms have become archaic. Today's discussions are more likely to refer to *concurrent* and *predictive* research designs—terms introduced in the 1954 *Technical Recommendations* (APA, AERA, & NCME, 1954). They are similar, but definitely not identical, to the ideas of present employee and follow-up research. The essential difference between concurrent and predictive designs is the time span for data collection, not the employment status of the research subjects. Predictive designs include a substantial time interval between the availability of predictor data and collection of subsequent criterion data; concurrent designs do not. Thus, a predictive design may use existing employees if the data to be evaluated can be collected from them at one time and criterion data collected some weeks or months later, but this procedure lacks much compared to the idealized follow-up study.

Does it matter whether the research design is concurrent or predictive? Opinions differ. I suspect that the answer depends partly on the traits studied. Concurrent and predictive studies of cognitive tests are likely to give similar results. Non-cognitive traits, especially personality traits, may be more influenced by experience on the job; there is no assurance that they would enjoy the same immunity to design differences as cognitive tests. Population differences (applicants versus employees) seem more important than time-span differences. In any case, correlation (the usual statistical method) says nothing about direction of causality, even if a causal relationship exists. The act of prediction, however, says something about timing. Without a time interval, even the direction of permitted prediction is uncertain; it is as appropriate to predict the trait from the criterion as to go the other direction.

Problems in Traditional Evaluative Research

The above recital of traditional personnel research is conventional, but it is a paradigm that needs to be re-examined. Despite its history of valuable use, it presents several potentially serious problems.

Changing Situation

The traditional paradigm fit well in the first half of the twentieth century and beyond; it still fits many situations. The fact, however, is that the world of work has changed, often dramatically, and many of the changes raise new questions not well answered by traditional methods. Computer use and digitalization have led to the globalization of work and to flexibility in work location (Friedman, 2006). Work has become less stable and more "volatile" (Landy, 2007, p. 415), more collaborative (Hough & Oswald, 2000), and more often done by contingent workers (Hulin & Glomb, 1999). Research methods need to go (and have gone) far beyond the simple bivariate paradigm correlating a single predictor with a single criterion.

Numbers of Cases

Tradition needs large numbers—situations where large numbers of people have been or will be hired for a given job or job family. It does not work for selection situations that arise only now and then, although the basic feature of the paradigm holds even for these: identify requirements, assess candidates, predict future contributions (even if only judgmentally), and make a decision.

We used to think 30 was a large number. Events since the 1964 Civil Rights Act have shown that "large numbers" may mean hundreds of research subjects. Conventional validation developed for hiring dozens or hundreds of workers for similar jobs each year. However, a major change in the American workforce, likely to continue, is that most people do not work in large corporations on jobs also done by hundreds of other workers. Over 20 years ago, Hodge and Lagersfeld (1987) reported that, even then, only about 10% of working Americans worked in organizations employing more than 1,000 people. Moreover, there is more differentiation of jobs; technological growth has produced a wider variety of jobs. Many employment decisions must now be made where only a few people are to be hired (perhaps only one). Further, more hiring is being done in professional, semi-professional, and managerial occupations, where the costs of error in individual selection decisions may be much higher than for the mass-market decisions, but where one person must be chosen from only a few candidates. The numbers for many less constricted decisions are nevertheless too small for reliable correlation coefficients. The traditional paradigm makes no provision for the small business, for the selection of the replacement for a retiring manager, or for hiring a unique specialist in even a large organization.

Inadequate Consideration of Prior Research

Traditional validation ignores prior research. The tradition developed when it was thought that validities of selection procedures are specific to, even unique in, the situation in which they are established. One of the more influential changes in the thinking of personnel researchers stems from *validity generalization* (Schmidt & Hunter, 1977), a method for quantitative analysis of the results of many independent prior studies of a given research hypothesis (e.g., that performance of clerical workers is predictable from tests of general mental ability).

Narrow Focus

The traditional focus in evaluating predictors and their use is too narrow. It centers on the psychometric and statistical bases of testing, not on the organizational issues the predictors are supposed to address. This may be a holdover from the days long ago when people spoke of "the validity of a test" in evaluating a test and its use. More recently, Cronbach (1971) argued persuasively that validity refers to *inferences* from test scores but not to the test nor to the scores themselves. The inferences may refer either to the descriptive, psychometric meaning attributed to test scores (what does this instrument measure, and what do the scores on it mean?) or to the relational inferences that may be drawn from the scores (how well is a person with a given score likely to do on the specified criterion?). The newer emphasis on a variety of intended score interpretations may be somewhat broadening (because it includes predictive interpretations as one sort of intention), but all of these take a purely psychometric point of view—and stop there. From an organizational point of view, however, a psychometric emphasis on how well things are measured, or how well they predict something else, is too limited. Evaluation should go beyond psychometrics and move on to the evaluations of actual decisions. It rarely does so (Wilk & Cappelli, 2003).

Kehoe (2002) may have moved in this direction by extending the idea of the *meaning of measurement* beyond descriptive validity. To him, the phrase required an understanding of the use of measurement for personnel decisions. The researcher and the decision maker may have widely different understandings, leading to nearly inevitable differences between research and operational procedures. How good are the decisions that are actually made? The evaluative focus needs to be expanded to an organizational level of concern. Multilevel research, mentioned below and discussed further in Chapter 10, seems to be another move in that direction.

Need for Judgment

The traditional paradigm is purely statistical; it is based on data, not judgments. In some respects, that is good. The view that human judgment yields better predictions than statistics is a myth (superstition based on hope), but it persists in spite of overwhelming evidence to the contrary. Such evidence was presented long ago by Meehl (1954), who later updated it by citing a "box score" in which, of 35 studies that compared statistical and judgmental predictions, the score was 35 to 0 in favor of statistics (Meehl, 1967). Nevertheless, statistical prediction is often impossible, infeasible, or insufficiently supported. The circumstances for a candidate at hand may differ enough from the research circumstances to make generalizing from the research questionable. The most obvious example lies in testing the skills of people with disabilities. One cannot intelligently (or legally in the United States) refuse to consider a blind applicant for a job in which vision is not a genuine requirement simply because the applicant does not match the research sample. One can, of course, modify the selection procedure (such as reading items orally), but the research does not apply to such nonstandard modifications. The decision maker must therefore make a judgment based on the applicant's performance on a procedure of unknown validity, on interviewer judgments of unknown validity, prior work experience of unknown validity, or on some random basis known not to have any validity. To disqualify an applicant because the possible assessment procedures have not been validated is likely to be illegal. Moreover, from an organizational point of view, it is probably stupid as well; how else can we describe a practice that would not let an organization hire an employee who might be superior to others because of special motivation, unusual skills, or other unresearched attributes—and all for no better reason than the applicant's failure to be ordinary?

Uniqueness and Prediction Error

Closely related is the more general fact that the traditional paradigm overlooks uniqueness or individuality, simply letting it slide into the category of prediction error. Prediction in traditional validation is based on an equation that considers everyone in a research sample alike in everything except the equation variables. The equation is a mathematical statement of averages; it says that, on average, people with a given predictor score will have a given criterion score. In fact, almost no one precisely fits this average; for most people in a sample, criterion scores will be *close* to the average for people with a given predictor score, but will miss it a little bit in either direction. A predicted criterion for some people will be far from the average. There may be many reasons: pure chance, measurement error, influence of other variables such as motivational levels, or simply that an individual person is unique. We can't do much about pure chance. We can take steps to minimize errors of measurement, we can try to include all important variables in the equation, or we can give more attention to individuality. Actually, people are alike enough in many ways that averages work pretty well, but nevertheless, we should give more attention to the fact of individuality.

> Psychologists have been slow to recognize that the patterning of activity is the most individual thing about a person. The study of individual differences has been almost exclusively concerned with the amounts of various components that are present . . . Organic chemists could never have distinguished between most of the complex substances that make up the biological world had they continued to do nothing except measure the amounts of carbon, nitrogen, oxygen, and rarer elements in organic substances . . . It was the discovery of the structure of the organic molecule, of the way atoms are linked to the hexagonal benzene ring, that constituted the real breakthrough. (Tyler, 1978, p. 107)

I do not know whether a structure in human behavior, analogous to the benzene ring, exists. If it does, however, the traditional validation research paradigm will not find it. There is a tension between the uniqueness of individual candidates and the commonalities that define research populations. It is strange, but the aspect of psychological research known as the study of individual differences, from which principles of assessment are derived, has become methodologically the study of averages. Only a few psychologists, at least in recent years, have examined human individuality, and their work seems not to have influenced personnel assessment. I do not know if uniqueness is genuinely important for the practical problems of making personnel decisions. I do know that two people may have precisely the same measured traits but have unmeasured differences, leading one to success on the job and the other to failure or mediocrity on the same job. Uniqueness offers no basis for statistical prediction, but it does, I think, require us to be less than arrogant about our predictions of future behavior.

A *whole person* view—the idea that people are more than bundles of independent traits, that assessments should look holistically at "the whole person"—implies recognizing uniqueness. Dachler (1989) suggested that selection be considered a part of personnel development, considering patterns of behavior rather than scorable dimensions, focusing more on probability of future growth and adaptability than on fitness for a particular job. There is much to recommend his position, especially where change seems to be the only constant. The emphasis on patterns is not so new (see, e.g., Cattell, 1949), but perhaps current realities will promote its serious consideration. Schmitt and Chan (1998) did so in calling for predictors that describe or reflect "dynamic interactions between the individual's repertoire of behavior and the situation's changing demands" (p. 244); their call seems to be for the whole person's repertoire and the whole situation's demands.

Dachler's view and traditional validation are not so far apart as they might seem. A guiding theme of this book is that a predictive hypothesis can be developed; that it can specify that people strong in a certain trait, or collection of traits, are likely to be strong in a certain aspect of performance or performance composite. Within this theme, a collection of traits can be a pattern of behavior, and growth and adaptability can be (and must be, if change is a ubiquitous situational feature) the preferred criteria. A problem with this (not an insurmountable one), at least in the United States; is the Federal regulation of personnel selection procedures (Chapter 4). These regulations follow traditional methods with no mention of alternatives such as holistic evaluation of people and their likelihood of adapting to change. I personally believe that the courts are not as rigid as the regulations—that courts will accept a well-reasoned, well-developed selection procedure that improves productivity without violating the values of the larger society. Maybe the main reason precluding a more holistic approach is that not enough people have thought about it often enough or deeply enough to develop a solid paradigm for its use.

Minimum Qualifications versus Best Candidate

The traditional paradigm does not face the question of minimum standards. In general, it assumes that a valid selection procedure is one in which, if some of the trait indicates good performance and more of the trait indicates better performance, then still more of it would indicate still better performance (known statistically as a *monotonic* relationship). This generally good assumption is the basis for top-down selection.

Suppose, however, that no applicant has scored very high. Will the job be offered (other considerations identifying no problems) to the one with the best score, or is the best score too low? How does one decide that a given score is too low? The determination of a qualifying standard, such as a minimum cut score, is difficult, requiring serious thought and research. In practice, minimum standards have been dictated largely by supply and demand, but some procedures (e.g., certification of competence in the performance of specific skills) require a more rational basis.

Static versus Dynamic Research Models

By the time a predictive validation study is completed, the applicant population, the job responsibilities, and the definition of success may all have changed. Yet tradition assumes that the conditions of the study will still be the conditions when the results are applied. As in the Gershwin song, "It ain't necessarily so." Maybe concurrent validation is the answer, but probably for only very stable cognitive abilities. New models are needed; happily, several have been introduced and are being explored.

Global or Specific Assessments

How general, or how narrow, should predictor or criterion variables be? A multiple regression equation permits narrowly specific predictors but requires a single, usually general criterion. Such an equation is sometimes criticized for being both too atomistic in its analysis of people and their traits and too general and nonspecific in its definition of criteria. Is either criticism justified? Should we seek global, general descriptions of traits or performance, or narrower, more specific ones?

Too much energy has been wasted on this question. Smith (1985) pointed out that measurement options always fall on a specific-to-general continuum. The options are not interchangeable. She said that specific criteria call for measurement of very specific traits, and that global criteria are probably better predicted by very general traits.

A Special Problem: The Level of Analysis

Traditional validation is done at the level of individual applicants and workers. Increasingly, attention is given to *multilevel analysis* (see Chapter 10) in research and theory crossing different organizational levels (Klein & Kozlowski, 2000). It is clear from nearly a century of research that selecting individuals on the basis of scores on valid predictors results in improved mean performance among those selected (Schmidt & Hunter, 1998). Intuitively, therefore, one might think that performance measured at higher levels of analysis (e.g., unit profitability) would also be improved, but that is a rather simplistic intuition. It ignores between-units differences and the concept of organizational systems (Schneider, 1996; Schneider, Smith, & Sipe, 2000).

Selection of Team Members

In a traditional work unit, although people in different positions may all work toward the same end (e.g., assembling something), different members of the unit have different responsibilities and do different parts of the work. Choosing people to form collaborative groups or teams, or to join existing teams, poses special problems, and the usual research at the individual level may not solve them. Roles within the group may be intended to be equal, but work may pile up for one member of the unit while another has a temporary lull. If people in the unit form a reasonably cohesive and congenial group, a person with available time may help the overworked one. Such help is common enough, and useful enough, that the idea of a discrete, unchanging division of duties is surely fictional; people who get along with each other tend to work collaboratively, and many organizations have intentionally made collaborative groups a fact of organizational structure (Beyerlein, Freedman, McGee, & Moran, 2003). Members of collaborative groups must have at least some versatility. Selecting the members, especially those to replace former members, may remain an individual process; if so, staffing research at an individual level of analysis is appropriate. At least two things distinguish group or team member selection from ordinary individual selection: (a) that versatility can be an individual level criterion and (b) that performance may be a team level criterion. Jones, Stevens, and Fischer (2000) distinguished teams from other collaborative groups such as crews or task forces; despite the distinctions, selection for any of them requires multilevel consideration.

Person–Organization Fit

An applicant for work in an organization expects to work with the people who are there. If a newcomer is not to remain an outsider long after joining an organization or group, he or she must somehow fit in. The term *fit in* has a disreputable history. A group of white males seeking a replacement for a departed member may reject a woman or an ethnic minority on the grounds of not fitting in; the term is often a surrogate for poorly disguised prejudice. Used in this way, it may also serve diagnostically to reveal a serious flaw of group identity. Like Mohrman and Cohen (1995), I think a well-functioning collaborative work group is one with a clear focus on the group's work goals—the tasks the group is supposed to accomplish. If "fitting in" is simply an expression of prejudice, it indicates people more self-centered than work-centered, preserving their social rather than their functional identities. "Fitting" a group committed to its work implies joining in that commitment—more than getting along pleasantly. The issue of fit is placed in a broader and clearer perspective when the fit is between the person and the organization as a whole. The problem is complex because the person's attributes are measured at an individual level, and the organization's attributes are measured at a more complex, multiple-person level.

The *attraction–selection–attrition (ASA)* model (Schneider, 1987; Schneider et al., 1995), mentioned earlier, describes relationships between individual people and the organizations that hire them. People are attracted to some organizations more than to others and apply to those they find more attractive. Whether the basis for attraction is factual or exists only in rumor or perception, organizations can choose only among those who are attracted enough to apply to them. If the basis for attraction was wrong, and people once in the organization find that the fit is poor, they leave. Schneider's contention is that the combination of initial attraction and subsequent attrition leads to greater organizational homogeneity; those who are attracted, hired, and stay tend to be alike. Such homogeneity can have a major, potentially negative impact on the organization's ability to survive and change in a rapidly changing world. Selection for fit may be counterproductive, even hazardous.

Failure to consider fit can also be hazardous. Deliberately selecting people with wholly different values and beliefs can result in newcomers who do not function well within the existing organizational culture, people who are not accepted by the dominant core already there and with whom they cannot clearly communicate. If newcomers are brought in specifically to turn around an organization (i.e., to change the way old-timers do things) they need to share at least some things with those they are expected to change (Schneider, 1987). Changing structures and organizational processes will not by themselves create change and organizational adaptability; the people in them must change, and that change occurs slowly. Maybe this is the reason so many organizational psychologists emphasize socialization efforts. Note also that socialization to a foreign culture may also be a question of fit, perhaps predictable from measures of adaptability or flexibility.

Some selection questions emerge. What attributes should newcomers share with most of those already in the organization? What newcomer attributes are most likely to increase organizational adaptability to external events and changes? Is the answer to this question dependent more on those external processes or internal needs? If we have answers to those questions, how are the relevant attributes to be assessed? These are, of course, questions for research, but when the consequences of error can be as great as an organization's failure to survive, the answers have enormous practical value—and the traditional validation paradigm seems unlikely to provide the answers.

THE ROLE OF POLICY IN PERSONNEL DECISIONS

Staffing decisions are usually made by managers, not by test developers, staff psychologists, or human resources specialists. Managers and testers occupy different worlds with different concerns. Managers, despite occasional talk about wanting the best people, are typically interested in making a decision to fill a vacancy with a satisfactory person as quickly as possible (Herriot, 1993); testers and other human resources people are concerned with matters such as validity, reliability, and compliance with government regulation (Heneman, Huett, Lavigna, & Ogsten, 1995). Managers may have had little or no training in psychometrics, may not understand the assessments, and may hold unwarranted views about tests. Some managers distrust tests and rely very little on test scores. What is worse (from a tester's perspective) is a manager who believes tests are great, who defers to test scores even when evidence shows them invalid, and who simply does not hear warnings or qualifications about them. Such true believers are surprisingly common and harder to work with than skeptics. To deal with both extremes, some staff psychologists establish rules for using tests or other assessment procedures in making decisions; these rules may have the weight of organizational policies. They might specify preferred score levels or patterns, circumstances that may justify overlooking poor scores, or limits to further information considered along with assessment scores.

In some organizations, individual managers are free to decide for themselves whether to use test information and, if so, how to use it. That seems an odd policy. If an investment has been made to develop and validate a systematic, standardized assessment program, it is strange to let unsystematic, individual whims determine how or whether the results of the investment will be used. Strange it may be, but it is likely when managers are not satisfied with established staffing procedures (cf. Heneman et al., 1995). Those responsible for the assessment portions of staffing programs must expect resistance, at least passively, from managers who do not understand or appreciate the applicable scientific and legal principles; nevertheless, *they should be held responsible for training the decision makers in the use of assessment data.*

Decisions are influenced by information, and personnel research should provide useful, understandable information. Decisions are also influenced by policies—policies of individual decision makers, of organizations, and of the society in which the organizations exist. Procedural justice requires that individual decision makers in an organization follow common policies and principles and use common sources of information.

Organizational Policies

Organizational goals need expression and ways to be achieved. Some paths toward achievement are procedural; others may be more general policies. Personnel decisions are relevant— or should be—for both. Policies are likely to be influenced by context. For example, if organization members have diverse skills, but the organization faces a need for major change, decision policies may well focus more on placement of existing personnel than on selection of new members from outside (Born & Jansen, 1997). Too often, organizational policies are not explicitly stated. As a result, bases for decision vary remarkably across time and across decision makers. Many kinds of policies might be developed, but here I concentrate on six that I consider especially important for personnel decisions.

Time Perspective

Is criterion performance to be predicted for the short-term or long-term future? With cognitive predictors, at least, criteria collected three months after hire will ordinarily be predicted more successfully than criteria collected after three years, but which time lapse is more important to the organization? Performance is also ordinarily predicted better for the immediate job than for one to which the person may later be promoted. Many organizations make initial selection decisions based on potential for growth into more responsible assignments. If this is the policy, personnel research should follow it with criteria that assess personal growth. A time perspective measured in years rather than months may make organizational sense, but it may also fail to provide good predictions. The short-term vs. long-term policy may not be organization-wide. For lower level jobs, promotion may be too rare to consider in decisions. For higher level positions, policy may favor a longer perspective.

A long-range policy makes several assumptions. First, it assumes that the skills needed for immediate value to the organization will stay relevant for a long time—even though the longer the interval between decision and outcome, the greater the opportunity for intervening events to reduce prediction accuracy. A further assumption is that decisions to hire, promote, or give special training are followed with appropriate developmental experiences. A genuinely long-term perspective is feasible only with genuinely integrated systems

(Schneider, 1996; Senge, 1990). In too many organizations, selection is left to one department, training to another, career development to yet another, and the systematic development of relevant managerial policies and practices to no one in particular. Such organizations would do well to stay with short-term objectives.

Governmental regulations in the United States favor short-term objectives. The *Uniform Guidelines* (Equal Employment Opportunity Commission, Civil Service Commission, Department of Labor, & Department of Justice, 1978) say that an employer may consider an applicant for a job at a level higher than the entry job if most people hired at the lower level will, within a reasonable time period of time, actually reach the higher level. An organization seeking a pool of qualified people from which to choose for a promotion-from-within policy, say five years from now, is not permitted under this rule to look beyond the job level attained by a *majority* of those remaining employed after five years. This provision should be reconsidered.

Decision Factors

On what basis—on what information about candidates—will personnel decisions be made? Let us dispense quickly with various forms of favoritism, even in countries where the term is not considered pejorative. Jobs and other special opportunities often go to friends, friends of friends, family members, or other favorites. Where favoritism rules, there is little point in assessing potential contribution to the organizational enterprise. Robert Bolda (personal communication, May 1989) reported that a distribution of valid test scores of recommended favorites was essentially normal with a mean close to the 50th percentile on national norms; selecting by favoritism, he argued, is like random selection. Standardized tests and inventories are generally useful predictors of job performance and much better than random selection.

Nevertheless, a first organizational policy decision is whether to use tests or not. Obviously, I favor testing. In my view, the answer depends on the purpose and whether, for that purpose, demonstrably useful alternatives are available. In the face of public pressure, the United States Department of Labor has at least twice abandoned tests (one a generalized civil service test and the other a test used by local employment services for referring candidates to local employers). They were abandoned without considering the relative merits of alternatives. To state it mildly, such policy decisions are seriously flawed.

In public discourse, testing has been perennially criticized by social critics and simultaneously touted by others as a magic solution to organizational and social problems. For example, some critics want to reduce or eliminate tests in schools while others want mandated testing to certify student or teacher competence. Critics have claimed variously that employment tests induce conformity, invade privacy, deceive applicants, or discriminate unfairly. The criticisms have enough core truth in them that organizational leaders need policies to provide some safeguards. Many organizations have written policies declaring the intent to be fair in using tests for decisions; some also have written policies against invasion of privacy or deception. Whether written policies are really applied in effect depends less on memos than on the behavior of key organizational leaders.

A researcher is tempted to suggest that personnel decisions be based only on information shown by research to be useful in predicting future performance. That limitation, however, might leave only random choice without research evidence. Policies need to guide use of assessments without traditional validation in situations such as (a) assessment of people with disabilities that preclude use of routine assessment methods, (b) choosing among those within a range or band of essentially similar scores, or (c) selecting for unusual jobs. Forming rational policies for such situations is not easy. The only cases I've seen personally do little more than sweep the dirty little problem of alternative assessments under the corporate carpet. Using an alternative to traditionally validated assessment requires a carefully and critically examined policy, based on as much evidence and logic as can be mustered.

Minimum versus Maximum Qualifications

Classical ideas of rational thought suggest that one consider all options, choosing the one that will maximize payoff. In a selection decision, this implies finding the candidate with the highest qualifications (e.g., the general argument for top-down selection). A common alternative settles for minimally qualified candidates. Simon (1979), discussing decision making, used the concept of *satisficing*. He argued that rational people, faced with a set of potential actions or decisions, each with its own outcome utility, will search until they find one with an outcome that is "satisficing"—one that will do. Under a satisficing model, personnel decision makers consider candidates serially until one is found who is expected to be good enough; to have acceptable, maybe more than minimal, but not necessarily high qualifications.

The satisficing point of view has pitfalls, such as having no definition of "good enough." An alternative policy, to search persistently for excellence, also has pitfalls, such as not finding it. If a job requires hiring decisions often, maybe nearly daily, the policy may be somewhat like satisficing but seeking the best of a limited number of candidates, but the best may differ from day to day. It is perhaps a fairness issue that a person rejected today actually has higher qualifications than one accepted yesterday. Making policy is not always easy.

Reporting Scores to Decision Makers

If tests are used, how should scores be reported to decision makers? Different policies may have different implications for designing evaluative research.

1. *Report actual scores.* The policy may require reporting raw scores (or perhaps percentile ranks or standard scores). Under this option, there is a technical and ethical obligation to train decision makers so that they become qualified to interpret scores and score differences.

2. *Report scores as passing or failing.* Many managers are more comfortable with the idea of a passing score. That preference, coupled with the belief of many staff psychologists that decision-making managers cannot be trained or trusted to interpret test scores, often leads to cut scores. Among candidates who have passed, the manager is free to choose at random or to base choices on any available information he or she *thinks* is valuable. This may help gain acceptance (although I do not know that it does), but it has a bizarre feature. Despite investment in testing and test validation (usually before setting a cut score), actual decisions are based on the chance availability of information that may be interpreted and valued differently by different managers.

3. *Report expectancies or predictions.* I know of no one who reports selection decisions based on predicted criterion levels rather than test scores, but it might be an idea

worth developing. It is, however, common to report scores and concomitantly provide *expectancy charts* for their interpretation (see Chapter 7). An expectancy chart estimates the probability of achieving a designated criterion level (e.g., an average production level or above) in various score ranges.

Developing such charts and teaching managers how to use them can promote competent use of assessments. Responsibilities of an organization's staff psychologist, in my judgment, include assuring that decision makers are trained in (a) the nature of the genuine qualifications for jobs and how they were determined, (b) the fundamental principles for evaluating their assessment, (c) the defensible and indefensible inferences from scores, and (d) acceptable limits of individual judgments to override ordinarily defensible inferences. Staff psychologists should also be responsible for giving managers judgment aids to use in making decisions. Expectancy charts can help with both responsibilities.

4. *Report score bands.* A *score band* is a range of scores in which score differences are deemed too trivial to consider. What is reported is not the score of an individual but the individuals whose scores are all the same or differ only trivially. The logic of the procedure is that decision makers choose among these on some basis other than the test score (see Chapter 12).

5. *Report only interpretations.* For higher level or non-routine jobs, expectancy charts and score bands are not likely to be feasible. Test scores and assessment ratings may be reported as narrative, descriptive interpretations rather than as scores or score ranges. Such a report can be a judgment aid and also serve instructional functions; it can define the qualifications assessed, distinguish them from other traits with which they might be confused, and provide detailed descriptions of the inferences that can (and cannot) be drawn from their assessment.

Conflicting Information

Managers are often impatient with probabilities; they want definite yes-or-no answers from assessments. They may be especially impatient if two or more predictions or probability statements are not compatible, as when the probability of being satisfactory on one criterion is high but is accompanied by a low probability of being satisfactory on another. For example, a candidate might be predicted to perform job tasks very well, but also present a strong likelihood of counterproductive work behavior.

Training in assessment use should stress the reality that people do not necessarily function at the same level in all aspects of work-related performance. A nice, cooperative person is not necessarily a good performer; one who works carefully and does not make any errors may not get much done. Incompatible predictions require reconciling judgments, not denunciation of the assessments or the predictions. Where the research program permits predictions of independent criteria, managers should be trained to expect some incompatibility and to use a predetermined policy to deal with it.

Monitoring Assessment Use

Training wears off. Personnel decisions like selection, promotion, or transfer are not everyday events for individual managers, and the training may be old when assessment results are reported. Human resources specialists, if themselves competently trained, can work with the manager, refreshing principles of interpretation, as part of the decision process.

Public Policy

Organizations function in broader environments, including the sometimes amorphous entity called public policy. Public policy may be enacted or decreed, or simply a *Zeitgeist* of currently dominant opinions. Equality of employment opportunity has been a dominant public policy in the United States since the passage of the Civil Rights Act of 1964. American debate about privacy as a constitutionally protected right has been illustrated in continuing concern that personality testing may be an unwarranted invasion of privacy, expressed long ago in Congressional hearings (Amrine, 1965).

Is it in society's best interest that each organization seeks only the very best applicants? For many western societies, and for productivity, it probably is, although that judgment is likely to vary from one culture to another. However, if the practice of selecting only the best became common enough in a given culture, it might create a chronically unemployed segment of society; people at the low ends of the distributions of qualifying characteristics would find jobs only in rare times of virtually full employment. Should criteria always be directly related to performance? Would it not serve a broad social interest to consider also predicting a criterion measure such as psychological well-being (Clegg & Wall, 1981)? Policy debates that focus on one special concern and ignore others, without considering balances and tradeoffs, are narrow and, in the final analysis, potentially counterproductive.

CONFLUENCE OF THEORY, RESEARCH, AND PRACTICE

Theories abound in law, in literature, in music, in philosophy—and in science. A scientific theory not supported by data is only a hunch—even if it is a logical hunch, derived from sensible premises. Scientific research is often designed more to find flaws in a proposed theory than to find reasons for accepting it; a theory is meant to be treated with informed skepticism. It is almost ritualistic to ask for more theory in industrial and organizational psychology. I join the call because good practice requires an understanding of what one is doing in developing, evaluating, or using assessment procedures and in making operational decisions based on them. Such understanding *is* theory.

Nevertheless, I'm always a tad uncomfortable with talk about theory. Too often what passes for theory seems to me merely facile verbalism. It is often glib, using words such as *theory* or *rationale* as labels for fragments of thought (or figments of imagination) in lieu of more carefully considered factual information.

A *theory*, to me, is a well-integrated collection of generalizable empirical observations and data (facts) and related ideas. A *hypothesis* is one of those ideas proposed to explain a relationship, an event, or some other state of nature. A *line of reasoning (rationale)* is specific more than generalizable; it may lead to hypotheses and, with enough supporting research, to a theory. Much of the theory proposed in applied psychology omits those lower steps toward it. I'm overly critical, of course, but in spite of my discomfort, I find that I, too, often bandy about such terms as "theory of the construct" when all I mean is a hypothesis (or *model* encompassing multiple hypotheses).

Research can lead to the development or revision of a theory as well as test aspects of one, but useful research is not limited to theory-related studies. It can be exploratory, maybe based on curiosity; it might be based on an unsupported hunch about the answer to a practical question or problem. Research on a question stemming from practice can lead to useful theories for further research. Sackett (2007) gave a good example; it began as a practical study of supermarket check-out cashier performance. "Off we went to conduct what we viewed at the time as a purely applied project" (Sackett, 2007, p. 179). Later, "We did not dream up [the typical versus maximum performance] theory and then go test it. What initially appeared on the surface to be comparable measures (items scanned per minute) came to be viewed as conceptually different when measured unobtrusively over the long term versus when measured by a supervisor standing over the test taker with a stop watch" (Sackett, 2007, p. 180).

Another example of research based on practice morphing into theory was provided by Dean and Russell (2005). They noted that biodata are often good predictors in practice, but that we don't really understand why. In time, a life stages theory and an ecology theory emerged from considering the empirical research; Dean and Russell did not consider these as competing theories. From their joint consideration of both theories, a theory evolved to be tested in their work. And it all began from the practical question of whether personal history could predict future job performance.

In short, research, even without formal, generalizable theory, can promote understanding of useful practices. Research and theory both need to focus more on promoting understanding of what is done in practice. Too much of what we know about personnel assessment and decision making, and therefore too much of this book, is limited to techniques. Better theories of work and work effectiveness—or of behavior generally—can sharpen, prune, and expand those techniques and improve decisions.

We must not forget that the purpose of research, theory, and practice is to optimize the process by which some people get rewards and opportunities and others do not. The central focus of this process—the one intended to reach the best possible outcomes—is a decision. Decisions are based on assessments, but they also imply judgment, preferably informed judgment. Some informing of judgment comes from on-site research, some from research literature, some from theory, and some from knowing organizational needs.

Theory and practice both begin with a need to be filled, a question to be answered, or an observation to be explained and understood. In assessment, the explanation typically invokes a hypothesized scientific construct, stemming perhaps from prior theory, hunch, or experience. In psychology, a *construct* is an idea or concept constructed or invoked to explain relationships between observations. A hypothesis about a construct is to be tested, not merely swallowed, and competing explanatory hypotheses are not only possible but likely. Theory development eliminates some of these competing understandings by targeted research studies, perhaps until only one is left. If all are eliminated, new ones must be sought; if several survive, a full understanding may require their integration.

Anderson (2005) reported wide concern about the growing divide between practice and research, and he is not alone. An unfortunate but growing gap seems to separate academic science from organizational practice. Academics often seem interested only in building theories. Practitioners tend to decry the triviality and impracticality they perceive in academic theories, yet some of the theories they decry could inform many practical decisions in their organizations. There is, or should be, a symbiotic relationship between theory and practice— between basic and applied research (Leibowitz, 1996). The dictum attributed to Kurt Lewin (nothing is as practical as a good theory) holds true. To be practical, however, a theory has to be a good one, internally consistent, supported by data, and tested in practice to find out how well it works beyond the boundaries of a research situation. Many ritual calls for theory ignore the symbiosis of theory and practice. Assessment practice should be guided by theory. To choose a variable to be evaluated as a predictor is a theoretical act, even if an unacknowledged one, and even if it is only at an early stage in theory development. The corollary, however, is that accumulated evidence of how well that variable actually predicts criteria of concern, and of possible influences on that prediction, should also inform, guide, and modify more formal and more complete theoretical development.

CONCLUDING NOTE

This chapter has been a rough overview of the issues to be considered in developing selection systems. Some issues are organization- or even job-specific; others require the development of broader generalizations. Together, the practice and science require more detail. The next chapter focuses mainly on practice. The one after that may seem to focus more on science. Don't be fooled; it focuses on the science that is the necessary basis for good practice. A clear return to practice issues comes with the legal ramifications in Chapter 4. After that, the book is an amalgam of science and practice.

2

Analysis of Selection Problems

Organizational problems exist. Sometimes the nature of a problem and a good approach to it are obscure and need to be discovered. Sometimes both problem and correction seem obvious, and sometimes they are. Sometimes, however, what seems obvious is wrong, even haphazard.

Haphazard problem identification is the unpublished background of a training study reported by Lindahl (1945).[1] Operators of a machine used to cut contact discs from tungsten rods often quit during training. Those who stayed often broke the diamond cutting wheels or cut discs that were unusable; the company's engineers saw no way to modify the machine. The call for help said the company "needed a test" to select better operators. Job analysis identified hand–foot coordination as crucial; analysis of foot pedal movements identified the successful kymograph pattern shown in Figure 2.1. Lindahl said it was a training, not a selection, problem; he trained operators to duplicate the pattern. Later, the engineers found they could make a cam to duplicate the pattern automatically, eliminating the hand–foot coordination problem. The need for a test, or for training, ended as a solved engineering problem.

Analysis of work performed should be systematic, both to understand a problem and to choose a corrective action. Traditionally, most jobs have had clearly defined boundaries separating one job from others. In many organizations, work is now more flexible, less clearly defined, and more collaborative; a change that leads many writers to use the term *work analysis* rather than *job analysis*. I see no need to take sides. Some jobs still have firm boundaries, others do not; people at work speak of having jobs, regardless of permeability of boundaries.

JOB ANALYSIS

Careful job analysis takes judgment. It is not science, even when it is used in scientific research or guided by scientific thought. Job analysis methods have been developed as information-gathering tools to help managers or researchers decide what to do next. If well-developed, it yields information that can lead to predictive hypotheses very likely to be supported empirically. Most of the job analysis methods described in this chapter are intended for practical purposes, such as selection, training, promotion, and similar personnel decisions. Those purposes require the insight into jobs and work to be done—insight achieved through factually *correct* information gained through *well-considered* job analysis.

---

[1] The background was told to later graduate classes of Joseph Tiffin and C. H. Lawshe, co-directors of Lindahl's dissertation.

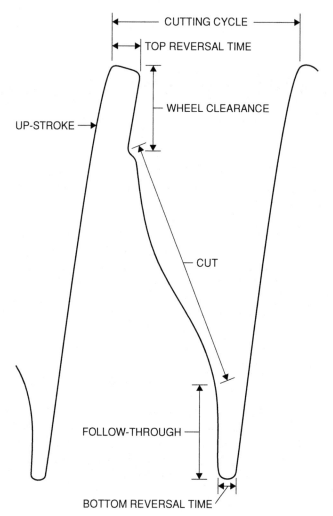

FIG. 2.1   Principal parts of foot action in a disc-cutting operation, as traced mechanically. Reprinted from L. G. Lindahl, (1945). "Movement analysis as an industrial training method," *Journal of Applied Psychology, 29,* 420–436. © American Psychological Association; used by permission.

Job analysis has a fairly standard vocabulary. Following McCormick (1979) and Brannick, Levine, and Morgeson (2007), with a few additions and liberties, I offer some common definitions.

- *Position*: Work done, at least potentially, by one person, defined by duties. It may exist as an open position even without an incumbent. There are at least as many positions in an organization as there are people.
- *Job*: A group of positions with the same major duties, tasks, and related behavioral expectations; the positions comprising a job are sufficiently alike to justify grouping them together within an organization or organizational unit. This definition does

not preclude flexibility. Different members of a self-contained work unit may have somewhat different work roles or assignments and may, on any given day, do different things. On another day, the job may require each member to do anything the group as a whole must do.

- *Occupation*: A class of roughly similar jobs across organizations and even different industries. Examples include attorney, computer programmer, mechanic, and gardener.
- *Job family*: A group of jobs similar in specifiable ways, such as patterns of purposes, behaviors, or worker attributes. Pearlman (1980) applied the *family* concept to occupations, but the term is equally applicable to sets of jobs within an organization.
- *Job analysis*: The study of what a jobholder does, what must be known to do it, what resources are used in doing it, with whom the incumbent interacts or shares functions, and the circumstances in which the work is done. What the jobholder does may be defined in several ways: tasks, classes of duties, activities, or patterns of behavior. What must be known includes job and organizational knowledge and job skills. Resources include tools and materials used (e.g., manuals or handbooks, supplies, or equipment), people who may be consulted for guidance or information, and the personal resources a person brings to the job: relevant experience, general abilities, or other personal characteristics.
- *Element*: The smallest component of work, maybe an elemental motion, or step in a complex task, or a broader behavioral category; there is little consistency in the meanings of this term.
- *Task*: A step or component in work performance intended for achieving job objectives. A task (unlike many duties and responsibilities) has a clear beginning and ending; it can usually be described with a brief statement consisting of an action verb and a further phrase.
- *Duties and responsibilities*: Activities and outcomes expected of an incumbent, including broad tasks where the choice of procedures may be left to the job holder. Duties are broader than tasks; whereas a job may require performance of 100 or more tasks, it rarely includes more than a dozen broad duties (Brannick et al., 2007).
- *Activity* (or *responsibility* or *duty*): A relatively large part of the work done in a position or job. The three words are redundant despite different nuances; duties and responsibilities may be considered less overt than activities. I tend to use *activity* to refer to a set of tasks related in time, sequence, outcome, or objective. Both activities and tasks are job components, but *activities* usually describe more general, broader components that are more likely to be shared; they may include organizational responsibilities beyond the boundaries of one's own work.
- *Essential function*: A term introduced in the *Americans With Disabilities Act (ADA)*, which defines a qualified candidate as one who "can carry out the essential functions of a position that the candidate holds or desires" (Schneid, 1992, p. 28). Equal employment regulations in the United States identify three conditions that may identify an essential function: (a) whether the position exists to carry out the function, (b) whether relatively few employees can perform the function, and (c) whether the function is so highly specialized that people are hired because of their special expertise in carrying out the function (Schneid, 1992).
- *Job description*: A written report of the results of job analysis. Job descriptions are usually narrative. They may be brief summarizing paragraphs; they may be more detailed. Descriptions based on survey methods may include listings of task

statements found to define or characterize the job being studied, along with statistical data.[2]

- *Job specification, or personnel specification*: Required qualifications for the job (or position), as revealed in the job description. Specifications can include legal requirements (e.g., age, licenses, residency), educational requirements (e.g., degree in engineering), or personal attributes (e.g., skills or knowledge).
- *Strategic work analysis*: Forward-looking planning for future work, whether at a position or broad level of work assignment, integrated with an organization's goals and operations. One distinction from work or job analysis is that it is less concerned with work observable at the time of analysis than with work as it is expected or intended to change. Previous definitions will fit under the rubric of strategic work analysis only if modified to indicate planning for the future rather than description of the present.

In job analysis, a job as a whole is analyzed into component parts. The level of detail can vary widely, depending on purpose. Detailed statements may be best for developing training programs, but general statements can be more useful for identifying criteria and predictors for selection decisions (Lawshe, 1987). Lawyers and courts often want more detail than is useful. Too much detail can muddle matters; what is needed is a clear enough understanding of the job to move on to the next step, the development of one or more hypotheses for predicting success on a job. Criterion development requires the wisdom and insight of people who know and understand the job—job experts—and those who understand the organization. Predictor choice requires no less from psychologists expert in individual differences and psychometrics. Highly detailed, cover-all-bases, formal job analysis may not be needed at all—except possibly for convincing others that the analysis was done and done well.

Information *needed* is not necessarily the information *desired*. In an age of litigation, analyses are governed as much by what is prudently filed away as by what is actually needed. Fine details may not be needed for any organizational purpose. Litigation requires evidence that a predictor is *job-related*. Failure to convince a trial judge that job analysis was thorough, preferably with results recorded in a lengthy job description based on statistical analyses, may lead to an adverse court decision (Kleiman & Faley, 1985).

METHODS OF JOB ANALYSIS

Fundamentally, job analysis (or work analysis) consists of observing what can be seen and asking questions about what cannot. A job analyst watches, questions, understands, and summarizes the resulting information in a job description. Some jobs can be adequately analyzed just by watching workers work; others require more.

The discussion here is incomplete, describing briefly only a few general methods. Most of them offer little for the emerging and important problems of analyzing work in collaborative work groups (Jones et al., 2000), or the analysis of work situations or of future needs. More

---

[2] In a peculiar pair of definitions, the *Uniform Guidelines* defines job analysis as "a *detailed* statement of work behaviors. . . ." And job description as "a *general* statement of job duties. . . ." (Equal Employment Opportunity Commission, Civil Service Commission, Department of Labor & Department of Justice, 1978, pp. 38307, italics added). Failure to see a difference between the process of analyzing something and the description of the results has caused mischief in some court cases.

detailed descriptions, and of many more specific methods, may be found in Gael (1988; a comprehensive, two-volume work) or Brannick et al. (2007); Voskuijl (2005) gave brief descriptions of methods not described here.

Observation and Interviews

Direct Observation

The most obvious way to learn about a job is to watch people work and to take appropriate notes. It makes minimal demands on, and causes minimal disruption for, the worker being observed. But it poses problems. The person may work differently in the presence of an observer, perhaps going more by the book than is necessary, or perhaps puffing up the job by adding things not ordinarily done, or perhaps failing to do some things because of nervousness about being watched. It is time-consuming and expensive, requiring a lot of time and skill to observe a sample of several workers. The biggest problem, however, is that much work is simply not observable. Questions must be asked and answered to augment and interpret what can be directly observed.

Direct observation can be supplemented by interviews or by video or computer monitoring. One advantage of the monitors is that the file can be studied over and over to verify the accuracy of job descriptions. Also, it is less intrusive and shows more typical behavior. In a study of checkout cashiers, both direct observation and unobtrusive observation of check-out activity (by a computerized system) demonstrated that computerized checkout and manual checkout were distinctly different jobs; the study also showed that obtrusive and unobtrusive observation result in different measures of performance (Sackett, Zedeck, & Fogli, 1988).

One might listen in to telephone conversations or check computer activity. One might try doing the job oneself for a kind of introspective observation, although such amateur efforts are often misleading. Introspective reports of incumbents may be useful, especially for identifying necessary sequences of job components and therefore of activities or tasks that are prerequisite to others and, in that sense, of major importance.

Interviews

Interviewing the person to be observed ahead of time can clarify the reason for the observation and reassure the person being watched. It can also provide a broad view of the job being observed and help in planning the observations. Is the work done all in one place, or will the observer need to move to different locations to see everything? Are certain crucial aspects of the work likely to be done so quickly that only an alerted observer will see them? Such questions, answered during an initial interview, can guide the analysis. Verification interviews after observations can verify (or modify) other information and may stimulate incumbents to mention things otherwise overlooked (Gael, 1988). More often, however, post-observation interviews are used to understand what goes on between things observed— the thought processes, perceptions, decisions, and reasons for occasional hesitations.

Interviews are not infallible. Results may describe an ideal rather than the way the job is actually done. Experienced incumbents may forget how they do parts of a job that they do automatically. Nevertheless, observations and interviews—and job analysis in general— can provide a lot of information. I offer a 10-item list of information to be obtained in any method.

1. A *descriptive job or position title that is locally meaningful and can make sense to prospective candidates.* If the title seems too broad for local purposes, choose a subtitle or limiting phrase to clarify initial communication about the job.

2. *The major tasks and activities of the job.* If the job requires solving problems, the type and difficulty of problems should be described, distinguishing decisions the incumbent makes independently from those requiring approval. Ways to identify components not directly or reliably observable might require some ingenuity (e.g., drawing diagrams, think-aloud procedures). Collaborative activities and the sequencing of work should be identified. It may be useful to identify things done daily, weekly, or as needed.

3. *Relationships to other jobs or positions.* What other jobs in the organization depend on the work done on this one? What tasks on this job depend on work done on other jobs? What aspects of the work require collaboration? To what job might the worker be promoted; from what background job might a qualified candidate be promoted to this one? What personal interactions are expected with people on other jobs? To whom (the role or position, not the person) is the incumbent to report? How closely is the work supervised, and with what sort of leadership? Does the incumbent supervise others; if so, does he or she make personnel decisions about those supervised or simply monitor the progress and quality of the work done?

4. *Machines, tools, equipment, and work aids used on the job and how they are used.* For which specific tasks or activities are they used? What training is needed for their use?

5. *Materials, products, or resources used on the job.* How they are used? For which tasks, activities, or problems are they are used, and how? Remember that other people may be resources for information or service or material, and that the worker's own relevant knowledge and skill are also resources. Identify resources available for use when needed even if not routinely used.

6. *Specialized terms used in the work.* How are they defined? Does failure to understand them disqualify a person for the job?

7. *Major characteristics of the work context.* These include the physical environment (particularly health or safety hazards), hours or shifts, social context, and any job-specific policy constraints. Work quality depends in part on worker characteristics but also on situational variables.

8. *Externally demanded qualifications and credentials,* such as licenses or bonds.

9. *Specific educational and experience requirements.* Expressing these requirements in terms of diplomas or degrees received or number of years is usually inadequate. Express educational requirements in terms of courses or course content used on the job, ranging from basic literacy to specialized academic programs. Express experience requirements in terms of expected knowledge or skill levels attained from prior experience.

10. *Knowledge, skills, abilities, or other personal characteristics (e.g., personality) required to do this work.* Are some abilities—cognitive, physical, sensory, social, or perceptual—demonstrably essential? What would be desirable, if not essential, and why? Do certain personal characteristics tend to reduce or to exacerbate hazards inherent in the work environment? Answers to most of these questions should be clearly relevant to performance of one or more of the major job activities or tasks; glittering generalities have no place in a job description.

The last four items in the list, as a set, help establish *job specifications (or personnel specifications)*. They identify candidate attributes to be assessed in determining qualifications for the job. As *hypothesized* predictors, research may be needed to establish validity and minimum qualifications, but some of them (such as the demand for a license) may be independent bases for selection or rejection.

Critical Incidents

Group interviews are typically, though not necessarily, used to get answers to a pair of questions, such as "Think back to a time when something was done that led to very good job performance or outcome; think back to a time when something was done that led to very poor job performance or outcome." This is not a comprehensive job analysis; it seeks only to find particular work behaviors that make a real difference. It may not be comprehensive, but it is enduring and important.

   In fact, the basic method may be useful even when the term *critical* is taken lightly. Some reports of critical incidents (e.g., in developing performance rating scales) may even seek incidents that describe routine or ordinary work behavior. It is harder to observe and to describe ordinary behavior than behavior that is especially good or poor; nevertheless, even with a lax definition of "critical," the basic method places an important emphasis on actual, observable behavior.

Functional Job Analysis (FJA)

A job analyst must distinguish what people do on the job from what gets done as a result; FJA provides a grammar for doing so. The noun in each sentence is always the worker, understood rather than repeated in every sentence. The verb—an *action* verb—is a *worker function*, something people do on the job. Worker functions are categorized under their direct objects, *things, data, and people* (TDP); the physical, mental, or social objects of the actions. Further phrases in the sentence more fully describe the overall task, as in Figure 2.2 (Fine, 1955, 1988; Fine & Cronshaw, 1999; Fine & Getkate, 1995). FJA evolves; changes

Sentence Element	Task Statement
Subject: Who?	(Always the worker; unstated)
Action verb: Perform what action?	Schedules
Object of verb: To whom or what?	Appointments, meetings, events
Phrase: Upon what instruction? Source? Specificity?	Supervisor, caller, or memo; usually a vague "set it up", perhaps with deadline
Phrase: Using what tools, equipment, work aids?	Calendar, appointment pad, telephone, or conference room schedule book as needed
In order to . . . : To produce or achieve what? (Expected outcome)	To assure presence of those expected to be present

Task Statement: Schedules appointments, meetings, or events according to instructions from supervisor or memo, or requests received from callers, using as needed appointment pads, calendars, telephone, or conference room schedule book in order to assure that all those expected to be present at the meeting or event will be able to do so.

FIG. 2.2   Illustrative task statement according to task sentence structure in functional job analysis.

TABLE 2.1
Worker Functions in Functional Job Analysis

Category	Action Verbs	Level
Working With **THINGS**	Precision working; setting up; operating–controlling	High
	Manipulating; operating-controlling; driving–controlling; starting up	Medium
	Machine tending Handling; feeding–offbearing	Low
Working With **DATA**	Synthesizing; innovating; coordinating	High
	Analyzing; computing; compiling	Medium
	Copying Comparing	Low
Working With **PEOPLE**	Leading Mentoring Negotiating Supervising	High
	Consulting; instructing; treating sourcing information; persuading; coaching; diverting	Medium
	Exchanging Information Taking instructions/helping; serving	Low

Note: Adapted from *Functional Job Analysis: A Foundation for Human Resources Management* (Figure 4.2) by S. A. Fine & S. F. Cronshaw, 1999. Mahwah, NJ: Lawrence Erlbaum Associates. Copyright, 1999, Lawrence Erlbaum Associates.

(usually minor) have led to new publications every few years. Instructions for using recent FJA models to develop an inventory of task statements are available in Fine and Cronshaw (1999) and Fine and Getkate (1995, pp. 29–41).

A small set of action verbs has been ordinally scaled for each of the three functional categories; the most recent version is given in Table 2.1. Some verbs have, in prior versions, been difficult to place in a consistent order, so Table 2.1 simply indicates the ordinal levels in terms of high, medium, or low. At the top of the *people* scale, the verb *leading* has been added in this version (Fine & Cronshaw, 1999).

Inventory Development

McCormick (1959) distinguished two types of inventories, *job-oriented* (or *task-oriented*) and *worker-oriented*. A job-oriented inventory is a set of brief task or activity statements each describing what is done and what gets done as a result. The inventory is a set of task statements, each with its action verb, direct object, and necessary delimiting phrases, for example, "translates correspondence from French to English," or "coordinates departing, *en route*, arriving, and holding aircraft by monitoring radar and communicating with aircraft and other air traffic control personnel." The action verb says what is done, its object identifies the target of the action, and further phrases flesh out instructions, resources, and outcomes. Developing the set of statements is usually an iterative process in which the preliminary statements are edited, perhaps several times, during the various phases of inventory development. The FJA grammar can be helpful in writing job task statements, even if its limits are not observed.

In contrast, worker-oriented inventories describe work in terms of behavior, not outcomes. McCormick's approach, instead of describing a candy maker's job as "makes fudge" (a job-oriented statement), describes activities with statements such as "manually pours ingredients into containers" and "observes condition of product in process" (McCormick, 1959, p. 411). The behaviors such statements describe might be required in a variety of jobs, for example, chemists, some quality-control inspectors, or bakers. In this section on inventory development, I emphasize task inventories, but common considerations apply in developing worker-oriented inventories.

Either sort of inventory is used in job survey research, especially in simultaneous studies of sets of related jobs in multiple locations; for example, in research consortia within broad industries. The life insurance industry, the electric power industry, and the petroleum industry have been among the sponsors of consortia for validating selection procedures. Job analysis in such research typically uses a job description checklist or inventory as a questionnaire.[3]

Survey instruments can be used to analyze a single job or position, but they are most useful where similar jobs (or jobs with similar titles) require people to do different things. Even within apparently standard jobs (e.g., patrol officer, firefighter, or data entry clerk), work performed may vary widely for different workers. A survey permits study of virtually all positions to determine whether there is enough uniformity among them to treat them as one job, or whether the positions should be grouped into different jobs with distinguishable patterns of activities and job specifications.

Survey methods are amenable to psychometric analysis. They call for inventories of statements that can be combined into internally consistent, scorable job *dimensions*. Dimension scores can identify differences or similarities of positions within jobs, quantify aspects (e.g., importance) of major duty categories, or help identify predictor constructs potentially most job-related. Quantification helps even for analysis of a single job or position in a single location when used to clarify the degree to which one job component is more important than another and therefore helpful in choosing criterion constructs.

Writing statements

Statements can be developed from training manuals, earlier job descriptions, organization charts, reference materials or manuals used in doing the work, or procedural guides and work aids. Information gleaned from documents can be augmented (or corrected) through

---

[3] In a checklist, one simply checks the statements that describe the job and makes no response to others. In an inventory, a response is given to each statement along a scale; the scale includes an opportunity to say the statement is not part of the job. I acknowledge the distinction, but I sometimes use these terms interchangeably.

on-the-job observations and interviews with job experts. Staff members or consultants may write statements; some may be written in conference by groups of job experts. They may be written at various levels of specificity. General statements are usually preferable to highly specific ones, but not always; what seems important is to keep the level at least somewhat similar across statements. In the absence of a standard method for doing so, I offer a suggested, but untested, method.

1. Write preliminary items, each on a card, without concern for level of generality.
2. Have job experts sort them, independently, into sets with fairly consistent content.
3. Conduct a consensus meeting to reconcile differences in items placed in the different content sets.
4. Within each set, have each expert arrange the items in a hierarchy from most specific to most general, placing the most general at the top of the stack with more specific statements below to illustrate it.
5. Conduct a consensus meeting for a final arranging of statements and to judge the similarity of level among statements topping the sets. If the experts think those statements are comparable in generality, inventory development may be complete, but items judged too general or too specific probably need editing; if the top item in a hierarchy is deemed excessively general, items lower in the arrangement may be more useful.

Using Job Experts

Job experts, meeting in groups, can write, add, delete, or edit statements. They may be incumbents, supervisors, engineers, quality-control staff, trainers, occupational safety officers, job evaluation staff, or others who have relevant knowledge about the targeted jobs. Some researchers call job experts *subject matter experts (SMEs)*, a term borrowed from research in education, but *job expert* is a more descriptive term.

Categories of Statements

Grouping statements into categories promotes clarity. Where the main purpose of an inventory, or a part of one, is to identify required traits or competencies to serve as predictors, items may be grouped into general kinds of requirements. The *Job Requirements Inventory* developed by Lawshe (1987) had 14 categories of items, grouped further under four more general categories, as shown in Table 2.2. A worker-oriented inventory, the *Position Analysis Questionnaire* (PAQ, described below) originally grouped items into information-processing categories. Categories might be broader for multipurpose inventories and more limited for those with specific aims.

Response Scales

Several options exist for the kinds of responses to be made. For a simple checklist, the response may be a check mark (or the absence of one) to show which tasks actually occur on the job. Even that simple response is ambiguous without clearer instruction. A checked statement can describe something the incumbent worker does occasionally, or does whenever the person usually responsible for doing it is not available. It might be something so trivial that any available person could do it, or so critically important that only people with specific expertise can do it.

TABLE 2.2
Outline of a Job Requirements Inventory

Performance domain	Number of items
Basic education proficiency requirements	
A. Understanding printed or written material	5
B. Performing calculations	9
Other proficiency requirements	
C. Understanding oral communication	4
D. Making oneself understood orally	4
E. Making oneself understood in writing	6
F. Understanding graphic information	3
Decision making and information processing requirements	
G. Exercising mechanical insight	7
H. Making estimates	5
I. Making choices and/or solving problems	5
Physical and sensory requirements	
J. Making visual or auditory discriminations	6
K. Using hands or fingers in work activity	4
L. Making gross body movements	4
M. Climbing or balancing	2
N. Exercising strength or endurance	12

Note. From *A Practitioner's Thoughts on Job Analysis* by C. H. Lawshe, 1987. Presented at Content Validity III, Bowling Green State University, Bowling Green, OH, November 15, 1984 (updated July, 1987). Used by permission.

A variety of response scales is shown in Figure 2.3. Responses define the measurement purpose of the scale; for example, a task difficulty scale may ask how long it takes to learn to do the task, and an importance scale may ask for responses ranging from trivial to crucial. Ambiguity remains. Distinctions between adjacent points on a scale may depend as much on a respondent's use of language, or on general response sets, as on the job.

Commonly, scales ask for ratings of importance, complexity, difficulty, frequency of task performance, or time required. Some response options show whether the task can be performed as soon as the worker is hired or only after extended training or experience. Multiple scales are used to get a variety of task information; they may also increase reliability of ratings by forcing greater attention to them. A problem with multiple scales, however, may be that distinctions seen by the investigator may not matter much to respondents. Task inventories often call for ratings of both importance and frequency of performance; correlations between these scales often approach 1.0, suggesting that they mean the same thing to respondents. Nevertheless, both scales may be necessary. The correlations approach unity, but they are not perfect. Some tasks *do* take up a lot of time, or recur frequently, but are not very important; some tasks *are* rarely done but are immensely important when needed. Their importance, as well as their rarity, needs to be known. For some statements, a scale indicating when the task is expected to be done (first day, first week, within three months, etc.) can indicate how quickly criterion data can be developed for predictive validation.

Some tasks may define jobs. A job-defining task might be one that (a) takes up the bulk of the respondent's work time, (b) is crucial to some important work outcome (something

Relative Time Spent Compared to Other Tasks
0- Never do task
1- Very small amount
2- Small amount
3- Same amount
4- Large amount
5- Very large amount

Importance
1- Unimportant
2- Minor importance
3- Important
4- Very important
5- Critical

Part of Job
1- Definitely not
2- A minor part
3- A moderately important part
4- A major part
5- A critical part

Task Difficulty—Absolute Scale
1- Short demonstration only (less than 1 hour)
2- Over 1 hour up to and including 8 hours
3- Over 1 day up to and including 1 week
4- Over 1 week up to and including 1 month
5- Over 1 month up to and including 3 months
6- Over 3 months up to and including 6 months
7- Over 6 months up to and including 1 year
8- Over 1 year up to and including 2 years
9- Over 2 years

Scales for Knowledge, Skill, and Ability Items

Relative Importance
0- Not important at all
1- Much less important than others
2- Less important than others
3- About the same as most others
4- More important than others
5- Much more important than others

Usefulness
1- Not useful
2- Slightly useful
3- Moderately useful
4- Very useful
5- Extremely useful

Scales for Job Demand or Job Characteristics Items

Frequency of Occurrence
5- Very often
4- Often
3- Sometimes
2- Occasionally
1- Rarely
0- Never

Characteristic of Position
1- Not characteristic
2- Slightly characteristic
3- Moderately characteristic
4- Almost completely characteristic

Degree of Involvement

1-	Assist	I aid or help someone else to perform the task, or I carry out the task under relatively close supervision. The other person(s) is primarily accountable for the action.
2-	Do	I perform the task independently or with very minimal supervision; I am primarily accountable for action.
3-	Do and Supervise	I perform the task and supervise others in the task performance.
4-	Supervise only	I give orders/instruction, followed up by personal observation/monitoring. Do not take part in the action itself but am accountable for its overall accomplishment.

FIG. 2.3 Examples of task inventory response scales. Reprinted from G. M. Drauden (1988), Task inventory analysis in industry and the public sector. In S. Gael (Ed.), *The job analysis handbook for business, industry, and government* (pp. 1051–1071). © S. Gael; used by permission.

would not result, or would not turn out well, if it were not done effectively), or (c) no one else does. For many purposes, selection among them, job-definers may be all one needs to know. I have come to use a response scale that combines all three. On a four-point response scale, the responses may be:

- I *do not do* the work described in this statement.
- This statement describes something I may *occasionally* do, but it is neither an important nor a frequent part of my work.
- This statement clearly *describes* my work; I do it, but it is neither very time-consuming nor as important as other things I do, nor unique to my job.
- This statement *defines* my job either because it is one of the most important things I do, or because it describes my work a lot of my time, or because no one else in my work unit is responsible for doing it.

The actual wording changes in different surveys because I want the job experts to choose wording they think communicates best for a given survey. Whatever the precise words, the scale is a composite of three scales and therefore may be ambiguous. However, it has a unifying theme, job definition, and job experts seem not to have been bothered by the ambiguity.

Inventory Research and Data Analysis

Pilot Studies

Inventories should be pretested for clarity and content and for effectiveness in standardization. Christal and Weissmuller (1988) said that not even changes in the wording of items should be made in established survey instruments "without extensive pretesting" (p. 1038). One kind of pretest asks a few people to read instructions and complete the inventory, "thinking aloud" throughout. In this process, ambiguities, unintended meanings, and other problems with items come to light. At some point, the draft inventory should be given to a sample of job incumbents. If possible, it should be completed in the presence of investigators so that problems with individual statements or response scales can be observed and recorded. The form of this preliminary inventory should include places for incumbents to identify additions, amendments, or corrections to the item list. Another pretest might preview the data analysis plans; statistical analysis can identify problem items requiring fixing.

Inventory Administration

Online administration is useful and increasingly widespread. If sampling is needed, typically in very large studies, people within units should be sampled. Systematic sampling might draw proportionately from different organizations, organizational units, responsibility levels, grouped job titles, or demographic groups to assure full representation of the variety of things people do.

The inventory may be given to both incumbents and their supervisors. The two levels may not provide the same information. In comparisons of inventory data from supervisors and their own supervisors describing the lower level supervisory job, Meyer (1959) found substantial disagreement; however, Smith and Hakel (1979) found little difference between supervisors, their bosses, professional job analysts, and a group of students. The 20-year period between the studies could account for the different findings, but maybe the divergence is due to questionnaire differences. Meyer developed an ad hoc one for his study; Smith and Hakel used the PAQ.

In any case, it is useful to gather data from both levels. People who have held a job a long time, with some autonomy, may create activities or methods not known to the supervisors.

Supervisors may expect some things to be done but either fail to make sure or to communicate clearly that expectation to the worker. A worker may inflate the nature of the job; a supervisor may disparage it. If worker and supervisor complete the survey questionnaire independently, the two versions of the job can be reconciled in meetings with job analysts. The resulting description can be more readily accepted as correct.

Sources of Error

If all incumbents give essentially the same responses to virtually all items, the job is considered the same for all of them. This rarely happens. One reason is statistical *sampling error*, inversely related to sample size. Another is *unreliability* of scaled responses; there are always some sources of measurement error (see Chapter 5). Respondents have their own sources of error—differences in values, perspectives, response styles, organizational status, or kinds of expertise—that influence responses almost as much as actual job requirements do. Questionnaire characteristics such as item ambiguities or phrases used may introduce error. Error cannot be wholly avoided, but careful development and pretesting can limit its extent. Wide differences in responses to groups of items might be attributed either to error or to real differences in jobs. Deciding which is correct requires informed judgment; there is no foolproof formula for it.

Data Analysis

Minimal analysis identifies means and standard deviations of responses to individual task statements. Statements with high means (or low, depending on scale direction) and low standard deviations are the best descriptions of the job or occupational group surveyed. However, more can be said with more analysis.

Response scales are typically short, rarely more than six levels. The proportion of responses at each level should be identified. If the distribution is bimodal, the statement may differentiate two classes of jobs among those studied, especially if there are several such statements and the differentiation is consistent across respondents. The five-point scale of importance in Figure 2.3 may call for more distinctions (e.g., between *important*, *very important*, or *crucial*) than a job analyst might need for a given purpose. If so, it might be dichotomized for that part of the analysis, putting the scale values of 1 or 2 in one category and scale values of 3, 4, or 5 in another.[4] Consolidation of categories might also be appropriate if more categories were available than were needed; for example, pilot studies may have shown that respondents preferred extra options providing minor distinctions.

Grouping Statements

Information obtained in a job analysis survey is generally used to make inferences of potentially useful (a) differentiation of jobs among those surveyed, (b) criterion variables, and (c) predictors. To facilitate these inferences, statements in a task inventory of 200–400 items—not uncommon—must somehow be grouped into reasonably independent, meaningful

[4] This may appear inconsistent with my position in later chapters, where I vigorously protest the dichotomization of variables in correlational analysis. I protest it in job analysis, too, if item responses are to be correlated with other variables or across items. However, where dichotomization leads to simplification of description, I am quite willing to advocate it.

categories. Items can be grouped before printing the inventory or after the response data are available. Data-based grouping can verify or suggest changes in a priori categories.

Statements may be classified by either judgmental or statistical methods (Drauden, 1988). Some researchers use cluster or factor analysis (Chapter 6) to describe categories of job functions or categories of specific skill requirements. Potential criteria can be inferred from job functions, and skill categories can suggest hypotheses about potential predictors. Factor analysis for job analysis inventories is widespread, but it was criticized by Cranny and Doherty (1988). Factors, they said, are defined not by task properties but by patterns of response disagreement. If everyone gives the same response to each of two statements, there is no variance, so there is no correlation; no factor can emerge. If different respondents report doing different things, or if respondents doing different things give systematically different scale responses to statements describing what they do, factor analysis of importance ratings *can* identify meaningful item groups. However, spurious correlations can result from variance in respondent values and response styles (i.e., error). Factor analysis of importance ratings does not tell whether factors reflect true position difference or spurious but correlated variance. Cranny and Doherty (1988, p. 322) concluded that the procedure is "totally inappropriate."

I prefer rational grouping. Again, I offer a procedure I think is useful, despite lack of systematic study.

1. When the list of task statements is available, and survey responses are at hand, use mean responses to identify the most critical or important or defining tasks.
2. Have a panel decide which two of these critical task statements describe the most clearly different tasks.
3. Have the panel sort the remaining statements (from Step 1) into one of three piles: like one, like the other, or like neither (presumably the "like neither" stack will be largest).
4. Repeat the process with the "like neither" pile until all of the most important or most critical task statements have been allocated.
5. Check for consistencies of responses across task statements within each group. Where inconsistencies are noted, either reassign the statement, edit it, or remove it from consideration.

Less critical items can be assigned to the groups identified from the more critical ones. This implies, of course, that the set of items seen by respondents were not grouped. If prior grouping is wanted, the same procedure can be used, omitting the first step, and asking the experts simply to identify the most disparate pair of items.

Linking Required Worker Characteristics to Activities

Inventories typically include questions about the circumstances in which the work is done and about resources required for effective performance. Circumstances include aspects of the physical environment, work schedule, safety or health hazards, and contact with other people. Resources may be physical resources (tools in a broad sense, materials, supplies and supply sources), financial resources (discretionary funds, noncash assets), people resources (people from whom information, advice, or help may be obtained), published resources (handbooks, technical manuals, job-related periodicals), feedback from work done (conformity to standards or specifications, results of inspections), or internal, personal resources such as knowledge, skills (cognitive, sensory, perceptual, or motor skills), work habits, various personality or temperament traits). Personal resources include such traits as adaptability to changed circumstances, social skills, and skill in using other resources. They also include job knowledge such as that drawn from training, written material, tables or schematic diagrams, or accumulated experience. They include special skills: how to operate a piece of equipment, how to perform a complex analysis, how to find needed information, how to use available resources—in short, how to do what the worker is paid to do. Figure 2.4 is an example of a job knowledge questionnaire.

Personal resources have come to be known widely as KSAs, that is, the Knowledges, Skills, and Abilities that may be required to do the work well. The term is often expanded to KSAPs or KSAOs (or SKAPs or KASOs for easier pronunciation), where either O or P stands for "other personal characteristics," recognizing the variety of traits that can be useful predictors of job behavior. I am not fond of these acronyms, but references to KSAs or KSAPs are so widespread, and such convenient syllables, that I use them anyway.

Many job inventories ask respondents to link KSAPs to tasks or activities. Figure 2.5 shows one way to record linkage judgments. The form from which it is drawn listed general duties in the left-hand column and offered selected skills and abilities as other column headings. Each cell represents a potential predictive hypothesis. Job experts put scale values in each cell, and the mean value was computed for each cell. A useful hypothesis might be identified if the mean value in a cell meets or exceed some arbitrary, previously chosen value.

Linkage matrices like Figure 2.5 can generate predictive hypotheses in several ways. If an overall performance criterion is to be predicted, a summary statistic for each ability column (e.g., a simple or perhaps a weighted average of importance) can help in choosing a battery of predictors. One might choose the KSAs having the most cells with mean ratings above an arbitrarily prestated value (e.g., 2.3 in Figure 2.5). If more than one criterion is to be predicted, these options can apply to groups of duties.

If job relatedness is to be determined by criterion-related validation, errors in assumed linkages will be corrected by failure to find satisfactory correlations. If job relatedness is to be determined by expert judgments, however, the duty and KSA definitions must be tested in pilot studies to assure common interpretations, and the rules for inferring job relatedness must be carefully considered in advance; any subsequent deviations must be justified, if indeed they can be, with very great care.

Job Families

Jobs can be grouped into job families using inventories. Developing selection procedures for one job at a time may be prohibitively time-consuming and expensive. Larger groups of similar jobs can save time and lower other costs if common procedures can be developed for them.

Job families can be developed in several ways. With surveys, statistical methods can be used. A variety of statistical techniques have been proposed, but the most useful seem to call on a form of hierarchical cluster analysis of responses to task statements (Harvey, 1986). Expert judgments have been used. Sackett, Cornelius, and Carron (1981) asked supervisors to rate pairs of jobs for overall similarity or difference on a seven-point scale. Analysis of these ratings gave job clusters similar to those obtained by rating task statements. Quantitative methods are elegant but not necessarily superior to purely rational methods used by genuine job experts. Statistical results are not invariant; they may depend on a variety of

KNOWLEDGE AND ABILITIES NEEDED
IN SOCIAL SERVICES OFFICE

POSITION _____ DEPARTMENT _____

Check if Needed	KNOWLEDGE OR ABILITY CATEGORY	Importance: 1 – Not at all 2 3 – Important 4 – 5 – Essential	Experience Required: 1 – None 2 – Some 3 – Moderate 4 – Substantial 5 – Extensive
	Ability to take notes accurately in interviews, telephone messages, conferences, or similar settings		
	Ability to read, understand, and use complex written materials such as guidelines, rules, regulations, agency policy, etc.		
	Knowledge of and ability to use standard programs for word processing		
	Ability to speak clearly and effectively in English		
	Ability to understand or empathize with people in stressful or emotional situations		
	Ability to understand, and to follow accurately and correctly, written and oral directions, instructions, and suggestions		
	Ability to choose, and use pertinent schedules, charts, tables, and other forms used in the agency		
	Ability to nd pertinent information in forms and records		
	Knowledge of, and ability to check for, required and acceptable information from materials and to identify inconsistencies in the materials		
	Knowledge of, and ability to perform, the four basic arithmetic functions and work with decimals, fractions, and percentages		
	Ability to use standard of ce equipment such as word processors, copiers, fax machines, and similar equipment		
	Ability to establish and maintain les in chronological, alphabetical, or policy section order		
	Ability to compare, evaluate, or develop information relative to established criteria		
	Ability to recognize signi cant changes in client circumstances		

FIG. 2.4   Selected items of knowledge, skills, and abilities from a job analysis form used in a social services agency.

Linkage of KSA Categories to Major Job Duties

In the table below, the major job duties have been listed down the left hand side. The KSA categories agreed upon have been listed across the top. Each job duty is a row in the table; each KSA is a column. The place where a row and a column intersect is a cell. The definitions for the brief phrases here are given in the help sheets; please keep those definitions before you all the time you are going through this exercise.

Each cell calls for your judgment about the relevance of the ability listed in the column to performance of the duty listed in the row. You should record your judgment as a 0, 1, 2, or 3 according to this scale:

   0 – not at all relevant to the performance of this duty

   1 – relevant, but only slightly, to performance of this duty

   2 – relevant to an important degree to performance of this duty

   3 – of the highest relevance to the performance of this duty

Job Duty	KSA				
	Verbal Comp	Clerical Sp & Acc	Interview Skill	Number Facility	General Reasoning
1. Questions clients					
2. Evaluates documentation					
3. Explains, answers questions					
4. Refers clients to resources					
5. Codes information					
6. Develops budget worksheet					
7. Calculates needs, allowances					

FIG. 2.5 Linkage of KSA categories to major job duties.

characteristics of job analyses, on the dimensions used for clustering, and certainly on the number of cases used in the analysis. Hartman, Mumford, and Mueller (1992) developed a large database (more than 1,200 people, more than 150 jobs) with job descriptions containing both task statements and job requirements; they found strong convergence of the clusters of job families based on tasks and on job requirements. That is, clustering task statements and KSAs, using large-scale survey responses, is likely to give stable results. This does not suggest that different clustering methods yield similar groupings, nor that quantitative methods should be used even when databases are small and homogeneous. In those cases, I suspect, job families based on the judgments of genuine experts will be more useful.

Inventories Based on Other Characteristics

A Bowling Green research group developed an inventory, the *Personality-related Position Requirements Form (PPRF)*, specifically intended to generate hypotheses about potential predictors among personality traits (Raymark, Schmit, & Guion, 1997). It is based on a list of 12 personality dimensions, shown, with definitions and contrasts, in Table 2.3. A sample page is shown in Figure 2.6. A companion personality inventory, the *Self-Descriptive Index*, was developed subsequently (Guion, Highhouse, Reeve, & Zickar, 2005) using work-related versions of items from the International Personality Item Pool (IPIP) database (Goldberg, 1999). Continuing experience with these instruments suggests that the PPRF is serving its purpose. However, certain social biases may influence the results of its use. Aguinis,

EFFECTIVE PERFORMANCE IN THIS POSITION REQUIRES THE PERSON TO:	Not Required	Helpful	Essential
Set 1			
1. lead group activities through exercise of power or authority.	☐	☐	☐
2. take control in group situations.	☐	☐	☐
3. initiate change within the person's work group or area to enhance productivity or performance.	☐	☐	☐
4. motivate people to accept change.	☐	☐	☐
5. motivate others to perform effectively.	☐	☐	☐
6. persuade co-workers or subordinates to take actions (that at first they may now want to take) to maintain work effectiveness.	☐	☐	☐
7. take charge in unusual or emergency situations.	☐	☐	☐
8. delegate to others the authority to get something done.	☐	☐	☐
9. make decisions when needed.	☐	☐	☐
Set 2			
10. negotiate on behalf of the work unit for a fair share of organizational resources.	☐	☐	☐
11. work with dissatisfied customers or clients to achieve a mutually agreeable solution.	☐	☐	☐
12. help people in work groups settle interpersonal conflicts that interfere with group functioning.	☐	☐	☐
13. help settle work-related problems, complaints, or disputes among employees or organizational units.	☐	☐	☐
14. negotiate with people outside the organization to gain something of value to the organization.	☐	☐	☐
15. mediate and solve disputes at individual, group, or organizational levels.	☐	☐	☐
16. negotiate with people within the organization to achieve a consensus on a proposed action.	☐	☐	☐
17. mediate conflict situations without taking sides.	☐	☐	☐
18. compromise to achieve organizational goals, even at a cost of personal or work unit advantage.	☐	☐	☐
19. negotiate with people outside the organization to settle conflict on behalf of the organization through agreement, synthesis, or compromise.	☐	☐	☐
20. settle disputes among subordinates or co-workers through negotiations and compromise.	☐	☐	☐
21. work beyond established or ordinary work period to perfect services or products.	☐	☐	☐

FIG. 2.6   A sample page from the Personality-related Performance Requirements Form (PPRF).

TABLE 2.3

Twelve Personality Dimensions Considered Relevant to Work

Dimension	Definition
I. Surgency	
I-A: General leadership	A pattern of visibility and dominance relative to others; the tendency to initiate action, to take charge of situations or groups, to influence or motivate behavior or thinking of other persons or groups of people to bring about or maintain work effectiveness.
I-B: Interest in negotiation	An interest in bringing together contesting parties through mediation or arbitration of disputes or differences in view or, as a contesting party, deal or bargain with others to reach agreement, synthesis, or compromise; a style of leadership characterized by an ability and willingness to see and understand differing points of view, and an interest in making peace and achieving workable levels of harmony.
I-C: Achievement striving	A strong ambition and desire to achieve; in competition with others, a desire to win and a continuing tendency to exert effort and energy to win or to do better than others; competition with one's self, a desire to exert effort to advance, to do better than one's own prior achievement in specific activities; a tendency to excel relative to others or to a personal standard; to go beyond what is expected and required in an attempt to become the best; not to accept satisfactory or good enough but to strive for excellent.
II. Agreeableness	
II-A: Friendly disposition	A tendency to be outgoing in an association with other people, to seek and enjoy the company of others; to be gregarious, to interact easily and well with others, to be likable and warmly approachable.
II-B: Sensitivity to interests of others	A tendency to be a caring person in relation to other people, to be considerate, understanding, and even empathic and to have genuine concern for others and their well-being.
III-C: Cooperative or collaborative work tendency	A desire or willingness to work with others to achieve a common purpose and to be part of a group; a willingness and interest in assisting clients and customers as a regular function of the person's work, or assisting coworkers as needed to meet deadlines or achieve work goals.
III. Conscientiousness	
III-A: General trustworthiness	A pattern of behavior that leads one to be trusted by other people with property, money, or confidential information; a pattern of honoring the property rights of others and general concepts of honesty, truthfulness, and fairness; a deserved reputation for following through on promises, commitments, and other agreements—in short, a pattern of behavior that leads people to say approvingly, "This person can be counted on."
III-B: Adherence to a work ethic	A generalized tendency to work hard and to be loyal; to give a full day's work each day and to do one's best to perform well—following instructions and accepting company goals, policies, and rules—even with little or no supervision; an approach to work characterized by industriousness, purposiveness, consistency, and punctuality.
III-C: Thoroughness and attentiveness to details	A tendency to carry out tasks with attention to every aspect, including attention to details others might overlook or perform perfunctorily; a meticulous approach to one's own task performance or the work of others, including careful inspection or analysis of objects, printed material, proposals, or plans.

TABLE 2.3   *(Continued)*

Dimension	*Definition*
IV. Emotional Stability	
IV: Emotional stability	A calm, relaxed approach to situations, events, or people; emotionally controlled responses to changes in the work environment or to emergency situations; an emotionally mature approach to potentially stressful situations with tolerance, optimism, and a general sense of challenge rather than of crisis; maturity in considering advice or criticism from others.
V. Intellectance	
V-A: Desire to generate ideas	A preference for situations in which one can develop new things, ideas, or solutions to problems through creativity or insight, or try new or innovative approaches to tasks or situations; to prefer original or unique ways of thinking about things.
V-B: Tendency to think things through	A habit of thinking, of mentally going through procedures or a sequence of probable events before actually taking actions; a tendency to seek information, to evaluate it, and to consider the consequences or effects of alternative courses of action.

Adapted and abridged from Table 1 in "Identifying potentially useful personality constructs for employee selection" by P. H. Raymark, M. J. Schmit, and R. M. Guion, 1997, *Personnel Psychology*, *50*, pp. 726–727. © 1997 by Personnel Psychology, Inc. Used by permission.

Mazurkiewicz, and Heggestad (2009) suggested several examples; they found bias, but they also found that frame-of-reference training seemed to be a workable solution to the problem.

The PPRF is only one example of a special-purpose job inventory. Another is the Job Adaptability Inventory (JAI), based on critical incidents related to adaptive performance (Pulakos, Arad, Donovan, & Plamondon, 2000). Others could be inventories of cognitive or social activities, specified environments (e.g., stress-inducing), or categories of work-related change. Rating traditional task statements for level of challenge, De Pater, Van Vianen, Bechtoldt, and Klehe (2009) identified one situational variable influencing assessments of candidate promotability, independently of current performance and time on current job. Inventories of a variety of environmental or situational challenges and facilitators might prove useful. (Moeller, Schneider, Schoorman, & Berney, 1988).

Position Analysis Questionnaire (PAQ)

The most widely used job analysis instrument, a worker-oriented questionnaire, is the *Position Analysis Questionnaire* (PAQ), developed and described by McCormick, Jeanneret, and Mecham (1972). It is an evolving document. Form C, made available in 1989, had 187 items, called *job elements*, each describing behavior. Earlier forms over a research span of more than 30 years included questionnaires under other names as well as two preceding forms of the PAQ. Most changes were additions, deletions, or modifications based on ongoing research. The most recent 2005 version (the "enhanced" PAQe) has incorporated major changes and brings the total number of items to 300.[5] Supplementary items included those for disability analysis, items based on the 2004 amendment to the Fair Labor Standards Act, and items covering previously omitted topics long believed to be important, such as physical

---

[5] I am indebted to Dr David J. Thomsen of PAQ Services, Inc., for providing a copy of the new form.

work positions required, stress-related items, and educational requirements. Most new items continue to describe what the worker does rather than the outcomes. A still developing addition is the PAQ Competency Library (www.paq.com, 2009), describing competencies of people from which position requirements may be inferred.

The 300 PAQe items are organized under eight major divisions, outlined in Table 2.4. The earlier emphasis on cognitive information processing (input–process–output) as a grouping principle seems less central than in earlier PAQ versions. This might be a problem for people coming to the PAQ without training, but the earlier insistence that job analysts be explicitly trained in PAQ use continues in this version.

Several differences distinguish PAQ statements from most task inventory items. A primary difference is that it is worker-oriented, not task-oriented. Each statement has only one response scale, but it is often different from one statement to the next; other inventories are likely to use a standard set of scales for all statements. Many response scales are lengthy

TABLE 2.4
An Outline of the PAQe Items

Supervisory and Managerial Responsibilities
  Leadership competencies
  Scope of supervision and management
  Coordination activities

World of Work (Environments; positions with which an incumbent interacts)
  Workplace diversity (multilingual; multicultural)
  Level and impact of position
  Organizational position (organizational requirements)
    Place within organizational structure
    Special demands relevant to organization in general
  Responsibilities
  Decision making, reasoning, planning, and scheduling (levels of responsibility)

Cognitive Skill and Ability Demands (Including KSAs, training, credentials, etc.)
  Mental knowledge and understanding
  Literacy and mathematics
  Mental and activity demands (largely demands requiring adjustment or adapting)

People Demands
  Personal and social aspects summary (Scaled "People functions" from FJA)
  Personal and social aspects and communications required
  Communications (one overall item)
  Oral communications
  Written or print communication
  Other communications
  Personal communication and interpersonal relationships
  Types of job-required personal contact

Information and Data Demands
  Information and data summary (Scaled "Data functions" from FJA)
  Visual sources of job information
  Non-visual sources of job information
  Sensory and perceptual
  Estimation of information
  Information systems

TABLE 2.4   *(Continued)*

Work Output
   Work output summary (Scaled "Things functions" from FJA)
   Use of hand-held tools or instruments
   Use of other hand-held devices
   Use of stationary devices
   Use of control devices on equipment
   Transportation and mobile equipment
   Manual activities

Physical Demands
   Full body activity—strength
   Full body activities, body positions and postures
   Manipulation and coordination activities
   Outside physical working conditions
   Indoor physical working conditions
   Physical hazards
   Other physical job activities
   Job work period

Enhanced Analysis Input
   Pay or income items
   Aptitudes
   Interests and sense of accomplishment

Taken from headings in PAQe and used by permission of David J. Thomsen and PAQ Services, Inc.

and detailed, with a variety of examples; many contain long or uncommon words. This may result in less ambiguity in PAQ items for respondents who understand them, but they can be a challenge to people who do not read well. Readability problems, coupled with a virtual change in instructions as response scales change, suggest that many respondents might find the PAQ hard to complete, reason enough for the recommendation that the PAQ be completed by specifically trained job analysts.

Worker Attribute Ratings

It is not yet clear how much of the research on earlier versions is directly applicable to PAQe; indeed, some of the early reports may be hard to find. Nevertheless, some early research, such as that on worker attributes, is still relevant to the development of predictive hypotheses. An example is research linking worker attributes to job elements.

Experts in the study of work and of individual differences rated the relevance of 76 worker attributes, on a six-point scale, to each PAQ statement (Marquardt & McCormick, 1972). Table 2.5 names a few of the attributes, just enough to suggest the broad scope of the 76×187 attribute-by-element matrix. Ratings of worker attributes for job elements (assuming the top of the response scale) appeared to be rather reliable. The median ratings for the various job elements filled the cells of the matrix. Median ratings ranged from 0.0 (*no relevance*) to 5.0 (*very strong relevance*) of the attribute for the job element shown. Table 2.6 offers only a small sample of the larger matrix, but it serves to indicate the range of importance of attributes for given dimensions. Moreover, it serves as a model for new research. New worker attributes (e.g., willingness to change or adapt to changed conditions, or ability to work collaboratively), with the added components of 21st-century work, expand the matrix.

TABLE 2.5
A Sample of Worker Attributes Matched to PAQ Job Elements

Aptitudes

Verbal comprehension: ability to understand the meaning of words and the ideas associated with them.

Divergent thinking: ability to generate or conceive of new or innovative ideas or solutions to problems.

Perceptual speed: ability to make rapid discriminations of visual detail.

Depth perception: ability to estimate depth or distance of objects (or to judge their physical relationships in space).

Ideational fluency: ability to produce a number of ideas concerning a given topic; emphasis is on the number, not the quality, of the ideas.

Stamina: ability to maintain physical activity over prolonged periods of time; resistance of cardiovascular system to breakdown.

Body orientation: ability to maintain body orientation with respect to balance and motion.

Continuous muscular control: ability to exert continuous control over external devices through continual use of body limbs.

Dynamic strength: ability to make repeated, rapid, flexing movements in which the rapid recovery from muscle strain is critical.

Interests or Temperament Traits, Characterized by Job Situations to Which People Must Adjust

Repetitive/short-cycle operations: operations carried out according to set procedures or sequences.

Influencing people: influencing opinions, attitudes, or judgments about ideas or things.

Sensory alertness: alertness over extended periods of time.

Prestige/esteem from others: working in situations resulting in high regard from others.

Dealing with concepts/information: preference for situations that involve conceptual or informative ideas and the possible communication of these ideas to others.

Selected from *The Rated Attribute Requirements of Job Elements in the Position Analysis Questionnaire* by R. C. Mecham and E. J. McCormick, 1969. Lafayette, IN: Occupational Research Center, Purdue University, January 1969, Report No. 1 [Under Office of Naval Research Contract Nonr-1100(28)].

McCormick, Mecham, and Jeanneret (1989) recommended computing a composite attribute score for each attribute using the equation

$$\text{Attribute score} = \Sigma AI/\Sigma I \qquad (2.1)$$

where A = the attribute relevance rating and I = PAQ job element response *for those job elements with ratings of 3 or above.* These scores can be converted, using normative data, to percentile ranks, but ipsative (i.e., within job) comparisons seem more useful for hypothesis development than normative scores across jobs.

Job Dimensions

Over the years, a series of principal components analyses has identified factors within each of the six divisions of Form C and for the PAQ as a whole.[6] Jeanneret (1990) reported an

---

[6] Note that the Cranny and Doherty (1988) objections mentioned in connection with factor analysis of importance ratings in task description inventories do not apply here. With 2,200 different jobs surveyed, much of the variance in responses must be attributed to individual differences among jobs, not simply to patterns of shared error among analysts.

TABLE 2.6

A Brief Abstract from the Matrix of Median Attribute Ratings for PAQ Job Elements

		Job element										
	VC	PS	DP	IF	St	BO	AM	SS	RO	IP	SA	DC
Information source												
1. Written	5.0	4.0	0.5	0.0	0.0	0.5	0.0	0.0	2.5	0.0	2.5	4.5
2. Quantitative	3.0	4.0	0.5	0.0	0.0	0.5	0.0	0.0	2.0	0.0	3.0	4.0
3. Pictorial	2.0	4.5	2.5	0.0	0.0	0.5	1.0	0.0	2.0	0.0	3.0	4.0
Mental processes												
39. Combining	4.5	2.5	0.0	4.0	0.5	0.0	0.0	0.0	0.0	0.0	3.5	5.0
40. Analyzing	5.0	2.5	0.0	3.5	0.0	0.0	0.0	0.0	0.0	0.0	3.5	5.0
49. Mathematics	3.5	2.5	0.0	2.5	0.0	0.0	0.0	0.0	1.0	0.0	0.5	4.0
Work output												
93. Finger manipulation	0.0	3.0	2.5	0.0	1.5	2.0	2.0	1.0	3.0	0.0	4.5	0.0
94. Hand–arm manipulation	0.0	3.0	2.5	0.0	3.0	3.0	4.0	2.5	3.5	0.0	4.0	0.0
Oral communication												
99. Advising	4.5	1.0	0.0	4.0	0.0	0.0	0.0	0.0	0.0	4.5	3.0	5.0
100. Negotiating	5.0	0.5	0.0	4.5	0.0	0.0	0.0	0.0	0.0	5.0	3.5	5.0
Job demands												
172. Set procedures	3.0	1.5	2.0	0.0	1.0	2.0	1.5	2.0	5.0	0.5	2.0	1.0
173. Time pressure	0.0	2.5	0.0	0.0	3.0	3.0	2.0	2.0	4.0	0.0	4.5	0.0

VC, verbal comprehension; PS, perceptual speed; DP, depth perception; IF, ideational fluency; St, stamina; BO, body orientation; AM, rate of arm movement; SS, static strength; RO, repetitive operations; IP, influencing people; SA, sensory alertness; DC, dealing with concepts. Selected from *Attribute Ratings and Profiles of the Job Elements of the Position Analysis Questionnaire (PAQ)* by L. D. Marquardt and E. J. McCormick, 1972. Lafayette, IN, Department of Psychological Sciences, Purdue University, June, 1972, Report No. 1 (Under contract no. N00014-67-A-0226-0016).

analysis based on more than 30,000 jobs. Factor scores, computed for each of the divisional and overall job dimensions, have several purposes. For the several attributes rated most relevant, the computed index can be a useful decision aid.

One study showed that people tend to go in, and stay in, lines of work in which their abilities fit the demands of the work done (McCormick & Jeanneret, 1988). If a job can be well described as acquiring and acting upon written information, it is more likely that people in the job do in fact have higher levels of verbal aptitude. This finding has major importance for PAQ-based job component (or synthetic) validity, described in Chapter 8. Another PAQ study found that the cognitive job demands moderate the validities of cognitive tests, but that psychomotor job demands have no such moderating effect (Gutenberg, Arvey, Osburn, & Jeanneret, 1983). Where cognitive demands are higher, cognitive tests are also more likely to be valid predictors of performance—an apparently obvious result—but psychomotor demands did not influence the validities of psychomotor tests.[7]

---

[7] Note that these studies were based on *factor scores*, not on scores merely representing items defining factors. Factor scores consider responses and factor loadings on *all* items, but representational scores typically use unit weights, adding the numerical responses for only those items with high loadings on the factor.

Direct Identification of Required Attributes

In most methods of job analysis, particularly the observe-and-question methods, required worker attributes are inferred from the analysis. Some task inventories include KSA lists to be judged by job experts as job requirements, providing a matrix like that in Table 2.6. With such methods, job analysis is the first link in a chain leading to specification of required attributes. More direct methods for identifying job requirements include the *Job Requirements Inventory* (Lawshe, 1987), already described, and the *Fleishman Job Analysis Survey* (F-JAS).

The heart of the F-JAS procedure is a set of 52 abilities (Fleishman & Reilly, 1992a), for which definitions and rating scales are provided, illustrated in Figure 2.7. The system

1. Oral Comprehension   This is the ability to listen and understand spoken words and sentences.

How Oral Comprehension is Different From Other Abilities		
Oral Comprehension: Involves listening to and understanding words and sentences spoken by others.	vs.	*Written Comprehension*: Involves reading and understanding written words and sentences.
		Oral Expression and Written Expression: Involve speaking or writing words and sentences so others will understand.

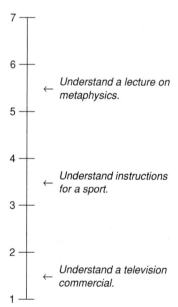

FIG. 2.7   Definition and rating scale for oral comprehension, one of the 52 abilities in the Fleishman Job Analysis Survey (F-JAS) Reprinted from E. A. Fleishman & M. E. Reilly, 1992; *Administrator's guide: F-JAS, Fleishman Job Analysis Survey.* Bethesda, MD: Management Research Institute. © Management Research Institute; used by permission.

distinguishes the defined ability from other abilities that might be confused with it. Each ability is rated on a seven-point scale with three commonly encountered tasks defining scale points. Each definer is a task recognized by virtually everyone from ordinary experiences. For each ability, one task has a high scale value, one low, one intermediate; the scale value is the mean of ratings assigned to the task by prior judges. Job experts compare the tasks required by the job with the three anchor tasks and assign ability ratings; the mean ratings define the job's ability requirements. For each of the 52 abilities, the ability is defined. The manual gives illustrations of tasks and jobs requiring the ability and, where available, examples of tests measuring the ability. Ratings are expected to be made by job experts, usually job incumbents. They might rate the job as a whole, or broad job dimensions, or selected tasks. Rating all 52 abilities is unnecessary; flow diagrams have been developed to help identify nontrivial ability requirements (Mallamad, Levine, & Fleishman, 1980).

O*NET: A Model for Occupational Analyses

The United States Department of Labor published several editions of the *Dictionary of Occupational Titles* (DOT), the first in 1933, for public employment office counselors. Counselors needed more information about occupational choices than their own experiences provided; and the various DOT editions described thousands of occupations. All editions emphasized work with specific duties, definable boundaries, and substantial stability. Changes in the labor force, employment patterns, and technology required a new approach to defining, describing, and classifying occupations. O*NET, short for *Occupational Information Network*, was that approach (Peterson, Mumford, Borman, Jeanneret, & Fleishman, 1999). Released in 1998, it officially replaced the DOT.

O*NET is intended to be a survey tool for comparing occupations in career exploration and counseling, not for job-specific descriptions. It includes comprehensive questionnaires that can be useful, and far more informative, for more narrowly focused job analyses; indeed, Frank Landy said, "No modern job analysis should proceed without a check on O*NET for the job title or family as a point of departure."[8] It combines the best of previously identified survey approaches, with both worker- and job-oriented sections, illustrated in Table 2.7[9] and the items in Figure 2.8. In its continuing national data collection program, O*NET collects information in six major categories in addition to information from a brief questionnaire on education and experience requirements. The names for individual questionnaires seem more traditional than those in the classification reported in Peterson et al. (1999); three of them are traditional KSAs. Many of the items, however, go beyond the traditional KSAs known and used for several decades. The headings in Table 2.7 include previously limited topics such as knowledge of administration, skill in critical thinking, and ability to recognize that something is wrong (problem sensitivity). Also less traditional, and very important, are the categories of work styles and work context.

O*NET is more than a set of questions; it is an extensive and continually developing database about occupations. For a given occupation, hundreds of local jobs may have been analyzed—but maybe only five or six. Reports about occupations in the database are based

---

[8] From personal communication by e-mail from Dr Frank Landy, August 8, 2008.

[9] I am indebted to Dr Jonathon Levine for providing a copy (current as of May, 2007) of the O*NET questionnaires and introducing me to www.onetcenter.org, where updated information is frequent. I am further indebted to him and to Dr Gary Carter for further helpful comments on an earlier draft of this chapter. I really appreciate them!

TABLE 2.7

Summary of Content of O*NET Questionnaires

1. *Education and Training Questionnaire*: (Questions on required educational level, experience, and special training)
2. *Knowledge Questionnaire*: (Questions on the importance and required levels of knowledge about general organizational functioning, such as administration, marketing, customer relations, HR, or production, and about general academic disciplines)
3. *Skills Questionnaire*: (Questions on the importance and required levels of skills needed, such as writing, critical thinking, equipment selection, equipment maintenance, judgment and decision making, time management, and management of personnel resources)
4. *Abilities Questionnaire*: (Questions on the importance and required levels of cognitive, perceptual, sensory, psychomotor, or physical abilities, such as written comprehension, problem sensitivity, memorization, reaction time, dynamic strength, stamina, night vision, and speech clarity)
5. *Generalized Work Activities (GWA) Questionnaire*: (Questions on the importance and level of activities such as getting information, evaluating information to determine compliance with standards, thinking creatively, performing general physical activities, handling and moving objects, interpreting the meaning of information for others, selling or influencing others, developing and building teams, monitoring and controlling resources)
6. *Work Styles Questionnaire*: (Questions on the importance of specified stylistic requirements such as persistence, social orientation, stress tolerance, integrity, and analytical thinking)
7. *Work Context Questionnaire*: (Questions on frequency or importance—or other scales depending on the nature of the item—of situational considerations such as requirements for face-to-face discussions, public speaking, or electronic communication; frequency of conflict situations; frequency of need to deal with unpleasant or even violent people; physical environments such as heat or cold, or indoor vs outside work; lighting conditions; hazards; physical requirements such as sitting or working in cramped quarters; and the nature of job demands)

Summary developed from O*NET questionnaires and items.

on averages; some averages are more dependable than others. This is not a serious problem; continuing data collection will assure that, in time, all of those averages will become more dependable. Moreover, it is not simply a matter of statistical reliability; it is also a question of the numbers of jobs with the same or similar titles. Clerical job averages may be fine for accounting clerks but not so fine for administrative assistants whose jobs are less common, less rigidly bounded, and more likely to vary greatly from one position to another even in different parts of the same organization.[10]

The O*NET questionnaires can do much to assist local analyses. Some items may be used without modification, some will require editing for local situations, some will suggest further items for local use, and some will be irrelevant to specific organizations or organizational units. O*NET has been shown to link individual job data, using ratings of jobs on the Generalized Work Activities (GWA) part of the questionnaire, to mean aptitude scores on the General Aptitude Test Battery, known to predict categories of job requirements (Jeanneret & Strong, 2003). Their results suggested that O*NET could be useful in applications of the general *synthetic validity* concept (see Chapter 8), more specifically as job component validity. LaPolice, Carter, and Johnson (2008) extended the idea using job components identified in O*NET analysis to predict performance in three different kinds of literacy

[10] Based on personal communication from P. R. Jeanneret, May 3, 2007.

From Knowledge Questionnaire

25. Foreign Language: Knowledge of a foreign language.
     A. How <u>important</u> is knowledge of a FOREIGN LANGUAGE to the performance of *your current job?*
     B. What <u>level</u> of FOREIGN LANGUAGE knowledge is needed to perform *your current job?*

From Skills Questionnaire

1. Reading Comprehension: Understanding written sentences and paragraphs in work-related documents.
    B. What <u>Level</u> of READING COMPREHENSION is needed to perform *your current job?*

From Abilities Questionnaire

6. Originality: Having unusual or clever ideas, or developing creative ways to solve a problem.
    B. What <u>level</u> of ORIGINALITY is needed to perform *your current job?*
48. Hearing Sensitivity: Hearing differences between sounds that vary in pitch and loudness.
    B. What <u>level</u> of HEARING SENSITIVITY is needed to perform *your current job?*

From Generalized Work Activities Questionnaire

1. Getting Information: Observing, receiving, and otherwise obtaining information from all relevant sources.
    B. What <u>level</u> of GETTING INFORMATION is needed to perform *your current job?*
19. Work with Computers: Programming, writing software, entering data, or processing information.
    B. What <u>level</u> of WORKING WITH COMPUTERS is needed to perform *your current job?*

From Work Styles Questionnaire

14. Independence: Working in one's own way, needing little or no supervision, and depending on oneself.

From Work Context Questionnaire

35. How much time in *your current job* do you spend <u>standing</u>?

FIG. 2.8   Sample O*NET items with abbreviated definitions of traits and activities. Items in Knowledge, Skill, Ability, and Work Activity questionnaires have two parts. **A** asks for ratings of *importance*; it is the same for all items in these questionnaires, so it is not repeated here after the first item. **B** asks for ratings of trait or activity *level*; these scales vary from item to item. Reprinted from questionnaires downloaded at www.onetcenter.org/questionnaires.html

(reading prose, documents with figures and charts, or quantitative documents). Both studies predicted mean test scores; the next step is demonstrating that GWA scores can predict measures of job component performance.

General Caveats and Comments on Job Analysis

Job analysis is not science in the sense of a hypothesis-testing, theory-challenging science —not even when it is used in scientific research or guided by scientific thought. It is an information-gathering tool to help managers or researchers make better judgments about what to do next. If well developed and used systematically, it yields reliable information that leads to logically defensible predictive hypotheses with strong likelihood of being supported empirically.

Often, too much is expected from job analysis. Insight is a legitimate expectation. Insight into jobs and their complexity is needed to choose criteria and predictors and procedural interventions that, if used, can improve organizational functioning; such insight is more likely if one acquires correct information through well-considered job analysis. The limiting adjectives—*correct* and *well-considered*—must be satisfied to have a fully convincing hypothesis.

Incorrect information is biasing. Not every job analysis must be comprehensive or even thorough, but they must be well considered. Things can go wrong in job analysis; here are some warnings to consider in preparing to do it.

1. *Different sources of information may yield different information, some of it wrong.* For example, observing one incumbent rather than another may give biased information. An unusually effective worker may do things differently from others with the same resources. People with strong verbal skills can describe tasks and resources more clearly than others—and, perhaps, embellish their jobs more.

   Job analysts using panels of job experts justifiably worry about information differences among experts with different characteristics. Research on the subject is neither extensive nor well replicated—nor wholly consistent—but some potentially influential characteristics have been studied. Examples include sex, race, performance level, and experience. Much more research is still needed on these and other respondent characteristics before concluding that any of them matter very much.

2. *One need not use* all *of the wealth of detail a complex job analysis provides.* Overall performance in any job, or any aspect of job behavior, can be optimally predicted by only a few predictors. After one or two variables—at most four or five—further variables rarely make more than trivial contributions to predictive accuracy. The temptation may be great to use all the predictor variables suggested by the job experts, but in the long run, careful choice among them is likely to yield more consistently good predictions.

3. *Job analysis tends to yield static descriptions of "the way we've always done it."* The usefulness of job analysis is not limited to describing a job as it is; it can describe how it might be, ought to be, or will be in the future. Job analyses, especially in human factors research, are sometimes used to determine needed changes in jobs and job structures, perhaps for work simplification or improved coordination across interacting jobs, but change has only recently seemed salient in analysis for selection research. Jobs are not static, they never have been despite static methods of analyzing them. Some changes over time—planned or not—can be dramatic. Less dramatic changes happen when a person adapts to change by changing procedures to fit his or her own set of skills, habits, or preferences. Job analysis should, and is beginning to, include planning for future contingencies and alternatives.

4. One approach was exemplified in a report by Arvey, Salas, and Gialluca (1992). A large inventory with both task and ability items was completed by more than 600 employees in diverse trades and locations; respondents rated both sets of items for importance to their jobs. Regression equations were developed to predict importance of ability factors from selected task statements and for developing a decision rule for predicting whether a particular job requirement would be necessary for a future job. The study was a demonstration of an idea, not a test of a hypothesis, but the demonstration seemed promising. So far as I know, it has not yet encouraged others to look for ways to forecast traits required for jobs that do not yet exist, but the problem is now more broadly recognized (Schippmann, 1999). Job analysis is a potentially useful tool for planned organizational change if it is used to redefine the way work gets done. I return to this topic after considering organizational needs analysis.

5. *Job analyses rarely recognize alternative ways to do or to qualify for the job.* Jobs can usually be done in more than one way. Early pioneers in work simplification sought a "one best way" to do a job, and most methods of job analysis generally describe

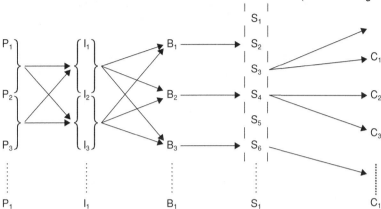

FIG. 2.9   A model for test validation and selection research. Reprinted from M. D. Dunnette (1963) A modified model for test validation and selection research, *Journal of Applied Psychology, 47*, 317–323. *Journal of Applied Psychology, 29*, 420–436. © American Psychological Association; used by permission.

one way, not necessarily the best. It is time for more attention to "if–then" hypotheses: *if* an applicant can be expected to do the job one way, *then* one set of attributes will provide the best predictors, but *if* another applicant is likely to do it differently, *then* a different set of attributes may be better. Dunnette noted the problem almost 50 years ago; he said that traditional prediction designs "grossly oversimplified" the prediction problem (Dunnette, 1963a, p. 317). His wisdom has too long been shelved because of preoccupation with the canonized oversimplifications enshrined in the *Uniform Guidelines* (see Chapter 4) and in the emphasis on means also enshrined in *meta-analyses* (see Chapters 7 and 8). It is long past time to look again at the Dunnette model as shown in Figure 2.9 and Figure 2.10. Unfortunately, job analysis methods have not emphasized options or provided the multiple hypotheses the model suggests. Meta-analysis might, but hasn't.

Figure 2.9 requires broad assessments of persons, settings, and outcomes. A score on predictor P_1 for individual I_1 may lead to consequence C_2 if I_1 behaves in a B_2 way in the S_4 setting. The same score for individual I_3 who behaves in manner B_3 in setting S_6 predicts a very different outcome. Is such complexity realistic? Many think not; in fact, the trend in validity generalization research suggests not. A conclusion is premature. Little effort has yet been made to develop appropriate data for testing the idea or for creating a more parsimonious model of it. Job analysis methods have not often looked for alternative ways to achieve a desired outcome, for equally desirable alternative outcomes, or for situational influences on either behavior or outcome. As work continues to become less structured, the likelihood that different people will approach the same responsibility in different ways seems to become greater; the greater it is, the more urgently needed is research on a contemporary version of the Dunnette model.

Figure 2.10 illustrates the kinds of judgments that might be made if an organization rejects both the "one best way" idea of job functioning and also the idea of "one best" predictive hypothesis and selection procedure. The emphasis in the lower right corner

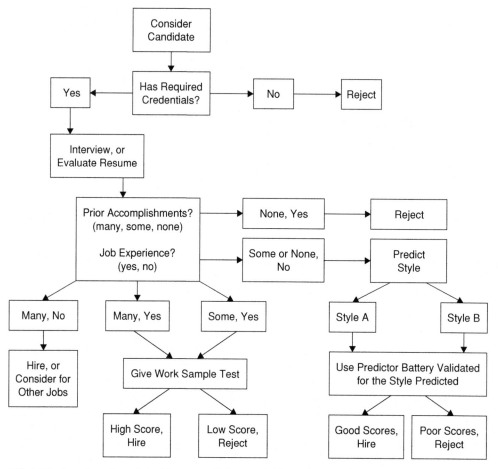

FIG. 2.10   An adaptation of the Dunnette *if–then* model for selection decisions.

of the decision path concentrates on the idea above that the assessments one might use for people expected (or predicted) to use one work style can differ from those for people expected to use a different one. The figure as a whole is based on the reality that employers make various kinds of judgments before formally testing applicants. Dunnette (1974) showed a similar picture for Equal Employment Opportunity (EEO) issues stemming from dissatisfaction with equal employment programs of the 1960s and 1970s. Likewise, a similar chain of individualized judgments could be based on disabilities (blind people might do the job using one set of abilities; sighted people may do it with another). A different chain could be based on different abilities; for a complex small assembly job, a person scoring low on a speed of hand movement might compensate with greater ability to plan sequences. Still another might be based on predicted (or otherwise likely) work styles; research might show that candidates likely to use style A will use different abilities in doing the job than another one likely to use style B. I don't know whether these if–then approaches will work or will be practical, but that's not the point. The point is that, decades after Dunnette proposed them, they still haven't been tried.

6. *Job analysis is typically descriptive, not prescriptive.* It might often be useful to describe *effective* ways to do a job. Traditional job analysis methods do not routinely distinguish between more effective and less effective things workers do on the job. They can, and should. I have seen people using traditional methods who first divide the workers to be observed and questioned into a group of highly effective performers and another group of less effective performers. Differences in resulting information in the two groups can highlight the actions and personal resources that lead to (or inhibit) effectiveness. It should be a much more common practice.

7. *No one method of job analysis is clearly superior to another.* Personnel researchers should not get carried away by a favorite approach to job analysis. Getting so involved in it that one is willing to argue that one's own method of choice is better than another is to lose sight of the main purpose. There are, of course, many reasons why people analyze jobs. For personnel research, the purpose of job analysis is to understand the job well enough to form sensible, rationally defensible hypotheses about measures that will predict criterion variables of interest. That purpose is not likely to be optimally met by any one method, nor is it likely to be met if one uses any method or set of methods exclusively or uncritically, so Brannick et al. (2007) called for hybrid methods, picking aspects of different methods that fit one's own purposes.

8. *This chapter has barely scratched the surface of the topic of job analysis.* Perhaps the most important caveat of all is to point out how little information is available to the reader whose knowledge of job analysis methods is limited to this chapter. Gael's job analysis handbook (Gael, 1988) fills two volumes and 1,384 pages of very small type; it contains methods not even mentioned here and gives more information on the ones that have been described—yet the descriptions are sparse enough that a user of the handbook would need to check out specific references to get adequate information for using any of them. Less daunting, but far more inclusive than this chapter, is the volume by Brannick et al. (2007).

ORGANIZATIONAL NEED ANALYSIS

Organizations face many challenges; only some of them call for improved selection or related decisions. Well-managed organizations see challenges as problems to be solved, and the first step is to analyze problems diagnostically to clarify their nature and to identify needed courses of action (if any). Organizational needs may be analyzed because of some problem to be solved, change in organizational goals, need to respond to new plans and expectations, or simply because it hasn't been done for a while. The purpose of the analysis is to generate plausible hypotheses about potentially fruitful courses of action. Some actions may do more good than others. For example, a specific human resources (HR) problem might be addressed, among other options, by improved selection, more training, job redesign, or organizational structure or policy changes; informed judgments of effectiveness (and costs) of the options can determine the focus of further study and action. Howard (1994) called this organizational *diagnosis for change.* I prefer an older phrase, organizational *need analysis,* because it carries no connotation of sickness; it doesn't matter much because the two terms mean the same thing.

Effective need analysis is organization-wide in scope. Organizations function as systems, and the needs and actions that appear to focus on only one aspect of the organization will also have implications for others (see, e.g., Schneider, 1996; Senge, 1990; Weisbord, 1991).

In the HR problem, the action chosen influences other HR activities, and the influence extends beyond HR functions. Effective need analysis is also forward looking; it looks for needed responses to change or it fosters useful organizational change. Senge (1990) described healthy organizations as *learning organizations*—those that not only adapt to external change but continue to learn and change in response to external events and internal experience.

If need analysis suggests that selection should be better, it also identifies criteria important enough to measure and predict—and maybe some candidate characteristics likely to predict them. It can identify a special selection problem to be targeted or one that cuts across organizational units and functions. It would be silly to select better qualified employees and put them to work with the same old inadequate training or equipment.

A General Approach to Need Analysis

Organizational need analysis is a managerial, not a scientific, function. Its immediate purpose is to generate information and options. The outcome of need analysis is a judgment (or a set of judgments) that can be framed as a hypothesis, and the quality of the judgment depends on the experience, knowledge, and wisdom of those who reach it. I offer five general questions to be considered, as carefully and with as much collaboration as possible, whatever analysis procedure might be used.

1. What work outcomes are most in need of improvement? At what organizational levels? What outcomes are most highly valued and not satisfactorily attained, and what ones are most deplored and too often seen? Whatever the answers, remedial action is needed; what priorities can be set for such remedies? Answers provide the criterion concepts for *any* hypotheses geared to improving the situation.

2. How widespread is the problem? Is it pervasive throughout an organization or organizational unit, or is it found only in specific instances (i.e., specific people or specific units)?

3. At what level of analysis (organization-wide, organizational unit such as plant or division, work unit, or individual) is the problem most accurately defined and approached? Consider, for example, a serious turnover problem. Should it be approached at the work unit level or the individual level or a broader organizational level? Should various levels be approached simultaneously? That is, is it a multilevel problem?

4. What kinds of corrective actions are plausible? What might reasonably be expected to help? What is the range or scope of sensible possibilities? Identifying a full range seems to call for the collective experience of people with a variety of backgrounds. Conferences with different people in the organization, and perhaps with outside consultants, can provide an initial list of plausible actions.

5. How effective have various options been in prior use, in the organization at hand or elsewhere? It is probably this question that gives some advantage to attempts to improve individual selection decisions when the problem is one of improving performance levels; most other activities lack the strong research base, with the relatively substantial levels of predictive power and usefulness, characteristic of the testing literature.

Insiders—people who know the organization intimately—are necessary participants in seeking the answers; this is not something that a manager can delegate to an outside consultant and merely await the report, although an outsider can facilitate the discovery of answers and the reduction of internal barriers to their expression. Collectively, participants must have a wide range of knowledge, of interest, and of technical expertise—more than is likely to be found in any one person. The best procedure for organizational need analysis may be to form a task force of bright people who know the organization from a variety of perspectives, augment them as necessary with appropriate external specialists, and let them study, question, argue, and arrive at their best collective judgments.

Goals, Outcomes, and Organizational Needs

An admittedly cynical view of the financial world of corporate mergers and takeovers is that it ignores the idea that organizations earn their existence by producing specific goods or services—the "strategic" in *strategic work analysis*, an important form of needs analysis. Long-term objectives such as brand loyalty, a reputation for excellence, long-term profitability, or even organizational survival seem to have been supplanted by short-term objectives (e.g., a good quarterly financial report). Organizational leaders may move sincerely to develop long-term mission statements, but organizational rewards that focus only on short-term objectives inhibit mission-defined progress. Such shortsightedness should concern the larger society. If long-range productivity is essential to economic growth and stability, a primary focus on the current quarter does little to foster it. Company identification and organizational commitment are not promoted by the disgraceful income disparities in some organizations but may be essential to achieving long-term goals. It may be overly romantic to say that organizations should contribute to the communities that support them—more than publicity-garnering "community service"—such as producing goods and services in the public interest. Nevertheless, inclusion of such long-term goals, and the identification of actions that help or hinder efforts to meet them, may make the attainment of the less "romantic" goals possible.

Work and Organizational Outcomes

Interventions—actions taken to improve some aspect of organizational functioning—try to achieve some outcomes or to avoid others. Economic outcomes at an overall organizational level may include profit or loss, stability or fluctuation of stock value, or market share. People-oriented outcomes may include performance (quality, quantity, and stability); workforce stability and dependability (exhibited in such statistics as turnover, absenteeism, or tardiness); worker well-being (or avoidance of worker stress, stress-related illness, or accidents); employee attitudes (job satisfaction, organizational commitment, willingness for or resistance to change, among many other examples); or responsible versus counterproductive or antisocial behavior (helping or mentoring others, acceptance of and commitment to organizational goals, or "self-starting" vs undesirable actions such as excessive use of alcohol or drugs, pilfering, theft, or even sabotage). Need analysis must ask questions to determine where the status quo might fall on a continuum from desirable to undesirable conditions.

What, in detail, is the nature of a precipitating performance problem? What morale indices are known? What is the state of equipment being used? Is selection systematic and based on valid information? Must supervisors train new people to do things they ought to know how to do before being put on the job? What kinds of work aids are available? Are they used? The answers to such questions may suggest their own corrective actions, but whether or not the suggestions are any good needs to be determined by more explicitly targeted study.

Some Approaches to Organizational Need Analysis

A systematic, comprehensive, and effective approach to analyzing organizational needs is elusive, partly because those who do it may be limited by habitual ways of thinking and long-held values. IO psychologists closely associated with social psychology emphasize the social aspects of organizational problems, human factors specialists emphasize equipment and process, and selection researchers emphasize individual differences. All of them emphasize people-oriented problems and solutions more than economists or engineers do. Defining needs depends on prior focus. Identifying a hierarchy of desirability (or undesirability) of potential work or organizational outcomes is an exercise in values clarification. What are the relative values of quantity and quality of production? Of production and employee health and safety? Of organizational well-being and the well-being of the community in which the organization exists? Organizational needs cannot be defined solely in terms of organizational self-interest; they must also be defined in terms of the social zeitgeist which, so far in the 21st century, includes great concern for the quality of life, the quality of work life, and opportunities for those whose opportunities have previously been limited. Because people responsible for different functions, or with different personal habits and values, are likely to view a precipitating issue or problem differently, methods of organizational need analysis must attempt to gain expression of different views and, to the extent possible, reconcile them.

Conference Methods

Dialogue among people with different views is an essential condition for clear identification and definition of problems—and their solutions (Schein, 1993). One method, then, gets knowledgeable people together to talk about an issue or problem.[11] Talking may range from argumentative to inhibited, whether it is called discussion, dialogue, conferring, or argument. It appears on the internet in the form of chat rooms and other sorts of virtual conversation (Stanton & Rogelberg, 2002). The approach is commonly aided by an outsider who can facilitate the process and its focus. The first product of the discussion is clearer and more honest identification and communication of differences. Others may include agreement to disagree after the different perspectives are understood. The most desirable conference product is consensual definition of the problem and priorities among alternative courses of action. The conference leader, or facilitator, works by asking general questions (often planned ahead of time), asking questions to explore or develop ideas contributed, assuring full participation, and summarizing discussion (especially during discussion when it begins to be repetitive). Conferences are not standardized.

Organizational Assessment Surveys

On the other hand, survey methods are often proposed precisely because they are standardized. Organizational surveys are used, either for assessing current situations and the members'

---

[11] Some conferences are often called *focus groups*. I use that term occasionally, but I prefer to call these meetings *conferences* because conferring has, for me, a greater implication of sharing and change in position, and possibly compromise on how best to achieve the intended end—and maybe because I have taught courses in conference leadership. Chat rooms may make less use of outside leaders; if so, that's unfortunate.

thoughts or attitudes about them, or for identifying and promoting organizational change (Kraut, 1996). Questionnaires can be developed after interviews and conferences, a sequence that assures that major questions are asked. They do not, of course, shout out the optimal corrective actions; appropriate action is inferred by people making informed judgments based on statistical results. The inferences may not be valid—they are necessarily influenced by the habits and values of those who draw them—but psychometric validity is not the main point. The main point is whether they promote broad, comprehensive thinking—the thinking that should take place before assuming that a favorite course of action, such as improving selection or training, is the needed course. The most useful need analysis helps people in organizations overcome force of habit in studying organizational problems.

Those of us interested in employee selection habitually think good selection procedures are always needed. The alternative—poor or random selection—makes no sense to us. The habit requires two qualifications. First, selection has only a chronological priority; it comes early in the employment process, before training or socialization or other steps in the achievement of organizational goals; later events and interventions enhance or destroy its benefits. Second, changes in selection or assessment practices may not be very effective; indeed, under some conditions (e.g., poor equipment), efforts to improve selection cannot work unless other problems are solved first.

Raising questions about unwanted outcomes should be systematic and ongoing (Beer & Spector, 1993). To some organizational experts, *systematic* requires careful measurement, and *ongoing* means periodic. Scheduled surveys can meet both requirements. Van de Ven and Ferry (1980) developed the Organizational Assessment Instruments (OAI) for survey research; with five components, or modules, as follows.

1. A *performance module* for recording data on performance efficiency at an overall organizational level, at work unit levels, and for individual jobs also provides a process for clarifying and assessing values and goals of organizational policy.
2. A *macro-organizational module* for studying organizational structure provides a procedure for recording data about the organization as a whole (e.g., organization chart, span of control at specific position levels); these data permit a measure of perceived authority or influence for different kinds of decisions.
3. An *organizational unit module* guides the study of tasks, structures, or processes in work units using questionnaires and records.
4. A *job design module* is a set of questionnaires for analyzing jobs or positions, incumbents, job functions, and employee attitudes. It helps in developing a task list and in identifying areas of specialization. It is more than an extensive job analysis form, seeking data on satisfaction, motivation, and salary. It also asks about individual differences among incumbents, apparently limited to the usual demographic variables and one personality variable (growth need strength); the instrument seems remarkably unconcerned with job knowledge, mental ability, or psychomotor skills.
5. An *interunit module* with questionnaires to study the control and coordination within and between interdependent work units or positions; some sample items and instructions are shown in Figure 2.11.

Organizational assessment is, like other forms of assessment, a measurement process, and validity concerns are relevant, but appropriate use of the OAI does not stop with simple scoring or tallying of responses. For example, if analysis indicated that one or more other units had "hindered" the work of the respondent's unit, further inquiry would be needed to

IN A PREVIOUS SURVEY, THE CONTACT PERSONS FROM THE FOLLOWING UNIT[S] IN XYZ FIRM REPORTED THAT THEY COORDINATED IN SOME WAY WITH YOUR ORGANIZATIONAL UNIT DURING THE PAST SIX MONTHS

UNIT 1. Name _____ Contact person _____

UNIT 2. Name _____ Contact person _____

UNIT 3. Name _____ Contact person _____

UNIT 4. Name _____ Contact person _____

WE WOULD LIKE YOUR PERSPECTIVE ON THESE INTERUNIT RELATIONSHIPS. PLEASE ANSWER THE QUESTIONS FOR EACH OF THE DESIGNATED OTHER UNITS INDIVIDUALLY. WRITE IN THE APPROPRIATE COLUMNS THE NUMBER FROM THE ANSWER SCALE THAT REFLECTS YOUR MOST ACCURATE ANSWER TO EACH QUESTION FOR EACH OTHER UNIT. BE SURE TO USE THE COLUMN WITH THE SAME UNIT NUMBER AS THAT DESIGNATED ABOVE TO ANSWER THE QUESTIONS FOR EACH OF THE OTHER UNITS. IF NO NAMES ARE WRITTEN ABOVE FOR UNITS 2-4, THEN LEAVE THOSE COLUMNS BLANK.

	UNIT 1	UNIT 2	UNIT 3	UNIT 4

1. *How well* are you *personally acquainted* with the *contact person* in this other unit?   _____ _____ _____ _____

NO PERSONAL ACQUAINTANCE	NOT VERY WELL	SOMEWHAT WELL	QUITE WELL	VERY WELL
1	2	3	4	5

5. During the past six months, *how much* was your unit involved with this other unit for *each* of the following *reasons*:

d. to receive or send *information* for purposes of coordination, control, planning, or evaluation?   _____ _____ _____ _____

NOT AT ALL	A LITTLE	SOME WHAT	QUITE A BIT	VERY MUCH
1	2	3	4	5

13. During the past six months, *how frequently* have people in your unit *communicated or been in contact* with people in this other unit?   _____ _____ _____ _____

NOT ONCE	1–2 TIMES	ABOUT MONTHLY	ABOUT EVERY 2 WEEKS	ABOUT WEEKLY	ABOUT DAILY	MANY TIMES DAILY
0	1	2	3	4	5	6

17. To what extent did individuals in this other unit *hinder* your unit in performing its functions during the past six months?   _____ _____ _____ _____

DON'T KNOW	TO NO EXTENT	LITTLE EXTENT	SOME EXTENT	CONSID- ERABLE EXTENT	GREAT EXTENT
0	1	2	3	4	5

FIG. 2.11 Sample items from the interunit module of the Organizational Assessment Instruments. Adapted and abridged from A. H. Van de Ven & D. L. Ferry (1980) *Measuring and assessing organizations*. © A. H. Van de Ven, used by permission.

determine whether the hindrance should be attributed to interunit conflict or to perceived ineptness in the hindering unit. Perceived ineptness might suggest, if supported by other information, a need for improved selection or training, but perceived conflict probably does not.

Despite the potential usefulness of instruments such as the OAI, the organizational assessment research literature seems strangely sparse. The problem may lie in the reluctance of top executives to participate in such assessments. Beer and Spector (1993), after offering several euphemisms, finally referred to *executive blindness* to describe the defensive attitudes of executives. At the executive level, "resistance to change" takes on a new and daunting meaning. Nevertheless, given the uncertainty created by global competition and domestic deregulation, organizational analysis is necessary and executive participation in it is essential to its success. It "must do more than simply add new information to the organization; it must help organizational members acquire the willingness, skills, and ability to discuss the undiscussable" (Beer & Spector, 1993, p. 644). There is no sure recipe for the "more" that is to be done. Another quotable: "It is tempting to think (or wish) that there is one best way to do a survey, but in fact there are many good ways" (Kraut, 1996, p. 149). Interestingly, the book he edited dwells not on descriptions of specific survey programs but on procedures and principles for developing and using them.

Continuous Diagnostic Monitoring

Howard (1994) and her associates told why changes may be needed (or perhaps inevitable) and ways to achieve them. In many organizations, a vague need for change (expressed by "Something's got to get changed around here") often results only in calling a meeting. Without intelligent leadership, conferences and surveys tend to focus on the precipitating problem and, like the proverbial frog in the pot, fail to notice slowly growing signs of trouble. Problems rarely happen overnight, so some organizations make need analysis an everyday part of doing business—daily monitoring of potential trouble-indicating events before they get out of hand. A variety of quality control measures may be recorded daily and trends observed. Customer complaints or commendations are recorded, accumulated, and evaluated, for individuals or for organizational units, as they are received. Personnel information (e.g., absences or other incidents) may also receive daily attention and evaluation. Elaborate change management systems are often adopted to anticipate assumed or anticipated needs, too often without preliminary diagnostic information. I'll describe two management systems, based on need or desire for change; others and their common backgrounds may be found in Landy and Conte (2007).

One of these is *Six Sigma.* According to Barney (2002), the system was developed at Motorola in 1986 because of a perceived quality problem; it was developed by a collaborative group of statisticians, engineers, and project managers. Their charge was to develop a system with extremely small chances for error; the "six sigma" refers to an event probability six standard deviations from the mean, that is, less than 3.4 incidents of poor quality per million chances to create one. Making the system work has required that employees and managers be extensively trained in a lot of specialties: statistics, some aspects of engineering and management (including cost control and waste management), and problem-solving methods. The approach has grown beyond quality control and cost reduction to encompass very nearly the entirety of organizational management.

A second system is *lean production.* Initially only an approach to manufacturing, it has also grown; it has influenced broader kinds of production in construction, education, health, and other service industries. It has been described as "a hybrid of both mass and craft productions systems" (Genaidy & Karwowski, 2003, p. 319). The system was intended to move as many tasks and responsibilities as possible from supervisory to production employees and to assign to each employee some of the responsibility for detecting defects and finding their causes.

Neither of these systems, nor their predecessors, quite qualifies as organizational need analysis, nor were they intended to. Explicit need analysis requires a return to the emphasis on diagnostics. Nevertheless, these systems do contribute more than clever names. Both of them, and several others, require continuous monitoring of diverse data, followed by routinely scheduled (Moeller et al., 1988) collaborative evaluation by people with diverse professional backgrounds. I would like to see more organization-wide programs of analysis move in such a systematic direction.

Identification of Work Facilitators or Constraints

Moeller et al. (1988) developed a *work facilitation diagnostic*—less an instrument or questionnaire than a model for diagnosing smaller work unit problems. They reported its use in work units in two kinds of organizations—university departments and sales units in a national telemarketing firm. It called for job or work unit experts to identify and reach consensus on things facilitating or inhibiting effective work within the units. The method combined the discussion and questionnaire procedures; questionnaires were developed specifically for each organization.

Another procedure, reported by Peters and O'Connor (1988), used a questionnaire to identify situational constraints that interfered with getting work done and done well. Here the emphasis was on the work of the individual rather than of the unit. The procedure considered 11 kinds of constraints, including problems associated with job information, tools and equipment, materials and supplies, budgetary support, and so on. Somewhat different principles and findings were reported by Olson and Borman (1989) in the development of a work environment questionnaire for the United States Army. Critical incidents were reported about especially effective or ineffective performance in Army jobs—emphasizing incidents attributable to situational factors not under the worker's control. Subsequent factor analysis of items suggested five factors: (a) general situational constraints, including both lack of resources and lack of information, (b) supervisor support, (c) training or opportunity to use skills, (d) job or task importance, and (e) unit cohesion and peer support.

These three studies investigate good ideas for improving job performance at individual and at unit levels, but they do not describe sources of facilitators or inhibitors or, indeed, whether inhibited performance calls for better selection or something else. If people hired by existing procedures or standards are thwarted in using their abilities, what gain can be expected from hiring people with even more ability to be thwarted? The question is mere rhetoric unless the consideration of options goes beyond human relations functions.

Work Design, Redesign, and Planning

Here we return to job analysis, but with much broader organizational perspectives. The term *work analysis* is itself a broader term. Many people still have traditional jobs with well-defined boundaries, but work in modern organizations is increasingly more flexible and less explicitly defined. It includes tasks, of course, but more and broader responsibilities as well. Work performed in one position may include a specific responsibility to represent the organization to the public. In another, it may require contribution to the attainment of vaguely defined organizational goals in ways left to incumbent cleverness. Systematic organizational need analysis can establish organizational tolerance for goal ambiguity, lead to planning for new or different ways of achieving organizational goals and, in turn, to planning or designing future work. Future work may include jobs not yet existing, or a redesign of existing work components for individuals or groups. Job or work design may be defined as "the process of bundling tasks or clusters of tasks into a collective called a job" (Brannick et al., 2007, p. 4). Duties and responsibilities, as implied tasks, can be included in this definition. Work design may occur at different levels: individual, team or collaborative group, and system. To Brannick and colleagues, it becomes system design when equipment is added to tasks (e.g., as in a man–machine system), but system planning and design can and should include social systems.

The Work Design Questionnaire

At the individual level, some aids are available. The *Work Design Questionnaire* (WDQ; Morgeson & Humphrey, 2006) is perhaps the most comprehensive, based on a wide-ranging literature survey and using careful psychometric procedures in development and evaluation. An existing job can be described with 21 different scores grouped under four major headings, as shown in Table 2.8. The authors reported research showing the correlation of WDQ scores with some outcome variables; job satisfaction, for example, was substantially correlated with all three of the autonomy scores. As a diagnostic tool for existing jobs, the WDQ can identify potentially promising areas for redesign. For as yet nonexistent jobs, it can be used as a kind of reality check when conferences have planned a new job with some specified tasks or responsibilities; the application of the 21 scales to the plan may show some implausible combinations and lead to revisions of the plan.

Redesign of Systems through Job Redesign

The WDQ was developed within a quantitative, psychometric tradition. For planning future jobs, especially at a local level, *qualitative research* methods may prove more useful. Qualitative studies collect data about research participants' experiences within natural settings (Lee, 1999, p. 27). The emphasis is on regular if not daily experience, and on collecting substantial amounts of data, much of it not quantitative, at a subjective level—attitudes, social perceptions, plans, aspirations, etc.—elaborated much more fully than questionnaire response. Qualitative research is more widely used than we usually think. *Talk-through* interviews as tests of proficiency are one example (Hedge, Teachout, & Laue, 1990). Work diaries and other incumbent introspective reports, performance monitoring, interviews and conferences (whether called focus groups or meetings of job experts)—these all call forth information about participant experience with the job or situation, and that information can inform efforts at job redesign.

Eliciting and using the ideas, and the nuances of those ideas, of people who know the setting can also prove useful in changing organizational systems. A case in point is the movement toward a major culture change in the operation of nursing homes, assisted living, and other long-term care facilities (Weiner & Ronch, 2003). A typical facility, like a traditional hospital culture, emphasizes standard rules, tasks, and procedures. Current efforts to change the culture emphasize the quality of life as defined by people who live in the facility; they become involved in planning their daily lives as part of *person-centered care (PCC)*.

TABLE 2.8

Factors of the Work Design Questionnaire

Characteristics of Tasks Performed
1. Autonomy in scheduling work
2. Autonomy in making decisions
3. Autonomy in choosing work methods
4. Variety or range of tasks to be performed
5. Significance or influence of job on others
6. Task identity; degree to which tasks are the whole, not parts, of something
7. Feedback from the job itself, permitting knowledge of how well the task was done

Characteristics of Knowledge Requirements
8. Job complexity; task difficulty
9. Need to process much information
10. Need to solve problems
11. Variety of skill demands for work completion
12. Degree of specialization required; depth of knowledge in specific areas

Characteristics of Social Context
13. Level of social support (opportunities for advice and help)
14. Interdependence; work done influences the work of others
15. Interdependence; work done by others influences work done on the job studied
16. Interactions outside the organization
17. Feedback from others

Characteristics of the Work Context
18. Ergonomics (appropriateness of required posture and movement)
19. Physical demands: strength, endurance, effort, or activity
20. Environmental characteristics such as extreme noise or temperature and hazards
21. Equipment: variety, technological complexity, etc.

Adapted by STM permission from tables and text in "The Work Design Questionnaire (WDQ): Developing and Validating a Comprehensive Measure for Assessing Job Design and the Nature of Work" by F. P. Morgeson and S. E. Humphrey (2006), *Journal of Applied Psychology*, *91*, 1321–1339. Actual scale titles used in the WDQ differ slightly from these.

The old concept of resistance to change is alive and well in such facilities where meal times and table assignments are set by administrators or kitchen staff, or where direct care workers (DCWs) are required to give a specified number of baths per day. The job of the DCW must be redefined as well as redesigned to make a system change from a management-oriented culture to a person-centered one.

Crandall, White, Schuldheis, and Talerico (2007) described such a project. The facilities participating in the project were definitely not chosen randomly. Representatives of 39 facilities attended an invitational conference to hear about the project; 16 facilities applied to be part of the project, and 10 were selected—in part on the basis of their plans to develop person-centered procedures in some aspect of their local operation. Teams from the selected facilities attended three two-day retreats for further training in person-centered care and also received on-site coaching on their projects during an 18-month period. During that time, one selected facility was closed because of too few residents. All facilities, even the one that closed, made some progress in developing actual PCC practices, and three of them were identified as *exemplars* that made major progress in changing toward a PCC culture. Characteristics of all three included: (a) increased communication, and therefore understanding, of what was important to those in their care, (b) talking with family members to support understanding, (c) flexibility in following residents' personal preferences in scheduling such things as bathing, getting-up time, dressing, and meal times, (d) direct care workers, with the clear support of others in the facility systems and at various administrative levels, were fully involved in planning changes, training others, and providing and participating in feedback to the local project teams, and (e) an organization that was predisposed toward change and improvement. Clearly, these changes could not have occurred without commitment at all levels and without subsystem support for the improved practices.

Conferences and Focus Groups

Useful culture change does not occur by chance. Someone or some group in an organization must see that things could be better and have at least a rough idea of the nature of changes needed to make them better—and the authority to initiate change. Developing that idea, and developing plans for making it happen in the organization's real world, requires work and commitment at all organizational levels. Problem-solving conferences and focus groups within an organization can define problems and objectives, plan programs and procedures for solving or at least modifying problems or for achieving objectives, and develop methods and measures for evaluating the plans. The meetings must themselves be well planned and have competent leaders. Leaders become competent by proper training and experience, but planning for the sessions may require a lot of creativity and skill in problem-solving. Most importantly, I doubt that results of these meetings would be helpful if the executives or managers who call for them have no prior intention of making use of the results.

Focus groups and consensus-oriented conferences can be useful in developing and consolidating ideas for planned change—or they might fail in the sense that their conclusions never result in organizational or system change. Here are some things to consider in planning for such meetings.

1. Be sure that participants represent a variety of points of view and of organizational roles. A group of true believers in redesign should be augmented by some skeptics. Otherwise, the skeptics can sabotage the effort.[12]
2. Plan multiple meetings. The first two or three meetings may only identify key design elements or assign problem components to specified participants. Consensus on a design will require many more meetings.
3. When a group is asked to create something new, one problem is a pie-in-the-sky enthusiasm, which can lead to new job designs that are utterly impractical or unreachable. This poses some danger, but perhaps no more than a rolling of eyes and here-we-go-again-if-we-just-be-quiet-this-too-shall-pass reaction. Multiple meetings, with clearer thinking between them, may promote some realism about proposed changes and, for true believers and skeptics alike, about what works, what doesn't work, what should be retained, and what needs to be fixed.
4. Negotiation is necessary. Organization officials may need to bite their collective tongues and allow consideration of some outrageous ideas (which, in spite of their

---

[12] Basically, these comments came in personal e-mail from Dr Diana White. For full disclosure, I identify Dr White as a research gerontologist—and my daughter, as well as my expert consultant on matters of qualitative research—and, along with Dr Tom Lee, responsible for my acceptance of, and even enthusiasm, for it.

concerns, might actually work). Group participants must recognize that some things, even unpleasant things, have to get done even in a new and improved culture.

5. Keep track during implementation. At frequent intervals, see how it is working and respond accordingly: fix what is not working or try something else; celebrate progress toward the intended changes, and celebrate the people who have made it happen.

6. Organizational support at all levels is essential if important changes are to be made. In the absence of any reason to anticipate such support, the groups might as well not meet. Organizational leaders, who are often managers or administrators, must be prepared to give up some of their own authority.

7. Consider, and plan for, systems to sustain successful changes.

Job Modeling

Identifying goals in the future of an organization or organizational unit makes it possible to develop models of jobs. Schippmann (1999) described this as *strategic job modeling*. As Schippmann clarified the term, "Strategic context variables are the array of characteristics that define the environment in which a business operates, *describe the collective aspirations for the future*, and detail the game plan from the current situation to the envisioned future state" (p. 20, emphasis added). Strategic job modeling was outlined in seven "steps" that are not necessarily sequential since some can occur simultaneously. The wording here is my very abbreviated and subjective choice; it may not match Schippmann's meaning at all:

1. Clarify organizational vision and strategies and desired outcomes. (Crucial, hence the above emphasis.)

2. Identify resources required to achieve the outcomes: for example, what information is needed, how to get it, and the targeted level of detail.

3. Decide which population of jobs (from executive level to hourly-paid) to target; identify associated sources of information about them.

4. Form questions to be answered in interviews or focus groups (going well beyond ordinary job analysis questions to far-reaching questions about context), and decide who will be asked to provide the answers (e.g., observers, incumbents, or visionaries).

5. Planning how information acquired from the interviews or focus groups will be organized, and how the results will be analyzed.

6. Develop and use survey questionnaires as follow-ups to interviews or focus groups.

7. Determine how survey responses will be analyzed and how results will be displayed, i.e., what empirical job models can describe work activities, competencies (or, I think, KSAPs), and their "strategic" context.

This is, obviously, a detailed procedure requiring a big investment of time and money. In a context of extremely rapid change, the whole pattern (as Schippmann recognized) may have changed by the time the models can be developed. But the basic questions this procedure asks can be asked in other procedures, and they reinforce several positions taken in this chapter: (a) that someone in authority must have and promote an idea—a vision, if you will—of how things in an organization could be improved, (b) that jobs can be designed or redesigned in ways that lead to such improvements, and (c) that the broad context in which work is done is as crucial to an understanding of that work as the activities, responsibilities, and tasks themselves.

CONCLUDING NOTE

Once upon a long time ago, a company owner or official could see that the organization needed some new members, line up potential employees, walk back and forth looking at them, and choose some just by pointing a finger at the chosen ones. No more. Jobs and organizations are more complex, and no one official is likely to identify among the available candidates those most likely to fit both. A first step now is to have a clear understanding of jobs, broader work activities, and organizational futures, and that understanding requires analysis of jobs and of organizational needs. This chapter has considered only that first step. In it, I have tried to make clear that the first step can be taken in a variety of ways; there is no "one best way" to analyze jobs or organizational needs for change; I've given a smattering of information about several approaches and, in any given situation, one of them may seem to work better than some of the others. The basic principle is to avoid tunnel vision. Intense focus on one problem to the exclusion of others, even related ones, may wind up with a solution that solves that one problem but also creates brand new, potentially worse problems elsewhere in the organization. A worse form of tunnel vision is to focus so much on one's own expertise that one is not able to recognize a variety of solutions and choose one (or some) that apparently promises better results. It may be decided that better personnel decisions (e.g., selection decisions) are needed. If so, job, work, and organization analyses identify the kinds of behavior or outcomes that are to be changed (for the better, of course)—and, it is hoped, the kinds of personnel assessments that may lead to such change. That moves us to the next chapter.

3

Developing the
Predictive Hypothesis

Most, but not all, personnel decisions are explicitly or implicitly based on predictions of work-related behavior or outcomes. An explicit approach to prediction calls first for a decision about the performance or results considered important (traditionally called the criterion) and then identifying one or more good bets among candidate characteristics for predicting it. Matching a criterion and probable predictor is a "predictive hypothesis," for example, that overall job performance is predictable from general mental ability.[1] In personnel psychology, we like to think that such a hypothesis focuses on individuals, but the focus is really on groups, such as groups of applicants. Within the group studied we may say, for example, that *in general* people who are assessed at some optimal predictor level perform better than those assessed at some sub-optimal level. *In general*, evidence may support the truth of what we say, but a specified person may perform much better or much more poorly than predicted by the general trend, and not always by chance.

Traditionally, such deviations are treated as errors; the inconvenient fact is that "errors" often occur because the simple hypothesis (one predictor, one criterion—a bivariate hypothesis) is inadequate. More accurate predictions might be based on alternative or more completely specified hypotheses. For the sake of clarity, this chapter emphasizes bivariate hypotheses, but be aware that more useful predictive hypotheses are likely to include multiple predictors and maybe even multiple criteria.

This chapter also emphasizes *constructs*—ideas "constructed" in an imagination informed by scientific data, general knowledge, or relevant experience—more than their measures. In that respect, it is somewhat conventional; measures tend to be assessments of traits or attributes. It is also limited to work-related predictions. Decisions may be based on policy, such as rewarding seniority when "deselecting" in downsizing, Legal requirements, such as licenses, are not based on explicit predictions, so they need no predictive hypothesis and are irrelevant to this chapter.

A predictive hypothesis describes an expected relationship extending over time; it suggests candidate characteristics at decision time potentially related to future behavior or achievement of those candidates. Typically, hypotheses are tested by correlation coefficients. Sometimes these statistics are not trustworthy (e.g., if based on only a few cases, having a defective criterion, or other data-collection problems), and sometimes they cannot even be computed in an operational setting. However, predictive hypotheses can and should be developed carefully even if they are not empirically testable.

---

[1] General mental ability, intelligence, and several other words seem interchangeable, although some people detect different nuances. Absence of a standard vocabulary is sometimes a problem, more often just an annoyance.

A predictive hypothesis is not simply a hunch. It is developed from a set of judgments. The first is a judgment of the kinds of work-related behavior or outcomes worth predicting; these are criteria. The second is a decision about how broadly or inclusively a criterion construct should be defined. The third is a choice of one or more descriptive constructs considered most likely to predict the chosen criterion. Possible criterion and predictor constructs stem largely from job and need analysis and from more general knowledge of the psychology of individual differences. This chapter describes general criterion and predictor constructs—in taxonomies when possible.

Most taxonomies describe broadly inclusive constructs; narrower may be more specific constructs, maybe facets of broader categories. Hypotheses are sometimes formed in broad categories, but sometimes with more narrowly defined constructs. For example, designers of animated computer displays do many different things, so a broad measure of overall job performance may be the valued criterion, predicted by general cognitive ability. If one aspect of performance is considered key to everything else, however, such as skill in detecting design inconsistencies, the narrower skill criterion may be predicted by more narrowly specified perceptual skill constructs.

Binning and Barrett (1989) provided a useful framework for developing a predictive hypothesis in a system for personnel decisions. It requires theoretically based inferences about relationships between predictors and criteria. With my own modifications in terms and numbering, Figure 3.1 follows their presentation for five of the inferences.[2]

- *Inference 1:* that a predictor *construct* is related to a criterion *construct*, a form of job behavior or a result of behavior. This describes the predictive hypothesis at a conceptual level, not directly testable.
- *Inference 2:* that a predictor *measure X* is related to *criterion* measure Y. It is an empirical relationship, expressible mathematically, and therefore empirically testable.

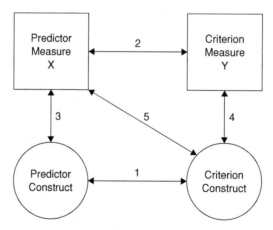

FIG. 3.1   Basic linkages in the development of a predictive hypothesis. Adapted from J. F. Binning and G. V. Barrett (1989). Validity of personnel decisions: A conceptual analysis of the inferential and evidential bases. *Journal of Applied Psychology, 74,* 478–494. © American Psychological Association. Adapted with permission.

---

[2] The full Binning and Barrett (1989) model has nine inferences; I have renumbered the five of them included in this limited discussion of the model.

- *Inference 3:* that a predictor *measure X* is a valid measure of, or reflection of, the predictor *construct*.
- *Inference 4:* that a criterion *measure Y* is a valid measure of, or reflection of, the criterion *construct*.
- *Inference 5:* that a predictor *measure X* is related to the criterion *construct* in a manner consistent with its presumed relationship to the criterion *measure Y*. This is the key inference for both theory and practice.

Much can be added to this framework. Binning and Barrett (1989) did so, but I stop here. Inference 5 (Inference 9 in their full model) is the basic operational hypothesis. It rests on the reasonableness of Inference 1, the inferred relationship between two hypothetical constructs not directly measurable, and of Inference 3, what I will call the psychometric validity of the predictor. Hypothesis development begins with the constructs of Inference 1. Constructs with a documented history of usefulness are often good choices, but familiar constructs may not seem quite right for the situation at hand. If so, informed imagination and creative thinking, plus relevant research, can lead to alternatives. Within an occupation, industry, or organization, folk-constructs (Borman, 1987) may arise within the setting. They should not be ignored in hypothesis development just because they do not seem to have research backgrounds (cf. Kelly, 1955).

BOUNDARIES OF A PREDICTIVE HYPOTHESIS

A predictive hypothesis is not likely to assert a universal truth. It may be intended to hold only within boundaries. It may be found to generalize widely across situations, but only after tests of similar hypotheses accumulate enough studies to justify comparison. Therefore, for practical purposes, the organization or organizational unit is a boundary condition. Specifying other boundaries requires understanding of the work to be done (from direct experience or job analysis), knowledge of the organization and its needs, and knowledge of relevant psychological and psychometric research and its implications. Within an employing organization, a predictive hypothesis does not necessarily depend on psychological theory. A predictive hypothesis can be proposed by workers or managers who may lack psychological and psychometric background but who know the work. It, too, can be worth testing.

Specification of Definitions

Predictors and criteria can be defined at two levels, conceptual and operational. Hypothesis formation begins with conceptual definitions of the constructs. At the level of Inference 1, for example, the hypothesis might be, "Quality of performance is a function of ability to make fine, precise manipulations of small objects." Performance quality is a criterion construct; the predictor construct is the ability to make fine, precise manipulations of small objects. The hypothesis, at this level, is not testable because no measurement operations are specified. If the predictor construct is more precisely defined as finger dexterity, its operational definition is usually a score on a standardized test. The term *finger dexterity* is more precise than it might seem. French (1951, p. 208) defined it as "the rapid manipulation of objects with the fingers" and distinguished it from "manual dexterity" (which involves larger arm movements not part of finger dexterity) and from "aiming" (which requires accurate eye–hand positioning).

Predictors may or may not be chosen to fit construct definitions. Inventories, interviewers' judgments, tests, and other predictors are often used because they seem appropriate intuitively or because they were useful somewhere else. I do not disparage predictors that work even without formal construct matching. I believe, however, that knowing what they mean can promote better measures and predictions—and help defend the choice in court.

Specification of Level of Analysis

At an individual level of analysis, each variable is measured for each person. At a work unit level, data describe units, not individuals. By definition, turnover is a work unit variable, the rate at which people leave the unit and must be replaced. Unit-level predictors might be group characteristics or situational variables with an impact on the group. Leaving the job (or not) is an individual level variable; a person quits or stays; predictors are individual traits. Turnover may be a multilevel relationship, with individual differences in traits and unit differences in turnover. A predictive hypothesis (but not a bivariate one) about reducing turnover by better selection might consider both individual traits that might lead people to stay or quit and group (or situation) characteristics that might cause them to stay or quit.

On this one relatively simple issue, therefore, at least three kinds of predictive hypotheses can be developed: individual level, group level, and multilevel. Hypothesis developers need to specify which kind they intend.

Specification of Population

To whom does the hypothesis apply? Anyone? Only experienced people? New entrants into the labor pool? People with required credentials (e.g., degrees or licenses)? Survivors of a hurdle, such as a basic screening test? In short, who is an applicant? The question has both legal and technical implications. Definitions of applicant populations are elusive, but the basic idea is a population to which research results should generalize, perhaps a demographic mix; or prior conditions, such as credentials or passing a screening test, or by intended assignments, such as assignments to work in other countries or cultures, among others.

Specification of Time Intervals

Usually (not always), criteria collected after a few months, or perhaps within a year or two, are predicted better than those collected after longer intervals. Murphy (1989) suggested that validities and most valid predictors change with changes in career stage from a *transitional* stage of new learning to a *maintenance* stage of doing more or less routinely what had been learned. Cognitive variables, for example, may be better predictors of performance in transitional stages and motivational predictors better in maintenance stages. Helmreich, Sawin, and Carsrud (1986) found that achievement motivation did not predict performance well until after a "honeymoon" period—akin to Murphy's transitional period. For some jobs, the learning period may go on and on; Ghiselli (1956) identified a job in which performance improved linearly for six years.

The "learning period" is a period of change in knowledge or skill. Individual differences in rate of learning may be expected in some jobs, so a concept of intraindividual change may be the criterion construct in some hypotheses. Chan (2002) discussed the implications of nine questions to be asked when developing intraindividual change hypotheses. With brutal abbreviation (and maybe distortion), they are:

1. Is observed change (or group differences in change) systematic or due to unreliability?
2. Is the change reversible? (In the case of new learning, is it quickly forgotten?)
3. Does change occur in a single path or in multiple paths?
4. Is it gradual or precipitate, or does it make sudden leaps (or drops) in successive periods of time?
5. Is it absolute on a constant scale, or on a person's own subjective scale, or is it a change in the construct?
6. Is it a phenomenon of the individual or of a group?
7. Can interindividual differences in intraindividual change be predicted?
8. Do cross-domain relationships change over time?
9. Do variables related to the change vary or do they remain consistent across groups?

Longitudinal modeling is uncommon in personnel research. Nevertheless, predictive hypotheses should give more attention to the fact that people can, and often do, change over time. Much has been said in recent decades about a lack of stability in jobs; they change. People change too, and the likelihood of change and of individual differences in change (as in Question 7) can be quite important in hypothesis formation.

Specification of Functional Relationships

The term *functional relationship* implies that the level of one variable Y varies "as a function of" variation in another variable X. The relationship (i.e., the function) can be expressed as a mathematical equation. Functions are discussed in more detail in Chapter 7, but two associated issues should not wait for that discussion.

One is the traditional assumption (deliberately or by default) that the function is linear. There are good reasons for the assumption, but there are also reasons for considering alternatives. Figure 3.2 shows four examples of simple but plausible functional relationships. Panel *a* describes the common linear function in which any difference in X always has a corresponding difference in Y; that is, adding a point to a score implies the same added level of criterion performance—identical whether the point is added to a low score, a moderate one, or a high one. In panel *b*, this is not true in the higher predictor levels; adding a point to the lower predictor scores is associated with a bigger criterion difference than at higher score levels where the curve may be asymptotic to some criterion level. Panel *c* shows a similar loss of advantage at both lower and higher score levels; that is, differences in actual predictor levels in either a low-scoring or a high-scoring range have only trivial counterparts in criterion performance, whereas predictor differences in the middle range are associated with substantial criterion differences. Panel *d* shows a functional curve where the very low scorers, and the very high scorers as well, perform more poorly than those in an intermediate range; this sort of functional relationship was found between certain "dark side" personality traits and leadership performance (Benson & Campbell, 2007). Failure to consider alternatives to linear functions in forming predictive hypotheses means that personnel research fails to test them. Investigations of nonlinear options have frequently appeared in recent literature, such as "growth trajectories" (Thoresen, Bradley, Bliese & Thoresen, 2004) or the "Eureka effect" (Keil & Cortina, 2001), both described in Chapter 10. Some are made possible by new statistical methods. A serious student of personnel assessment should move beyond the simple curves of Figure 3.2.

A second issue, mentioned in Chapter 2, is the oversimplification inherent in assuming a single best way to do a job. A variety of traits may be relevant to performance, and it may

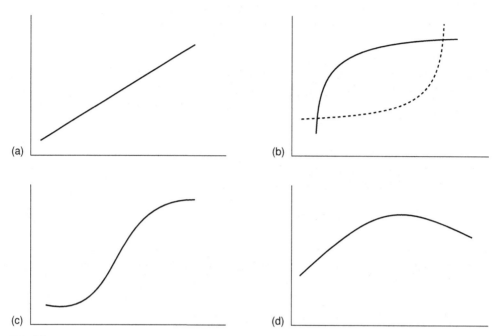

FIG. 3.2   Four examples of functional relationships.

be that different traits are helpful to different people. For example, older typists may make fewer keystrokes per minute than their younger colleagues, yet they may type just as much material by absorbing more when they scan the text.

Symbiosis of Theory and Practice

Professional practice is central to applied psychology, but continued application without understanding never improves. Theory is understanding—or the attempt to understand. The Binning and Barrett (1989) model is theoretical in calling for understanding, beginning with the constructs. Defining constructs with some clarity leads to understanding *why* assessment of a certain trait should predict subsequent performance. If it does *not* predict as logically expected, one must change one's understanding of the criterion, the predictor, or both; progress results. Figure 3.1 illustrated inferences in the abridged Binning and Barrett theoretical model it presented.

Inference 2 in Figure 3.1 implies criterion-related validation, but tests of it, even if possible, are not always necessary. What *is* always necessary is support for Inference 5. That support requires, first, a clearly formed, rationally defensible predictive hypothesis (Inference 1 in Figure 3.1). Second, it requires evidence that the predictor measure is a valid measure of the predictor construct (Inference 3). That is generally called construct validity, "the *sine qua non* of theory development" (Hackman, 2009, p. 312). If Inferences 1 and 3 can be defended well, local validation research for Inference 2 may be superfluous at best and misleading at worst. The supported theory of Inference 5 is much more convincing.

Some selection procedures are intended to be samples, not predictors, of actual performance content. Even a defined content domain to be sampled is a kind of theory in that it includes some components, and excludes others, because of ideas about the domain to be sampled. "The resulting domain definition can be considered, in rather overly-elegant terms, a 'theory of the attribute.' It may not be a particularly elegant theory, it may not be based on extended prior research, but it does need some thought about the boundaries of the meaning of scores describing performance on a resulting content sample" (Guion, 1987b, p. 208). A theory of an attribute (a construct) defines, among other things, a content domain, a critically important part of criterion designation (Ilgen & Schneider, 1991).

I'm often a tad uncomfortable in ambiguous conversations about theory. I relieve that discomfort a bit by using and ordering my own definitions of related terms. I see *theory* as an integrated collection of generalizable data (facts) and related ideas. A *hypothesis* is one of those ideas about a relationship or an event, whether empirically supported or not yet tested; it, too, should be somewhat generalizable. A *rationale* is a logical line of reasoning, not necessarily with empirical foundation. I think of hypotheses and rationales as steps in theory building; either, if logical and at least partially supported, can lead to a broader theory. There is a point to this digression: developing a predictive hypothesis for a given situation may be informed by existing, general theory, by a tentative narrower theory, by a limited but general hypothesis, or by a rationale informed by careful work analysis. These all require serious thought. Developing the hypothesis is not a chore to be taken casually.

CRITERIA: WHAT TO BE PREDICTED

A *criterion* is a "dependent variable, the variable to be predicted" (English & English, 1958, p. 130). Some criteria are construct-related. Others are work-related. Others are candidate-related (Guion, 1997). Construct-related criteria are used in hypotheses to confirm or disconfirm the meaning of scores intended to be measures of specified constructs (e.g., eye–hand coordination). These differ from work-related criteria (e.g., production errors) to be predicted as a basis for personnel decisions; a work-related criterion is deemed organizationally important enough to predict and is hypothesized to be predicted from measures such as test scores but not "redundant" to them (Austin & Villanova, 1992, p. 838). Candidate-related criteria are focused on candidate well-being such as job satisfaction or stress avoidance (for more, see Schuler, Farr, & Smith, 1993; Warr, 2007). The focus here is on work-related criteria.

A criterion on which nearly everyone performs at about the same level does not allow different predictions from different scores. Predicting individual criterion performance requires individual differences—variance. With little or no variance, and therefore little or no correlation, something different is needed, such as better training or job redesign.

The "Criterion Problem"

"The criterion problem continues to lead all other topics in lip service and to trail most in terms of work reported" (Wallace & Weitz, 1955, p. 218). More than half a century later, it is still true. It is still commonplace to bemoan the criterion problem. What, exactly, is the problem? Austin and Villanova (1992) surveyed the criterion problem since 1917; my discussion of it draws from them and is also influenced by the writings and speeches of, and conversations with, S. Rains Wallace, who believed that too much emphasis is placed on criterion usefulness and too little on understanding (Thayer, 1992). The problem is, at root, a long history of doing things backwards, that is, of choosing a test or other predictor and then trying to decide what it might predict (Guion, 1997). The result is accepting any performance measure that might be lying around as the criterion, caring little about its meaning.

Early studies reported a variety of criteria, and the validity of a predictor depended on the criterion measure used (Severin, 1952). Should the criterion be narrow and homogeneous, or should it be as inclusive and general as possible? Nagle, citing Toops (1944), considered a single, unitary criterion "indispensable" (1953, p. 278). However, Toops also said that criteria are *not* unidimensional—that efforts should be made to predict *profiles* of success. This widely ignored view still seems worth developing.

Some writers have been impatient with insistence on a single, overall criterion. Long ago I urged simultaneous, independent prediction of several criteria, arguing that (a) dimensions of job performance and performance consequences are often too independent for meaningful combination, and (b) "the relative importance of these independent criteria ought not be judged prior to validation research—as is so commonly done in the development of 'composite' criteria—but ought to instead be judged *after* the empirical data are in, at the time these data are to be used" (Guion, 1961, p. 149). Similarly, Dunnette called on researchers to give a higher priority to understanding than to prediction, arguing that much "research has gone astray because of an overzealous worshiping of *the* criterion with an accompanying will-o-the-wisp searching for a best single measure of job success . . . I say: junk *the* criterion! Let us cease searching for single or composite measures of job success and proceed to undertake research which accepts the world of success dimensionality as it really exists" (Dunnette, 1963b, p. 252).

To round out these historic quotations, however, a differing one is needed. A personnel researcher "should, ideally, weight criterion elements, regardless of their intercorrelations, into a composite representing an economic construct in order to achieve his practical goals, and, at the same time, he should analyze the relationships between predictors and separate criterion elements in order to achieve his psychological goals" (Schmidt & Kaplan, 1971, p. 432).

Practicality is in the eye of the beholder. Long-range planning committees, financial officers, design engineers, production engineers, and marketing or human resources managers may all have different views. An organization has many constituencies; differences in their practicalities may require different predictive hypotheses, each with a different criterion (Villanova, 1992). Maybe the pendulum really is "swinging again" toward multiple criteria (Guion, 1998, p. 110).

Criterion Constructs

Criteria are measures of behavior, performance, or results important to the organization and to the decisions to be made. Events and results of behavior worth counting, recording, and predicting may include accidents, quitting, completion of training, or receipt of letters of commendation. The meanings of such measures are often unclear.

Absence (or absenteeism) illustrates the problem. The number of days at or away from work, or the number of absences over a stated time period, is hard to explain in construct terms. Absence was once thought to mean *withdrawal from an aversive situation*, especially if the number of days absent approaches the total number of absences. In this view, being late is a mild form of withdrawal, being absent is a stronger form, and quitting is the ultimate withdrawal. Other interpretations have included poor socialization, failure to adapt to job demands, or a deliberate choice to go to work or not. In self reports of reasons for absence, nurses in two hospitals most often cited minor illness; tiredness and family demands were also named (Hackett, Bycio, & Guion, 1989). Reasons for absence may not be readily apparent. Even classifying absences as necessary or avoidable is difficult. The day after a major blizzard in my town, a custodial employee responsible for maintaining chemical balance in the campus swimming pool managed to walk across nearly two miles of car-high snow drifts to get to the pool. He got to work, so were the absences of others avoidable?

Why would an organization want to predict something with such questionable meaning? One reason is economic; absence is expensive. It is still psychological, but is escape from work clearly indicated by absence? Probably not; it may depend as much on the situation as on the person. A candidate's history of withdrawal, with many possibly avoidable absences, may be explained by a general tendency to escape unpleasantness. Or perhaps the construct of relative responsibility is the construct of interest, but absenteeism may not measure it well.

Starting with the measure (e.g., counting absences), and then trying to determine what it means, is the wrong way to go. To form the hypothesis, it makes more sense to specify first the criterion *concept* or *construct*. Only when the concept is reasonably clear can a measure of it be proposed, tried, and evaluated. With a construct as complex as responsible work behavior, a composite of several measures (maybe including attendance) may be useful. Predicting one component, in short, may be less useful, and less well done, than predicting a *pattern* of behaviors tapping a common and clearly defined construct.[3]

Many criterion constructs have been used. Table 3.1 lists 11 performance dimensions (constructs) suggested by Ng and Feldman (2008) and Van Iddekinge and Ployhart (2008), among others. Many of these constructs are complex, convenient composites of behavior or

TABLE 3.1
Work-Related Criterion Constructs Used in Recent Research

- *Performance of Core (Assigned) Tasks:* the level of success in doing the things the organization pays one to do.[a]
- *Adaptive Performance:* the degree of change in work behavior in response to changing work demands.[b,c]
- *Creativity:* the degree to which new and useful ideas for improvements are generated.[a]
- *Performance in Training Programs:* the rate of learning new material in relatively formal training.[a]
- *Organizational Citizenship Behavior:* the extent of engagement in a variety of behaviors supportive of the organizational environment.[a,b]
- *Safety Performance:* the extent of compliance with safety rules and the demonstration of safe workplace behavior.[a]
- *General Counterproductive Work Behavior:* the extent of behavior disruptive to smooth organizational functioning.[a,b]
- *Workplace Aggression:* the existence, extent, or severity of behaviors at work or in the workplace that intentionally harm coworkers, former colleagues, or previous employers or that intentionally harm the reputation of the employers or organization.[a]
- *Substance Abuse:* use of illegal drugs or alcohol on the job or at the workplace.[a]
- *Tardiness:* habit of being late for work.[a]
- *Absenteeism:* frequency of failure to show up for work.[a]

Explicitly suggested in [a] Ng and Feldman (2008) or [b] Van Iddekinge and Ployhart (2008). [c] See also Table 3.3.

---

[3] Criteria may be economic; reducing costs, such as absenteeism or other unwanted events, can be immensely practical. However, the principle applies to economic as well as to psychological constructs. There are differences in the kinds of costs to be controlled and in the mechanisms for controlling them. A clear definition of a construct, economic or psychological, permits more valid measurement of it.

outcomes deemed important and reasonably similar. They are informed by prior research, as seen by two pairs of reviewers. Table 3.1 can not be viewed as a systematic, comprehensive list—but it is a practical thought starter.

Theories of Performance

An early theory, or model, of performance was proposed by Hunter (1983). Stripped to essentials, the model stated that performance depended largely on job knowledge, which depended largely on cognitive ability. Job experience (seen as opportunity to learn) was a later addition to the model, influencing both job knowledge and performance on work samples (Schmidt, Hunter, & Outerbridge, 1986).

Campbell, McCloy, Oppler, and Sager (1993) proposed a theory of individual performance, defining it as cognitive, motor, psychomotor, or interpersonal behavior controllable by the individual, relevant to organizational goals, and conceptually varying in proficiency. The definition excluded work outcomes, effectiveness (defined as evaluation of outcomes), and productivity (considered a group, not an individual, construct). The excluded categories may be predictable and valued criteria, but they are not what Campbell et al. meant by *performance*. Their definition of performance differed from an earlier definition in the SIOP *Principles*, "the effectiveness and value of work behavior and its outcomes" (Society for Industrial and Organizational Psychology, 1987, p. 39). Under any reasonable definition, however, performance is not unidimensional; it may have many components. Ranking employees by level of proficiency in one component may differ from the rank order on another component.

Performance Components and Determinants

The theory suggested eight general factors of performance. With modification and abbreviation, they are shown in Table 3.2. Note that these are called "higher order" components, meaning that they are general aspects of performance with subordinate subsets, or facets, likely under each term. Some of them may not be relevant to a given job (e.g., many jobs have no supervisory component); many may require a finer definition to be operationally useful for specific jobs (e.g., a job in which the incumbent must communicate effectively to widely differing constituencies might require more specific communication components). They provide, however, a framework for criterion construct definition. Campbell et al. (1993) also suggested three determinants of proficiency in any performance component: *declarative knowledge* (actual knowledge and understanding of things one must do), *procedural knowledge* (skill in doing them), and *motivation* (the direction, degree, and persistence of effort in doing them).

Adaptive Performance

Adaptability to change might be considered a personality trait, but as a criterion, it is known as *adaptive performance* (Hesketh & Neal, 1999; Pulakos et al., 2000). A related construct proposed by Dorsey, Cortina, and Luchman (2010) is *situational awareness*. It calls not only for changed behavior in response to changed situations but also for changed behavior in attempts to change the situation. Related terms include *continuous learning*, persistently acquiring job knowledge and skill throughout a career as performance requirements change (London & Mone, 1999), or the well-established reverse concept of *resistance to change*

TABLE 3.2
A Proposed Taxonomy of Higher Order Performance Components

1. *Job-specific task proficiency.* How well the person does major substantive or technical tasks central to the job, i.e., job-specific behaviors differing from one to another. Joining two pieces of half-inch wood with dovetails and glue, and joining 2×4 studs and sills, are different core tasks for the cabinetmaker and the carpenter.

2. *Non-job-specific task proficiency.* Tasks performed by virtually everyone in an organization, or at least virtually everyone in a job family. In the construction example, virtually everyone at a job site—cabinetmaker, carpenter, plumbers, electricians, and various helpers—must be able to make rough cuts, drill holes, hammer nails, and clean the work area.

3. *Written and oral communication task proficiency.* Tasks requiring formal oral or written presentations to an audience, whether of one person or many. The critical, differentiating performance component is proficiency in writing or speaking to an audience. Examples vary from formally telling the boss of the results of a planning conference to the presentation of technical data to an audience of hundreds.

4. *Demonstrating effort.* Consistency of effort, frequency of expending extra effort when required, and the tendency to keep working even under adverse conditions.

5. *Maintaining personal discipline.* Avoidance of negatively valued behavior: alcohol and substance abuse at work, violating laws or rules, excessive absenteeism, etc.

6. *Facilitating peer and team performance.* Supporting peers, helping them, or acting as a *de facto* trainer; being a good model for facilitating group functioning by keeping the group goal-directed, and reinforcing participation by other group members.

7. *Supervision/leadership.* Influencing subordinate performance through direct interpersonal interaction: setting goals for subordinates, teaching or training, modeling appropriate behavior, and rewarding (or punishing) in appropriate ways.

8. *Management/administration.* Management activities distinctly differing from direct supervision.

Adapted from "A theory of performance" by J. P. Campbell, R. A. McCloy, S. H. Oppler, and C. E. Sager, pp. 35–70. In *Personnel Selection in Organizations*, N. Schmitt and W. C. Borman, Eds. (1993), San Francisco: Jossey-Bass. Copyright 1993 by Jossey-Bass. Adapted with permission.

(Coch & French, 1948; Oreg, 2003). It is unwise in a rapidly changing world to accept resistance to change without trying to overcome it—and predicting those most likely to resist change may be feasible. I consider it more useful to predict *acceptance of change*, preferably enthusiastic acceptance. This may be implied in *learning work tasks, technologies, and procedures*, one of eight dimensions of adaptive performance in the taxonomy proposed by Pulakos et al. (2000), supported by exploratory and confirmatory factor analyses, and summarized in Table 3.3.

Organizational Citizenship Behavior

Regularly coming to work on time, keeping the job rather than quitting, staying overtime if needed, helping others, reducing conflict within the group, training or mentoring newcomers, justifying trust, or simply providing a good model for others—all of these form a different view of performance, concerned less with task performance and more with supporting the organization and unit where work is done. An addition to the Campbell et al. (1993) taxonomy was first proposed by Borman and Motowidlo (1993) as *contextual performance*. It was similar to *organizational citizenship behavior* (*OCB*, Smith, Organ, & Near, 1983), and the two lines of inquiry have merged as OCB (Borman, 2004; Organ, Podsakoff, & MacKenzie, 2006). Several overlapping terms have appeared, but hierarchical research by Coleman and

TABLE 3.3

Eight Dimensions of Adaptive Performance

Dimension	Abridged Definition
Handling emergencies or crisis situations	Reacts with urgency in life-threatening or emergency situations, weighs options and makes emotionally controlled and clear-thinking decisions; steps up to take action as necessary and appropriate.
Handling work stress	Stays cool in difficult circumstances or with work loads and schedules; does not overreact to unexpected events; manages frustration by directing effort to constructive solutions, avoids placing blame; showing resilience in stressful situations and a settling influence on others.
Solving problems creatively	Analyzes complex situations uniquely and with innovative ideas, seeks fresh approaches; integrates seemingly unrelated information; entertains possibilities that others miss; thinks "outside the box."
Dealing with uncertain and unpredictable situations	Takes effective action without having to know all of the facts; readily changes gears in response to changed events; effectively changes plans, actions, or priorities; refuses to be paralyzed by uncertainty or ambiguity.
Learning work tasks, technologies, and procedures	Shows enthusiasm for new ways to do the work and keeps knowledge and skills current; quickly learns and adjusts to new procedures; anticipates changes and prepares for them.
Demonstrating interpersonal adaptability	Is flexible and open-minded with others; listens to and considers views and opinions of others and alters own opinions when appropriate; works well with diverse personalities; has insight into others' behavior and tailors own behavior to persuade, influence, or work with others.
Demonstrating cultural adaptability	Takes action to learn and understand needs and values of other groups, organizations, or cultures and is comfortable with them; shows respect for others values and customs.
Demonstrating physically oriented adaptability	Adjusts to challenging environmental states such as extreme heat, humidity, cold, or dirtiness; pushes self physically to complete strenuous or demanding tasks; makes physical changes to perform physical tasks as necessary on the job.

Adapted and abridged from "Adaptability in the workplace: Development of a taxonomy of adaptive performance" by E. D. Pulakos, S. Arad, M. A. Donovan, and M. E. Plamondon, 2000, *Journal of Applied Psychology, 85*, p. 617. Copyright 2000 by American Psychological Association. Adapted by STM permission.

Borman (2000) reduced the list to three general constructs, which I abbreviate as helping others, helping the organization, and making a conscientious effort to do one's job well. These can be, and were, subdivided into finer facets. I particularly like, and reproduce as Table 3.4, the summary in Dorsey et al. (2010).

OCBs support the development and continuation of a work environment that helps people accomplish organizational and job tasks. One difference between OCB and task performance is that task activities are things people are hired to do; OCB is desirable but rarely demanded. Other differences exist, but this one poses a special problem. It is a good idea to base personnel decisions on predictions of job performance, but should such decisions be influenced by predictions of desirable behavior that is not required? Doing so may

TABLE 3.4

Facets of Organizational Citizenship Behavior: Criteria Worth Predicting

Personal Support

Helping	Helping others by offering suggestions about their work, showing them how to do hard tasks, teaching them useful knowledge or skills, performing some of their tasks, and providing emotional support for personal problems.
Cooperating	Accepting suggestions of others, following their lead, putting team objectives over personal interests, informing others of things likely to affect them.
Courtesy	Showing consideration, courtesy, and tact in relations with others.
Motivating	Applauding achievements and successes of others; cheering others on as needed, showing confidence in them, and helping them overcome setbacks.

Organizational Support

Representing	Representing one's organization favorably to outsiders by defending it when it is criticized, promoting its achievements and positive attributes, and expressing one's own satisfaction with the organization.
Loyalty	Showing loyalty by staying despite temporary hardships, tolerating occasional difficulties, handling adversity cheerfully and without complaining, and publicly endorsing and supporting the organization's mission and objectives.
Compliance	Complying with organizational rules and procedures, encouraging others to do so; suggesting procedural, administrative, or organizational improvements.

Conscientious Initiative

Self-Development	Taking courses on own time to increase knowledge and skill, volunteering for developmental opportunities, trying to learn new knowledge and skills from others or in new job assignments.
Initiative	Without push from others, do what is necessary to accomplish team or organizational objectives even if not part of one's own duties, correcting non-standard conditions when encountered, finding extra work to do when one's own work is completed.
Persistence	Persisting with extra effort despite difficult circumstances, accomplishing more difficult and challenging goals than usual, getting work done on time even with short deadlines, and performing at levels beyond ordinary expectations.

Adapted from "Adaptive and citizenship-related behaviors at work" by D. Dorsey, J. M. Cortina, and J. Luchman, Figure 22.1 in *Handbook of Employee Selection* by J. L. Farr and N. T. Tippins (Eds.) (2010). New York: Routledge. Copyright 2010 by Taylor & Francis. Adapted with STM permission.

be distasteful, potentially unethical, and maybe counterproductive (Borman & Motowidlo, 1993). Of course, some OCBs *are* generally required. For example, virtually all employees on a production line are to be at work on time and to stay there as scheduled; all employees must *avoid* stealing cash or merchandise. In choosing a contextual criterion, a first question is whether it represents required behavior for everyone, or whether it is merely desirable. A further question is whether the desired behaviors are more likely and more safely elicited from day-to-day managerial influence than from traits people carry with them (e.g., see Organ et al., 2006). A different, and very serious, question was posed by Bergeron (2007). Because rewards tend to stem more from task performance than from OCBs, is time being good organizational citizens detrimental to individual rewards and career progress? My question is focused differently: why choose OCB as a criterion if it is not valued enough to be rewarded?

Hypotheses Based on the Theories

With eight factors of performance and three kinds of determinants in the Campbell et al. theory, 24 generic hypotheses can be formed. Table 3.4 names at least three general OCB dimensions to be added, bringing the total to 72 hypotheses. They are not equally sensible; it would be hard, for example, to rationally defend a hypothesis that procedural job knowledge predicts conscientious effort. To hypothesize that conscientious effort is a function of motivation, however, permits forming a more specific predictive hypothesis, defining more precisely the form of effort and plausible motivational variables.

I don't worry about possibly senseless combinations because any entry in the list can be a starting point for developing more sensible hypotheses development. Nor do I want hypothesis development to be limited to these taxonomies. Organ et al. (2006) added other useful citizenship constructs without placing them formally within a theoretical structure; examples include cheerleading, peacemaking, and self-development. Others might include empathy and generalized affect, offering some more possible generic hypotheses as starters in developing more explicit predictive hypotheses. Still more can be added from general psychological theories having implications for work and working. Hypothesis development can be iterative, starting with constructs that may be too broad but, with careful thought and definition, can lead to genuinely relevant hypothesis for a situation at hand. For the broadly knowledgeable psychologist, manager, or HR specialist, there is no shortage of possible hypotheses to consider.

Performance Outcomes

Psychology and psychologists concentrate on behavior. Introductory psychology textbooks once uniformly defined the field as the scientific study of behavior. Definitions now include much more, but explaining, modifying, or predicting behavior (including "latent" behavior and behavioral traits) is still the core of the discipline. Work-related criteria are likely to be measures of performance, generally defined as behavior.

Not so for managers who may hire psychologists in the expectation of improved, organizationally relevant results. Examples include how much gets done, or how well it is done, or others like those in Table 3.5. Pulakos and O'Leary (2010) returned to and expanded

TABLE 3.5
A Few Examples of Outcome or Results Criteria

Production Outcomes
Average time required to complete repetitive tasks
Units produced per day (or week, etc.), e.g., sales volume
Rates or costs of errors
Deviations from standards
Customer complaints (or commendations)

Behavioral Outcomes
Time in training to reach standard proficiency
Rate of growth in production outcomes
Number of absences (or of days absent)
Tardiness
Accidents
Length of service (how long before quitting or termination)

---

the notion of management by objectives, with individual objectives being the result of organizational level goals "cascading" (not trickling) down, selectively, through intervening organizational levels.

Managers' and psychologists' criteria have much in common. Results stem from behavior, things people do in their work. Results stem from other things, too, but the ideal logic of personnel research starts with candidate information, uses it to predict behavior, and then predicts organizationally important outcomes from that behavior. All too often, actual research is a two-step, not a three-step process: the candidate information is used to predict *either* performance or outcomes, not both. Outcomes predicted directly from candidate information provide coefficients that seem unimpressive because so many other things influence the outcomes. One influence may be differences in worker behavior. If the job is at all complex, not all people on the same job do it in the same way or perform at the same level.

Let's digress with some speculation about a possible direction for personnel research, one using the *if–then* model (Dunnette 1963a, discussed in Chapter 2)—*not* a bivariate prediction model. Focusing first on understanding how results come about, insofar as an individual employee achieves them, can lead to hypotheses about behaviors that contribute to them. It would not be surprising to discover, particularly in complex work, that different people use different behavior to get similar results. Computerized technology, new statistical technology, and willingness to use different models can combine to make *if–then* research feasible. The result can be a comprehensive staffing system based on a set of interconnected predictive hypotheses. The system will be evaluated, not individual predictive hypotheses.

Results-oriented criteria tend to be explicitly task-related, such as the average time a troubleshooter takes to locate a source of trouble, the number of new advertising accounts per month, the rate of scrap or breakage or use of expendable material, or the number of customer complaints per month. These are, or could be, matters of record. Each involves measurement simply by counting things in the record. Each represents a way to order employees according to their contributions to the organization. However, it is often more important to predict prerequisite behavior—behavior that produces a desired outcome—than to predict the outcome itself because outcomes are influenced by many variables not under the control of the worker. The distinction was made clearly by Wallace (1965), who pointed out that the "results" concept of an insurance agent's sales volume differs in meaning and in predictability from the behavioral concept of getting out of the office and looking for prospects.

Counterproductive Work Behaviors

Undesirable behaviors such as theft, willful destruction of equipment or products, loafing on the job, coming in late (or not at all), or harassment of other employees are, in many employment settings, important enough to predict and to try to control. The variety of such behaviors covers a range of problems from petty but disagreeable nuisances to major expenses and even crimes (Mount, Ilies, & Johnson, 2006). The rash of top executive illegal activity reported in news during the years straddling the turn of the century was surely counterproductive in the extreme (Daboud, Rasheed, Priem, & Gray, 1995). All of this variety is gathered under terms such as organizational misbehavior (Vardi & Weitz, 2004), dysfunctional behavior, counterproductive work behavior (CWB, Sackett, 2002), or simply bad behavior (Griffin & Lopez, 2005), all referring to intentional employee behavior having negative consequences for other people or for the organization or work environment.

TABLE 3.6

Examples of Counterproductive Work Behavior

- Theft and related behavior (theft; steal cash or property; give away goods or services; misuse employee discount).
- Destruction of property (deface, damage, or destroy property; sabotage production).
- Misuse of information (reveal confidential information; falsify records).
- Misuse of time and resources (waste time, alter time card, conduct personal business during work time).
- Unsafe behavior (fail to follow safety procedures; fail to learn safety procedures).
- Poor attendance (unexcused absence or tardiness; misuse sick leave).
- Poor quality work (intentionally be slow or do sloppy work).
- Alcohol use (use alcohol on the job; come to work under the influence of alcohol).
- Drug use (possess, use, or sell drugs at work).
- Inappropriate verbal actions (argue with customers; verbally harass coworkers).
- Inappropriate physical actions (physically attack coworkers; make sexual advances toward coworker).

Adapted from "The structure of counterproductive work behaviors: Dimensionality and relationships with facets of job performance" by P. R. Sackett, 2002, *International Journal of Selection and Assessment, 10*, pp. 5–6. Copyright 2002 by Blackwell Publishers. Adapted with permission.

Sackett described 11 categories of CWB, shown in Table 3.6, in a list that is not exhaustive but shows the variety of CWBs.

Do they all reflect the same, underlying construct? Probably not, but there does seem to be some unity among them. Viswesvaran (2002), studying absenteeism and its correlates, found it reasonable to consider CWB a general construct. Sackett and DeVore (2001) proposed a hierarchical model, illustrated and organized by Landy and Conte (2007, p. 179). Other possible components have been suggested (e.g., Griffin & Lopez, 2005; Vardi & Weitz, 2004) and are included in the first level in Figure 3.3 (18 at the first level, going beyond Sackett's and DeVore's 11 categories). Are these terms somewhat independent or are they redundant? I don't know. Do they fit together under the second-level constructs? Maybe. Do they suggest important constructs for some predictive hypotheses? I think so.

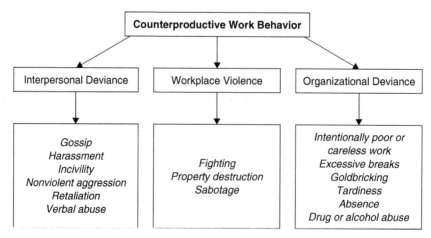

FIG. 3.3   Categories of counterproductive work behavior.

Figure 3.3 is not a factor analysis report, but factor analytic terms fit. The basic categories, similar to the 11 described in Table 3.6, are like the narrowest, most explicit factors, grouped under three more general categories, all under the still more general factor of counterproductive behavior. The basic 11 were supported as correlated factors by Gruys and Sackett (2003). Further work showed that people tend to see the different categories as somewhat likely to occur together, although not so likely as to suggest that if a person does any one of these things, that person would be particularly likely to do any of the others. I chose labels for the three general categories from earlier studies, but they are not inconsistent with the factors (production deviance, property deviance, and personal aggression) reported by Stewart, Bing, Davison, Woehr, and McIntyre (2009). Vardi's and Weitz's (2004) terms were (a) deviance from social norms, ranging from goldbricking to property destruction, (b) aggression, whether directed toward individuals or the organization itself, and (c) political action, primarily within-organization politicking. Landy and Conte (2007) seemed to have interpreted these categories in a different but equally useful way: self-gain (e.g., theft); organizational gain (e.g., misstating profit, over-billing); and destructive behavior. These two sets of terms are interesting particularly because politicking (organizational gain), whether local or wider in effect, can fit executive crime as well as misbehavior at lower levels, and because they include ideas not ordinarily included in other discussions. Figure 3.3 treats internal politicking as a narrow, specific form of CWB, and intentional cheating ("inappropriate organizational gain") as ultimately destructive to the organization.

Warren (2003) pointed out that deviant behavior—that is, deviating from the normal or routinely accepted behavior—may be destructive or constructive. For example, goldbricking is negative but putting forth out-of-the-ordinary effort to get a job done on time is positive. In this section the emphasis is on CWB, but Warren's distinction points out that especially productive work behavior also occurs, deviates from a norm, and may be predictable.

Trainability and Other Important Criteria

Trainability is a frequent and important criterion construct. The rate of learning complex tasks may be especially important when people must adapt to changing technology or assignments (Hesketh & Neal, 1999), but it differs from adaptive performance. The idea that anyone can become expert given enough time is a myth; those who take a long time to learn a task generally do not reach the level of proficiency after training reached by those who learn it more quickly (Goldstein & Ford, 2004; Jones, 1966; Woodrow, 1938). It is organizationally useful to select or promote people who will learn their duties quickly or adapt quickly to job changes.

A related criterion is the idea of *performance growth trajectories*, discussed in Chapter 10 as "idiosyncratic patterns of systematic performance growth across a specified period of time or a series of performance observations" (Thoresen et al., 2004, p. 836). This concept recognizes "longstanding evidence that performance is dynamic" (p. 835) despite the ubiquitous assumption otherwise. Traditional selection research uses one criterion, collected at one time—a single frame in a movie. If the performance rank order changes substantially over time, the validity of performance predictions may be quite different for performance predicted earlier or later. Perhaps the rank ordering of workers *is* consistent over time, but no one will ever know unless data are collected to find out.

Consider a few other performance constructs suggested in various sources, as follows.

- *Self-management in learning.* Voluntarily taking action to acquire additional work-related knowledge and skills (Campbell, 1999; London & Mone, 1999).

- *Personal support.* Making helpful task-related suggestions to others or providing emotional support—the antithesis of CWB; also accepting suggestions or putting group or team objectives ahead of personal interests, etc. (Coleman & Borman, 2000; Hanson & Borman, 2006).
- *Organizational support.* Favorably representing the organization, defending and promoting it and supporting organizational goals. (Coleman & Borman, 2000; Hanson & Borman, 2006).
- *Proactive work behavior.* Taking charge, preventing problems, being self-starting; not passive about problems or about the implementation of ideas and procedures (Parker, Williams, & Turner, 2006).

There is no dearth of ideas about performance and performance outcomes or consequences worth predicting; moreover, I have not even mentioned criterion constructs specifically relevant to team-centered or global operations. Researchers and practitioners need to use careful thought to choose criterion constructs from the multitude of options available for this first component of a predictive hypothesis. With all these options, it should not be forgotten that criterion constructs form hierarchies of generality. Although often true, overall job performance (OJP) gets an undeserved bad rap as something used only for ratings and only by those who don't know how to be specific. OJP can be carefully developed and well defined—supported by careful rational thought and by careful research—and useful across different jobs and settings (Campbell, 1999; Viswesvaran, Schmidt, & Ones, 2005). Predicting components of OJP may, however, speed up understanding what is in it that is or is not predicted.

Status Quo, Change, and Criterion Choice

Organizations grow and adapt through change. Chosen criteria should promote effective change, maintain useful stability in the face of change, and help develop an organization that continues to function effectively in a changing world (Friedman, 2006; Kanter, Stein, & Jick, 1992; Murphy, 1999). Simpleminded adherence to status quo does not keep organizations lively or alive. Long ago, social critic Whyte (1957) criticized American organizations saying that they chose, largely through personality testing, conformers who resist change. Many of his arrows were off target but, in fact, many criteria, if predicted well, do tend dangerously to maintain the status quo (Schneider, 1987). I cannot accept mindless adulation of change for its own sake or an overly enthusiastic pursuit of every innovation. Nevertheless, new ideas to improve products, services, or ways of doing things promote organizational growth and progress; the people who imagine and develop them are valuable to organizations and to society and should be sought at all organizational levels. Innovation should be evaluated—and rewarded. New ideas sometimes solve problems; sometimes they create new problems. Some of them simply do not work. Measures of innovativeness should consider quality as well as quantity in evaluating ideas produced; if not, the innovations may not hold up over time (Murphy, 1999).

Not all organizations need or experience rapid change; some work is relatively untouched by the most publicized technologies. For these settings, a somewhat static criterion may be useful and still profit from new thinking about it. If only for this reason, these lists of criterion constructs—not exhaustive but selected either because they've been remarkably useful or because they interested me—can be important for developing new criteria for evaluating the work of organizational members and procedures for selecting them.

ISSUES IN FORMING CRITERION CONSTRUCTS

Refining a criterion construct requires some judgments and choices, some of them controversial. For clarification, despite oversimplification, some choices are described as dichotomies.

Typical versus Maximum Performance

A criterion can reflect either what a person *can* do under some circumstances, or what the person *will* do (is likely to do) under typical circumstances. The distinction is related to that between maximum performance and typical performance tests (Cronbach, 1970, p. 35). Sackett et al. (1988) studied supermarket cashiers. In the first part, supervisors observed speed of operation with stop watches; in a second part, scanning machines recorded aspects of performance as well as sales. The two methods were compared—and they did not agree very well. With the supervisor near by, performance was about as good as it could get—maximum. With only the scanner and the customer near by, performance was ordinary—typical. Can-do and will-do performance are not highly related, so either decide which construct is more useful or establish different hypotheses to predict the two independently.

Complexity versus Simplicity

Construct Complexity

Here the dichotomy is a choice between multidimensional and unidimensional criteria, between predicting composites of somewhat related components and predicting the components themselves; that is, a choice between predicting a single overall criterion and predicting several independent criteria. Schmidt, Ones, and Hunter (1992), who would surely consider this chapter so far to be much ado about not much of anything, are among those who argue for overall, general criteria. With characteristic firmness, they said, "Criterion measures have long been considered critical because of the assumption that the nature of the criterion measure determines which predictors will be deemed valid and which invalid. It is now clear that for criteria of overall job performance . . . and tests of cognitive ability, this assumption is incorrect . . . there are no documented cases of an aptitude or ability test being valid for one such criterion measure but not for another (i.e., zero validity)" (Schmidt et al., 1992, p. 656). Much research evidence supports their view.

I have a serious quibble, however. The statement seems to treat a criterion as something having no purpose other than test validation. This, I contend with my own characteristic firmness, is to miss the entire point of personnel testing. The point is to effect improvement at some level of the organization, and the kind of improvement needed should determine the choice of the criterion. If broad, sweeping change is needed, or if improvement is to be seen at higher organizational levels, an overall performance criterion at the individual level may make more sense. Improvement within a narrow boundary, however, calls for a more narrowly specified criterion. An idea that different criterion components may require substantially different predictors requires explicitly different hypotheses for the different components. If this presumption is wrong, the error will be shown if the different criteria are predicted about equally well by any of the sets of predictors. On the other hand, an a priori presumption of no such differences gives no opportunity to test the assumption and find it wrong.[4]

Static versus Dynamic Criteria

Ghiselli (1956) introduced the idea of dynamic criteria, in which relative rank order on any given performance dimension changes over time. If the rate of change in criterion performance differs for different people, validity changes over time. Ghiselli reported that some validities were stable over time, others gradually decreased, and others changed in cycles. Subsequent reports offered further evidence of systematic validity change (e.g., Bass, 1962; Ghiselli & Haire, 1960; Thoresen et al., 2004). As the fact of change has become more salient, the thought of a fixed, never-changing criterion level has become much less attractive. Much ink has been spilled in arguments over dynamic criteria, but an emerging view notes "longstanding evidence that performance is dynamic" (Thoresen et al., 2004, p. 835).

Simplex Matrices

Validity decreases over time. In a correlation matrix showing validity coefficients with successive times of criterion collection, coefficients may be systematically smaller as they depart from the principal diagonal. Such a matrix is termed a *simplex* (Guttman, 1955; Humphreys, 1960), illustrated in Table 3.7. Determining the likelihood of simplex validity matrices is a research line long overdue. Practical validation research offers few if any examples of such series of repeated criterion measures, but pairs of validity coefficients are sometimes reported, one with an early criterion and the other with a later one. Lower predictive validity for later criteria has often been found, so the assumption that early criteria are more predictable than remote ones has become commonplace. For some predictors, however, later criteria may be more predictable (Helmreich et al., 1986). Research on the simplex could test the notion and further evaluate the dynamics of criteria.

TABLE 3.7

A Simplex Matrix of Correlation Coefficients

Variable[a]	1		2		3		4		5		6		7
1	r_{11}	>	r_{12}	>	r_{13}	>	r_{14}	>	r_{15}	>	r_{16}	>	r_{17}
2			r_{22}	>	r_{23}	>	r_{24}	>	r_{25}	>	r_{26}	>	r_{27}
3					r_{33}	>	r_{34}	>	r_{35}	>	r_{36}	>	r_{37}
4							r_{44}	>	r_{45}	>	r_{46}	>	r_{47}
5									r_{55}	>	r_{56}	>	r_{57}
6											r_{66}	>	r_{67}
7													r_{77}

[a] Let variable 1 be a predictor. Variables 2–7 are the same criterion variable collected at six successive times.

[4] Responding to a statement in the *Smithsonian* to the effect that no litmus test exists for distinguishing positions grounded in scholarship from those grounded in ideology, Doering (1992, p. 14), said, "there is a simple and reliable test. Scholarship admits the possibility of error." My view is that a hypothesis that can be shown to be wrong is preferable to hiding error.

PREDICTORS AND PREDICTIVE HYPOTHESES

People with different backgrounds may infer different predictor constructs. That's OK; no one hypothesis has a lock on good prediction. Psychologists may choose constructs from factor analysis or from general theories. Managers and job incumbents may rely on their experience; job experts convened for job analysis may rely on their analyses. Ignoring ideas based on experience risks ignoring some very good bets, but good bets, maybe better bets, can also stem from knowledge of past research and theory.

Several research-based taxonomies are available as practical starting points for predictor choice. The *Handbook of Human Abilities* (Fleishman & Reilly, 1992b) lists 52 cognitive, psychomotor, physical, and sensory/perceptual abilities. For each one, it offers a conceptual definition, sample tasks, jobs requiring it, and some examples of ways to measure it. Various lists differ in details but overlap in descriptions of the major explanatory constructs. Choosing constructs for predictors depends on logical analysis of the work, understanding of the potentially relevant constructs, and knowledge of prior research.

COGNITIVE ABILITIES

Cognitive abilities are abilities to perceive, process, evaluate, compare, create, understand, manipulate, or generally think about information and ideas. Common work-relevant cognitive activities include reading verbal or graphic materials, understanding the principles that make things work, planning events or procedures, solving problems, or perceiving signs of trouble (e.g., in equipment, in human interactions, or in contradictions in plans). Mental abilities are diverse and somewhat overlapping. More than 50 years of factor analytic research, however, has clarified and defined (though not without controversy) many components of mental abilities.

Cognitive Factors

Factor analysis (discussed in Chapter 6) examines intercorrelations among measures to infer underlying latent constructs. Several lists of mental abilities have been based on factor analyses, beginning with the seven "primary mental abilities" (*verbal comprehension, word fluency, spatial ability, perceptual speed, numerical facility, memory,* and *inductive reasoning*) identified by Thurstone (1938).[5] Subsequent research made finer distinctions, taking the number well beyond seven. Spatial ability, for example, split into *spatial relations* (ability to perceive spatial patterns accurately) and *visualization* (ability to imagine movements or manipulations of objects in space); the perceptual speed factor has both *speed* and *accuracy* components (French, 1951), although they are rarely measured separately in practice. French provided detailed information for nearly 60 factors, some with large noncognitive components, in his 1951 monograph, and the number considered well established has grown much larger (Carroll, 1993).

---

[5] Beware of names given to factors; they can be misleading because they can mean different things to different hearers. Factor analysts often avoid names, preferring to define factors by specific measures of them. My intent here is to indicate the variety of factors, not to provide detailed definitions from individual researches.

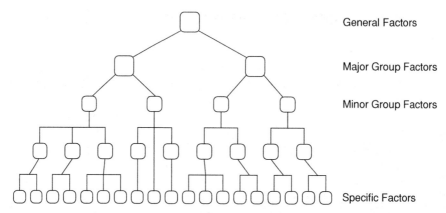

General Factors

Major Group Factors

Minor Group Factors

Specific Factors

FIG. 3.4   A hierarchical model of the factorial structure of human abilities. From R. M. Guion (1965a).

Basic factors

One way to organize factor analytic research is hierarchical, as shown in Figure 3.4. The lowest level of the hierarchy defines the basic, most explicitly and narrowly defined factors; higher levels are more general. Organizing results at the basic factor level is simple listing. A very different organization was the *structure of intellect* model (Guilford, 1956), classifying cognitive factors according to a three-way data matrix: by intellectual *operations*, test *content*, and *product* of the thinking process. The operations category has been the most enduring; it includes remembering, knowing, evaluating, and both the convergent and divergent production of ideas. The model is now archaic but illustrates an organizing principle that may, like the original periodic chart in chemistry, point to potentially new constructs that may fit a situation better than old ones do.

Various taxonomies list 10 to well over 100 cognitive factors (Anastasi, 1988); Carroll (1993) suggested that the number could approach infinity! It would be pretentious to offer a comprehensive list of basic cognitive factors used in personnel research; so I offer only an illustrative (*not* definitive) short list of factors frequently encountered.

- *Verbal comprehension*: the ability to understand words and their meanings, and to apply such understanding in verbal communications. At some level, it seems necessary in nearly all work. Some authors distinguish factors for understanding oral and written communication.
- *Fluency*: the ability to produce a lot of ideas or associations quickly. Different jobs may require different kinds of fluency, such as verbal fluency, ideational fluency, or number fluency. It seems to be involved wherever creativity is a criterion component.
- *Perceptual speed*: the ability to identify figures (such as numbers, letters, pictures, or names), make comparisons, or match visually perceived figures quickly and accurately. Perceptual speed is a generally useful predictor of clerical performance and also in some technical work where spotting errors is critical.
- *Flexibility and speed of closure*: the ability to restructure visual perceptions and to do so quickly; for example, to remember and find a previously perceived figure embedded in distracting material, or to perceive a perceptual field as a whole, even where missing details must be supplied by the perceiver. I have found flexibility and speed of closure useful for patrol officers who, from only quick and incomplete glimpses of

things, must have enough of an idea of the whole to know when further investigation is warranted.

- *Spatial orientation and visualization*: the ability to perceive spatial patterns, to orient oneself (or an object) relative to objects in space, or to alter spatial patterns mentally into altered patterns or arrangements. Engineers, mechanics, and others who must work from drawings need such ability; I suspect that drivers, pilots, or travel planners probably need it as well.
- *Number facility*: the ability to do elementary arithmetic operations quickly and accurately. Computers and calculators do not eliminate the need; it is easy to get vastly wrong answers with such aids, and some mental arithmetic lets one at least approximate the correct answer and evaluate the answer given by the gadget.
- *General reasoning*: the ability to understand relational principles among elements of a problem and to structure the problem in preparation for solving it; it is also the ability to work toward a conclusion or solution and to test the soundness of conclusions reached, perhaps by comparing the soundness of one conclusion with that of other possible conclusions. The very complexity of the definition attests to the complexity of the concept. Many factor analyses have identified more than one reasoning factor; distinctions, however, tend not to be very clean.
- *Problem recognition*: the ability to tell from early and perhaps subtle warnings that something is wrong, or may go wrong, in work with equipment, people, social systems, or data. Sensitivity to potential or existing problems seems useful in jobs such as physician, air traffic controller, or monitors of machinery operation.
- *Associative memory*: the ability to recall bits of information previously associated with unrelated information; for example, to remember numerical information associated with names.
- *Memory span*: the ability to recall in proper sequence a series of items (numbers, words, symbols) after a single presentation of the series, for example, looking up a telephone number and remembering it.

General factors

The earliest factor analysis was reported by Spearman (1927), who proposed a two-factor theory of intelligence. Every mental ability test score, he said, was determined by two factors. One of these was general *intelligence*, called *g*; the other was a factor specific to the individual test. (A later incarnation of the theory made room for *group factors*, less general than *g* but influencing scores on groups of tests and making room for a three-level hierarchy.) Sternberg and Detterman (1986) asked several experts to define intelligence; the disparate set of definitions included core concepts such as reasoning, symbolic representation, problem solving, and decision processes. Different authors, with different perspectives, emphasized different features of behavior called intelligent. One comprehensive definition was *Intelligence is the resultant of the processes of acquiring, storing in memory, retrieving, combining, comparing, and using in new contexts information and conceptual skills; it is an abstraction* (Humphreys, 1979, p. 115). It is an unwieldy definition. So is the broad concept of intelligence, however defined.

The terms *general factor* and *g* are not interchangeable. A general factor may be identified in a specific analysis. The term *g* is a theoretical construct of general intelligence. A general mental ability score is a score on a test. For example, an intelligence test may have many item types but not be a sufficient measure of *g*. One item might be a verbal analogies item, the next a number series, the third a mental manipulation of two-dimensional depictions of three-dimensional objects, the fourth an arithmetic story problem, and the next four a repetition of the same four item types at a slightly higher difficulty level, and so on (the so-called *spiral omnibus test*). If an overall score is the total number of items correctly answered, with no regard for the kinds of items most likely to be answered correctly, the score may be called a general mental ability score even if the test omits many kinds of mental ability items, reflecting neither a general factor nor *g*.

Some test scores are called intelligence quotients, or IQs. In adult testing, an IQ score is a standard score with a mean of 100 and a standard deviation somewhere between 12 and 20, depending on the idiosyncratic preferences of the test developer. IQ scores depend on the ability distribution in the standardizing sample, on the standard deviation chosen, and on the content and structure of the particular test. Thus a person can have several different IQ scores if tested with different tests. The term IQ is venerable, but it should be retired. I get upset when people—especially psychologists, who should know better—refer to IQs as traits, as in "how well he will do in life depends on his IQ." Such verbiage confuses the test score, IQ, with the construct, *g*. Because an IQ score depends so much on test-specific things, IQ is clearly *not* a characteristic of the person tested. Because of its excess semantic baggage, *the term IQ should be firmly and finally dropped.*

R. B. Cattell (1963) argued that general intelligence has two major components, *fluid intelligence* (*Gf*), involving basic reasoning and other aspects of information processing, and *crystallized intelligence* (*Gc*), based on learning and measured by tests such as vocabulary; eventually, he claimed five second-order (general) factors, adding general visualization (*Gv*), general fluency (*F*), and general speediness (*Gs*) (Horn & Cattell, 1966). Carroll (1993), in his encyclopedic re-analysis of mountains of factor analytic studies, also proposed a three-stratum model. The first stratum consisted of first-order factors somewhat like the list of basic factors above—but more of them and more precisely defined. The second stratum included at least six general factors such as fluid and crystallized intelligence and adding general visual and auditory perceptions, broad speediness, retrieval ability (readiness to produce several kinds of responses from long-term memory), and a broad memory factor from more basic memory and learning factors. The third level corresponded pretty well to Spearman's concept of *g*.

Two major issues center on the generality of factors. First, how important is a general factor in determining scores on tests of cognitive ability? Second, are general factors or more specific factors better bases for personnel decisions? I do not answer either question clearly. Neither does a survey of the members of the Society for Industrial and Organizational Psychology (SIOP), reported by Murphy, Cronin, and Tam (2003). On an item asserting that general mental ability is the most important single construct, 44% agreed and 41% disagreed. From their review, Carretta and Ree (2000) claimed that almost all of the predictive validity of cognitive tests comes from *g*, and Salgado et al. (2003) found that the effectiveness of performance predictions based on general cognitive ability applied as well in the European Union as in the United States. Nevertheless, subdivisions of general mental ability can be extremely important in the performance of specialized tasks and for a variety of predicted criteria.

Alternative Constructs

Cognitive science may provide useful alternatives to factor analytic constructs, but it has not yet done so in systematic taxonomies. One cognitive scientist, proposing a "triarchic theory," divided intelligence, like Gaul, into three parts: (a) componential, in which cognitive tasks are analyzed into component processes, such as performance and knowledge acquisition, (b) experiential, in which dealing with novelty differs from the automatized responses likely with well-known things, and (c) contextual, in which both practical and social intelligence are invoked (Sternberg, 1985). The two forms of contextual intelligence limit my enthusiasm for the theory; both have long psychometric histories of failed attempts at measurement, and I still see no historic change. The usefulness of the theory does not reside in influencing currently practical assessment procedures, however, but in pushing concepts of intelligence beyond traditional psychometric constructs. The value of theories based on cognitive research lies in the emphasis on intellectual *processes*, usually considered less static than traits.

The study of individual differences in cognition has not yet broadened the scope of abilities measured, a "leading priority for the intelligence tests of the future" (Sternberg, 1991, p. 265). That future seems reluctant to arrive, but there is enough ferment among people interested in concepts of intelligence that some of the constructs they develop, insofar as they differ from traditional ones, will eventually be measurable in employment and other non-laboratory contexts. Personnel researchers should follow basic research on individual cognitive differences attentively, both for new constructs and for psychometric measurement. An example of the latter is the interest in item generation theory, where item development is typically based on cognitive theory (Embretson, 1998; Irvine & Kyllonen, 2002; see Chapter 10).

Kyllonen (2002) described a *cognitive ability measurement* (CAM) taxonomy, an information-processing measurement model, containing seven processing components (working memory, processing speed, declarative and procedural knowledge; declarative and procedural learning, and timing) operating in three content domains (verbal, quantitative, and spatial). The resulting 21 categories are surely ripe for predictive hypotheses, and they are independent of factor analytic constructs. A "new" structure of intellect model suggested by Carroll (1976) represented a marriage of factor analytic factors and components of cognitive processing rather more complex than CAM.

Useful constructs can be inferred by experienced job experts, without relying on factor analysis or on cognitive science. Managers, incumbents, and other job experts have their own working folk constructs. Using them, psychologists can modify well-known, well-established scientific constructs for particular responsibilities. Ad hoc constructs stemming from local wisdom, refined by an infusion of research-based knowledge, can be useful. Some folk constructs can be refined by data, especially by identifying component factors. Many of these are *compound predictors*, defined as a "combination of basic . . . traits that do not necessarily covary" (Hough, 2003, p. 298).

Creativity is an example. Creativity is more complex than the usual first-order (basic) factors but less general than typical second-order factors. Carroll (1993, pp. 423–431) described a general originality–creativity group factor requiring both fluency and flexibility in the production or invention of things, procedures, or ideas. It may also have a motivational component, a desire to do or try things that are different or unusual. It may also, in given situations, imply an ability to capitalize on serendipity, seeing opportunities in unplanned events or situations. George and Zhou (2001) said it might involve personality variables such as openness to experience or conscientiousness.

Problem-solving ability is a convergent thinking ability to find a right or best answer to a problem. Unlike creativity, it is a divergent thinking ability. It includes such components as (a) problem definition, (b) systematic data gathering, and (c) planning an approach to problem analysis. Troubleshooting is an example; good troubleshooters understand the problem domain, have detailed knowledge of the systems or equipment in trouble, and follow a clear plan rather than jump willy-nilly from one possible solution to another. Most moderate- to high-level jobs involve at least some problem-solving activity. Raaheim (1974) suggested that solving a problem depends on prior experience with its components and with the tools available for solving it; the strong experiential component suggests that it might be related to specific job knowledge.

Planning ability seems to be an ability to arrange a set of likely events, things, or processes in a logical sequence. It may also involve an ability to see implications of alternative decisions, a matter of foresight.

Wisdom is a term rarely encountered in psychometric literature, but Sternberg (1990) devoted an entire book to it. Contributions of various chapter authors conceive of wisdom in terms of problem finding, of affect, of judgment, of *knowing in the face of uncertainty* (Kitchener & Brenner, 1990). The book focuses primarily on developmental issues but has implications for work. Folk theory often holds that older workers compensate for loss in physical and sensory abilities with increased wisdom.

Ability to learn from experience seems relevant to any job with a lot of nonroutine activities. Long-term memory is probably a component, as is ability to see the implications of the knowledge it represents or perhaps an ability to restructure knowledge.

Verbal expression—the ability to communicate, either orally or in writing (Fleishman & Quaintance, 1984, p. 322), may include verbal comprehension, but it is clearly more. It may include memory for past effective communication or sensitivity to the targets of the communication, among other things.

Speed of information processing is probably much more general than the perceptual speed factor usually discussed. It's surely more than simple *reaction time*. Carroll (1993, pp. 613–619) identified a second-stratum factor of *broad speediness*, encompassing a wide array of primary speed factors. Is such ability related to how quickly (and perhaps how thoroughly) people can grasp complex information in such settings as briefings? If so, it would be relevant to performance of executives, cab drivers, and fighter pilots. Reaction time may be influenced by the ability to focus or to divide attention. There is a strong literature on vigilance (focus), but not much on speed of response where attention must be divided.

Common sense is included in this list because the term is so common and the evidence of it so rare. Different people often mean different things by it. When job experts invoke the need for common sense, the psychologist should question them closely about what they mean. They may mean the construct called *tacit knowledge* (Sternberg, 1997; Sternberg, Wagner, Williams, & Horvath, 1995), an experience-based knowledge. Tests of tacit knowledge have been shown to be valid predictors and to offer incremental validity beyond general mental ability. It seems similar to declarative knowledge in the Campbell et al. (1993) theory of performance.

The list could go on. All of these examples are broad, moderately general constructs. They illustrate the kinds of constructs people may infer about work requirements.

Job-Specific Knowledge and Skill

"Know-how" is a folk construct. People who have it—who know and understand thoroughly a job's requirements—may be better workers than those with less of it. For hypothesis building, however, the term needs cleaner definition. Job knowledge may be general or be limited to specific information or skill. As background for developing the O*NET system of occupational information, Mumford, Peterson, and Childs (1999) found seven categories of basic and cross-functional occupational skill: content skills (e.g., writing and speaking), process skills (e.g., learning and critical thinking), problem-solving skills, social skills, a wide variety of technical skills, systems skills (including detection of changes in a system or identifying long-term outcomes of changes), and resource management skills. Basic skills (the first two categories) are partially acquired in school but are further developed through experience; they help in learning other types of material. Cross-functional skills are those useful in a wide range of occupations.

On a continuum from general to specific, the nearer a particular skill or knowledge is to the basic skills, it seems, the more likely it is to be expected of all qualified candidates; the more job-specific it is, the more likely it is to be the content of in-house training programs. For organizational entry, hypotheses usually emphasize more general skills and knowledge; for promotions, they may emphasize skills and knowledge specific to the work to be done. Job knowledge is often a "predictor" if the performance to be predicted is nearly immediate, as in predicting whether the person will be able to do major parts of the job on the first day at work.

PERSONALITY CONSTRUCTS

From the 1960s to the 1980s, the use of personality traits as predictors was rare. Some researchers (e.g., Schneider & Hough, 1995) have attributed the demise of such research to a review that concluded that personality test validities had not been demonstrated (Guion & Gottier, 1965). That is quite different from saying that inferences from personality test scores were not valid. Two other influences were probably greater. First, the Civil Rights Act of 1964 explicitly permitted the use of "professionally developed ability tests" but said nothing about personality inventories. Because such inventories were severely criticized by social critics, many employers quietly stopped using them, fearing litigation. Second, the view of Mischel (1968), that behavior is determined more by situations than by traits, was widely accepted. For whatever reason, personality predictors went underground but reappeared in the 1980s.

Traits

A *trait* differs from *a state*, a temporary condition or mood; one may be in a good or poor mood at a given time, without the consistency implied by *trait*. A *personality trait* is a habitual way of thinking or doing in a variety of situations. It may be a general value, goal, or behavioral tendency to seek or to avoid certain kinds of situations or experiences. It might be a persistent need, even a metaphorical need. It may be a role that one habitually plays—the role of leader, clown, scholar, teacher, or an unnamed role stemming from other traits (e.g., learned helplessness). It may be a pattern or combination of traits, a syndrome or type. The O*NET taxonomy does not refer to personality traits but to "work styles" (Borman, Kubisiak, & Schneider, 1999).

Most personality inventories provide scores for several traits. Consider the variety of constructs implied in this partial list of scales in some existing personality measures: alienation, anxiety, coping styles, emotional empathy, hopelessness, level of aspiration, perceptions of daily hassles and uplifts, response style, rigid type, risk-taking orientation, self-confidence, self-esteem, stress tolerance, team builder, Type A, and vigor. So, many possible constructs must overlap; they require some means of reduction; commonly, factor analysis is the means chosen.

The Five-Factor Model

Languages have thousands of words describing individual personalities. Many words have overlapping meanings; for example, *timid*, *shy*, *nervous*, and *irresolute* all describe people who tend to falter in social situations. Meaningful distinctions can be made among these terms, but the more general idea of social faltering can be inferred from the similarities. This example is an "armchair" factor analysis. Actual factor analysis, considering larger samples of descriptive words, has often resulted in five factors, the so-called Big Five. The lexical five-factor solution (more formally, the five-factor model, FFM) has dominated much of personality research on both sides of the millennial divide.

The Five Factors

Different names have been given to the factors by various researchers, as in Table 3.8 (Digman, 1990). Some of these differences in preference can be attributed to bipolarity, with some names describing the positive and others describing the negative end of a bipolar scale. Some depend on acceptance of neologisms. Some are due to the different descriptive terms used in different lexical studies. Mainly, however, name differences seem to reflect the different nuances different researchers think most worthy of emphasis. As Goldberg (1995) said, a single descriptive term cannot capture everything in a factor defined by a whole set of descriptive words.

My preference for Factor I is *Surgency*. It suggests the interpersonal aspect of the factor associated with extraversion, but it also includes the dominance and visibility implied by wave-like "surging"; its positive end is partly defined by such adjectives as aggressive, assertive, unrestrained, daring, and even flamboyant (Hofstee, de Raad, & Goldberg, 1992). It seems especially relevant to leadership, especially emerging leadership. However, *Extraversion* seems to be the name of choice for most recent writers. Goldberg's early work spoke of Surgency, but with his colleague Saucier, he came to speak of Extraversion (Saucier & Goldberg, 2003).

For Factor II, I prefer *Agreeableness*. It encompasses likeability or friendliness without putting much emphasis on conformity or compliance or implying emotional attachment to others. It is the term commonly used.

TABLE 3.8

Interpretive Names Given to the Five Recurring Personality Factors

- *Factor I:* social adaptability, extraversion, surgency, assertiveness, exvia, social activity, sociability and ambition, power, activity, positive emotionality, interpersonal involvement.
- *Factor II:* conformity, psychoticism, agreeableness, likeability, cortertia, paranoid disposition, friendly compliance, love, sociability, level of socialization.
- *Factor III:* will to achieve, psychoticism, dependability, conscientiousness, task interest, superego strength, thinking introversion, prudence, work, impulsivity, constraint, self-control.
- *Factor IV:* emotional control, neuroticism, emotionality, emotional, anxiety, emotional stability, affect, negative emotionality.
- *Factor V:* inquiring intellect, culture, intelligence, intellect, intellectance, openness, independent.

Adapted from "Personality Structure: Emergence of the Five-Factor Model" by J. M. Digman, 1990, *Annual Review of Psychology, 41*, p. 423. Copyright 1990 by Annual Reviews, Inc. Adapted with permission.

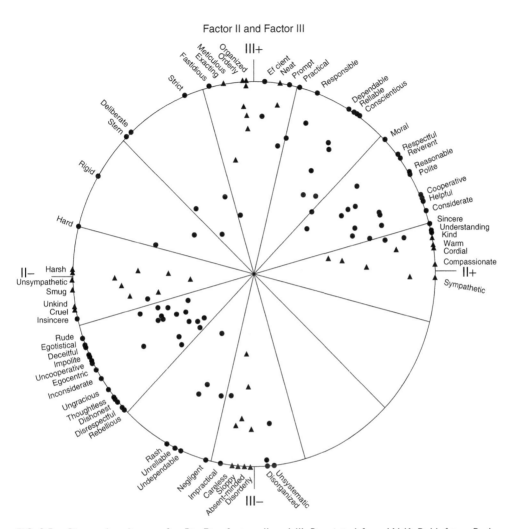

FIG. 3.5   Circumplex diagram for Big Five factors II and III. Reprinted from W. K. B. Hofstee, B. de Raad, and L. R. Goldberg (1992). Integration of the Big Five and circumplex approaches to trait structure. *Journal of Personality and Social Psychology, 63*, 146–163. © American Psychological Association. Reprinted with permission.

For Factor III, I prefer *Conscientiousness*, the usual term. The factor is somewhat ambiguous. One set of key terms defining this factor, identified by Hofstee et al. (1992, p. 158), includes *organized, neat, precise, exacting*; another includes terms such as *conscientious, responsible*, and *dependable* clustering together, as shown in Figure 3.5. The figure is a *circumplex*, a graphic depiction of the projection of pairs of factor loadings on the circumference of a circle. Words such as *orderly* help define only Factor III. Words such as *conscientious* help define both Factor III and, secondarily, Factor II. An emphasis on orderliness alone, implied by the first set of terms, may imply obsessive attention to detail; such attention to work details has organizational value only if accompanied by conscientious regard for results, as in inspection or proofreading.

This factor merits special attention. Employee theft of cash or merchandise is so common that screening of job applicants for honesty or integrity is widespread. At first these terms seem to mean "theft-potential," but that is too narrow. A person of integrity is not simply a nonthief but one whose word can be trusted; whose work is careful and effective even without monitoring; who, in short, can be counted on to do the right or good thing. Moreover, an often-replicated study by Barrick, Mount, and Judge (2001) found measures of this factor to have some validity in all criterion and occupational categories they studied. Even higher validity is likely for some criteria if narrow, specific aspects of conscientiousness are added to the predictor mix. Subordinate facets of conscientiousness (achievement, dependability, order, and cautiousness) identified by Dudley, Orvis, Lebiecki, and Cortina (2006) offered incremental validity beyond that obtained by global conscientiousness alone.

For Factor IV, I prefer *Emotional Stability*. It (a) is a familiar term, measured well by many inventories, (b) is positive, not negative, (c) seems free of controversy, and (d) is often a valid predictor.

Naming Factor V is not merely a matter of preference; substantive differences exist in the factors identified. "Openness to experience" is substantively different from "intellect," and neither reflects the central traits very well. In fact, Saucier (cited by Goldberg, 1995) suggested that the factor is better captured by terms such as "imagination." I think the most useful of several proposed terms is *Intellectance*; it seems to imply, as does the collection of terms in Table 3.8, finding pleasure in thinking about things, whether they be within the culture or personal experience, problems to be solved, or things to be created.

As Figure 3.5 shows, each of the Big Five factors includes many descriptive adjectives at different levels of abstraction. John, Hampson, and Goldberg (1991) identified three- and four-level hierarchies of terms such that each level above the lowest includes those below it. For one illustrative hierarchy, they cited the terms *tactful, polite, considerate,* and *nice.* Nice people are considerate (among other things), considerate people are polite (among other things), and polite people are tactful (among other things). For some jobs, there is a growing view that the facets below the Big Five level may describe traits more directly relevant to particular criteria or job categories.

Criticisms of the Five-Factor Model

The number of factors with major billing is often criticized. Eysenck (1991) said three dimensions were all that were needed. R. B. Cattell (1986) considered a set of 23 primary traits and 12 second-order factors necessary to describe normal personality. The FFM is more often criticized for not including enough factors than for having too many. This is much more than a quibble about numbers of traits; it reflects the serious question of the adequacy of those five factors for specific purposes, such as diagnosis or providing predictors for personnel decisions. The criticism usually suggests additional factors (or proposed factors) deemed necessary for those purposes.

The scientific merit of the FFM has been questioned. In a special issue of the *Journal of Personality* on the FFM, one author wrote that identifying five reliable factors is good, but a more important task is "to understand and specify the components within (and perhaps between) the five factors" (Briggs, 1992, p. 282). Block (1995) criticized the FFM for, among other things, excessive reliance on factor analysis without experimentation, prolonged observation, or concern for explanatory theory.

The five-factor model is more complex than a recitation of five factor names implies. Goldberg and his colleagues, major advocates of lexical research and the Big Five, also see shortcomings in available research, saying that "Lexical studies . . . are not the entire enter-prise" (Saucier & Goldberg, 2003, p. 13). I join their call for greater attention to alternatives to the Big Five and for comparing it to its alternatives. In personnel research, enthusiasm for the Big Five has been based on meta-analyses of validity coefficients; meaningful meta-analytic comparisons with alternatives will have to wait until there is a much larger pool of primary studies of the validities of the alternatives. It is worth noting that Saucier and Goldberg called for new lexical studies of nouns as well as adjectives.

Alternatives to the Big Five Structure

An alternative especially relevant to selection decisions is the original nine-factor taxonomy of the Personnel Decisions Research Institute (Hough, 1992, pp. 144–145), shown in Table 3.9 with abbreviated definitions. It was superseded by a quite different, more comprehensive model (Hough & Ones, 2001), but the earlier model seems relevant to the Block (1995) criticism that the FFM relies too heavily on factor analysis, because it easily illustrates a

TABLE 3.9
Nine Personality Constructs in the Personnel Decisions Research Institute Taxonomy

Dimension	Definition
Affiliation	Degree of sociability shown: liking to be with people; outgoing, participating, friendly vs. shy, reserved, and preferring to work alone.
Potency	Degree of impact, influence, and energy shown: forceful, persuasive, optimistic, energetic in getting things done vs. timid about opinions or giving directions, lethargic, and pessimistic.
Achievement	Tendency to strive for competence: hard worker, with high standards, concentration on and persistence in task completion, high self-confidence vs. low ego-involvement in work, self-doubting, little belief in value of hard work.
Dependability	Degree of conscientiousness: disciplined, well-organized, planful, respectful of rules, honest, trustworthy, orderly, thinking before acting vs. unreliable, impulsive, and rebellious.
Adjustment	Emotional stability and stress tolerance: calm, even in moods; thinking clearly and rationally, with composure, in stressful situations vs. nervous, moody, irritable, worrying, functioning poorly under stress.
Agreeableness	Degree of pleasantness shown in interpersonal relations: likable, tolerant, tactful, helpful, easy to get along with vs. critical, fault-finding, defensive, generally contrary.
Intellectance	Degree of culture shown: open-minded, esthetically fastidious, imaginative, curious, independent in thought vs. unreflective, artistically insensitive, and narrow.
Rugged Individualism	Degree of fitting stereotypically masculine vs. feminine characteristics and values: action-oriented, independent, unsentimental vs. sympathetic, sensitive to criticism, subjective, feeling vulnerable.
Locus of Control	Perceived level of control over rewards and punishments: belief that people control what happens to them by what they do vs. belief that what happens to people is beyond their personal control.

Table developed from text of "The Big Five personality variables—Construct confusion: description versus prediction", by L. M. Hough, 1992, *Human Performance*, 5, pp. 144–145.

different approach to taxonomic development. Beginning with a rational look at the five factors, Hough (with her colleagues at PDRI) divided *Surgency* into two categories, *Affiliation* and *Potency*, not unlike the *Hogan Personality Inventory* (Hogan & Hogan, 1992). On the average, measures of these categories were poorly correlated, suggesting that combining them into a single entity was unwise. Beyond that, however, Hough analyzed an array of validity coefficients within predetermined classes of variables. Some of the coefficients did not fit any of the classes and were collectively called *Miscellaneous*; from a judgmental examination of patterns of the Miscellaneous correlation coefficients, she and her colleagues identified three additional constructs: *Achievement, Rugged Individualism* (avoiding the historical label of Masculinity–Femininity), and *Locus of Control*—terms often prominent in personality research.

The 2001 report (Hough & Ones, 2001) follows the principle, with expanded sets of correlations, of identifying nomological networks of relationships of different measures of different constructs to different "other" variables. When such nomological webs for two concepts of personality, suggested as different constructs and given different names, are highly similar, the pair of concepts offer only two different names for a single construct. Hough[6] called this taxonomy a "work in progress" because much new data must be obtained before it can be fully implemented. Their tentative model offers constructs and a catalog of measures for each of them. It stays somewhat with the Big Five taxonomy but adds specific facets, most of which are collected from facets proposed in a variety of sources; the "working model" (minus the measures) is shown in Table 3.10. The global or more general constructs stay pretty much as five-factor theorists have identified them; the subordinate constructs are the proposed facets (or taxons, or constructs) accompanied by a selection of terms that seem to me to clarify the intent of each taxon. Make no mistake: they are not proposing a simple model as an alternative to or expansion of the five-factor model. They are proposing no less than a gigantic research program for the next few decades.

One alternative to the FFM is the O*NET Inventory of Work Styles. It includes 16 constructs that, like those in the Hough–Ones nomological web, are informed by but not directly based on factor analyses; these, plus one other *(Energy)*, were previously grouped under seven broader headings: Achievement Orientation, Social Influence, Interpersonal Orientation, Adjustment, Conscientiousness, Independence, and Analytical Thinking (Borman et al., 1999). The 16 style constructs are shown in Table 3.11. Some of them seem not to be very independent or to be defined with much precision, but these are judgments that must be held pending future research. When that research is available, expect some entries to be combined, some divided further, and some abandoned.

Table 3.12 is different. The traits in it describe personality flaws measured in the Hogan Development Survey to predict managerial incompetence or derailment of managerial careers (Hogan & Hogan, 2001). These constructs are not necessarily dysfunctional; people described by some of them would seem desirable candidates. Some of them (e.g., imaginative, diligent) actually do have desirable or bright sides—but also dark sides that can surely derail a career, possibly with termination or demotion. The three divisions of these traits allude to a theoretical background. A factor analysis identified three categories of scales that Hogan and Hogan said paralleled Karen Horney's themes of flawed interpersonal traits; they correspond to the obtained factors and are shown as headings of the three divisions.

---

[6] Personal communication from Leaetta Hough, August 23, 2007.

TABLE 3.10
Personality Constructs in a Proposed Nomological Web Taxonomy

Emotional Stability (Global)
   Self-Esteem (*self-confidence; freedom from feelings of inferiority*)
   Low Anxiety (*a trait, not a temporary state*)
   Even-Tempered (*calm; not hyperactive or excitable*)

Extraversion (Global)
   Dominance (*ascendant, assertive, taking leadership*)
   Sociability (*affiliative, gregarious, outgoing*)
   Activity/Energy Level (*energetic, vigorous, generally active*)

Openness to Experience (Global)
   Complexity (*preference for complexity; seeking it*)
   Culture/Artistic (*cultural taste; artistic; interest in esthetics*)
   Creativity/Innovation (*tendency to generate ideas—perhaps a set to be different*)
   Change/Variety (*experience-seeking; change-oriented*)
   Curiosity/Breadth (*being curious about many things*)
   Intellect (*original thinking; theoretical orientation; interest in working with ideas*)

Agreeableness (Global)
   Nurturance (*caring, altruistic, empathic tendencies*)

Conscientiousness (Global)
   Achievement (*achievement striving, seeking mastery; work orientation*)
   Dependability (*responsible, dutiful; seeks to avoid trouble*)
   Moralistic (*virtuous*)
   Cautiousness vs. Impulsiveness (*cautious and restrained vs risk-taking*)
   Order (*orderly; conscious of details*)
   Persistence (*endurance*)

Adapted from "The structure, measurement, validity, and use of personality variables in industrial, work, and organizational psychology" by L. M. Hough and D. S. Ones, 2001 (Appendix) in N. Anderson, D. S. Ones, S. N. Sinangil, and C. Viswesvaran (Eds.), 2001, London/Thousand Oaks, CA: Sage. Copyright 2001 by Sage Publications, Inc. Adapted with permission.

Situational Influences

Situational variables are often appropriate for multivariate predictive hypotheses, usually in interaction with predictor traits. Results are often inconsistent or negligible, maybe because many situational variables are poorly defined. Tett and Guterman (2000) proposed a theory of trait activation, suggesting that situations can activate or inhibit trait expression. It is not a brand new idea; Tett and Guterman outlined its history from 1928. It became obscure in personnel research after the mid-1960s, but Tett and his colleagues are reactivating it with a general model of trait-based job performance (Tett & Burnett, 2003). The direct link between a trait and subsequent behavior, according to their model, is moderated by trait-relevant cues from the task, social or organizational environments, including evaluation and reward systems. I offer this inadequate synopsis simply to point out that the theory is clear in requiring situational variables be explicit in hypotheses about trait–situation interactions. Explicit specification of trait relevance should reduce capricious variability in results across studies.

Variability will remain, but it can be more systematically understood. Mischel (1977) distinguished weak and strong situations. Situational strength has been shown to moderate personality-performance relationships (cf. Mischel, 1977).

TABLE 3.11
The O*NET Taxonomy of Work Styles

Work Style	Definition: When Job Requires
Achievement/Effort	establishing and maintaining personally challenging achievement goals and exerting effort toward mastering tasks
Persistence	persistence in the face of obstacles
Initiative	willingness to take on responsibilities and challenges
Energy	exerting energy and the stamina to get things done
Leadership	willingness to lead, take charge, and offer opinions and direction
Cooperation	being pleasant with others on the job and displaying a good-natured, cooperative attitude
Concern for Others	being sensitive to others' needs and feelings, and being understanding and helpful to others on the job
Social Orientation	preferring to work with others rather than alone, and being personally connected with others on the job
Self-Control	maintaining composure, keeping emotions in check, controlling anger, and avoiding aggressive behavior, even in very difficult situations
Stress Tolerance	accepting criticism and dealing calmly and effectively with high-stress situations
Adaptability/Flexibility	being open to change . . . and to considerable variety in the workplace
Dependability	being reliable, responsible, and dependable, and fulfilling obligations
Attention to Detail	being careful about details and thorough in completing tasks
Integrity	being honest and ethical
Independence	developing one's own ways of doing things, guiding oneself with little or no supervision, and depending on oneself to get things done
Innovation	creativity and alternative thinking to develop new ideas for and answers to work-related problems
Analytical Thinking	analyzing information and using logic to address work-related issues and problems

Adapted from "Work styles" by W. C. Borman, U. C. Kubisiak, and R. J. Schneider, 1999, Table 13-2 (pp. 218–219). In *An Occupational Information System for the 21st Century: The Development of O*NET*, by N. G. Peterson, M. D. Mumford, W. C. Borman, P. R. Jeanneret, and E. A. Fleishman (Eds.), 1999, Washington, DC: American Psychological Association. Copyright 1999 by American Psychological Association. Adapted by permission.

Further Personality Constructs

Personality constructs defined in the context of trait taxonomies can help clarify constructs and the distinguishing differences between them. However, the contemporary emphasis on taxonomies may not be merited. Matching the *behavioral* content of criterion and predictor constructs in hypothesis formation will, I think, yield better predictions and decisions. It may reduce the general-vs.-specific problem. Broad criteria call for broad, general constructs as predictors. Narrower criteria may be harder to match with lower levels in the trait taxonomies. Some personality predictors from uncategorized, "miscellaneous" lists of variables may give better matches. Some may be borrowed from the nomological web model (Hough & Ones, 2001). Other examples include specific orientations such as *work orientation* (Gough, 1985), or *service orientation* (Hogan, Hogan, & Busch, 1984), or the breakdown of the Type A personality construct into *achievement striving* and *impatience–irritability*, each predicting different sorts of outcomes (Spence, Helmreich, & Pred, 1987).

TABLE 3.12
Personality Constructs in the Hogan Development Survey

Moving away from People	
Excitable	Moody and hard to please, expecting to be treated badly; prone to disruptive emotional displays
Skeptical	Cynical, distrustful, and suspicious; retaliate openly and directly to perceived mistreatment, perhaps with confrontation, violence, accusations, or litigation
Cautious	Avoidance of risk of rejection or blame; respond to possible criticism by being very cautious or by taking no action at all
Reserved	Detached, uncommunicative; seemingly self-focused and indifferent to feelings or opinions of others
Leisurely	Independent, insistent on working at own pace; often have social skills for hiding annoyance so that peevishness and foot-dragging are hard to detect
Moving against People	
Bold	Arrogant, unusually and even excessively self-confident, with strong sense of entitlement and expectation of success; take more credit than due for success and refuse to acknowledge failure or error
Mischievous	Risk taking, testing of limits, exploitive; self-confident and feel invulnerable, with some problems telling the truth; tend to be unpredictable in responses
Colorful	Expressive, dramatic, seeking notice and the center of attention; fun to watch but impulsive and unpredictable
Imaginative	Creative, sometimes odd; generally desirable characteristics but can also be eccentric and confusing to others because of sudden and unusual changes of direction
Moving toward People	
Diligent	Meticulous, perfectionistic, inflexible; tend to be critical of the performance of others; can be good role models, but can also be fussy and overly controlling with subordinates
Dutiful	Eager to please but not to take independent action or go against the flow; alert to signs of disapproval, and tend to ingratiate themselves

Developed from tables and text in "Assessing leadership: The view from the dark side" by R. Hogan and J. Hogan, 2001, *International Journal of Selection and Assessment*, pp. 40–51. Copyright 2001 by Blackwell Publishers. Adapted by permission.

Theoretically based constructs are available. Some are recently proposed, such as *other orientation* (Meglino & Korsgaard, 2007). Existing personality inventories may suggest many others with longer histories. The *Edwards Personal Preference Schedule* and Jackson's *Personality Research Form* have scales based on Murray's (1938) catalog of psychogenic needs. The *Embedded Figures Test* was based on the field-dependence–field-independence construct, the tendency to disassociate perceptions or ideas from the context in which they occur. The Jungian-based *Myers–Briggs Type Indicator* classifies people into personality types based on four dimensions: extraversion versus introversion, sensation versus intuition, thinking versus feeling, and reliance on judgment versus perception. A typology of personality types and matching types of work environments is assessed by Holland's *Vocational Preference Inventory* and its matching job analysis form, the *Position Classification Inventory*. The Millon theory, developed originally to assess abnormal behavior but subsequently for normal adults, has 24 scales for 12 bipolar constructs in the *Millon Index of Personality Styles* (MIPS). These are only a few of literally hundreds of constructs purportedly assessed in inventories reviewed in publications such as the Buros Institute's *Tests in Print* and *Mental Measurements Yearbooks* or the Test Corporation of America's *Tests* and *Test Critiques*.

Personality constructs tend to be interpreted as unobservable descriptions of what people *are*, not what they *do*. Perhaps the emphasis should be reversed, defining personality constructs as characteristic responses to broad environmental demands, such as those at work or at school. Pointing out that the psychology of college sophomores may be in part a function of the common demands they face, Dawes (1991) suggested that research questions should be rephrased to reflect those demands, asking for description of acts rather than of traits. Botwin and Buss (1989) did so; they developed act-content inventories for 22 categories. Their research supported the five-factor model quite well, *but only when they controlled for a general activity level*. General activity level is itself a construct of probable importance for many kinds of work, but few taxonomies include it. It may be only one obvious example of work-relevant constructs not commonly assessed. Perhaps further research should identify and classify things people persistently do in their work as much as or more than latent traits.

COMPETENCIES

Competency analysis (or competency modeling) is often described as a part of, adjunct to, or even replacement for job analysis (Morgeson, Delaney-Klinger, Mayfield, Ferrara, & Campion, 2004; Roe, 2005; Vosquijl, 2005). Competencies may be criteria, inferred from job analyses that include competency analysis (Bartram, 2000; Blancero, Boroski, & Dyer, 1996; Morgeson et al., 2004), or they may be cast as predictors (Chan & Schmitt, 2005; McClelland, 1973; Russell, 2001).

The problem of definition seems especially elusive for competencies; Morgeson et al. (2004, p. 676) called it "one of the most vexing issues." McClelland (1973), apparently the first to use the term as an attribute to be assessed, did not offer a definition, but he was clear that he meant something other than intelligence. For Russell (2001), competencies meant combinations of personal traits and characteristics of work to be done, but Brannick et al. (2007) identified them as broad human attributes "not linked directly to specific tasks" (p. 137). A common theme is that competency is a multidimensional construct that can be decomposed into less inclusive components (Chan & Schmitt, 2005). Risking derision, I offer a short definition: *A competency is a learned ability to accomplish a complex task and do it well*. That is, a competency is itself complex, applicable to broad classes of tasks (not necessarily familiar ones), and an acquired ability—without specifying any particular avenue of learning.

Eastman Kodak used competency analysis to transform the HR function. In some ways it seemed a subjective, group-think process, but sensible and well thought out. The groups agreed on three kinds of competencies. *Core competencies* were rated as essentially universal across HR work roles. *Leverage competencies* were considered important for selecting or developing people for some roles but not all of them. *Role-specific competencies* were rated as essential for one or maybe two roles but not necessarily for others (Blancero et al., 1996).

Bartram (2005b) said that competencies, if defined in terms of observable behavior at work, provide the basis for differentiated criteria representing different aspects of performance and "a more sophisticated understanding of the factors underlying OJP ... [and] allow better prediction of job performance for a particular role once the competency requirements for the role were understood" (pp. 1185–1186). From this perspective, Bartram described eight (the "great eight") performance variables defined as behavioral competencies and

TABLE 3.13
Bartram's Great Eight Competencies

Competency Title	Domain Definition
Leading and deciding	Takes control and exercises leadership. Initiates action, gives direction, and takes responsibility.
Supporting and cooperating	Supports others and shows respect and positive regard for them in social situations. Puts people first, working effectively with individuals and teams, clients, and staff. Behaves consistently with clear personal values that complement those of the organization.
Interacting and presenting	Communicates and networks effectively. Successfully persuades and influences others. Relates to others in a confident and relaxed manner.
Analyzing and interpreting	Shows evidence of clear analytic thinking. Gets to the heart of complex problems and issues. Applies own expertise effectively.
Creating and conceptualizing	Works well in situations requiring openness to new ideas and experiences. Seeks out learning opportunities. Handles situations and problems with innovation and creativity. Thinks broadly and strategically. Supports and drives organizational change.
Organizing and executing	Plans ahead and works in a systematic and organized way. Follows directions and procedures. Focuses on customer satisfaction and delivers a quality service or product to the agreed standards.
Adapting and coping	Adapts and responds well to change. Manages pressure effectively and copes well with setbacks.
Enterprising and performing	Focuses on results and achieving personal work objectives. Works best when work is related closely to results and the impact of personal efforts is obvious. Shows an understanding of business, commerce, and finance. Seeks opportunities for self-development and career advancement.

Note: Selected content from "The Great Eight competencies: A criterion-centric approach to validation" by D. Bartram, 2005, *Journal of Applied Psychology, 90*, Table 1, p. 1187. Copyright 2004 by SHL Group plc. Reproduced by permission of SHL Group Ltd.

summarized in Table 3.13. I view them as relatively specific constructs to be included in Campbell's higher-order category of job-specific task proficiency.

NONCOGNITIVE PREDICTORS

Personality measures are often said to be "noncognitive," despite recognized cognitive components. Here I use that term to discuss traits with even less cognitive contribution to total score variance, if any at all.

Physical and Sensory Traits

It is hard to say whether vision, hearing, strength, and speed of physical movement are no longer important in modern work or whether they have simply gone out of style, as personality assessment did for about a quarter of a century. Maybe the Americans with Disabilities Act (ADA) and the Civil Rights Act of 1964 (as amended) reduced interest in using physical and sensory abilities for personnel decisions. For many kinds of work, however, they are potential predictors and may be genuine prerequisites for competent performance of some jobs.

Physical Characteristics

Anthropometric characteristics (mainly height and weight) may be directly useful as predictors on some jobs or indirectly useful as moderators or mediators (Judge & Cable, 2004). Physical traits *can* be relevant to work outcomes, and accommodation for physical differences may not be as simple as it might seem. Remodeling or computerizing a work area might be prohibitively expensive. Providing a work aid (such as a simple stool) for one person might create hazards for another (who might stumble over it). Job analysis should show just how important apparent physical requirements really are and how the job might be done differently; it should form a foundation for imaginative thinking about potential methods of accommodation. Hogan and Quigley (1986) reported that height and weight requirements had been approved in litigation only where there was no adverse impact or where job-relatedness was clearly demonstrated. Common sense or the mere appearance of relevance is not and will not be enough evidence of job-relatedness. For many jobs, redesigning the work environment may be more productive than selecting people to fit the environment as it is.

Physical Abilities

Many jobs, not merely laboring jobs, require physical skills. Mail carriers, fire fighters, power line repairers, tree trimmers, construction workers, and paramedics are among those for whom strength, endurance, and balance are relevant. Nevertheless, few psychologists have studied physical abilities and their relevance in employment practices; most of what we know has come from the work of Edwin A. Fleishman and his associates, summarized as follows in Fleishman and Reilly (1992).

- *Static strength*: Ability to exert continuous muscular force for short periods of time. Used in pushing or lifting heavy objects.
- *Explosive strength*: Ability to exert muscular force in short bursts. Used in running, jumping, throwing things, or striking them (as in splitting logs with an axe).
- *Dynamic strength*: Ability to use repeated or sustained muscular force over long periods of time; muscular endurance, resistance to muscular fatigue. Used in tasks requiring climbing or digging.
- *Trunk strength*: Ability of stomach and lower back muscles to support parts of the body in repetitive tasks or over long periods of time. Used when working with tools while partially sitting or moving heavy objects while bent over.
- *Extent flexibility*: Ability to bend, stretch, twist or reach out; a matter of degree, not of speed. Used when working in awkward, cramped settings or extending arms to reach something.
- *Dynamic flexibility*: Ability to bend, and so on, quickly and repeatedly. Used in tasks such as shoveling substances (snow, coal, etc.) to move them.
- *Gross body coordination*: Ability to coordinate movements of arms, legs, and torso when the whole body is in motion, as in swimming.
- *Gross body equilibrium*: Ability to keep or recover one's balance in unstable positions or conditions. Used in construction work, or in walking on ice.
- *Stamina*: Ability to maintain challenging physical exertion over long time periods without getting winded; an aerobic ability. Used in fighting fires or in making extensive deliveries by bicycle or on foot.

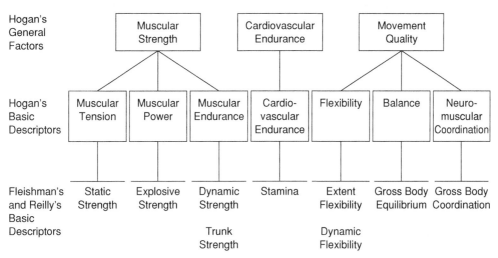

FIG. 3.6   A model of physical abilities, based on the Hogan (1991a, 1991b) and the Fleishman and Reilly descriptors.

Joyce Hogan (1991a, 1991b) considered seven of these sufficient in personnel selection, arguing that static and dynamic distinctions rarely made sense in job descriptions. She identified three general fitness factors: (a) muscular strength, the ability to apply or resist force by contracting muscles; (b) cardiovascular endurance, or aerobic capacity, and (c) and coordination or quality of movement. A comparison of her taxonomy and Fleishman's is shown in Figure 3.6. Different terms for similar abilities reflect slightly different emphases. She later combined strength and endurance factors; apparently, the physical requirements of jobs could be defined with but two general factors, (a) muscular strength and endurance and (b) physical skill in movements (Hogan, 1991b). Either Hogan or Fleishman may disagree with the comparison, but precision in naming the traits is not the point here. The point is that different measures of physical abilities may measure different components of work.

The different measures have predicted work sample criteria very well, but they can also serve as instruments of unfair discrimination (Hogan, 1991a). Some of the significant validities for combined groups of men and women were not significant in either group by itself. Perhaps the overall correlation is spurious, created by combining data from groups with substantially different means on both variables. If so, the apparent "validity" merely capitalizes on the mean sex differences, enough so that sex by itself might predict as well. If so, litigation seems likely.

Possible sex discrimination was background for research reported by Arnold, Rauschenberger, Soubel, and Guion (1982). In earlier times, only men were steel mill laborers, doing all the heavy physical work. Women applicants posed two problems. First, on average, they had less strength, suggesting probable adverse impact and subsequent litigation. Second, abandoning physical testing (to assure that those hired were strong enough to do the work) risked serious on-the-job injuries—and litigation under other laws. Traditional criterion-related predictive research was absurd. If avoiding personal injury is the purpose of the research, it would be worse than silly to hire lots of people and simply wait for people to hurt themselves, just to provide a criterion group! Arnold et al. abstracted elementary physical tasks from the various labor jobs and correlated them with performance on a general work sample. An arm dynamometer test was the best single predictor; other tests added little predictive power. The muscular strength measured by the arm dynamometer seemed the most general of the strength tests.

Physical ability, especially strength and flexibility, can be developed by special training and exercise. When physical abilities are predictors, opportunities for compensatory ability development and subsequent retesting should be considered. Arnold et al. were adamant that weaker applicants should be rejected, but they also insisted that those screened out be told to develop strength to improve their chances of being selected at a later time.

Sensory Abilities

Vision and hearing ability are not unitary; "good vision" or "good hearing" means quite different visual or auditory skills for different jobs. Fleishman and Reilly (1992b) listed 12 different visual and auditory abilities, including, in addition to near and far visual acuity, such specialized abilities as night vision, color vision, depth perception, and a corresponding variety of sounds related to hearing. Military and postwar vision research for work settings was reviewed in Guion (1965a); little has been added since. No comparable research history is available for hearing. For both vision and hearing, occupational use probably must include strong cognitive as well as sensory components. A certain pitch with low volume might be emitted from a piece of machinery; two people may have the acuity to hear it, but the better worker is the one who understands its implication.

Accommodation

One or more of a candidate's abilities may have been permanently impaired by trauma, surgery, illness, or birth defects. Inspiring stories have been told of exceptional people overcoming such problems, but accommodation is often needed for people of impaired physical or sensory ability. Even for undramatic problems, such as the average lower strength levels of women, redesign of equipment to reduce strength requirements is often more useful than selection practices that might be deemed discriminatory.

Accommodation is not just something the organization does. The best accommodation may be made by the person. We tend to forget how very adaptable people are. Impairment in one ability is often compensated by increased skill in another. Formal hypotheses developed for most candidates may need to be replaced by job trials for a disabled candidate to see how he or she is differently abled.

Psychomotor Abilities

The term *psychomotor ability* implies a combination of cognition, sensory processes, and muscular activity in task performance. Dexterity, coordination, steadiness, precision and speed of movement, and motor response latency are examples. Fleishman and Reilly (1992b), relying on Fleishman's earlier factor analytic work, distinguished hand dexterity from finger dexterity. Both require quick and accurate movements, but hand dexterity requires larger arm muscle groups. Early on, Bourassa and Guion (1959) failed to confirm the distinction. The two factors may be combined in complex competencies, where the distinction is unlikely to make much difference.

Experience, Education, and Training

The word *construct* does not fit some predictors; specified training or experience requirements are among them. The hypothesis justifying such requirements, if actually thought out, is that people with the desired credentials are the only ones who can do the job, or, in a less extreme view, the ones who can do it better. Credentials required by law, such as some licenses, are a necessary basis for decision, but no prediction is involved. Other requirements, such as years of experience or education, are rarely useful. Too often those with fine credentials do not have the competencies to match. Education requirements might be justified if (a) the job requires extended knowledge comparable to that of recognized professions, (b) the knowledge and ability requirements are hard to evaluate by other methods, (c) the consequences of *not* requiring a specific degree and academic major are likely to be severe, and (d) the educational program is virtually the only way to acquire the knowledge demanded by the job (Ash, Johnson, Levine, & McDaniel, 1989). Similar training or experience requirements *can* be useful, if systematically specified, evaluated, and based on job analysis (Gibson & Prien, 1977; McDaniel, Schmidt, & Hunter, 1988b).

Seniority is too often a basis for personnel decisions. It may be required by union contracts, although they may include provisions for considering qualifications as well. The justification, other than expedience, is the assumption that, as experience in the job increases over time, ability to do the job also increases. This is a linear or monotonic view (terms defined in Chapter 7), a view not supported by data (Jacobs, Hoffman, & Kriska, 1990). Staying on the same job a long time may mean doing it too poorly to be promoted.

Nonlinearity may have resulted in underestimates of correlation in the relatively few empirical studies of seniority. Some research suggests that length of experience on a job, up to a few years, can be a useful consideration (Jacobs, et al., 1990; McDaniel, Schmidt, & Hunter, 1988a). McDaniel et al. (1988b) suggested a limit of about five years, and, in a meta-analysis, found generally low but positive validity coefficients for length of service but high ones where the mean experience in the sample was relatively brief.

CONCLUDING NOTE

This chapter mentions many predictor constructs but does not suggest any "best bet" predictors for designated criteria. Linking predictors to criteria is still a local hypothesis, based on local job and need analyses. Better national or global hypotheses await massive, cross-industry, cross-occupational, cross-cultural research and meta-analyses. The ideal of an empirically developed matrix of such linkages has not yet been achieved; its achievement would require a massive research program.

Without it, hypothesis development is necessarily local or organizationally specific. Criterion constructs, other than overall performance, seem dictated by organizational needs. Choosing predictor constructs requires knowledge of both the organization and job, and it is surely aided by scientific knowledge. The balance of scientific ideas and local situations can get one in trouble. Too much unrestrained scientific excitement leads to the use of esoteric constructs only because they are interesting and currently popular topics—and to overlooking constructs with good records. The best rule is for multivariate parsimony, the development of predictive hypotheses with relatively few predictors chosen from different categories, done with careful job and situation analysis and extensive knowledge of the relevant research. Cognitive constructs, I suspect, should always be included; more often than is typical, hypotheses should include personality and other noncognitive constructs. And always, the hypothesized predictors ought to make good sense to scientists and managers alike and be defendable in litigation.

Making good sense includes questioning things we think we know. We think that defining a construct also defines a single continuum—that people at the high end of it have lots of the construct and those at the low end have very little of that same construct. Hackman (2009) pointed out that positive and negative affect have been shown to be qualitatively different, involving different neural systems. It does not seem strange to suggest that high and low absenteeism might also be qualitatively different—or any of the other trait constructs that have been described. For now, the kind of thinking described as required in developing predictive hypotheses is still our best approach, but we need to be aware, in practice, in theory development, and in reading this book, that alternative approaches are likely to be on the horizon. They may or may not be better than the approaches we now know. Serious effort is needed to find out.

This chapter has alluded, sort of in passing, to legal problems and possible litigation. In countries with statutory prohibitions against employment discrimination, every predictive hypothesis should be formed with a strong enough logical foundation, preferably based on a history of theory or data or both, to help defend in court subsequent employment procedures. That takes us to Chapter 4.

4

The Legal Context for Personnel Decisions

Few organizations have full discretion in making decisions. Laws often limit employers' actions. Some occupations require licenses. Limitations may be specified in union contracts. Interlocking directorates are illegal in the United States under the Clayton Act. Discrimination in personnel decisions is prohibited by several laws. These laws are commonly discussed primarily as prohibiting discrimination in hiring practices, but only 4% of the charges filed with the Equal Employment Opportunity Commission (EEOC) in 2005 were based on hiring. Discharge, various sorts of harassment, and other decision issues accounted for more (Goldman, Gutek, Stein, & Lewis, 2006).

Some laws mandate consideration of characteristics not relevant to job performance; others require that other irrelevant characteristics *not* be considered in employment decisions. A required irrelevancy in many American civil service jurisdictions is veterans' preference. The most frequently litigated prohibited irrelevancies are based on race, sex, age, or disability. These legal requirements are based on a social policy that transcends the interests of individual employers. Most such policies are more concerned with prohibiting discrimination *against* members of designated groups than with promoting discrimination *favoring* certain groups. Laws permit going to court for a variety of reasons, and Americans seem increasingly willing to sue. In this age of litigation, personnel decisions based on whim, stereotypes, prejudices, or expediency are just plain foolish.

This chapter emphasizes American laws promoting equal employment opportunity (EEO), partly because I know them best and because they've been around so long. Ethnic minorities have been a fact of American life for centuries, but they were not salient in Europe until the 1950s immigration wave (Evers, te Nijenhuis, & van der Flier, 2005). Much (but certainly not all) legislation and research on employee selection on both continents stemmed from the American Civil Rights Act of 1964, as amended. That act and its progeny have dominated practice in the United States for more than four decades and form a guide for anti-discrimination laws in many other countries with similar cultures. American EEO laws apply anywhere in the world where United States citizens are employed by an American-controlled company. Businesses incorporated in other countries are subject to American laws for their operations in the United States, and American businesses operating in other countries may be subject to laws that may differ greatly from American laws and customs. For example, in India, many organizations must *reserve* a specific number of places for so-called "backward classes" (Parikh, 1997). Discrimination is a growing issue, and related research grows as well, as other countries and cultures consider the problem; so, "future researchers literally have an entire world in which to investigate these issues" (Goldman et al., 2006, p. 817). For a more global perspective, see the review of legal environments in 22 different countries by Sackett et al. (2010).

A BRIEF HISTORY OF EEO REGULATION IN THE UNITED STATES

Some regulation is traced to the Bill of Rights, collectively the first 10 amendments to the US Constitution. Religious discrimination is barred under the First Amendment. A person with a vested property right in employment can sue under the Fifth Amendment's protection against deprivation "of life, liberty, or property, without due process of law" if a personnel decision results in loss of employment. The Thirteenth, Fourteenth, and Fifteenth amendments, adopted during the reconstruction era and accompanied by Civil Rights Acts in 1866, 1870, and 1871, provide collectively that all persons within the jurisdiction of the United States (citizens and noncitizens alike) shall have the same rights under the law, including property rights. Enforcement of these provisions was dormant during most of the 20th century. However, they were dusted off in the late 1960s to bring suits against state and local jurisdictions, exempted under the 1964 Civil Rights Act until its 1972 amendment (Baker v. Columbus Separate School District, 1971; Baker v. Columbus Separate School District, 1972; Washington v. Davis, 1976).

Executive Orders

Different EEO regulation came in a series of Executive Orders (EOs) dating back to the Second World War. The first (EO 8802), issued by President Roosevelt, required federal agencies to include provisions in defense contracts obligating contractors to hire without regard to race, creed, or national origin. Similar orders were issued by Presidents Truman, Eisenhower, and Kennedy. EO 11246 was issued by President Johnson in 1965, providing that contractors (a) will not discriminate on the basis of race, color, or religion, (b) will take affirmative action to avoid such discrimination against employees or applicants, (c) will comply with the Order and with rules, regulations, and orders issued by the Secretary of Labor under its provisions, (d) will impose the same requirements on all subcontractors or vendors, and (e) will lose the contract and be declared ineligible for future government contracts in the event of noncompliance.[1]

EO 11246 had a major impact on employment procedures in the United States. The Office of Federal Contract Compliance (OFCC, now the Office of Federal Contract Compliance Programs, OFCCP) was established in the Department of Labor to enforce its provisions, which are applicable even to employers who do not have written contracts with a federal agency (United States v. New Orleans Public Service, Inc., 1974). Affirmative action was a major feature of the Order. Enforcement regulations required contractors and subcontractors to develop affirmative action programs with detailed analyses of minority and female employment in the organization and, where such representation was weak, to establish "specific goals and timetables," that is, for setting up targets or, arguably, quotas for specific subgroups or "affected classes."

---

[1] Subsequent Executive Orders relevant to this discussion are not described here save to say that they have brought other groups under their protection, prohibiting, for example, discrimination based on sex, national origin, age, or conditions of handicap. Not all Executive Orders are as comprehensive as 11246; for example, reporting requirements and sanctions are not specified in EO 11141, banning age discrimination.

EO 11246 was issued *after* the effective date of the Civil Rights Act (*Civil Rights Act*, 1964). The Executive Order may seem an odd redundancy, but its affirmative action requirement went beyond the Act, then considered by many EEO advocates to be too weak and too slow in providing remedies. In contrast, the Executive Order seemed like an executioner's order—swift and fatal for the employer who relied on federal contracts for business survival. In retrospect, the argument was flawed; very few contracts have ever been canceled.[2]

The Civil Rights Act of 1964

Reconstruction era attempts to provide equal rights under law had virtually disappeared by the end of the 19th century. Segregation was supported by law and the courts in much of the country—by custom in most of the rest of it. The Civil Rights Act (1964) was to social policy in the US what the continental divide is to the flow of rivers. It put the full power of the federal government to work on behalf of black citizens for equal access to schools and public accommodations as well as for employment opportunities. During Congressional debate, in a misguided and unsuccessful effort to derail support for the proposed Act, an opponent of the bill offered an amendment (in a jocular manner) to include sex as a pro-scribed basis for decision; another amendment added national origin. Both were accepted by the bipartisan management of the bill through Congress and became part of the Act. The Act's importance as a signal of a shifting concept of government cannot be overemphasized. Previously, the federal government had regulated things and standards (e.g., food and drugs, weights and measures). This Act regulated behavior (White, 1982).

Unlawful Employment Practices

Title VII of the Act specifies several unlawful employment practices.

1. Employers may not fail or refuse to hire, or discharge, anyone on the basis of race, color, religion, sex, or national origin.
2. They may not segregate or classify employees or applicants so as to deprive anyone of employment opportunities on the basis of race, color, religion, sex, or national origin.

---

[2] The social objective to be met, whether by Executive Order or legislation, has never been clearly or precisely defined. EEOC and OFCC initially had different time tables for meeting it. The first OFCC Director, Edward Sylvester, asked a former colleague of mine, Dr Richard Shore, of the Policy and Planning Division of the Department of Labor, to draft an order concerning employment testing. It was done, and I was asked to comment on it. In doing so, I told Mr Sylvester that I thought that the issuance and enforcement of such an order could "eliminate unfair racial discrimination within a generation." He deemed this an appropriate and reasonable objective, and work toward issuance of the order went forward. Others, notably the staff of EEOC, argued that discrimination should be ended immediately—specifically by July 2, 1965. Legally, they were correct. Psychologically, time was needed to change attitudes, skills, knowledge, educational foundations, and many other conse-quences of centuries of slavery and segregation. I believed that evidence that people were finally being hired on the basis of their qualifications would encourage minority youth to seek qualifications for useful and satisfying occupations, and that such an encouraging view was necessary for genuine equality in employment. That belief was a minority view (without pun) among agencies charged with fostering fair employment, a view eventually swept aside in the OFCC as well as the EEOC in favor of goals and timetables leading to group parity as quickly as possible.

3. Employment agencies may not fail or refuse to refer candidates on the basis of any of these characteristics. This holds as well for labor unions with regard to membership or influencing employers to discriminate.
4. All provisions apply equally to employers, labor organizations, or joint labor–management committees controlling training programs.
5. Advertising employment or training opportunities may not indicate preferences for any group under any of these designated characteristics.
6. It is unlawful to retaliate against people who have opposed unlawful employment practices under the Act.

Exemptions

The Act does not "apply to the employment of aliens outside any State." Nor does it prevent religious organizations from hiring their own adherents to carry out religious work. Some preferential hiring is explicitly endorsed, such as preferential hiring of American Indians on or near reservations, or veterans' preference. Bona fide seniority systems are also protected. The Act does not prohibit or discourage discrimination on the basis of actual qualifications to do a job.

The Use of Employment Tests

In 1963, during Congressional debate on the Civil Rights Bill, a fair employment case in Illinois (Myart v. Motorola, 1964) went into the state court system, national headlines, and Congressional debate. The dispute arose when Mr Myart, a black applicant, was allegedly refused a job, despite previous and presumably relevant experience, because of an unsatisfactory test score. He filed a complaint with the Illinois Fair Employment Practices Commission charging racial discrimination. The Commission concluded that Mr Myart should be offered the job and that use of the test should be discontinued. It further concluded that the future use of any other test should consider the possible effects of cultural deprivation on test performance. The decision was subsequently overturned by the Illinois Supreme Court, but it engendered heated public debate. Many applauded the attack on testing, but many in Congress feared that a federal agency to be created under the bill would interfere with the rights of employers to establish employment standards.

In this context, the Tower amendment (Senator John Tower proposed the original version of the amendment) was added to the legislation as Section 703(h) (*Civil Rights Act*, 1964). It says in part, "nor shall it be an unlawful employment practice for an employer to give and to act upon the results of any professionally developed ability test provided that such test, its administration or action upon the results is not designed, intended, or used to discriminate because of race, color, religion, sex, or national origin."

The Tower amendment is ambiguous in that it refers to "professionally developed *ability* tests," but not to tests (or inventories) of knowledge, personality, behavioral habits, or life history. It is silent on the evaluation of experience or motivation. It does not specify the requisite profession of the test developer. (May a work sample test of welding ability be developed by professional test developers or by professional welders?) In practice, courts have considered many kinds of assessments of qualifications, ranging from basic ability tests through personality inventories to assessment centers without reference to this phrase. The emphasis is usually on determining whether the assessment procedure has had the effect of discriminating against the protected groups or has that effect without being sufficiently job-related.

The Equal Employment Opportunity Commission

The Act established the Equal Employment Opportunity Commission (EEOC) and empowered it to investigate charges of prohibited employment practices; to dismiss charges deemed unfounded; to use conference, conciliation, and persuasion to eliminate practices where charges were found to be true; and to work with authorities in states or other jurisdictions where the practices are prohibited by local law. Where there is a finding of "reasonable cause" to believe the charge is true, the EEOC can file suit in the federal courts. Early in EEO history, working together through "gentle persuasion" lost out procedurally to the adversarial posturing of litigants.

The Right to Sue

The Act empowers aggrieved persons to bring suit in the federal courts with or without an EEOC finding of reasonable cause. It expressly gives federal courts authority to establish appropriate remedies, including "such affirmative action as may be appropriate."[3] It gives the Attorney General the authority to bring suit, without EEOC participation, under some circumstances.

Establishing Rules and Regulations

The Act created the EEOC. EO 11246 created the OFCC in the Department of Labor. Other statutes placed EEO enforcement obligations in the Departments of Treasury, Education, and Health and Human Services. The nation's largest employer, the US Civil Service Commission (CSC, forerunner of the Office of Personnel Management), issued its own rules. Rules and regulations were not always consistent across these entities.

1972 Amendment of Title VII

The Act was amended in 1972 to bring governmental employers (federal, state, and local) under its aegis. The 1972 amendments also created the Equal Employment Opportunity Coordinating Council (EEOCC, abolished in 1978), consisting of heads (or their deputies) of the Civil Rights Commission and of the four major enforcement agencies: the EEOC, the OFCC, the CSC, and the Department of Justice. It was supposed to promote efficiency, eliminate contradictory requirements for employers, and avoid duplication of effort among enforcement agencies. Its efforts culminated in the *Uniform Guidelines on Employee Selection Procedures*, abbreviated here as "the Guidelines" (Equal Employment Opportunity Commission, Civil Service Commission, Department of Labor & Department of Justice, 1978).[4]

---

[3] I think this implies a broader concept of affirmative action than the "goals and timetables" (or "quotas," depending on political leanings) typically implied in subsequent regulations.

[4] As this is written, in 2009, the Uniform Guidelines still remain in force despite technical problems. As I said before (Guion, 1998), I still see no sign of plans to revise them.

Orders and Guidelines

Guidelines were issued from 1966 through 1974 to help employers comply with the law and tried to reflect views of a diverse group of contributors.[5] Their development was characterized by controversy and acrimony about specific provisions. Moreover, each agency tended to be interested in developing regulations only when a published rule would have helped its case in current litigation. When the crisis-at-hand ended, whether by settlement or evaporation, so did regulatory progress.[6]

Equal Employment Opportunity Guidelines, 1966

The 1966 EEOC Guidelines (Equal Employment Opportunity Commission, 1966) were written as a booklet to help confused employers unfamiliar with things like validity. In general, it presented orthodox requirements for the choice and evaluation of personnel selection tools, mainly tests. However, it included two not widely recognized departures from the orthodoxy of the time. One was that the concept of a test could include many other kinds of assessment. The other was the notion that validities might differ for different subgroups (e.g., blacks and whites) and that tests should be used only for subgroups for which they were valid.[7] However, distribution of the 1966 document attracted little notice.

Office of Federal Contract Compliance Testing Order, 1968

Work culminating in the 1968 Testing Order (Office of Federal Contract Compliance, 1968) began in 1965. The first draft was brief, terse and, I thought, clear, but it met with strenuous resistance. Later an Advisory Committee on Testing and Selection was appointed, on which I served,[8] successively longer versions were developed and critiqued, and a final version was issued as a "Testing Order" in 1968. The Order is no longer in effect, but its form and many of its provisions substantially influenced the Uniform Guidelines, so its history may help in interpreting that document and its flaws.

[5] I would like to overlook or even deny my involvement in this history, but honesty seems the better policy. It requires the use of "we" or "I" where it would be pleasant to say "they." My involvement was primarily in the early development of the OFCC Testing Orders of 1968 and 1971 and tangentially in the EEOC Guidelines of 1970. I was a consultant to OFCC in the beginnings of discussions about the proposed OFCC Order. I resigned but subsequently returned as a member of an advisory committee that eventually drafted the 1968 and 1971 Orders. Despite admitted involvement, I do not accept full responsibility for the final content of these documents—and certainly not for later interpretations of them. However, that involvement did give me some unfortunate insights into the processes by which they were developed.

[6] I may be over-generalizing here. The statement is true with regard to the development of the 1968, 1970, and 1971 documents. I believe, without first-hand knowledge, it was true in later developments.

[7] This departure became prominent later, was studied extensively, and was later dropped as scientifically unsupportable. I consider it more fully in Chapter 9.

[8] The committee was jointly chaired by an academic, Raymond A. Katzell of New York University, and an industry-based psychologist, Howard C. Lockwood of Lockheed Corporation. Other members were Lewis E. Albright (Kaiser Aluminum and Chemical Corporation), Robert D. Dugan (Life Office Management Association), J. Robert Garcia (Plans for Progress, on leave from Sandia Corporation), Robert M. Guion (Bowling Green State University), C. Paul Sparks (Humble Oil and Refining Company), Mary L. Tenopyr (North American Aviation), and E. Belvin Williams (Teachers College, Columbia University).

Its principal thrust was that contractors should validate any tests or other instruments used in selection decisions if they had an adverse impact on any group protected under EO 11246. *Adverse impact* exists if members of a protected group are proportionately less likely to be hired, that is, have a lower *selection ratio* (SR), than members of the group with the highest SR. A working definition of adverse impact was needed. Defining it in terms of statistical significance seemed unlikely to help employers, but committee discussions led to a simple rule of thumb for a reasonable approximation: *Adverse impact exists if the selection ratio in one group is less than 80% of the selection ratio in the group with the highest selection ratio.*[9] Despite problems, this is still a common definition of adverse impact, although many courts now consider evidence of statistical significance as well, often in distinction from practical significance.

Adverse impact was not considered evidence of discrimination; it merely triggered the validation requirement. Real qualifications may differ in different groups; affirmative action efforts, such as special recruiting, can exacerbate adverse impact. Nevertheless, if the 80% rule was not met, the Order required evidence of validity for the procedure producing the adverse impact. Under the Order, virtually any quantitative selection procedure was subject to validation; nonquantitative selection procedures, such as interviews, could be challenged under the adverse impact concept and subsequently quantified (e.g., by ratings) and validated. If the 80% rule was satisfied, the employer had no validation obligation under the Order.

It was important to assure that contractors knew what was meant by *validity* and *validation*. To avoid writing a textbook, we referred readers to the *Standards for Educational and Psychological Tests and Manuals* (American Psychological Association, American Educational Research Association, & National Council on Measurement in Education, 1966) which recognized three aspects of validity: *criterion-related validity*, emphasized in employment practice; *construct validity*, important in clinical testing; and *content validity*, important mainly in educational testing. Although these terms had been introduced earlier, implications of the last two for employment testing had not been explored. Recognizing, albeit hazily, the inclusion of construct and content validity in the *Standards*, we added, with virtually no serious deliberation, that "evidence of content or construct validity may also be appropriate where criterion-related validity is not feasible" (Office of Federal Contract Compliance, 1968, p. 14392). With this not-very-helpful addition, we moved on to other topics.

EEOC and OFCC Regulations in 1970 and 1971

In the 1968 Presidential campaign, Richard Nixon pledged to consolidate federal EEO enforcement. Early in the Nixon presidency, the OFCC and EEOC each named one attorney and one psychologist to a subcommittee, which drafted a common document.[10] We took the document back to our respective agencies. It did not satisfy the OFCC committee, which sent several objections to the EEOC. Apparently, it did not satisfy the EEOC either; there was no response until the EEOC independently issued a new set of Guidelines (Equal Employment Opportunity Commission, 1970). It differed from the draft in major details and added provisions objectionable to the OFCC and its advisory committee. It added

---

[9] This definition appeared first in employee testing guidelines issued in the State of California. Dr Mary Tenopyr, who served on both the OFCC advisory group and the California FEP committee, developed the tables subsequently approximated by the 80% rule.

[10] William Enneis and Philip Sklover were EEOC psychologist and lawyer, respectively; I was the psychologist representing the OFCC advisory committee, but I no longer have records identifying OFCC's attorney.

ambiguous requirements (e.g., that validation must result in a "high degree of utility") and the logically impossible requirement that a user must demonstrate that *no* "suitable" alternative procedure existed. Reactions to the new Guidelines produced a concentrated effort in OFCC to issue a revised Testing Order (Office of Federal Contract Compliance, 1971). It contained a widely unnoticed footnote stating that it was consistent with the 1970 EEOC Guidelines, differing only because of differing legal authority or for clarification. The footnote was tactful; many "clarifying" changes were corrections. The impossible clause (proving the absence of an alternative) was simply omitted. Both documents acknowledged construct and content validity defenses, but neither treated these topics very well. Both documents required employers to do and to act on differential validity studies if there were enough data for the research.

Civil Service Commission Regulations, 1972

The federal government and local jurisdictions receiving federal funds are required by law to select employees on the basis of merit. *Merit* is usually defined by scores on competitive examinations, but "merit systems" include procedural components. To assure fair selection systems, the United States Civil Service Commission issued its own regulations in 1969 and again in 1972.

The 1972 version (United States Civil Service Commission, 1972) differed substantially from the EEOC Guidelines and the OFCC Order. Adverse impact was not a reason for requiring validation. What EEOC and OFCC documents called criterion-related validation was, in the CSC document, called "statistical validation," and a combination of content and construct validation within CSC tradition was called "rational validation." The main conflict between the CSC on the one hand and the OFCC and EEOC on the other lay in their preferred approaches to validation. Rational validation was preferred by the CSC, largely because it had a long history of use in the CSC evaluative procedure for civil service examinations. The EEOC and the OFCC preferred criterion-related validation because of its apparent objectivity and wide professional acceptance. This difference, more than others, set the stage for difficulties in developing a truly uniform, consensus document that could be endorsed both by hiring agencies and by EEO enforcement agencies.

Federal Executive Agency Guidelines, 1976

The EEOCC issued for public comment a first draft of "uniform" guidelines in 1973. It received an "almost universally negative" reaction (Miner & Miner, 1978, p. 47); a 1974 revision fared little better. Differences of opinion were strong; Labor, Justice, and the Civil Service people endorsed a draft in 1975, but the EEOC would not. The CSC said it (and other employers) could not afford criterion-related validation; EEOC and the Civil Rights Commission felt that endorsing other validation procedures weakened existing regulations. The impasse persisted. In 1976, the 1975 draft was issued as the *Federal Executive Agency Guidelines* and the EEOC reissued its 1970 Guidelines, defiantly distancing itself from the other agencies.

The spectacle of the US government issuing two sets of conflicting regulations, after spending so much time trying to develop a single set, seemed to stimulate further effort; two years later, the *Uniform Guidelines* appeared (Equal Employment Opportunity Commission et al., 1978). The Uniform Guidelines and related case law now define "the legal context" for personnel decisions.

MAJOR PROVISIONS OF THE UNIFORM GUIDELINES

Judicial and administrative decisions have modified some interpretations of the Uniform Guidelines. Some of them recognize later developments in professional knowledge and practice. Because things change, decision makers and their advisors must get and remain current in their understanding of the legal context within which they work as well as the scientific and professional context. Here, I treat the Guidelines as a special case in the development of the legal context—special because it remains official, has been in effect longer than its predecessors, has influenced similar documents in other countries, often guides federal actions *vis-à-vis* other laws, and seems unlikely to be revised or superseded in the near future.

Adverse Impact and Disparate Treatment

Discrimination may be charged and litigated under two distinct legal theories. One is *adverse impact*, or *disparate impact*, in which an employment practice considered discriminatory is said to affect different groups differently; it may reflect "unintentional" discrimination (cf. Landy & Conte, 2007, p. 286). Although the purpose of the law and its enforcement is to protect individual citizens from discrimination based on group identity, adverse impact is a group-level statistic. Evidence that the practice results in a group as a whole being less likely to be hired is preliminary (prima facie) evidence (but no more than that) of discrimination against group members. In court, the plaintiff (the party charging discrimination) has the initial burden of proving adverse impact; if that is successful, the burden of proof shifts to the defendant (the employer) to show job-relatedness. If that is successful, the burden shifts back to the plaintiff to show an alternative that is as job-related as the challenged practice and has less adverse impact.

The most commonly invoked measure of adverse impact, the so-called 80% rule, brings up an unsettled question of definition: Who is an applicant? As a member of the OFCC advisory group, Paul Sparks raised the question repeatedly, with no answer from OFCC officials or advisory group members. He raised the question because, in those early days, employing companies wanting more minority representation in their organizations targeted minority communities in intensive recruiting activities. Far more responses came from those communities than routine recruiting provided, and more of these responses came from people without basic qualifications for employment. So, who was an applicant? Everyone who responded? If that were the definition, the minority SR would be drastically reduced, and adverse impact drastically inflated. To be considered an applicant, would a person responding to the enhanced recruitment have to meet some sort of basic qualification? That itself raises new questions.

This is a question that did not go away. The rapid increase in online recruiting and job seeking exacerbated the problem and forced a definition, at least of an "internet applicant," as anyone meeting four requirements: (a) submits (by internet or other electronic means) expression of interest in employment, (b) is considered for a particular position by the employer, (c) has indicated in the expression of interest basic qualifications for that position, and (d) does not remove himself or herself from consideration (or indicate that he or she is no longer interested) before decisions have been made. For the most part, omitting from the expression of interest the special provision for electronic statements, this would seem to be a useful general definition of "applicant." It still leaves some unanswered questions (e.g., who defines the basic qualifications, and on what basis might they be challenged?).

The second legal theory refers to *disparate treatment*, evidence that a candidate from a protected group is *intentionally* treated differently from other candidates in the employment process. In principle, all applicants should receive the same treatment. Singling out some people for special interviews, tests, waivers, and so forth, is different, or disparate, treatment. The provision goes further, including as disparate treatment requirements imposed "now" (at the time of negotiation or litigation) that differ from those that were imposed when alleged discrimination occurred. Even if employment standards have changed, victims of prior discrimination are not normally to be held to a higher standard than existed at the time the discrimination occurred. This would imply that a rigorous but valid employment test adopted to replace a less valid procedure determined to be discriminatory—one that made it harder to qualify for a job—could not be used to bar the victims of the prior discrimination without stringent proof of business necessity.

The Uniform Guidelines retained the principle (mandated by the Supreme Court) that adverse impact requires justification in terms of business necessity. That term does not imply something necessary for the survival of the business; rather, it means that a selection procedure must be related to job behavior or performance—usually that it is a valid predictor of an important criterion—and therefore serves a useful business purpose not as well served by a known alternative with less adverse impact.

The 80% (four-fifths) rule was retained as an enforcement trigger. It lacks the force of law, and it must be interpreted in the light of other information. One employer might have an adverse impact ratio (AIR) well under 80%, a sign of potential discrimination, only because of vigorous recruiting as affirmative action. Another employer may have an AIR above 80% because of the chilling effect of a reputation suggesting that application to that employer would be futile for members of certain demographic groups. Although a "chilling effect" argument requires substantial proof to succeed in court (cf. Dothard v. Rawlinson, 1977), its inclusion in the Guidelines emphasizes that the 80% rule is subject to interpretation in specific contexts.

According to the Guidelines, a selection procedure having adverse impact on any protected group may be modified, eliminated, or justified by validation. These options are more easily stated than used. Modification can be expected to modify psychometric characteristics, including validity, reliability, or average difficulty level; therefore, the modification option should be undertaken only with carefully designed research. Elimination is not an acceptable option for procedures with demonstrable, useful levels of validity; to abandon a valid selection procedure because of fear of litigation is to return to essentially random selection—not a wise way to run an organization (but see Ricci v. DeStefano, below). Of the three, validation in support of the business necessity defense is the only sound option. In fact, the organization itself should routinely demand that recommended selection procedures have a record supporting claims of validity before they are put to use in selecting people—quite apart from litigation issues. If validation fails to show that a selection procedure serves an important business purpose, the procedure should not be adopted or, if it is in fact being used, should be replaced. Statistical validation is not the only way to show job-relatedness. Early case law includes cases accepting the business necessity defense on rational, "common sense" grounds (Day, Erwin & Koral, 1981, p. 41). Now, with the accumulation of case law, I would dislike trying to defend in court a "common-sense" argument of validity, although a thoroughly well-thought-out validity *argument*, (a) stemming from job analysis, (b) moving step by step through justification of the predictive hypothesis, (c) specifying the logic of predictor choice and development (requiring reference to prior data and theory), and (d) reaching a logical conclusion of valid assessment and prediction might be effective.

When validity is safely claimed, the Guidelines offer three options for using a valid selection procedure: (a) use *cut scores* to screen out only those deemed unqualified, (b) group people into *bands* or ranges of scores or predicted performance levels, and (c) rank people for *top-down* selection. The different procedures may have differing degrees of adverse impact; the Guidelines assert that the probable level of adverse impact is least for cut scores and greatest for ranking.[11] If a cut score is used, and if adverse impact is shown, the cut score must be defended. If ranking has an adverse impact, the principle of alternatives (as presented in the Guidelines) requires the employer to consider the use of a minimum cut score as an "alternative procedure" likely to have less impact. The Guidelines say nothing about the fact that it will surely have substantially less validity.

The Guidelines call for a further option (often invoked by plaintiffs) of substituting an alternative selection procedure of essentially equal validity but with less adverse impact. Again, sound practice requires considering alternatives from the outset, when a predictive hypothesis is formed and when the predictor construct and its assessment method are chosen. Prior literature should be considered, especially that presenting evidence of validity and adverse impact, along with evidence of other challenges to the validity of the potential predictor. Alternatives *are* considered, in good practice, independently of legal considerations.

Unfortunately, good practice is often pushed aside by the pressures of day-to-day demands; a legal challenge to existing selection procedures often leads to searches for post-hoc evidence of validity. Records rarely exist of alternatives considered when the challenged test was introduced, or even why it was chosen. It is simply there, like ambient air. Section V of the Guidelines says further, "The employer cannot concentrate solely on establishing the validity of the instrument or procedure it has been using in the past" (Equal Employment Opportunity Commission et al., 1978, p. 38291). Alternatives must also be considered, including any that an enforcing agency might suggest: "Whenever the user *is shown* an alternative selection procedure with evidence of less adverse impact . . . the user should investigate it" (Equal Employment Opportunity Commission et al., 1978, p. 38297, emphasis added). In short, the list of alternative procedures to be considered includes not only those that the employer's own judgment considers worthy but also those suggested by an adversary; the accepted investigation might require major research activity, more than would have been required at the outset. The suitable alternative requirement was surely written with criterion-related validity coefficients in mind, without much concern for building validity arguments. The Guidelines are not much help for validity coefficients either. Are coefficients substantially equal if they do not differ significantly? If so, how much statistical power is required to test for the significance? Such questions are not answerable from the Guidelines, nor is there any recognition that even small differences in validity coefficients may indicate substantial differences in the savings the test and its alternatives make possible.

The section on alternatives has another disquieting feature: a requirement, for a given procedure, to study "alternative methods of using the selection procedure which have as little adverse impact as possible" (Equal Employment Opportunity Commission et al., 1978, p. 38297). The practical effect of this requirement for many employers has been to try to reduce adverse impact through such methods of use as differential norms, or setting up

---

[11] The list does not include or mention another option, historically used rather widely. This option, in its simplest form, involves transforming scores to percentile ranks, independently, for score distributions in majority and minority groups, and then ranking applicants according to percentile scores. This would be a top-down procedure with minimal adverse impact. Separate norms, however, were prohibited by the 1991 amendment to the Civil Rights Act.

score intervals (usually called "banding"), or adding constants to scores of members of certain subgroups with little or no concern for the impact such methods have on the validity of the procedure. Of these, only banding has been legally acceptable since the 1991 amendment.

If a procedure has been in use, and the user is then shown (probably in or in anticipation of litigation) "an alternative procedure with evidence of less adverse impact and substantial evidence of validity for the same job in similar circumstances, the user should investigate it to determine the appropriateness of using or validating it in accord with these guidelines" (Equal Employment Opportunity Commission et al., 1978, p. 38297). On the face of it, this provision simply requires the employer to give thoughtful consideration to a suggested alternative. In my experience, however, I have been involved in court cases where compliance agencies have actively (and not always subtly) promoted the adoption of favored tests or other alternative procedures—with greater concern for "as little adverse impact as possible" than for "substantially equal validity."

The entire issue of suitable alternatives arises because of several court cases in early litigation under Title VII in which it was quite reasonable to infer that the employer chose certain tests to be the instruments of illegal discrimination, apparently believing that they could be justified under the Tower amendment simply because they were professionally developed. That line of legal argument is no longer available, but the possibility of pretext remains real enough that plaintiffs must have the alternative procedure argument available to them. Given the ambiguities of the Guidelines' provisions, however, it seems unnecessarily burdensome to require routinely under Title VII that all employers consider all alternatives others may suggest.

Requirements for Validation+

The Guidelines' requirements for criterion-related validation were generally sensible approximations of the conventional professional views of the time. New research evidence, and new thinking stimulated largely by EEO, has made some of these conventional views obsolete. The Guidelines were inconsistent with many other professional views of the time, and the divergence is greater now.

In one respect the professional community and the Guidelines authors are in full agreement; the Guidelines state, "Under no circumstances will the general reputation of a test or other selection procedures [sic], its author or its publisher, or casual reports of it's [sic] validity be accepted in lieu of evidence of its validity" (Equal Employment Opportunity Commission et al., 1978, p. 38299). Here there is no equivocation and no ambiguity. Data, not reputation or hearsay, establish validity—or its absence.

Criterion-related validation is preferred but may not be technically feasible. Three conditions are required for feasibility: (a) adequate samples (it is unclear whether this refers to sample size, representativeness, or both), (b) adequate predictor and criterion score ranges, and (c) an acceptable criterion (i.e., unbiased, reliable, and relevant). If it is determined that criterion-related validation is feasible, the study must meet the following requirements.

1. Criteria must be based on review of job information or job analysis; a criterion must "represent critical or important job duties, work behaviors or work outcomes" (Equal Employment Opportunity Commission et al., 1978, p. 38300). A fully-fledged job analysis is not required if the importance of the criterion used can be shown without it; examples include production rates, errors, and absences.

2. "The possibility of bias should be considered" (Equal Employment Opportunity Commission et al., 1978, p. 38300) in choosing criteria. The Guidelines do not define bias, but the inference comes readily that the agencies consider any mean difference in criterion or predictor scores of different demographic groups as bias. This is unfortunate; mean differences may reflect true population differences stemming from effects of differential experience, differential recruiting, or any of a host of other factors.

3. Research samples should be like the relevant labor market for the job in question. The Guidelines are concerned with demographic similarity; professional practice is concerned with other similarities. In considering concurrent studies, for example, employers should also consider whether those in the sample have skills or knowledge acquired through experience that might influence the validities of potential predictors.

4. Relationships between predictors and criteria should be statistically expressed and should be statistically significant, typically at the 5% level of confidence (but see Chapter 7).

5. Validity should not be overstated. The provision refers to a study using several criteria, finding a significant relationship of a predictor with only one of them, and then ignoring the possibility of a chance relationship. It also explicitly criticizes the use of multiple coefficients of correlation obtained in a sample without recognition of expected shrinkage in other samples. It is silent on population estimates from sample statistics.

6. If, in general, the results show that a selection procedure is a valid predictor of an important criterion, studies of fairness should be conducted (where technically feasible). This requirement marks the greatest difference between professional opinion and the Guidelines. As shown in Chapter 9, the statistical models of so-called "fairness" are contradictory (if test use is "fair" by one statistical definition, it will necessarily be "unfair" by another), the Guidelines are ambiguous about the definition of fairness to be used, and the fairness models assume racial, ethnic, or sex differences in validity or prediction—differences that have rarely been reliably found.

The Guidelines' provisions on content validity (and on construct validity) are confused and confusing. The definition in the glossary seems to contradict the technical standards in the text. The glossary definition seems to suggest a limited content domain, but the main text suggests a more inclusive one. Further confusion comes in the statement that arguments of content validity are inappropriate for content that may be learned on the job—a provision potentially ruling out selection based on job experience (Day et al., 1981, p. 159).

In the face of confusion, obsolescence, and naiveté, it is hard to say unambiguously what the Guidelines require for evidence of content validity. I can do no more than give my view, with all the fallibility that implies:

1. A content domain must be defined by a thorough job analysis that identifies tasks, resources used in doing them, and their relative importance. This implies that acceptable content validity arguments are job-specific or at most job-family-specific. That is, organization-wide content domains are unlikely to be acceptable.

2. If the defined job content is but a portion of the job, it must be critical to overall job performance.

3. The content of selection procedures must somehow match the content defined by the job analysis.

4.   Reliability estimates should be given for assessment scores (and perhaps judged according to a higher standard than required for tests developed on other grounds, particularly if adverse impact is substantial).

5.   Required prior training or experience may be justified as valid content if its content closely resembles the content of the job, as identified by job analysis.[12]

6.   Selection procedures defended only on the basis of content validity may be used only with a minimum cut score; although words in the Guidelines refer to circumstances where ranking is permitted, they imply criterion-related data. I have given the requirement as I understand it, but I must add that I consider it silly. In a typing test based on content validity, for example, it is silly to say that applicant A cannot be preferred over applicant B, who scores just above the cut score, even if A completes the test without error in half the time declared acceptable. The requirement also fails to acknowledge that relationships between test scores and criteria, where they can be examined, are almost always linear or at least monotonic (terms discussed in Chapter 7). Unless there is compelling evidence to the contrary, this means that persons with higher scores can nearly always be predicted to do better on relevant criteria than those with lower scores—even if the predictor is defended by content validity alone.

7.   For a defense invoking construct validity, the Guidelines also specify job analysis as the first step. It should identify behavior required for effective performance and constructs believed to underlie effective behavior. Such constructs should be clearly named, defined, and distinguished from other constructs, and selection procedures chosen should be supported with empirical evidence that they are related to the intended constructs. These requirements, so far, are excellent from a professional point of view.

Unfortunately, the Guidelines go on to say, "The relationship between the construct as measured by the selection procedure and the related work behavior(s) should be supported by empirical evidence from one or more criterion-related studies involving the job or jobs in question which satisfy the provisions [for criterion-related validation]" (Equal Employment Opportunity Commission et al., 1978, p. 38303). In short, despite some words supporting the use of construct validity arguments, and despite the apparent understanding of them, this provision effectively rules out construct validity arguments. It is impossible to say whether this is due to the limited understanding among the Guidelines' authors, to a more Machiavellian manipulation, or simply to the fact that this is a committee-generated document with all the contradictions and confusions that implies. A more benign interpretation of this provision is that the establishment of construct validity requires a correlation between test scores and construct-related criterion. It would be a plausible idea, but the implied distinction is not made elsewhere in the document. Whatever the reason, the Guidelines' approach to construct validity is confused and psychometrically unsound (see Chapter 5).

---

[12] Requiring "close resemblance" may be both unlikely and unwise. A requirement for certain kinds of training, such as engineering training, is a requirement for knowledge that might not be applied on a given job (Guion, 1974). A mechanical engineering student, for example, takes courses in English and chemistry that may have little bearing on the design of particular pieces of heavy equipment, yet most employers hypothesize that people with engineering degrees are likely to be better at designing such equipment than people without the degrees. Although the hypothesis can be tested, it would be a silly employer—and a potentially dangerous one—who would hire a lot of nonengineers to design the equipment merely to provide data for criterion-related validation.

Use of Valid Personnel Selection Procedures

"Transportability" of Validity Information

Acceptable evidence of validity may be based on validation research done elsewhere, but only with restrictions. The question is whether the outside research generalizes to the user's situation; some people refer to such generalizing as "transporting" the validity evidence. This provision predates the development of validity generalization research, and discussing it now seems rather quaint; it is still, however, part of the legal context, and some test users still rely on it. Guidelines requirements for transportability include (a) evidence of the similarity of the job at hand and the job in the original study, identified by the same methods of job analysis, (b) a criterion in the original study appropriate for the local job, and (c) similar demographics of the applicant pool or research sample in the original and the new situation.

Certainly the key characteristics of the job—those for which criterion data will be sought—should match in the two situations. It is less certain that broader similarity is truly necessary, and very nearly certain (from research done in the 1970s) that demographic similarity is *not* necessary. However, these requirements still define part of the legal context for personnel decisions.

Testing for Higher Level Jobs

Employers often seek people who will move up in the organization. The desire is defensible, but predictability of behavior tends to deteriorate over time. Moreover, too often such advancement is rare, and hiring for the higher level may in effect be a pretext for discrimination. Employers may consider applicants for later, higher levels only if (a) the majority of those still employed after "a reasonable period of time" (rarely more than five years) move to the higher level job, (b) the higher level job will continue to require largely the same skills, and (c) employees are not likely to develop requisite knowledge or skill on the original job.

Use of Scores

Four methods of score use are recognized: top-down, banding, pass–fail with a cut score, and in composites combining scores with scores on other predictors. Little is said in the Guidelines about combining predictors, but cut scores, especially low ones, are clearly preferred. Ranking requires justification by criterion-related validation. Although wording suggests that content or construct validity arguments are acceptable, the justification requirement nullifies them. The idea of passing a test seems so ingrained in a society using cut scores for awarding licenses, diplomas, grades, and certificates that reference to passing or failing scores seems natural.

Where there are differences in mean scores of demographic subgroups (and there usually are), and where variances are about the same (and they often are), the level of a cut score is necessarily related to the degree of adverse impact. A cut score can be set so high that virtually no one in the lower scoring group can pass it. The way to reduce adverse impact, therefore, is to lower the cut score. How low? The Guidelines do not say, but some enforcement agencies in some situations have argued that the cutoff should be at the score level of the lowest-scoring satisfactory employee. This position ignores such matters as possible third variables (e.g., motivation), or hiring and retention of employees through affirmative action programs. It ignores the statistical realities of monotonic relationships between test scores and performance. It ignores Congressional intent, in Title VII, affirming employers' rights to set qualifications, or that selection procedures are developed to improve workforce proficiency—not simply to maintain an unacceptable status quo.

It also ignores real selection procedures. In civil service jurisdictions, the typical pattern is to rank candidates by test score, select first at the top of the eligibility list, and then select others down the rank order list until the list is "exhausted," or frequently until it gets hard to find people on it still interested in the job. Even with an established passing, score, actual practice makes the de facto passing score somewhat higher.

In the private sector, the difference between a minimum cut score, if one is even considered, and the de facto passing score is even greater. Hiring rates differ with the times. In a period of recession, for example, a company may do little hiring. When it does hire someone, it will choose from the best of the many applicants; the lowest score among those hired may be quite high. When unemployment is very low, when virtually "any warm body" will do rather than leave a job unfilled, the de facto cutting score is reduced drastically. Such variability seems to be unacceptable to the authors of the Guidelines; they seem to assume that, unless ranking is justified, a fixed cut point will be established. Nothing is said about selection above that point. If more people score above the cut score than can be hired, how are new employees chosen? At random? The Guidelines do not say.

Reporting and Record Keeping Requirements

The Guidelines specify stringent record-keeping requirements. Although not matters of psychological or psychometric principle, records are important to legal defenses. They are so important to litigation that any employer affected by the Guidelines should study them in great detail and with informed legal counsel. Moreover, various agencies have issued (and revised) record-keeping requirements independently of the Guidelines. Reports must be on time, complete, and accurate, based on employment or other records providing information that the Deputy Assistant Secretary of Labor deems necessary. Failure to report as directed represents noncompliance.

CASE LAW FROM MAJOR EEO COURT DECISIONS

A *statute*, such as the Civil Rights Act, is a set of words adopted after legislative debate, compromise, and amendment. Application of these words to a specific instance is not always clear. Each party in a dispute may honestly believe the words to be on its side. The courts have the responsibility of applying the words and their legislative history to the specific case. In the United States federal courts, the dispute is first heard by the judge or jury in a District Court; the judge is the "trier of fact" who determines the facts of the case and interprets them in the light of the relevant statutes and prior court decisions. Attorneys' arguments, testimony from witnesses, and study of the law and interpretation developed in prior cases all contribute to the judge's decision. When a jury is involved, the judge instructs it as to the law. In the end, one party prevails; the losing party may appeal the decision to a Circuit Court of Appeals (the appellate level), which has jurisdiction over District courts in its geographical area. At the appellate level, lawyers present their cases to a panel of judges; these judges do not hear witnesses or determine facts but hear and study arguments to determine whether an error of procedure or of legal interpretation has occurred. The decision of the lower court may be confirmed, reversed, or remanded for reconsideration or retrial. Decisions at the appellate level become binding precedents for the district courts of that circuit; that is, those decisions guide district court judges in future cases involving the same or similar legal issues. A district judge does not always follow precedent, but strong and compelling reasons, based on the facts of the case and their differences from the facts in the precedent case, are needed to justify deviation. The highest level of appeal is to the United States Supreme Court. Decisions at this highest level are binding precedents for all other federal courts—with the same possibility that the triers of fact in a new case may find important differences justifying a different legal path.

At all three levels, decisions rendered become part of *case law*—the body of judicial interpretations of the statute. The relative weight of decisions in case law is greater at the higher judicial levels, so I concentrate this review mainly on a few decisions from the Supreme Court, listed chronologically. I do not give details of cases, only some implications for personnel practices. See books by Arvey (1979), Gutman, Koppes, and Vodanovich (2010), Miner and Miner (1978), or Lindemann and Grossman (1996) for more on EEO case law.

Griggs v. Duke Power Co.

The *Griggs* decision (Griggs v. Duke Power Co., 1971) was the first Supreme Court decision under Title VII. When the Civil Rights Act of 1964 was enacted, the Duke Power Company had 95 employees in a North Carolina facility, 14 of whom were black. The plant had five departments, including a labor department. The company had required a high school diploma in all departments except labor, the only department hiring blacks. On July 2, 1965, the effective date of the Act, the company extended the high school requirement to the labor department and required acceptable scores on two aptitude tests installed at that time.

The unanimous Supreme Court decision included many far-reaching provisions, as follows.

1. *Business necessity*: The Court said that the Act prohibits the use of practices that appear to be fair but have discriminatory effects. "The touchstone," it said, "is business necessity." The idea of business necessity may have seemed clear to the writers, and no definition was offered. The Court seemed to equate business necessity with job-relatedness, but other cases were needed to clarify the concept.
2. *Job-relatedness*: Whether job-relatedness is sufficient to show business necessity was not clear from this one decision; that it is a requirement for justifying use of a selection procedure was not in doubt. The Court said that the educational and test requirements were both adopted "without meaningful study" to relate them to performance. Does job-related mean valid? Is traditional validation "meaningful study"? The decision did not clearly say.
3. *Intent versus effect*: Unequivocally, questions of intent were said to be irrelevant under Title VII—that good intentions cannot excuse the use of procedures that establish special obstacles, unrelated to performance, for minorities. It is the consequences of a practice, not the motive behind it, that is important. Referring to tests, the decision itself italicized the relevant words in quoting from the Tower amendment permitting tests that are not "designed, intended, *or used* to discriminate."
4. *Deference to Guidelines*: The 1966 EEOC Guidelines were available when the case was first heard, but not subsequent regulatory documents. The Court said that the EEOC Guidelines were "entitled to great deference." That did not give them the force of law, but their provisions were to be carefully considered in Title VII cases.

5. *Tests of job qualifications*: The Court found in reviewing the legislative history of the Tower amendment affirmation of employers' rights to insist that everyone, regardless of demographic identity, meet applicable job qualifications. The history declared that the specific purpose of the proposed law was to require that selection decisions be based on qualifications rather than on race or color. The Court concluded that the EEOC requirement that employment tests be job-related was entirely consistent with Congressional intent. Its decision said that tests are obviously useful but cannot have "controlling force unless they are demonstrably a reasonable measure of job performance. Congress has not commanded that the less qualified be preferred over the better qualified simply because of minority origins. Far from disparaging job qualifications as such, Congress has made such qualifications the controlling factor, so that race, religion, nationality, and sex become irrelevant."[13]

Albemarle Paper Co. v. Moody

The court in Albemarle v. Moody (1975) supported class-action suits. It held that, as a remedy for prior discrimination, back pay could be awarded to people not individually named in the suit, who did not themselves file charges, but who were members of the affected "class." The class might, for example, be all women who had unsuccessfully applied for employment for a specified job or group of jobs between specified dates. Obviously, losing a class-action suit can be a very expensive proposition for the defending organization.

The decision also strengthened the "great deference" posture *vis-à-vis* the EEOC Guidelines. Those Guidelines were central in the court's determination that the validation research done by the company's consultant was defective, especially regarding criterion ratings and numbers of cases for specific job titles. In a separate but concurring judgment, Justice Blackmun was concerned about "the Court's apparent view that absolute compliance with the EEOC Guidelines is a sine qua non of pre-employment test validation." He further suggested that "too-rigid application" of those Guidelines would necessarily lead to quotas—an early expression of judicial concern about quotas.

Washington v. Davis

Washington v. Davis (1976) was not a Title VII case. It began before the 1972 amendment brought governmental agencies under Title VII scrutiny, so it was tried as a constitutional case. It was particularly important, however, because it showed some discontent within the Court against rigid applications of its own prior decisions. In this case, the Court emphasized validation over adverse impact. Adverse impact was clearly shown; the test (for police officer selection in the District of Columbia) was validated against scores on the final examination in a long, intensive training program. A rigid extension of prior decisions would have denied the acceptability of the validation study because the criterion was not actual job performance; because the training program had a clear relevance to job performance, the Court held that it was an acceptable criterion and declared the test to be job-related.

---

[13] The phrase "demonstrably a reasonable measure of job performance" is poor. No "measure of job performance" can exist for an applicant who has not yet performed the job. Therefore, in the context of the rest of the decision, I interpret the phrase as meaning *demonstrably and reasonably related to job performance*, implying both data and logic.

Dothard v. Rawlinson

The Alabama legislature had established minimum weight and minimum height requirements (120 lb; 5 feet, 2 inches) for employment as prison guards. A woman was rejected for a guard trainee position because of failure to meet these requirements; she sued. These requirements would exclude about one third of American women but only a bit over 1% of American men. Accepting these statistics as evidence of adverse impact, the Court in Dothard v. Rawlinson (1977) said the burden of proof then shifted to the defendant to show job-relatedness, a position consistent with the history of testing Guidelines. Virtually all federal EEO regulations had taken the position that adverse impact triggered a demand for a showing of validity; the shift in the burden of proof that was implicit in *Griggs* and *Albemarle* became explicit in *Dothard*.

Regents, University of California v. Bakke

Regents of University of California v. Bakke (1978) was heard under Title VI, the educational section of the Civil Rights Act, and the 14th amendment, but it had major implications for debates of future amendments of Title VII. California had two independent admissions programs, a regular program for most applicants and a special one for minorities who claimed disadvantaged status. Bakke, a white applicant to the Medical College of the University of California at Davis, was rejected in each of two years when minorities with substantially lower scores were admitted, and he sued successfully in California courts. The United States Supreme Court affirmed that the admissions system was unacceptable and that Bakke should be admitted, but it reversed the judgment that race cannot be legally considered. Its view was that racial diversity among medical students might be a legitimate consideration among others, but that the two-track system used at Davis violated constitutional protections.

Connecticut v. Teal

In a multiple-hurdle selection system, a candidate is not hired without passing all stages. A "bottom line" concept is that adverse impact is calculated on the basis of the selection ratios at the end of the chain. The Guidelines accepted the bottom line concept for avoiding adverse impact, albeit reluctantly and only as a matter of prosecutorial discretion. Connecticut v. Teal (1982), however, ruled against the idea even when the final stages showed no adverse impact. In this case, the first hurdle for promotion was a written test. Those who passed were placed on an eligibility list from which selections were based on prior work performance, recommendations of supervisors, and (lightly) seniority. Test results had clear adverse impact under the 80% rule, but at the end, the percentage of blacks promoted was higher than the corresponding percentage for whites. That the bottom line statistics could, at least on their face, support a charge of adverse impact against whites entered neither the decision nor the sharply worded dissenting opinion.

The Court's view was that Title VII assured each *individual* equal opportunity, not overall equality across racial groups. From that perspective, a black applicant who failed the test would not be comforted in seeing that those who passed it had equal chances for the promotion. The court ultimately held that *any component* of the overall process with different effects in different demographic groups is subject to adverse impact analysis and the subsequent requirement for evidence of job-relatedness.

This decision was extremely important in organizations—and there are many—using a *multiple hurdles* approach to personnel decisions. In a common practice in on-campus college recruiting; for example, the first hurdle is a recruiter's interview and credential-based decision, followed for some with a home-office visit for further assessment. Arguably, this first hurdle might not survive a validation study.

Watson v. Fort Worth Bank & Trust

Regulatory agencies had long tried to regulate subjective assessments as well as scored tests. Watson v. Fort Worth Bank & Trust (1988) examined supervisors' subjective recommendations for promotion. The Court knew its dilemma. Requiring adverse impact analysis for such practices could lead to hidden quotas, but not requiring it could hide discriminatory effects. The plurality decision (only eight justices heard the case) held that the standards of proof were rigorous enough to avoid quota-producing "chilling effects." Two standards of proof of prima facie discrimination were required: identification of the *specific practice* challenged, and convincing statistical data showing that the practice *causes* loss of equality of opportunity. Moreover, a "burden of persuasion" does not transfer to a defendant because the defendant can criticize or refute either the data or the causal inference.

The Court also said that the cost of alternative procedures is a factor to be considered; cost had not heretofore seemed to be a matter of much concern to the Court or to enforcement agencies. Similarly, for the first time, the Court also said that expensive validation studies were not needed, even for tests, when common sense and good judgment affirmed the job-relatedness of the practice. Indeed, in matters of judging job relevance, lower courts were urged to defer in many matters to the greater expertise of employers in questions of business practice.

Wards Cove Packing Co. v. Atonio

Wards Cove v. Atonio (1989) affirmed most of the decision in *Watson v. Fort Worth Bank*. It affirmed the extension of adverse impact analysis to subjective procedures, the need to specify the practice being challenged, and maintaining the burden of persuasion on the plaintiff. It added a further requirement that evidence of adverse impact compare the demographic data *on a specific job* to the available supply of people for that job; that is, adverse impact statistics must be based on relevant labor markets. The Court also reduced the "business necessity" language to "business justification"—implicit, I think, in earlier decisions—saying that a practice need not be essential to survival of the business or in some other sense indispensable.[14]

---

[14] Many observers, including some in Congress, decried this as "reversing" *Griggs*. In my judgment, which is far from legally trained, I cannot see that it is. From *Griggs* on, business necessity has been equated with job-relatedness; the word *necessity*, insofar as it ever had anything other than rhetorical value, has always seemed to me to imply only that a procedure was deemed "necessary" (or not) for sound business practice. Reading a "plant-closing" implication has always seemed to me a fanciful, out-of-context extension of the word "necessity." Relevant labor market statistics have long been demanded in statistical evidence of adverse impact, so I am not at all sure that this represents anything drastically new, either. Detractors of the Court, however, saw the *Watson* and the *Wards Cove* decisions as severely watering down Title VII enforcement.

Wygant v. Jackson Board of Education, and Richmond v. J. A. Croson Co.

These cases make a common point despite situational differences. Wygant v. Jackson Board of Education (1986) involved teacher layoffs; Richmond v. Croson (1989) involved awards of construction contracts to minority-owned businesses. Both were 14th Amendment cases. In *Wygant*, the contract between the school board and the teachers' union agreed that teacher lay-offs would be based on seniority—if the percentage of minorities laid off is no greater than the percentage employed at the time of lay-off. In some years, nonminority teachers were laid off but no minority teachers were. The school board and the lower courts had held that the contract was constitutionally permissible as a remedy for "societal discrimination" and to encourage black "role models." The plurality decision of the Supreme Court held otherwise, saying the school board had not shown convincing evidence that the contract remedied prior discrimination by the board or its predecessors and, moreover, without such evidence, vague concepts such as *societal discrimination* and *role model* could not justify a race-conscious action as remedy. In *Richmond*, the Court's argument was similar, recognizing a "tension" between the 14th amendment equal protection clause and race-based decisions intended to remedy effects of prior discrimination. The city of Richmond had a "Plan" requiring contractors with the city to subcontract at least 30% of the contract dollars to minority businesses. The Croson company had difficulty reaching that target and sought a waiver, denied by the city.

In both cases, the Court applied the concept of "strict scrutiny," looking closely at the relevance of the evidence presented. "Strict scrutiny" requires (a) direct evidence that the alleged discriminating entity had indeed discriminated systematically against an identifiable group of people, and (b) evidence that any remedy proposed or used is "narrowly tailored" to make up explicitly for that prior discrimination. In both cases, the Court found no direct evidence of prior discrimination to compel governmental interest in the remedy invoked. Broad national statistics do not supply compelling evidence of discrimination in specific governmental organization. Without such strong evidence, no remedial action is needed, especially if it harms other individuals. In *Richmond*, the mandatory 30% for minority businesses was seen as failing to consider the rights of individual "persons" denied contracts *only because of their racial identity*. The opinion reaffirmed *Wygant* in stating that the findings submitted did not provide the city "with a strong basis in evidence for its conclusion that remedial action was necessary."

Ricci v. DeStefano

To eliminate the potential for litigation because of severe adverse impact, the Civil Service Board (CSB) of New Haven, Connecticut, refused to certify the results of a firefighter promotional exam (Ricci v. DeStefano, 2009). Its use would have excluded from promotions all black and most Hispanic candidates. Adverse impact was not disputed. District and appellate courts upheld the refusal, but that judgment was overturned by the Supreme Court. This case seems to be the first to consider adverse (or disparate) impact and disparate treatment together. Disparate treatment, prohibited in the original 1964 Civil Rights Act, refers to intentionally discriminatory treatment of individuals. Adverse impact, codified and prohibited in the 1991 amendment, refers to unintentional discriminatory effects of a practice. The CSB argued that it had a statutory obligation not to use a test known to have severe adverse impact. Petitioners (nonminority firefighters) argued that the refusal violated the disparate treatment provision of Title VII.

I won't describe the opinions in the case in much detail. The principal issue was whether the CSB had a *legal motive* for its refusal to certify and if not, whether there was a *"strong basis in evidence"* for having a racial motive. The majority opinion asserted that the tests were valid (i.e., clearly job-related) but that the city had not known an alternative method equally valid and with less adverse impact. Without doing so, the city had no "strong basis in evidence" for its expectation of adverse impact litigation. There was some evidence, but it did not meet the Court's standard of a "strong basis," that is, the evidence was not deemed compelling under "strict scrutiny." It did, however, citing procedures in test development, deem the evidence compelling that the tests were indeed job-related (valid). Apparently, given an adverse impact situation (which seems clear), the city could have argued successfully for the validity of the test and the burden of proof would have shifted to the petitioner–plaintiffs to point to acceptable alternatives with less adverse impact. Therefore, because refusal to certify was based on a racial argument, or perhaps because individual candidates had worked so hard to prepare for the test, the refusal to certify constituted disparate treatment.

It is not clear to me how this decision clarifies matters comparing disparate treatment and disparate impact. I'm not alone. Gutman and Dunleavy (in press) devoted much of their review of the case to the "anomalies" in the opinions. I expect this to be the first of several cases dealing with the issue.

THE 1991 AMENDMENT TO THE CIVIL RIGHTS ACT

Differences in opinions about fairness in employment were neither resolved nor clarified by 25 years of EEO enforcement and litigation. If anything, they froze as polar opposites, held not as reasoned policy but as deeply held emotional or political commitments. For some, Supreme Court decisions such as those in *Watson* and *Wards Cove* seemed overdue statements of sanity in the EEO arena. To many others, they seemed to signal a weakening of basic EEO principles, including the Court's standards in *Griggs*. Never mind that clarification of the *Griggs* ambiguities had required nearly 20 years. Never mind that subsequent decisions failed to clarify other fundamental issues. Perception determines action, and perceptions led to acrimonious exchanges among columnists, political pundits, members of Congress and, ultimately, to efforts to "rein in" the Supreme Court by amending the Civil Rights Act to reverse some 1980s decisions legislatively. A first, unsuccessful attempt in 1990 was passed in both houses of Congress and vetoed by the first President Bush; Congress failed to override the veto. Opponents argued that the bill called for quotas; proponents said it did not. Neither view was correct, although both were loudly proclaimed. The bill did not call for quotas, but it could have led to efforts by employers to avoid litigation by actions resembling de facto quotas. It had happened before. Soon after passage of the 1964 Civil Rights Act, many—maybe most—employers demanded that personnel directors "get the numbers right," that is, hire enough minorities and women to avoid litigation. Given the ambiguities of the 1990 bill, similar efforts to get the numbers right were virtually certain, and the right numbers are most easily obtained by using a surrogate for a quota if not a quota in fact. This problem could have been avoided by more carefully crafted language. So-called debate was hot if not well informed or well intended. In my cynical view, based on personal correspondence with Senators, the debaters were less concerned with defining and fixing a problem than with attempts to gain partisan advantage.

The *Civil Rights Act of 1991* was passed and signed into law, amending Title VII. Worries about quotas were to be put to rest by prohibiting "race-norming," a way to get the numbers right by using percentiles within score distributions for different racial subgroups and using top-down selection based on group percentile ranks rather than raw or standard scores. Shortly before the Congressional debates, controversy erupted over the practice in state Employment Services referrals using the United States Department of Labor's General Aptitude Test Battery (see Hartigan & Wigdor, 1989). Race norming does not seriously affect mean job performance, but making it illegal quieted charges that the amendment was a quota bill. Of the Supreme Court decisions opposed in the 1990 bill, only the *Watson* view that defendants did not have a "burden of persuasion" was changed by the 1991 Act. Definitions of business necessity and of job-relatedness were to have been codified by the 1991 Act. Nevertheless, they remain as ambiguous (or "flexible") as before. Another provision addresses intentional discrimination, providing even for jury trials and for compensatory and punitive damages. Good sense requires organizations to make sure that intentional discrimination on irrelevant grounds, or even the appearance of it, does not occur.

AFFIRMATIVE ACTION

Employers not only must avoid unlawful discrimination but must take affirmative action to reduce the effects of prior discrimination. Early examples of affirmative actions included recruiting efforts, special training programs, direct mentoring, or extended probationary periods. Some affirmative action programs are voluntary, but many are imposed by court orders or consent decrees. Affirmative action is not a requirement under Title VII, although it is in the Guidelines and, in fact, in Title VII as a statutory remedy. It has been a requirement for government contractors under the various Executive Orders (including the still effective 11246) since 1961. It has been controversial since the development of the Philadelphia Plan in 1969, and the controversy is usually emotional.

The Philadelphia Plan

The affirmative action requirement in EO 11246 posed a special problem for the building trades: contractors do not generally have their own crews of skilled employees; they hire those sent by unions for contracted projects. OFCC investigations found few minorities in trade unions in the five-county Philadelphia area, despite a substantial minority population, so the Secretary of Labor issued an order calling for increased proportions of minorities in each of six trades in each year of a four-year period. Any building contractor submitting a bid for a federal contract was required to submit with it an affirmative action program to show goals within standard ranges and a plan for reaching them.

Reverse Discrimination

Affirmative action was initiated not to provide favoritism for groups of people, nor to reward (as veterans' preference rewarded prior service), but to compensate partially for the effects of past discrimination. When courts find that an employer has a history of discrimination, affirmative action programs (AAPs) or even outright quotas may be mandated as remedies. When an employer independently sees evidence of adverse impact on a particular job or set of jobs, that employer may voluntarily establish an AAP with goals and timetables. Doing so, however, runs the risk of a reverse discrimination charge, and the plan must explicitly intend to correct prior discrimination (see Weber v. Kaiser Aluminum & Chemical, 1977, 1979).

Developing Affirmative Action Plans

To establish a local affirmative action program, the employer should first identify jobs with evidence of either adverse impact or disparate treatment. For such jobs, the responsible practices should be identified and corrective plans developed. The plans need not be (and probably should not be) restricted to hiring intentions. They may include special recruiting, educational or training programs, and plans for identifying and advancing those whose abilities are underutilized in their current positions. They should not go beyond correction of prior adverse impact or disparate treatment either from a desire to "do good" or from fear of litigation.

Affirmative Action as Social Policy

Employment discrimination, sometimes by law and often by general practice, was unrestrained before 1964. Since then, social policy in the United States has deemed discriminatory practices wrong and that employers should work "affirmatively" to right the wrong. Differences in public opinion, however, question whether an affirmative action plan (AAP) is compensating for prior discrimination or affirming a policy of preferential hiring. Public opinion, or social policy, defining social justice differs in different countries and cultures. At least three kinds of cultural norms can be identified. Much of western Europe, North America, and some other regions are likely to emphasize individualistic norms and rewards for individual achievement. Some countries (notably Germany, Sweden, and other social democracies) emphasize equality of opportunities and other characteristics of the social order. An Asiatic perspective may offer models of justice based on need.

AAPs are not unique to the United States, nor are they necessarily restricted to specific ideals of justice. In Canada, the Employment Equity Act was established in 1986, and its Ministry of Labour is required to report annually on the progress in reaching parity between representation in the labor force and "availability" in the labor market for the protected *groups*: women, aboriginal peoples, persons with disabilities, and members of visible minorities. In 2006, representation of aboriginal peoples progressed only slightly, women's progress was better but below availability, and representation of the disabled was in some occupations at or better than par (*Employment Equity Act, Annual Report 2006*, 2007). South Africa passed its Employment Equity Act in 1998 and the Promotion of Equity and Prevention of Unfair Discrimination Act in 2000 (Dupper & Strydom, 2004). Under Section 8 of the Employment Equity Code of Good Practice, issued by the South African Department of Labour, affirmative action measures should be developed as part of an employment equity plan; moreover, steps should be taken to change corporate culture so that it affirms diversity (South Africa, Department of Labour, 2004). These are individualistic, not collectivist, cultures.

Perhaps the oldest affirmative program is in India, culturally quite different in perspective. It differs from most of those in North America and Europe in that it specifies quotas or "reservation policies" (Parikh, 1997; Weisskopf, 2004). The principle of reserved places dates at least to the British 1892 amendment to the Indian Councils Act of 1861; after Indian independence, it was formalized in the 1950 constitutional call for reservations for "Scheduled Castes" and "Scheduled Tribes," holding a "certain number of seats or positions, in a desirable institution or occupation, for members of groups that were under-represented in such positions" (Parikh, 1997, p. 4).

Diversity

Greater diversity among organizational members is generally accepted as desirable, despite the lack of evidence (Sacco & Schmitt, 2005). Most arguments about diversity, and most research on the topic, concentrate on demographic diversity, especially on demographic categories protected by law (race, sex, age, etc.). Diversity could include more than these categories. Cascio (2003) discussed it in terms of diversity in knowledge and perspectives in management teams and in terms of mixing corporate cultures in the wake of mergers or international networks. Harrison and Klein (2007) pointed out that some studies have included diverse values, skills, personality, and pay levels, and that the volume of research on something called diversity has doubled about every five years, but with precious little payoff in the form of generalizable results.

Authors frequently and casually use the term "diversity" and synonyms such as heterogeneity, dissimilarity, and dispersion. Yet the precise meaning of diversity is not clear. "Casting a deliberately broad net . . . We use the term *diversity* to describe *the distribution of differences among the members of a unit with respect to a common attribute, X, such as tenure, ethnicity, conscientiousness, task attitude, or pay*" (Harrison & Klein, 2007, p. 1199, emphasis in original). Harrison and Klein go on to say, first, that diversity is a variable describing units or groups of people, not individuals differing from others; diversity, they say, is not just one thing but three: *separation*, referring to differences in opinion or position; *variety*, referring to differences in kind in such things as education, knowledge, or experience; and *disparity*, referring to differences in valued assets such as pay or status. The implications of this model go beyond legal issues or others associated with organizational membership. Nevertheless, its implications for theory and research methods relevant to those issues deserve close attention.

Demographic diversity need not be confused with affirmative action plans. It may be valued in its own right. It may be a goal in organizational planning; AAPs are mandated plans to be submitted to governmental entities. It may be unrelated to efforts to fix the effects of past discrimination. It may lead to outcomes such as more creative plans or solutions to problems. However, it may also lead to bickering, tension, turnover, or even outright feuding among demographic subgroups. So far, it is not clear that creating demographic diversity is necessarily a mediating criterion in selecting new organizational members for such unit criteria as workforce stability, productivity, or cost-effectiveness.

AGE DISCRIMINATION

The Age Discrimination in Employment Act of 1967 (29 US 1967) prohibits discrimination against anyone 40 years of age or older, enforced through the EEOC. It encourages personnel decisions about older people on the basis of ability, not age. It applies to hiring, early retirement programs and their promotion, benefits packages, and more. Worth noting is the thought that rejecting a so-called "overqualified" applicant may be rejected by courts as a violation of ADEA (Cascio, 2003). Also worth noting is that, unlike Title VII, this Act does not compare predefined groups, such as over 40 versus under 40; it is concerned with older versus younger. If someone at 45 replaces someone who is 60, a court could determine that the older person's termination was due to age bias; the fact that both parties are in the protected age bracket is no defense (Gutman, 2000, p. 197).

Several exceptions are in the law: (a) executives in high policy-making positions, with good annual retirement packages can be retired at age 65, (b) state laws specifying mandatory retirement age for law enforcement officers and firefighters are not affected by the Act, and (c) state and local policy-making officials, whether elected or appointed, are subject to mandatory retirement at the age determined by state and local laws (Gutman, 2000, p. 199).

Many ADEA litigation suits involve terminations—firing, reductions in force, or involuntary retirement—although many other cases have been related to promotion, opportunities for special training, and compensation. A few companies have openly had age limits for jobs involving public safety (e.g., bus drivers), defended as bona fide occupational qualifications (BFOQs). Courts (at least initially) were more receptive to such arguments in ADEA cases than in cases of racial or sex discrimination, apparently because employers should not have to experiment with the safety of third persons (e.g., passengers) to develop empirical proofs (Faley, Kleinman & Lengnick-Hall, 1984). Where someone aged 40 or over brings suit under ADEA, a defense must show that factors other than age were determining considerations. For promotions, transfer, or terminations, the other factors are usually performance ratings. Several reviews have considered the role of performance appraisals in the outcome of such cases, but with inconsistent conclusions (e.g., Faley et al., 1984; Feild & Holley, 1982; Miller, Kaspin & Schuster, 1990).

Systematic procedures of performance evaluation have been helpful for employers. In promotion or demotion cases, employers' defenses have been strengthened where established procedures were shown to be regularly used. Where employees were victors, decisions expressed reservations about the quality of the supervisory judgments even in formal evaluation systems. In cases involving layoffs or retirement, an advantage was found in formalized systems where performance could be compared to that of others. In cases involving outright discharge, however, the question has not been one of relative performance but of whether the employee bringing suit has failed to perform adequately. This, concluded Miller et al. (1990, p. 571), "will generally be the employer's only legitimate defense. Minimal performance, rather than relative performance, is the primary issue."

This is a sobering conclusion. Performance evaluations are usually lenient, often unrealistically so. It is unpleasant to give a poor rating, especially if it is to be discussed in a face-to-face interview. It may be administratively burdensome as well, especially where special procedures are required to justify negative ratings. All too often, a rating of "minimally acceptable" is given when actual performance is really not at all acceptable. Such a rating, if routinely used, effectively rules out evaluating performance relative to performance standards.

Adverse impact cases under ADEA are rare; one circuit court was said to have declared adverse impact "categorically unavailable" under ADEA (Smith v. City of Jackson, 2005). A claim of adverse impact is very hard to evaluate. Age is different from other protections. People get older (but not less male or less white), and a great many other things are associated with getting older (e.g., percentage of change in compensation, frequency of promotions, or likelihood of seeking special training programs). Cohort analysis would be required, but it would be hard to decide which associated variables need to be controlled.

In *City of Jackson*, and later in Meacham v. KAPL (2008), the Supreme Court supported a defense against charges of adverse impact by finding evidence that it was explainable by reasonable factors other than age, as permitted by the Act. In *City of Jackson*, the "reasonable factor" was that newer hires had been paid less than their more senior counterparts and that larger percentages of compensation increases for them were needed to maintain stability in the police force. In *KAPL*, it was based on performance, assessed by a combination of ratings on performance, flexibility, and critical skills plus years of service as an added factor. Together, these cases show strong differences between the defenses needed under title VII and ADEA.

DISCRIMINATION AGAINST DISABLED PERSONS

The Americans with Disabilities Act of 1990 (Bureau of National Affairs, 1990) prohibits discrimination against qualified people with disabilities. A *disabled person* is one with a physical or mental impairment that substantially limits one or more major life activities, or who has a record of such impairment, or who is regarded as having such an impairment. *Major life activities* include caring for oneself, walking, speaking, seeing, hearing, and working. *Impairment* might be a physiological or mental condition, cosmetic disfigurement, anatomical loss, mental illness, retardation, or learning disability. The Americans with Disabilities Act (ADA) does not protect people whose employment on a given job would threaten the safety or property of others. *Has a record of* is intended to protect against decisions based on unwarranted assumptions that prior disabling conditions still exist or on inaccurate records of disability. Recovering alcoholics, or people whose prior blood pressure or cardiac arrhythmia has been controlled, are still defined as disabled to prevent employers from using their history as a reason for adverse decisions. *Regarded as having* includes the protection of those at risk because of appearances or associations with others.

The law requires employers to focus on what a candidate can do, not on disabilities. For a job to be filled, the employer must be able to distinguish *essential functions* of the job from those that, even if important, may not have to be performed by every incumbent. Essential functions are fundamental job duties, things an incumbent must do to perform the job. These are functions of the *job*, not of the person doing it; the focus is on purpose of the function. How it is ordinarily done by other people, or by tradition, is irrelevant. A disabled person may need to carry out the function in a quite different way, perhaps with some gadget to help. For example, any worker on a certain job may be required to retrieve items from a moderately high shelf, one out of reach for someone in a wheel chair. That person may be able to retrieve those items, and easily, if provided with a telescoping grabber. Special tools need not create a burden for the employer; indeed, they may suggest to local production engineers better ways for everyone to carry out the essential job functions.

Essential functions also define a *qualified* candidate. A clerical job, for example, may require operation of certain machines, filing materials in or retrieving them from a five-drawer file cabinet, and delivering occasional materials to people in other offices. If any one of these is identified as an essential function of the job, a qualified candidate must be able to do it. ADA prohibits only discrimination against *qualified* candidates with disabilities. It does not require preferential hiring of qualified but disabled candidates; in fact, it explicitly encourages hiring the candidates *most* qualified to perform essential functions, irrespective of disabilities.

Reasonable Accommodation

Employers must offer *reasonable accommodation* to overcome barriers that a disability may pose for an otherwise qualified candidate—if the candidate requests it. Candidates often will

TABLE 4.1

Accommodations under the Americans with Disabilities Act

Accommodation 1:	Making facilities available
Accommodation 2:	Job restructuring
Accommodation 3:	Use of part-time work or modified work schedules
Accommodation 4:	Reassignment of a disabled person to a vacant position
Accommodation 5:	Using or modifying equipment used to perform job functions
Accommodation 6:	Modifying employment tests, training materials and/or work policies
Accommodation 7:	Providing readers or interpreters
Accommodation 8:	Other similar accommodations

Reprinted from A. Gutman (2010), *EEO Law and Personnel Practices* (3rd ed.). New York: Taylor & Francis. © Taylor & Francis. Reprinted with permission.

not ask for it despite the law because they fear being perceived as unable to do the job or because of stigma or because of unwillingness to assert rights and then be perceived as threatening (Baldridge & Veiga, 2001). A very short person may be considered disabled. The disability may be a barrier to the essential filing function if file drawers or shelves are too high, but a stool may be enough to help a short person to carry out the function. Thinking of accommodation as a major architectural change is often unwarranted. Congress, EEOC, and the courts have stressed reasonableness; accommodation is not required if it would impose an undue hardship on the organization.

ADA offers plain language to clarify what it means by "reasonable" accommodation (Gutman, 2010). The eight accommodations are shown in Table 4.1. The first of these is pretty nearly universal, and the eighth simply says that the other six are illustrative rather than exhaustive. The rest are relatively low cost actions and not very disruptive—although accommodation in testing can cause psychometric problems. In any case, accommodation differs from affirmative action. Affirmative action refers to extensive programs for distinctive groups of people; accommodation is individual in focus, applied to one person at a time (Gutman, 2010).

Job Analysis

Job analysis is not required by ADA, but it has long included ascertaining which tasks or functions are important to effective performance and which are less so. Under ADA it is prudent to ask whether every worker must carry out all critical activities. The distinction needs to be made between important activities that are critical in the sense that they must be carried out by at least some persons on the job and those that are essential in the sense that everyone on the job must be able to do them. Job analysis procedures need to assure that essential functions, as the term is used in the ADA, can be unambiguously determined before the determination is needed.

General Employment Procedures

Some organizations need to change procedures to be sure they comply with the ADA.

1. Medical examinations or background checks are frequent parts of the employment process. The ADA permits these procedures only after making a conditional job

offer (i.e., conditioned on or depending on satisfactory results of such post-offer procedures).

2. Candidates may not be asked on application forms or in interviews about disabling conditions, although questions about their abilities to perform essential functions are permissible. Those with known disabilities may be asked to describe or demonstrate how they might (with or without accommodation) perform those functions, but they may not be questioned about the disability itself.

3. Reasonable accommodation applies to application forms and interviews as well to the job and job environment; accommodation might include providing application forms with large type, completing them orally while someone else fills in the blanks, providing an accessible interview location for people with mobility problems, providing an interpreter to sign for deaf candidates, or readers for blind ones, and so on.

Putting off the medical examination until a tentative decision is made poses problems for some kinds of testing. Psychomotor tests might be used in medical diagnosis, or personality inventories to diagnose other disabilities, but for personnel decisions, both are usually used as predictors. With evidence that such tests have been validated for predicting performance on essential job functions, they need not be treated as part of the medical examination. However, a different use of personality measures seems not to have been addressed: use for organization-wide rather than job-specific criteria (e.g., person–organization fit). Measures of conscientiousness, for example, may serve these more general purposes, but courts may not accept the predicted criteria as performance of essential functions.

Testing

Any individual may request accommodation based on a disability. Although an interviewer may not ask a candidate about visual impairment, for example, the candidate may request a test in large type, or even Braille. Tests given to people with a specific impairment must not actually measure the impaired skill, rather than other KSAs, unless the job specifically requires it. A written test given to a candidate for work as a road equipment operator may be unduly difficult for a dyslexic person, but it is not intended to assess dyslexia, and the dyslexia might not interfere with performance of essential functions. Such a test would be deemed inappropriate without special accommodation, such as oral administration.

Other kinds of accommodation might include relaxed time limits, alternative modes of test presentation (oral, on computer, etc.), permitting alternative methods of responding (e.g., using a tape recorder rather than filling in circles), simplified language, more frequent rest pauses, providing isolated space (for those whose disabilities make them susceptible to distractions), using alternative methods of assessment, or simply waiving the assessment. In any case, the word "reasonable" remains operative. Philips (1993) described court cases that suggested limits on required accommodation, holding that granting the requests would amount to preferential treatment rather than the elimination of a disadvantage.

What does accommodation do to the validity of the interpretations of the test scores? The question can rarely if ever be answered. The only safe assumption is that scores obtained under nonstandard conditions do *not* have the same meaning as scores obtained under standard conditions. Accommodation by nonstandard procedures may be about the same as accommodation by waiving the test requirements: in either case, one may have no valid assessment of an important trait. Campbell and Reilly (2000) has a much more thorough discussion of available research and court actions related to accommodations in testing.

OTHER LEGAL LIABILITIES

Negligent Hiring

EEO law has dominated the legal context for a generation or so, but other kinds of laws are also part of it. Among these are laws of *torts*, that is, wrongful acts resulting in injury. If an employee does something resulting in injury to a coworker, a customer, or some other third party, the employer can be sued for damages. The suit might be based on the doctrine that an employee carrying out assigned duties is an agent of the employer. More often, in states where they apply, the doctrines of negligent hiring and retention are being used. These hold that an employer can be found negligent in hiring or keeping an employee if (a) an injury was caused by an employee acting "under the auspices of employment," (b) the employee is shown to have been unfit for the job, (c) the employer knew or should have known about the unfitness, (d) the injury was a foreseeable consequence, and (e) the hiring or retention of the employee was the *proximate cause*[15] of the injury (Ryan & Lasek, 1991).

Grounds for Action under Negligent Hiring

There must be an injury. In most litigation, the injury is physical (results of assaults, accidents, rapes, or other physical violence). A consequence of criminal behavior such as theft may be the injury. Emotional or psychological injuries might be litigated.

The "auspices of employment" is rarely at issue. It is not restricted to carrying out actual job duties as the employer's agent; the activities or event causing injury may include more than assigned task performance (Shattuck, 1989), although liability seems restricted to activities carried out while the employee is on the job or in some sense representing the employer (e.g., wearing the employer's uniform). An employee on his or her own time, or commuting from work to home, is not acting under the auspices of employment (Ryan & Lasek, 1991).

Showing that an employee is "unfit" is not necessarily showing incompetence on the job. Much litigation in this area involves violence, so a person with a history of violent reactions to interpersonal frustrations may be deemed "unfit" for employment in jobs where potentially frustrating contact with others is likely. Being "unfit" includes (from case law) not only mental or personality disorders but also more ordinary deficiencies. An employee's competence in driving may be considered in determining fitness in a job in which driving ability is hardly a defining characteristic (e.g., a social worker) but in which the employee must drive from one site to another. Would checking for a valid driver's license be enough to avoid liability for an employee at fault in an injury-producing accident between sites? I do not know, but a finding of unfitness seems likely if the employee had a history of multiple at-fault traffic accidents.

A typical negligent hiring and retention case asks whether the employer should have foreseen the possibility of unfitness. Maybe checking for a license is a sufficient precaution, but greater care would be shown by checking accident or driving records or insurance papers or perhaps giving a special driving test. It is prudent to identify possible consequences if a

---

[15] Proximate cause means that the injury must be a reasonably expected or probable consequence of things done or not done by the employer. If an employee with a long history of lying causes injury by threatening a potential customer, failure to learn of that history is not a proximal cause of the injury; there is no necessary or prudent connection between being a liar and threatening people (Ryan & Lasek, 1991).

TABLE 4.2
Job and Personal Characteristics to Consider in Liability Analysis

Requirements and Activities	Judgment Needed
Job Activities	
Drives company vehicle	Frequency, mileage
Receives cash or checks	Frequency, amount
Receives goods from shipper, others	Frequency, cost
Responsible for property of others	Frequency, cost
Enters customer homes, customers present	Frequency
Enters customer homes, customers absent	Frequency
Works where children are present	Frequency, circumstances
Works with general public	Proportion of time, risk
Works with hazardous materials	Risk, risk factors[a]
Works nights	Risk, risk factors
Responsible for work of others	Degree shared
Personnel Requirements	
Must hold license or other certification	Compliance
Must operate specific equipment	Nature of equipment, risk
Must have specific product knowledge	Nature of product, risk
Must have specific education or training	Nature, risk

Table developed in part from text in C. A. Shattuck (1989), "The tort of negligent hiring and the use of selection devices: The employee's right of privacy and the employer's need to know", *Industrial Relations Law Journal, 11*, p. 5. © 1989 by the Regents of the University of California. Adapted from *Industrial Relations Law Journal* (now *Berkeley Journal of Employment and Labor Law*), Vol. 11, No. 1, by permission of the Regents of the University of California.

[a] "Risk" refers to a judgment about the nature of potential risks of injury to third parties; "risk factors" refers to judgments about personal or situational characteristics that might enhance the potential of risk.

person who is unfit in any specific way is put on the job. Shattuck (1989) listed several considerations in job analysis; most of these are shown in Table 4.2, with some modifications.

Appropriate Methods of Assessment

Most writers on negligent hiring emphasize reference checks and background investigations—advice easier to give than to follow. Another legal doctrine, known as defamation, has made reference checks all but worthless. About the only information prudent employers give when asked about former employees is confirmation or disconfirmation of dates of employment and last job held, and some refuse even that. There is safety in the refusal. To be actionable under a charge of defamation, information given by the previous employer must be shown to be false, but the burden of proof falls on the employer, who must show that the statement made is true. Saying that an employee was discharged because of the supervisor's *opinion* that the employee was not trustworthy can be true if the opinion is a matter of record; it is therefore not defamatory. The same information given in a context of innuendo permits the inference, without factual support, that the employee did in fact violate trust, and it may be defamatory under the principle known as "slander *per quod*." Statements that do not hold up under legal scrutiny, whether false, partially true, or unsupported, may also serve as the basis for suit for wrongful discharge (Ryan & Lasek, 1991). All in all, the risks are usually deemed too severe to take on behalf of inquiry from outside the organization.

Background investigations run similar risks and may also violate a candidate's rights of privacy. Many kinds of public information can be tapped, but always with some risk that the information is erroneous. Questions of validity of references and background investigations are not new (Guion, 1965, p. 409). Moreover, some resulting information cannot be used for employment decisions. Courts have repeatedly ruled against the use of arrest records, for example, to deny employment to those in demographic groups experiencing unusual arrest frequency—although convictions may be used. There is always a question of cost. Thorough background investigations are likely to be fruitless for young applicants and very expensive for older ones with a long background to investigate.

Retaliation

Retaliation for employee actions may be illegal. For example, firing a "whistle blower" may be retaliatory. Statutory and case law, as well as interpretations of constitutional civil rights amendments, have developed a concept of *protected actions*. A plaintiff charging retaliation must present evidence (a) of having engaged in a protected activity and (b) subsequently suffering a *materially adverse action*, and (c) of a causal connection between the protected action and the claim of retaliation. Retaliation charges are generally likely to involve such personnel decisions as termination, unwanted transfers, or failure to assign a complainant to special training opportunities.

At the close of their chapter on retaliation, Gutman et al. (2010) listed recommendations for reducing the risk of litigation. They pointed out that the various laws are not meant to be general codes of civility. Nevertheless, they said, civility in dealing with employee complaints is likely to be more productive than trying to get even.

Immigration Law

The Immigration Reform and Control Act of 1986 had been fallow until political issues in 2006–2008 over "illegal aliens" and "guest worker" proposals heated up interest in it. The political heat is likely to flare up again in this century's second decade. Those issues center largely on undocumented workers, but they could have included issues in recruiting and hiring highly skilled or educated people from other countries. Cascio (2003) summarized the main features of the Act under four categories: (a) it prohibits hiring, or continuing to employ, anyone not legally authorized to work in the United States by citizenship or by "green cards," (b) it requires verification of the identity and work authorization for every new employee (even if the employer has only one employee), (c) discrimination on the basis of national origin is prohibited, except that it permits hiring a US citizen in preference to an alien if the two are equally qualified, and (d) aliens living in the US continuously from 1982 to the effective date of the Act, November 6, 1986, were granted amnesty.

Immigration law, which many pundits contend is not adequately enforced, can be a major issue for employers and applicants alike. Given the political steam that has accumulated in discussing it, it is hard to say what the situation will be by the time the polemic rhetoric has frozen attitudes and prevented clear reasoning.

CONCLUDING NOTE

This chapter omitted much. It could have included record-keeping requirements and other regulatory rules, requirements for federal employment of part-time people, laws for the use of polygraphs, state laws, and related laws in other countries. What *is* described here is brief, barely scratching the surface. Moreover, changes in laws, regulations, or court decisions can be expected.

Personnel decisions must be made according to existing laws. The law is dynamic, ever-changing, and varies by state or local jurisdiction. Changes follow or accompany (or are accompanied by) changes in the ideas and attitudes of society in general, whether emerging spontaneously or in response to leadership. Even imperfect law is an expression of, and an instrument of, social policy. Perhaps, then, the objective of this chapter is better described as trying to emphasize that personnel decisions must be made not only according to organizational policies and interests but according to social policy and interest insofar as it can be understood. Having a good lawyer who keeps track of civil rights legislation and case law is important to any organization.

It seems clear that compliance with the law and successful defense of challenged practices requires thorough records of decisions made in forming predictive hypotheses, in choosing or developing constructs and operations for their assessment, and in providing meaningful evidence of the validity and other psychometric attributes of those assessments for their intended purposes. This takes us into Part II, focusing on principles of measurement and of data analysis.

II
PSYCHOMETRIC AND STATISTICAL FOUNDATIONS

This is the most technical part of the book. Chapters 5 and 6 present measurement theory, both classical and modern. Chapter 7 introduces the simple, conventional approach to correlation and statistical prediction, bivariate regression, used to evaluate assessments for assessment-based decisions. Bivariate regression allows prediction of one criterion from one predictor; bivariate correlation indicates the strength of relationship of these measures. Together, these are the basic statistical tools for criterion-related (or criterion-oriented) validation.

Bivariate regression is simple and conventional, but it has serious limitations and interpretive ambiguities. I present it in detail, not because it is such a great evaluative tool, but because its assumptions, logic, and data are basic to more complex (and often more useful) statistical prediction. It is becoming increasingly clear that predicting the behavior of real people in real work situations takes more than a single predictor, and maybe more than a single criterion. Chapter 7, therefore, questions the conventional criterion-related approach, and Chapter 8 describes the basics of more complex but often more useful multivariate methods. Chapter 9 introduces the twin problems of bias and fairness, in which bias is seen as a multivariate statistical problem, requiring still more complex analyses; fairness is seen as a judgment based on values as much as on data.

5

Basic Concepts in Measurement

Measurement starts with the idea that *anything that exists, exists to some degree, and therefore can be measured.* Constructs exist, at least as ideas. Some things that exist differ in kind, not in degree. Stevens (1946) identified four kinds of measurement scales: *ratio* scales (those with a true zero and equal intervals, permitting multiplication of scores, e.g., one score is twice as much of the variable as another), *interval* scales (with equal intervals but no true zero, permitting addition), *ordinal* scales (with neither zero nor equal intervals, permitting only relative ordering of scores), and *nominal* scales, which are not scales at all (if "scale" implies quantity) but categorical classifications.[1] Personnel assessment procedures fall into all four categories, but the measurement theory guiding their development and evaluation is primarily quantitative and generally assumes at least interval scales. Classical test theory (CTT), or classical psychometrics, began about a century ago with simple, basic equations; over the years it has grown into a more complex theory. This chapter presents the basics and the evolution of basic CTT concepts.

Measurement and related terms are sometimes ambiguous. I offer definitions here to try to reduce ambiguity, at least within this book. (I don't promise consistent use of my own definitions, being easily influenced by the use of words in other reading.) To *measure*, a verb, is to use a procedure to express numerically the degree to which a specified characteristic describes a person or object. A *measure*, a noun, is the numerical value determined by the act of measuring. *Score* and *measure*, as nouns, are treated as synonyms even for procedures that are not tests. *Measurement* is the process by which different scores can be ordered, with relatively fine gradations, according to a fairly well-defined continuum. *Assessment*—a broader term including measurement—includes both order and classification, often concerned more with what can be said about the people assessed than about precisely defined scales or scale units. *Assessment* as a noun also includes *measure* or *score*. Measurement seeks precise units, but some procedures settle for approximations where precision is either unnecessary or unlikely. *Measurement theory* (*psychometric theory*) is the rational foundation for developing and evaluating procedures providing somewhat precise scores—scores on at least an interval scale. There is no corresponding theory for purely nominal scales, but some aspects of psychometric theory apply to them as well.

---

[1] A delightful and thoroughly readable discussion of these scales is presented by McDonald (1999, pp. 410–419).

BACKGROUND OF PSYCHOMETRIC THEORY

Psychophysical and Psychological Scaling

Psychophysics

Psychophysical scaling relates magnitudes of physical stimuli to scales of associated psychological experience (perception). A precursor to psychophysics was the development of the equal-tempered musical scale in the late sixteenth and early seventeenth centuries (Guion, 1973). Notes at a higher pitch are associated with higher frequencies, but it is not a one-to-one association. Units of the musical scale (octaves, intervals, or steps) are perceived as equal whether high notes or low, but higher notes require greater differences in physical frequencies at different scale levels, as shown for octaves in Figure 5.1. Physical frequencies relate to the perception of an octave in a 2:1 ratio; the frequency of *A* above middle *C* is twice that of *A* one octave lower, which is twice that of *A* another octave lower. Psychophysical scaling was one of the earliest research areas in experimental psychology.

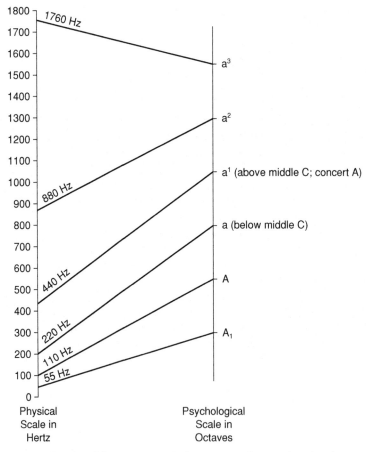

FIG. 5.1   The physical scale of frequencies and the associated musical scale of octave differences in tone.

Its smallest unit was a just noticeable difference (*jnd*); the *jnd* varied across observers. Equations were found for individual observers and averaged to develop general laws of sensory perception, formal models of the psychological processes, and scales with equal psychological intervals.

Attitude Scaling

Attitudes form psychological scales without functionally related physical scales. The *law of comparative judgment* (Thurstone, 1927) was derived from psychophysics, stating a mathematical theory of the separation of stimuli in a purely psychological scale. It is a theory of judgment, not of attributes. Judgments—whether of attitudes or of the relative merit of approximations to correct answers—are typically collected by ranking or by comparing pairs of statements or objects.

In psychophysics, differences noticed equally often are assumed psychologically equal. Applying the principle to groups gave rise to the *method of equal-appearing intervals* for developing scales to measure attitudes or values (Thurstone & Chave, 1929). A different approach to attitude scaling, known as the *method of summated ratings*, was developed by Likert (1932). Both methods of scaling are still used, described further in Chapter 13.

Reaction Times and Individual Differences

"The Personal Equation"

In the eighteenth century, clocks at Greenwich Observatory were set on the basis of the time that stars passed a cross-hair in a telescope. Near the end of the century, the Royal Astronomer fired an assistant for consistent errors, but it was subsequently learned that professional astronomers also disagreed because of individual differences in their reaction times. "Personal equations" were developed by which the observations of one astronomer could be equated with those of another with a different average reaction time. The chronoscope, invented in the nineteenth century, allowed more precise computation of individual reaction times and, therefore, more exact personal equations (Boring, 1961).

Although astronomy moved on to better measurement, the problem attracted the attention of Wilhelm Wundt, a founding father of modern experimental psychology. His "mental chronometry" measured components of mental processes in seven levels of complexity, each requiring lower levels as prior steps. The time required to carry out a given step was determined by measuring how long it took to complete the process *through* that step (level), measuring how long it took to get *to* that step, and subtracting. This line of research was abandoned, partly because of poor technology, but it has resurfaced in modern cognitive psychology. If task times are discrete and not overlapping, reaction times, historically and currently, provide measures of the duration of psychological processes.

Psychological Testing and the Normal Distribution

Adolphe Quetelet, a Belgian astronomer and mathematician, noted that, if the center of a distribution of measures represented perfection, then nature erred equally often in either direction. He later found that distributions of social and moral data also followed this "normal law of error." That idea was important to Galton's studies of the inheritance of genius and later to the development of the product–moment coefficient of correlation. It treats the standard deviation of a more or less normal distribution as a useful unit of measurement (Boring, 1961); it is still the assumed unit in most psychological measurement.[2]

James McKeen Cattell (1890) and others of his era developed several perceptual and sensory tests and tests of memory, which Hull (1928) considered academic aptitude tests. Employment tests were developed by Munsterberg at Harvard, clinical tests by Kraepelin in Germany, and intelligence tests by Binet, Simon, and Henri in France (Anastasi, 1988; Hull, 1928). Paper-and-pencil mental ability tests of the early twentieth century used Binet's question and answer approach. Projective personality tests and standardized school achievement testing were introduced during the same period. By mid-century, a group of test experts, concerned about the proliferation of tests and test use, developed a set of "technical recommendations" to identify for test users and test developers acceptable standards for reporting information about tests and about selecting and using them (American Psychological Association, American Educational Research Association, & National Council on Measurement Used in Education, 1954). These recommendations were revised and expanded in 1966, 1974, 1985, and 1999 by publications generally known as *APA Standards*, regardless of the order of listing the three associations as authors. Since 1975, the Society for Industrial and Organizational Psychology has followed each edition of the *Standards* with *Principles for the Validation and Use of Personnel Selection Procedures*, most recently in 2003 (Society for Industrial and Organizational Psychology, 2003). These documents focus somewhat on testing but extend psychometric concepts to other forms of measurement and assessment as well. *Standards* is more general across uses of measurement in various disciplines and each individual standard is more like a rule to be followed when appropriate to a given use. *Principles* is specific to personnel testing and other selection procedures and is more interpretive and guidance-oriented. A third document is the *Uniform Guidelines*; it is the official United States governing document in legal affairs but is psychometrically archaic.

Different kinds of psychological measurement have all emphasized individual differences in perceptions, abilities, or personality attributes. Some have emphasized theories of psychological processes. A few have offered theories of attributes measured. Usually the technique came first, followed later by questions of what the measures mean. Reliability was the dominant topic in measurement during the early part of the twentieth century; later, validity became the dominant concern. In employment practice, validity often refers to effectiveness of prediction, but psychometric theory is more concerned with score meaning (Cronbach, 1988; Messick, 1989, 1996).

RELIABILITY: CONCEPTS OF MEASUREMENT ERROR

I treat reliability and validity separately, at least in beginning this chapter, as if they were independent. I know better, but I do it because, frankly, it is traditional. The interdependence will be emphasized later. For now I simply point out that people differ, and so do measures of

[2] Boring (1961) pointed out, first, that one cannot assume that a mathematical function such as the "normal law" applies to a particular variable until it has been demonstrated empirically, which Galton and most of his followers failed to do. He went on to say, "The *a priori* assumption that the normal law applies to biological and psychological variables, and therefore provides a device for changing ordinal scales into equal intervals has continued well into the present century. The scaling of mental tests in terms of standard deviations . . . in some ways preserves this ancient fallacy" (p. 123). Yes, indeed.

the ways in which they differ. Some of the difference in measures is due to error, such as flaws in measurement, the vagaries of chance, or traits measured—including extraneous traits not intended to be measured. Flaws, chance, and unintended traits are errors in measurement.

Measurement Error and Error Variance

Measurement errors happen. Two people using the same yardstick to measure the same table may get different results. A chemist using sophisticated equipment may weigh a crucible several times, with apparently trivial differences, and settle for the average as the "true" weight. Mental measurements are even more subject to error. Measurement error always exists, but despite it, scores usually reflect fairly well the level of the trait being measured. It is sensible to infer, despite error, that one who scores high on an arithmetic test really is pretty good at arithmetic. The basic assumption of psychological testing is that any measure contains an error component and a component that is consistent (termed "true"). Classical test theory begins by assuming that any measure X (obtained score) can be "mysteriously parsed" (Zickar, Cortina, & Carter, 2010) into the algebraic sum of a true measure (true score) t and a measurement error (error score) e, or

$$X = t + e \qquad (5.1)$$

Further assumptions are (a) that true scores and error scores are not correlated, (b) error scores in one measure are not correlated with error scores in another, and (c) error scores in one are not correlated with true scores on something else. Together, these assumptions say that error scores happen randomly. In fact, however, some errors are not purely random. In ordinary language, a "true" score, if really true, has no error, but the CTT language defines it as *the mean of an infinite number of a person's obtained scores on* parallel (equivalent) measures *of the same trait* (Thurstone, 1931), that is, measures with the same means, standard deviations, and distributions of item statistics. But if every obtained score in that infinite set of replications contains a consistent error for each person, the person's theoretical mean score might intuitively be considered "true" plus or minus the consistent error. The *theoretical* error score does not include errors made consistently over repeated testing; it includes only inconsistent error. If all errors were inconsistent, the mean of even less than infinitely repeated measures would approximate an intuitively "true" score. However, the influence of constant error for each person influences the mean of repeated measures precisely as it influences each individual measure. In CTT, "true" does not mean literally correct; it means consistent.

I once had a thermometer with a glass tube attached by staples to a board showing the scale. My son (at age 4) liked to slide the tube up and down; the temperature reading depended on where he left the tube—a random error. However, if we pushed the tube down as far as it would go, we got a reading about 20° too low. It was inaccurate, but it was *repeatedly, consistently* inaccurate, always with that 20° *constant* error.

Distinguishing systematic, repeatable errors from errors that vary randomly across repeated measures allows rephrasing the basic CTT equation as

$$X = s + e \qquad (5.2)$$

Equation 5.2 considers an individual's actual score X to consist of s, a composite of a true score and any systematically consistent error affecting the person, and e, random or inconsistent error. The s score includes the person's private constant error. These personal errors differ for different people, so a set of them has some variance. If an error is consistent for everyone in the set, it systematically influences all measures in the set equally and therefore has no variance. Classical reliability theory is concerned with data sets and variances, so the equation can be expanded to one describing variance in X:

$$\sigma_x^2 = \sigma_s^2 + \sigma_e^2 \tag{5.3}$$

where σ_x^2 is the total variance in a set of scores, σ_s^2 is the variance due to systematic causes, and σ_e^2 is variance due to inconsistency.

Reliability

The word *reliability* often describes a nice personality trait, a characteristic of those who can be counted on to do desirable things. The term could also be applied to a chronic liar who can be counted on to tell lies if they are more convenient or fun. With the tube pushed all the way down, that thermometer could be counted on to be consistently (reliably) wrong by 20°.

Psychometrically, reliability is consistency in sets of measures. Equation 5.3 shows where the consistency comes from: from the trait being measured and individual systematic errors. If the thermometer tube is wherever the child left it, the measurement errors are inconsistent, not predictable. Eliminating the random error created a large constant error, but it also created consistency. As a basic concept, then, *reliability is the extent to which a set of measurements is free from error variance.* In equation form,

$$r_{xx} = 1 - \frac{S_e^2}{S_x^2} \tag{5.4}$$

where r_{xx} is the reliability coefficient, S_e^2 is the variance of the inconsistent errors, and S_x^2 is the total variance, in the set of scores. The smaller the error variance relative to total variance in obtained scores, the more reliable the measures in the distribution. In discussions of reliability, "measurement error" refers to inconsistency.

We could also define reliability as the proportion of total variance attributable to systematic sources, but it is important to recognize that it is *not* defined as the proportion of total variance due to variance in the trait to be measured.

Reliability Coefficient and Index of Reliability

If one actually knew the systematic scores in a distribution, a correlation coefficient, $r_{sx'}$ could be computed between systematic scores s and obtained scores X. Such a coefficient is purely hypothetical, but important to reliability theory; it is the *index of reliability*, and it helps clarify the reliability concept. Of course, the index of reliability cannot be computed directly, because error scores and systematic scores are purely theoretical, but methods exist for estimating reliability. They require empirical correlations of two sets of observed measures of the same construct, from the same people, under the same (standardized) conditions—replicated measures. They might be scores on the same items at two different times, or scores on two parallel test forms, or scores on two more or less parallel halves of a test. The correlation coefficient approaches unity to the extent that each individual score is in the same relative position in each of the two score distributions. It will be less than perfect to the extent that the relative position of the people in the two sets of data are inconsistent. The computed coefficient is a *coefficient of reliability*, r_{xx}. It is literally the correlation between two sets of obtained scores, but it is best understood as a statement of the level of variance shared in the obtained X distribution and the theoretical s distribution. It is therefore interpreted directly (without squaring) as the coefficient of determination of the theoretical index of reliability, estimating the proportion of the total variance accounted for by systematic sources.[3] The relationship between the computed coefficient of reliability and the theoretical index of reliability is stated as

$$r_{xx} = r_{sx}^2 \tag{5.5}$$

or

$$\sqrt{r_{xx}} = r_{sx} \tag{5.6}$$

A reliability coefficient estimates the degree to which variance in a set of scores is systematic. The meaningfulness, and the usefulness, of a reliability coefficient for evaluating measurement depends on the sources of variance treated as systematic or random (consistent or inconsistent) in computing it.

Validity

Reliability is often termed the *sine qua non* of classical measurement theory; if a test is not reliable, it cannot have any other merit. However, evidence of reliability is not in itself sufficient evidence that a construct has been measured well or that it will be useful. There is still the very important question of whether systematic sources of variance are relevant to the purpose of measurement. This is a matter of validity. Validity is the major consideration in test evaluation; reliability is important because it imposes a ceiling for validity. The theoretical relationship of reliability to validity is shown by the equation

$$r_{\tilde{x}\tilde{y}} = \frac{r_{xy}}{\sqrt{(r_{xx}r_{yy})}} \tag{5.7}$$

where $r_{\tilde{x}\tilde{y}}$ is the theoretical correlation that would exist if predictor x and criterion y were perfectly reliable, r_{xy} is the validity coefficient actually obtained, and r_{xx} and r_{yy} are the respective reliability coefficients. This is known as correcting the validity coefficient for *attenuation*; that is, for unreliability.

It may be important for theoretical purposes to ask what the correlation would be if the two variables were measured with perfect reliability. That question is rarely important in personnel research. We have a test (or other means of assessment). It is imperfect. We use it anyway, use something else, or improve its reliability; inevitably, we use a less than perfectly reliable test. It is useless to dream about validity we might have had if only we had a perfectly reliable test.

---

[3] For a mathematical proof, see (Guilford, 1954) among other statistics or psychometrics texts. Derivations of equations are important for a full understanding of them, but they are not presented in this book.

In some situations, however, it is useful to know the level of validity with a perfectly reliable criterion; that is, to know how much of the *reliable* criterion variance is associated with predictor variance. We can find out by correcting only for criterion unreliability:

$$r_{x\tilde{y}} = \frac{r_{xy}}{\sqrt{r_{yy}}} \tag{5.8}$$

where y is the criterion, $\tilde{y}$ is the perfectly reliable criterion, and x is the test. Assume an obtained validity coefficient of .40—good, better than many, but not great. Assume also a criterion reliability coefficient of .25—a terribly low reliability. Substituting in Equation 5.8, $r_{x\tilde{y}} = .40/\sqrt{.25} = .40/.5 = .80$, the estimated correlation with a perfectly reliable criterion. The coefficient of determination for this hypothetical correlation is .64; 64% of the total *explainable* criterion variance is "accounted for" by (shared with) the test. A validity coefficient expressed as the relationship of the predictor to the explainable criterion variance is a more standardized statement than the uncorrected coefficient, is less subject to the vagaries of random criterion variance, and generally makes more sense. 64% should describe a pretty useful prediction, but don't get excited about it. That very low reliability estimate may be a fluke—a gross underestimate. Suppose a better reliability estimate were .81; then the corrected coefficient would be .44, not very different from .40. In using Equation 5.8, overestimating criterion reliability gives a more conservative estimate of corrected validity.

A general, but unwarranted, attitude is that Equations 5.7 and 5.8 have been handed down from Olympus as eternal verities. In fact, they were created early in the twentieth century specifically assuming (a) that both predictor and criterion were samples from theoretically infinite sets of parallel forms and (b) that validity was adequately defined by a validity coefficient. The past half-century and more has seen alternative concepts of validity, and Equation 5.7 may not fit or even be possible for use in limiting validity according to some of them. Consider, for example, the definition of validity as the extent to which a test measures what it "purports" to measure. No r_{yx} value exists to fit the definition directly. Moreover, different methods of estimating reliability treat some sources of variance as systematic and others as essentially random, so the limitation depends on how reliability is estimated (more on this later).

Later in this chapter I reiterate the notion that validity is inference and that the inference requires not only numbers but a logical, evidence-based argument. The correction attempted by Equations 5.7 and 5.8 is based only on numbers. Nevertheless, despite these reservations about the equations (see Putka & Sackett, 2010, for more), I still hold to the logical implications of the principle: validity arguments are suspect to the degree that the scores are unreliable.

Accuracy

Accuracy should not be confused with reliability.[4] A thermometer or test may provide reliable but exceedingly inaccurate measures. Nor should accuracy be confused with validity. Consider the thermometer example. To determine its accuracy, a set of temperature readings could be paired with criterion readings obtained for the same situations using instruments

---

[4] Many authorities have treated reliability and accuracy as synonyms, but they should not be treated so. They differ in the nature of the correlated variables and in the specification of the constants in the linear equation.

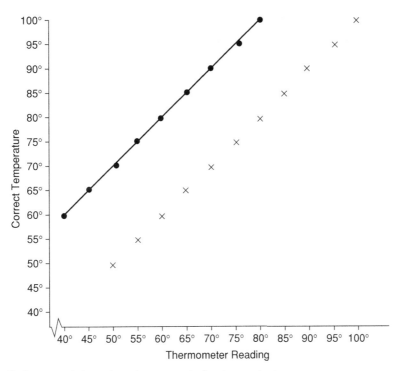

FIG. 5.2 Perfect correlation where inaccuracy is due to constant error.

in the Bureau of Standards. If the correlation between flawed thermometer readings and the standard readings were high, we could conclude that the thermometer gives "valid" measures of temperature—but not necessarily accurate ones. The thermometer with the 20° constant error could be perfectly valid, as shown in Figure 5.2: the connected dots show perfect correlation despite the constant error. The unconnected crosses show both perfect correlation and perfect accuracy.

To be perfectly accurate, a measure must be perfectly correlated with a standard measure of the same thing, and the relationship must be linear. The general formula for a linear relationship (as in Figure 5.2) is

$$Y = a + bX \tag{5.9}$$

where a is a constant amount that must be added to (or subtracted from) predictors in predicting Y, and b is a constant amount by which each value of X must be multiplied to predict Y. For perfectly accurate measurement, $a = 0$ and $b = 1$, indicating perfect correlation, and the regression equation is simply $Y = X$. How accurate is imperfect measurement? The answer depends on (a) the degree of correlation of a test instrument and an accepted standard (i.e., how close the constant b is to unity); (b) the absence of the constant a (indicating constant error) in the regression equation.

This is all very well for physical measures; we can refer sensibly to the accuracy of predictions or of measures defined by standards in something like a bureau of standards. There is, however, no such bureau for cognitive or temperament or other psychological traits. The concept of accuracy, therefore, is meaningless for most psychological constructs.

SOURCES OF VARIANCE IN RELIABILITY ESTIMATION

Thorndike (1949) pointed out that reliability, or the lack of it, depends on the reasons for individual differences in test performance. He did not consider reliability a property of the measuring instrument (test). Rather, he considered it clear that a test is a stimulus and that score variance stems from individual differences in responses people make. Even situational considerations such as heat or humidity may influence reliability if they influence the responses people make. The sources of variance in mental measurements are sources of variance in human performance.

Thorndike's categories were based on distinctions between long-lasting and temporary characteristics of people and between characteristics that are very general, influencing behavior in a wide variety of situations, and those that are more specific to a test or item. In a later discussion of the sources of variance, Stanley (1971) pointed out that random errors can arise from aspects of test administration and scoring. He therefore added another category of variance sources, and I follow his lead. Table 5.1 shows, in reduced form, the sources of variance as identified by Thorndike and extended by Stanley. The following outline expands Table 5.1 and is adapted from the Thorndike and Stanley presentations. It describes why people get different scores; with some verbal modification, it applies also to the variety of other kinds of assessments. Zickar et al. (2010), for example, were as focused on ratings as on tests, and their views are reflected in the outline.

Reasons for Individual Differences in Test Performance and Ratings

   I.   *Reasons that are more or less permanent and apply in many measurement situations*

   A. Some traits are general; they influence performance on many different kinds of test. For example, intelligence may influence performance on verbal, numerical, spatial, or job knowledge tests.
   B. Some people are more test-wise than others; that is, because of more experience or special training or insights in taking tests, they come closer to their maximum potential scores in *any* kind of test situation.
   C. Some people are quicker to understand instructions, and do so more completely, than other people. Some flounder through several items before catching on—if ever.

TABLE 5.1
Sources of Unreliability in Measures

I.	Lasting and general characteristics of the person
II.	Lasting but specific characteristics of the person
	A. Specific to the test as a whole
	B. Specific to individual test items
III.	Temporary but general characteristics of the person
IV.	Temporary and specific characteristics of the person
	A. Specific to the test as a whole
	B. Specific to individual test items
V.	Factors in the administration of the test or in the scoring of performance on it
VI.	Chance (variance not otherwise accounted for)

D. An individual rater may have certain styles, habits, or biases (conscious or otherwise) that function consistently across ratings of individual ratees.

II. *Reasons that are more or less permanent but apply mainly to the specific test being taken*

    A. Some of these reasons apply to the whole test or to any equivalent forms of it.

        1. Some people have more of the ability or knowledge or skill or other trait being measured by the test.

        2. Some people find certain kinds of item easy while others may be more confused by them. For example, some people are good at "outguessing" true–false items.

        3. In ratings, differences in rater traits (habits, styles, etc.) produce inconsistencies within the aggregated overall ratings for a specific ratee and across ratees.

        4. The number of observations or test items influences score or rating consistency; more being more reliable than few.

    B. Some reasons apply only to particular items on a test. Of all items that *could* be included, only a small number actually *are* in the test. There is an element of luck here; if the test happens to contain a few of the specific items to which the person does (or does not) know the answer, that person will have a higher (or lower) score than someone else who is less lucky (or luckier) in the specific questions faced.

III. *Reasons that are relatively temporary but would apply to almost any testing or rating situation*

    A. A person's health status may influence the score or ratings.

    B. A person may not do as well when he or she is particularly tired.

    C. The testing situation is challenging to some people; they want to score high (or rate accurately) so that they can enjoy a feeling of achievement; others may feel less, just want to get done.

    D. Individuals react differently to emotional stress. Ratings by a stressed rater, or the scores of stressed examinees or those tested by a stressed examiner or rater, are likely to differ, but inconsistently, from those expected in emotionally secure conditions.

    E. There may be some relatively temporary fluctuations in test-wiseness, or attention to cues.

    F. A person varies from time to time in readiness to be tested; such differences in set produce differences in attention to and comprehension of the test situation and, therefore, differences in scores. Readiness begets better scores. Situational variables may similarly affect rater readiness to rate.

    G. People respond differently to physical or other ambient conditions (light, heat, social pressures, etc.); those with the same abilities may score differently because of differences in their reactions to unusual or perhaps adverse physical conditions.

IV. *Reasons that are relatively temporary and apply mainly to a specific test or testing situation*

    A. Some reasons apply to the test as a whole (or to equivalent forms of it).

        1. Some reasons are time-limited (Zickar et al., 2010), including conditions or incidents occurring in one testing situation that would not occur in

           another, such as a health emergency or malfunctioning heating equipment. People also differ in how well or how quickly they understand a specific set of instructions; understanding may come more readily at one time than at another.

      2.   Some tests require special techniques; some people may "stumble" sooner into certain insights useful in tackling a particular test than would others.

      3.   Differences in the opportunities for practicing skills required in test performance (or in rating others) produce score differences.

      4.   A person may be "up" for a test or "ripe" for it more at one time than at another; individual differences in readiness cause differences in scores.

    B.   Some reasons apply only to particular test items or persons being rated.

      1.   Momentary forgetfulness or lapses of memory while taking a test make a person miss an item that might otherwise be answered correctly. Similarly, forgetting observations can also influence ratings.

      2.   Momentary changes in level of attention or carefulness have the same effect.

      3.   The term *transient error* refers to "momentary and nonrepeating factors" (Becker, 2000, p. 370). Such error may apply more generally than to specific items if the "moment" lasts long enough to influence responses to several items.

  V.   *Reasons implying influence of the situation or other persons.* For measures involving interactions between examiner and examinee (e.g., individual assessment), or for measures using open-ended responses to be evaluated using a complex protocol, as in ratings (e.g., performance evaluations, evaluations of work samples)—such things are ambient conditions, not characteristics of the examinee or ratee, and they can influence scores or ratings.

    A.   Conditions of testing may vary in strictness or accuracy of time limits, in lighting, in distractions, or other conditions intended to be standard or controlled.

    B.   Interactions between examiner and examinee characteristics (e.g., race, sex, age, or personality traits) may enhance performance for some examinees and interfere for others.

    C.   Bias or carelessness in taking a test, in scoring responses, or in rating people.

  VI.   *Pure chance.* Some reasons just cannot be pinned down; after taking everything else into account, unexplained individual differences persist. For example, sometimes a person may simply be luckier in guessing than at other times.

Errors Reflected in Reliability Coefficients

Reliability is traditionally estimated by a correlation between two sets of measures presumably measuring the same thing in the same sample of people in the same way (i.e., replicated measurement). Different methods of estimation reflect different sources of error. In traditional CTT, the two sets of scores may be (a) two different but equivalent forms of the same test, or (b) scores on a test administered at different times, or (c) scores on two halves of a test administered once. For each person, the two systematic scores are expected to be the same; systematic variance therefore causes, improves, or at least maintains correlation. Error scores

TABLE 5.2
Allocation of Variance in Different Estimates of Reliability

Estimate Method	Treatment of Sources of Variance[a]							
	I	IIA	IIB	III	IVA	IVB	V	VI
Immediate test–retest	S	S	S	S	S	E	E	E
Delayed test–retest	S	S	S	E	E	E	E	E
Immediate equivalent forms	S	S	E	S	S	E	E	E
Delayed equivalent forms	S	S	E	E	E	E	E	E
Split half	S	S	E	S	S	S	E	E

[a] S = systematic variance; E = error variance.

are *not* the same, being inconsistent, so error variance comes from conditions or personal characteristics that differed, and therefore inhibited or lowered correlation in the two sets of scores. If the effect of a source of variance is consistent in the two sets of scores, it is *treated as* a source of systematic variance. If it is inconsistent, it is *treated as* a source of error variance. Different ways to estimate reliability *treat* different sources of variance as systematic (correlation-causing) or as error (correlation-reducing). Oversimplifying to make the point, Table 5.2 shows five traditional methods of estimating reliability and the way they treat the different sources of variance.

Category I variance (general and long-lasting) is necessarily systematic, maintaining if not causing correlation between the two sets of scores for any of the five methods.

Category IIA (long-lasting but fairly general) characteristics include the trait being measured—surely a source of systematic variance if the trait itself is stable—but the category also includes other characteristics that maintain correlation regardless of the method of estimation.

Category IIB (long-lasting but more specific) focuses narrowly, even on specific items. The score of a person who, by chance, happens to know the proper response for a particular item will be somewhat higher than the score of one of equal ability who happens not to know it. This is surely a source of systematic variance in a quick retest. It would not be if reliability were estimated by correlating two equivalent forms of the same test (i.e., two forms built to the same logical and statistical specifications but with different specific items). A person who knows a specific fact required for the first form does not necessarily have that advantage in the second one, so the category is treated as a source of error reducing correlation by any of the equivalent forms methods.

In Category III (temporary but general), some circumstances are more temporary than others. I think of these as changing slowly enough that the change will not be noticed within a testing session but rapidly enough that the change may be pronounced before a second session. These are treated as sources of systematic variance if the time interval is too short for change to occur; otherwise the category is treated as correlation-reducing error variance.

Category IVA (temporary but less general) is concerned with temporary traits, so, as with Category III, the time interval determines how it is treated in reliability estimation. The shorter the interval, the more likely it is that Category IVA variance is treated as systematic or maintaining correlation.

Category IVB (temporary but specific to particular items) is treated as error variance in almost any method of estimating reliability. Momentary fluctuations in set, mental blocking, and other temporary characteristics have their influence on specific test items or groups of items. Such momentary characteristics are largely unpredictable and should be treated as error.

Category V includes some sources that may contribute to systematic variance, but most of them are more likely to be treated as sources of error. Consider test time limits. It is unlikely that the same error in timing would be made twice; timing errors are properly treated as sources of error variance. Specific biases of an examiner, however, may be long lasting; if the same examiner tests all examinees, examiner characteristics may contribute to systematic variance (i.e., they do not reduce the correlation). If different examinees are tested by different examiners, however, examiner differences are likely to be treated as error variance. Ratings are subject to a variety of rater differences, so rater characteristics are usually sources of error. If a single rater is involved, of course, that rater's quirks are treated as systematic.

Category VI represents error variance in its purest form, reducing correlation.

OPERATIONAL DEFINITIONS OF RELIABILITY

Reliability estimation methods vary in designs for data collection and in computational procedures. Each one is a specific set of procedures for defining what is meant by reliability—an operational definition of reliability. Different operational definitions, as shown in Table 5.2, emphasize different sources of error variance. A conservative reliability estimate (usually desirable except when used to correct for attenuation) treats many characteristics of persons and settings as sources of random error. A generally preferred procedure would therefore seem to be the delayed equivalent forms method, which considers Categories I and IIA as systematic and all other categories as sources of error. However, differences in intended uses of scores and in item domains properly influence judgments of how different sources of variance should be treated. If a test is to be used to assess current readiness for training, long-term stability may not be important. If a test of job knowledge is based on a small item domain, so that all possible items appear in one form of the test, item sampling is not a source of error. Operational definitions should be sensitive to the most serious sources of error for the situation at hand. I follow here the old-fashioned classification (dominant in much of the literature) of these definitions. A more comprehensive view is considered in the next chapter under *generalizability theory*.

Coefficients of Stability

Stability means scores are consistent over time. A coefficient of stability defines random error as individual differences in score change (inconsistency) over an appreciable time period. Retesting with the same test form is useful if item sampling is not a problem. Retest correlation may be spuriously high if previous responses are remembered. (Immediate test–retest after a few minutes or hours is often encountered but rarely appropriate.) Testing with an equivalent form after the time interval increases variance attributed to error, eliminating memory and other item-specific considerations as irrelevant sources of systematic variance.

Coefficients of stability are useful for psychomotor or sensory tests if intervals are long enough to counteract practice or fatigue effects. Longer time intervals are needed for cognitive tests. The appropriate time interval depends on how long people remember particular content and how often the content is practiced. A lot of skill, practice or use of specific information produces overlearning; individual differences in benefits of practice are appropriately treated as error variance.

Stability is important in performance ratings but hard to assess. Memory creates a spurious impression of stability; ratings are easy to remember, particularly when there are few ratees or when they are burned in memory in feedback sessions. Performance itself may not be stable. How much do coefficients of stability reflect stability in measurement compared to stability in the trait measured? Measures should not be considered unreliable if they detect changes in characteristics being measured. High stability may show only that the measure is not sensitive to change.

Coefficients of Equivalence

Virtually all measurement is based on data sampling. Accident frequency is sampled, for example, during a specific time period. Even a measure of one's weight is a sample of the day's varying circumstances such as heat or humidity, intake of fluids or salt, food consumption, or weight of clothing.

When two samples come from the same specifications and correlate well, the question of equivalence arises. Theoretically, two test forms with different items are considered equivalent, or parallel, if they can be assumed to have identical true score (systematic score) distributions. For practical purposes, they are considered equivalent if they (a) have matching content (each has the same number of each kind of item), and (b) yield essentially similar score distributions (at least means and standard deviations that are essentially alike). Equivalent forms are developed by specifying logical and statistical properties (item type and content; item difficulties, validities, or intercorrelations; or test means and standard deviations) to which each of them will conform. Such item matching should yield correlated forms with essentially the same "true score" distributions.

Conceptually, a coefficient of equivalence defines reliability as the extent to which a set of measures is free from errors due to sampling a test content domain. Actually, because genuine equivalence is hard to achieve, reliability coefficients computed as correlations between equivalent forms are rather conservative. The conservatism is not so great with tests of well-defined content such as vocabulary or arithmetic, but it may seriously distort reliability estimates for less well-defined areas such as temperament and motivation or for measurement by ratings. Coefficients of equivalence are useful reliability estimates for test-like performance measures such as work samples or simulations or observer checklists when equivalent forms can be developed. Equivalent forms of achievement tests are likely to be needed in situations where retesting is likely (a concern to be revisited in Chapter 10).

Coefficients of Internal Consistency

The degree to which a test or other measurement procedure consistently reflects the intended characteristic can be described at various levels. Peak (1953) introduced the term *functional unity* to suggest a level of similarity among items or groups of items sufficient to suggest that the various parts all seem to be measuring pretty much the same thing. Related terms are *internal consistency* and *unidimensionality*. These terms are hierarchical; I consider them different degrees of homogeneity, although some authors use the terms *homogeneous* and *unidimensional* as synonyms (Schmitt, 1996). Of them, unidimensionality most strongly implies homogeneity; internal consistency describes how well items can all be ordered along a single scale—it implies homogeneity but not necessarily unidimensionality; the consistency might be due to common mixes of dimensions in different sets of items. A test has functional unity, even with clearly distinguishable components, if the components are clearly positively related. For any of these, reliability estimation is called *internal consistency analysis.* Coefficients of internal consistency treat variance due to variations in item content as a major source of error variance, and they show how much the variance is systematically based on a common concept measured by the test as a whole. They are widely used because they are convenient; they need only one administration with just one test form. They are inappropriate for tests with time limits because different examinees taking a timed test actually respond to different numbers of items.

Split-Half Estimation

The oldest—and probably the most used—reliability coefficient, often described as an estimate of internal consistency, is based on deriving separate scores for two halves of a test. Strictly speaking, split-half methods do not really estimate internal consistency; they are more like coefficients of equivalence. They assume not homogeneity of item content, but equivalent heterogeneity in the two halves; they do assume that the test as a whole is at least a functional unity. Splitting into halves must be carefully done. In most cognitive tests, items are arranged according to item type, content, and difficulty. A first-half versus last-half split does not give equivalent halves; the first half is likely to be easier than the second. A common alternative puts odd-numbered items in one half and even-numbered items in the other. With forms so thoroughly intermixed, a temporary characteristic must be *very* temporary not to influence both scores, so Category IVB variance is treated as systematic variance, giving a spuriously high estimate of reliability—useful for criterion measures because it adds caution to a correction for attenuation (i.e., "correction" of an obtained correlation coefficient for measurement error). A time period for recording job performance is, in effect, a single administration, and the weeks or days of a year's production are analogous to items in a test. An odd–even split can smooth out seasonal variations with even-numbered weeks in one half and odd-numbered weeks in the other. It is preferable, however, to select items (or days or weeks) for the two halves randomly. Random selection tends to balance errors, making the halves more nearly equivalent; it also reduces somewhat the tendency to overlook heterogeneity encouraged by an odd–even split. Moreover, the number of consecutive items appearing in either half is variable, so more of the IVB variance is treated, properly, as error.

A correlation between half-scores needs correction because reliability is in part a function of the number of items or observations. Correlating half-scores gives a coefficient of equivalence for half as many items as are in the full test. The relationship between reliability and test length is shown by the general *Spearman-Brown prophecy formula,*

$$r_{nn} = \frac{nr_{xx}}{1 + (n-1)r_{xx}} \tag{5.10}$$

where r_{nn} is the reliability expected for scores based on n times as many items or observations as those at hand, and r_{xx} is the reliability coefficient for the test as it is. If $n = 2$, as in estimating the reliability coefficient of a full test from that computed for a half-test, the formula simplifies to

$$r_{xx} = \frac{2r_{\frac{1}{2}\frac{1}{2}}}{1 + r_{\frac{1}{2}\frac{1}{2}}} \tag{5.11}$$

where $r_{\underline{11}}$ is the correlation computed between the two half-test measures and r_{xx} the coefficient expected for the full-length test. This is often described as a Spearman-Brown "correction."

A different split-half technique (I think preferable, although it is not often used now) is the Rulon method (Rulon, 1939), it stems directly from the conceptual definition of reliability. It seeks a direct estimate of random error variance by treating score differences on the two halves as error and applying the definitional equation

$$r_{xx} = 1 - \frac{S_e^2}{S_x^2} \qquad (5.12)$$

Where S_x^2 is the total variance in measure X and S_e^2 is the variance attributed to the error. $S_e^2 = \Sigma d^2/N$ and d is the difference between the scores on the two halves. Note that Equation 5.12 repeats Equation 5.4. The assumption of equivalence in the two halves remains; this plan assumes that, if the two halves are truly equivalent, scores on them differ only because of variable error. Squaring these differences and dividing by N (number of cases measured) estimates the variance of assumed errors. Error variance divided by total variance is the proportional statement, returning us to the original concept of reliability as the extent to which measures are free from random error variance. No Spearman-Brown correction is needed.

Kuder–Richardson Estimates

Techniques involving analysis of item variance are more literally estimates of internal consistency. The most common of these methods was presented by Kuder and Richardson (1937) in a series of formulas; these formulas require the assumption of homogeneity (Cureton, 1958). The Kuder–Richardson formulas may be considered averages of all the split-half coefficients that would be obtained using all possible ways of dividing the test. The preferred formula (Richardson & Kuder, 1939) known as *Kuder–Richardson Formula* 20 (KR 20) from the numbering of equations in the original derivation, is

$$r_{xx} = \left(\frac{n}{n-1} \right) \cdot \left(1 - \frac{\Sigma_{pq}}{S_x^2} \right) \qquad (5.13)$$

where n is the number of items in the test, p is the proportion of correct responses to a given item, $q = (1 - p)$, and S_x^2 is the total test variance. Note that error variance is given as the sum of item variances, pq. This is a harsh assumption and may indicate why KR 20 is considered a lower bound estimate of reliability (Guttman, 1945).

Coefficient Alpha

Cronbach's coefficient alpha (1951), applicable to a wider variety of assessments than KR 20, is more commonly reported:

$$\alpha_n = \left(\frac{n}{n-1} \right) \cdot \left(1 - \frac{\Sigma S_i^2}{S_x^2} \right) \qquad (5.14)$$

where α_n is $r_{xx'}$ the reliability coefficient called alpha for a test of n components (items or sets of items), S_i^2 is the variance of item responses or other component scores, and S_x^2 is the total score variance. If item responses are dichotomous, then $S_i^2 = \Sigma pq$, and the equation for alpha is the same as KR 20. Coefficient alpha is appropriate for most norm-referenced tests of abilities because these are typically constructed to provide internally consistent sets of items. It is not appropriate for domain-referenced tests constructed to represent a heterogeneous content domain. Under appropriate circumstances, alpha can be used for items with response scales, ratings, or scores on small sets of dependent items such as a set of items based on a single passage or illustration.

Researchers should *not* use alpha merely for its convenience. The choice of a method for estimating reliability should always be based on the kinds of error most critical for the project at hand. Alpha is often considered a measure of unidimensionality, as distinguished from equivalence or stability or more forgiving levels of homogeneity, but it is not. A relatively high alpha can be obtained, given enough items, in a distinctly multidimensional test (Cortina, 1993), meaning only that split-halves, on the average, correlate well enough to have some functional unity. It still requires other data to determine whether the test as a whole is unidimensional, or if not, what mix of constructs make up a total score.

Internal Consistency for Speeded Tests

Internal consistency estimates require tests to be untimed; these methods assume opportunity to respond to every item. For speeded tests, a split-half reliability can be used only if the two halves are separately timed.

Interrater or Interscorer Agreement

Category V sources include errors attributable to raters or scorers. Two different observers seeing the same behavior or product may evaluate it differently—a source of error variance. With tests and rating scales scored by observer judgments, such errors can be large. The score depends not only on the person or thing observed and rated, but also on perceptual sets and other characteristics of the scorer or rater.

Interrater reliability, like other operational definitions, is often expressed as correlation. If there are several raters or scorers, a correlation matrix can be computed and an average determined, or intraclass correlation can be used. With dichotomous ratings, it may be expressed as the percentage of agreement between pairs of raters.

Comparisons among Reliability Estimates

I consider the differences among the various estimates important. Some experts disagree; estimates by various methods are often similar. If variance in a set of measures is generally systematic, with little of it attributable to random error, different operational definitions of reliability should agree fairly well; variance Categories I and IIA should account for the bulk of the variance in any method of estimation. However, different methods make different assumptions, procedural and mathematical, and define error differently; I believe researchers, test developers, and test users should use estimates that make sense for the circumstances they face. When a test is used to predict performance over a long period of time, stability is more important than internal consistency. If retesting is common enough to justify equivalent forms, coefficients of equivalence are needed. If production should be consistent month in and month out, an alpha coefficient over a period of several months is appropriate. The absolute values of stability, equivalence, and alpha coefficients may

TABLE 5.3
Proportions of examinees with retest scores differing by designated amounts for various
levels of reliability

	Percentage of cases differing by more than		
Test Reliability	0.5 SD	1.0 SD	1.5 SD
.00	72	48	29
.60	58	26	9
.70	52	20	5
.75	48	16	3
.80	43	11	2
.85	36	7	1
.90	26	3	0.1
.92	21	1	0
.94	15	0.4	0
1.00	0	0	0

Adapted from Wainer and Thissen (1996). Copyright (1996) by the American Educational Research Association.
Adapted by permission of the publisher.

not differ very much, but small differences in reliability can make great differences in the
appropriateness of decisions about individual people, as shown in Table 5.3 (from Wainer
& Thissen, 1996). Reliability coefficients of .94 or .92 are usually considered very good. If
one method gives an estimate of .94 and another gives .92, and both imply some sort of
retest, then the test and retest scores differ by more than a half standard deviation for 15%
of the cases; 21% of the retest scores differ that much with a coefficient of .92, an increase
of 40%. If one method fits the intended use and the other does not, the difference is less
trivial than a difference of .02 suggests.

Standard Error of Measurement

So far, reliability has been defined and discussed in terms of distributions of data sets.
However, the basic datum is always a single measure, and the reliability of an individual
score may be important. Its importance is greatest in those situations in which only one
position is to be filled, or in which "reasonable accommodation" for disabled applicants
requires a unique, unstandardized assessment procedure. The standard error of measurement,
expressed in test score units, may serve such purposes when there is a reasonable estimate
of group reliability. If so, we can rearrange the definitional equation for reliability to get

$$S_e^2 = S_x^2(1 - r_{xx})$$ (5.15)

or

$$S_e = S_x\sqrt{(1 - r_{xx})}$$ (5.16)

where S_e is the standard error of measurement, sometimes abbreviated to SEM. If such
computations are possible, an individual score can be given a range of plausible scores
(e.g., $X \pm 1.96\,S_e$) to see if the range is largely above some minimally acceptable level. Where

there are two or more candidates for a single position, S_e permits a test of statistical significance for the difference between their scores.

A further use is to determine whether scores discriminate differently (i.e., are more or less reliable) in different score intervals. In most large-scale selection programs based on assessments, candidates assessed very favorably (i.e., scoring very well) will, barring disqualifying information, be offered employment. Those assessed unfavorably will not receive offers. Between these assessment ranges are the cases where decisions are not so automatic, where the hard decisions are made. The standard error is not very important in the very high and very low intervals, but in this interval for hard decisions, it can be a crucial determinant of the usefulness of the assessment procedure; given a large enough database, S_e may be computed independently in different intervals. This use should be more common in evaluating assessment procedures than it is; one evaluation of a test can ask whether the SEM in the crucial decision-making range is relatively and acceptably low.

INTERPRETATION OF RELIABILITY COEFFICIENTS

Some people simplify reliability interpretation by stating a minimally satisfactory coefficient. It is not that simple. Interpretation must consider other information, including intended use. For basic research, high reliability may not be critical. Decisions about individuals, however, require highly reliable measures. A reasonable level for "highly reliable" may depend on the history of a particular kind of measurement; "high" is usually lower for interviews than for standardized tests. Several other factors need to be considered in interpreting coefficients.

Homogeneity of Sample

The size of any correlation coefficient depends in part on the extent of individual differences in the sample. In relatively homogeneous groups, where all scores are pretty much alike, total variance is small. Because error scores and true (systematic) scores are uncorrelated, homogeneity does not influence the size of the error variance; error variance is about the same whether the data include only a limited range of scores or the total possible range. It is the ratio of error to total variance that counts (see Equation 5.4). If reliability data are collected from a select group of employees, it is necessary to estimate the reliability expected in a more variable applicant group. If we can estimate total applicant variance, we can estimate reliability for applicants by the formula

$$r_{nn} = 1 - S_o^2 \frac{(1 - r_{oo})}{S_n^2} \tag{5.17}$$

where the subscript n refers to a new, more variable group, and the subscript o refers to the old, homogeneous group.

This equation can rarely be used in criterion measurement. Such measures can be obtained only from selected groups of people who are hired and stay long enough to provide criterion data. There is usually no way to estimate "unselected criterion variance," hence no basis for the correction. A criterion reliability coefficient is, therefore, likely to be an underestimate—a crucial point in interpreting a validity coefficient corrected for criterion unreliability because the underestimate leads to a spuriously high correction.

Average Ability Level

The average ability or other trait level in the group studied also influences the reliability coefficient. Error variance is likely to be larger in lower-level groups where luck can influence scores. It is poor practice to use data obtained from people at one level to estimate reliability for people at a different level. A test for selecting unskilled helpers should not be evaluated by reliability data from skilled journeymen.

Sample

A reliability coefficient computed from a handful of cases is no better than any other statistic based on inadequate data. Increasing the number of cases does not have a systematic effect on the size of the coefficient, but it does affect its own dependability. Moreover, adequacy is not just a matter of numbers. The sample should represent the population for which the measure is to be used. The reliability of a temperament test planned for industrial applicants cannot be adequately determined by giving the test to mental patients or college sophomores or even employees already on the job.

Length of Test

Reliability is generally influenced by the length of a test or period of observation, as described by the Spearman-Brown formula. This generality, like others, has exceptions; added length can, in fact, decrease reliability if the added items or observers add only random variance to the pool (Li, Rosenthal, & Rubin, 1996). Reliability may also be decreased if, as in many new forms of testing, the added items have strong local dependencies, as in sets of items all referring to the same reading passage or problem situation (Wainer & Thissen, 1996). Within the generality, however, simple algebra permits transforming the Spearman-Brown formula to answer the question, "How long must the test—or criterion time period—be for adequate reliability?" The transformed equation is

$$n = \frac{r_{nm}(1 - r_{xx})}{r_{xx}(1 - r_{nn})} \tag{5.18}$$

where n is the number of times the existing test must be multiplied for a desired level of reliability, r_{nm} is that level, and r_{xx} is the reliability coefficient before lengthening the test. Use of the equation assumes that increments are equivalent to the existing procedure. It may be applied only to coefficients of equivalence or of internal consistency.

Reliability improvement improves validity. Properly increasing test length by a specific value of n, estimated validity will be shown by

$$r_{x_n y} = \frac{r_{xy}}{\sqrt{\frac{1}{n} + \left(1 - \frac{1}{n}\right) r_{xx}}} \tag{5.19}$$

where $r_{x_n y}$ is the validity expected for the lengthened test x, and n is the factor by which the test is to be lengthened (Thorndike, 1949). Using selected values in this equation will show that, where a test is reasonably reliable to begin with, not much added validity will be gained through lengthening the test. Where, however, a low validity coefficient is due to low test reliability, lengthening the test can be useful. In any case, all of the caveats about the relationship between reliability and validity associated with Equations 5.7 and 5.8 apply to these equations as well.

Item Characteristics

Ambiguous items, or those giving extraneous hints, reduce reliability. Items with optimal difficulty levels (about .50) are more reliable than extremely easy or extremely hard items. Relatively high inter-item correlations, or high correlations of item responses with total scores (discrimination indices), are needed for high internal consistency coefficients. In short, building reliability into a test (or any other measurement procedure) begins with good test development (see Chapter 11).

VALIDITY: AN EVOLVING CONCEPT

Validity is another ambiguous term. The ambiguity is due partly to changes in its meaning over time as the varied uses of assessment have changed or expanded. Thurstone (1931) defined validity conceptually as the correlation of test scores with a criterion *that is a better measure of the trait* than the test being evaluated. The better measure may be hard to get or otherwise costly. Hull said the best aptitude criterion is "the test of life itself" (Hull, 1928, p. 1). This notion of validity used criteria only to evaluate tests as trait measures. A test, it was generally said, "purports" to measure something, and validity is the degree to which it measures "what it is intended or purports to measure" (Drever, 1952, p. 304).[5] This view was common in educational measurement. A different view came with the growth of personnel testing in the 1930s and 1940s: validity was effectiveness in predicting a criterion assessing something more important than the predictor. Personnel testers of that period did not recognize a distinction between evaluating test scores as trait measures and evaluating them as predictors. Both evaluations were commonly called validity, results of either are called validity, and data collected for one of these evaluations may be (but often are not) useful for the other.

Three Troublesome Adjectives

Early attempts to clarify the validity concept (American Psychological Association et al., 1954; American Psychological Association, American Educational Research Association, & National Council on Measurement Used in Education, 1966) described criterion-related, content, and construct validity as *aspects* of validity—without defining validity in general. Criterion-related validity (divided into predictive and concurrent in the 1954 version) was the relation of test scores to an external criterion. Content validity implied fidelity in sampling a content domain in test construction. Construct validity required empirical data and logic showing that a particular construct could be inferred from scores and that scores were not contaminated by other constructs. The three came to be treated as if they were different *kinds* of validity, not aspects, an error of interpretation forcefully criticized by Dunnette and

---

[5] I chose this dictionary because in 1952, to personnel selection people, validity meant correlation with a job-related criterion; other test users (e.g., in education or clinics) thought of validity in terms of "purported" meaning.

Borman (1979) and by me as an unholy psychometric trinity (Guion, 1980). The terms seemed useful when introduced in the 1954 Technical Recommendations, but they were quickly troublesome, especially when inappropriately enshrined in the Guidelines and rigidly interpreted by some courts.

Constructs and Construct Validity

At least since Cronbach (1971), validity concepts have emphasized the *meaning* of scores, and the meaning is often encapsulated in ideas we call constructs—or, at least in assessment, traits. Such ideas, even if vague, govern the development of assessment methods and evaluation of score interpretations or relational inferences from them. For more than half a century, a notion of a construct being validly measured has been central in discussions of validity (Braun, Jackson, & Wiley, 2002; Loevinger, 1957). The term *construct validity* has expanded during the past two or three decades. For personnel decisions, the expansion is due in no small part to the Binning and Barrett (1989) model. Constructs and the validity with which they are assessed are basic to the model; the simple correlation coefficient of inference 2 (in the partial model in Chapter 3) is not a sufficient evaluation. Without a logical reason to match predictor and criterion constructs, without evidence that both predictor and criterion constructs are validly measured (i.e., evidence of construct validity for both), the coefficient is not interpretable. References to "test validity" are misleading and inadequate—misleading because judgments of validity are evaluations of inferences and interpretations from scores, not of the test per se, and inadequate because the evaluation must include much more than a so-called validity coefficient (American Educational Research Association, American Psychological Association, & National Council on Measurement in Education, 1999; Cronbach, 1971; Putka & Sackett, 2010).

Interpretive and Relational Inferences

Interpretive inferences describe examinees in terms of specified attributes or other constructs. *Relational inferences* interpret scores in terms of different but related examinee characteristics. These are not wholly independent. A descriptive inference might be based on the assessment content, or it might depend on relationships defining a descriptive construct.

In a relational inference, one infers from a score a corresponding level on a different variable—either an alternative variable measuring the same construct or a variable measuring something to be predicted. There is almost always more than one possible inference from a well-understood test score. To be sure, a test can be designed to yield scores that do no more than predict a specified criterion—to be an ad hoc, empirically developed measure, heterogeneous in content, and wholly atheoretical, having no meaning at all if the criterion changes. A change in the job or technology or context can destroy such a limited relational inference, and no one will know why; what has been measured, if anything, remains a mystery.

Usually, several constructs can offer plausible descriptive interpretations. One may be intended by the user or developer; others may be unwanted contaminants. If data show that scores can sensibly be interpreted in terms of the intended meaning, but not in terms of the intrusive others, then the intended descriptive inferences are surely valid.

Because inferences can be very different (the terms interpretive and relational inferences are not exhaustive), the idea of construct validity has grown remarkably beyond its 1954 origins, so much so that the term has become excessively ambiguous. The 1999 *Standards* emphasized the variety of inferences to which the generic term *validity* can be applied, leading many writers to say that validity is a unitarian concept that has outgrown its trinitarian heritage. I argue, instead, that the many different kinds of inferences users intend to draw from scores imply multiple validities—far more than the four in 1954 or the three in 1966—and that the concept of validity is far broader than a single term can describe.

Psychometric Validity

Multiplicity of validities, and the evolution leading to it, suggests a brief definition of generic validity: *Validity is the evaluation of intended inferences drawn from measures.* I distinguish evaluating (validating) descriptive inferences from evaluating relational ones.[6] With apology for yet another adjective, I have called the evaluation of any descriptive inference *psychometric validity*. In that term, I collapse the older descriptive concepts of construct and content validity, among other considerations, as components of a basic understanding of the meanings of scores. The latter I prefer to call *job-relatedness* (for personnel assessment), or, more generally, *usefulness*. This chapter emphasizes psychometric validity because it is the basic concept in classical test theory. It is intended to examine the evaluative component of classical psychometric theory, looking beyond the comfortable limits that corral validity within a correlation coefficient to the less limited idea of domain sampling—whether of construct or content domains. The distinction between psychometric validity and job-relatedness is one I continue to make. For both, however, validity is not a number; it is itself an inference—a conclusion reached from a logical consideration of many pieces of information, data, and theory.

The simple, fundamental question of psychometric validity is, "How confidently can the scores resulting from the measurement be interpreted as representing varying degrees or levels of the intended characteristic?" There is never a simple answer. Answers are judgments, supported by data and logical argument. They depend on the relative weight of evidence— the weight of accumulated evidence supporting an interpretation relative to the weight of accumulated evidence opposing it. One looks not at single bits of information but at the preponderance of the evidence, and this all applies, not incidentally, equally well to the validity of relational inferences.

VARIETIES OF PSYCHOMETRIC VALIDITY EVIDENCE

Gathering evidence from which judgment about validity can be developed is the essence of what is broadly designated *validation*, the design and use of data collection procedures, followed by logically or theoretically "connecting the dots," to determine whether an intended inference from the scores can be supported and justified by the logic and the data obtained (Kane, 2001).

---

[6] After making this distinction for more than three decades, I've discovered that it is not so new. Cureton (1950b) made even finer distinctions for usefulness. He referred to the correlation between observed test and criterion scores as *predictive power*, reserving the word *validity* for the correlation between observed predictor scores and criterion true scores (i.e., corrected for criterion unreliability). Correction for unreliability in both measures (i.e., correlation between predictor true scores and criterion true scores) gave what he called *relevance*. I have long admired Dr. Cureton, but not until I read the Angoff (1988) history and the Cureton reference did I realize that the distinction I've been preaching originated with him.

Validation is more than the accumulation of research findings and careful judgment to justify (or to reject) an intended inference. The accumulation, carefully arranged, is a logical argument that justifies (or fails to justify) a particular use, inference, or interpretation of scores (Cronbach, 1988). Validation is the process by which a validity argument is developed, and as Kane (2001) would have it, is preceded by the development of an interpretive argument. For predictions, my understanding of Kane's position is that the predictive hypothesis must first be developed as a justifying argument based on job analysis, prior research, and some consensus in the judgments of job experts as the foundation for further development of a validity argument.

Cronbach (1988) went further. Testing is not a private matter between the tester and the client. Tests are widely challenged. Cronbach identified challenges from five perspectives: (a) potential usefulness, (b) political purposes, (c) relevance of assessment operations to proposed uses, (d) economic implications of assessment-based decisions, and (e) an explanatory perspective that has dominated psychometric evaluation at least since 1954. Collecting and looking at evidence and logical connections from multiple perspectives—going beyond psychometrics—is a good, even necessary, way to find flaws in one's validity arguments.

In pointing out that the three-aspect notion of validity "is an idea whose time has gone," (Cronbach, p. 4) went on to say, "A favorable answer to one or two questions can fully support a test only when no one cares enough to raise further questions." For those who care enough, the 1999 *Standards* viewed validation as considering many questions in developing a validity argument. Two points need emphasis: (a) validation is complex, requiring evidence in response to many questions, and (b) validation is never finally complete—it should be reviewed frequently to see if new evidence changes the evaluative judgment about the intended inferences.

Maybe the term *validity* has outlived its usefulness. I would be happy to retire the word to the scrapheap of overused terms dying of terminal ambiguity (but I have not yet done so). Instead, we should refer to *evaluation* of tests and test uses (as Kane, 2001, does); the very term requires us to ask questions and seek answers in making evaluative judgments. I doubt the feasibility of the change even as I declare its appropriateness; the term *validity* is too deeply embedded in governmental regulation and professional prose.

I offer, under four headings, some questions a decision maker might try to answer in developing a validity or evaluative argument about inferences from an assessment procedure. Answers require professional judgment; they often require forming and testing ancillary hypotheses (Landy, 1986). The questions below do not form a checklist to be completed by stamp collectors or bean counters. Indeed, in various speeches, articles, and book chapters, I have offered lists of evaluative questions deliberately differing in number, ranging from 4 to 14 questions, covering the topics more thoroughly (e.g., Guion, 1983, 1987a, 1991, 1998). This list has eight (the earlier edition had nine), or more if you count those in italics. I hope the inconsistency in numbers of questions confounds any simplistic, bureaucratic tendency to insist on a specific checklist.

Evidence Based on Test Development

Formal measurement consists of rules for assigning numbers to represent real relationships. For example, suppose that oranges have more of some property (e.g., acidity) than apples (they *can* be compared!) and that apples have more of it than bananas. These relationships are transitive, meaning also that oranges must have more of the property than do bananas. The rules for assigning numbers become a mathematical model of the real relationships implied. Measures are meaningful if the numbers fit the model and the model is faithful to the reality of transitive, quantitative relationships. One can never prove either, but one can show that the procedure was developed to reflect relationships consistent with the model. Validity is not usually invoked in evaluating formal measurement procedures, but evidence of it is found when intelligent efforts have failed to prove that the measures do not represent reality (Coombs, Dawes, & Tversky, 1970).

Evaluative Questions

Because psychological measurement is rarely based on formal models, some questions need to be asked in evaluating the development of a procedure.

- **Did the developer of the procedure have a clear idea of the attribute to be measured?** The developer of the procedure must have had something in mind to be measured. It may have been a well-established construct or just a vague idea of a continuum along which people or objects can be ordered. It is a small but positive piece of evidence of validity if development was guided by a clear conception of the construct to be measured. It is a large, negative piece of evidence if the developer has not bothered or is unable to describe the attribute measured, how it matches or differs from other attributes, or whether it is an attribute of people, of groups of people, or of objects people do something with or to. A theory of the attribute is basic for developing measurement procedures, whether as predictors, descriptors, or criteria (Guion, 1987b). The developer of a measurement procedure should have an idea of the boundaries of the attribute, the sorts of behaviors that exhibit the attribute (or do not), or some variables with which the attribute may be correlated and some with which correlations would not be expected. This is less than the grand nomological network envisioned by Cronbach and Meehl (1955), but it suggests testable hypotheses about the attribute or construct to be measured (Dunnette, 1992).
- **Are the mechanics of measurement consistent with the concept?** Most psychological measurement is based on the responses people make to standard stimuli presented according to standard procedural rules. If the developer had a clear idea of what was to be measured, it should have governed a development plan, and further questions like these need answers:
  - *Is the presentation medium appropriate?* Is printing a test on paper, showing it on a computer monitor, or recording it on a DVD consistent with the definition of the attribute to be measured? Has the developer actually thought about the question and come to supportable answers—or only followed habit or current fads in choosing the medium?
  - *Are there rules of standardization or control, such as time limits?* If so, were they dictated by the nature of the trait being measured or merely convenient or a habit?
  - *Are response requirements appropriate?* For example, it is not appropriate to use a recognition-based multiple-choice item type for a construct defined in terms of free recall.
- **Is the stimulus content appropriate?** If the attribute to be measured taps a specific content domain, such as the content of a training program, then content-oriented test development—with its insistence on domain definition and rules for domain

sampling—constitutes good evidence of validity. But the principle applies also to more abstract constructs such as those developed by factor analyses. For tests of factorial constructs, evidence should show that the item type chosen has tapped the factor satisfactorily.

In some few cases, sampling a well-defined domain may be ample evidence without further study. Content sampling alone is enough to justify test use if five requirements are met:

1. The content must be, or be rooted in, behavior with a generally accepted meaning, such as the field test portion of a driver's license test.
2. The content domain must be defined unambiguously. Are its defined domain boundaries clear enough that informed observers can agree on whether a given topic or action falls within them, even if disagreeing with the definition?
3. The content domain must be directly relevant to the measurement purpose. The distinction here is between a *sample* with consistent behavioral implications and a *sign* supported only statistically (Wernimont & Campbell, 1968).
4. Qualified judges must agree that the domain has been properly sampled. Two key words are *qualified* and *properly*. "Properly sampled" may require sampling proportional to some aspect of the domain (e.g., time spent or importance). The measurement content must avoid irrelevant content *not* in the defined domain.
5. The response content must be scored and evaluated reliably.

- **Was the test carefully and skillfully developed?** After determining that the developer had a clear idea in mind at the outset, and that it stayed in mind long enough to plan the measurement operations and content, what evidence suggests that the plan was (or was not) carried out well? More detailed questions include these:
    - *Does the final set of items fit the original plan?* Any departures from that plan should be satisfactorily explained.
    - *Were pilot studies done to try out ideas* about item types, instructions, time limits, ambient conditions, or other standardizing aspects of the test, especially if they are unusual?
    - *Was item selection based on item analysis?* Were appropriate item statistics computed and used? Did the data come from an appropriate sample or from what I insist on calling a "scrounge sample"? (The term is blunter but a better description than the polite "sample of convenience.") Was the sample large enough to yield reliable statistics? Does the final mix of selected items fit the original plan, or is there some imbalance? Was the item pool big enough to permit stringent criteria for item retention?
    - *Were methods of test construction*, particularly sophisticated methods such as item response theory (described in Chapter 6), *carried out with full awareness of the assumptions and constraints of the method?*

Creating Validity

These questions consider the likelihood that justifiable inferences can be drawn from scores on a test, a likelihood built into the test in its planning and construction. No one has said it better than Anne Anastasi:

Validity is thus built into the test from the outset rather than being limited to the last stages of test development . . . The validation process begins with the formulation of detailed trait or construct definitions, derived from psychological theory, prior research, or systematic observation and analyses of the relevant behavior domain. Test items are then prepared to fit the construct definitions. Empirical item analyses follow, with the selection of the most effective (i.e., valid) items from the initial item pools. Other appropriate internal analyses may then be carried out, including factor analyses of item clusters or subtests. The final stage includes validation and cross-validation of various scores and interpretive combinations of scores through statistical analyses against external, real-life criteria. (Anastasi, 1986, p. 3)

Evidence Based on Reliability

- **Is the internal statistical evidence satisfactory?** Classical item analysis looks for two item characteristics: (a) difficulty level, usually expressed in the reverse as the percentage giving the correct item response, and (b) discrimination index, often expressed as the correlation of item responses to total scores. With an appropriate sample, distributions of item difficulty can show variability and average difficulty among items. Both should be appropriate for the anticipated measurement purposes. A test that is too easy or too hard for the people who take it will not permit valid inferences about them. Item statistics should be evaluated, of course, in the light of the circumstances that produced them. Their usefulness may depend on such things as sample size, appropriateness of the sample to the intended population, and probable distributions of the attribute in the sample and population.

  Discrimination indices should suggest a reasonable level of internal consistency. Responses on all items should at least be somewhat related to total score; otherwise, no clearly definable variable is measured.
- **Are scores stable over time?** Evidence of stability over a reasonable time period (e.g., the time between selection and obtaining criterion data) seems essential.

Evidence from Patterns of Correlates

- **Does empirical evidence confirm logically expected relationships with other variables?** A theory of the attribute will suggest that good measures of it will correlate with some things but not with others, and at least some of these hypotheses can be tested. Evidence supporting them also confirms the validity of the scores as measures of the intended attribute. One might hypothesize from one's theoretical view of mechanical aptitude that those with high scores on a test of it will do better in an auto mechanics school than will those with low scores. To test the hypothesis, scores are correlated with grades in the school. A significant, positive correlation is evidence of validity for both relational and descriptive inferences. Testing other hypotheses, perhaps showing correlations with the number of correct troubleshooting diagnoses in a standardized set of aberrant pieces of equipment, or the speed with which a bicycle is taken apart and reassembled, gives further evidence of psychometric validity. Every such hypothesis supported gives further confirming evidence of the validity of interpreting scores as measures of mechanical aptitude as defined. Failure to support hypotheses casts doubt (a) on the validity of the inference or (b) on the match of the theory of the attribute with the assessment procedure. Along with *confirmatory* studies, however, studies deliberately designed to be *disconfirmatory* should often be included among the bits of evidence considered. Evidence of psychometric validity is stronger if confirmatory evidence is accompanied by *disconfirmatory* evidence failing to confirm or ruling out alternative inferences or interpretations of scores—evidence that relationships *not* expected by the theory of the attribute are in fact *not* found.

A simpler form of statistical evidence, one that pleases some people remarkably well, but essentially ignores psychometric validity, is a nice relational *validity coefficient.* Most people, and many courts, place far too much faith in a single validity coefficient. An impressive validity coefficient might stem from a common contamination in the instrument being validated and the criterion. Suppose that performance ratings of school principals are contaminated by a general stereotype that a good principal is physically tall, imposing in stature, looks like a scholar, and speaks in a low, soft voice. If the measure to be validated is an assessment center rating of administrative potential, and if these ratings are influenced by that same stereotype, there will be a nice validity coefficient. It does not necessarily follow that the assessment ratings provide either good descriptions or good predictions of administrative ability.

Another problem with a single validity coefficient is that it seeks only evidence confirming (or failing to confirm) a specific, usually narrow, inference. It says nothing to confirm or to disconfirm alternative inferences. Other problems, such as unknown third variables, are discussed in Chapter 7. Validity coefficients are, of course, valuable bits of evidence in making judgments about validity, but *one should not confuse validity coefficients with validity.*

- **Is the empirical evidence of validity based on strong research programs?** In practical terms, this means ruling out contaminations. Cronbach (1988) identified two approaches to construct (or psychometric) validation, a "weak program" and a "strong" one (pp. 12–13). A weak program is exploratory; it casts about for evidence wherever it may be found and considers it in judging the validity of score interpretations. Such a program, he said, has some merit. If pursued doggedly, it seems bound to yield better interpretations of scores on existing tests and better techniques for developing improved ones.

A strong program requires a more explicit theory of the attribute, one that goes beyond simple trait theory. It develops deliberate challenges to the theory, confirmatory hypotheses that seriously risk not being supported and alternative interpretive hypotheses that risk confirmation rather than disconfirmation. Whether through experience, challenge from others, or one's own fertile imagination, such hypotheses identify and competently evaluate plausible rival inferences.

Strong programs improve the march of science; weak ones do too, but largely by luck. Where on the continuum does the personnel decision maker want to be? In a litigious environment, trying for a strong program seems sensible. Potential plaintiffs can challenge tests by posing rival interpretations of the scores. By anticipating the more plausible rivals, and disconfirming them, one develops a defense. Anticipating them, and confirming them, is good reason to find another basis for decision before someone sues.

CONCLUDING NOTE

This chapter has focused on psychometric validity. It should. Determining whether the intended descriptive inferences to be drawn from a set of test scores are defensible is a good

(I think necessary) first step in evaluating assessments for operational situations—a good first step in developing a strong argument to defend the use of an assessment procedure for personnel decisions. The need for the argument is not limited to the defense of the procedure in adversarial litigation or contract negotiation. It may be needed when arguing the case for initiating or maintaining the procedure as a budget item, or when facing competing demands for space or personnel.

Determining whether validity arguments can support or defend relational inferences—predictive hypotheses proposed as potential bases for personnel decisions—is also important. The traditional correlational focus in evaluating the use of predictors is too narrow; it settles for the statistical components of a potential argument more than the organizational issues the predictors are supposed to address. Long ago, people (including professional testers) spoke of "the validity of the test" in evaluating both the test and its use. Less long ago, Cronbach (1971) argued persuasively that validity refers to *inferences* from scores, not to the test, and not to the scores themselves. The first stage in the validation of a personnel assessment procedure is to assure that it fits the predictor construct in the predictive hypothesis—that it permits valid descriptive inferences. What does the test measure? Is that what was intended in the predictive hypothesis? What else might the measures mean? The second stage is to assure that specified relational inferences are supported. On average, how well is a person with a specified score likely to do on the criterion to be predicted? By how much do predictions miss actual criterion performance? Does the statistical model used fit the specifications of the predictive hypothesis? If not, why not?

The first stage, evaluating descriptive inferences, may get skipped in settings where something must get done and intended descriptive inferences seem safe enough—or when no one has a clear idea of traits to measure. In these situations, one puts together a mish-mash of things various people in an organization think might work, develops an empirical key for "scoring" it, finds the correlation between scores and a criterion of interest, and—if that correlation is a nice one—declares a procedure of uncertain meaning properly validated. The second-stage focus on evaluating predictors and their use, even those describing clearly understood attributes, is often too narrow. Too often it is limited to a focus on psychometric and statistical procedures, not on the logical basis for a predictive hypothesis. This second stage in validation should be more than a statistical exercise; it should be based on a thoughtful approach to developing and testing a predictive hypothesis.

I've reiterated these things because I believe it is time to move to a third stage. Even if the second stage is carefully and intelligently carried out, it is still too narrow because it takes only a limited view—in the selection of a criterion—of the organizational issues the predictors are supposed to address. From an organizational point of view, *the focus needs to move on to the validities of the decisions themselves.* The intriguing title of a recent chapter is "The Validation of Personnel Decisions in the Twenty-First Century" (Landy, 2007). Under that title, he said that "changes in both scientific thinking and research and the nature of work have presented new challenges to the concept of establishing the validity of inferences" (Landy, 2007, p. 409). Unfortunately, the chapter did not say much about the validity of decisions as such. Kehoe (2002), however, had earlier extended the idea of the *meaning of measurement* beyond the idea of descriptive, construct validity to encompass an understanding of the organizational implications of the use of measurement in making personnel decisions. These implications seemed to involve evaluations of the decision processes as surely as the measurements and the predictive inferences drawn from them are themselves evaluated.

In an e-mail cycle of nontrivial duration, Landy and I explored the potential meaning of the phrase, *validity of personnel decisions.* I have come to see it as a third level, or stage, of a sequence of evaluative concerns. I see evaluation as needing an increasingly broad focus, somewhat like changing the narrow focus of a camera's telephoto lens to the broadest focus through its wide-angle lens. In evaluating assessment, the first—narrowest—level focuses on the predictor itself: how well does it measure the construct hypothesized as important in a predictive hypothesis, that is, the psychometric validity of descriptive inferences? The second, intermediate level is the evaluation of how well the chosen criterion (or criteria) can be predicted from those scores, that is, the operational validity of relational inferences. Traditional talk and research about validity stops here. The third level, for me, evaluates the decisions that actually get made, recognizing the all but inevitable differences between research and operational procedures. That is, the focus must not stop with the navel-gazing inferences of traditional validation; it's time to expand the notion of validity argument to an organizational level of concern. It's an idea that needs more thought to be useful, even though it's admittedly a strange way to end a chapter on traditional thinking. It is my view of future issues in evaluation. Landy's is quite different.

On one point, however, we are in full agreement: This view of the expanding focus must not be allowed to become institutionalized like the 1954 Technical Recommendations were; it must not become beans for the bean-counters or spaces in the albums of stamp collectors. I'm not particularly worried; measurement theory, as will be shown in the next chapter, has gone beyond the traditional theory described in this one.

6

Further Concepts in Measurement

Classical psychometric theory has served well and is sufficient for many practical uses. Extensions of classical theory, and alternatives to it, have been developed. They are useful, but some of them may require more resources than most personnel researchers have (big subject pools, opportunities for repeated measurement, etc.). Even if practical limitations make newer approaches infeasible, they can influence thinking even when using the older ones. Chapter 5 described classical psychometric theory as it has evolved, not as formulated early in the twentieth century. This chapter describes the basics—the beginnings—of three areas contributing to measurement theory: factor analysis (not at all new but an area that has influenced others), generalizability theory, and item response theory.

TEST CONSTRUCTION

Although relevant to all psychological measurement, classical psychometric theory has developed mainly for testing. Test construction is described a bit more fully in Chapter 12, but an introduction here can provide the context for the theoretical and methodological developments to be described.

In constructing an ability test, the ability to be measured needs at least rudimentary definition. Components of a proposed test, usually items, are created to fit that definition. A pool of potential items is administered to a sample of the population in which the test is to be used; item responses are analyzed statistically. The simplest, oldest analyses compute indices of difficulty[1] and discrimination. *Item difficulty* may be expressed as the proportion of those responding who gave the "right" (correct or keyed) response to an item. An *item discrimination* index refers to the *relationship* of item scores to the trait being measured, such as a correlation coefficient. Concepts, theories, and methods discussed in this chapter extend these simple indices. Neither index makes much sense unless the test score implies a position on a scale measuring a single attribute. Classical test construction aims at scores approaching unidimensionality (or functional unity) closely enough to provide *transitivity* in measurement, necessary for consistent score interpretation.

In a transitive, quantitative scale for measuring a single trait, if $x > y$ and $y > z$, then necessarily $x > z$. The intrusion of a different construct (whether another trait or systematic error) may prevent transitivity of scores (perhaps finding $z > x$). In real-life psychological

---

[1] *Difficulty* is an appropriate term for ability test items, but it seems a bit weird when used for measures of personality or interest. Don't worry about it; *difficulty* as defined here usually is the consistent term for this item characteristic, whether in measuring ability, personality, or something else.

testing, one person, A, may have a higher score on a measure of trait X than another person, B, and that can have many causes. It *might* be that A does in fact have more of X; alternatively, A *might* have less of trait X but have a higher score anyway because of the additive influence of some sort of error. Systematic error may stem from the effects of measurement methods, but it seems more likely to stem from various extraneous traits inadvertently part of the score mix. In this sense, systematic error can reduce psychometric validity just as surely as transient error does.

The first topic in this chapter, *factor analysis*, investigates dimensionality, or structure, in measurement. The second topic, *generalizability theory*, recognizes multidimensionality and the possibility of multiple sources of systematic error. Both are best viewed as extensions of classical theory. The third topic, *item response theory* (IRT, earlier called *latent trait theory*) has contributed the idea that individual test scores can be meaningfully described independently of the score distribution in a sample. If the sample is truly representative of the population from which it is drawn, distribution-dependent statistics may offer reasonable estimates of population values. However, "The usual rule applies: We hope—and *hope* is the operative notion—that the convenient sample obtained behaves sufficiently like a random sample not to invalidate statistical estimates" (McDonald, 1999, p. 32). Where sample distributions differ markedly from population distributions, sample statistics are likely to provide poor estimates of population values. IRT reduces this problem.

FACTOR ANALYSIS

An early method of factor analysis (Spearman, 1927) tested the proposition that scores on each test in a set of tests were primarily influenced by a general factor, *g*. Subsequent methods (cf. Thurstone, 1947) enabled researchers to identify various sources of systematic variance (constructs termed *factors*) having common influences on scores of two or more tests in the set of tests studied. Factor analytic and related procedures allow study of the internal structure of test scores and other assessments, and they can also guide development of tests that maximize intended sources of variances and minimize others. The systematic variance intended for one test may be systematic error for a different one; verbal comprehension may be the intended trait in a reading test and a contaminating source of systematic error in an arithmetic test.

Cluster Analysis Methods

Cluster analysis was seen early by Robert Tryon as a "poor man's factor analysis" (Tryon & Bailey, 1970, p. vii). He noted that variables measuring the same thing not only correlate well but tend to have the same patterns of correlations with other variables. If one draws a profile on translucent paper showing the correlations of a given test with each of the other tests in a set, and superimposes that profile on one for another test in the set, the two profiles may be quite congruent.[2] If they are not, the two tests measure different things. The principle of profile similarity governed the development of the Tryon's BC TRY computer system, now no longer available on modern computers or statistical software. The visual look-and-see approach is easy enough with only a few variables. It is harder for larger correlation

---

[2] Find a fairly sizable correlation matrix and try it! You will find that congruent profiles explain a great deal.

matrices. Khattree and Naik (2000) included a chapter on a variety of cluster analysis methods that can be carried out using SAS software.

As with factor analysis, the objects of measurement can be anything for which a data matrix can be formed, among them, tools, foods, work products, buildings, or (most often) people. Unlike factor analysis, cluster analysis does not identify underlying latent structure of measures; instead, it classifies or identifies categories in which the members (e.g., people) are alike in definable ways (e.g., similar profiles of specified variables) and, as a group, different from other subgroups (e.g., groups with identifiably different profiles). The most common measure of similarity is the Euclidean distance measure:

$$d(a,b) = \sqrt{[\Sigma(a-b)^2]} \tag{6.1}$$

where a and b are scale values for two objects (people) on each variable in the set being studied; these differences (squared) are summed across all variables in the set. Some writers (e.g., Sharma & Kumar 2006) prefer to use d^2; the choice makes no practical difference in defining clusters.

Methods of cluster analysis share the common goal of finding clusters of tests or people that are largely homogeneous groups and that have minimal correlation with other clusters or outlying cases. Every variable, whether measures, people, or other entities, is assigned to a class or cluster, or as a misfit belonging with (or congruent to) virtually no other variable. Those assigned to a given cluster of similar profiles are considered to be alike in the dimensions of the profiles, but identifying defining dimensions is less important in cluster analysis than developing or identifying a category different from other categories.

Partitional Clustering Methods

Several methods have been used to partition or divide the people in a data set into a predetermined number of clusters. The number of clusters may be based on a subjective analysis of a scatterplot, a prior theory, or a judgment of the number of groups that may be practical in the specific situation, or any other a priori information. Partitioning methods typically use an iterative procedure beginning with a more or less random identification of data points to represent a first guess about cluster centroids (an "average" person or object—the means of all variables in the set). Cluster membership is first assigned by similarities of specific cases to the arbitrary centroids. Then the centroids are recalculated, cluster membership is changed accordingly, and centroids are recalculated again. This continues until a specified stopping rule applies. The most commonly used method of partitioning is known as the K-means method; it minimizes the distances within clusters (Omran, Engelbrecht, & Salman, 2007).

Hierarchical Methods

Hierarchical clustering links predefined clusters to form a cluster tree (*dendrogram*) shown in Figure 6.1. Discussions of these widely used methods generally tend to overlook the fact that the initial clusters must somehow be determined; I discussed partitioning methods first because, if a rather large number of initial clusters is specified, these clusters can inform the beginning for hierarchical clustering. Elementary linkage analysis is another way to make a preliminary guess (McQuitty, 1957), and its results often match those of less elementary methods. Clustering methods range from a simple "nearest neighbor" approach, in which

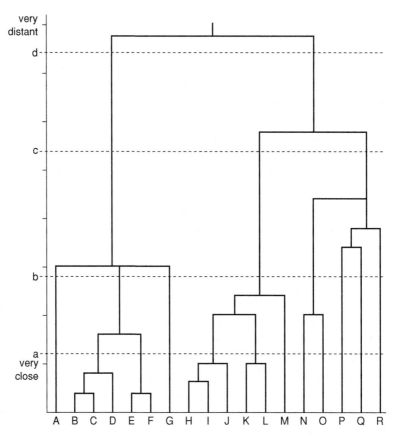

FIG. 6.1   A cluster tree for hierarchical cluster analysis.

the clusters with the two nearest neighbors are linked first, to a more complex variance-based system known as Ward's method (see Khattree & Naik, 2000; Omran et al., 2007).

Related Methods

Multistage Euclidean grouping (MEG), introduced by McDermott (1998), validates the homogeneity and replicability of clusters resulting from various methods. A similar index was provided in the now obsolete BC TRY system. I have not found a related procedure in modern software, but see Omran et al. (2007). In MEG, each person is represented by a profile with at least two attributes (and usually more) expressed as standard scores. The process moves forward in stages, beginning with the division of the data set into blocks (not to be confused with preliminary clusters) leading in the third and final stage to a number of clusters deemed "correct" by a preset criterion. Homogeneity coefficients (Tryon & Bailey, 1970) are computed "for each cluster, for each profile variable, and for the overall solution" (McDermott, 1998, p. 679).

Model-based cluster analysis (Raftery & Dean, 2006) is based on a statistical model, partially based on the Bayesian principle that an observation belongs in a specific cluster if the posterior probability that it belongs in one group is greater than the probability that it belongs in any other. It simultaneously selects variables, the number of clusters to result, and the cluster models. This method (and others using density estimation; see Khattree & Naik,

2000) shares much with what has been called latent profile analysis (LPA; Mun, von Eye, Bates, & Vaschillo, 2008). The term *latent*, in this context, refers to a latent *categorical* variable defining cluster membership, not to the observed variables making up the profiles. The method specifies density, orientation to Cartesian axes, and shape individually for each cluster.

An alternative model-based approach uses structural equations, specifically models postulating a mixture of latent classes or groups (structural equation mixture models, SEMMs). A description of the approach by Bauer and Curran (2004) details some mathematical foundations of the method, especially relative to "common" factor analysis and latent profile analysis, but it emphasizes the applied usefulness of the method. It matches other methods of subgroup identification by directly identifying the number and nature of relatively homogeneous groups within a heterogeneous population. It goes beyond that, however; indirectly, it makes it possible to deal with such typically difficult issues as distributions that are not normal and other limiting assumptions. For example, latent curve models can be used to specify individual nonlinear growth curves around curves defined at the level of group means—an application fitting the distinction between transition and maintenance phases in complex work.

The use of clustering techniques is, as several authors have noted, widespread and growing —but not in personnel research. Many recent articles have used clustering or profile analysis in widely diverse fields of inquiry. Examples include health and medicine, personality and personality disorders, educational psychology (including counseling, developmental, and school psychology), brain research, and engineering, but not often personnel assessment or decision making. Nevertheless, I include the topic for two reasons. First, there does seem to be a growing recognition that personnel research needs to identify distinguishable subgroups on grounds more psychologically fundamental than mere demography; perhaps this section can pique the curiosity of potential researchers who need to subgroup the cases in their samples. Second, it offers a clearer way to approach the concepts of factor analysis, an infrequent approach since BC TRY became obsolete in the 1980s.

Elementary Concepts in Factor Analysis

Factor analysis identifies underlying hypothetical variables, or *factors*, causing correlation of scores on different measures.[3] So do other procedures, such as cluster analysis, linkage analysis, canonical correlation, and several methods of multidimensional scaling. These procedures are all based on the idea that variables with similar patterns of correlates are pretty much the same, measuring the same factors. Factors are *constructs* that vary quantitatively; dimensionality is implied because some people may "have" less or more of the construct than other people, so factors are seen as dimensions along which objects of measurement (e.g., people) may be ordered. A dimension may be broad, such as intelligence, or more restricted, such as perceptual speed, or very narrow, such as any one of the 120 factors of mental ability postulated by Guilford (1959). Factor analysis identifies dimensions in a set of tests by finding groups of highly correlated variables which are minimally correlated with other groups of variables. It begins with variables all measured in the same sample (of people or of other objects of measurement), forming a matrix of correlations or covariances and analyzing them to identify dimensions called factors that account for systematic variance.

---

[3] Factor analysis is not new; most graduate students can use more complex forms of it than presented here. Those who know it well can skip ahead, but this most elementary of introductions might arouse a few forgotten insights.

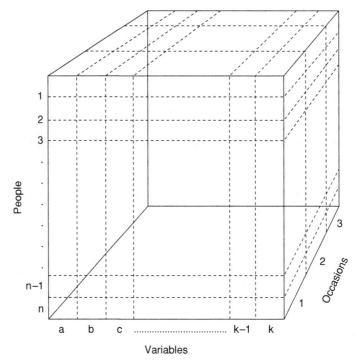

FIG. 6.2   The basic form of a data matrix; cells would contain scores from each of *n* people on each of *k* tests on three different occasions.

It is useful to visualize a data matrix in which each cell contains a quantified observation. A three-dimensional data matrix is shown in Figure 6.2. In it, variables are the columns, individual people are the rows, and occasions are the successive layers from front to back. A correlation matrix can be computed for any slice of the data matrix. We can compute correlations of test scores across persons, that is, between the columns of the face of the matrix; this is the most common slice for factor analysis. We could also compute correlations between persons across tests (e.g., between the rows of the face of the matrix), clustering people rather than tests. Or we could correlate scores over occasions. Any such matrix of correlation coefficients can be the basis for a factor analysis if (a) observations or measures are reasonably reliable, (b) there are enough of them to permit reliable correlation coefficients, (c) enough variables are included to permit clear identification of factor structure, and (unless using more complex procedures than described here) the assumption of linear correlation makes sense.

Usually, research interest calls for a matrix of correlated variables. To get really elementary (and to violate harshly the principle of enough variables), a tiny, made-up matrix is shown in Table 6.1. The variables are four different tests; each cell in the matrix shows the correlation coefficient computed for a pair of them. Making up data confers omniscience, so Figure 6.3 explains the correlations in terms of five commonly encountered factors. It is easier to understand what happens in factor analysis if we work backwards from a solution; that is, from the knowledge of the underlying, latent factors and their contributions to scores on each test, as in Figure 6.3. Even without Table 6.1, we can tell that Test A would correlate well with Test B because a big part of the total variance in each is due to individual differences in ability to use language. The correlation between Tests A and C may be even higher; more of the total variances from these tests stem from common dimensions—in this

TABLE 6.1
Correlation Matrix of Assumed Relationships among Four Tests

	A	*B*	*C*	*D*
A	–	.62	.63	.15
B		–	.52	.00
C			–	.17
D				–

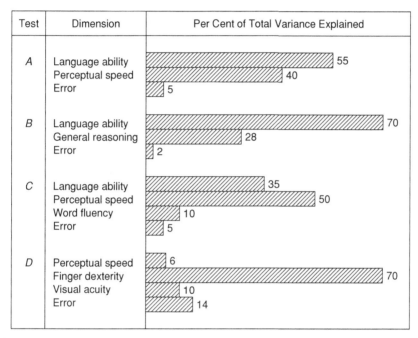

FIG. 6.3 Dimensions contributing to total test variance in each of four hypothetical tests.

case, two of them. Test D correlates only slightly with A and C (only small common sources of variance) and not at all with B (because they measure nothing in common). Error, of course, refers to the unreliable component of scores attributed to transient or inconsistent error which, by assumption, should be uncorrelated across the four tests.

This backward approach is, of course, unreal. In practice, we know only the intercorrelations, and we draw inferences about the factor structure of the tests from those correlations. Table 6.1 shows a matrix of correlations for such tests. Actually, the matrix in Table 6.1, although based on Figure 6.3, would not allow us to know the full structure of these tests. In a matrix this small, one can look at the correlations and know that Tests A, B, and C are all measuring the same thing to some degree, and that Test D does not measure it. Knowing something about these tests, we can look at the matrix and infer the nature of that "same thing." If Test A is a general mental ability test, B is a vocabulary test, and C is a test of reading speed, these tests obviously have a common requirement to understand verbally expressed ideas. It is plausible to infer that the ability to satisfy this requirement is one underlying cause of the correlations observed; that's enough to tag it "language ability" without further refinement.

The matrix is too small, and merely looking at it is insufficient. In factor analysis, at least two variables, and preferably more, should be included in the matrix for each factor anticipated.

Because three of these tests, according to Figure 6.3, require at least some perceptual speed, an actual factor analysis could identify perceptual speed as a factor. General reasoning ability, word fluency, finger dexterity, and visual acuity are also sources of variance in the matrix, but each of these influences scores on only one test, so factor analysis of this matrix could not identify them. Although I specified them as systematic sources of variance in creating the example, factor analysis of such an inadequate matrix would treat them only as sources of error variance—as if the variance they produce were random. At a bare minimum, four more tests would have to be included in the set for these factors to be identified.

Figure 6.3 illustrates a basic principle: choose tests for factor analysis as if testing hypotheses about them. By making educated guesses about likely factors influencing scores on tests (variables) of special interest, one can choose other variables for the analysis that are likely (and some that are unlikely) to measure such factors. A good factor analysis poses hypotheses about the structure of scores of interest and then chooses variables to test these hypotheses—potentially to confirm or to disconfirm the hypotheses.

Multiple Factor Analysis

Few standard, universally accepted measurement instruments exist in psychology. If someone develops a way to measure a new form of reasoning, someone else will see a somewhat different and presumably better way to do it. If both get used a lot, someone else will see a reason for a third version. Different investigators may have similar ideas about a construct but give it different names and use different ways to measure it. Worse, different measures of a popular construct, all under the same name, may not correlate at all well. For whatever reasons, there is a great deal of redundancy in psychological measurement, and it does not always occur where it is expected or wanted.

When two apparently different measures correlate well, how can the correlation be explained? McDonald (1999) offered three possible answers: (a) one variable may cause change in the other, (b) both variables may be effects of a common cause, or (c) the two variables may measure something in common. Factor analysis is interested in the third option.

Multiple factor analysis reduces redundancy in a set of measures by creating a smaller set of clearly distinguishable variables called factors (or components). Again, a high correlation between two measures is assumed to be caused by a common source of systematic variance, a latent construct or factor. Unlike clustering methods, factor analysis seeks factors undergirding a matrix of correlations that explain variance in the individual tests.

It is not my purpose to show how factor analyses are done or to discuss fully their many purposes; see Bobko (1990), McDonald (1999), or Pedhazur and Schmelkin (1991) for more comprehensive information. Instead, my purpose is to offer clues for understanding and evaluating reports of factor analytic research.

Tables of Factor Loadings

Results of factor analyses are presented in tables of *factor loadings*, the hypothetical correlations of tests with underlying, or latent, factors identified by the analysis.[4] Table 6.2

---

[4] For most methods of factor analysis there can be two such tables. One of these is the result of the basic computations which, in many commonly used factor analytic methods, depends on an arbitrarily chosen starting point. The other consists of rotated factor loadings. I think rotation, discussed in the next section, gives more interpretable information.

TABLE 6.2
Rotated Factor Loadings

Test	I	II	III	IV	V	h^2	r_{xx}
Minnesota, turning	.61	.05	−.06	.27	.14	.47	.85
Minnesota, placing	.73	.12	−.06	.17	.18	.61	.88
Dowell manipulation	.60	−.04	.14	.33	.33	.60	.87
Purdue Pegboard, nonpreferred	.68	.17	.13	.03	.01	.51	.80
Purdue Pegboard, both hands	.63	.06	−.02	−.17	.17	.46	.87
O'Connor Finger Dexterity	.50	−.03	.09	.14	.43	.46	.83
Placing test, finger	.28	.08	.05	.25	.26	.22	.49
O'Connor Tweezer Dexterity	.22	.05	.34	.17	.42	.37	.85
Pin moving	.32	.10	.00	.41	.31	.38	.68
Bowling Green Tweezer	.37	.04	.20	.00	.53	.46	.71
Placing test, tweezer	.37	.03	.28	.37	.15	.38	.82
Depth perception, Ortho-Rater	.18	.57	.12	.04	.08	.38	.88
Depth perception II	.00	.53	−.09	.05	.34	.41	.57
Near acuity, left eye	−.19	.62	−.08	.14	.40	.61	.90
Near acuity, right eye	−.08	.65	.00	.16	.36	.58	.86

From "A factorial study of dexterity tests" by Bourassa, L. M. and Guion, R. M., 1959, *Journal of Applied Psychology*, *43*, p. 203. © 1959 by American Psychological Association. Reprinted with permission.

is an example from a small study done a very long time ago (Bourassa & Guion, 1959) when gigantic computers were very new. It identifies the variables (tests), the resulting factors (by Roman numerals) accounting for parts of the total variance among the measures, the factor loadings of each variable on each factor, a common variance value h^2, and a reliability estimate for each variable. I describe this study and its implications, partly because I remember it well, partly because I can describe it bluntly, and partly because it clearly illustrates, with a matrix small enough to comprehend easily, important aspects of factor analytic research too often unrecognized by users of computer programs.

The Study

The research was designed, as all such research should be, to answer specific questions. It is technically an *exploratory* factor analysis (as opposed to *confirmatory* factor analysis, which came along much later), but it posed and tested specified hypotheses about the factors explaining variance in the set of variables.

In the factor analytic middle ages, factor analysts spoke of "discovering" the factors describing admissible inferences from test scores—as if the factors discerned from a sample of measures described invariant and enduring psychological building blocks for general behavior. What a factor analysis discovers is the factor structure "put there [in the matrix] by the tests psychologists choose to invent" (McDonald, 1999, p. 167). It is too easy to overlook the fact that dimensional structure applies to a specific matrix, not to mankind in general. But that's OK. Having chosen to develop certain tests, we do not imply that their intercorrelations truly describe real psychological processes. "Some of these [processes] may indeed reveal themselves through the dimensional analysis of individual differences. Some processes may not depend for existence or detection on individual variability" (McDonald, 1999, p. 168). Indeed, some traits may be revealed only by situations that stimulate them (Tett & Burnett, 2003).

Well-designed factor analytic research, like other research, is built on prior findings. Prior research had distinguished two dexterity factors found in many matrices, a hand dexterity factor involving arm and hand motions, and a finger dexterity factor involving finer movements of the fingers without arm movement (French, 1951). Experience with transistor assemblers of the time suggested that manipulating tiny objects with tweezers might be an independent, even finer form of dexterity. Moreover, with those assemblers, a dexterity test requiring tweezers correlated highly with visual depth perception. Although French had excluded vision from the dexterity factors, we (i.e., Bourassa & Guion, 1959) believed that vision was involved in the dexterity demands of ordinary work. The study was based on two hypotheses: (a) that a tweezer dexterity factor could be identified that differs from either hand or finger dexterity, and (b) that visual factors and these psychomotor factors would be correlated; that is, that visual factors (depth perception and near point visual acuity) would be more highly correlated with dexterity as the muscle movements became finer; that is, least with hand dexterity and most with tweezer dexterity. The study was driven by these hypotheses, but the results did not support them. Expected factors did not emerge, and those that did emerge were not correlated. All in all, it was a thorough disconfirmation of our hypotheses; more sophisticated modern methods could not have disconfirmed them more emphatically.

Nevertheless, the study illustrates how variables can be chosen. At least two tests are required to define a factor; the tests in this study had frequently defined one of the four factors established in prior research. When a previously unknown factor is proposed, new measures must be developed and pilot tested for fit to the expected characteristics of the factor. Four tests requiring tweezers use, three of which were developed for this study, were included as possible definers of tweezer dexterity.

Factor Rotation

The term "rotation" is archaic, describing pre-computer graphic procedures. Thurstone (1947) developed a *centroid factor analysis* method. In it, the starting point was arbitrary; different people analyzing a matrix from different starting points would end up with different tables of factor loadings. Rotation made the factor loadings less arbitrary, more consistent across researchers, and more interpretable.

Given a center, or origin, Cartesian coordinates show the correlation between any two variables as the cosine of an angle; like correlation, a cosine varies between plus and minus 1.0. The cosine of 90° (or 270°) is zero, so a right angle represents zero correlation; two variables or factors described with a right angle (or a zero correlation) are said to be *orthogonal*. The cosines of 0° and 180° are +1.0 and −1.0, respectively, representing perfect positive or negative correlation. Cartesian coordinates, drawn at right angles at the origin, represent two orthogonal factors (graphic rotation studies two factors at a time). Intermediate correlations, positive or negative, can be depicted by intermediate angles, so any correlations between factors can also be depicted graphically. That is, factors on the tests in the analyzed matrix can be described graphically, two factors at a time, by placing each variable in its appropriate relation to the factors (axes) and to each of the other variables (appropriate in the sense that the angle between them, at the origin, has a cosine equal to the correlation coefficient). Placing the coordinates on translucent paper gives an overlay that can be rotated to provide a less arbitrary placement of the axes, such as minimizing the angles between an axis and points representing the tests. In that way, one places axes where the resulting factor loadings will be as close as possible to either zero or 1.0—a rule that maximizes variance of loadings on a factor, or *varimax* rotation. Other rotational rules have been used. The advantage of rotation is to provide a more easily interpreted structure. Note that rotated factors by this procedure are orthogonal—uncorrelated. Sometimes, however, it makes more sense to think of the factors as being correlated. We (Bourassa and I) expected correlated factors.

Graphic rotation also allows moving one axis at a time so that angles between axes are permitted to vary; this is known as *oblique* rotation and can indicate correlations between factors. The degree of correlation may depend on characteristics of particular samples of situations, subjects, or measures chosen for research and therefore be unreliable. However, a matrix of correlations among oblique factors can be factor analyzed to look for a higher level of generality, *second-order* or *general factors*.

The point was demonstrated in the Thurstone (1947) box study. Twenty measurements were taken from each of a sample of boxes; they included functions of the basic three dimensions, such as the square of the width, the perimeter of a side, or the diagonal across an end. Correlations were computed and the resulting matrix was analyzed. Three basic dimensions resulted—length, width, depth. Clearly, these are dimensions of physical space and may be considered independent, that is, uncorrelated (orthogonal). However, oblique rotation showed them to be *not* independent. Moreover, considering the logic of the study, we really should not expect them to be. The study was based, not on physical objects in general, but on boxes. Boxes have an expected shape. Most of them, opened from the top, have less depth than width, less width than length. Because of this common tendency, the three dimensions are correlated in a population of boxes.

Many early factor analysts preferred orthogonal rotation (at least in exploratory analyses) because it clarifies differences between factors and because it yields more reliable factor loadings. However, oblique rotation can help avoid over-interpretation of factors and their distinctions. I often recommend oblique rotation. If it's not a good idea, then the estimated factor correlations are trivial, and orthogonality can be accepted. Although the logic of the Bourassa and Guion (1959) study demanded oblique rotation, the data did not conform; the factors turned out to be orthogonal despite the hypothesis. Others recommend no rotation at all in certain situations. Carretta and Ree (2000), referring explicitly to factor analysis of cognitive abilities, argued that the first unrotated factor is the general cognitive ability, *g*.

> When factors are rotated, it seems as though the first-factor variance disappears. In reality, it has become the dominant source of variance in the new rotated factors. The result is that these other factors become *g* plus something else. When the rotated factors are interpreted, the 'something else' usually determines the factor name, while the general component is not acknowledged. (Carretta & Ree, 2000, p. 228)

However, if the purpose of the analysis is to identify the components of a domain, as was Thurstone's original purpose in developing multiple factor analysis, then the emphasis on the "something else" correctly interprets the results.

The word "rotation" continues to be used, but rotation by manipulating charts is not. Most computer packages offer several approaches for either orthogonal or oblique rotation. Programs for hierarchical factor analysis avoid some of the pitfalls of oblique rotation and subsequent analysis of factor correlations. Methods of rotation—indeed, all of the methods and models of factor analysis—have changed since the early days.

TABLE 6.3

Tests with Significant Loadings (≥ .30) on Factor V

Test	Loading
Bowling Green Tweezer Dexterity Test	*.53*
O'Connor Finger Dexterity Test	.43
O'Connor Tweezer Dexterity Test	*.42*
Ortho-Rater, near acuity, left eye	.40
Ortho-Rater, near acuity, right eye	.36
Depth perception	.34
Dowel manipulation	.33
Pin moving	.31

Italicized loadings are the highest loading for that test. Reprinted from Guion, R. M. (1965) *Personnel Testing* (p. 59). New York: McGraw-Hill. © Robert M. Guion.

Factor Loadings

Factor loadings are interpreted like other correlations; squaring them gives a coefficient of determination. The loading of "Minnesota turning"[5] on Factor I in Table 6.2 is .61; the coefficient of determination is about .37. That means that about 37% of the total variance in scores on that test is due to variance in Factor I. Almost none of the variance on this test can be attributed to Factor II. Factor I represented a merger of the three hypothesized dexterity factors, identified as manual dexterity; Factor II was a similar merger for a general "good vision" factor, which we named visual sensitivity (but hindsight considers it a method factor).

The nature of a factor is inferred from characteristics of the measures with the highest loadings; its boundaries exclude characteristics of those with low loadings. Naming or otherwise interpreting factors is subjective. (Early factor analysts railed against descriptive names for factors, using Roman numerals instead because numerals carry no unwanted semantic baggage.) In interpreting a factor, variables may be listed in the order of their factor loadings down to some arbitrary value considered important enough to consider (usually .30), as in Table 6.3.

Bourassa and Guion (1959) named Factor V *Visual Feedback* and defined it as the ability to use fine visual cues in the manipulation and placement of small objects. The three tests at the top of the list all called for placing small objects into holes. Two of them, but not all three, called for the use of tweezers. The inclusion of a non-tweezer test in this list, and the failure of a reliable tweezer placing test to appear (a factor loading of .15 is pretty low), mean that the factor, whatever it might be, is not the hypothesized tweezer dexterity factor. The inclusion of the three vision tests, and the fact that the dexterity tests with significant loadings required examinees to look closely at the objects in picking them up and placing them, made visual feedback a better interpretation of the skill represented by this factor. This example shows how nonsignificant loadings can contribute to understanding constructs.

No such factor had been identified in previous factor analyses, so it was identified as "tentative," subject to verification in further research. So far as we know, no such research has been done, and, even though this is an old study, the lack of confirming or disconfirming

---

[5] The Minnesota Rate of Manipulation Test has two parts, turning and placement. In one the objects (comparable in size to checkers) are turned over; in the other, they are placed in holes in a board.

evidence means that the factor can neither be accepted nor rejected in forming a taxonomy of sensorimotor skills.

Factors III and IV were considered spurious and not interpreted. Factor III has only one loading above .30; the three for Factor IV form no interpretable pattern.

Communality and Uniqueness

The total variance, s^2, of any variable in a correlation matrix is a function of (a) sources of variance shared with other variables in the same set and (b) variance due to sources unique to the variable (i.e., not found in any of the others in the matrix):

$$s^2 = h^2 + u^2 \qquad (6.2)$$

where h^2 is the *communality* of the variable and u^2 is its *uniqueness*. Communality is the proportion of total variance in a distribution of scores on a test (or other variable) explained by the factors identified in the matrix studied, the sum of the squares of all of its factor loadings. In Table 6.2, for example, the communality of the Minnesota turning test is .47; 47% of its total variance is explained by the factors identified in the study (including, alas, the uninterpretable ones). The remaining 53% of its total variance, u^2, is not common to other measures in the battery; it is unique. Part of its uniqueness is due simply to unreliability; inconsistent errors of measurement, according to the reliability estimate in Table 6.2, contribute about 15% of the total variance. That leaves 38% (53%–15%) of the total variance as systematic specific factor variance, unique to this one test, at least in this battery.

For the finger placing test developed for the study (halfway down the column), the communality is only .22; 78% of its variance is unique. Is variance in these scores sufficiently explained? The reliability estimate is important in answering this question. Uniqueness for the Minnesota turning and the specially developed placement tests is, respectively, 53% and 78%. These seem quite different, at least until we look at the test–retest reliability estimates. These estimates show 85% of the turning score variance treated as systematic, potentially explainable, compared to only 49% for the placing test. The five factors from this analysis accounted for 55% (.47/.85) of the *explainable* variance in the turning test scores and for 45% (.22/.49) in the placing test scores. Clearly, these tests do not differ as much in systematic variance as the communalities alone might suggest. Factor analyses rarely account for large proportions of systematic variance, especially in psychomotor tests. There are always unrecognized, untapped sources of variance in the matrix analyzed. There is, however, reason to believe that effort expended to improve reliability could also improve communality and, perhaps, the factor loadings of the home-grown finger placement test on the three interpreted factors.

Some uniqueness may stem from failure to include in the study variables tapping the same sources of variance. Look again at Figure 6.2. 70% of the variance of Test D was due to variance in finger dexterity, a source of variance not present in any of the other three tests. The only source of communality in that test—in that four-test battery—comes from the 6% of its variance attributable to perceptual speed. However, adding a fifth test, one also measuring finger dexterity, would substantially increase communality. The same logic applies to the finger placing test.

A *factor score* is an index of the level of a person's ability (or other attribute) at a factor level rather than the level of an individual test score. It is computed by multiplying the raw score obtained on every test in the study by its factor loading on every factor and then summing the products. A very different alternative score for a factor construct is to simply add the scores on those tests that are assumed to have significant loadings on the factor (i.e., *unit-weighted scores*). The difference between a factor score and the more common unit-weighted score for the same factor is not trivial. Factor scores maintain maximum independence between the dimensions; those based on unit weighting are usually correlated, even when rotation was orthogonal.

Multitrait, Multimethod Research

Research to clarify the justifiable interpretations of scores on specified tests (or other measures) moved forward with the introduction of the multitrait–multimethod (MTMM) matrix by Campbell and Fiske (1959). In such a matrix, two (preferably more) different traits are assessed by two (again, preferably more) different methods, forming a matrix with correlation coefficients in the cells. Worth noting is that a table of factor loadings is a kind of MTMM matrix; the factors are traits, and the different measures are different replications of those traits. Evidence of *convergent validity* is found when correlations across measures of the same trait by different methods are relatively high. Evidence of *discriminant validity* is found when the correlations of different traits measured by the same method are relatively low. Evidence of *method variance* is also found by MTMM analyses, although Williams, Ford, and Nguyen (2002) criticized its use. They (and most other statisticians) argued that method factors can be hypothesized (and therefore controlled) separately from substantive trait factors by using confirmatory factor analysis. It is a different model of multivariate research directly permitting evidence of all three of these.

Confirmatory Factor Analysis

In the early days (sometimes, unfortunately, even now), some people "explored" available data sets with no discernible clues about the factors they might find. From the beginning, the best factor analytic research began with hypotheses about constructs, how they might be measured, or what other constructs ought to be different. A battery of measurement instruments would be assembled and include reference or marker variables with a history of high loadings on factors postulated for the matrix being developed. It would be administered to people in an appropriate sample, analyzed, and the results compared subjectively to prior expectations. Even a hypothesis-testing factor analysis used an exploratory method—as if the researcher had started with nothing more than curiosity.

Confirmatory factor analysis (CFA) methods have long been available and accessible. These methods do a stronger job of dividing total variance into components such as the variance due to a construct of interest, to systematic sources other than that construct (e.g., that due to method variance), and that due to random error. Exploratory methods are often unable to distinguish random from systematic error variance; CFA can do so (Lance & Vandenberg, 2002; Williams, et al., 2002).

CFA differs from exploratory multiple factor analysis in several other ways (Raykov & Marcoulides, 2008). For one thing, it is more systematically based on previous research and theory; from prior knowledge, a hypothetical model of the structure of a specified or anticipated data set is created. A CFA model is far more detailed than the set of hypotheses generally recommended for governing the choice of variables for exploratory analyses. Components, or parameters, of the CFA model may be constrained in the light of prior knowledge. For example, factor loadings of some measures may be constrained to be zero where prior data or reasoning suggest trivial or nonsignificant loadings; others may be constrained to be perfect to suggest that, for interpretative purposes, a solution needs to assume absence of transient error or systematic covariance with other factors. The defining distinguishing characteristic is that the model fails to be supported if there is no unique solution to the analysis; if one exists, the method also permits (better, requires) that the procedure estimate how well the model fits the data analyzed. CFA also eliminates the need for rotation or for argument whether factors are or are not correlated; the model can specify where correlated factors are expected.

To illustrate a plausible CFA model, consider a highly detailed, cognitively difficult job requiring innovation and creativity. Suppose that job analysis leads us to believe that performance on the job can be predicted from measures of a slightly compulsive facet of conscientiousness—but not from a different facet suggesting dependability in following rules. Because these are both facets of conscientiousness, we would expect factors suggesting them to be correlated. We would expect the compulsion to get the details right to relate to job performance, but we would not expect reliable obedience to rules and procedures to do so. The model, shown as Figure 6.4, identifies three measures expected to reflect each of the three factors; it also shows that some error variance (perhaps transient error) independently influences each of the measures. Suppose also that one of the three hypothesized factors is general or overall performance of job duties, also measured in three different ways. From a practice perspective, the model is in part a test of a predictive hypothesis and in part a psychometric test of the plausibility of the suggestion of those two factors within the more general factor of conscientiousness. In the context of this chapter, we are mainly interested in the psychometric importance of CFA. I know of no examples in which CFA has been used to test a predictive hypothesis, but I also know of no reason why it could not be.

In any case, the final step is to determine how well the hypothesized model fits the data. A CFA research model requires precision in theoretical statements. It specifies expected latent variables. It may specify specific model parameters (factor loadings, variances, or covariances) or the existence of correlation among factors. Data are collected from a representative sample, parameters of the model are estimated, and statistical tests are used to check on the goodness of fit between the a priori model and the data (see Lance & Vandenberg,

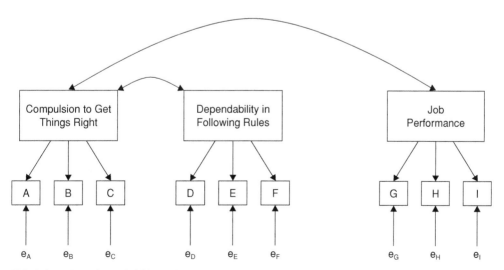

FIG. 6.4 A hypothetical CFA model suggesting that variance in nine measures (including aspects of performance) stems from three factors.

2002). The fit of data to an a priori model confirms (or disconfirms) the model. This is, of course, like other statistical hypothesis testing. The model may be confirmed only in the sense that the null hypothesis is not rejected. That is, one does not really *confirm* the correctness of a model; one only fails to *disconfirm* it. Nevertheless, confirmatory factor analysis can indicate how well the model fits the data, and a well-fitting model is a great aid to understanding the measures used.

Factor Analysis and Personnel Decisions

Chapter 3 stressed the centrality of the predictive hypothesis for assessments intended as aids to personnel decisions. A simple predictive hypothesis includes at least two constructs, a predictor and a criterion, and both should be validly measured. Factor analysis, especially CFA, is an important tool for evaluating psychometric validity. If it identifies tests with strong loadings on a factor fitting the construct of interest, with little variance attributable to either random or systematic error, then such tests are appropriate in testing the predictive hypothesis. CFA applications are broader. CFA is used often where structural equations are to be used later as a first step in clarifying the measurement model. It has also been used to clarify multitrait–multimethod matrices (see Chapter 8 for these applications). A major use in personnel selection can be to determine measurement equivalence over groups or time periods, and an especially interesting potential use is in growth modeling or the measurement of change over time. *Measurement equivalence* (sometimes called measurement invariance) is an important theoretical concept. A test used in two or more different groups, different times, or different media should mean the same thing in those different conditions (Meade, Johnson, Braddy, & Johnson, 2008); that is, if the researcher wants to compare groups, or the same group tested at different times or with different media, the relationship of test scores to underlying traits should be the same across such conditions. The discussion of item response theory, later in this chapter, may clarify the concept. We will not discuss ways to evaluate such equivalence; a useful discussion of them was presented by Meade et al. (2008).

GENERALIZABILITY THEORY

Generalizability theory examines limits or boundaries for consistent meaning of test scores. Assessments are made in specific circumstances—by a certain person, on a certain day or time of day, in a certain room or other location, with specific ambient temperature or noise or distractions, and so on. If score interpretations were limited to any single combination of such specific circumstances, they would have little interest to anyone. Such circumstances should be matters of indifference, variables that have at most a trivial influence on assessments. We want to generalize the inference to the one we would have made from assessment of the person on another occasion, in another setting, or with another administrator or ambience.

Many kinds of generalization are important. The question of generalizing from sample to population is familiar. Cook and Campbell (1979) referred to *external validity* to mean the problem of generalizing research findings to "target" populations of people, settings, tasks, or times. Schmidt and Hunter (1977) referred to meta-analysis results as "validity generalization," indicating generalization of research findings in one set of studies to situations not included in that set. Generalizability theory is different from these; it was developed to test the limits of the generalizability of descriptive inferences from trait measurements (Cronbach et al., Gleser, Nanda, & Rajaratnam, 1972).

I present only the basic logic and some simple research designs. Brennan (2001) and Shavelson, Webb, and Rowley (1989) offer much more. As with factor analysis, I use a technologically ancient example because of its simplicity in presenting some basic concepts.

Elements of the Theory

Generalizability theory is an analytic method with implications for measurement theory. It goes beyond classical random error to offer a conceptual framework for considering other potential sources of error, systematic and random, and it provides evidence for evaluating psychometric validity. Putka and Sackett (2010) saw it is an extension of reliability theory and seemed to urge replacing classical approaches to reliability estimation with the kind of analysis implied by generalizability theory, considering more sources of error in measurement.

Classical test reliability estimation inquires into limited kinds of generalizability. Internal consistency coefficients refer to generalizing across the various items or observations. Stability coefficients tell whether inferences generalize across occasions or subgroups of examinees. A generalizability study can answer both kinds of question by collecting data using analysis of variance designs. It can simultaneously estimate variance attributable to different sources, such as persons, items, and occasions. In a given study, if all items are administered to all persons on all designated occasions, the design is "fully crossed," expressed as $p \times i \times o$, and shown by Venn diagrams as the top part of Figure 6.5. The bottom part depicts a design in

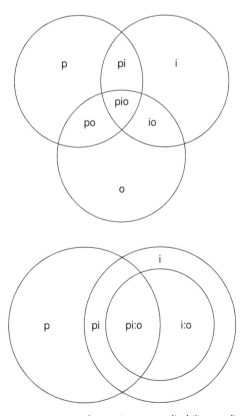

FIG. 6.5 Two designs for person, item, and occasion generalizability studies.

which two sets of items (presumably equivalent in some sense) are used on two occasions, as if using equivalent forms in a test–retest reliability study. Items would be "nested within" occasions, expressed as a $p \times i{:}o$ design. These are only two of the many different designs one might choose for studies of two sources of variance other than the traits of the people assessed.

Generalizability of a Job Analysis Scale

The 20-item scale of job involvement (Lodahl & Kejner, 1965) was central to a survey stimulated by apparent ambiguity in the construct itself. Tombaugh (1981) wrote 64 more items tapping various facets of involvement. The survey was administered in group sessions, some by the researcher and some by a company official. Items (i) were one facet of the design (independently and again in sets fitting three previously identified factors). Another facet was employees nested within group leader ($e{:}g$). A third facet was occasions (o); two administrations of the questionnaire were scheduled two months apart. (The design was $i \times o \times e{:}g$.) Variance components were calculated for the 84 items (and for the original 20 items), and for three item factors, employees, group leader, and occasions. Much happened during that two-month interval. Wage and salary increases were given, an anticipated temporary plant shutdown resulted in substantial overtime during the three weeks preceding the second occasion, and union contract negotiations had begun. None of these things were anticipated when the schedule was set; their cumulative effect seemed likely to be substantial. It wasn't. The only substantial variance component was for individual differences across employees. Variance components for items, for the three item factors, administrators, and even occasions were zero or very nearly so. Tombaugh concluded that the original Lodahl–Kejner scale allowed highly generalizable, internally consistent and clear inferences, despite alleged ambiguity.

Basic Concepts in a Hypothetical Application

Definition of Construct Measured

Consider an eight-item behavioral checklist an interviewer uses to assess friendliness in positions calling for extensive public contact; for example, receptionists. The first thing to do is to spell out in some detail what "friendliness" means in this context—our "theory of the attribute." It may consist of smiling a lot, giving undivided attention to those who come in, and showing interest in them or sympathy with their problems. The theory excludes emotional involvement with others, long-term relationships, or altruism.

Sources of Variance

What circumstances might influence the behavior—but ought to be irrelevant? Time of day might be one. Morning grouches may be more likely to be friendly in the afternoons, and it may be more likely in the mornings for morning chirpers, but the time of day of the interview ought to be irrelevant. Also irrelevant is the specific rater who completes the checklist. The demeanor of the person greeted might be an influence—an obnoxiousness factor. The checklist behaviors (ratings) should account for most of the assessment variance. Time of day, specific observer, and even obnoxious behavior of the other person should account for very little of it.

Variance Components

A generalizability study examines specified sources of variance. The example includes four obvious sources of variance: individual differences among the people observed (p), time of day (t), rater (r), and the obnoxiousness factor (o). The design might be fully crossed, $p \times t \times r \times o$. The meetings of receptionists and visitors might be taped so that maybe six raters might complete the eight-item checklists. Perhaps 20 people employed as receptionists might each be taped twice, once in the morning, once in the evening. Several actors playing visitors could be used with scripted levels of pleasantness and obnoxiousness. Other designs might eliminate the need for taping, but they would not be fully crossed. This design is, in that each of the 20 people is rated at both times of day with both kinds of visitors by all six observers. The 20 people are the *objects of measurement*. People are the usual objects of psychological measurement, but other objects might be jobs or work products. The other elements of the design (time, visitors, and raters) would be called factors in most discussions of analysis of variance, but in generalizability theory they are known as the *facets* of the design to avoid confusion with the factors of factor analysis. Each facet in the design has two or more *conditions* or levels: two time periods, two levels of visitor demeanor, and six raters. (We do not ordinarily refer to the object of measurement as a facet in the design; if we did for this illustration, a people facet would be said to have 20 conditions.)

There are 15 sources of variance, not just four: the four main effects, p, t, r and o; there are also six two-way interactions, pt, pr, po, tr, to, and ro; four three-way interactions, ptr, pto, pro, and tro; and the residual four-way interaction confounded with random error, $ptro$. Note that nothing has been said about the significance of the effects. Generalizability analysis is not concerned with statistical significance; the interest is only in the proportion of total variance attributable to each source in the design.

If the attribute is well measured—that is, if the inferences from the checklist scores generalize well across the conditions of measurement—most of the total variance will be due to individual differences among the people. A substantial variance component for time of day might mean that friendliness, as defined, is not a particularly stable attribute. A substantial variance component for visitor demeanor might suggest that the definition is erroneous in totally disregarding emotional involvement. A substantial variance for raters might suggest a need for more rater training or, perhaps, for averaging across a set of observers.[6] (In fact, generalizability analyses include estimates of the numbers of observations needed for acceptable generalizability, analogous to the use of the Spearman-Brown equation.)

Sampling

Classical psychometric theory is based on the idea of *parallel* forms (i.e., with identical "true" score distributions). Generalizability theory requires only *randomly parallel* forms; that is, forms based on loosely random sampling from the various levels or conditions of the facets. I stress loosely; like Wood (1976, p. 249), I consider sampling in generalizability studies more closely related to the Brunswikian idea of a representative sample than the random sampling of probability theory. In this case, occasions should sample realistic interviewing times, not all possible ones.

---

[6] Averaging treats the set of observers as a fixed facet so that decision makers can generalize only for this set. That is not a disadvantage; in fact, it is wise to evaluate the observers at hand without generalizing to a universe of unknown observers.

Universes and Universe Scores

The relevant facets depend on the researcher's definition of a *universe of admissible observations*. The definition depends on the researcher's theory of the attribute, and different researchers developing similar assessment procedures may differ in specifying what belongs in or lies outside that universe. Admissible observations can include those conditions that the researcher considers matters of indifference. In the example, one researcher might consider time of day irrelevant; observations at any time of day are admissible. A different theory of the attribute might treat friendliness as dependent on the time of day, so that only observations at specified times (depending on the theory) are admissible. Occasions of observation and rating might be defined in several ways, such as the day of the week or now versus later. In defining a universe of admissible observations for generalizability analysis, the facet conditions to study are those that researchers think should be irrelevant but pose threats to psychometric validity.

In the example, checklist items define one component of a universe of admissible observations; they constitute the observations relevant to the researcher's theory of the attribute. Admissible observations must fit the definition of the construct being assessed. Many possible kinds of behavior in an interaction of receptionist and visitor might reveal the level of friendliness, but only those that fit the construct definition are admissible.

Researcher preference influences the definition or restriction of the rater facet of the universe of admissible observations. One researcher may consider any reasonably intelligent observer–rater acceptable and use volunteers from an introductory psychology class. Another may consider experience as a supervisor of receptionists essential and limit the universe to supervisors, letting choice of supervisors be a matter of indifference. The important thing is clarity in defining the observations that are or are not admissible in measuring an attribute.

The universe of admissible observations is necessarily broad. Cronbach et al. (1972) also identified a different, more restricted concept, the *universe of generalization*, the set of conditions within which a decision maker wants to make generalizations. In view of the limitations of real data, the universe of generalization is likely to be substantially narrower than the universe of admissible observations. It must not be larger. Defining a universe of generalization that goes beyond the universe of admissible observations implies either hypothesis testing, analogous to criterion-related validation, or just plain overgeneralization.

Cronbach et al. (1972) distinguished between a *G-study* and a *D-study*. A generalizability study (G-study) investigates facets and conditions of a universe of admissible observations, mainly those that have a bearing on the meaning of scores. A decision study (D-study) investigates facets and conditions involved in decision making, whether decisions about the measurement procedure or about the objects of measurement. It is based on the universe of generalization important for the intended decision making. In a D-study, a decision maker might find it useful to obtain estimates of *universe scores* for the objects of measurement. These are somewhat analogous to true scores. A person's universe score is the mathematical expected value of that person's mean performance over the facets that define the universe. As a result, the person can have as many universe scores as universes defined. A work sample test, for example, may have one universe of generalizability defined by a quality control expert and a different one defined by a production supervisor.

Multiple Sources and Concepts of Error

Classical psychometric theory divides the total variance in a set of measures into true score variance (i.e., consistent, systematic variance) and error variance. The term "true" score variance stretches the concept of "true" beyond reasonable lexical limits, and the classical idea of error variance is simplistic, allowing only for random or transient error or, as Putka and Sackett (2010) would say, inconsistent sources of variance. These limits of classical theory have long been recognized, but most of us have adapted to the linguistic nonsense. As Thorndike (1949) pointed out, we can mean different things by *true* or systematic and *error*, depending on which category we think a source of variance fits. Gulliksen (1950b) and Lord and Novick (1968) acknowledged multiple sources and concepts of error within the true score language, but both of these classics continued to refer to two categories. Generalizability theory extends classical theory by methodically and statistically considering multiple sources of systematic error, different kinds of error in the estimation of universe scores, and the idea that the purposes of measurement properly determine what is considered an error. Facets of the defined universes also define different sources of systematic error; they identify specific, nontrivial, potential systematic sources of error. Many studies may be needed to cover all facets in a universe of admissible observations, and still further studies may be suggested when a developer or user of the procedure accumulates experience with it and finds previously unrecognized problems.

Errors in Estimating Universe Scores

Estimates of true scores in classical theory are based on regression equations where observed scores are adjusted for regression to the mean:

$$t = X + r_{xx}(X - M_x) \tag{6.3}$$

where t is the traditional "true" score, X is the obtained score, M_x is the mean of all scores in the set, and r_{xx} is the reliability estimate. Estimates of universe scores in generalizability theory are also based on regression equations, but they are necessarily more complex. In addition to considering the person's observed score position relative to an overall mean, it must also be considered with reference to the means for the various conditions of the various facets of the universe of generalization. Cronbach et al. (1972, p. 138) offered several alternative equations for different D-study designs. True score estimates are rarely computed when working within classical psychometrics because it considers observed scores and estimated true scores perfectly correlated. Estimates of universe scores, however, are *not* perfectly correlated with obtained scores, largely because of weaker assumptions (e.g., the assumption of randomly parallel forms instead of strictly parallel) and, in some designs, because the necessary slope parameters cannot be determined.

Estimating a specific point value by a regression equation necessarily involves some error of estimates. In the statistical prediction of a criterion variable, for example, we may compute a standard error of estimate to measure the extent of prediction (estimation) errors. The generalizability theory error of estimate is analogous, but a universe score is also subject to two other kinds of error, known as *absolute* error and *relative* error. The absolute error is the difference between the observed and universe score, on the original raw score scale. It is important when decisions are made about people on the basis of domain-referenced interpretations of their own scores (see Chapter 11), without reference to their relative standing in a distribution of scores. Relative error is the difference between observed and universe scores expressed in deviation score units. It is important when relative standing is used as the basis for decision, as in norm-referenced measurement (Shavelson et al., 1989).

In classical theory, errors are assumed uncorrelated. In generalizability theory, the three kinds of error are correlated, but imperfectly; knowing the magnitude of one of them does not shed much light on the others. The relative magnitudes of these three errors, however, are known. Absolute error is greatest, and error of estimate is least. The order suggests considerations for test use in practice (Viswesvaran & Ones, 2005): Domain-referenced interpretations are likely to be less reliable than norm-referenced interpretations; universe score estimates based on regression are likely to be more reliable than observed scores.

Why, then, are such estimates so rarely used in personnel decisions? One reason is the belief that scores for everyone should be interpreted in the same way, with no differentiation of subgroups according to various conditions of measurement. Moreover, the overall rank order of candidates by observed scores is precisely the same as the rank order by estimated true scores. Suppose, however, that the assessment procedure is scored by observer ratings (as in interviews, individual appraisals, or assessment center exercises) and that a generalizability study found a strong variance component for an observer facet. In this case, the classical assumption that error is random does not hold, and estimating universe scores by taking observers into account would provide a different but more reliable rank ordering of people seen by different observers. If the conditions of facets resulted in socially sensitive subgrouping, with most women or minorities in a particular subgroup, the increased merit of estimated scores might not have practical value, but this implication of generalizability theory should not be overlooked.

Error and the Purposes of Measurement

From classical theory, we habitually think of measurement error as only the random or inconsistent error. We know (even as we ignore it) that estimates of inconsistent error variance always depend on how our research has treated certain sources of variance (Thorndike, 1949). We know also that some sources of variance are not wanted, even though they are not random; these are treated by our methods of reliability estimation as systematic sources of variance, tied to the amorphous concept of "true" scores and forgotten. Perhaps the big advantage of generalizability theory is that it forces serious thought about likely sources of variance, distinguishing those that should be considered sources of error and those that fit the theory of the attribute.

The Use of Generalizability Theory

Interest in and use of generalizability theory, at least within the psychology of work, has decreased in the past couple of decades. Some reasons for the decline were identified by DeShon (2002), among them the tendency to limit the theory to studies of individual differences. Putka and Sackett (2010) thought it might be due to too much jargon. Maybe it is because the approach is more often applied in educational measurement and therefore appears in literature not commonly perused in IO psychology. Another reason is that researchers have not seen it as a major advance from classical theory. In fact, Viswesvaran and Ones (2005) seemed to argue that generalizability theory and classical test theory are redundant if "appropriate data are collected and analyzed" (p. 369). They may be right, but they did not convince me. I consider it a worthy extension to classical theory, and it has much to offer the evaluation of measurement, whether in terms of reliability or validity.

Its decline in the IO literature is regrettable and may be reversed by the cumulative effect of recent articles and book chapters. This extension of classical theory has much unused promise for all topics in the psychology of work but especially for personnel assessment. I see promise in clearer understanding of allowable inferences from test scores not only in currently routine assessment situations but also in some that are not yet routine. Examples might include studies of systematic error that might be found in aspects of user interface in computerized assessment, or studies of systematic error in cross-cultural or cross-national testing, or in studies to examine the possibility of systematic error producing nonlinear regression or growth trajectories (discussed in Chapter 10).

ITEM RESPONSE THEORY

Item response theory (IRT), once known as latent trait theory, "is a rubric for a family of measurement models that describe the relationship between an individual's performance on a test item and his or her standing on a continuous latent trait" (Reise & Waller, 2002, p. 88). It is based on the commonsense idea that people with a lot of a specific ability are more likely to give the right answer to an item requiring that ability than are people with less ability. Those with the most favorable attitudes toward something are more likely to give item responses that reflect their positive attitude than are those with less favorable attitudes. Whatever the nature of the underlying latent trait measured by an internally consistent set of items, a systematic relationship can be assumed between levels of the trait and the likelihood of a specified response. The relationship can be modeled and charted as a mathematical function, or equation, known as an *item response curve* (IRC).[7] Knowing the equation parameters for the different items and knowing a person's responses to the items, that person's level of the trait can be estimated. This is quite different from classical test theory, in which a test score typically reflects only the number of items answered correctly (with or without weighting responses or making some correction for guessing), without taking account of differences in item characteristics such as difficulty and discrimination indices.

Many IRT models have been proposed: multidimensional and unidimensional, linear and nonlinear, or dichotomous and polychotomous responses, such as points on scales or classification categories (Ellis & Mead, 2002; Embretson & Reise, 2000; McDonald, 1999). The simplest IRT models assume unidimensional traits, dichotomous responses, and non-linear item response curves; this introduction to IRT is limited to such models.

Local independence is generally assumed in IRT models, meaning that a person's response to one item is not affected by the response given to any other item. Local independence does not mean uncorrelated. Overall, item responses must be correlated or there can be no internal consistency, let alone unidimensionality. At a specific level of ability, however, item responses should be uncorrelated (Hambleton, 1989, p. 151).

Item Response Theory Compared to Classical Theory

Classical test theory is based on the idea of sampling from a population. Statistics derived from the available sample are used to estimate population parameters—and to estimate the variance of "true scores" in that population. In contrast, IRT is based on mathematical models of the relationship of the underlying latent trait to be measured by a test and specified

---

[7] Earlier, an IRC was called an *item characteristic curve, ICC.* The curve models item responses, so IRC seems more descriptive, and I will use it. Many articles referenced here, however, refer to ICCs.

properties of individual test items. That relationship is *not* assumed to be linear, and distributions of scores are *not* assumed to be normal; freedom from these restrictive assumptions permits IRT estimates of item parameters and person trait estimates to be *invariant*, that is, free from dependence on the distribution of ability in a specific sample (Ellis & Mead, 2002).

It is common to begin a discussion of IRT by recounting the shortcomings of classical test theory (CTT). Some authors have gone so far as to assert that IRT replaces CTT, an idea not quite shared by Zickar and Broadfoot (2009), who pointed to situations where CTT is to be preferred as well as others where IRT is necessary. Similarities as well as differences were shown by comparing the two theories using 10 "new rules" of IRT matched point by point to 10 "old rules" of classical theory (Embretson & Reise, 2000, pp. 14–39). I will describe the respective rules for only four of the rules both theories address, but I strongly recommend Embretson and Reise's lovely book for a better and more comprehensive introduction to item response theory.

Measurement Error

Both theories necessarily deal with measurement error, but they do so in quite different ways. Classical test theory assumes (and computes) a standard error of measurement (SEM). The SEM is often considered constant across score levels (Equations 5.15 and 5.16). The assumption is generally recognized as a bit absurd; it makes sense to expect more measurement error at low ability levels than at high ones. If the sample is large enough, SEMs can be estimated for different ranges within the distribution (Lord & Novick, 1968). In many employment settings, those with quite high scores are virtually certain to get offers of employment without comparisons to other individuals; those with quite low scores are pretty sure to be rejected. In between is a range within which comparisons and difficult decisions are made. Knowing the SEM in the high and low ranges is not very important, but it can be vitally important in that range of difficult decisions where decision makers should know whether assessments distinguish people reliably. Even where the SEM can be computed explicitly for that range, however, the assumption is still made that it is constant for all scores within the range.

In contrast, IRT effectively replaces the constant SEM with an information function. The level of information (or, conversely, error) differs across different scores but generalizes across populations. IRT uses an information function to show the differing precision of trait estimation at different levels.

Item Properties

Classical psychometric theory uses two item statistics, a difficulty index and a discrimination index.[8] These statistics describe item responses in a specific sample and depend on the distribution of the trait in that sample. In a high-ability sample, higher on average than the relevant population, a difficulty index erroneously suggests an easy item; the same item in a low-ability sample appears hard. If shape and level of a sample distribution differs substantially from the population distribution, item discriminability statistics underestimate

---

[8] I often refer to it as a *discriminability index* to avoid some of the social and legal implications associated in personnel testing with the word *discrimination*, but *discrimination index* is more commonly used in psychometrics.

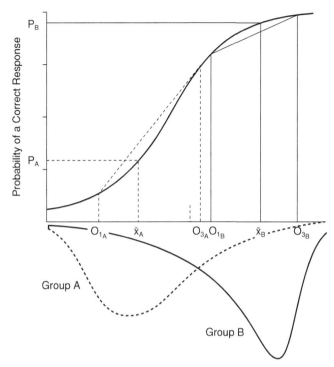

FIG. 6.6   Differences in item statistics in two groups in which the probability of giving a correct response is the same for people at any given level of ability. Reprinted from Guion, R. M., and Ironson, G. M. (1983). Latent trait theory for organizational research. *Organizational Behavior and Human Performance, 31*, 54–87. © Elsevier Science and Technology Journals. Reprinted with permission.

population values.[9] Samples that differ from each other in the shape and level of the underlying trait distributions yield different item statistics.

The point is illustrated in Figure 6.6, showing an IRC. The abscissa (horizontal axis) is a theoretical scale of the latent ability, designated theta, θ; the ordinate (vertical axis) is the probability of a correct response. Distributions of ability in two groups are shown below the abscissa. The mean ability in Group B is much higher than the mean ability in Group A, therefore the proportion of correct responses is much greater; that is, CTT item difficulty statistics, designated P_A and P_B, are quite different in the two groups. The first and third quartiles (Q_1 and Q_3) in each group are also shown. The straight line connecting these points for either group has a slope proportional to the CTT discriminability index. The slopes differ substantially, so traditional discriminability indices in the two samples also differ. The total set of cases, divided into two samples, yields two sets of item statistics. Dividing the total into still more groups would yield still more statistics, all differing.

Any functional equation, whether the linear equation in classical theory or the equation for the IRC, is characterized in part by its parameters, the constants of the equation (e.g.,

[9] In theory, but not often in practice, sample variance may be greater than the population variance, and the value obtained may be an overestimate. Even in such a case, a discrimination index is a correlation statistic, subject to the same vagaries as any other correlation statistic relative to the population correlation.

the a and b parameters of the linear equation $Y = a + bX$). In IRT, the fit of existing data to the mathematical model of the relationship between item responses and the underlying latent trait permits simultaneous estimation of item and ability parameters, and these estimates are more stable than the CTT item characteristics in research samples. The IRC item parameters are said to be *invariant*. In any sample, regardless of mean ability level, the IRC is essentially the same and specifies the probability that a person of a given trait level, θ, will give a keyed response; that probability depends on the form and specific properties (parameters) of the curve, not on the number of people at that trait level or at any other. Parameters of the IRC are also independent of the distribution of the trait in the population of interest (Hambleton, 1989). The probability of a correct item response is therefore not a normative statement but an invariant one given the individual's estimated trait level; groups of subjects with substantially different distributions of the trait will provide substantially the same parameters, at least within a linear transformation. It is parameter invariance that makes IRT a substantial advance in psychometric theory.[10]

Parameter invariance permits applications not feasible under classical test theory. Large pools of items can be assembled and calibrated (i.e., have individual IRC parameters determined) by giving smaller item sets to different groups of people; it makes virtually no practical difference whether a given item was calibrated in Group A or Group Z. This fact, in turn, makes possible adaptive testing, described more fully in Chapter 12, or a more scientifically meaningful approach to adverse impact, described later in this chapter.

Scale Definition

One way to scale test scores is the simple raw score scale of the number of items answered correctly. This has little meaning beyond the specific test. Interpretation depends on both the number of items in the test and its overall difficulty. Tests developed by classical methods are often scaled in terms of the distribution of scores in a specified sample—a normative scale. It might be a scale of the percentile equivalent of obtained raw scores, or a set of z-scores (or a linear transformation of it) showing distance of a raw score from the sample mean in standard deviation units. In either case, the scale is not on a common metric. If one person is assessed with one set of items and another person with a different set, their scores cannot be compared unless the two sets of items are truly equivalent. In IRT, however, the theta scale provides a common metric regardless of the specific item set used.

Test Length

In classical psychometrics, the Spearman-Brown formula is one defining characteristic of the theory: reliability increases as the length of the test is increased (by parallel segments, of course). In contrast, in IRT, improved reliability may be achieved with fewer rather than more items. Specifically, in adaptive testing methods, items are selected from a pool sequentially tightening the trait estimate for a specific examinee. Thus, fewer items selected on the basis of item parameters can yield more information (i.e., more reliable scores) than a fixed set of items developed by traditional procedures.

---

[10] As pointed out later, invariance exists within linear transformations; the exact values of the parameters may differ.

Item Response Curves

An item response curve can take many forms. Examples include linear functions, discontinuous functions such as Guttman step functions, and ascending or descending curvilinear functions, either monotonic or nonmonotonic. Use of a linear function assumes that, for a given unit change on the trait scale, there is a constant amount of change in the probability of a correct (i.e., keyed) response—a probability change that is the same for a unit change anywhere on the trait scale. A step function assumes discontinuities such that the probability of a correct response may be fixed, but only up to a specific trait level, at which it changes to a different value (higher or lower). A monotonic curve assumes that the probability of a correct response continually increases (or continually decreases) with theta level, but not necessarily at a constant rate. People in a low ability range may have little likelihood of giving a correct or keyed response, regardless of where they are in that range. The slope of the curve in that range is very slight, possibly asymptotic to a zero or very low probability. In midrange ability, the change in probability increases sharply with increasing ability increments—maybe up to a certain point—after which further but progressively smaller changes may be seen; that is, the slope of the curve may be increasingly steep up to a *point of inflection*, after which it begins to return to a more gradual slope until, at higher score ranges, the slope (and therefore the probability difference) is again trivial and asymptotic to a slightly greater probability (see examples in Figure 6.7). A generally ascending nonmonotonic curve is usually similar except that, in a very high ability range, the probability of a correct response may drop a bit.

What form is appropriate? Lord (1980) considered it an empirical matter. With enough subjects, a first approximation of an IRC can be drawn by plotting conventional item difficulty statistics against total score. In most psychological measurement, the result will look most like the positive monotonic curve. A well-established mathematical model of such a curve is given by the equation for a normal ogive, familiar from cumulative frequency distributions; much of the early research on IRT problems used that equation. It is, however, rather complex. A simpler equation, the logistic function, provides a close approximation to the normal ogive and, in one form or another, is the model most commonly used.

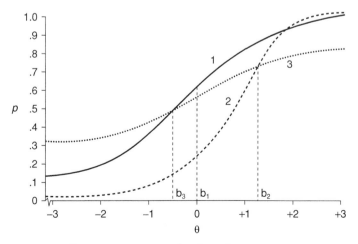

FIG. 6.7 Three-parameter item response curves for three items.

Three-Parameter Logistic Model

The three-parameter logistic equation is

$$p_i(\theta) = [c_i + (1 - c_i)]/[1 + e^{[-Da_i(\theta - b_i)]}] \tag{6.4}$$

where $p_i(\theta)$ is the probability that someone with an ability level, θ, will give a correct response to item i, where a_i, b_i, and c_i are parameters of the curve, and D is an arbitrary constant (usually set at 1.7 making the resulting curve virtually interchangeable with the normal ogive).

The three parameters in the three-parameter model are the a, b, and c constants. Values of θ, however, are additional parameters in the equation; if there are 500 subjects in the research sample and 20 items, then there are 560 parameters to be estimated: 500 values of theta and the three IRC parameters for each of the 20 items. It is easy to see why practical use of IRT had to wait for modern computers and computer programs.

The b parameter is the value of theta, θ, at the point of inflection where the slope of the curve is at its maximum; it is called the difficulty parameter; the larger the value of θ, the more difficult the item. The a parameter is a value, expressed in θ units, proportional to the slope of the curve at the point of inflection. It is usually called the *discrimination parameter*, the higher values indicating greater discriminability among examinees. The c parameter is the lower asymptote of the curve, the probability of a correct response from a subject at an infinitely low trait level. In ability testing, it is sometimes (although imprecisely) known as "the guessing parameter." In attitude measurement, it might reflect some sort of response bias (Drasgow & Hulin, 1990). If the value of c is zero, the b parameter is the value of theta corresponding to a probability of a correct answer of .5.

Figure 6.7 shows three-parameter IRCs for three different items. Items 1 and 3 are easy items with relatively low values of b; Item 2 is clearly more difficult, requiring a higher level of ability to have a 50–50 chance to answer the item correctly. It is also the most discriminating item, as shown by the steeper slope at its point of inflection. There is, moreover, very little likelihood of getting it right by chance, as indicated by a near-zero value of c. Items 1 and 2 have desirable IRCs in that neither item is unduly easy or unduly hard, neither is easily answered correctly by chance, and both discriminate different levels of ability well in a fairly large range of ability. Item 3 is not a useful item. The probability of a correct answer by chance is high, and a correct answer is less than certain even at the highest ability level. The slope is slight, indicating that the probability of getting it right does not differ much among people of different ability levels. It suggests an ambiguous item.

Parameter invariance is not absolute. The zero point on the θ scale is commonly set at the sample mean, and the range from −3.0 to +3.0 depends on sample variability; the computed values of the parameters will actually be different for samples differing in mean or variance. The shapes of the IRCs will be congruent, however, and the scale used in one sample can be transformed by a simple linear equation to the scale used in the other; parameters set on one scale can be transformed to the other scale. An illustration is shown in Figure 6.8. A regression equation of $B' = 1.11A + 0.6$ permits the transformation of b parameters in Group A to the scale for b parameters computed in Group B; the correlation for these data is .989—a good but not unusual correlation. In this sense, parameters are said to be invariant within a linear transformation.

The correlations between b parameters calculated in different samples can be expected routinely to exceed .95. Correlations for the other parameters are lower, dipping to .30

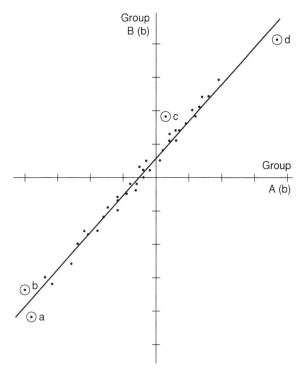

FIG. 6.8 Scatter plot of *b* values for 40 items computed independently in two hypothetical samples.

and below for the *c* parameter. The relative unreliability of *c* estimates is not surprising; the number of cases at the extremely low end of the ability distribution is quite small even in a large sample. For that reason, it is usually recommended that *c* be set at a common value or constrained not to exceed a given value (such as .25 on a four-option multiple choice examination).

Figure 6.8 identifies four items that are outliers, without which the correlation would be still higher. Items circled as *a* and *b* are extremely easy, and item *d* is extremely hard. Most test developers would consider deleting these items simply because they are so extreme. Item *c* is different. It is in a middle range of difficulty in both samples, but it is a whole lot more difficult in Group B than in Group A. Its *b* parameter is not invariant; the item functions differently in the two groups. Why? Feasible answers include the possibility that the item is biased against Group B, that it is ambiguous, that some group-related characteristic of test administration was especially important for the item—and others not yet thought of. Whatever the reason, the item does not have an invariant difficulty parameter and (I think) should be deleted from the test.

Alternative Models

If estimates of a *c* parameter are so unstable, why have them? If guessing or response bias is irrelevant to the trait measured, what value does a *c* parameter have? Questions like these, and the fact that for many measurement purposes the *c* parameter is not theoretically meaningful, have led many investigators to use two-parameter models, omitting the *c* parameter

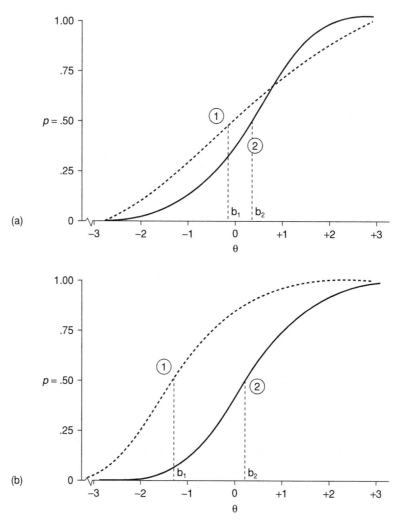

FIG. 6.9   Comparison of two-item examples of item response curves under (a) two-parameter model and (b) one-parameter model.

from Equation 6.4 by setting it equal to zero. The a and b parameters are the two IRC parameters estimated.

If parameters like c can be ignored, why not ignore another, such as a? Some investigators do, and others do for some purposes. The result is a single-parameter model in which only the difficulty parameter is computed. Figure 6.9 illustrates the difference between the two-parameter and one-parameter models. Part (a) of the figure shows the two-parameter model with two overlapping IRCs. Item 2 is considered more difficult because its point of inflection is at a higher point on the theta scale. (Note that, because $c = 0$, the value of b corresponds to $p = .5$.) It is also the more discriminating item because it has a steeper slope at that point. However, in the high ability range, the probability of a correct answer to Item 2 is greater than for Item 1, that is, Item 1 is harder for high-ability people. Stated differently, Item 1 is harder for some people and Item 2 is harder for others.

In contrast, in the one-parameter model shown in part (b), the relative difficulty of the two items remains the same; there is no crossing of the curves, and crossing is impossible under the assumption of equal discriminability.

The one-parameter model is also known as the Rasch model. It was developed independently by Georg Rasch (1980). Rasch's equation has been shown to be transformable to a logistic form in which there is no c parameter ($c = 0$) and a substitution permits the assumption of equal values of a across items (Hambleton, 1989). Despite the mathematical equivalence, most proponents prefer to call it the Rasch model rather than the one-parameter logistic to distinguish it from the family of logistic models.

There is ample reason to consider it independently, beyond the fact that it was independently developed. The logic of the Rasch model is not merely that a three-parameter model can be simplified, but that the Rasch model, and not a two- or three-parameter model, truly promotes objectivity in psychological measurement. According to the Rasch model, the unweighted sum of the number of items a person answers correctly will suffice to measure the trait for that person; moreover, it is the only latent trait model consistent with scoring tests in terms of the number items answered correctly (Wright, 1977, p. 102). Wright criticized the "guessing parameter" as confounding item characteristics and person characteristics and the a parameter for permitting IRCs to cross, contending that it is not truly objective measurement if one item is more difficult than another for some people and easier for others.

Logically, these points are well taken. Empirically, however, and in practical assessment use, some items do tend to promote successful guessing, and items do in fact frequently differ in discrimination power. My view is that the question is an empirical one. Using the three-parameter model will show whether the two less reliable parameters (a and c) differ to any important degree from equality or zero. When the differences are not substantial, the logically and mathematically simpler Rasch model may be chosen, and items not conforming to it may be deleted.

Test Characteristic Curves

A *test characteristic curve* (TCC) can be computed or drawn as an average of the IRCs of its individual items. For any given level of θ, the mean probability of a correct response can be determined across the set of items; it is an *expected true score*, defined as the expected proportion of right answers for people at the θ level of ability.

If the TCC is steep, meaning that the test as a whole distinguishes well between people of different ability, true score variance is high. If the curve is shallow, the true score distribution will have less variance, and people with similar true scores may differ a good bit on underlying ability. If there is a specific region of ability within which test scores should distinguish ability levels as much as possible, items from a calibrated pool can be chosen for maximum discrimination at the desired levels.

If item parameters are invariant across different distributions of ability, it follows that TCCs would stay the same regardless of ability distributions. Ironson, Guion, and Ostrander (1982) demonstrated this by dividing a set of more than 1000 cases into two groups. One, a high-ability group, consisted of 350 cases scoring above the median and 167 further cases selected at random from the full distribution. The other, a low-ability group, consisted of the remaining 518 cases, most scoring below the median. This created two distributions, one positively skewed and the other negatively skewed; the overlap was deliberate to match realistic distributions rather than make the more dramatic comparison of those above versus those below the median. Despite substantial distributional differences, the two resulting TCCs were very nearly identical.

Test and Item Information Functions

The concept of reliability is replaced in IRT by the concepts of item and test information. IRT seems to offer a better way to think about reliability problems, especially those associated with the classical concept of the standard error of measurement. Internal consistency is not much of a problem in tests constructed by IRT analyses. Many of the relevant computer programs use iterative models, alternately estimating person and item parameters. If items do not form an internally consistent whole, the iterative processes may take a long time to converge.

In classical test theory, the standard error of measurement (SEM) is a generalized index of the precision of measurement, that is, the degree to which error around a value is constricted. It is score-based, depending on both the sample of examinees and the sample of items used, and it can be considered a kind of average of SEMs at the different scores levels throughout the distribution. IRT indicates the precision of measurement at different ability levels through the *item information function*, a function indicating the degree of precision at any given value of θ. Each IRC has a corresponding information curve; see Figure 6.10. For any value of θ, the amount of information (the value of the information function at that point, the opposite of *un*reliability) is proportional to the square of the slope of the item's IRC. Note that the IRT and CTT approaches to measurement precision are conceptually quite different. Classical reliability begins with components of total score variances attributable to true variance (including other systematic variance) and random error variance. IRT starts at the item level and is concerned about imprecision (the effect of error, whether random or systematic) at every trait level and in responses to every item.

At points on the IRC where the slope is slight, the information level is low. Where the slope is steep, the information level is high. (The actual value of the information function also depends on the conditional variance, *pq*, at that value of θ.) Thus, in Figure 6.10, the information functions of both items peak at the point of steepest slope (the point of inflection) of their IRCs, and information is particularly high for Item 2 for high-ability people.

Not everyone with a specified level of theta has the same obtained score. We are dealing with probabilities. Even someone with a probability of .9 that he or she will answer an item correctly may get it wrong. Even if someone has a low probability of getting an item right, the item may call for information he or she just happens to have. Because of such happenstance, obtained scores are not mere transformations of theta; measurement is imprecise, subject to error. The extent of imprecision in overall test scores can be estimated from the *test information function*. A test information curve is obtained by summing, not averaging, the item information functions. Test information is inversely proportional to the classical SEM, but unlike the SEM, it can be estimated at any given value of θ. For a θ associated with a high level of test information, the expected true score will be approximated closely by the obtained score.

More technical detail about IRT may be found in chapters by Drasgow and Hulin (1990), Ellis and Mead (2002), Hambleton (1989), or Reise and Waller (2002) or in books by Embretson and Reise (2000), or McDonald (1999) among other sources.

Applications of Item Response Theory

Validity questions are not removed by using IRT, but finding that items fit an IRT model is pretty useful evidence of psychometric validity. It is rather difficult to obtain a set of items that fit the model chosen without having a fairly clear idea of the nature of the construct

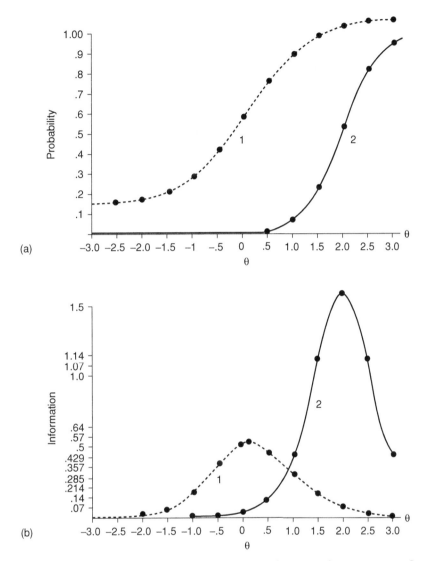

FIG. 6.10 (a) Two item response curves and (b) their corresponding item information curves. Reprinted from Guion, R. M., and Ironson, G. M. (1983). Latent trait theory for organizational research. *Organizational Behavior and Human Performance, 31*, 54–87. © Elsevier Science and Technology Journals; reprinted with permission.

and without preparing items with that theory of the attribute in mind. It may be assumed, therefore, that most items in an **IRT** pool do in fact tap the construct to some degree. If the history of the development of the item pool makes that assumption reasonable, then the method can be trusted to weed out items that do not fit the intended construct.

Computerized Adaptive Testing

Think of an examinee on one side of a table and a test administrator, with a very large deck of cards, on the other. Each card has on it a test item and, in ink visible only to the test administrator, the item's b parameter and information at that level. The administrator chooses an item where $b = 0$. If the examinee answers it correctly, the administrator chooses a second, harder item with a positive b value. If the first answer is wrong, the second item chosen is easier. A few more items are similarly chosen to identify the likely region of θ. Then a few more items are chosen having maximum information in that region. The result can be a very precise estimate of θ for that person with only a few, carefully chosen items.

The scenario is unlikely. The idea of someone sitting with a large deck of cards picking out items defines boredom. The scenario is not at all unlikely, however, if the examiner is a computer and the cards are entries in its data bank. A computer program can do, almost instantly, precisely what I have described. The result is called computer adaptive testing (see, e.g., Wainer et al., 1990), discussed further in Chapter 11.

Rating Scales

The discussion so far has emphasized testing, with occasional wording to recognize that IRT is applicable to other forms of measurement, ratings among them. Models are available for graded scales such as the common five-point response scales, for nominal response categories (e.g., county of residence), or continuous scales such as work quality.

Rating scales are used for many purposes. Performance in general may be assessed by performance rating scales completed by a supervisor or peers. Performance on a simulation, work sample, or business game might be rated by observers; judges may be asked to rate products of work samples or simulations. The use of an appropriate IRT model can identify the kinds of observational items that distinguish performance at different levels very well and have maximal information at critical scale levels. Adaptive rating scales, analogous to adaptive testing, have been developed with IRT for managerial performance measures (Schneider, Goff, Anderson, & Borman, 2003).

Analysis of Bias and Adverse Impact

IRT is useful for EEO concerns because item parameter estimation is independent of the ability distribution in the sample studied. If the trait measured is not itself correlated with sex, race, or idiosyncrasies of a particular culture, then subgroups based on sex, race, or culture should yield the same invariant IRC parameters within linear transformations. IRT analysis is in fact sometimes used to identify items that function differently in different demographic subgroups. Differential item functioning is a frequent topic in the study of bias and is discussed in Chapter 9.

Adverse impact needs to be reexamined in the light of principles in IRT and other modern measurement approaches. The 80% rule for defining adverse impact is subject to many criticisms, among them that it fails to distinguish between adverse impact ratios (AIRs) due to bias, those due to unequal recruiting practices, and those due to genuine differences in the trait measured. One method suggested for reducing adverse impact when the 80% rule suggests adverse impact is to use a procedure with less adverse impact. The suggestion is seriously flawed, not the least flaw being that a measure chosen to measure a trait rationally hypothesized to predict an important criterion is often replaced by a measure of another trait not fitting any well-developed hypothesis. More technically, the flaw lies in the failure to assure measurement equivalence (or measurement invariance). In IRT, equivalent measurement requires essentially the same TCC parameters. (Meade et al., 2008, advocated CFA for the purpose.) Significance tests replacing the 80% rule are also flawed, especially where

TABLE 6.4
Selection Ratios and Adverse Impact Ratios for a Hypothetical Case

Basis for Decision	Proportion Selected[a]		Adverse Impact
	Group 1	Group 2	Ratio
True ability	.72	.62	.86
Method A	.76	.58	76[b]
Method B	.67	.67	1.00

[a] Assume all "qualified" candidates are selected. [b] Adverse impact under the 80% rule. Reprinted from "Adverse impact from a psychometric perspective" by Ironson, G. H., Guion, R. M., and Ostrander, M. (1982), *Journal of Applied Psychology, 67*, p. 420. Copyright 1982 by the American Psychological Association. Reprinted by permission.

multiple demographic groups are to be compared or where the comparisons are made in multiple locations; in these cases, the statistical probability of "finding adverse impact" increases dramatically when in fact no true differences exist between groups (cf. Roth, Bobko, & Switzer, 2006), simply because measurement is not equivalent—scores do not mean the same things—in the groups compared.

An AIR depends on candidate sample characteristics that change from sample to sample and from time to time; it is therefore unstable. To repeat, AIRs do not consider true population differences. Table 6.4 illustrates the problem. If we knew the true ability distributions, we would know that Group 1 has a higher proportion of qualified candidates than does Group 2. Selection ratios based on true abilities would be truly different, although the AIR would be greater than 80%. In classical procedures, we can estimate true test scores but this is not at all an estimate of true trait level. Table 6.4 does have two different methods of measuring the ability, and we can assume that they have hypothetically magnificent psychometric validity—and give fallible results anyway. Method A results in adverse impact under the 80% rule; Method B does not (Ironson et al., 1982). But is Method B truly superior? Observed selection ratios under either method differ only trivially, yet only Method A implies adverse impact. In fact, it can be argued that Method B adversely affects employment opportunities in Group 1 because it fails to recognize Group 1's greater likelihood of having truly qualified members. We revisit this article and its implications in Chapter 9.

Using IRT logic, Ironson et al. (1982) argued that adverse impact should be defined in terms of the distortion—the overstatement or understatement—of any actual subgroup ability differences *at the ability level where decisions are made*. (The emphasis in that statement is to counter the frequency with which researchers have spuriously and erroneously assumed that differences between subgroup means indicate adverse impact.) The basis for the Ironson argument lies in the relationship of expected true scores to theta, and it recognizes and tests the possibility of true trait differences between groups. Depending on the TCC, a subgroup score difference may either exaggerate a true difference or understate or even hide true differences. To illustrate, four examples of distortions of true mean differences are shown in Figure 6.11. In the top half of the figure, the two tests compared have identical subgroup means but different TCC slopes. Test A, with the steeper mid-range slope, exaggerates true ability differences; Test B, with a relatively slight slope, constant throughout the ability range, minimizes those differences. In the lower half of Figure 6.11, the slopes are the same, but subgroup test means differ. Test C is easier than Test D. An easy test masks true differences; a hard test exaggerates them.

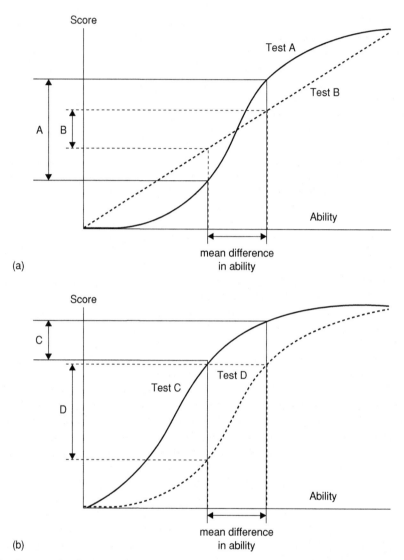

FIG. 6.11 Distorted reflections of true ability differences between groups using different tests when (a) tests are equated for ability but differ in slopes of their test characteristic curves, and (b) tests are of unequal ability but have test characteristic curves with identical slopes. Reprinted from Ironson, G. H., Guion, R. M., and Ostrander, M. (1982). *Journal of Applied Psychology, 67,* 419–432. Copyright 1982 by American Psychological Association. Reprinted with permission.

These TCC effects generally hold true in any specified test score range, but they are important mainly in the range where actual employment decisions are made. Discussion of subgroup mean differences in these illustrations of distortion is merely a convenience, unrelated to a either a legal or a psychometric definition of adverse impact. Adverse impact depends on the level of scores where decisions are made. If one is trying very hard to maintain or improve workforce quality, the region of decision is in the above average ability range. If one is trying to fill as many positions as possible while maintaining some minimal sense of standards, the region of decision is lower. In either case, it is the distortion of proportional differences at a specific ability or score level that defines adverse impact, not the distortion at the level of group means. This psychometric approach to defining adverse impact has attracted almost no attention, but now that more IRT studies are being done, and with better software, it may become more feasible as well as technically preferable.

CONCLUDING NOTE

The methods described here have been used more in theory-testing research and in test development than in practical personnel selection programs. Except for simple, exploratory factor analysis, little in this chapter has been widely used in personnel selection. That is unfortunate; those who fail to get familiar with up-to-date, modern psychometric theories and methods condemn themselves to mediocrity in personnel research. Without knowledge of the purposes, points of view, logic, and language of relatively new theories and methods, they will continue to use old, traditional approaches to measurement and other assessments.

Personnel decisions should be based on assessments of characteristics rationally hypothesized to be important to job performance and other relevant behavior at work—the predictors in predictive hypotheses. The assessments, however made, should be evaluated critically—and often comparatively. Chapters 5 and 6 have focused on ideas and procedures for the evaluation of tests and other assessment procedures. They have both emphasized, in particular, the essential and evolving concept of measurement error. It has evolved from a concept of essentially random error producing unreliability to the broader concept of multiple sources of error, whether consistent or inconsistent. For systematic error to be taken seriously, traits must be clearly defined, and methods of assessment must be designed explicitly for them, applying jointly the relevant substantive theory and psychometric methods (Embretson, 1985). With no theory to define a construct and distinguish it from others, the necessary item properties are not adequately identified, and the descriptive value of a test presumed to measure it cannot be fully evaluated.

Design and evaluation have been more demanding for tests than for other methods of assessment. Nevertheless, principles developed for testing apply as well to other forms of assessment: constructs should be specified, assessment procedures should be relevant to those constructs, and the resulting scores should be influenced by avoidable error as little as possible. Evaluation of any assessment procedure must focus on the permissible inferences to be drawn from scores, whether relational or descriptive; they are inferences about the people being assessed, not about the assessment tool. The research methods and the concepts and issues that led to them are, at all levels, intended to make score-based inferences more justifiable—or more justifiably abandoned.

For many people, the notion of a construct is mysterious, grand to the point of grandiose, and something identified only after extensive research. As pointed out earlier, a construct may be little more then an idea about how people differ in some important way, it should have enough unity (without necessarily being unidimensional) that transitivity is conceptually sensible, and it should be distinguishable from other constructs about how people might differ. Even Cronbach (1980) disavowed the most highfalutin concepts of constructs and construct validity, which he, with Meehl, had introduced in a less mysterious form (Cronbach & Meehl, 1955).

Factor analysis and related approaches to identifying dimensionality in measurement are tools of description, describing the several constructs that might influence a test score. Generalizability analysis is a tool for clarifying description by identifying potential contaminants of trait descriptions and by identifying the limits of generalizability of descriptive statements. Item response theory is a tool for examining psychometric properties of responses to items that have "substantive properties" relevant to the descriptive construct being measured (Embretson, 1985, p. 4). In short, the topics touched on in Chapter 6 augment those of Chapter 5 because they have introduced further, perhaps better, ways to evaluate descriptive inferences from numerical results of assessments. They are important additions to the personnel testing portfolio, and they should be used more often than they are.

So far, however, the discussion has centered on psychometric understanding more than on prediction. The next two chapters focus more on statistical tools for evaluating relational or predictive inferences.

7

Bivariate Prediction of Performance

If the criterion predicted is organizationally sound, the most important single fact about an assessment method is its predictive validity. A validity coefficient is proportional to predictive accuracy. Higher coefficients are associated with greater accuracy, meaning less error in prediction—the essence of relational validity. Correlation is *proportional* to predictive accuracy, but *only* proportional, not a direct measure of it—a fact too often ignored in personnel research. The employment process is future-oriented, and I think evaluating predictive accuracy—the match of predicted to actual performance in a cumulative record—is at least as important as evaluating the degree of co-variation of assessments and performance. Traditional criterion-related validation[1] computes a coefficient of co-relationship. If it considers the question of predictive accuracy, it settles for computing the standard error of estimate (discussed later). Even that is rarely reported, and it says nothing about the magnitude of error when it is.

The two previous chapters emphasized the validity of interpreting scores as measures of something—psychometric validity. This one and the next emphasize the validity of interpreting scores as predictions of something—relational validity, that is, the strength of the relationship between predictor scores and the particular criterion used in the analysis.

If the criterion is job-related rather than construct-related, this concept of validity differs from that described in Chapter 5 as psychometric validity. With a job-related criterion, validation is an evaluation of the job-relatedness of the predictor. The term *criterion-related validity* serves as an index (but not a measure) of the accuracy of the statistical predictions based on a specified regression equation.

Criterion-related validation answers two basic questions. First, what *kind* of relationship exists between a predictor and the criterion predicted? This question is answered by a regression line, straight or curved, or an equation. Second, what is the *degree* of relationship? Is there any relationship at all? How strong is it? Is it strong enough to be important? How accurate are predictions based on it? Except for that last question, which does not get much attention in this chapter,[2] answers are based on validity coefficients and associated regression

---

[1] Occasionally, someone will abbreviate the term "criterion-related validity" and speak or even write about "criterion validity." This vulgarization of language causes mischief in communication and should be avoided; logically, "criterion validity" refers to the validity of a criterion, i.e., to the psychometric evaluation of a criterion measure, *not* to the statistical concept of the degree of relationship between a criterion and another variable (or collection of variables) that predicts it.

[2] My friend Frank Landy said recently that my style is that of a common scold. My comments in this chapter about predictive accuracy will verify his description.

functions, used in tandem to show the nature and strength of a relationship—even if gremlins lurk in the validity evidence.

This chapter considers only *bivariate prediction*, the prediction of one variable *Y* from another variable *X* (although either may be a composite of related variables). The use of just one predictor is not likely to be optimal. It may even be seriously deficient, but the simple bivariate case illustrates most of the relevant statistical issues.

VALIDATION AS HYPOTHESIS TESTING

Bivariate criterion-related validation directly tests the predictive hypothesis that a criterion *Y* is a function, mathematically, of a predictor *X*. There are many ways to test a predictive hypothesis (Landy, 1986), but bivariate analysis offers a way to begin exploring validation and its meaning. A close look at the problems and procedures of bivariate validation aids understanding of other ways to evaluate assessments for personnel decisions. Moreover, bivariate validation provides building blocks for more comprehensive procedures.

The first, essential requirement for good criterion-related validation is a well-chosen, well-measured criterion. Further, it must be important to the organization and to the decisions to be made, have substantial variance, and be reliably and validly measured—requirements often overlooked in the habit of using any available criterion. Statistical validation should not merely assume that the criterion measure is valid. The psychometric validity of inferences from it should be evaluated using the same principles (Chapters 5 and 6) used to evaluate other measures.

Generalizing from a research sample to an applicant population requires caution. Part of the problem is that sample size keeps shrinking as an inevitable result of realism; Kirchner and Dunnette (1959) described the situation resulting in a sample of roughly half of a delightful potential of 862 sales applicants—without getting into the problem of dividing those remaining into different kinds of sales jobs or company division subgroups. Research samples are rarely drawn randomly, as many statistical procedures assume, and they might not even be clearly representative of a plausible population in the Brunswikian sense (Brunswik, 1956). Figure 7.1 illustrates how an actual research sample can be somehow biased simply by the chain of events in the employment process. The outer circle represents all plausible applicants—an applicant population. Some job seekers are not interested in the open job or in the location; others would be disqualified on a basis other than test scores. These are not plausibly part of the applicant population. A plausible population might include serious job seekers within a defined commuting distance, those who might be at least marginally qualified, interested, and looking for work. The dot in the center represents a mean statistic in that population. Only some of those in this imagined population will present themselves for consideration, and collectively they may differ substantially from the population. Not all of them will actually be tested, and of those tested, only a subset—certainly not a representative subset—will be hired (even if scores on the assessment do not influence hiring decisions), and it is unlikely that all of these will stay on the job and provide criterion data. At each stage in this progression, the ever shrinking sample may be as far off center as each circle in Figure 7.1. Nonrandom forces are likely to determine the composition of the group at each step, so a research sample is usually biased to some unidentified degree. The sources of bias may not be known and, therefore, the researcher cannot know what to do about them. Researchers should try to specify and match as well as possible

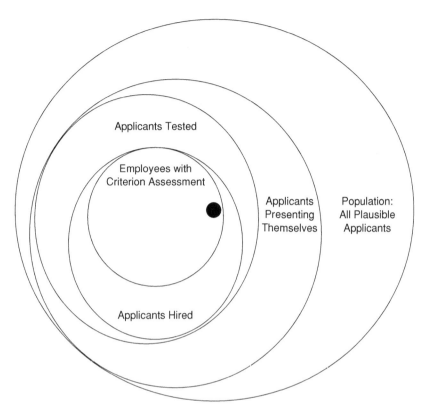

FIG. 7.1   Chain of events in assessment and hiring that can lead to bias in a research sample.

the defining characteristics of the population to which their results should generalize, but they must also acknowledge that the research sample is not likely to match the applicant population precisely.

The research procedures should also match the way the predictor will be used in practice. Most validation assumes a one-stage decision process when, in fact, most decisions involve two or more stages. In such cases representation of the total applicant population is inappropriate; second-stage samples should be representative of those who pass the first hurdle (De Corte, Lievens, & Sackett, 2006).

BIVARIATE REGRESSION

Regression refers to the clustering of measures around a central point. A *scatterplot*, graphically showing a point for each pair of X and Y values, will show a distribution of Y values for any given value of X. Values of Y for each X are distributed about a central point; usually, most of them are near that central point. It is convenient to think of the scatterplot as divided into columns and of distributions of Y within columns as normal, around the column mean or some other designated central point.

If the two variables are related, the central point in each column changes systematically with changes in the predictor variable. The pattern of change can be shown graphically with a smoothed regression line or curve that describes the relationship.[3] The pattern can also be described algebraically with a functional equation, $Y = f(X)$, stating that Y is a function of X. Of the many possible functions, some may fit the data better than others. The central points are identified by the equation, line, or curve used to describe the relationship; prediction is based on the central point of that equation, line, or curve for a given score.

Performance of those who score high on the predictor is usually better than that of those whose scores are low. This general statement is based on the typically reasonable assumption that the relationship is *positive* and *monotonic*. A relationship is positive if higher predictor scores are associated with higher criterion scores. It is monotonic if that statement (or the converse negative statement) is true throughout the predictor score distribution. It is both positive and monotonic if the central points in the criterion distributions are consistently higher for successively higher values of the predictor—if the smoothed curve always goes up, even if only a little bit in some places.[4] If the functional relationship is both positive and monotonic, more of X implies more of Y throughout the score range. If the relationship is negative and monotonic, more of X implies less of Y throughout the range.

If specific criterion levels are to be predicted, the *kind* of relationship may be empirically determined, or may be only assumed. Two different kinds of positive, monotonic relationship

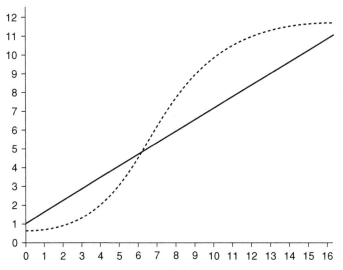

FIG. 7.2   Straight line (linear) and curved (curvilinear) regression for predicting a criterion from scores on a predictor.

---

[3] It may be some kind of discontinuity, not smooth. The statistical training of psychologists is typically limited to functional equations in which the graph of the equation is smooth—a smooth straight line or a smooth curve. As a rule, the possibility of discontinuous relationships is ignored. There may be a threshold ability level that must be reached before any functional relationship can be found, and at the threshold, perhaps, the predicted performance level might jump from nearly zero to some low but distinctly nonzero level. Such thinking is purely speculative, but not necessarily foolish speculation. Such discontinuities, if found, might provide a rational basis for minimum cutting scores.

[4] The emphasis on the smoothed curve is because random variations occur in the pattern of column means (commonly used as central points); literally connecting them ordinarily yields a jagged pattern. When I refer to a consistent increase, I refer to the trend of change in central points in a functional equation or in a smoothed line or curve.

are shown in Figure 7.2. The equation for the straight line relationship is $Y = 0.6X + 1.0$. In a linear relationship, the incremental difference in predicted values of Y for successive values of X is constant throughout the range of scores in X. In the straight line in Figure 7.2, a difference of 1 point in X is always matched by a difference of 0.6 in the predicted value of Y.

The broken line curve in Figure 7.2 describes a different kind of relationship. I have not determined the equation for it, although it could be done. This is a simple freehand curve, drawn to represent a smoothed pattern approximating the mean values of Y for narrow intervals of X. Using such a curve, predicted values of Y differ very little for different values of X in either the low or the high end of the X scale, but the predicted values of Y differ a great deal from one score to the next in the midrange of the X scale. The curve is not fanciful. A similar curve was hypothesized and found by LaHuis, Martin, and Avis (2005).

Linear Functions

In the general linear regression equation, $Y = a + bX$, the constant b is the *slope* of the line, the incremental increase in Y with each unit increase in X, and a is the Y *intercept*, the expected value of Y when X equals zero. Values of a and b (the parameters of the equation) can be determined for a given data set by solving a simple pair of simultaneous equations:

$$\Sigma Y = Na + b\Sigma X$$
$$\Sigma XY = a\Sigma X + b\Sigma X^2 \tag{7.1}$$

In personnel research, linear regression is typically assumed and rarely questioned. Some justifications frequently offered for assuming linearity are:

1. In computations based on the same data set, the linear regression constants, a and b, and the associated statistics such as correlation coefficients, are more reliable (vary less across samples) than their counterparts in nonlinear equations.
2. Linear regression is "robust"; its relevant statistics, a and b, do not seem to fluctuate much from sample to sample even where data violate the basic assumptions.[5]
3. Evidence of nonlinear relationships is relatively rare, maybe because it is rarely sought. Hawk (1970) and Coward and Sackett (1990) found them with about chance frequency in studies of the Generalized Aptitude Test Battery (GATB). Currently, researchers are more likely to consider nonlinearity and finding and reporting it, and citing supportive research in other kinds of data sets (Benson & Campbell, 2007; LaHuis et al., 2005; Tupes, 1964).
4. Some nonlinear functions can be transformed to linear ones (e.g., with logarithmic transformations).
5. Departure from linearity may exist without being important. The curve in Figure 7.3, for example, is slightly higher than the straight line for values of X from 3 to 9; it is slightly lower at each end of the X distribution. The two regression patterns do not differ dramatically in midrange values of X; the largest difference is about .5 on the Y scale. (For some criteria, this could be an important difference; for others it may not be.)

---

[5] The assumptions are linearity of regression, normal distributions of X and Y, errors are not correlated with either variable or across the variables, and homoscedasticity, meaning equal Y variances in the different values of X. These will be discussed further later in the chapter.

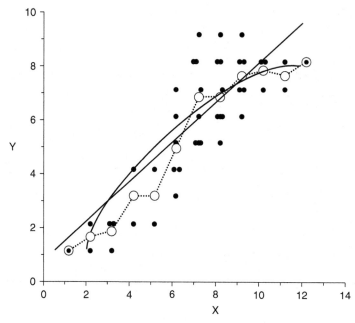

FIG. 7.3 Straight line and free-hand curve fitted to common data (hypothetical). Column means are circled and connected by a jagged regression line.

6. Correlation coefficients based on the linear assumption are required in many statistical analyses following bivariate validation. Multiple regression, factor analysis, meta-analysis, and utility analysis are a few examples of procedures that are usually based on linear regression for bivariate components.

Nonlinear Regression

Nevertheless, it is silly to assume linearity automatically, without further thought. Scatterplots should be routinely examined for regression patterns. A nonlinear pattern may fit better and make more sense. Ghiselli (1964) reported a nonlinear regression that withstood several cross-validations. With such a finding, there is little reason to use a repeatedly inferior linear regression, especially if the curve makes good sense.

An Example

Consider Figure 7.4; each part plots the data in Table 7.1. The criterion Y is based on supervisory ratings of performance expressed in standard scales (mean = 50); the predictor X is the score on a vocabulary test. The best fitting linear regression in (a) is nearly horizontal. No matter what the test score, the performance predicted by the linear equation is about the same (Guion, 1965a). The same scatterplot is repeated in part (b), where it is marked off in columns. An x in each column shows the mean rating and mean test score for the column. A freehand curve was drawn to smooth out the jagged line connecting those column means. Low-scoring people tend to get low ratings—and so do high-scoring people. The highest ratings go to those with moderate test scores, the so-called *inverted-U* effect.

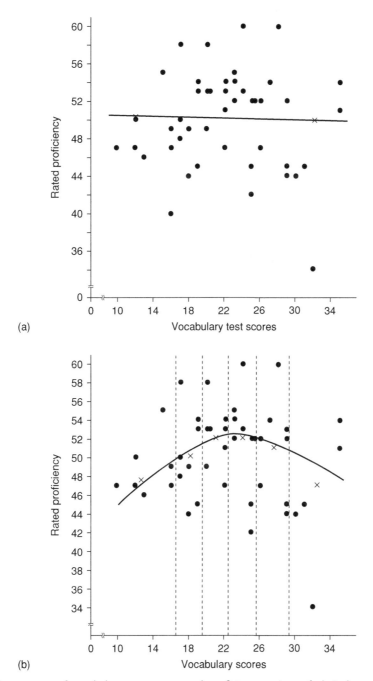

FIG. 7.4 Scattergram of vocabulary test scores and proficiency ratings of clerical workers in the home office of a large organization: (a) the best fitting linear regression; (b) a smoothed, freehand curve approximating column means. © R. M. Guion, 1965.

TABLE 7.1

Vocabulary Score and Rated Proficiency of Office Workers

X[a]	Y[b]	X	Y	X	Y	X	Y	X	Y
19	45	22	54	16	40	12	47	10	47
24	53	29	45	30	44	23	55	29	53
15	55	23	52	17	58	22	53	26	52
22	47	26	47	35	51	31	45	16	49
24	60	28	60	25	52	20	53	29	52
23	56	25	52	17	48	20	53	12	50
18	49	13	46	22	51	27	54	25	42
29	44	19	54	17	50	32	34	16	47
20	58	18	44	20	49	35	54	25	45
19	53								

[a] Scores on the word meaning section of the Purdue Clerical Adaptability Test. [b] Supervisory ratings of job proficiency two years after hire. From *Personnel Testing* (p. 133), by R. M. Guion, 1965. © R. M. Guion.

Does such a relationship make sense? It can. If authoritarian enough, supervisors may be annoyed by subordinates who are brighter than they—and give them lower ratings than they deserve. If so, the ratings are not valid and the predictions are questionable. On the other hand, inferences of proficiency based on these ratings may be valid, but the job may require only moderate verbal intelligence. People with low scores may not have enough verbal ability to do the job well; those with high scores may be too bored by it to do it well. This is plausible in the small community where these data were gathered. No other employer paid as well, so overqualified people may have stayed but worked perfunctorily.

In such a situation, nonlinear regression should not be accepted without replication and without considering the relative reasonableness of proffered explanations. If results were replicated, and if evidence that the ratings were valid was strong, then a hiring strategy might prefer those with moderate scores, hiring only enough high-scoring people to provide a pool from which promotions might later be made. This is a situation where decisions could be based on more than one prediction, considering both the prediction of rated performance and a prediction of the likelihood of staying on the first job long enough to be considered for promotion.

A different example, reported by Benson and Campbell (2007), also found the inverted-U effect. It was done in a large multinational firm with more than 300 managers. Predictors were scales of the Hogan Development Survey (HDS), a set of 11 scales for assessing the *dark side* of personality. Two composite scores were *moving away from people* (withdrawal or avoidance) and *moving against people* (dominant and intimidating behavior). Criteria were five leadership performance ratings, aggregated across two groups of raters. The relationship of the moving-against composite to each of the five performance factors was consistently in the inverted-U form.

Departures from Linearity

Revisit Figure 3.2, showing some curve types to compare to linear regression. If freehand curves seem somehow unscientific, one can fit exact regression equations (Ezekiel, 1941;

Guilford, 1954; Lewis, 1960).[6] However, it is not necessary to compute equation parameters precisely when data sets are large enough that decision rules based on freehand curves differ only trivially from those based on statistically fit curves.

Polynomial trend analyses (cf. Pedhazur & Schmelkin, 1991) are used by many researchers to consider possible departures from linearity. A first-order polynomial is a simple linear equation with the term bX. A second-order polynomial is the same equation plus an additional term, cX^2, a quadratic equation describing a parabolic function where the curve bends once. A third-order polynomial adds yet another term, dX^3, a cubic function with two bends. Each term raises X to a higher power and has its own constant. The more "bends" in the curve, the higher the power of the final term. Trend analysis determines the portion of total criterion variance explained at each polynomial level. If a trend (e.g., linear or quadratic) accounts for enough variance (by the researcher's standards), the analysis stops. If not, the analysis continues by determining the additional variance contributed by the next trend level.

Trend analysis is popular, but I do not use it. I consider the nature and accuracy of the predictive function more important than the variance it may explain. For example, in most monotonic relationships, a linear trend accounts for most of the variance, but a well-fitting curve may be a more useful decision tool, even when accounting for little of the remaining variance, if it works more effectively at some score levels than the linear trend—and is replicated.

Logistic Functions

In item response theory, an item response curve based on a logistic function describes the probability of a correct answer at specific ability levels. A similar logistic function relating ability (as measured by test score) to the probability of achieving a specified level of success on a specified job describes a *job characteristic curve* (Raju, Steinhaus, Edwards, & DeLessio, 1991). With a two-parameter logistic regression model of the relationship of ability to the probability of job success, they found that the proportion of people at each score level actually classified as successful was quite close to the predicted proportion. Of course, a single report by itself does not demonstrate generalizable value of logistic regression. I mention it because (a) the logistic model has been useful in other applications and (b) it makes sense in personnel selection situations where applicants vary widely in predictor scores and where performance differences among those scoring very high or very low are likely to be trivial. In short, it is better to consider nonlinear functional relationships that make sense in a given situation than to assume linearity through mere force of habit.

Too many researchers automatically discount the possibility of nonlinear regression, either because linearity generally accounts for most of the variance in trend analysis or because linear regression has been so common in traditional studies of cognitive predictors. I consider the automatic rejection of nonlinearity, without so much as plotting the data, essentially unscientific. Benson and Campbell (2007) may agree; they considered it possible that the relationship of performance and noncognitive variables such as personality (especially its "dark side"), or the prediction of leadership performance, might be more complex than the simple linear model. In two studies, they found, and plotted, nonlinear, inverted-U regression. These two studies were reported together, but they used different personality measures and different settings, and quite different criteria. Such differences suggest that at least some generalizability can be found, even for nonlinear regression.

---

[6] I offer old references in the hope that readers will learn from them how to do something like fitting curves before relying solely on computer software to do it for them.

CONTINGENCY AND EXPECTANCY TABLES

Contingency Tables

Highly differentiated predictions are often unnecessary. Predicting a broad performance category (e.g., OK, good, excellent) from a contingency table may serve organizational purposes quite well. The example in Table 7.2 was created by merging and simplifying data from two actual situations in which job incumbents customize and install a technical product and help customers learn to use it. Training is self-paced through three levels; the criterion is the level reached within a specified period. The predictor is a four-category classification of prior work experience. The columns in Table 7.2 represent different categories of experience; rows represent training level reached. Each cell tells how many of those with a given category of experience actually reached a training level and how many (in parentheses) were expected to do so on the basis of marginal totals. Where the discrepancies between observed and chance cell frequencies are larger, the prediction is better. Customer service experience appears to be the best background for learning this job; about twice as many of those with that background, compared to candidates in other categories, completed Level 3 in the allotted time, and only two people (compared to theoretical frequency of 9) failed to go beyond Level 1. Neither technical nor sales experience seems very helpful, although people with a sales background have a good record of completing Level 2.

Contingency tables provide a practical compromise between an overly simplistic pass–fail use of predictors and statistical regression; broad categories rather than precise numerical values are predicted, but the categories are more informative than those in a simple dichotomy. Cell entries can be frequencies, percentages, or criterion means.

Expectancy Charts

Expectancy charts typically show the percentage of those scoring in a given interval who have been (or are predicted to be) in some sense successful on the job. The criterion is a

TABLE 7.2
Hypothetical Data for Prediction from Categorical Variables

| | Principal Experience Category | | | | | | | | | |
| Training level completed | Clerical | | Customer service | | Technical | | Sales | | Marginal total | |
	f^a	%	f	%	f	%	f	%	f	%
Level 3	3	12	15	56	9	25	5	20	**32**	**28**
	(7)		(8)		(10)		(7)			
Level 2	4	16	10	37	12	33	15	60	**41**	**36**
	(9)		(10)		(13)		(9)			
Level 1	18	72	2	7	15	42	5	20	**40**	**35**
	(9)		(9)		(13)		(9)			
Marginal Total	**25**	**100**	**27**	**100**	**36**	**100**	**25**	**100**	**113**	**99**

[a] The presumably observed frequencies are shown on the first line for each level. Below the "observed" frequency, in parentheses, is the chance frequency expected on the basis of marginal totals.

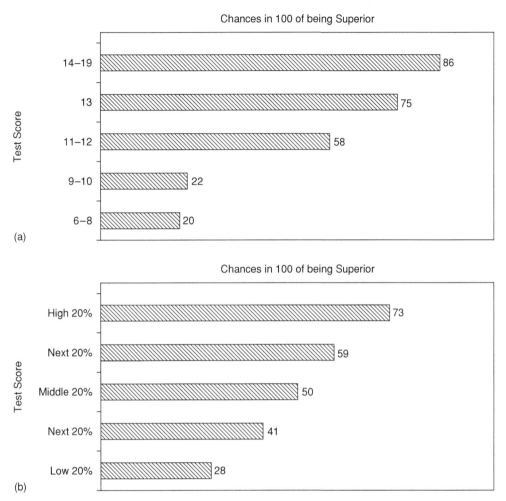

FIG. 7.5   Expectancy charts: (a) an empirical expectancy chart reporting obtained proportions; (b) a theoretical expectancy chart based on a bivariate normal distribution where r = .40. © R. M. Guion, 1965.

dichotomy—or artificially dichotomized continuous variable (e.g., superior vs. some category less than superior, satisfactory vs. not satisfactory). Three to six predictor intervals are typical. Intervals are usually chosen so that each interval contains about the same number of people. The expectancy chart in Figure 7.5(a) shows the likelihood or *expectancy* of success for people scoring in each interval, assuming that future people will pretty much repeat history. Data in (a) actually show past history; each bar in the bar graph shows the proportion of people in that score range (in the research sample) who actually did achieve a level of performance deemed superior. It is possible to use properties of correlation coefficients to produce a *theoretical* expectancy chart showing theoretical expectancies that are freed from the specific errors in the research sample, much like the smoothing of a regression line (Lawshe, Bolda, Brune, & Auclair, 1958; Guion, 1965a, 1998). The theoretical expectancy chart for the same data is in Figure 7.5(b).

Expectancy charts are useful for decision makers. They offer a sense of the kind and strength of the relationship. They do not demand understanding regression or correlation statistics, but they do promote understanding of the practical usefulness of predictors and offer help in making decisions about applicants. It's nice to report correlation coefficients to one's statistically trained colleagues, but most decision makers will be helped more by good visual presentations (see especially Wainer, 2005, for examples of both clarifying and misleading visual aids).

Group Mean Differences

Researchers often want to compare group means; the difference between the mean score in one group and the mean score in another may imply a correlation between the scores and group membership. Groups might be defined by performance quality. If Group A consists of superior performers and Group B consists of everyone else, one expects the mean test score in Group A to be higher than the mean score in Group B. The effect size is d, the mean z-score difference, and is discussed in more detail in Chapter 9.

MEASURES OF CORRELATION

A coefficient of correlation describes how closely two variables are related. It is based on the tightness with which criterion values cluster around the central points that define the regression function. Various kinds of correlation coefficient describe degrees of relationship; they may differ on the kinds of relationship assumed, on data distributions, or on kinds of measurement scales, but they have important common characteristics.

Basic Concepts in Correlation

Any coefficient of correlation is based on a specified regression pattern. If the pattern does not fit the data very well, but is assumed in computing a coefficient, the coefficient understates the relationship. The degree of understatement can range from trivial to dramatic.

If correlation is perfect, the research subjects have identical rank orders on predicted and actual criterion scores, and the scale distances between measures of any pair of people is the same on both scales. Perfect correlation is rare, even in cooked-up data; departures from perfection are expected. The lower the correlation, the greater is the prediction error. Regression functions permit prediction; correlation coefficients permit inferences about the degree of prediction error when prediction is based on the specified regression function.

Residuals and Errors of Estimate

A *residual* is the difference between the observed value of Y for an individual case and Y_c, the predicted criterion level for the value of X in that case; Y_c may be found from the regression equation or from a graph of it. If a less than optimal regression function is used, such as the linear pattern in Figure 7.4, the absolute mean and variance of the residuals will be relatively large. Anyone really interested in the accuracy of prediction will want to know both the absolute mean and variance of residuals, but neither gets reported very often.

A General Definition of Correlation

The basic defining equation for all correlation is

$$\text{Coeff} = \sqrt{1 - \frac{S_{res}^2}{S_y^2}} \qquad (7.2)$$

where "Coeff" is used in place of a more specifically identified coefficient to emphasize the generality of the equation, S_{res}^2 is the variance of the residuals, and S_y^2 is the total variance of Y. The coefficient of correlation is a measure of *effect size*, a general term used to indicate the strength of the effect of an independent variable in research. Most coefficients of correlation can range between 0 and +1.0; or 0 and −1.0, depending on whether high scores are associated with good or poor performance. A negative slope can be changed to positive by the simple expedient of reversing the scale of one of the variables, so this discussion of basics is limited to positive values. A coefficient of 1.0, then, indicates a perfect relationship in which every data point falls directly on the regression line or curve with no residuals at all. The ratio of residual variance to total variance indicates the degree of imperfection in the strength of relationship. If S_{res}^2 equals S_y^2, that ratio is 1.0 and the coefficient is 0.0.

Coefficients of Determination

If Equation 7.2 is squared (i.e., the square root is not taken), the result is the *coefficient of determination*. It estimates the proportion of shared variance in the two variables, typically expressed by saying that the proportion of variance in one of them (usually Y) is "accounted for by" the variance in the other. This means common or associated variance, but the usual parlance includes terms such as "variance explained by" or "variance accounted for" despite their unwarranted causal implication. Even the term itself—determination—inappropriately implies causation.

If a validity coefficient is .30 (not uncommon), the coefficient of determination is .09, or 9% common variance. Attorneys and their witnesses are fond of intoning in such a case that "less than 10% of the criterion variance is explained by the predictor," slurring over (or omitting) the word variance as if it were unimportant. Many researchers, too, are obsessed with coefficients of determination, as if they were meaningful measures of effect size. They are not.

Variance is important in statistics. Variances can be added; their square roots (standard deviations) cannot be. The standard deviation is more descriptive because it is a kind of average of individual differences. However, it has limited mathematical usefulness. You cannot add (or subtract, multiply, or divide) the standard deviation of one measure to the standard deviation of another because standard deviations are square roots of other numbers. It is true that $3 + 3 = 6$; it is equally true that $\sqrt{3} + \sqrt{3}$ is *not* equal to $\sqrt{6}$.

A correlation coefficient is a more useful description of co-relationship than common variance, and it *is* a measure of effect size. An even better descriptive statistic is the slope of the regression line; it is more meaningful because it gives the expected change in Y associated with a change in X (Pedhazur & Schmelkin, 1991, p. 380). Historically the validity coefficient was the end product, often the only product, of criterion-related validation. Researchers are now increasingly skeptical of a lone correlation coefficient as evidence of predictor value.

Third Variables

A further caveat is familiar: correlation says nothing about causation. It is easy but wrong to presume that the variable obtained first somehow produces the second one. To do so is to forget the third variable problem. Both the X and the Y may be effects of some common third variable or collection of variables. Gulliksen (1950a) gave a delightful example. He said that the number of storks' nests built each year in Stockholm correlated .90 with the annual birth rate in the city. Few people believe that storks bring babies, or vice versa, in Stockholm or elsewhere. The correlation is reliable, so one might speculate about third variables that may explain it, such as economic variation or perhaps the varying severity of winters. Other speculation is possible, but the only sure thing is that a causal interpretation of the correlation is wrong.

The Product–Moment Coefficient of Correlation

Most software statistical packages include procedures for computing *product–moment coefficients* (also known as Pearsonian coefficients). Different programs use slightly different equations, but all are derived from the basic product–moment definition:

$$r_{yx} = \frac{\sum z_x z_y}{n} \tag{7.3}$$

This basic equation looks simple but is too complex for practical purposes. It requires transforming every value of X and Y to z-scores (once called the "moments" of a distribution), multiplying each pair of z-scores, and finding the mean of the products. A more useful computational equation works from raw scores:

$$r_{yx} = \frac{n\sum XY - \sum X \sum Y}{\sqrt{[n\sum X^2 - (\sum X)^2][n\sum Y^2 - (\sum Y)^2]}} \tag{7.4}$$

where r_{yx} is the product–moment coefficient for the regression of Y on X, X and Y are the raw scores, and XY is the product of the raw scores, for each person, and n is the total number of cases (usually persons) in the sample studied. In correlational research, sample data are used to estimate population values. Several things influence a product–moment correlation coefficient. Some of them have statistical methods for estimating population values from sample statistics, including distributional statistics and the correlation coefficient, but most do not.

Intractable Sources of Error in Coefficients

The sources of error described here are "intractable" in the sense that no statistical corrections exist for them. Errors in obtained sample coefficients can be corrected statistically in some cases; such errors and corrections are discussed in the next section.

Nonlinearity

A product–moment correlation coefficient assumes linear regression. Operationally, it is not often an unreasonable assumption. However, to the degree the assumption is violated, the coefficient will underestimate the degree of relationship. Where evidence of nonlinearity is questionable or trivial, the linear assumption is still preferred, but the assumption needs to be checked. If it is violated seriously, the product–moment correlation will seriously understate the degree of relationship. The solution is to plot data and fit an appropriate curve.

Heteroscedasticity

It also assumes *homoscedasticity*, that is, equal residual variances (equal prediction error) in different segments of the population predictor distribution. If the outline of the scatterplot is approximately an oval, the assumption may not be seriously violated. Again, serious violations cause *serious* understatement of the relationship. The assumption of homoscedasticity is almost universally accepted without question, and the product–moment coefficient seems moderately immune to violations (Greener & Osburn, 1980). Ignoring the assumption, many researchers act as if residual variance were fixed throughout a distribution. It's not; an overall statement of residual variance is best considered an average of different residual variances in different score intervals.

Lord and Novick (1968) noted that violation of the assumption is likely. They considered *heteroscedasticity* (i.e., unequal residual variance) to be mainly a sign of nonlinearity; they considered logistic functions more likely than linear ones to fit real data. In personnel selection, a different and common source of nonlinearity, for which a logistic function is *not* a solution, is shown by a triangular scatterplot as in Figure 7.6. Note that the triangular pattern necessarily forces the regression to be nonlinear. The data are clearly heteroscedastic; residual variance is greater at high score levels than at lower scores. This happens if relative lack of a trait (e.g., an ability) prevents criterion effectiveness, but abundance of the trait makes effectiveness possible without assuring it.

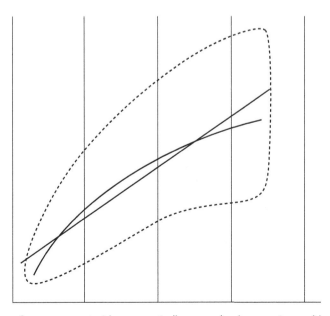

FIG. 7.6 Outline of a scattergram with systematically unequal column variances. Note especially that the triangular pattern forces nonlinearity of regression.

Heteroscedasticity can be a more serious problem than usually recognized because it can result in linear coefficients severely understating the predictive value of a hypothesized predictor. If the most critical decisions are made at low score ranges where residual error is least, the predictor may be more useful than the linear coefficient suggests. It may work the other way. If only top candidates are to be accepted (i.e., if hard decisions are to be made at the high end of the distribution where residual error is great), a correlation based on linear regression can be extremely misleading, suggesting continually increasing validity in score levels where, in fact, the predictor has stopped being useful.

Correlated Error

Measurement errors are assumed to be uncorrelated with each other and with scores on the two variables. If only random errors are meant, violations may have little effect on the correlation of reasonably reliable measures. Safeguards against major influences of correlated errors include both maximizing reliabilities of both measures and replicating studies in new samples.

Systematic errors of measurement are also assumed uncorrelated, and violations of this assumption create more serious problems. A source of systematic contamination common to both variables may produce a spurious increase in the coefficient, as shown in Figure 7.7. Area *a* (including area *d*) represents common test and criterion variance, which is the source of any criterion-related validity of the test scores. Area *b* (including area *d*) shows variance common to the test and a third variable. Area *c* (including area *d*) represents variance common to the criterion and the third variable. Area *d* represents variance common to all three measures. If it is very small (i.e., if variance common to all three is small), the third

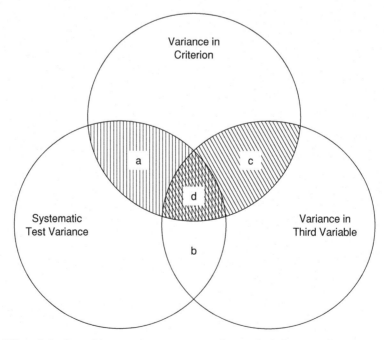

FIG. 7.7   Effect of third variable on test–criterion correlation; shaded areas indicate relative levels of common variance.

variable is no more than a minor nuisance. If area d is very large, however, it augments whatever common variance of test and criterion may exist, and the whole of third variable variance may account for more criterion variance than the test does. The larger that common variance, the greater is the difficulty in accepting the test as valid. The problem is that, looking only at the bivariate correlation, we never know how important "third" variables might be. Where correlated systematic error is plausible, generalizability theory (Chapter 6) can give more information than bivariate correlation can offer.

Extreme Distributions

Product–moment coefficients require no assumption about distributions, but some interpretations of them assume an underlying normal bivariate surface. Extreme skewness in one variable but not the other produces nonlinearity and consequent correlation reduction; in fact, any time the two distributions differ markedly in shape, correlation is markedly reduced (Edwards, 1976).

Questionable Data Points

Plotting data sometimes identifies one or more *outliers*. An outlier is a data point that stands out from the other data points and "may lead to serious distortion of results" (Pedhazur & Schmelkin, 1991, p. 398). Figure 7.8 illustrates two effects, exaggerated for emphasis. Outlier (a) spuriously reduces correlation if it is included in computing the coefficient; in a small sample, it could turn an apparent positive relationship to a negative one. Including outlier (b) would inflate the correlation.

Many personnel researchers believe that all data points should be retained in the analysis (cf. Orr, Sackett, & DuBois, 1991), but I think outliers should be investigated. Outliers

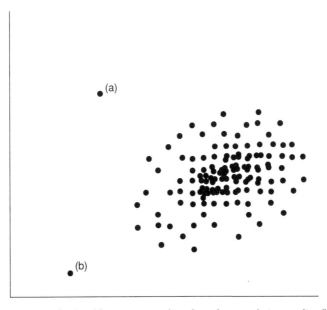

FIG. 7.8   Effects of outliers: Outlier (a) may spuriously reduce the correlation; outlier (b) may spuriously increase the correlation.

occur for many reasons; careful thought might indicate substantive reasons for them. A best guess is that they fit some other construct, or some other parameter of the regression function, that had not been recognized. Such "careful thought" should occur before excluding these data points from correlation analysis. Point (a) in Figure 7.8 might be from one who performs well on the criterion but did not line up the test answer sheet properly. Point (b) might represent incomplete data. Some outliers may be due to correctable errors, such as an incorrectly scored test. The solution is obvious: correct the error and do the analysis over. Some may be due to errors that are not correctable; for example, an examiner may misread instructions and give one person nearly double the standard time. Not much can be done here beyond deleting the errant data point and doing the analysis over without it. Unfortunately, deleting outliers has potentially unpleasant consequences, among them rationalizations to excuse deleting troublesome data not actually due to error. Research reports should identify any deletions and the reasons for them; it is the researcher's obligation to investigate outliers, to decide what to do about them, and to report fully. When in doubt, keep the outlier in the data set.

Questionable data points may be outliers, sometimes called "klinkers," or, with more dignity, "defective observations" (Abelson, 1995, p. 68). They can mess up an analysis, even if not clearly outliers. They are often too ambiguous for one to be sure whether they qualify as klinkers. A common practice is to do an analysis once with the possibly defective observations retained and again leaving them out. Typical practice is to report one analysis fully and to relegate the other to a footnote, usually saying that it made no difference. Beware of such footnotes unless they are somewhat detailed, such as reporting the amount of difference in effect sizes or p values.

Group Heterogeneity

Some researchers will do almost anything to build a large sample, such as combining small, disparate samples including groups of people that differ in important ways. Combining them into a single large group can hide differentiating characteristics and distort correlational information. Subgroups in the overall sample may have different means on one or both variables or different correlations. Figure 7.9 shows some strange effects of such combinations. The groups in (a) have the same predictor statistics and the same correlations (which look pretty good) but different levels of criterion performance; combining them results in an approximately zero correlation. Each group in (b) also has a strong positive correlation, but different levels on both the criterion and the predictor; combining them would produce an aggregate negative coefficient. The group interaction shown in (c) would result in an overall coefficient of about zero and a triangular scatterplot. The most serious distortion is (d); here an overall correlation would be positive and probably strong despite the fact that the two variables are not related in any of the groups; the apparent correlation would be due only to the correlation of group means.

Statistical Adjustments

Unreliability

As described in Chapter 5, unreliability, in either variable, reduces correlation. The effect is systematic and therefore correctable. Predictor unreliability is simply a fact in assessment-based decisions. Criterion unreliability, on the other hand, influences research findings but

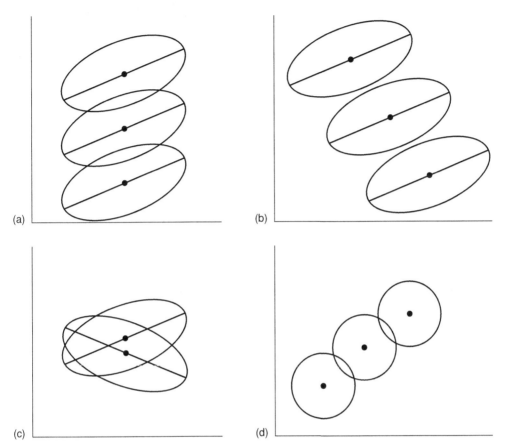

FIG. 7.9   Possible effects of combining groups with different means in the predictor, the criterion, or both.

not individual decisions. For operational purposes, coefficients should therefore be corrected only for criterion unreliability. This adjusts the correlation coefficient by accepting observed predictor reliability and postulating perfect criterion reliability:

$$r_{y''x} = \frac{r_{yx}}{\sqrt{r_{yy}}} \tag{7.5}$$

where $r_{y''x}$ is the expected correlation between a perfectly reliable Y and the fallible predictor X. This is known as the *correction for attenuation* in the criterion only.[7] It is an estimate, albeit a questionable one, of the correlation in the population; it is more questionable to think the population criterion is without random error.

Realism and custom dictate other actions. First, overestimate criterion reliability; a low estimate would unduly inflate the resulting correction. Spuriously high corrections "may not only lead one into a fantasy world but may also deflect one's attention from the pressing

---

[7] Of course, it can be "corrected" or adjusted for unreliability (attenuation) in both variables, but that adjustment has little practical value for personnel decisions.

need of improving the reliability of the measures used" (Pedhazur & Schmelkin, 1991, p. 114). Second, correct only coefficients that are statistically significant. Adjusting very low and statistically insignificant correlations can be seriously misleading and is a bad practice.

An unidentified reviewer reacted negatively, wisely, and correctly to the old and often-repeated advice in that second recommendation because such an emphasis on significance is inconsistent with the general objections now given to significance testing (which I join in a later section). The comment went on to ask why one correlation would be corrected but not another that differs only by decimal dust but doesn't quite reach an arbitrary level of significance. The comment pointed out that "This practice would surely distort information on effect sizes."

The point is a good one, but it responds to a different problem. The old advice was coined in the days of local, situation-specific validation where only one test–criterion correlation was obtained in an operational setting, and the personnel researcher had to decide how one could justify making a statistical "correction" that may inflate an obtained, trivially low correlation to a much higher level. The old answer is to correct only a statistically significant coefficient.[8] The problem stimulating the reviewer's position may stem from meta-analysis (also discussed below), in which a substantial set of validity coefficients may be analyzed to determine what, if any, is the generalizable average effect size across the whole set. Meta-analysis generally makes the corrections the pooled data allow, but the average effect size would surely be overstated if only those correlations meeting a pinpointed significance level were corrected.

A serious problem with correcting for criterion unreliability occurs in the most common of validation situations, the use of a supervisory rating (i.e., just one rater) as a criterion. Reliability estimation for ratings is at best precarious; with a single rater, it overcorrects substantially, according to Van Iddekinge and Ployhart (2008). In their review of recent literature, they argued that generalizability theory is potentially a better way to validate. Its use requires careful advance planning, with multiple dimensions rated by multiple raters. Facets of the design should indicate multiple sources of error and of systematic influences on scores; appropriate generalizability coefficients could serve as estimates of validity without returning to the restrictive assumptions of classical test theory.

Reduced Variance

If variance on either variable is substantially less in the sample than in the population, the sample coefficient underestimates population validity. *Reduced variance*, or *restriction of range*, is often associated with truncation of one or both variables. Strict truncation occurs when a rigid selection rule (e.g., a rigid cut score) keeps poorly scoring candidates out of the sample. Reduced variance also occurs when people in the sample have been selected by other (so-called third) variables correlated with either the criterion or the predictor.

The problem of a reduced range of scores *cannot* be solved by meddling with the measurement scale, such as turning a five-point rating scale to a nine-point scale. (I have seen it happen!) The problem is not the range of the measurement scale; it is the disparity between sample and population variance in the scale used. Anything that truncates the sample distribution reduces variance and, therefore, correlation. Several things can happen to produce

---

[8] Current wisdom, however, prefers statements of effect size over statements of significance; better advice is to decide in advance the approximate level where corrections seem likely to be seriously misleading.

a research sample with lower than population variance, and corrections are available for only some of them:

1. If score variances are known for both the unrestricted group (considered an estimate of variance in the applicant population) and the restricted group (those hired), the corrected correlation coefficient can be obtained by the equation

$$r_n = \frac{r_o \cdot \dfrac{S_{xn}}{S_{xo}}}{\sqrt{1 - r_o^2 + r_o^2 + \dfrac{S_{xn}^2}{S_{xo}^2}}} \tag{7.6}$$

where r_n is the new estimate of the coefficient for an unrestricted sample, r_o is the old (obtained) coefficient for the available restricted sample, and S_{xn} and S_{xo} are the predictor standard deviations for the unrestricted and restricted groups, respectively (Thorndike, 1949, p. 173). Sometimes the "old" standard deviation is not known. In this equation and the two that follow, estimating it can be based on available national norms. Sackett and Ostgaard (1994) recommended an estimate 20% lower than national norms.

2. The organization may accept all applicants on probation and then terminate or transfer people below some criterion cut point. Then a test may be given and concurrently validated. The direct restriction is on the criterion, not on the predictor, but the estimated unrestricted correlation coefficient can be found by reversing the roles of predictor and criterion in Equation 7.6 (Ghiselli, Campbell, & Zedeck, 1981, p. 300).

3. Indirect truncation of the predictor occurs if prior selection is based on a correlated third variable. If selection has been based on one test, another test is being validated, and scores on the two tests are correlated, variance on the new test is restricted. Let X and Y be the new test and the criterion, and Z a third variable. Thorndike (1949, p. 174) offered the following equation for correction:

$$r_n = \frac{r_o + r_{zy} r_{zy} \left(\dfrac{S_{zn}^2}{S_{zo}^2} - 1 \right)}{\sqrt{\left[1 + r_{zx}^2 \left(\dfrac{S_{zn}^2}{S_{zo}^2} - 1 \right) \right] \left[1 + r_{zy}^2 \left(\dfrac{S_{zn}^2}{S_{zo}^2} - 1 \right) \right]}} \tag{7.7}$$

Statistical correction is not a panacea. Sample variance may be lower than population variance just by chance. But one would not know, and statistical correction would make an inappropriately large estimate. Unknown factors may have reduced variance indirectly. No correction exists.

Correction equations can be used in cases of reduced variance even with no clear point of truncation. Instead of an explicit cut score, for example, there may be a region—a score interval with fuzzy boundaries—below which no one was hired, above which most applicants were hired, and within which decisions were mixed. Several reports by Linn (e.g., Linn, 1968; Linn, Harnisch, & Dunbar, 1981) have verified that reduced variance, even without mathematically precise truncation, is associated with reduced correlation—perhaps drastically reduced in highly selective situations—reinforcing the need to correct for the effect. Equation-based corrections are conservative, giving underestimates of population values (Linn et al., 1981).[9]

Corrections in Tandem

Can a coefficient be corrected both for unreliability in the criterion and for reduced variance? Lee, Miller, and Graham (1982) studied the effect in a large Navy sample and found most corrections somewhat higher than the population values. Subsequently, Bobko (1983) approached the question analytically, providing an equation that makes the corrections simultaneously. Using the previous notation,

$$r_n = \frac{\dfrac{r_o}{\sqrt{r_{yy}}} \cdot \dfrac{S_{xn}}{S_{xo}}}{\sqrt{\left(1 - \dfrac{r_o^2}{\sqrt{r_{yy}}}\right) + \left(\dfrac{r_o^2}{\sqrt{r_{yy}}} \cdot \dfrac{S_{xn}}{S_{xo}}\right)}} \tag{7.8}$$

With small selection ratios, small samples, and low criterion reliability, the difference between r_n and the population value can be great. On the average, this tandem correction still provides underestimates (Bobko, 1983). The analytic approach assumed the normal bivariate surface and samples of 100 or more. It has its own assumptions usually violated by real data. Nevertheless, tandem correction for criterion unreliability and predictor range restriction—whether sequentially using traditional equations or with Equation 8—seems a generally safe and conservative way to a workable estimate.

Artificial Dichotomies

Dichotomizing continuous variables is common, especially in setting cut scores. The result is some loss of validity. The "cost of dichotomization" (the title of an article by Cohen, 1983) is minimal if the variable is split at the mean, resulting (if the distribution is normal) in two equal intervals. If the product–moment correlation of X with Y is r, dichotomization at the mean results in a biserial coefficient of correlation of $.798r$, where $.798$ is the value of a multiplying constant e. The *utility* of a selection procedure (see Chapter 8) is directly proportional to r, so assessment with a cut score at the mean is about 80% as useful as using continuous scores (if other effects on utility are the same). The loss is greater the further dichotomization strays from the mean. If the cut score is 0.5 *SD* from the mean, $e = .762$. At 1.0 *SD*, $e = .662$. Clearly, a really restrictive cut score (or a terribly lenient one) can cause horrendous damage to the value of selection assessments. If it is known or anticipated that a continuous predictor distribution of scores will be dichotomized for a cut score, *a biserial coefficient of correlation, not the product–moment coefficient, should be used as a validity coefficient.*

Suppose commendable validation research yields a validity coefficient of .30 against a very good criterion and that appropriate corrections are estimated. A report of the research

---

[9] Reporting both the corrected and uncorrected coefficients is absolutely essential. Standard 1.18 in the 1999 *Standards* repeats the statement in the earlier edition, "When statistical adjustments, such as those for restriction of range or attenuation are made, both adjusted and unadjusted coefficients and all statistics used in the adjustment should be reported" (American Educational Research Association et al., 1999, pp. 21–22).

should be comprehensive. It should include full information on research design and procedures followed, evaluation of the criterion and the logic of a predictive hypothesis, the statistical analyses, both the obtained and corrected coefficients, and a regression equation and standard error of estimate (or alternative information) used by decision makers to make more or less precise predictions with known margins of error. The report should be filed (and be accessible) as justification for the selection procedure, and it would be impressive. But suppose further that, for operational use, a cut score is set at a level that will reject a bit more than 15% of the applicants, that is, about 1 *SD* below the mean. We now have a binary distribution of scores of 0 and 1 where we once had (and based the report on) a continuous distribution of scores, and we now have a de facto validity coefficient of .662 × .30, or about .20. Under a challenge to the use of the test, the nice research report fails to support that selection procedure *as it is actually used*. The validity of interpretations based on a selection procedure is the validity as it is used, not the validity of some hypothetical use that might have been.[10]

Estimates of Product–Moment Correlation

A product–moment correlation coefficient is computed with two continuous variables, linearly related, with somewhat similar distributions. Occasionally one or both variables are dichotomies, but product–moment coefficients can be estimated. The *biserial coefficient of correlation*, r_{bis}, is used if one variable is continuous and the other a dichotomy assumed to be imposed on an underlying, normally distributed continuous variable:

$$r_{bis} = \frac{\bar{X}_p - \bar{X}_q}{S_x} \cdot \frac{pq}{y} \tag{7.9}$$

where $\bar{X}_p$ and $\bar{X}_q$ are the predictor mean scores for the two criterion groups, p and q are the respective proportions of the total sample, y is the ordinate of the normal curve at the point marking the separation of p and q, and S_x is the standard deviation of the full predictor distribution.

If no underlying continuum is assumed, or if it is but the assumption of normality is really questionable, the *point-biserial coefficient of correlation*, r_{pbis}, offers an estimate:

$$r_{pbis} = \frac{\bar{X}_p - \bar{X}_q}{S_x} \cdot \sqrt{pq} \tag{7.10}$$

using the same notation. In most computer programs, r_{pbis} is simply computed as r with the dichotomized variable treated as a continuum having only the values 1 and 2.

If both variables are dichotomized and have normally distributed underlying continua, and the assumption of linear regression is appropriate, r may be estimated by the *tetrachoric coefficient of correlation*, r_{tet}. The equation is complex, with an infinite progression of successively smaller terms, and is not presented here; most statistics packages provide programs for it.

---

[10] Recall Whittier's words from *Maud Muller:* "For of all sad words of tongue or pen, the saddest are these: 'It might have been!'" Users of cut scores based only on the desire for convenience or the distrust of decision makers' abilities might frame these words and post them where they will be seen daily. (Thanks, Gary Carter, for identifying the poem!)

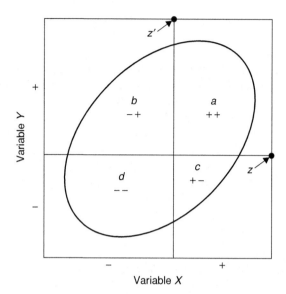

FIG. 7.10   Form of contingency table for computing a phi coefficient.

The *phi coefficient*, φ, may be computed for "true" dichotomies in both variables. Speaking strictly, phi is not an estimate of *r*, but it uses a data table like that in Figure 7.10. It is found by the equation

$$\phi = \frac{ad - bc}{\sqrt{(a + b)(a + c)(b + d)(c + d)}} \tag{7.11}$$

where *a*, *b*, *c*, and *d* are the frequencies in the cells as designated in Figure 7.10.

How good are the different estimates of *r*? To make comparisons, I tinkered twice with a real data set. The first time, I exaggerated the criterion skewness already present. The second time, distributions in both variables were made more nearly normal. The skewed distribution (except for phi) was dichotomized with about a third of the cases assigned a score of 2 and the others 1. Normalized data were dichotomized as close to the means as possible on both variables. Median splits were approximated to set up the matrix for phi. Product–moment correlation coefficients provided standards for comparing the various estimates shown in Table 7.3. The product–moment correlations were, by intent, virtually the same in the two data sets (one rounded up to .41, the other rounded down to .40).

The "estimates" differ from these values, in some cases substantially. They should; dichotomizing continuous data reduces correlations (Cohen, 1983; Thorndike, 1949). Biserial correlation is much lower than *r* in both sets, especially the skewed data. The assumption of normality must be taken seriously; merely "normalizing"—moving toward normality—is not enough. The point biserial coefficient requires less stringent assumptions; it appropriately underestimates *r* for the skewed data, but it inappropriately *exaggerates* r for the "normalized" criterion. Note that the computer approach treating the dichotomized criterion as continuous values of 1 to 2 exactly duplicates r_{pbis} by formula. The bottom two lines of Table 7.3 use 2 × 2 dichotomies. Phi computed by its own equation is identical to *r* with two 2-point distributions. It seems somewhat reasonable but, in general, estimating deserves skepticism.

TABLE 7.3
Variety of Correlation Coefficients from the Same Data

Coefficient	Skewed	Normalized
Product-moment[a]	.41	.40
Biserial r, by equation[b]	.15	.22
Point biserial r, by equation[b]	.30	.44
Product-moment r, 1 dichotomy[c]	.30	.44
Product-moment r, 2 dichotomies[c]	.32	.30
Phi coefficient, by equation	.32	.30

[a] Standard computation using GB-STAT statistical package. [b] r_{bis} and r_{pbis} computed by equations 9 and 10, respectively. [c] 1 dichotomy: only criterion is dichotomized. 2 dichotomies: both variables are dichotomized. Both coefficients computed as product–moment correlations. [d] Computed by Equation 7.11.

Nonlinear Correlation Coefficients

Curvilinear regression rarely appears in the validation literature or in-house reports, maybe because it is rarely looked for or discussed in statistics textbooks. That's unfortunate. Nonlinear regression may be more complex and less reliable than linear, but not so much more complex, nor so much less reliable, that it merits being ignored.

Some curvilinear functions can be transformed to linear ones (Edwards, 1976), but the most likely curves for employment use are not among them. If plotting shows nonlinear regression, and a free-hand curve is drawn, the correlation coefficient can be computed by Equation 2 by computing the residuals and their variance. If the best fitting function is unclear (e.g., a logistic curve vs. a quadratic), the choice can be made comparing residuals.

No symbol for nonlinear correlation coefficients is consistently used. I use r_c for a sample statistic and ρ_{cv} for a population value. This superficial problem highlights the lack of attention to nonlinear regression. Even in the APA Publication Manual (American Psychological Association, 2001, p. 144), a long list of statistical symbols mentions only η^2 (residuals computed only from column means as central points) and identifies it only as a "measure of strength of relationship," as the closest thing to a nonlinear coefficient.

Sampling Error and Error in Sampling

A statistic obtained from a sample is subject to sampling error. Sampling error is a statistical term, not an implication of anything done wrong in sampling. Essentially, it is the inverse of the size of the sample. But errors *are* made in drawing or accepting samples, and they can cause errors in regression equation parameters. The sample may be unrepresentative of the population—perhaps grossly so. Representative sampling (distinguished from random sampling) presents its own dilemma: it and other nonprobabilistic sampling methods do not permit estimation of sampling errors or, indeed, inferences of population relevance (Pedhazur & Schmelkin, 1991); statistical inferences and population parameter estimates are probabilistic.

Another problem in sampling is that correlational statistics assume that measurement error is at least somewhat random; even if the assumption is reasonable for the population, it is not necessarily reasonable for the sample. Populations are rarely precisely known; unless made up by the researchers. In personnel selection, the researcher may define applicant populations in tangible terms, such as demographics or certification of some sort, but potentially biasing characteristics associated with such tangible ones are rarely considered in the definition.

Standard Error of Estimate

The problem of predictive accuracy needs careful examination. Many writers (among them illustrious psychometric theorists such as Gulliksen, 1950b) equate accuracy with measurement precision. I do not. Precision of measurement is indicated by a standard error of measurement approaching zero; accurate measurement would be indicated (where external measurement standards are available) by a near-zero mean measurement error.

So with prediction. Precision in prediction is indicated by the standard error of estimate:

$$s_{yx} = \sqrt{\frac{\Sigma\,(Y - Y')^2}{n - 2}} \tag{7.12}$$

where the numerator under the radical is the sum of the squares of the residuals. The s_{yx}^2 is an index of precision in prediction, but it gives no corresponding statement of accuracy. Predictive accuracy can be described by the absolute mean of the residuals (the mean itself is necessarily zero). Both the absolute mean and variance of residuals, of course, are proportional to the correlation coefficient, and both can be applied and interpreted in either linear and nonlinear regression.

Prediction Problems in Bivariate Regression

Many assessments (e.g., biodata) often give good empirical predictions, even when no one (including the researcher) knows why. The absence of a theoretical basis can be one reason why assessments like biodata fail to be as useful as their full potential (Dean & Russell, 2005). One cannot judge the psychometric validity of a measure without defining the variable being measured (an act of theorizing). Without understanding the acceptable construct interpretations of both variables, predictions based on them cannot be fully understood (Carretta & Ree, 2001). Even with theoretical understanding, however, many statistical problems associated with bivariate analyses conspire to make bivariate regression and correlation hard to understand or to explain.

Traditional validation for about a century has relied on bivariate correlational analysis. Bivariate analysis, whether correlational, quasi-experimental, based on contingency tables, or something else, is much less complex than the real life circumstances in which predictions and personnel decisions must be made. Folks harried by demands that they do something about a problem—that they provide a good test or decision rule—seek simplicity themselves and in the process tend to forget things they should know. For example, every student of elementary statistics learns that causal interpretations of correlations or their matching regressions are not justifiable, at least without much more data than a single correlation coefficient. Nevertheless, "it is surprising how causal implications nonetheless sneak insidiously into interpretations of correlations" (Abelson, 1995, p. 181). Abelson went on to discuss the *third variable* problem. After giving the usual objections to causal inferences because of unconsidered third variables ("single, isolated correlations are always doomed to ambiguity," p. 182), he pointed out that such inferences are legitimately argued if there is a *pattern* of covariation. Such a pattern is discovered, however, by multivariate techniques that can investigate plausible third variable explanations.

Don't take the notion of a "third" variable too literally. The term was basic in drawing Figure 7.7 because it made the point that variables exist beyond the X and Y variables and can influence correlations, predictions, and decisions. The point is not the number—it may be much greater than 1.0. Any extraneous variables, alone or in concert, can violate basic assumptions. Classical test theory applied to correlation and regression assumes that measurement errors in a predictor are not correlated with much of anything, including systematic or true scores. Many relevant variables, omitted or ignored in bivariate regression, become systematic errors in the predictor, the criterion, or both. The influence of these unconsidered variables is hidden in the consistent error components of the score distributions, perhaps reflecting other constructs, with *effects typically not known or knowable in bivariate research.*

Regression analysis (but not correlation) assumes essentially normal score distributions, not the severely skewed ones often seen in personnel research. Severe skewness leads to spurious, inexplicable nonlinearity. A more serious problem, however, is that the practical use of regression analysis, whether bivariate or multivariate, assumes stability in the job and in performance. In fact, performance changes, and not at rates constant for all workers. Without considering individual differences in criterion growth curves, or individual differences in reactions to situational change, bivariate regression can be especially misleading. In spite of "longstanding evidence that performance is dynamic" (Thoresen et al., 2004, p. 835), most validation studies continue to assume stable performance patterns and static performance measures. A single criterion measure, even one that tries desperately to be all-inclusive, is simply not the complete, stable, truly general sign of performance typically assumed in the old-time validation religion. Using Murphy's (1989) distinction between maintenance and transitional stages of performance on a job, Thoresen et al. studied personality predictors relative to individual "growth trajectories" defined as "idiosyncratic patterns of systematic performance growth across a specified period of time or a series of performance observations" (Thoresen et al., 2004, p. 836). Classic bivariate validation is a lot simpler in methods of data collection and analysis, but the notion of individual differences in a growth trajectory seems a lot more realistic. It is worth much further, serious study in real work situations over realistic time spans.

Another major problem is the time it takes to do a truly predictive validation study. "Why bother to validate a selection method or procedure against a criterion which is already out of date by the time the study has been completed? Validation cycles . . . are becoming of increasingly dubious value" (Herriot & Anderson, 1997, p. 23). They called for *compressed validation cycles.* The idea is one that has never, so far as I know, been fully articulated. It is hard to operationalize, but it deserves careful thought.

Many things can influence or distort a bivariate correlation coefficient, including its regression form, or pattern, on which it is based. Sometimes the direction of error is plain, but some influences may lead to unknown or unknowable error. Some with knowable effects can be corrected, but many of them are like incurable aches and pains: you simply have to live with them. Living with them, however, should induce caution. One should not place undue faith in a single bivariate validity coefficient. It can offer some evidence—even good evidence—of validity, but potential distortions should be considered in evaluating that evidence. One may need to gather new data, either through replications or new research to investigate possible explanations.

Bivariate research is useful; one should not discount it recklessly. Bivariate correlation is a necessary component in many multivariate analyses, it may provide a first step in investigating a plausible hypothesis, and it is more readily interpretable in large sample studies, but it must be recognized as inherently ambiguous.

SIGNIFICANCE, CONFIDENCE, AND EFFECT SIZE

"The correlation was (or was not) statistically significant at the 5% level of confidence." Such a statement is common in research reports, based on rejection of the *null hypothesis* (that variables are not related at all). If a large coefficient occurs in a large sample, it is not likely to have occurred by chance; the null hypothesis can be rejected at a specified probability level, usually $p = .05$. The researcher's decision is a dichotomy; the researcher either rejects the null hypothesis or fails to do so. Failure to reject null does not mean accepting zero as "true," nor does rejecting it imply acceptance of any nonzero value. The whole idea has become trivial; a former editor of the *Journal of Applied Psychology* said, "It is hard to recall a single article out of several thousand submissions in which the outcome of a 'significance' test made a great deal of difference to the interpretation of the study's findings" (Murphy, 2002, p. 119). Nevertheless, readers of the research literature will encounter significance testing, so read on.

Computing and Interpreting Statistical Significance

Correlation analyses compute p using the standard error of a zero correlation,

$$SE_{r=0} = 1/(n - 1)^{1/2} \qquad (7.13)$$

If the obtained correlation is 1.96 standard errors or more from $r = 0$, it is said to be "significant at the 5% level of confidence," based on areas under the normal curve. Other significance levels can be used—10%, 1%, etc.; I've seen authors use as many as five levels of confidence in a single report, treated as if they were measures of something substantive, measured by the number of asterisks used.[11] If significance testing is done at all, it is more defensible to establish a priori an acceptable p level for the dichotomous decision to accept or to reject the hypothesis of no relationship.

Correct decisions are made when (a) rejecting the null hypothesis when it is really false, or (b) not rejecting it when it is really true. A distinction is made between *Type I* and *Type II* errors. A Type I error occurs if the null hypothesis is true but is rejected; a Type II error occurs if it is not rejected when it is false. In personnel research, a Type I error is related to the likelihood that personnel decisions will have the effect of random selection, being based on an invalid assessment procedure. A Type II error is related to the likelihood that a valid assessment procedure will be discarded, particularly in EEO litigation, where validity under the *Uniform Guidelines* is virtually synonymous with statistical significance at the .05 level.

Obtaining correlation coefficients from many different samples from the same population would result in a distribution of coefficients ranging from very low to very high. Coefficients from any two samples will differ, maybe trivially, maybe substantially. After the research is finished, can future samples be counted on to give coefficients of about the same size as the one obtained in the research study?

That is a good question, but it is not answered by significance testing. Significance testing goes at it in a reverse (or perverse) process; it tests the null hypothesis that the correlation coefficient in the population is precisely zero. Rejection of null does not imply that the

---

[11] My predecessor as editor of the *Journal of Applied Psychology*, John P. Campbell, set a rule of no more than two significance levels! It was a good rule; I followed it, but the associate editors during my term did not.

sample coefficient at hand is a good estimate of the population coefficient, and failure to reject null does not mean that it is a stable one. Literally, the null hypothesis "is *always* false in the real world" (Cohen, 1990, p. 1308; emphasis in original). Part of the perversity of significance testing is that it gives no useful clue to the probability that a correlation approximately like that obtained in the research sample would be found in the next sample when assessment-based hiring actually begins; it asks only whether the probability of a coefficient as large as or larger than that obtained in the research sample is lower than some prestated probability level.

The Irrelevance of Significance Testing

Significance testing is not wholly irrelevant. It may be useful in exploratory research intended to try out a new idea. It may be relevant to a statistical correction of an obtained correlation coefficient when it is so low that it does not deserve to be made to look good by "correcting" it. It seems to be necessary for publication of research findings. Mostly, it has little relevance, if any, to the researcher's substantive interest, and it can even be misleading (Kline, 2004). "A null hypothesis test is a ritualized exercise of devil's advocacy" (Abelson, 1995, p. 9). The ritual has become so encrusted with false implications that a hard look at the subject has long been needed. As a matter of fact, it has long been provided—by nearly a century of criticism from people who understand logic, statistics, and practical statistical implications (e.g., Boring, 1919; Hunter, 1997; Kline, 2004; Morrison & Henkel, 1970; Murphy, 2002; Nickerson, 2000). Meehl listed 10 "obfuscating factors" that render nearly any failure to reject null, at least in areas like test validation, "largely uninterpretable" (Meehl, 1991, p. 17).

Significance testing grew from controlled agricultural experiments. If one divides a wheat field into plots and systematically uses a treatment in some plots but not others, it is important to ask if the treatment actually influences yield. The amount of effect may matter less than whether the effect exists. In designing a controlled experiment, one specifies in advance a significance level sufficient to justify a causal inference. The results are neatly dichotomized as reaching that preset level or not. It is this that Abelson called "devil's advocacy"; even in controlled experiments, reality does not dichotomize itself so neatly, and the "terms 'accept' or 'reject' . . . are semantically too strong" (Abelson, 1995, p. 9).

Neither dichotomous significance tests nor probabilities of deviance from null (p) answer the important questions. Neither recognizes the improbability of null. Neither recognizes that effects can be trivial even if not null (cf. Murphy & Myors, 1999). Neither addresses the more practical question about the likely size of the coefficient that might be expected in the next sample after the research is done. While admitting that significance testing may help avoid manuscript rejection or large penalties in EEO litigation, many authors have concluded that both the asterisk count and the p levels are irrelevant to personnel decisions. So what should be done?

Schmidt (1996) argued that null hypothesis testing in individual studies should be abandoned—not even taught in graduate programs—and replaced by point estimates of effect sizes and confidence intervals (likely range of effect size values around the estimate). While many would not go so far (graduate courses should teach it, critically, so that students will recognize it for what it is), a growing number of researchers share the view that effect sizes and confidence intervals are far more informative.

Kline (2004), acknowledging that significance tests will not soon disappear, gave three recommendations to researchers, on which I superimpose my own views. First, don't treat them as informative; they do not answer major questions. Second, don't imply (as a writer) and don't infer (as a reader) that nonsignificant results suggest a population value of zero; all such a result means is that zero cannot be ruled out entirely. Third, and most important, both effect sizes and confidence intervals should routinely be reported. Moreover, effect sizes should be "interpreted and evaluated for their substantive significance, not just reported" (Kline, 2004, p. 15). Effect size, and its likely stability, is far more relevant to personnel decisions than is significance level (cf. Kirk, 1996). A fourth was in a later section of Kline's book, directed to researchers, reviewers, editors, EEO litigants and judges, journalists, and others getting exercise from conclusion jumping: "No matter how intriguing a result from a single study, *it must be replicated before it can be taken seriously*" (Kline, 2004, p. 58, emphasis added).

META-ANALYSIS AND VALIDITY GENERALIZATION

Science asks what is generally so (even if not invariably). Scientific generalization is not based on isolated studies; it depends on (a) *replications* or (b) a set of similar findings, even if not strictly replications. A strict replication repeats a study in detail—sampling from essentially the same population and using the same measures of variables in the hypothesis, the same set of controls, etc. Results are said to be replicated if they are reasonably similar to those in the original study. Most replications are less strict, perhaps changing one control, a measurement method, or some other feature of the original study. Strict replications are unlikely in personnel research, where merely changing to a different organization might change a host of features. In a "set of similar findings," where no single study closely replicates another, studies may form a set if they all consider a similar hypothesis.

Meta-analysis seeks all studies of a broadly common hypothesis (or as many as possible) to see if they form a set of similar findings. It looks at the historic accumulation of effect sizes across research on that hypothesis, more or less precisely defined. It is commonly used in many fields of experimental and correlational research. Bivariate validation tests the relational hypothesis that a trait X is related to a criterion Y. It is usually an isolated study, done in just one setting with specific predictor and criterion measures. Such isolated support for the hypothesis does not make it "generally so." Over time, other studies like it will be done, testing roughly the same hypothesis. Affirming the generality of a relationship requires a research history supporting it in different settings with different details.

Ghiselli (1966) surveyed hundreds of bivariate validity studies and found wide variation in validity coefficients for given combinations of test type, occupational group, and criterion category. That was not surprising; variation among findings, if not the reason for it, was well known. Conventional guesses attributed it to unknown and perhaps unknowable local influences. Pleasantly surprising was that many *mean* validity coefficients were high. If the mean uncorrected coefficient is .40 or more, the chance of finding validity in one's own situation seems good. Validities for such job–test–criterion combinations could even be considered "generalizable" (Lawshe, 1952).

The idea of generalizable validity was dormant for years. Schmidt and Hunter (1977) revived it by showing that variability in validity coefficients in different situations could be attributed to statistical and procedural variables—they called them "artifacts"—in individual studies. They introduced *validity generalization*, a specific form of meta-analysis; an informal, readable, history of their work is available in Schmidt and Hunter (2003). *Meta-analysis*, in all forms, looks quantitatively for conclusions that have been generally so in independent research on the same basic hypothesis. Traditional literature surveys had the same objective but were verbal rather than quantitative, often imprecise, and subjective. Subjectivity remains in meta-analysis, primarily in coding information, but procedures are systematized and results are quantitative. Of several approaches to meta-analysis, the one known also as *validity generalization* (VG) is the most directly appropriate to personnel testing. It is the method that gives the greatest attention to psychometric issues (Hunter & Schmidt, 2004; Rothstein, 2003). Although Murphy and Newman (2003, p. 421) suggested, for good reasons, changing the term to "psychometric meta-analysis," I choose to stay with VG as a simpler abbreviation not likely to be associated with any other concept.

Principles of Validity Generalization

Validity generalization starts with a set of independent validation studies of the same hypothesis, usually with correlations as effect sizes. It differs in purpose from most other methods of meta-analysis. Instead of intending only to summarize related studies, VG seeks "to estimate what the results *would have been*" had all the studies been conducted without methodological limitations or flaws" (Hunter & Schmidt, 2004, p. xxv, emphasis added).

In VG, correcting for such limitations creates a new distribution of effect sizes and new estimates of the population parameters, specifically mean and variance. The estimated population mean is *not* the simple mean of reported coefficients; it is the mean of coefficients corrected for at least some of the artifacts. After adjustments, the variance of the distribution exceeds zero only to the degree to which samples come from different samples or even different populations, or to which results stem from different systematic influences or are influenced by different uncorrected artifacts or other sources of error. The essential idea in VG is that the criterion-related validity coefficient would be the same in all tests of the research hypothesis within an applicable population if it were not for artifactual influences on the results of individual studies. Coefficients can be corrected statistically for some artifacts. Corrections for others are applied to the estimated variance of the distribution of corrected coefficients. If that variance can be explained largely after these corrections, then validity is said to generalize across the diverse situations from which individual coefficients came. If not, then generalization is appropriate only where potentially specifiable influences exist.

VG tests two explicit hypotheses about the relational predictive hypothesis. The *situational specificity* hypothesis is that criterion-related validity depends in part on unknown influences within research settings; it can be rejected if corrections substantially reduce the variance of the validity coefficient distribution. Corrections cannot be made for unknown or unreported artifacts, so Schmidt and Hunter (1977) advocated a rule of thumb that rejects situational specificity if 75% or more of the variance is explained by known artifacts, and they have continued to recommend that rule (Hunter & Schmidt, 2004). Their argument was that unknown artifacts may account for the rest, so the corrected mean correlation may be treated as the population value across all studies. The Pedhazur–Schmelkin caveats about nonprobabilistic samples and populations also apply to VG.

The *validity generalization* hypothesis is not simply the obverse of situational specificity, although rejecting the hypothesis of situational specificity is a necessary first step. Generalized validity is supported when nearly all of the coefficients in the distribution are at or above a nontrivial level and in the same direction (all positive or all negative). Many VG reports identify a *credibility* value, the point in the distribution above which 90% (or another value) of the corrected validity coefficients lie. A credibility value should not be zero, and it should not be trivial. If validity generalizes, the mean of the distribution of coefficients (after corrections for artifacts) is the best estimate of criterion-related validity in the kinds of job sampled in the accumulated research.

TABLE 7.4

Study Artifacts that Alter the Value of Outcome Measures (with Examples from Personnel Research)

1. *Sampling error:* Study validity varies randomly from the population value because of sample size.
2. *Measurement error (criterion):* Study validity is systematically lowered to the extent of random error in the measurement of performance.
3. *Measurement error (predictor):* Criterion-related validity of test is systematically understated because of test unreliability.
4. *Dichotomization of a continuous criterion:* Study validity is understated because of dichotomization. Turnover at the individual level is often dichotomized as "more than" or "less than" an arbitrary time (e.g., one year) of staying with the organization.
5. *Dichotomization of a continuous predictor:* Study validity is understated because of dichotomization, as in setting cut scores or dichotomizing interviewer judgment into "acceptable" versus "reject."
6. *Range variation in predictor:* Study validity is systematically lowered to the extent that the predictor variance is lower among those hired (and therefore having performance data) than among applicants in general.
7. *Range variation in the criterion:* Study validity is systematically lowered to the extent of systematic, variance-reducing criterion attrition, as when good workers are promoted and poor workers are fired.
8. *Imperfect construct validity of the predictor:* Study validity is reduced if the factor structure of the test differs from the structure expected in measures of the same intended trait.
9. *Imperfect construct validity of the criterion:* Study validity is reduced to the extent that the criterion is deficient or contaminated.
10. *Reporting or transcriptional error:* Reported study validity may differ from actual study validity when data are inaccurately coded, computational errors are made, errors are made in reading computer data entry or output, typographical errors, etc. These errors can be very large.
11. *Variance to due extraneous factors ("third variables") that affect the relationship:* e.g., study validity is systematically lowered if incumbents differ in job experience when performance is measured (because job experience affects job performance).

Adapted from *Methods of Meta-Analysis: Correcting Error and Bias in Research Findings* (2nd ed.), by Hunter, J. E., & Schmidt, F. L. (Eds.), 2004. Thousand Oaks, CA: Sage. © 2004 by Sage Publications. Adapted with permission.

Table 7.4 presents a list of artifacts that may influence validity coefficients and their distributions. In reading the table, assume that, "in the book of the recording angel" (a phrase taken from Stanley, 1971, p. 361), a "true" validity coefficient exists and describes the relationship of predictor to criterion constructs. Measurement errors, of course, always exist (Artifacts 2, 3, 8, and 9). Procedural errors in the design or conduct of the study (Artifacts 4–7 and 11) are also likely. Merely taking a sample suggests a result different from the "true" result; the smaller the sample, the greater the error (Artifact 1). There is a nonzero likelihood of error in recording, analyzing, or reporting what was done and found (Artifact 10). Not all sources of variance in reported coefficients are artifactual; some of the accumulated data may include samples from different populations with different "true" validity coefficients. The eleven artifacts, however, are potential sources of variance in the set as a whole, and validity generalization research estimates appropriate corrections for one or more of them.

To summarize VG procedures: corrections for artifacts provide a "corrected" distribution of coefficients. Its mean is an estimate of the hypothetical "true" or population validity, and the variance of these estimates is less than that of the uncorrected coefficients. If the corrected variance approaches zero, the specter of unknown situational influences is exorcised. When coefficients in a corrected distribution are both positive and negative (and not close to zero), the kinds of predictors in the analysis do *not* have generalized validity; failure to reduce variance substantially by the corrections argues that something does in fact systematically influence validities across situations.

Three different results can occur in a VG study. It may (a) refute (or support) the situational specificity hypothesis by showing (or not) that the variance of the distribution of corrected coefficients approaches zero, (b) support (or refute) the validity generalization hypothesis by showing (or not) that all or nearly all validity coefficients across diverse situations are nontrivial in size and in the same direction, and (c) if situational specificity is rejected and generalization is supported, an estimate of population validity is the mean of the corrected coefficients ($\bar{r}_c$). "Estimate of population validity" is a longer, more cumbersome phrase than "true validity," but it is more accurate. Some people accept the phrase "true validity" as a term in their everyday vocabularies, but I prefer to resist it. We cannot know the mythical truth, but we can know estimates of what it might be in the population implied. The estimate itself is subject to failures or oddities in corrections and also to the fact that, even if searches for studies to be included are extensive, the studies summarized are but a sample of those that might have been. The quality of VG findings depends first on the quality of the original studies, and then on how many of the artifacts the analysis has been able to correct and on how well the corrections have been made. Original research reports rarely give all the information needed for the corrections. Despite problems, meta-analytic results are nevertheless more dependable than single-study results.

Methods of Analysis

I describe here only the simplest method, omitting most of the controversy, modification, and options in a rather extensive literature. The first step is to search thoroughly for both published and unpublished research reports. Some experts recommend purging the file of bad research; others seek the most nearly complete file possible. Each report is read and coded for data points and associated information. Each validity statement is one data point. If two or more data points are reported from a sample (for the hypothesis at hand), they are not independent. A decision about handling the problem must be made early in the process; options include randomly choosing one data point from the lot or averaging them. Ignoring the problem is a poor choice.

Coding includes classifying and recording information about the various artifacts. Distinctive job characteristics, industry in which the study is done, sample demographics, or characteristics of work environments may also be coded. If situational specificity is rejected, much of this information will not be used, but it is practical to anticipate its use at the outset, before objectivity-destroying biases or mental sets develop. A major frustration in meta-analysis is the failure in many research reports to give even basic information. In a study of reliability generalization, 628 articles were found that studied the same measure; of these, nearly two-thirds made no mention at all of reliability (Vacha-Haase, 2003, p. 208), an appalling finding in a research literature—appalling because reliability is basic psychometric information; besides, if sample size, reliability, and range restriction are all given, individual correlation coefficients can be corrected so that the distribution of coefficients is a distribution of population estimates, not of raw coefficients. However, if not, judgments based on the literature can often be made about artifact distributions to get plausible values to use for corrections.

Interpretation of results is evaluative and in some respects personal. Meta-analyses with only a few data points are often evaluated unfavorably. Even an excellent, well-reported analysis may be rejected as irrelevant to one's own purpose if the hypothesis, jobs studied, or criteria do not fit it. Equations used in corrections may be criticized, although choice among optional equations seems trivial relative to the advantage of the method in general (see, e.g., Linn & Dunbar, 1986; Raju & Burke, 1983).

"Bare-Bones" Analysis: Correction for Sampling Error Only

The simplest form of meta-analysis corrects only for sampling error, the biggest artifactual source of variance in most sets of correlation coefficients. This "bare-bones" analysis offers the simplest description of validity generalization. In correcting only for sampling error, other artifacts are ignored; ignoring them, of course, does not get rid of them, and the analysis should be more comprehensive if possible. Sampling error is present in every study, but so also is measurement error; in practice, corrections for both of these ubiquitous errors should be made in every meta-analysis. However, the bare-bones analysis makes it easier to describe the process in elementary terms.

Table 7.5 presents hypothetical correlation coefficients presumably from 10 independent studies, all testing roughly the same hypothesis. The sample size is known for each study, but no information related to other artifacts has been devised; thus, only a bare-bones analysis is possible. Each study may be considered a replication of the others in the sense that each is concerned with the correlation between the same two constructs. The best estimate of the population correlation across replications is an average. Data points based on large samples are more reliable estimates of population correlations than those from small samples, so each one is weighted by the size of the sample from which it came:

$$\bar{r} = \frac{\Sigma(N_i r_i)}{\Sigma N_i} \qquad (7.14)$$

TABLE 7.5

A Hypothetical Set of Correlation Coefficients from Ten Independent Studies of the Same Hypothesis

(i) Study Number	N_i	r_i	$N_i r_i$	$N(r_i - \bar{r})^2$
1	23	.17	3.91	.1863
2	217	.23*	49.91	.1953
3	68	.53*	36.04	4.9572
4	141	.30*	42.30	.2256
5	92	.08	7.36	2.9808
6	30	.15	4.50	.3630
7	45	.03	1.35	2.3805
8	101	.19	19.19	.4949
9	309	.32*	98.88	1.1124
10	54	.39*	21.06	.9126
Sum	1080		284.50	13.8086

* Significantly different from 0.00 at the .05 level of confidence.

where $\bar{r}$ = mean correlation coefficient across studies, weighted for sample size, N_i = the size of the sample in study i, and r_i = a correlation coefficient observed in study i. Substituting the data in Table 7.5, $\bar{r}_r$ = 284.50/1080 = .26. Note that these correlation coefficients have not been transformed to Fisher's z'. An average correlation, based on the z' transformation, tends to overestimate population values, even at the modest levels of most validity coefficients.

The variance across these studies is best described in terms of the average squared deviations, weighted by the sample sizes:

$$s_r^2 = \frac{\sum N_i (r_i - \bar{r})^2}{\sum N_i} \qquad (7.15)$$

where s_r^2 = variance of observed correlation coefficients across samples, weighted for sample size, and the other notation is as before. Substituting data in Table 7.5, s_r^2 = 13.8086/1080 = .0128. If one looks only at the range of coefficients, from .03 to .53, one might think results differed substantially. No one adequately trained in statistics would look only at those values, however, because the end points of distributions are notoriously unreliable. Further noting that half of the correlations are nonsignificant, one might have serious doubts about the generality of support for the hypothesis. However, the significance tests are also misleading. Although small, there is some variance among these correlations. The question is whether that variance approaches zero when artifacts are considered—whether the "corrected" variance, s_{rc}^2 (variance of corrected coefficients, r_c, in the set of studies) is close enough to zero. A prior question is the variance due to sampling error, s_{ec}^2. Unless there is an anomalously large sample in the data set, Hunter and Schmidt (1990, p. 108) recommend the equation

$$s_{ec}^2 = \frac{(1 - \bar{r}^2)^2}{\bar{N}_i - 1}. \qquad (7.16)$$

Substituting in Equation 16, s_{ec}^2 = (1 − .0676)^2/(108 − 1) = .008. Subtracting this from the estimated total variance from Equation 15, s_{rc}^2 = .0128 − .008 = .0048. In short, when sampling error is the only source of error considered, the variance of the distribution of population estimates in the 10 studies of Table 7.5 shrinks to .0048 from an initial variance of .0128— sampling error has accounted for 62.5% of the initially observed variance across studies. That does not meet the 75% rule of thumb, so this simple analysis does not permit rejection of the situational specificity hypothesis and the question of validity generalization does not arise.

Correcting for More than One Artifact

With real data, other correctable artifacts such as unreliability and range restriction should be reported. Further corrections can lead to different results. It is usually not possible to correct for all artifacts in Table 7.4. Even individual studies that provide full statistical information rarely offer information about such matters as transcription or reporting error, so they cannot be considered in the analysis; however, we cannot rule out (or, for that matter, rule in) the possibility that these artifacts may account for a nontrivial portion of the variance.

By the rule of thumb, if more than 25% of the original variance remains after the ordinary corrections, we are justified in searching for moderators. In a sense, meta-analytic moderators are variables that suggest different population-defining characteristics. The search is limited by the information coded from the original studies. Procedures for estimating variance of corrected coefficients are given in Hunter and Schmidt (2004). Because conventional equations seem to provide underestimates, improved procedures have been proposed by various authors. The refinements are seen as more accurate and more likely to lead to rejection of situational specificity.

Using Artifact Distributions

Research reports in this imperfect world often provide no information about things that might have influenced the results. In any given set of studies to review, some will report certain kinds of information, but others will not. Some kinds of information (such as codable information about criterion construct validities) are not at all likely to be reported—or perhaps not even known to the study authors. Where little or no information is available across studies, an artifact is consigned to the abyss of unknown influences—influences that may be large or small, positive or negative, common or uncommon, but contributing in unknown ways and degrees to the variance of correlation coefficients.

From VG to Personnel Decisions

Meta-analyses in general, and VG in particular, create a stronger scientific foundation for personnel research and personnel decisions. A local predictive hypothesis can be helped by identifying predictors commonly used in a relevant meta-analysis. From what is becoming a vast meta-analytic literature, many broad, general hypotheses have been supported well enough that many researchers believe that local decisions can be based on the kinds of assessments included in a given analysis. Probably the best example is the array of findings in support of general mental ability tests as predictors of performance in virtually all jobs, although some hesitation in fully accepting this generality has been suggested from time to time (see especially Landy, 2003). Nevertheless, the path from scientific generality to local application often is neither satisfactory nor clear. Brannick (2001) pointed out that pooling validity studies necessarily helps in estimating local criterion-related validity, but "the difficulty is that unless the variance due to situations is virtually zero, the global estimates do not answer the question, 'What do we expect the test-criterion correlation to be in this local context?'" (Brannick, 2001, p. 468). He went on to develop and describe empirical Bayesian meta-analysis to allow a new study to provide information that, when combined with prior information from the meta-analysis, can lead to a new estimate of the population effect size and a new estimate of the uncertainty surrounding it.

Is a new local study always advisable? Probably not. "When the estimated mean true validity is large and the estimated variance of that validity is small . . . it would take a large sample with a negative local r to render a judgment that the test is not useful in the local context" (Brannick, 2001, p. 479). With less pleasing meta-analytic results, adding a local validation study to the mix, if it is feasible, is a good idea.

Evaluating a Prior Meta-Analysis

Murphy and Newman (2003) lauded the Brannick article for bringing about a "reemergence" (p. 409) of Bayesian approaches to VG that the early Schmidt–Hunter articles seemed to prefer. When we go beyond VG to the larger context of personnel selection, Brannick's article means more than bringing something back. Bayesian statistics have rarely been invoked in personnel research, and the Brannick contribution emphasizes that they should be. Nevertheless, the local adequacy and appropriateness of a given VG study as a Bayesian prior needs closer examination. Several questions need to be answered in deciding that a given meta-analysis is both adequate and appropriate. Briefly, here are a few.

1. Is the generalized validity level useful, that is, is the 90% credibility value positive, nontrivial, and strong enough to guide local personnel decisions?
2. Are individual validity coefficients themselves reasonably stable? Are the numbers of cases in the studies reviewed large enough to assure a distribution of stable data points? I am skeptical of meta-analyses of studies with samples of only 10–20 cases, even with an awful lot of them. Words like *reasonably* and *an awful lot* are far too ambiguous to be helpful; what is reasonable, or enough, probably depends on how desperately one needs help in finding a potentially useful predictor construct.
3. Has the analysis been carefully done? Have the researchers been systematic and objective and reliable in establishing and using categories for coding the various studies?
4. If situational specificity has not been clearly rejected, have plausible moderators been investigated? Or even suggested? (Moderators are discussed in the next chapter.)
5. Most important of all, are the constructs embedded in the meta-analysis the same constructs specified in the local predictive hypothesis? Perhaps that is too much to ask, but the locally important constructs should at least be commensurate with those in the prior distribution. Brannick and Hall (2003) identified the commensurability problem as one where the various correlations in the distribution use different measures, perhaps measuring different things. They pointed out that computing the mean of all correlations published in a given journal over a given time period would mean nothing at all; it would be based on "many constructs X and many constructs Y, and this is exactly the problem," and further, "each measure of X [and each measure of Y] should be saturated with the same construct" (Brannick & Hall, 2003, p. 350).

However, for the local user, there is a further commensurability problem, the commensurability of the local predictive hypothesis and that examined in the otherwise admirable VG study. The two sets of constructs are unlikely to be identical, but the VG constructs should encompass the constructs of interest to the local study.

Choosing Predictors from Meta-Analyses

The conclusion that too many people seem to reach from a VG study, one that supports generalizability of a useful hypothesis, is that any operational definition of a predictor construct and any operational definition of a criterion construct will be as good as any other in operational use. This is a silly conclusion, and I'm fairly sure that most meta-analysts would at this point say, "Whoa; wait a doggone minute!" In any large meta-analysis, however, a few of the measures used in the primary studies are likely to be junk. I mean by "junk" measures with little or no psychometric validity for the construct investigated, measures with items varying wildly in difficulty or power (if any) to distinguish among examinees with varying trait levels, or including items subject to more-than-usual sources of measurement error. My point here was best made by Murphy and Newman (2003, p. 421), who said "Care about quality: Meta-analyses that attempt to be comprehensive usually end up giving more weight to bad studies than to good ones, simply because there are so many bad ones out there."

A different problem is meta-analysis in which one measure (e.g., test) dominates. Even with a few others claiming to measure the same or closely related constructs, the results of the analysis may apply clearly only to that measure—and leave it to other analyses to see if conclusions apply to alternative measures. The "few other" measures may have been used in "good" studies (or maybe among the "bad" ones) without enough influence in the entire distribution of correlations to override the general finding. In any case, the isolated measure in a set of studies, most of which used a specified but different measure, cannot be declared "as good as any other" with much assurance. If most (maybe all) of the primary studies in the meta-analysis have used the same single predictor, it may have generalizable validity, but other, less commonly used alternatives might prove better—or worse. Such meta-analyses are not much help in choosing a predictor for a local selection situation. One reason, and I think a major reason, has nothing to do with the logic or quality of meta-analysis in general but with the reporting. Several authors (e.g., Hunter & Schmidt, 2004; Rothstein, 2003) have given useful advice on information to be included in reporting meta-analytic studies and their results, but they have virtually nothing to say about reporting the predictors, their frequency within the distribution, descriptions of criteria they may have predicted, or other information making it possible to identify specific measurement operations that might be chosen for a local project. Meta-analysis is supposed to be science, not practice, but science should influence practice.

So I conclude that even a solid meta-analysis supporting one's predictive hypothesis at the construct level may not offer much help in choosing a test that operationally defines the generally valid construct, and I firmly reject the idea that a finding of generalized validity means that any predictor claimed to measure the construct for a predictive hypothesis is as good as any other. Judgment is always required in choosing predictor constructs and ways to measure them; the judgment is simplified but not eliminated by an adequate and appropriate meta-analysis, that is, one that shows the generalized validity of a relevant hypothesis. The constructs of the local hypothesis are often narrower than those of a meta-analysis, but the meta-analysis constructs, to be appropriate, must include if not match those of local interest. And, of course, the user needs to be sure that the evidence supporting psychometric validity for the predictor chosen is satisfactory.

Issues in Validity Generalization

Some matters still at issue, at least for me, can be reviewed quickly. I endorse wholeheartedly the delightful suggestions made by Murphy and Newman (2003), reproduced in Table 7.6, but I have a few additional concerns, as follows.

1. Does meta-analysis oversimplify the search for generalizations? Too much emphasis on the general can obscure important exceptions. "Generalizations are important to any scientific area, but so too are the exceptions . . . Our task is not only to seek generalizations, but to find and attempt to understand exceptions" (Linn & Dunbar, 1986, p. 232). Is meta-analysis misdirecting research? Yes, if it causes people to stop doing research on exceptions or rejects as myth or superstition the search for trait–situation interactions. These are not, however, necessary consequences.
2. Validity generalization is fundamentally a bivariate process, most often concerned with the relationship between one predictor and one criterion. It is not, at least as

TABLE 7.6

Five Suggestions for Improving Validity Generalization Research and Applications

---

Become Bayesian: In most areas of research, there is some variability in study outcomes that cannot be explained by statistical artifacts. Schmidt and Hunter were right in 1977 to think of the problem of interpreting study outcomes in Bayesian terms, and it is time to get back to our Bayesian roots.

Define the Population: There is no such thing as *the population*, and it is the researcher's job to define the population he or she wishes to generalize to and to justify that definition. It always pays to be skeptical in evaluating these definitions.

Care about Quality: Meta-analyses that attempt to be comprehensive usually end up giving more weight to bad studies than to good ones, simply because there are so many bad ones out there. The excuse is that evaluations of study quality are subjective. They are. Get over it. Ten good studies are usually more useful than sixty bad ones.

Change the Name: It is time to retire the jersey "Validity Generalization." Psychometric meta-analysis conveys the idea quite nicely.

Reform the Language: Stop calling parameter estimates *true*. They aren't.

From "The past, present, and future of validity generalization" by K. R. Murphy and D. A. Newman, 2003. In *Validity Generalization: A Critical Review* (Table 14.1, p. 421), by K. R. Murphy (Ed.), 2003, Mahwah, NJ: Lawrence Erlbaum Associates. Copyright 2003 by Lawrence Erlbaum Associates. Reprinted with permission.

described in this chapter, concerned with the "third variable" problem—the possibility that correlation may be *inflated* with contaminants common to the variables. Table 7.4 lists many artifacts that reduce correlation, but it seems silent on the third-variable question, the question of pervasive contamination.

3. What is learned from a meta-analysis of consistently flawed data? If an entire body of research is subject to one or more common flaws, the issue centers on the confidence one can have in that entire body. The allegation of universal flaws is not likely, of course, but the question may lead to better research designs, even to a need for a new set of studies for a new meta-analysis. A more likely allegation is that all the studies are flawed but in such different ways that the flaws cannot emerge as moderating influences. This is a partial reprise of the quality issue, but the early computer warning, GIGO (garbage in, garbage out), seems equally applicable to meta-analysis.

4. I once knew a delightful lady who declared the overwhelming principle of test use to be, "Don't use rancid data." Meta-analysts should follow her dictum. Very old studies should perhaps be excluded because their methods, measures, or subjects (jobs) are so outmoded that their results have no contemporary relevance. How far back in the history of research on a topic can a meta-analysis go without getting rancid data? For a research topic active over a long time, one VG analysis could provide a corrected mean correlation for old studies and a different one could compute it for new (relatively) ones, and the two could be compared for consistency. In the effort to find all studies related to a meta-analysis, researchers conscientiously gather much old, rancid data. The most often cited generalization is that cognitive tests are related to job performance; most of the evidence for that generalization was based on studies of the GATB (General Aptitude Test Battery) collected more than three decades ago. Much has changed, in work and in testing practices, during those decades. Because of modern technology, some jobs have developed a stronger cognitive component, but others have lost much of the cognitive demands of the work they did

because the technology has created automatic procedures to replace their previously complex work.[12]

5. A related problem is that VG procedures do not acknowledge the possibility that validities might change over time; old, outdated studies can be dubious. Responding to this idea, Schmidt, Pearlman, Hunter, and Hirsh (1985, p. 722) said, "Anyone advancing the hypothesis that validities change or have changed over time should present evidence supporting this hypothesis." I consider that response essentially unscientific, because very little research has studied the stability of the sources of validity over time or the effect of specific environmental change (e.g., technological change) on test–criterion relationships. Almost as an aside, Sackett and DuBois (1991) re-analyzed a race-of-rater, race-of-ratee meta-analysis reported by Kraiger and Ford (1985); one moderator studied was year data were gathered, dichotomized as before or after 1970 (an appropriate year considering the timing of OFCC and EEOC regulations); effect sizes were substantially different, although only eight studies in all were in the analysis. For the more typical meta-analysis, Frank Landy suggested that studies done before and after 1985 be compared because the nature of work began to change dramatically about that time from the influences of technology and the nature of organizations.[13] Another controversy raises the question of whether a single meta-analysis should include studies in which the time interval between predictor and criterion measurement varies from zero to a very long time. This controversy was discussed in Chapter 3 in the discussion of the possibility of dynamic criteria. The possibility should not be ignored. Perhaps a mean validity coefficient, once established, is as permanent as the aqueducts of Rome, but the open-minded researcher will consider effects of circumstances that might prove an exception.

6. Meta-analysis examines sets of independent research findings for the same basic hypothesis. In practice, it is often hard to identify the variables of "the same basic hypothesis" and to know if different studies are properly considered replications. How precisely, or how generally, should the variables be defined? Most definitions of meta-analytic constructs are rather amorphous—if offered at all. In a meta-analysis of studies of unspecified constructs, the mean corrected coefficient, r_c, is still the correlation between a couple of unspecified constructs. But even if the substantive meaning of the mean correlation is obscured or imprecisely understood, the result is nevertheless a supported generalization, and a broad one, and it can have practical implications. But is an understanding resulting from clear construct definition an impractical luxury?

7. When is situational specificity safely rejected? Simply by accounting for most of the variance with artifacts? The 75% rule? When the confidence interval around r_c is small? How small? Many meta-analytic studies have searched for moderators, and many moderator variables have been reported. Is situational specificity to be rejected when a search for moderators fails? What if no one moderator is common enough in even a large set of studies to provide much variance? The notion that unidentified variables in local situations influenced the size of validity coefficients was invoked early in history to explain the wide differences in validity coefficients found in apparently similar settings. The notion went untested for years, largely because there

---

[12] The point was made in detail by Neal Schmitt in an address to graduate students at Bowling Green State University, November 7, 2009.

[13] Personal communication August 25, 2008.

was no known way to test it. Meta-analysts provided and applied a method, and situational specificity has typically been found wanting; indeed, some proponents of meta-analysis at any cost have declared situational specificity dead and ready for burial—at least for cognitive assessments. Work has consistently shown that the variability among validity coefficients is less than previously supposed, but it has not convincingly demonstrated that validity variance necessarily reduces to zero. "It is hard to believe that context has no effect on test validity other than that which arises as purely technical artifacts of measurement" (Hedges, 1988, p. 200).

8. VG is still concerned with bivariate relationships, at least as far as it has been described in this chapter. Advances in meta-analysis to be described in the next chapter include multivariate considerations, but many extant summaries of validity studies are purely bivariate, with all the interpretation issues that implies.

In spite of these issues, validity generalization must be recognized at least as one of the major methodological advances in personnel research in the lives of most current researchers.

CONCLUDING NOTE ON BIVARIATE PREDICTION

In regression analysis, the predicted value is a specific point on the criterion scale for a given predictor score. A specifically identified person will perform at that level, or above it, or below it; there is a distribution of criterion levels at any specified score level. An interval, based on the standard error of estimate, can be determined within which the criterion value for an individual may be expected at a given probability. To simplify the statistical language, we can say that, *on the average*, people with a certain score will perform at the predicted criterion level, and most people are not going to perform at that precise average. Most researchers and practitioners know both things, but in their statistical zeal, they tend to forget them and focus only on averages. Together, these statements say that the predictor variable itself leads us to expect a certain criterion performance, but that chance or events or situations or related "third" variables may lead a particular job candidate to perform at a better or poorer level than the average for the score. Most research reports, and most operational personnel decisions, are content to predict the simple, central point value associated with a candidate's score. I insist that predictions should routinely include confidence intervals around that point, both for making personnel decisions and for primary research studies, as well as in meta-analyses.

Moreover, we must get over our history of blind acceptance of the notion that predictive inferences from assessment are as valid as a bivariate correlation describes them; no more, no less. It simply is not true. Too much remains unexplained after the coefficient is computed, and the explanations—and both the theoretical and practical understanding of the predictive relationship—require systematic consideration of other variables. If personnel researchers stop behaving like three blind mice, they will do thorough, well-planned multivariate research. That is the next topic.

8

The Use of Multivariate Statistics

Most jobs are complex—complex enough that effective performance requires more than just one trait. Prediction is usually better with more than one predictor. It can be improved by using specific combinations or patterns of trait measures and sometimes by including situational characteristics as well. Methods of prediction may use predictors and make predictions sequentially. Many options exist, and choosing among them requires both statistical considerations and professional judgment.

Evidence of validity, as now understood, consists of data and inference used to develop a validity argument. The first step in argument development is a clear, rationally supportable predictive hypothesis that an organizationally important criterion construct is related to a hypothesized predictor construct. It becomes a testable hypothesis when operational measures are chosen for both constructs. Testing a bivariate hypothesis may not provide adequate evidence. The bivariate hypothesis may be deficient, omitting equally important traits. Measures may be systematically contaminated by irrelevant traits, or may simply fail to measure the intended construct well. Evidence of validity, therefore, often requires the tests user to understand what is being (or not) measured. One aspect of validity is relational or predictive. Another is interpretive, a matter of meaning. Employment test validity arguments need evidence of both predictive and psychometric aspects.

This chapter begins with compensatory multiple prediction models in which a candidate's strength in one predictor can compensate for a weakness in another. The most commonly used multivariate approach to prediction is the compensatory model known as multiple linear regression (MLR), also called ordinary least squares (OLS) regression. This I discuss at a very basic, elementary level because the basics are so often forgotten in handing over the computational work to computer software. Other prediction models are introduced and described briefly; this chapter does not try to teach statistics, but it does try to expand statistical horizons beyond the common boundaries. My intent is to introduce (or at least mention) methods often overlooked in the habitual (and sometimes inappropriate) use of MLR. Some of them are relatively new and have been introduced and used more in other disciplines than in personnel psychology, but they deserve to be considered in trying to improve personnel decisions.

COMPENSATORY PREDICTION MODELS

Scores on predictors can be combined in any of several models. In a linear, additive model—the most common kind of model, of which MLR is a common example—scores are summed to form a composite, often assigning different weights to different variables. The several predictors are assumed to be linearly related to each other in the composite, and the composite is assumed to be linearly related to the criterion.

269

TABLE 8.1

Composite Scores for Three Traits for Three Hypothetical Candidates

	Trait			
Candidate	1	2	3	Sum
Without different weights				
A	10	10	10	30
B	8	10	12	30
C	15	0	15	30
With different weights				
Weights	2	3	1	
A	20	30	10	60
B	16	30	12	58
C	30	0	15	45

An additive model is *compensatory*; a person's strength in one trait may compensate for relative weakness in another. Consider Table 8.1. Candidate A has equal strength in all three traits. Candidate B is weaker than A in Trait 1 but may have enough added strength in Trait 3 to compensate. Candidate C is extremely deficient in Trait 2 but strengths in the other two may compensate. All three form the same composite score by adding the three component scores. This is called *unit weighting* because each score can be regarded as multiplied by 1.0 (a unit weight). However, if some traits are deemed more important than the others, they may have more weight (i.e., be multiplied by larger values) in forming the additive composite, as in the lower half of Table 8.1. If Trait 2 is considered so important that C's deficiency in it is unacceptable despite other scores, a purely additive (compensatory) model is inappropriate. Many ways have been proposed and used for additive combinations, and for alternatives to additive models, to use multiple measures to predict and to understand criteria of interest. I will describe some of them, but quite briefly, in the hope that the references provided will be consulted for fuller discussions of those that seem especially appropriate for specific personnel predictions.

Regression Equations

Multiple regression analysis, specifically MLR, is the most commonly used linear additive model. It finds optimal weights for the several predictors—optimal in the sense that the composite scores formed have the best possible correlation with the criterion in the sample studied. (Nearly all standard texts in statistics offer a fuller discussion of multiple regression; the discussion here is a brief summary emphasizing features that appear in other methods or that the other methods hold in contrast to multiple regression.) The composite score permits prediction or estimation, with minimal error, of the expected criterion value for each person. Those optimal weights are optimal *only* in the research sample. In a different sample, even from the same population, different "optimal" weights would be found. The best to be expected—the best to hope for—is that the weights computed in one sample will approximate those computed in most other samples.

If weights are assigned subjectively, as in Table 8.1, they are *nominal* weights, and they may differ from *effective* weights, a distinction discussed later. MLR regression weights are statistically computed, for use with either standardized or unstandardized scores, but computed and effective weights may also differ substantially unless scores are standardized before computing presumably optimal weights. Unstandardized weights depend on relative variances, so standardized regression has the effect of controlling variances across measures. To retain the notation used in Chapter 7, I shall continue to use the letter b as the weight computed for standard scores (instead of the conventional β). In raw score form (with simple subscripts), the multiple regression equation for n predictors is

$$Y = a + b_1X_1 + b_2X_2 + \ldots + b_nX_n \tag{8.1}$$

where a is the Y *intercept* of the weighted predictor composite and b is a regression coefficient, providing optimal weights for multiplying predictors, as identified by subscripts, to maximize the slope of the composite regression equation (i.e., maximize correlation). A composite score C is the sum of b_nX_n products, and the equation can written in the familiar bivariate $Y = a + bC$ form, where b = the slope of the regression of Y on the composite score C. In the two-variable case, regression coefficients can be computed directly from the relevant correlation coefficients and standard deviations:

$$b_1 = [(r_{yx_1} - r_{xy_2}r_{x_1x_2})/(1 - r^2_{x_1x_2})]\cdot(s_y/s_{x_1})$$

and $\tag{8.2}$

$$b_2 = [(r_{yx_2} - r_{yx_1}r_{x_1x_2})/(1 - r^2_{x_1x_2})]\cdot(s_y/s_{x_2})$$

where values of r are correlation coefficients, specified by subscripts, and s refers to a standard deviation, as indicated by the subscripts. These equations work fine for a two-predictor case; beyond that, they get unwieldy.

If $r_{x_1x_2} = 0$, the regression weight of either predictor is its validity coefficient reduced by the ratio of the criterion standard deviation to the predictor standard deviation.[1] If raw score distributions are standardized, all standard deviations are 1.0, so standardized regression weights equal the validity coefficients. If the two validity coefficients differ, the predictor with the higher validity has the greater weight, and the disparity increases as the inter-correlation ($r_{x_1x_2}$) increases. If $r_{x_1x_2} = 1.0$, one predictor is enough; the other adds nothing.

Multiple Correlation

Predictions are based on regression equations, but the accuracy or precision of those predictions is indicated by correlation coefficients. Correlation indicates the strength of the relationship of the predictor composite to the criterion. It can be computed as a bivariate r, with the optimal composites as X, or from existing correlation coefficients. For the two-predictor case,

---

[1] That ratio is necessarily 1.0 or less. With perfect correlation, predicted and actual criterion values will be the same and so will their standard deviations. With imperfect correlation, $r_{yx} < 1.00$, there is always some regression to the mean, meaning that predicted criterion values regress (move) toward the criterion mean, resulting in a lower variance or standard deviation. Because less-than-perfect correlation is always expected, regression weights are lower than the validity coefficients.

$$R^2_{y \cdot x_1 x_2} = \frac{r^2_{yx_1} + r^2_{yx_2} - 2r_{yx_1}r_{yx_2}r_{x_1x_2}}{1 - r^2_{x_1x_2}} \tag{8.3}$$

Where the square root, $R_{y \cdot x_1 x_2}$ = the coefficient of multiple correlation for two X variables predicting Y; the various product–moment correlations are defined by the subscripts. The equation shows general principles of multiple correlation: (a) the validity of the composite is proportional to the validities of the components, and (b) the validity of the composite is inversely proportional to the intercorrelations among components.

Suppressor and Moderator Variables

Suppressors

By those principles, each test in a well-developed battery is a valid predictor of the chosen criterion and has low correlations with other variables. A generally valid predictor may contain an invalid, contaminating variance component. A variable that does not predict the criterion but is correlated with the contamination may improve prediction. To see how this works, look again at Equation 8.3. If $r_{yx_2} = 0$, even if both of the other two correlations are greater than zero, then the numerator of that equation becomes simply r_{yx_1} (the other two terms being zero). The denominator is less than 1.0 (because $r_{x_1x_2}$ is *not* zero); therefore, $R_{y \cdot x_1 x_2}$ is *greater* than the validity of the one valid predictor alone. The reason is that variable X_2 removes from the composite (suppresses) the unwanted variance in X_1 not associated with the criterion. In a regression equation, it has a negative weight. The effect is possible even if the intercorrelation is greater than zero; it can be identified by different signs for the regression weight and the correlation.

The effect is typically not great. If $r_{yx} = .30$ for the valid predictor, and if $r_{x_1x_2} = .40$—these are not unrealistic numbers—the multiple correlation coefficient is raised only to .33. With a higher intercorrelation, the suppressor effect is greater; it is also clearer if all three coefficients are first corrected for range restriction and criterion unreliability. Suppressor effects are rare, but not as rare as once thought (Tzelgov & Henik, 1991), and perhaps less rare with better models for variable selection (cf. Shieh, 2006).

Moderators

Moderator variables influence the relationship between other variables; they are correlated with correlation. Frederiksen and Melville (1954) found better prediction of academic performance from interests for noncompulsive students than for those classed as compulsive. Although it is easier to think about validities in subgroups, variations in correlations associated with a continuous variable like compulsiveness "should vary continuously . . . not jump from one value to another at some arbitrary level of compulsiveness" (Saunders, 1956, p. 209). That is, validity should change systematically and continuously as the level of the moderating variable changes. Saunders suggested adding a term to regression equations multiplying predictor scores by moderator scores. Where there is a moderator effect to investigate, the suggested regression equation for one predictor and one moderator has the form

$$Y = a + b_1 x + b_2 z + b_3 xz \tag{8.4}$$

where Y = the criterion, x = the predictor, z = the moderator variable, and xz = the product of scores on x and z, the interaction or moderator term, weighted in the composite by b_3. In Equation 8.4, variables X and Z are expressed in deviation score units (e.g., $x = X - M_x$), with means of zero, unlike the linear Equation 8.1. *Moderated multiple regression* is an additive (compensatory) model, but it is not linear because of the multiplicative term. A significant interaction term says that, for every value of z, there is a different slope of the regression of y on x, even though the difference may be small and gradual (for more complex interactions, see Aiken & West, 1991).

Deviation scores (or perhaps z-scores), not raw scores, should be used when variables are multiplied. The effect of raw score computation in regression analysis is to standardize all components, including the product term. Aiken and West pointed out that standardizing products of raw scores (instead of the scores themselves) results in sometimes dramatic changes in the linear regression terms of the component variables themselves.

The introduction of the moderator concept more than a half-century ago induced an initial surge of enthusiasm. Researchers made sweeping searches for moderators in whatever data pool was available, and such reliance on empirical but thoughtless exploration was rarely rewarded. Searching for demographic moderators (as solutions to fairness problems) was no more fruitful. Searches for moderators in the validity generalization paradigm did no better. For several years, many selection specialists gave up on moderators. However, as patterns of research became more thoughtful and relied less on empirical serendipity, moderators seemed to be less elusive; recently, Sackett and Lievens (2008) said that research is moving more toward the explanatory power of moderators (and mediators) than to the emphasis on main effects of prediction *per se*.

Two of the five-factor personality traits have frequently shown predictive value by themselves. Conscientious workers tend to be organized and disciplined; conscientiousness has been found related to performance in many jobs, but with considerable variability among validity coefficients. Agreeableness has been found valid in a more restricted kind of job, those where necessary collaboration is a more likely component. Theoretical arguments suggest that people high in conscientiousness but low in interpersonal competence might not perform well, leading Witt, Burke, Barrick, and Mount (2002) to propose that agreeableness, especially in occupations requiring some degree of joint functioning, might moderate the predictive validity of conscientiousness. Figure 8.1 illustrates the effect they found in a fairly large sample of clerical workers who worked with customers and interdependently with coworkers. In five of seven samples, substantial moderator effects were found, and in all of these, some worker interdependence was a job characteristic. In two others, one a sample of cross-country truck drivers and the other a group of managers whose work with others was more hierarchical than collaborative, low levels of agreeableness were less likely to cancel out the predictive value of conscientiousness. Why? In some jobs, but not in others, "substantial interaction with others and cooperation are critical for success at work . . . the conscientiousness–agreeableness interaction is likely to have less . . . impact on performance when frequent interaction with others is not an important part of the job" (Witt et al., 2002, p. 168).

Some failures to find moderators are due to methodological errors (e.g., use of raw scores), but many more seem due to trying variables as moderators without a logical basis for trying them. The Witt et al. research was not based on a hope for serendipity; it proceeded from serious thinking, hypothesizing, and theory formation. The field of industrial and organizational psychology is big, with many activities and concepts expected to influence a variety of work outcomes. A systematic consideration of such variables surely should be a rich source of reasoned moderator hypotheses.

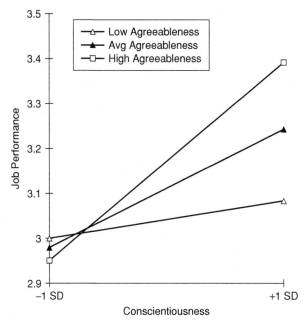

FIG. 8.1   Job performance regressed on conscientiousness scores for three levels of agreeableness scores. Reprinted from Witt, L. A., Burke, L. A., Barrick, M. R., & Mount, M. K. (2002). The interactive effects of conscientiousness and agreeableness on job performance. *Journal of Applied Psychology, 87*, 164–169. © 2002 by American Psychological Association. Reprinted with permission.

Another source of an apparent (rather than a real) failure to find moderators is the use of inappropriate measures of effect size. Often, no measure of effect size is attempted beyond looking at the regression weight for the interaction term. Aiken and West (1991), following Cohen (1988), offered the f^2 statistic as a measure of effect size for interaction terms. Few researchers report effect sizes, perhaps because most computer packages seem to offer only eta squared (η^2) as an effect size statistic; η^2 is an absolute maximum correlation capitalizing on chance fluctuations and errors in the measures. The f^2 statistic is "the proportion of *systematic variance* accounted for by the effect relative to *unexplained variance* in the crite-rion" (Aiken & West, 1991, p. 157, emphasis in original); i.e., unexplained by main effects. The equation assumes homogeneity of error variance across subgroups when interacting variables are categorical rather than continuous (Aguinis & Pierce, 2006). Noting that an equation for f^2 that corrects for violations of the homogeneity assumption is quite complex, Aguinis and Pierce offered a simplified program for computing it and provided an internet source.

Other Additive Composites

Multiple regression is only one way to form a composite, and reasons for forming compos-ites are not limited to criterion prediction.[2] Reasons might include, for example, weighting

---

[2] This section is taken more or less verbatim from Guion (1991), based largely on the unjustifiably but generally ignored work of Richardson (1941).

predictors to promote an organizational policy. "The general problem of the combination of measures has been obscured by the indiscriminate adoption of the multiple correlation technique as the 'best' solution, *and by the failure to investigate the properties of various weighting systems*" (Richardson, 1941, p. 379, emphasis added). With computers and mindless use of software, the problem is even more obscured than Richardson suspected; it is now easy to compute regression weights, appropriate or not.

Effective versus Nominal Weights

Decision makers frequently prefer to assign subjective weights to the variables they will combine. In any weighting method, the weights one *thinks* one is using can differ from the actual contributions of component variables to the composite: "It does not follow that test variables with equal linear weights have actually been weighted equally. The mischievous character of arbitrarily assigned weights depends on the fact that the actual *effective* weights turn out to be quite different from the *nominal* weights originally assigned" (Richardson, 1941, p. 380). This discussion of the "mischievous character," like Richardson's, is limited to linear, additive models with either zero or positive correlation (i.e., no variables with negative correlation).

Suppose we have three variables to combine. The effective weight of each is its contribution to the total variance of composite scores. Assuming perfect reliability for simplification, these general principles govern effective weights:

1. If component variables are in standard score form, they have equal variances of 1.0; if they also have zero intercorrelations, their effective weights are proportional to the *squares* of the nominal weights. If variable *A* is to be weighted twice as heavily as *B* or *C*, the nominal weights are 2, 1, and 1, but the effective weights of uncorrelated standard scores are 4, 1, and 1, respectively.
2. If intercorrelations are zero, but variances are not equal, the effective weight of a component is proportional to the product of the square of its nominal weight (V) and its variance s^2.
3. If nominal weights and variances are unequal, and if variables are positively correlated, the effective weight of a component is proportional to the product of its nominal weight and the weighted sum of its correlations with other variables. (Treating reliability as perfect, the self-correlation is 1.00 in these computations.) The equation for total composite variance, s_t^2, is:

$$s_t^2 = V_1 s_1 \Sigma V_i r_{1i} s_i + V_2 s_2 \Sigma V_i r_{2i} s_i + \ldots + V_n s_n \Sigma V_i r_{ni} s_i \qquad (8.5)$$

where V, r, and s refer to nominal weight, correlation, and standard deviation, respectively, the subscripts $1 \ldots n$ refer to the variables, and the subscript i refers to all other variables; so, r_{ni} refers to the correlations of variable n with each of the other variables.[3] Table 8.2 shows nominal weights, standard deviations, and intercorrelations in a three-component situation; relative nominal and effective weights are also shown. (Relative weights are computed by summing weights for all variables and dividing each weight by the sum.) Relative nominal and effective weights differ substantially.

---

[3] If you miss seeing weights and standard deviations squared, see Richardson's derivation (1941, p. 383).

TABLE 8.2

Data for a Hypothetical Three-Variable Composite

Variable	V	s	Correlations			Relative Weights	
			A	B	C	Nominal	Effective
A	1	1	1.00	.50	.80	.167	.067
B	3	2		1.00	.60	.500	.460
C	2	3			1.00	.333	.473

Modified and reproduced from Guion, R. M., Personnel assessment, selection, and placement, in *Handbook of Industrial and Organizational Psychology, 2nd Edition, Volume 2*, by Dunnette, M. D. and Hough, L. M. (Eds.). © by Nicholas Brealey Publishing; used by permission.

4. If all other considerations are equal, and if the assumption of perfect reliability is not made, the effective weight of a component is directly proportional to its reliability. It used to be common to weight variables nominally by the inverse of their standard deviations. This works if differences in variances are caused by differences in construction (e.g., when one test has 10 items and another has 100). If differences in variances are associated with differences in reliabilities, the inverse of the standard deviations (or unit weighting z-scores) the anomaly of giving the highest effective weight to the least reliable component can happen.

Each of these situations has assumed either positive intercorrelations or zero. What if they are negative? To deal with that issue, we must recognize two quite different purposes in weighting variables. One is predictive. With standardized measures, we know that regression coefficients ("optimal" weights) are inversely related to intercorrelations and, if intercorrelations are zero, the regression coefficients are the same as the validity coefficients. Throwing a negative correlation between variables into Equation 8.2 increases the regression coefficient still further, and improves R^2. A negative correlation between two variables, each positively related to the criterion to be predicted, will improve prediction. But, for this purpose, weights for optimal prediction are more likely to work if they are empirically, not subjectively, determined.

The other purpose is to create a composite measure that is at least somewhat internally consistent and interpretable—a composite that means something—such as weighting items in a test or biodata inventory. One might want to weight items according to their judged importance. Weights might be assigned to maximize reliability, overall variance, or common factor variance (see, e.g., Green, 1950, and, for a different view, Horst, 1966). For such purposes, component correlations should be positive; in trying to create a measure of something, it makes no sense to combine unrelated things, let alone those that are negatively related. Combining negatively related components provides a composite with little or no psychological meaning.

A weighting scheme matters if only a few variables form the composite. In these cases, it should be based on rational or theoretical grounds rather than on computations alone. One important rational principle is simplicity. Studies long ago cast doubt on the value of weights determined by very sophisticated methods. Ghiselli and Brown (1949), using arbitrary weights based on results from an unrelated study, reported a high validity coefficient. Lawshe and Schucker (1959) reported predictions as good for sums of raw scores as for more formal methods, including multiple regression, supposed to maximize predictive accuracy.

Often, psychometric and statistical assumptions are not met in applied settings; it is not wise to take excessive pride in an impressive weighting system. It is wise to see if the effective weights make sense.

Unit Weighting

Unit weighting means simply adding scores or standard scores, literally multiplying by 1.0, as in the top of Table 8.1. Dawes and Corrigan (1974) insisted, and demonstrated, that use of more complex models offers no more than slight improvement over simple weights, whether equal or differential, in accounting for criterion variance; their finding held even with randomly chosen weights. Others have supported the finding (Einhorn & Hogarth, 1975; Wainer, 1976). However, Cattin (1978) said that regression weights may predict better than unit weights if (a) patterns of intercorrelations among the predictor variables differ, (b) the regression-based multiple R is high, (c) different predictors have substantially different weights, and (d) the ratio of subjects to variables is large. He recommended an empirical comparison, computing both a cross-validated R (discussed later) and the correlation for the unit-weighted composite—and using whichever is higher. I suggest a third option to try: unequal weights that approximate or are somewhat proportional to the optimal regression weights (analogous to smoothing a curve). In general, carefully computing weights to several decimal places gives only the appearance of precision; simpler nominal weights may do as well or better if variables are carefully selected, are positively (but modestly) correlated with each other, and do not differ greatly in criterion-related validities or reliabilities. In any case, the message of Richardson's essay holds clear: Find effective weights and see if they reasonably represent the nominal weights your judgment called for.

Logistic Regression

Criteria may be constrained to fit within specified parameters. A common example is group membership, the constraint being integers, as many integers as groups. If the criterion is the probability of being in a designated group, its range is limited to values within the range of zero to +1.0, or perhaps a simple dichotomy. Harrison (2002) referred to such criteria as *limited range dependent variables (LRDVs)*, including highly skewed criteria or discrete variables with two or more categories. Dichotomies pose special constraints; a person is either in a specified condition or situation or is not—a yes or no constraint. It may be that an event has occurred (such as an example of CWB), or it has not. It may be a matter of personal choice made or not made (e.g., quitting; applying for special training). It might be a change in something, such as being promoted within a specified time frame or changing status, as from apprentice to journeyman in a trade. Such criteria are clear dichotomies, usually coded as binary data (either 0 or 1), have firm constraints, at least by definition, with the category of major interest likely to be coded 1. These examples are *yes* or *no* categories: yes, required training is completed versus not completed; yes, the person quits within two years; or yes, the person engages in specific counterproductive (or, more useful) customer-pleasing behavior.

Multiple regression *can* be used to predict such criteria, treating the 0 and 1 categories as points on an underlying continuum, but it does not give very satisfactory information. Regression coefficients are often very peculiar and hard (even impossible) to interpret sensibly. To understand the problem, consider the simple case of linear bivariate regression, with the criterion changed to a continuous probability criterion, limited by zero and +1.0.

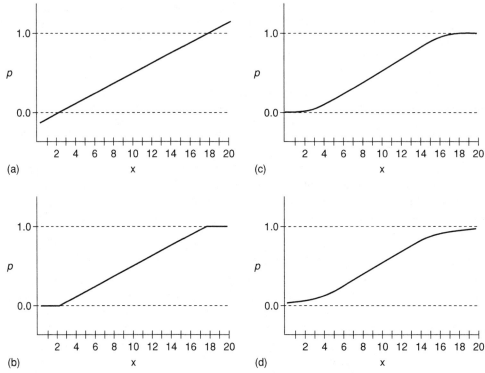

FIG. 8.2 Effects of constrained criteria on linear regression: (a) ordinary linear regression permitting prediction outside of the criterion limits; (b) predictions forced to be level at criterion limits despite regression equation; (c) somewhat smoothed version of curve in (b); (d) a curve fitted to the logistic model with retained linearity in the middle of the X distribution.

The regression coefficient refers unambiguously to the slope of the regression line. A unit change in the predictor is associated with a specific amount of change in the criterion, the amount being defined by the slope. With linear regression, the amount of criterion change per unit of predictor change is constant—the same for low, moderate, or high scoring people. However, if the criterion has limits of zero and 1.0, as a probability criterion does, linear predictions for people with extreme scores are likely to fall outside those limits—greater than 1.0 or less than zero—as in Figure 8.2a. Of course, for practical purposes, predictions are kept within the limits by treating people (in Figure 8.2a) with scores of 0–2 as if the predicted criterion were zero, or those with scores of 14–16 as if the predicted criterion were +1.0. This is shown in Figure 8.2b. The sharp angles in (b) seem unrealistic; the regression seems more likely to change slope from 0.67 to zero gradually, as in (c), with extreme scores asymptotic to the criterion limits. Computing a nonlinear regression, such as a logistic curve with a point of inflection somewhere in the midrange, is more clearly interpretable. That, of course, cannot be done if the criterion is a dichotomy, predicting either yes or no for the category of interest.

It seems, however, that most researchers stick with the dichotomous criterion (e.g., quitting or staying in the first year). That approach, as with biserial correlation, predicts for each person only whether he or she will be a member of the group that stays or the group that leaves. It allows no differentiation within either group. A more useful criterion would be the corresponding probability, pretty much as given in an expectancy chart. When the criterion is the probability of staying, it is a continuous variable permitting differentiation of the probability of being in the group of interest all the way through the predictor scale. The curve in Figure 8.2c, visually smoothed, is appropriate for any yes–no criterion for which a continuous probability (e.g., of *yes*) can be determined and predicted, although it retains the rigid linearity within most of the range defined by the boundaries of zero and 1. Figure 8.2d, *a logistic regression*, is preferable because it is computed from equations, and its point of inflection identifies the predictor score where the likelihood of category membership changes.

The transformation of dichotomous data to probability data is not always easy, but it is often possible and sensible to assume that a continuous underlying latent variable (e.g., propensity to quit) exists and accounts for or explains membership in the observable category of interest. DeMaris (2004, pp. 251–255) offered a readable mathematical foundation for the transformation. A logistic function is one of several functions, probably the most commonly used, for describing the relationship of the underlying latent probabilities to predictor variables, and DeMaris describes one of these—probit regression—in tandem with logistic regression.

An approximation of the logistic function can be developed heuristically with simple arithmetic—less precise than formal equations but showing the basic logic. Table 8.3 shows make-believe scores on an assessment X for 50 people assessed and hired. Of these, after time, half are classified as "yes" in a yes–no dichotomy. Remember (from IRT) that a logistic curve is a good approximation of an ogive, such as a cumulative frequency ogive. Figure 8.3 shows that ogive for assessment X. In the psychometric middle ages (i.e., 1940s and 1950s), data from 50 people would have been considered a good-sized sample, but not now and not for the present purpose. Even with such a small data set, however, probabilities of a "yes" score can be computed, even if not reliably. A modicum of reliability

TABLE 8.3
Frequency Distributions for Test X and Probabilities of Being Classified in Group I ("Yes")

X	f	cum f	f_{yes}	p_{yes}	p_{yes} in score group
24	1	50	1	1.0	
23	1	49	0	0.0	
22	1	48	1	1.0	0.8
21	2	47	2	1.0	
20	3	45	2	0.7	
19	4	42	3	0.8	
18	7	38	4	0.6	0.6
17	9	31	6	0.7	
16	8	22	5	0.6	
15	5	14	1	0.2	
14	3	9	0	0.0	0.3
13	2	6	0	0.0	
12	2	4	0	0.0	
11	1	2	0	0.0	
10	1	1	0	0.0	0.0
9	0	0	0	0.0	

can be achieved, however, by grouping scores, as shown by dashed lines in Table 8.3. Plotting the five resulting points in Figure 8.3 shows the development of a curve roughly similar to an ogive or logistic curve. It does droop for the final segment at the top, but that average is based on only three cases; adding another one or two cases could make that final segment go in virtually any direction, including horizontal! If the curve is drawn and smoothed, even with only four data points, it is possible to estimate the probability for any given score.

A logistic curve is neither a linear model nor additive. Additivity requires linearity for each predictor—that the change in Y associated with a change in X be constant throughout the range of scores. This is obviously not true in nonlinear regression. With two or more predictors, each with its own functional relation to Y, any combination of predictors is likely to "inherently" violate the additivity assumption and makes predictors interactive (Pampel, 2000, p. 8). Even so, part of the attractiveness of logistic regression is that it can be used for prediction of discrete, limited range criteria in a variety of applications and contexts, such as event history analysis (Allison, 1984; Yamaguchi, 1991) or multilevel research (Gelman & Hill, 2007).

Although logistic regression cannot be included among the linear, additive models, its multivariate form can be considered a compensatory model. However, it is necessary to transform the probability of each Y_i into a *logit*, a transformation of the logistic function into a more tractable linear one. The statistical genealogy of logistic regression was more likely to express likelihood as *odds* than as *probabilities*, so it is useful to distinguish the two terms. The odds of an event occurring (a horse winning a race) might be something like 2 to 3 (written 2:3), meaning that if there are two chances it will occur, then there are 3 chances it will not. It is more meaningful, and necessary for computing logits, to express the odds as so many to 1. Odds of 2:3 are therefore expressed simply as 0.67, interpreted as 0.67:1. Statements of odds are not limited. Probabilities, values of p_i, are limited to the range from zero to 1.0; odds range from $+\infty$ to $-\infty$, definitely out of the LRDV category!

If the probability that individual i will be classed as *yes* is p_i, then the probability that individual i will *not* be classed as *yes* (i.e., will be classified in criterion category *no*) is

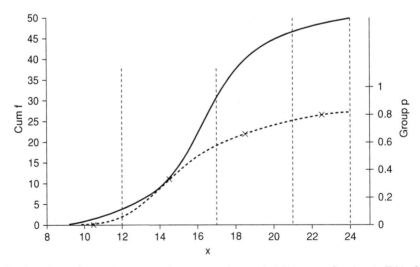

FIG. 8.3   Cumulative frequency ogive and corresponding probability curve for data in Table 8.3.

$1 - p_i$. The odds that the person will be classed as *yes* are defined by the ratio of these probabilities; the natural logarithm (logarithm to the base e) of the odds is a logit, designated here as L_i:

$$L_i = \frac{p_i}{1 - p_i} \tag{8.6}$$

If individual i has a one in four chance of being in the *yes* category, assigned a binary value of 1 ($p_i = .25$), that value transforms to a logit of 1.10, the natural logarithm of the odds ratio, $p_i/(1 - p_i)$. Notice in Table 8.4 that a probability of .5 refers to even odds and a logit of zero. Smaller probabilities have negative logit values; those above .5 translate to positive logits. More important, the relative change from one probability value to another is much less than the corresponding change in logits. For a .2 jump in probability from .5 to .7, the change in L_i is less than 1.0; the jump of .2 from $p = .7$ to $p = .9$ has a change in L_i greater than 2.0, a substantially different change in value. But a change in probability from .99 to .999 (a much smaller difference of .009) is associated with a still greater change in L_i. It is not surprising, from a cursory examination of Table 8.4, that the logit range is from $-\infty$ to $+\infty$. Table 8.4 illustrates these major characteristics of logits associated with several other values of p_i (not shown are the logarithms of 0 and 1, respectively, at negative and positive infinity). This transformation permits the logistic regression function to be linear, so that regression coefficients are interpreted as they would be in bivariate or multivariate linear regression. The constraints imposed by predicting probability with linear regression are, for practical purposes, virtually eliminated by predicting logits instead so that

$$L_i = a + bX_i \tag{8.7}$$

a *log-linear* form, and, for multivariate prediction,

$$L_i = a + b_1X_1 + b_2X_2 + \ldots b_nX_n \tag{8.8}$$

The logit, when predicted, can be converted back to a probability by turning the logarithm on its head. That is, we let the linear equation for a logit become the exponent of the base e; the equation is:

$$p_i = 1/(1 + e^{-L_i}) \tag{8.9}$$

Linear functions are what we think we know best and understand most easily. They offer predictions that have been useful. So why go through all this business of trying to convert criteria from dichotomies to continuous frequencies and subsequently to probabilities, odds, and logits? One reason is that by transforming the expected value of Y (EY|X in bivariate

TABLE 8.4
Transformation of Probabilities to Logits

p_i	.0001	.001	.01	.1	.3	.5	.7	.9	.99	.999	.9999
$1 - p_i$	.9999	.999	.99	.9	.7	.5	.3	.1	.01	.001	.0001
Odds	.0001	.00	.01	.111	.429	1.0	2.33	9.0	99.0	999.0	9999.0
L_i	−9.21	−6.91	−4.60	−2.20	−.847	0	.847	2.20	4.60	6.91	9.21

regression) to a logit, we have overcome the constraints of the dichotomous criterion and can actually "pound out predictions and test structural hypotheses" using our familiar linear hammer (Harrison, 2002, p. 448)—and do so with more precision and with recognition that individual differences still exist among people in a given category. Another is that log-linear forms have grown to include a variety of useful models for personnel decisions: e.g., (a) dependent variables with multiple categories from which discrete choice is made, that is, one to be chosen from a set of options (polytomous models), and (b) a whole class of models for predicting discrete counts over time (such as number of absences or number of grievances filed) which yield distinctly skewed distributions and for which OSL multiple regression is therefore inappropriate (Harrison, 2002, p. 473).

Plotting for Understanding

Long ago, Pat Smith (my colleague, known in the literature as Patricia Cain Smith) put a sign behind her desk so any student entering her office could see it. I've reproduced it (as well as memory allows) as Figure 8.4. It is clear, succinct, and something any supervisor of graduate research might want to post. Clearly, data plots, histograms based on two- or three-dimensional contingency tables, pie charts, and scattergrams with smoothed regression curves drawn relative to column central points can be useful in explaining statistical finds to people without statistical training, but the same graphic displays can also help the re-searchers themselves. They can help identify anomalies in the data such as outliers, subgroup differences in means or regression, heteroscedasticity, nonlinearity, sampling problems, or silly inferences.

Wainer (2005) illustrated a silly inference from some early nineteenth-century research studying longevity in different occupations. Death certificates had been studied for dates of birth, dates of death, and occupations. Mean age at death in each field was determined as an index to the safety or dangerousness of the occupation. "Student" was the most danger-ous occupation according to an average age at death of 20.7 years! A 1997 follow-up by Wainer's son checked dates of birth and death on tombstones in the local cemetery from birth dates in 1700 to 1980. A smoothed curve showed a somewhat consistent longevity until about 1920 when the curve dropped dramatically. "Obviously, the reason for the decline is nonrandom sampling: people cannot be buried in the cemetery if they are not already dead. Relatively few people born in the 1980s are buried in the cemetery, and [none of them] could have been older than seventeen" (Wainer, 2005, p. 144). Given the ages of people in my cohort still living, it seems that the Wainers may have to wait until 2080 or so to plot the data for the 1980s cohort! Retelling a Thurber fable illustrated that useful inferences can be drawn from nonrandom data—but with difficulty and great care and, I would add, a dose of skepticism. Plotting the data helps show where useful inferences cannot be made. Plotting subgroups in a single chart can identify situations in which a common regression

> HAVE YOU PLOTTED YOUR DATA?
>
> If Not, Go Away
>
> Don't Come Back Until You Have Done So

FIG. 8.4   Patricia Cain Smith's greeting to her students.

is inappropriate. Plotting, and other graphic displays, should become routine, especially when multiple predictors are used.

Utility Analysis

Multiple variables do not necessarily mean multiple predictors. The evaluation of a validity coefficient for a single predictor may require consideration of a great many other variables as well. The usefulness of a valid predictor depends on more than the size of the coefficient. It has long been known that the usefulness of a predictor depends on a combination of r, criterion variability and base rates, and the selection ratio. Taylor and Russell (1939) developed tables that measured usefulness by the increase in the proportion of employees considered satisfactory. Later, Brogden (1946, 1949) and Cronbach and Gleser (1957) developed utility analysis (so-called Brogden–Cronbach–Gleser model incorporating both psychometric and organizational variables). The basic equation (as presented by Boudreau, 1983) is

$$\Delta U = (N)(r_{yx})(\bar{Z}_x)(SD_y) - C \tag{8.10}$$

Where ΔU = the increase in payoff (in dollars) stemming from the predictor use, N is the number of employees selected by the procedure, r_{yx} is the validity coefficient, $\bar{Z}$ is the mean z-score of those selected, SD_y = criterion standard deviation, in dollars, without the predictor, and C = total cost, all things considered, of selection.

Much has been done in utility analysis since the development of the above equation, but this demonstrates its multiple considerations. In many organizations, the estimated utility is quite high—so high that many executives view it skeptically. Because individual selection decisions are not based on it, I do not go on to describe newer developments, but the basic principles (that utility is directly proportional to r, to the number hired under the procedure, to the mean qualification level, and to the criterion standard deviation) still holds.

NONCOMPENSATORY PREDICTION MODELS

It seems unlikely that a specific predictor is so important to performance that no other predictor can compensate for a weakness in it. Psychologically, people generally learn to live with their deficiencies and make up for them. Statistically, the idea of an absolutely essential, noncompensable attribute seems to suggest a discontinuous function, one with no performance overlap across the point of discontinuity. I know of no such finding. Even so, nonadditive, noncompensatory prediction models can be useful (e.g., Brannick & Brannick, 1989; Einhorn, 1971; Mertz & Doherty, 1974) if their implications are not taken too literally.

Multiple Cutoff Methods

A multiple cut (or multiple hurdles) approach sets a cut score for each of two or more predictors. An applicant scoring below the cut score on any one of them is rejected; each test is a "hurdle" to clear. Two situations may justify the method: (a) if each trait is so vital to performance that other personal strengths cannot compensate adequately for weaknesses in it, or (b) if the best, most experienced workers have a high enough score mean on a trait, coupled with low variance, to indicate importance of the trait. These are uncommon conditions; in general. Objections to cut scores in bivariate prediction apply even more to multiple cut scores, where even very low cut scores can result in rejecting too many candidates. A cut score about 1.5 *SD* below the mean of a normal distribution will reject about 7% of the candidates. If a similar cut score is set on another, uncorrelated measure, 7% will be rejected by it also. Some people might be in the low 7% on both tests, but the percentage of the total group being rejected will approach, even if it does not reach, 14%. More hurdles mean more rejections. Many of those passing all of the hurdles will do so with scores too low to suggest any genuinely useful qualifications at all. Cut scores high enough to assure people qualified on each trait may mean that no candidate qualifies on all of them.

A strict multiple cutoff approach is justified only when predictors are perfectly reliable (Lord, 1962, 1963). If practical considerations demand cut scores, the model can be modified as a partially compensatory model (Lord, 1963). Selection effects using compensatory, noncompensatory, and partially compensatory models are shown in Figure 8.5, in which cut scores on two variables are quite low. Those scoring above (or to the right of) the lines for the model in use may be offered employment (or other opportunity); those scoring below or to the left of the relevant line would be rejected. A partially compensatory model seems less arbitrary, less susceptible to false assumptions, and more likely to be justifiable than a rigidly noncompensatory model.

Sequential Hurdles

In a *sequential hurdles* approach, those who "pass" one or more preliminary steps are assessed later on other characteristics. The cut scores for preliminary assessments may be intended only to reduce the size of the group to be assessed by costlier methods. If it is set

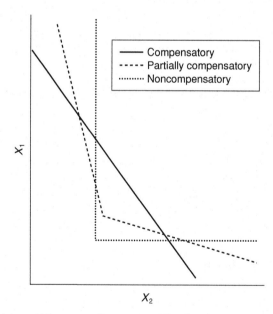

FIG. 8.5 Areas of decision within two-predictor scatterplots for compensatory, partially compensatory, and noncompensatory decision models. In each case, the area above or to the right of the line is the score area in which a decision to select is appropriate; those scoring below or left of the line are appropriately rejected. Reprinted from Guion, R. M., 1965, *Personnel Testing*. New York, McGraw-Hill. © R. M. Guion

pretty low, there may be no legal requirement for validation; that is, there may be no adverse impact. If it is high, however, it is important to recognize that a fixed cut score transforms scores to a binary dichotomy: 1 (pass) or 0 (fail). Adverse impact may exist, and it may be severe. Validation of this preliminary measure may appropriately use a criterion based on outcomes at a subsequent stage rather than on-the-job performance or other behavior, and it should use the dichotomous pass–fail scoring. Alternatively, the entire sequence, with its decision rules for progressing through the sequence of hurdles, may be considered a "personnel selection program" subject to program evaluation (considered below as a form of quasi-experimental research). I do not recall any examples of this alternative in operationally-focused personnel research, but the procedure deserves serious attention.

Moving on from the early hurdles may not be based on a fixed cut score; instead, a fixed number of candidates more qualified than others may move to the next stage. In this case, validation of and prediction from assessments at the various stages may appropriately be based on actual scores.

Conjunctive and Disjunctive Models

The following equations identify jointly one definition (there are others) of conjunctive and disjunctive *decision rules* (not literally predictions):

$$\text{Conjunctive: } Y = \min(b_1X_1 + a_1, \ldots, b_kX_k + a_k) \tag{8.11}$$

$$\text{Disjunctive: } Y = \max(b_1X_1 + a_1, \ldots, b_kX_k + a_k) \tag{8.12}$$

They suppose a battery of k predictors with a linear bivariate regression equation for each predictor (although other functions might be justified). The conjunctive decision rule bases decisions on the predictor that minimizes the estimated criterion value; there is no cut score. No other score in the set, no matter how high, compensates for an unsatisfactory prediction based on the minimum score. A disjunctive decision rule, similarly, is based on one predictor, the one with the highest estimated value of Y. No matter how poorly one performs on some other variable, the decision is based on the candidate's strength. These models should be considered much more often. The typical multiple regression model, with its emphasis on dispersions around mean values of Y, is a one-size-fits-all model; conjunctive or disjunctive models make decision making a bit more individualized.

Identifying Situations for Noncompensatory Models

Brannick and Brannick (1989) identified six possible prediction models, two of them using equations developed earlier by M. T. Brannick (1986). He saw that conjunctive and disjunctive models dealt with profiles in which points are scattered about a central level and developed equations for detecting nonadditive (i.e., noncompensatory) components in prediction.[4] The simpler of the two Brannick equations is

$$Y = a + \Sigma b_iX_i + b_{k+1}[\Sigma(z_i - \bar{z})^2]^{1/2} \tag{8.13}$$

---

[4] It should be noted that all of these are properly recognized, like logit regression, as examples of multiple regression, even though the organization of this chapter has largely limited the term to the common linear, additive model.

where Y is the predicted criterion value, the phrase $a + \Sigma b_i X_i$ is the conventional multiple regression term, and $\Sigma(z_i - \bar{z})^2$ is proportional to the standard deviation of the variables, expressed in z-scores, within the profile; $\bar{z}$ is the mean of the z-scores in the profile. If the scatter term adds significantly to the variance explained by the linear term, a noncompensatory model is suggested. The more powerful equation is

$$Y = a + b_i X_i + b_{k+1}[\Sigma B_i(z_i - Y^*)^2]^{1/2} \qquad (8.14)$$

where $a + \Sigma b_i X_i$ is the usual multiple regression equation; the full scatter term, $[\Sigma B_i(z_i - Y^*)^2]^{1/2}$, is proportional to within-profile variance, differing from the scatter term of Equation 8.13 in weighting the variables within the profiles according to their contribution to the predictions. Remember that the standardized regression coefficients, in bivariate relationships, are the same as the correlation coefficients. Here they are designated B to distinguish them from the unstandardized coefficients designated b (and from the linear β weights). The central tendency in Equation 8.13 is the profile mean z-score, and the profile points are straightforward z-scores. In Equation 8.14, it is the Y score predicted for the profile values, Y^*; the differences between profile z-scores and that central tendency are weighted before summing by their standardized regression coefficients (i.e., weights). In practice, use of Equation 8.14 requires three computational steps:

1. In standard score form, estimate standardized regression coefficients and standardized criterion scores from the ordinary least squares regression equation.
2. With Y^* as a central tendency of the standardized profile of variables, z_i as the standard score of variable i, and B_i as its corresponding standardized regression coefficient, compute the scatter term, $[\Sigma B_i(z_i - Y^*)^2]^{1/2}$. (This term, despite the use of standard scores, is not itself in standard score form, so it does not have unit variance.)
3. Then, in simultaneous regression, apply Equation 8.13. A new set of linear regression coefficients, the unstandardized b_i, will be computed as will the regression coefficient for the scatter or profile term, b_{k+1}.

In both Equation 8.13 and Equation 8.14, the scatter term suggests a nonadditive model if it adds significantly to the multiple correlation. In some uses, notably in predictions of judgments, the significance test is inappropriate because of within-judge dependencies, but even in such cases, Brannick and Brannick (1989) recommended heuristic use of the significance test. Note that Equation 8.14 provides a basis for estimating criterion variance associated with the scatter term, and that the degree of relationship can be estimated by correlating actual and expected values of the criterion. It does *not*, however, tell the decision maker how to use the information the scatter term provides. It might be used as it is, simply as a term adding significantly to prediction. It might be used conjunctively or disjunctively, or in some other nonadditive combination. Various algorithms might be tried to see which gives the maximum R^2. One such algorithm might be: *If X_1 is below a standard level, predict from X_2.*

I sympathize with frustrated readers at this point. I have said nothing about the relative benefits of these or other models that could be discussed, such as profile matching (Cattell, 1949; Guion, 1965a) or prediction from categorical variables (Guion, 1954; Wickens, 1989). Nevertheless, I am convinced that a variety of prediction models—particularly models avoiding the one-size-fits-all uniformity—are needed in this era of change and diversity more than ever before. I recommend strongly that personnel researchers study, develop, evaluate, and clarify uses of existing and new noncompensatory models.

REPLICATION AND CROSS-VALIDATION

Error is a fact of psychometric life. Each assessment and each statistic contains error—some inconsistent, some consistent. An additive composite holds hope that random errors may cancel each other. Hope may spring eternal, but it is not always rewarded. When scores are added, systematic errors may also be added, some random errors may be too big to be canceled by others, and some errors of either kind may by chance be correlated with error in the criterion. A simple additive combination can give a large validity coefficient in one sample that is never repeated in another. The problem is worse with complex weights, lots of variables, or peculiar nonadditive or nonlinear components. Because high validities encourage new personnel procedures promoting or requiring organizational change, it is unwise to rely on a one-shot coefficient that might have capitalized on errors. Results of validation, especially a multivariate one, need to be repeated—replicated—in a new sample.

Multiple regression requires cross-validation. Loose use of language sometimes treats cross-validation and replication as interchangeable, but they are different.[5] Cross-validation applies multiple regression weights obtained in one sample to data obtained in a different one to see whether the multiple R found in the first sample holds up in a second or whether it was inflated by sample-specific error. Replication refers to a repetition of an original study—with or without systematic change in weights, measures, or procedures—to see if independent results are similar.

Cross-validation is required in multiple regression studies because the composite-forming regression equation developed in one sample has the highest possible correlation with the criterion *in that specific research sample.* In another, independent sample from the same population, using the same equation, the new correlation is almost always lower. *Shrinkage,* the reduction in the size of the multiple coefficient of correlation in another sample, is expected. If shrinkage is negligible, the weights are considered stable; if large, the weights are not reliable and the composite is not recommended.

Double cross-validation combines replication with cross-validation. A regression equation is developed in each of two independent samples and cross-validated in the other. Predictors with strong weights in both equations have done well twice, and they can enter a new equation based on all cases, combining the two samples.

The logic of cross-validation calls for independent samples. A common but poor practice draws a sample and divides it, either into two equal samples or into one larger sample for initial research and a smaller "hold-out" sample for cross-validation. This practice may be better than no cross-validation at all, but it lacks independence. When a sample is randomly divided into two parts, any systematic error in one part is probably repeated in the other, making weights more similar than is likely in genuinely independent samples. Moreover, the research sample is smaller, so weights have more sampling error than if they had been obtained with the total sample. A cross-validated coefficient is sometimes higher than in the research sample—the opposite of shrinkage. Such an anomaly is more likely with interdependent samples. The practice was denounced by Murphy (1983), who titled it "Fooling Yourself With Cross-Validation: Single Sample Designs."

Dividing a single sample is ill-advised, but it may not be feasible to draw two large samples. An alternative is to estimate shrinkage from a single sample by formula estimation. Wherry (1931) offered the most commonly used equation for estimating the shrunken

[5] *Mea culpa.* In Guion and Gottier (1965), we used the term *cross-validation* when we were referring to simple replication.

coefficient from a single sample. As presented by Claudy (1978) but with notation used earlier, and in squared form, it is

$$\bar{R}^2 = 1 - [(n - 1)/(n - k - 1)]\cdot(1 - R^2) \tag{8.15}$$

where $\bar{R}$ = the estimate of the shrunken coefficient, R = the computed coefficient, n = sample size, and k = the number of predictors in the equation. Other equations have been offered. Results differ little among them; simplicity is a useful basis for choosing. Conceptually, $\bar{R}$ derived by formula differs somewhat from the empirically determined shrunken coefficient in two-sample cross-validation. It does not estimate correlation in a second sample; it estimates the population multiple correlation. Given the option, replication is preferable.

"Synthetic" Validity

Lawshe (1952) introduced the term *"synthetic" validity*, distinguished from generalized or situational validity, for testing procedures in small businesses where conventional validation was not feasible. "Synthetic" is in quotation marks because validity is not synthesized; validity is inferred or developed or discovered, but it is not synthetic. The term was borrowed from industrial engineering and synthetic time charts based on prior motion and time studies. What is synthesized is a valid test battery. Synthetic validity permits inferring validity for a test battery by (a) analyzing work into elements or component parts, (b) choosing tests and determining their validities for these elements, and (c) combining tests valid for components into batteries valid for the job as a whole (Balma, 1959; Scherbaum, 2005). I discuss it in the context of replications in the sense that prediction of one component may or may not be replicated with another. The basic idea is depicted in Figure 8.6, with seven job components and six predictors; the cells with Xs suggest a validity coefficient meeting some criterion (e.g., specified minimum effect size). A target job might consist mainly of components 1, 4, and 7. An appropriate test battery may, therefore, consist of predictors A, B, D, and F. This illustrates the concept; I purposely ignore practical issues (such as how to weight the different predictors, or whether to use just a couple of them) to concentrate on the ideas that have emerged from the original introduction of the term.

Job Component	Predictor					
	A	B	C	D	E	F
1	X			X		
2		X	X			
3					X	X
4	X	X				
5	X					X
6			X		X	
7				X		X

FIG. 8.6 Model of predictor–component validities for synthetic validity.

Some Personal Background

For full disclosure: I was an early enthusiast whose enthusiasm ebbed, but it may flow again. Some personal history may provide a context for the vacillating consideration to follow. I was a student of Lawshe's when he proposed the concept. Later, I was able to try it in a small business organization; the trial was reported only as an illustration because the sample was too small, even for that era (Guion, 1965b). Nevertheless, it was encouraging; however, three subsequent studies, with moderate to large samples, were deemed failures. Even though the synthetic batteries predicted overall job performance well on the different jobs, they did no better than the predictions made by lumping all jobs together and using a common battery; hence the ebbing enthusiasm. It ebbed further when I was on a monitoring committee for the US Army's Synthetic Validity Project (Wise, Peterson, Hoffman, Campbell, & Arabian, 1991). I'll describe the project below, but at the time, although the results pleased most committee members, I considered them too much like those I had written off as failures, partly because there was no discernible discriminant validity. An equation developed for one occupation could be applied just as well to others. Validity coefficients were as high as could reasonably be expected—and discriminant validities as low as anyone could fear.

I made two mistakes in judgment. One was too much emphasis on small business, not enough on small or rare jobs. Lawshe's original proposal was made during a symposium on small business, but nothing he ever said suggested small business as a restrictive venue for the approach. Even an organization as large as the US Army has jobs filled by so few people that traditional validation would not be feasible; Johnson (2007) and Scherbaum (2005) reported other examples. The other mistake was a failure to see that synthetic validity did not have to be better; it merely had to be useful. Remember that validity at the time of Lawshe's proposal was limited mainly to what later came to be called criterion-related validity. If only a few people are hired for a specific combination of job components, and if synthesized batteries can be valid enough to be useful, it doesn't matter whether that validity is greater than could be obtained by aggregating different jobs sharing some of the components but in different degrees.

My third mistake was different—an error in timing, not judgment; most of my early experience with the topic predated meta-analysis and validity generalization, now widely accepted (cf. Johnson, 2007; Scherbaum, 2005; Steel, Huffcutt, & Kammeyer-Mueller, 2006). When the Army project was condensed to a single chapter (Peterson, Wise, Arabian, & Hoffman, 2001), in which validity generalization was acknowledged as an alternative to synthetic validity, I saw the concept from a different perspective. I hope to be more realistic now.

Approaches to Synthetic Validity

At different times, different people have viewed synthetic validity from different perspectives and with different approaches. Despite the differences, the results generally support the idea that a valid test battery can be synthesized. Any approach begins with, and depends on, thorough work analysis. The emphasis is on *analysis*, not on *job*. The jobs, or work, may be defined with limitations (perhaps all machine-shop work) or to be wholly comprehensive ("all non-management jobs in the organization," Johnson, 2007, p. 127). The analysis, whatever its scope, must be thorough in the sense that major and (I think) somewhat independent components of the work to be done do in fact emerge by the end.

Steel et al. (2006) summarized the many approaches in two categories, *job requirements matrices* (JRM) and *job component validity* (JCV). I follow their precedent with a different term for JRM. I refer to the same concept as *prediction of component performance.* Scherbaum (2005) called this "Guion's approach," but I think it was Lawshe's original plan. For each emerging component, it requires at least a rudimentary predictive hypothesis for which measures (criterion and predictor) are chosen or invented. Traditional regression equations and/or validity coefficients, or (*mea culpa*) significance levels, are determined. In the Guion (1965b) demonstration, the two best predictors for each component were identified (in terms of probability of being rated superior in overall performance) and the predictive usefulness was indicated in an expectancy chart. Expectancies were translated into a simple scale from +3 to −3. Scale values for the components identified for a given position were added; a positive sum identified a person likely to be identified as a superior worker. Better data analysis methods (e.g., correlation coefficients) can be used if justified by available data. Whatever the statistic, the traditional function of $Y = f(X)$ describes the prediction.

A different order of prediction characterized the JCV approach using the PAQ (McCormick et al., 1972). Assume (as is characteristic in synthetic validity designs) that a specific job component identified in one position is like that seen in another, both in evaluating performance on that component and in the employee attributes required. Assume further that over time people tend to gravitate to positions that fit their personal attributes (i.e., KSAPs). From these assumptions, one can go on to determine the linkage of job component performance and personal attributes by the function $X = f(Y)$ as well as by the opposite but more traditional statement. That is, by defining the job components with a well-established analysis method such as the PAQ, one can predict in advance the predictor attributes fitting each one. If data permit a choice between using synthetic validity (specifically, JCV) or validity generalization, the two approaches yield very similar results if uncorrected VG mean coefficients are used in the comparison (Hoffman & McPhail, 1998). That finding is helpful because situations still exist where JCV can be used where VG reports have not yet been done.

Hollenbeck and Whitener (1988) sought a procedure that would (a) provide an overall validity coefficient, (b) rely like JCV on a standardized, worker-oriented job analysis, and (c) be based on empirical prediction to establish the linkage of test to job component performance. Their approach integrates three prior synthetic validity methods, JRM and JCV, and a third, the J-coefficient, a precursor of the JCV approach (Primoff, 1953). The principal goal for J-coefficients was to develop a mathematically correct expression of validity based on supervisory ratings of the importance of job elements and previously validated "beta" weights of the ratings for a test (Primoff, 1959).

The Hollenbeck–Whitener method requires two person-by-job component matrices. In the first, each cell shows (a) the product of the person's z-score on a proposed test for the component and (b) the weight assigned by job analysis to that component. The second shows the products of the ratings of performance of components (in z-scores) and the weight given to each component. Sums of the products are summed for each matrix, and a Pearson coefficient is computed using these values.

The US Army Approach

The US Army's Synthetic Validity Project (Peterson et al., 2001; Wise et al., 1991) was a large study, and it integrated parts of prior methods while creating its own. They chose a procedure that (a) involved establishing a taxonomy of job components accounting for performance content in the range of jobs for which the results should be applicable, (b) used criterion-related validity (or expert judgments, if necessary) with performance in the various components serving as the criteria to estimate validity of potential predictors for each component, and (c) for each job, put together a predictor battery by combining predictive equations for each of its components. Each of these carries with it some critical warnings. First, the taxonomy of job components must be nearly exhaustive for the job population of interest; researchers must be careful not to overlook any actually or potentially important component. Second, equations for predicting component performance should be independent and different for different job components. If they are not—if all predictors predict component performance equally well across jobs—the final predictive equations will be the same for all of the jobs and validity generalization would be more meaningful. Third, the concept of a single, overall performance criterion based on summed component performance must be a sensible construct.

Psychologist subject matter experts (SMEs), familiar with the predictors and with Army jobs, estimated probable correlations between predictors and performance components (performance on both task categories and more general job behaviors). Army SMEs judged the relevance of each performance component to each of three criterion constructs. Equations were developed by a variety of empirical and judgmental (or combined) methods for predicting actual validity coefficients and for establishing discriminant validity.

The findings were fairly typical. Synthetic validity worked, in that test batteries created for particular sets of job components gave composite scores that correlated well with established criteria, but without much discriminant validity across jobs. The evaluation of these results depends on whether selection or placement is the purpose of testing. Extrapolating beyond the Army situation, we might say that selecting people for a new job, never previously filled, or for one with infrequent hiring, may be helped by a synthetic validity approach. The Army equations predicted performance well, one might say indiscriminately, across jobs. With poor discriminant validity, placement is not helped, but with highly correlated criterion components, discriminant validity is not critical when performance is truly general. Perhaps greater discriminant validity would be found for predictions of remote criteria, such as performance on jobs to which entry-level people are promoted. Perhaps discriminant validity is not necessary; maybe its absence can be interpreted as successfully replicating an assessment-based prediction across components.

Developing a Selection System

After reading decades of articles proclaiming the promise of synthetic validity, and after doing several promising studies, Johnson (2007) declared that synthetic validity was no longer merely a technique of promise but "a technique of use (finally)" (Johnson, 2007, title). The chapter is a more readily accessible account, in some detail, of a study reported by Johnson, Carter, and Tippins (2001) as part of a symposium. The title of the original presentation reveals a major difference between this approach and others that have been proposed: "A synthetic validation approach to the development of *a selection system for multiple job families*" (emphasis added). Whereas much of what is written on the topic follows Lawshe's emphasis on small business, the work summarized in the Johnson chapter described a system looking at roughly 400 different non-management jobs. It points out that 400 independently conducted validity studies would not be particularly feasible, even if the jobs were grouped into families, and that these jobs were not static, in any case; jobs change, and new ones pop up. The final step in their approach specifies procedures for using existing data to develop test batteries for new jobs as they develop.

Unlike JCV, this approach identified job components as clusters of similar work behavior and job families as clusters of jobs with similar work requirements. A table linking 26 job components to 11 job families showed that some (only six) components were found in all families. Predictors were chosen for each component, and predictor batteries were selected for each job family. Correlations to identify level of validity were empirically developed (see Johnson, 2007, for details).

Looking Ahead

I think the merit of synthetic validity will be realized, not in scattered studies in small business, but in comprehensive, large-scale VG projects providing a general matrix of personal traits related to performance in work components. For any job, including those in which hiring is rare or some that are quite new, that matrix can be the basis for synthesized test batteries that will, a priori, be valid. Admittedly, this is still a dream (despite Johnson's "finally"), but is a realizable one; Marquardt and McCormick (1972) developed a similar matrix long before computers and validity generalization showed the way; it's time to reprise their study.

A generalized, large-scale system was also envisioned in the review by Steel et al. (2006), who also saw the advances in developing taxonomies of generalized work behavior or criteria, and the development of validity generalization, as providing a stimulus for further development of synthetic validity. In Guion (1998), I imagined an idealized, systematic approach to personnel decisions; a slightly different imagining is described in Chapter 12. The Johnson et al. procedure is far more realistic, but it moves toward an overall system that may define personnel decisions policies and procedures for an entire, complex organization. Keep the idea of synthetic validity in mind to bring it out again there. It just might work!

CAUSAL OR CONFIRMATORY RESEARCH

The hypothesis that changes in one independent variable (or a set of them in concert) *causes* changes in another one, a dependent variable, generally requires carefully controlled experiments in which only the dependent and independent variables are allowed to vary; everything else stays constant, including directions and timing of measurements. The concept of causality, and research on the concept, has broadened. Two complementary conceptualizations of the concept were described in a series of articles in *Psychological Methods* introduced by Maxwell (2010).

We are taught from our first exposure to it that correlation has nothing to say about causation; correlated variables simply covary, and most personnel research is correlational, not experimental. In correlational research, it is not strictly proper to describe variables with words such as *dependent* and *independent*; the hypothesis generally is that variation in one variable (or set of them) *is related to* variation in another one without the causality implied by those terms.

Even so, lurking in a predictive hypothesis is the apparent implication that criterion performance is caused by the predictor trait, even though the implication is untested in conventional validation. A causal chain is implied, even if neither strictly true nor easily tested, when a test is used to predict success in training and training success is assumed to predict later job performance. The plausibility of causal chains (or more complex causal networks) can be investigated by *structural equation models*, most simply by *path analysis*. Path analysis does not demonstrate causality, but its results can refute causal hypotheses by showing that a path in the chain simply does not function as a causal model requires (i.e., the data do not fit the model).

Path analysis and quasi-experimental field research are among so-called *causal* or *confirmatory* research methods. In this context, the term "causal" is used loosely; Pedhazur and Schmelkin (1991) reviewed the pitfalls of the term, citing so many contradictory quotations that I use it fearfully. It is, however, conventional to refer to structural equation modeling as causal modeling, so let's use the term without taking it too seriously—remembering that causal research does not confirm or prove causality; it merely tests the plausibility of a causal model.

Structural Equations

Scientifically, structural equation models are worth investigating when a construct is not well understood. Developing and testing a theory about the construct and its associations with other constructs is useful, not only to science but also to practice; a causal chain can identify variables or conditions (like the success-in-training variables above) that mediate predictions. Structural equation modeling of causal assumptions is a powerful method of confirmatory statistical analysis. A brief glossary can help introduce the general concept, as follows.

- *Structural equations*: a set of equations specifying a mathematical model representing "a network of hypothesized linear relations among a set of variables" (Millsap, 2002, p. 257).
- *Model specification*: The first step in developing the model. It is the identification and description of components of the theory basic to the model. That means specifying all variables the theory assumes to be related to the one at the end of the path, and specifying the place of each variable within that theory. Structural equations, and the models they serve, are necessarily multivariate; a well-specified model will include more than one—probably much more than one—variable along the path, and may also include more than one criterion.
- *Specification error*: Usually, the omission of relevant variables. A specification error means that the model of reality represented by a set of equations is wrong—to some degree, and in some sense. Usually, leaving out an important variable is what is wrong, but errors of overspecification—including variables that do not belong in the model—may also occur. A fully specified model is sometimes called *self-contained* (James, Mulaik, & Brett, 1982).
- *Identification*: information within the model necessary to represent the parameters of the equations in the model. Models are *just-identified*, *overidentified*, or *underidentified*. A just-identified (or *saturated*) model is one that provides the information needed to estimate the parameters (e.g., the right number of equations for the number of unknown parameters to be estimated). Such a model cannot be tested because it has no degrees of freedom, no redundancy. An underidentified model is untestable because necessary information is lacking. Only an overidentified model can be tested, but knowing when a model is overidentified presents problems and controversy among experts. When results yield negative variances or correlations greater than 1.0, identification problems may be the culprit. The concept is confusing. Pedhazur and Schmelkin (1991) acknowledged that even their unusually clear explanation probably produced a "sense of frustration, if not helplessness" (p. 704).

- *Fit*: Results of goodness-of-fit statistics to see how well the parameters estimated fit the theoretical model.
- *Exogenous* and *endogenous* variables: Exogenous variables are those the model accepts as given; explaining variance in these variables lies outside of the model itself. I think of them as defining a context from which the model emerges. Endogenous variables are those whose variation is explained, according to the theory modeled, by other variables within the model (including exogenous variables).
- *Mediating variable*: A variable in an intermediate position in a causal chain, a mediator can be distinguished from a moderator in function, although a variable *can* serve in both roles within a model (James & Brett, 1984).

Path Analysis

A predictor–criterion link, even when validated, is often only part of actual selection programs. Over time, many different people make decisions about different candidates. Perhaps, as a matter of policy, valid predictions may inform decision makers without dictating their decisions. Decision processes are often more complex than simply giving a test and then using an explicit, score-based decision rule (such as a top-down policy). Steps in the process evolve or are developed in the belief that they will produce clear and measurable benefits. That is a causal statement: that the benefits are the effect of the program—with or without tests—causing them. It calls for specifying the links in a potential causal chain between assessment (in a first step) and criterion, which may be followed by systematic differences in training, work environments, or other potential mediating or moderating influence. Again, the causality in that chain cannot be unambiguously determined, but its plausibility might be investigated using causal or confirmatory research.

Development of Path Models

Path analysis is theoretical; it studies a systematic theory of the events or variables that may produce one or more outcomes of interest. It is not exploratory but confirmatory; the theory precedes data and then the data are analyzed to see if (or how well) they support the theory; that is, one does not do a path analysis and then develop a likable theory to explain the result (Millsap, 2002). The theory need not be grand, but it should be comprehensive enough to avoid specification errors. Any thoughtful development of a multivariate predictive hypothesis is, in a sense, theory development.

Suppose one wants to predict how long it will take people to learn to repair malfunctioning electronic equipment. The traditional predictive hypothesis is typically limited to personal traits. For this task, traits might be knowledge of electronic theory, cognitive flexibility in developing and trying out possible problem solutions, and achievement motivation. The hypothesis might add something that happens after hiring, such as the skill level of (or time with) a trainer or mentor. The traditional predictive hypothesis says nothing, however, about potential causal links among these four predictors; their interrelationships are considered only in terms of intercorrelations. Figure 8.7a illustrates this traditional research model in a "single stage model" (Pedhazur & Schmelkin, 1991, p. 311) in which the dependent or criterion variable is related to each one in a set of more or less intercorrelated variables. The model implies causality in the direction of the arrows, but only because the four independent, exogenous variables existed or were measured first.

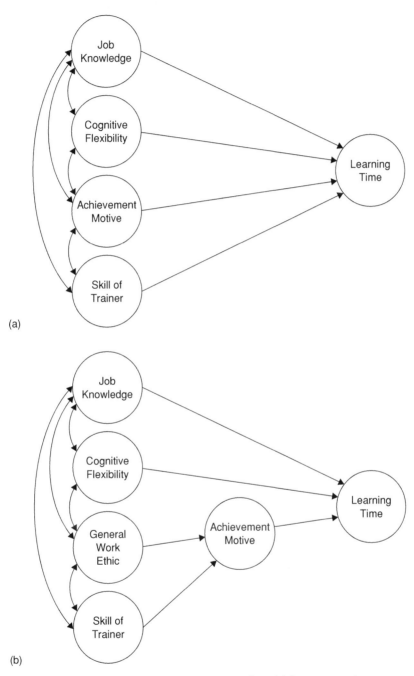

FIG. 8.7   Transformation of predictive hypotheses to a causal model. Some arrows between exogenous variables are omitted for simplification.

Suppose, however, we propose that the motivation to achieve in this learning situation is an endogenous variable caused (or at least influenced) by both the work ethic the person brings to the job (an exogenous variable) and the exogenous skill of the trainer. The model in Figure 8.7b hypothesizes achievement motivation as a direct influence on learning time and an effect of a general work ethic and trainer skill; it functions in the model as a mediating variable. It also assumes that learning time is directly influenced by three learner traits but not by trainer skill. Given the content of this paragraph, the model is misspecified because the amount of one-on-one time is not included, and there is no reason in theory or in practice for ignoring it.

A properly specified model need not include every variable in the causal chain, nor does a model of the effect of personnel decisions require specification of every independent variable that might influence criteria. To model a causal understanding of a given selection program, one tries to understand how various program elements contribute to an intermediate decision, trait, or condition, and whether that intermediate variable has an influence on one or more criteria. The issue is whether the program itself has been fully specified.

An Example

Schmidt et al. (1986) reported a path analysis for data collected from people in four military specialties; a synopsis of the model and the results they obtained is shown in Figure 8.8. According to the model, amount of job experience influences level of job knowledge and

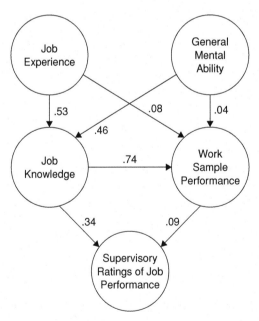

FIG. 8.8   Path coefficients for incumbents in four military specialties. Adapted from Figure 3, p. 437, in Schmidt, F. L., Hunter, J. E., & Outerbridge, A. N. (1986). Impact of job experience and ability on job knowledge, work sample. Impact of job experience and ability on job knowledge, work sample performance, and supervisory ratings of job performance. *Journal of Applied Psychology, 71,* 432–439. © 1986 by American Psychological Association; adapted by permission.

ability to do the job, as shown on work sample tests. General mental ability also influences knowledge and work sample performance, and both of these influence supervisory ratings. Beside each path arrow in Figure 8.8 is a path coefficient, a standard partial regression weight, showing the strength of the influence in that path.[6]

The model as a whole is said to be confirmed, but general mental ability has little direct impact on work sample performance. It does, however, influence work sample performance via the mediating job knowledge variable. According to these results, supervisory ratings are influenced more by job knowledge than by job performance as measured by the work sample.

Field Experiments for Program Evaluation

Campbell (1957) introduced such evaluation as *quasi-experimental research*, but a more general term is *field experimentation* (Shadish & Cook, 2009), including both randomized experiments and various nonrandomized approaches, including quasi-experiments. An assessment procedure or selection program in a field setting (as opposed to a laboratory setting) has the role of an independent experimental variable, and it can be evaluated as "causing" (i.e., having direct influence on) the dependent variable (criterion) with carefully designed experimental or quasi-experimental research. In a traditional experiment, people are assigned at random to the experimental conditions or treatments to control for individual differences. The dependent variable in a well-controlled experiment is the hypothesized effect of the treatments. In a quasi-experiment, a causal inference is desired but not assured because, among other things, the people studied are not randomly assigned to treatments. Nevertheless, quasi-experimental research, like path analysis, can either confirm or disconfirm the plausibility of causal hypothesis. Disconfirmation is less ambiguous.

A Quasi-Experimental Study

In three groups of discount stores, records of terminations for "gross misconduct" were kept for 15 months (Paajanen, 1988) before a testing program was started in two of them, and for nine months after starting it. All three groups had clear downward trends over time. The control group would not please a laboratory experimenter; these stores had noticeably less termination for misconduct at the outset than did the other two. For both experimental groups, a discontinuity was seen in the trend when testing began. These two groups of stores had an immediate drop in terminations for misconduct, and the downward slope continued— more steeply, and with less random fluctuation. That testing *per se* had an effect is a plausible inference, but questions remain unanswered. Why the downward slope in all three? The downward slope was much more pronounced in one experimental group than in the other; why? Why were more terminations experienced in the two experimental groups than in the control? Were actions being taken, independently of the assessments being evaluated, that also effectively reduced misconduct?

---

[6] Partial correlation and partial regression weights have not been mentioned in this book (see Pedhazur & Schmelkin, 1991). In the original report, Schmidt et al. (1986) provided two sets of path coefficients, those reported here and another set for data in which the nonlinear relation of job experience to work sample performance was transformed to a linear coding of a grouped distribution. The purpose here is simply to illustrate path analysis, so only one set is given.

Some Quasi-Experimental Designs

Validity and Research Design

It is not enough simply to do something (such as introducing testing) and noting change in something else. That might be described as correlational research but not as field experimentation even with "quasi" as a prefix. Field experiments generally require more careful planning to assure the validity of the results. Validity of quasi-experimental results differs from validity of assessments. Readers frustrated by my distinction between the validity of measurement and validity of prediction should be braced for further frustration. Donald Campbell, who introduced and has been a major figure in quasi-experimental design, and his associates have in several articles identified four aspects of the validity of causal inferences that need evaluation. *Statistical conclusion validity* refers to statistical significance. No one should ascribe excessive importance to statistical significance, but it seems prerequisite to inferences of causality. *Internal validity* requires that the manipulated variable or "treatment" be the only plausible explanation of an outcome. Design flaws that permit other explanations of the outcomes threaten internal validity and may invalidate the entire research. *Construct validity* refers to interpretations of the meaning of outcome and treatment variables—largely the same meaning as before except that the constructs may not be explicitly measured. *External validity* refers to the generalizability of research findings beyond the specific study itself. Campbell (1957) originally identified eight kinds of "threats" to these various validities, but over the years the list has grown; Shadish, Cook, and Campbell (2002) expanded the list to 37!

Design descriptions here are illustrative but terribly brief. For better descriptions, consult Cook, Campbell, and Peracchio (1990) and Shadish et al. (2002). Using the early notation, the letter X designates the treatment (or program) and the letter O designates outcome, the criterion in regression analysis. Subscripts indicate the relative sequence of outcome observations.

Three Generally Interpretable Designs

None of these three simple designs is a sure bet—each is subject to possible threats to validity—but if done well, their results can be interpretable.

- *Design 1: Untreated control group with pretests and posttests:*

$$O_1 \quad X \quad O_2$$
$$O_1 \qquad O_2$$

In this common design, two groups are identified and initial dependent variable observations, O_1, are made in both. Only one group gets the experimental treatment. Subsequently the dependent criterion variable, O_2, is again measured in both groups. Four possible outcomes were described by Cook et al. (1990), the most clearly interpretable being an outcome with no outcome change in the control group but with a clear increase in the treatment group. Interpretations of the other possible results were more ambiguous, permitting alternatives. They do, however, allow statistically significant results to be interpreted as treatment effects, even if somewhat less convincingly.

- *Design 2: Two groups with switching replications*

O_1 X O_2	O_3
O_1	O_2 X O_3

This is essentially Design 1 with replication in which the roles of the groups are reversed. If the treatment (e.g., installing an assessment center) works, results should be that $O_2 > O_1$ in the top group and $O_3 > O_2$ in the bottom group, with other differences trivial. An improved design would use another group without the treatment.

- *Design 3: One group removed treatment design*

O_1 X O_2 X O_3 noX O_4

Sometimes, doing something, no matter what, is followed by improvement. Recall the Hawthorne studies in which lighting at the work place was enhanced through several levels, each improvement followed by higher production. When illumination level was subsequently decreased, production stayed level if not better (Roethlisberger & Dickson, 1939, pp. 14–18). Design 3 generalizes the chance that uncontrolled variables (what I have called third variables, such as basking in the attention of the experiment), might account for changes in the dependent variable. Suppose production was observed at O_1, after which X was introduced, followed by an increase in production at O_2 and a further increase at O_3 after adding still more X, perhaps a more complex treatment. One might think that X caused the production increases unless the final step is taken: returning to the original condition. If O_4 is not about the same level as O_1, the results cannot be causally interpreted; if it is, a causal relationship is plausible—at least not disconfirmed.

Pragmatism and Program Evaluation

It must be kept in mind that a lot goes on in an organization unrelated to the experiment being done. In structural equation terms, the quasi-experiment is nearly always underspecified. Even with far more comprehensive designs, evaluating an assessment program for personnel decisions will not be wholly confirmatory. It takes place in a context with other processes and procedures. But unknown exogenous variables may have a positive as well as a negative effect. An old example, circa 1940, for which I've been unable to recall or find a reference, found that the mere introduction of a testing program improved the assessed quality of candidates who applied. Such outcomes should be considered in designing these studies. The designs described here may be inadequate for the questions raised in many programs; a much broader program of evaluation, with tighter specification, is likely to be needed (cf. Berk & Rossi, 1990, Edwards, Scott, & Raju, 2003; Shadish et al., 2002). Program evaluation is not easy, it is not likely to uncover unintended consequences; nevertheless, developing, evaluating, and understanding broad programs for personnel decisions merit far more thought and attention than I have so far seen.

Moreover, these things merit a broader variety of considerations than I have given here; covering so many things in a single chapter requires a fairly clear if elementary description of one apparently useful approach. Despite the comparisons of Campbell's and Rubin's views on causation in the *Psychological Methods* special section (Maxwell, 2010), I have stayed with the Campbell approach—not because of any assumption of its superiority, but because it has a stronger emphasis on issues of design and measurement. Nevertheless, I urge reading that section; particularly, I urge reading the "reflections" article by Rubin (2010) for people who enjoy good writing as much as the learning they get from it.

META-ANALYSIS AND VALIDITY GENERALIZATION

The basic concepts of meta-analysis were described in Chapter 7. The raw material of validity generalization is a set of bivariate correlation coefficients. The corrected mean correlation in the set may be generalizable, but it is still a bivariate correlation. The bivariate logic can be extended to a multivariate approach in either of two ways. One is to identify variables that moderate the relation (usually when validity does *not* generalize); the other is to collect sets of data summarizing research that has combined at least two specified constructs or construct categories.

Moderators in Validity Generalization

When the variance of corrected coefficients is too large to permit inferences of validity generalization, situational specificity cannot automatically be assumed. There is always a possibility that population differences do exist within the set of studies. Such differences may not be so pronounced that each study can be taken as a sample from a unique population in a unique situation (which the pre-1977 situational specificity hypothesis generally accepted), but subgroups of studies may define populations that differ from those in other sets of studies. When results suggest such a possibility, the task of meta-analysis changes from seeking generalizations to searching for moderators.

The validity generalization rule of thumb implies that, if more than 25% of the original effect size variance remains after the ordinary corrections, we are justified in searching for moderators. Use of a rule of thumb in a topic rich in the statistical examination of data is somewhat disconcerting. It would be useful to have a statistical basis for estimating population variance in correlations within the sample summarized, but the statistical power for detecting such variance is extremely low in sets of correlation coefficients based on small samples (Oswald & McCloy, 2003). This is, of course, revisiting the primacy of sampling error, the culprit limiting the reasons to search for moderators in many meta-analyses. Even when the researcher seeks evidence of moderator effects, the search is limited by the information coded from the original studies. That information may provide one or more variables, continuous or categorical, that may be associated with differences in corrected coefficients—in short, a moderator.

Early rhetoric in the promotion of validity generalization made bold assertions like this one: "Professionally developed cognitive ability tests are valid predictors of performance on the job and in training for all jobs . . . in all settings" (Schmidt & Hunter, 1981, p. 1128; the ellipses merely replace references). Schmidt and Hunter were not shy; the assertion is early in the second sentence of the article, right up front. A lot of less-than-close readers widely interpreted it as a claim that all tests are equally valid predictors everywhere for all jobs, but the statement does not say that. The word *equally* is neither printed nor implied, either for validity coefficients or job settings. And it does not say or imply that "cognitive ability tests" refers only to general mental ability tests or *g*; in fact, a footnote said that the term included measures of verbal and quantitative abilities, mechanical comprehension, spatial ability, and reasoning abilities as cognitive ability tests. Notice, the sentence does not say that tests of distinguishable cognitive abilities are all equally valid. Too many inferences from the sentence—and the article—were blatantly false (Landy, 2003, p. 172).

From the outset, the meta-analytic concept of validity generalization expected that some moderators would be found. And they were. Hunter and Hunter (1984) demonstrated the moderating effect of job complexity for the criterion-related validity of cognitive tests for predicting overall job performance. They did a re-analysis, using validity generalization methods, of the original Ghiselli (1966) data and classifying the jobs into groups relatively homogeneous in job complexity. The corrected validity estimates ranged from a high of .61 for the group with highest job complexity to .27 in the least complex jobs—considering the variance in that range, a clear and persuasive moderator effect. Job complexity was also a moderator for psychomotor tests, although in the opposite direction; psychomotor tests were most valid in predicting performance on precisely the kinds of job families where cognitive ability tests were least useful. Salgado et al. (2003) studied mental ability tests across 12 occupational groups, essentially replicating Hunter and Hunter, within the various countries of the European Community. They reached the same basic conclusions, showing that the generalizations of mental ability tests for predicting overall performance, as found in the United States, also generalize "to other continents, countries, and cultures" (Salgado et al., 2003, p. 1076). Although the cognitive complexity of some of the European jobs was greater than in the United States, so were the validity coefficients higher in those jobs. The inclusion of "culture" in the quotation interested me; apparently they see different EC countries as having nontrivial cultural differences but with no finding of country or culture as another moderator.

The search for moderators has become almost routine in meta-analytic research. A search for a moderator that fails to find one is more definitive than a study that fails to find one because it wasn't even considered. McDaniel, Morgeson, Finnegan, Campion, and Braverman (2001) found that situational judgment tests based on job analysis were better predictors of performance than those without the job analytic foundation. A field study reported by Ferris, Witt, and Hochwarter (2001) found that the relationship between general mental ability and rated job performance was moderated by social skills; although this was not a meta-analysis, meta-analytic work might well look for opportunities to investigate social skill as a more general moderator, particularly with ratings as criteria. Gully, Incalaterra, Joshi, and Beaubien (2002) reported that level of analysis moderated several correlations with team performance; effects were stronger at the team level than at the individual level.

Many more potential moderators might be investigated in meta-analytic studies if the primary studies had reported situational information, especially situations related to moderating or mediating interventions. "To advance research related to the situation, we need theory about how different settings influence relationships between personality and behavior" (Barrick, Mitchell & Stewart, 2003, p. 61). One such theory, that of trait activation, has been reported by Tett and Burnett (2003), and it can (and should) guide new research. I do quibble a bit with the quotation from Barrick et al. (2003); my view is that we need more data than theory at this stage of considering situational moderators. With more data considered, more comprehensive theories can be developed.

Combining Predictors

Meta-analysis can lead to multivariate generalizations in at least two ways: (a) through analysis of regression-based data using two or more kinds of predictors, and (b) through contributions to path analysis.

Regression and Correlation

Hunter and Hunter (1984) raised the question: does adding other variables to ability to form a predictor test battery offer any improvement over the validity of ability alone? At the time, they found too few studies with appropriate combinations to answer the question with meta-analysis, but an analytic approach suggested to them that incremental validities were likely to be trivial. Nearly 25 years later, it still seems that meta-analysis is not soon going to provide definitive answers. Schmidt and Hunter (1998) lamented the absence of precise estimates of the generalized intercorrelation of general mental ability measures and alternative assessment procedures.

Hunter and Hunter (1984) did, however, manage to report, from various sources, the multiple correlation estimates for some 19 two-variable composites, six of which are given in Table 8.5. A recent meta-analysis of multiple correlations for three composites, also of general mental ability plus an alternative assessment, reported by Potosky, Bobko, and Roth (2005) is also summarized in that table. (The three alternative assessments in the Potosky et al. study were chosen because they have commonly been suggested as ways to reduce adverse impact.) In all three combinations, the bivariate validity coefficient for general mental ability (GMA) alone was .51, based on prior validity generalization. The table suggests that the combination of GMA and a structured interview offer the best improvement in predictive efficiency, and the work samples are also useful; it raises serious question about biodata and assessment centers, suggesting that they add little incremental validity.

TABLE 8.5
Meta-Analytic Validities of Six Two-Predictor Composites

Additional Predictor	From Potosky et al.[a]		From Schmidt & Hunter[b]	
	r for Added Predictor	Multiple R	r for Added Predictor	Multiple R
Conscientiousness	.22	.55	.31	.60
Structured interview	.48	.61	.51	.63
Biodata	.32	.53	.35	.52
Work sample			.54	.63
Job knowledge			.48	.58
Assessment center			.37	.53

[a] Data in these columns are drawn from "Forming composites of cognitive ability and alternative measures to predict job performance and reduce adverse impact: Corrected estimates and realistic expectations", by Potosky, D., Bobko, P., and Roth, P. L. (2005). *International Journal of Selection and Assessment, 13*, pp. 308–309. © John Wiley & Sons; adapted by permission. First predictor in each pair is a cognitive ability test.

[b] Data in these columns are drawn from "The validity and utility of selection methods in personnel psychology: Practical and theoretical implications of 85 years of research findings", by Schmidt, F. L., and Hunter, J. E. (1998). *Psychological Bulletin, 124*, p. 265, Table 1. © 1998, American Psychological Association. Adapted by permission. First predictor in each pair is a test of general mental ability.

The problem of the database of original studies remains. Before meta-analysis can reach its potential, even for two predictor composites, a lot of housecleaning is needed for the original research studies entering the analysis. Ideally, a meta-analysis casts light on the generalizability of a predictive hypothesis, which (as described in Chapter 3) is a hypothesis about a predictor construct (a trait or characteristic or attribute of a person or setting) that is related to a criterion construct. What construct is assessed in an interview, structured or otherwise? A biodata inventory? A work sample or assessment center? These are methods for assessing constructs, not the constructs themselves. Much of the primary research studied in meta-analyses, and many of the meta-analyses themselves, deal with methods of assessment, not constructs—a comment made more often than heeded over the years (e.g., Bobko & Roth, 2003; Hunter & Hunter, 1984). We hear of studies of "the" interview or "the" assessment center, as if these were fully standardized and interchangeable. They are not; there is no such thing as a standard interview or assessment center across individual research studies.

It will take several years of accumulated research, using specific protocols, before meta-analysis can clarify the value (or its lack) of using combinations of predictors. First, the methods of assessment (interviews, biodata, etc.) need to be carefully examined to determine and pull out the constructs imbedded in some of them. Second, a reasonably standard list of predictor constructs, and of the methods for assessing them, needs to be identified. Third, new meta-analyses need to nail down explicit generalizations about the relationships between these constructs and more explicit criterion constructs (i.e., more explicit than the usual glibness of "overall job performance"). Then, finally, the generalizable intercorrelations among them, and the correlations of each predictor construct with each criterion construct, need to be identified (and that, of course, means having them reported in the primary data) so that generalized information needed for computing regression equations can be used. Eventually, perhaps actual meta-analyses will give definitive information about two- or even three-predictor composites. Did I say several years? Maybe several decades would be closer to the truth. But I'm sure someone will find ways to abbreviate such a research prescription.

CONCLUDING NOTE ON STATISTICAL ANALYSES

Chapters 7 and 8 have offered many equations relevant to the evaluation of predictors. Clearly, personnel researchers need extensive training in data analysis. A much wider variety of data analytic techniques than the limited sample in these chapters is available to statistically well-trained people, and different situations may favor different methods of analysis. Traditional statistics permit inferences of statistical reliability but are not generally well suited to seeing how well real data fit either organizational needs or theoretical models. Research related to personnel decisions, perhaps due in part to the freezing of the field early in the EEO era, has given relatively little attention to newer, theory-confirming or -disconfirming methods. Those who will improve the empirical evaluation of assessment-based personnel decisions must develop a larger repertory of confirmatory techniques and models.

Researchers need an inclusive knowledge of statistical procedures, but there is an important caveat: *Statistics is a tool, not a religion.* Too often, researchers appear to have a blind faith in the results of statistical analysis, especially when they have abdicated responsibility for understanding what a computer program is doing. Statistics is a guide to judgment, not an alternative to it; results of statistical analysis merit thoughtful evaluation, not automated acceptance. No matter how elegant the statistics, applying them to lousy, ambiguous data does not suddenly convert them, like converting "lead into gold (i.e., to extract high quality information from low quality studies)" (Murphy & Newman, 2003, p. 419). Perhaps with more dignity, Wilkinson and the Task Force on Statistical Inference (1999) urged use of *minimally sufficient analysis* and said, "If the assumptions and strength of a simpler method are reasonable for your data and research problem, use it. Occam's razor applies to methods as well as to theories" (p. 598); they cited Fisher (1935), an earlier and authoritative source, for the advice. They went on to say that nothing is wrong with using state-of-the-art statistics, and that there *is* something wrong with desperately clinging to obsolete procedures. The whole argument has been updated deliciously by Peterson (2009).

Accounting for error and exceptions deserves more serious attention than ordinarily happens. Ghiselli (1960b) started to investigate systematic reasons for errors of prediction in his notion of the *prediction of predictability*, later known as the moderator concept; moderator research faltered because (a) researchers studied demographic factors extensively, concluded that they did not serve as moderators, and with magnificent illogic concluded that therefore there are no moderators, and (b) the era of pure empiricism led researchers to try any old variable at hand as a moderator—with or without, and usually without, any systematic reasoning behind the effort. Because the moderator concept involved an accepted statistical operation (moderated regression), and because that statistical operation had not had a lot of success, the prediction of predictability became a lost idea. Neither statistical failures nor statistical successes should be accepted on faith.

9

Bias, Group Differences, and Adverse Impact

Are tests biased? It is a simple question, but it can't be answered simply with a yes or a no. By the end of the chapter, you will find it harder to answer than it is now.

The question, an important but difficult one, is made unnecessarily obscure by the persistently ambiguous use of the word *bias* in general conversation. "Bias" is often used as a synonym for prejudice, which is more a characteristic of people than of tests. In measurement and assessment, bias is a technical term for a psychometric or statistical problem. Many descriptions of bias, in the popular press and in psychometric literature, refer to concepts that may be important and relevant but are in fact different. A statistically significant difference in group mean scores is important and might be relevant, but it is not evidence of bias. Adverse impact—especially as defined by the 80% rule—is important and might be relevant, but it is not evidence of bias.

We need to clarify the term, *adverse impact.* In the regulatory language of the Uniform Guidelines (Equal Employment Opportunity Commission, Civil Service Commission, Department of Labor, & Department of Justice, 1978), adverse impact is a consequence of something; because selection procedures, primarily testing, are the things regulated (and because personnel psychology emphasizes testing), adverse impact is more commonly considered an effect of testing than of other potential causes—of which there are many. Unfortunately, the same term, adverse impact, is also used to describe tests or test use, as in the insistence in the Guidelines that, if a test is used and adverse impact occurs, the test must be replaced by an "equally valid test with less adverse impact." That is, the term has two different meanings: (a) adverse impact as differences in the probability of being hired for a specified job, and (b) adverse impact as a characteristic of a test (or other assessment device) having an effect on that probability. A test "with less adverse impact" often seems to mean either that a level of adverse impact is an inherent property of a test, invariant across situations, or that tests or test use *cause* adverse impact. We can distinguish the *operating effect* from a *psychometric problem* contributing to the effect. The problem might be differences in group distributions (e.g., means and variances) or on technical evaluations (e.g., reliability and validity). This chapter focuses on measurement issues, but many other considerations may contribute to operating adverse impact.

This chapter should unravel some of the confusion brought about by group differences in test score distributions and about group differences in the way people in different groups respond to different items. We will look further at adverse impact, but from a psychometric rather than a regulatory or legal point of view. At the end, the opening question may be clarified, but the clarification may raise more questions for which answers are elusive.

BIAS IN MEASUREMENT

A Brief History of Employment Fairness

Before the national Civil Rights Act in 1964, various cities and states in the United States had established agencies to promote "fair employment" in their communities. Discrimination in employment had a long and accepted history. Each new national group of immigrants faced it, as did women, and it was mandated by some of the so-called "Jim Crow" laws enacted in the former slave-holding states after slaves were freed. By the middle of the twentieth century, a growing national conscience was declaring that such discrimination was not fair, and cities and states established agencies given such names as "Fair Employment Practices Commission."

The word stuck. A large *test fairness* literature developed in the 1970s proposing "fairness models" of prediction. The models were group-oriented, focusing on groups protected under law. Unfairness, sometimes considered a property of the test, was more typically seen as a matter of the way a test was used.

Group Parity Models

Several fairness models, all defined in terms of correlation and regression analysis, were proposed during the 1970s. Thorndike (1971) said that a fair test requires that the proportion in each subgroup that would have been hired on the basis of criterion performance, had it been known in advance, be matched by the proportion of those actually hired on the basis of test performance. To achieve that ideal, cut scores would have to be used and manipulated in the different groups. Cole (1973) went further, proposing that, to be fair, employment in the groups compared would have to have the same conditional probability of selection given success. To achieve fairness, as with the Thorndike model, the effective cut scores in the groups need to be adjusted. Both models are included in the term *group parity*.

The Regression Model

In linear regression, the sum of the residuals is zero. If a total sample is divided into two groups, but is used, the subgroups' sum of residuals from the total sample's regression line is not necessarily zero in a subgroup and may be substantially nonzero. Cleary (1968), in perhaps the first of the fairness models, defined a test as "biased" if criterion prediction, based on a common regression line, is consistently too high or too low within subgroups. The concept was also known as *differential prediction*[1] or *differential validity*. (For some obscure reason, the two terms, although referring to different things, were used almost interchangeably at the time.) It also became known as the *regression model*, or the *Cleary model* of fairness or, conversely, of bias. Under this definition, test use was considered fair if the sum of residuals from the common regression line is zero in the subgroups. With different subgroup regression (usually parallel), fairness under Cleary's definition requires use of the group's own regression line to predict criterion performance. The 1985 *Standards* replaced the term *fairness* with the term *selection bias* (American Educational Research

---

[1] The term was used in the Second World War, with a different meaning, when validity coefficients differed for performance predictions differed for different jobs (Humphreys, 1952).

Association et al., 1985). *Predictive bias* was the preferred replacement term in the 1987 *Principles* (Society for Industrial and Organizational Psychology, 1987) and the 1999 *Standards* (American Educational Research Association et al., 1999).

By the 1990s a consensus had formed within the personnel testing community that differential prediction for different ethnic groups was rare and unlikely for cognitive tests. Because corresponding evidence for personality measures was sparse, Saad and Sackett (2002) used Project A data to study three personality predictors of five different criteria in nine military occupations. Evidence of differential subgroup prediction was found in a third of the regression pairs, mainly in intercepts (the number of differences in slopes was about at chance level), and it seemed to depend mainly on specific criteria in specific jobs. This was a thorough study, and it suggests two conclusions: (a) when it happens, the reasons for prediction differences are rarely as clear as they were in this study—and they were not always clear in this one—and (b) differential prediction *per se* presents a pair of dilemmas. In the first place, when parallel regression functions are found, they usually are not found in the earlier expected pattern. Conventional wisdom in the 1960s, when differential prediction was widely supposed, expected use of a common regression equation to *underpredict* minority criterion performance. Accumulated data, however, did not support that expectation, typically finding that common regression lines *over*predicted performance in minority groups. Even the expected underprediction presented a legal dilemma in that it followed Guidelines but produced heavier adverse impact. The Civil Rights Act of 1991 seems to have made that action subject to litigation for "manipulating" scores and treating assessment in the protected group differently from the treatment in other groups. It is not clear whether the Congressional prohibition of race norming can extend in case law to other protected groups.

The Fates of the Models

The various fairness models are incompatible. Except under the unlikely condition of perfect correlation, fairness under one model is unfair under another. For a specific example, if score distributions are approximately normal in the groups compared, a fair test under the Thorndike model will be unfair under the Cleary model. Many other models were proposed (for a summary, see Petersen & Novick, 1976), any one being inconsistent in some respects with the others.

Inconsistency is only one reason for the demise of the arguments over fairness models. A special issue of the *Journal of Educational Measurement* (Jaeger, 1976) may have stilled the debate; it demonstrated the futility of looking to statistical models for answers to political or social questions. Most participating authors looked to more rational, explicit values and the development of decision algorithms to maximize both organizational and social utilities. IRT was not yet widely known. If debates had not already been stilled well before the 1990s, Congress would have stilled them with the Civil Rights Act of 1991. It outlawed anything that seemed likely to become a quota system, including the use of different norms for different demographic subgroups. Still another reason for the apparent demise of debate is that the Cleary model won it among psychometricians. Except for attempts in the regulatory agencies to match Guidelines requirements to group parity definitions, the regression model was officially accepted in the *Standards* and the *Principles* as predictive bias. Its acceptance is not simply historical; a quite recent chapter on "bias and fairness" was based on the concepts of predictive bias and group mean differences (Evers et al., 2005).

Note that the fairness models were models of test use, not models of bias inherent in test scores or assessment instruments. Note that they were introduced well before the introduction of validity generalization replaced the concept of situationally specific correlation. At the time, the issue was whether the use of a given test in specific selection situation led to biased predictions in that situation, not whether the test inherently produced some sort of general bias regardless of specific uses. Moreover, the models are more likely to raise questions of cutting scores, whether literally set or *de facto*, and their effect on predictive bias. The chapter's opening question was not answered by the fairness models, although they led to concern over differential prediction—an important concern.

Differences in Group Mean Scores

Assumptions and Explanations in Comparing Mean Scores

A pervasive finding in personnel testing is that comparing two or more demographic groups shows differences in mean scores on tests that assess genuine job qualifications. These differences may occur because (a) essentially random score differences occur, even where the groups compared show no differences in true scores or latent abilities, (b) different recruiting practices were used for the groups compared, (c) score differences reflect real differences in the distributions of ability (or other construct) in the groups compared, or (d) measurement is not equivalent in the groups compared, even if latent construct distributions may be the same. This latter explanation is especially important: observed mean differences are not unfair if they validly reflect mean differences in the distributions of the latent construct assessed.

Evaluation of these optional reasons may help in understanding the problem of measurement bias, especially when placing them in the historical context. Explanation (a) was offered mainly in the immediate aftermath of the passage of the 1964 Civil Rights Act, before much research was done on comparisons of test use in different demographic groups. When a substantial body of research had been reported, differences with practical implications had occurred far more often than could be attributed to chance, eliminating explanation (a). Explanation (b) also disappeared in time, at least from professional discussions. Early in the Civil Rights era, it made some sense because the comparisons, usually of black and white applicant groups, were based on groups formed by very different recruiting practices: highly varied, concentrated recruiting for black applicants but no special recruiting for whites.[2] Employers hoped to find and hire enough women and black applicants to "get the numbers right," that is, to have hired enough women and blacks to approximate their proportions in the local labor market. Of course, such recruiting efforts contributed to adverse impact under the 80% rule because they brought in disproportionately larger numbers of unqualified recruits. Because of growth in the numbers of qualified applicants in the protected classes, increased attention to other demographic groups, the mounting body of case law, computerized recruiting, and perhaps a growing sophistication and social awareness among organizational leaders, among other things—for whatever reasons, the level of disparity in recruiting for different demographic groups seems to have dropped. And good riddance: explanation (b) implied that distributional differences were due to biased recruiting and tended to ignore other possible explanations. Explanations (c) and (d) came later, after development of modern measurement theory permitted both of them

[2] This was quite different from the "targeted recruiting" proposed by Newman and Lyon (2009), who advocated, as in their study, targeting for general mental ability and conscientiousness (i.e., qualifications) as well as for diversity.

to compare systematically *ability* (or other latent trait) distributions and corresponding *score* distributions.

The question, "Are tests biased?" does not ask about bias in test use; it asks about inherent bias in test scores. I suggest that *test score bias (measurement bias) exists when a distribution of obtained scores or expected true scores differs systematically from the distribution of ability estimates.* Bias, by this definition, is not a matter of opinion; it can be detected empirically, and it can be defined more succinctly in terms of measurement equivalence, the requirement that measurements in the groups have the same psychometric properties in each—that a given score means the same thing in either group. So, *bias exists when the measurements compared are not equivalent across the groups compared.* Explanations (c) and (d) consider this concept of bias. Explanation (c) suggests that mean differences, as one aspect of the distributions, arise because of real group differences in the underlying construct, differences that *must* be reflected if the construct is validly measured. Explanation (d) considers the case in which distributions of latent ability estimates are alike in the two groups but some aspect of the score distributions (e.g., means) differs from the same aspect in the compared ability distributions; in such cases, it is likely that the measurements in the groups compared are not equivalent (Drasgow, 1982, 1984).

A different concept of bias is expressed in interaction terms, offering a statistical but not a psychometric definition of bias. In moderated multiple regression, a predictor is one independent variable. A second variable might be demographic group membership, and a third variable is the interaction between these two. If the regression constant for the interaction is statistically and practically meaningful, bias is sometimes defined as an interaction of test scores and group membership.

The "Other Variable" Problem

The psychometric definition of bias, like the raw fact of differences in group means, also evades the question of why it happens. To be understood, the source of statistical or psychometric bias must be discovered. A discrepancy between score distributions and distributions of ability estimates (or estimates of other latent constructs of interest) might not be a function of an entire test or assessment procedure; it might be due to properties of individual components, such as items or item sets, within the test. Perhaps these properties are perceived differently in the groups compared and therefore have different group response characteristics. Still, the question of "why" remains: what in the nature of a demographic group is likely to produce different responses to an item? That may still be the wrong question; it might be too narrow. A broader question: what personal or situational influences on members of specific groups may produce the different responses? That is, the difference may be more likely to stem from some form of the "third" or unknown variable problem.

The so-called "third variable" problem, as introduced in connection with bivariate regression, is better described in multivariate research as a "further variable"—or even better, an "omitted variables" problem, if we look again at multiple regression and moderators. One assumption in multiple regression is that the model represented by the regression equation is "fully specified"—that it includes all important predictors. Assume that predictors A and B predict criterion Y and that they are virtually independent—not much correlation between them. Assume also that an evaluation of these predictors requires investigation of differential prediction. If we tested each predictor separately, we would have an omitted variables problem in each. "Failure to simultaneously examine both predictors can result in a misspecified model . . . If an omitted variable correlated with the criterion is also correlated with subgroup membership, the [regression] coefficients for subgroup membership and for the subgroup–test interaction may be biased . . . this bias can lead to changing conclusions about the presence and nature of differential prediction" (Sackett, Laczo, & Lippe, 2003, p. 1047).

The Sackett et al. Monte Carlo study demonstrated the effect with generated data. Distributions for 1000 cases were created for variables A (termed ability) and B (termed conscientiousness) and a performance criterion with random error; A and B were uncorrelated. A minority group of 100 cases was randomly selected to create a surrogate for race by reducing each of the ability scores in the minority group by a full standard deviation. That is, A (ability) was correlated with performance and with group membership; B (conscientiousness) was correlated with performance but not race.

The first analysis looked for differential prediction from variable A using moderated regression (predictors including A; group, presumably race; and the $A \times$ group interaction). For the regression of performance on variable A, there were no slope or intercept differences based on group membership. The second analysis replaced variable A with variable B. If group membership is based on race, then the omission of a variable such as ability, correlated with both the criterion and race, is tantamount to saying that the shared variance of ability and race is attributable to race. The result created different intercepts for the two groups, in spite of the fact that the study was designed to make variable B free from bias.

A third analysis, in two parts, was a fully specified model. Both predictors, group membership and the group $\times B$ interaction, were entered in the first part. The second part made a composite of A and B and included group and the group by composite interaction. In both parts, no differential prediction occurred, that is, neither group membership nor the interaction term had significant regression coefficients. The Monte Carlo study was followed by a similar analysis using data from Project A. The effect found in the simulation was replicated with actual data.

The effect of these analyses is anticlimactic but potentially revolutionary for traditional practice. I believe they render moot most of the differential prediction research done for about three decades. At the very least, they point up the error in following the insistence of American regulatory and case law that each predictor be independently analyzed for adverse impact (and, by inference, for differential prediction). What may prove revolutionary is their effect on forming the traditional predictive hypothesis. According to Chapter 3, traditionally a criterion is chosen first, and then predictors are chosen that seem likely to correlate well with it. Within the tradition, the criterion is likely to be broad and complex. A fully specified model for such a criterion may include many predictors. If the predictive hypothesis suggests a few predictors, but is nevertheless underspecified, preliminary data may suggest that some predictors are especially promising. Turning tradition around, the alternative to a fully specified model "is to seek a narrower, focused criterion that focuses exclusively on the workplace manifestation of the construct tapped by the predictor" (Sackett et al., 2003, p. 1055). My personal interpretation of this statement suggests a two-stage process. First, identify a construct that is clearly and logically relevant to a narrowly defined aspect of performance. Then identify assessment methods *and criterion measures* that clearly measure that construct. This is not a totally new idea; in a slightly different context, I have long advocated narrowly defined criteria, arguing that the relative importance of essentially independent performance components should not be judged before validation research (by somehow combining components) but after the research has been done and decisions about individual candidates are to be made (Guion, 1961, p. 149). What seems almost revolutionary is to require evidence of the psychometric validity of both variables—"almost revolutionary" because, despite decades of lip service to the idea, evidence of relational validity (with criterion and predictor sharing common sources of variance) remains too often the only kind of evidence sought.

GROUP MEAN DIFFERENCES IN SCORES

Researchers often want to know how people in one group compare, on the average, with people in a different group. In experiments, one group may get an experimental treatment; the treatment is withheld from the other group. Outcomes are measured and mean outcomes are compared across the groups. The experimenter's main interest is in the *focal* group, the group getting the treatment. The other group, a *reference* group (or *control* group) pretty well matches the focal group in everything except the treatment; that is, hardly anything, including group size, is allowed to vary across groups except the treatment. Studies of bias are not necessarily experimental, but group outcome means are typically compared.

When a mean score for candidates in one group is lower than the mean score for candidates in another group, some people would say that the test is biased. Others (some psychologists and statisticians) might agree, but only if the difference is statistically significant. Neither jump to conclusion is justified. An observed difference between the means of score distributions in two groups of people says nothing more than that, *on the average*, people in the two groups score differently. The observation of a mean difference, statistically significant or not, is not enough by itself to support an inference of test bias; it may instead (or maybe not) lead to an inference of bias, or of adverse impact, or of differential validity, or of differential prediction based on test use. These are possible explanations of group mean differences, but an equally plausible, perhaps more plausible, explanation is a misspecification in the research design—the effect of "other variables" omitted from the research.

In correlational terms, a mean difference exists if the regression lines predicting performance in the two groups are different but parallel. In that case, the predictions are equally valid in the two groups, despite the difference in means. That is, slopes are equal; but intercepts differ, and so do predicted criterion levels for any given score. If the regression lines cross (i.e., different slopes), validities are not equal, a fact obscured when considering only mean differences, especially if the lines cross somewhere near the X and Y means. Whether the mean difference signals adverse impact or not depends on the selection ratio, and adverse impact may also occur with low selection ratios and disparate group variances—even if there is no mean difference at all (cf. Cascio, Jacobs, & Silva, 2010).

The difference between group means is a measure of *effect size*, but the effect is hard to interpret if expressed in raw score units. Standard scores permit a common evaluation of differences by permitting interpretations in standard deviation units. This rather glib statement begs the question of which standard deviation should be used in the transformation. I prefer to use the standard deviation of the distribution in the combined group when homogeneity of variance permits it, partly because it is easier and partly because it minimizes sampling error. When variances in the groups are different, each group's own standard deviation is used. Some meta-analysts use the standard deviation from the reference group (or control group) only. Whichever value is chosen, the effect is described as a *standardized mean difference*, indicated by the italicized letter *d*. If $d = .33$, the two groups differ by about a third of a standard deviation, transformed if it is useful to the raw score scale. Differences between groups, especially where one group is protected by law, are often expressed in standardized mean differences. The larger the difference, the greater the *potential* for adverse impact, but even with a large mean difference, demonstrable adverse impact as an operating effect still depends on the selection ratio and other considerations.

Since the early research after passage of the US 1964 Civil Rights Act, a general assumption has been that the standardized mean difference in ability test scores of black and white employment candidates is about a full standard deviation ($d = 1.0$), larger than other demographic comparisons. Hough, Oswald, and Ployhart (2001), in a thorough review, found many less extreme *d* values. Examples from two of their tables, consolidated here in Table 9.1, show that the effect of group membership varies widely from a full standard deviation down to no mean difference at all, depending on the groups compared and the constructs measured.

TABLE 9.1

Means of Standardized Mean Differences across Various Group Comparisons on Measures of Frequently Assessed Constructs

	Groups Compared					
Construct Assessed	Black/ White	Hispanic/ White	Asian/ White	American Indian/White	Women/ Men	Older/ Younger
Cognitive						
g (GMA)	−1.0	−.5	−.2	−	0	−.4
Verbal ability	−.6	−.4	−	−	.1	−
Quantitative ability	−.7	−.3	−	−	−.2	−
Science achievement	−1.0	−.6	−	−	−.2	0
Spatial ability	−.7	−	−	−	−.4	−.2
Memory	−.5	−	−	−	0	−
Mental processing Speed	−.3	−.4	−	−	0	−.6
Personality						
Extraversion	−.10	−.01	−.15	−.10	−	−
Affiliation	−.31	−	−	−	−	−
Surgency	.12	.01	−.01	−.11	−	−
Conscientiousness	−.06	−.04	−.08	−.14	−	−
Achievement	−.01	.04	.13	−.09	−	−
Dependability	−.11	−.11	−.29	−.19	−	−
Adjustment	.04	.01	−.08	.03	−	−
Agreeableness	−.02	−.06	−.01	−.13	−	−
Openness to experience	−.21	−.10	−.18	0	−	−
Scales						
Integrity	−.04	.14	.04	.08	−	−
Managerial potential	−.30	−	−	−.07	−	−
Social desirability	−.05	.56	.40	.03	−	−

A negative value indicates that the first-named group in pair has lower mean scores. The Asian group in the studies of cognitive constructs is limited to east Asians. The three scales are more complex constructs than the others listed. Adapted from "Determinants, detection, and amelioration of adverse impact in personnel selection procedures" by L. M. Hough, F. L. Oswald, and R. E. Ployhart, 2001, *International Journal of Selection and Assessment, 9,* Tables 1 and 2. © 2001 by John Wiley & Sons. Adapted with permission.

Requirements for Group Comparisons

Simple Corrections

The *d* statistic is algebraically transformable to a biserial coefficient of correlation, so the principles of correcting or adjusting for correlation coefficients can also be applied to mean differences. A simple requirement is to correct for range restriction. Failure to consider this difference in the groups compared can lead to an underestimate of the group mean difference (Roth, Van Iddekinge, Huffcutt, Eidson, & Bobko, 2002). If range restriction has occurred because of a screening device used prior to the assessment being considered, comparisons of group differences in the first and second hurdles can be misleading. Corrections for measurement error (unreliability) are less common but can also be applied.

Measurement Equivalence

As mentioned before, the more vital requirement is measurement equivalence or invariance across the groups (Drasgow, 1984; Raju, Laffitte, & Byrne, 2002; Stark, Chernyshenko, Drasgow, & Williams, 2006). For a meaningful comparison the measurement method should yield scores that are interpreted in the same way in the different groups. This is more than test form equivalence in classical test theory, requiring the same means, variances, and other distributional characteristics in the parallel forms. IRT comparisons of subgroups ask for none of these; they require that the relationship of observed scores to underlying ability is the same across groups, specifically that the test characteristic curves (TCC) have the same parameters in all compared groups, within linear transformations.

Drasgow (1984) pointed out bluntly that the only cure for nonequivalence is revision of the instrument, by either improving or replacing items that contribute to it. Perhaps the test could be thrown away and replaced with another that *would* provide equivalent measures. *There is no point in going ahead with the comparison if measures are not equivalent across groups* because there will be no way to know whether an observed difference is attributable to the instrument, its use, the way it is perceived, or a difference in whatever latent trait is measured. Methods for demonstrating equivalence have been proposed by Raju et al. (2002) and Meade, Lautenschlager, and Johnson (2007), among others. Because equivalence can be demonstrated empirically, it should not merely be assumed—as would be necessary if relying on classical test theory. Group comparisons without measurement equivalence seem not worth doing, bringing to mind the adage that something not worth doing is not worth doing well. Some meta-analyses on group comparisons have been reported, but apparently without separating studies with evidence of equivalent measurement from those without it.

In a study of test type and ethnic differences, Schmitt and Mills (2001) gave five traditional tests and a 6-skill computerized job simulation to nearly 1000 job applicants; constructs in the two types of assessment were "similar but not identical" (Schmitt & Mills, 2001, p. 456). Standardized mean differences between black and white mean scores were about twice as big for traditional tests as for the job simulation. Validity coefficients for the 51 applicants hired were also higher for the traditional tests, though less dramatically.

Two major reviews, one a meta-analysis, offered many hypotheses related to group differences. Hough et al. (2001), in a very thorough narrative review of research related to adverse impact, including meta-analyses, identified many variables that sometimes accounted in part for group differences. These variables included, besides constructs measured (as in Table 9.1), "measurement method, culture, test coaching, applicant perceptions such as test anxiety and perceptions of the validity of the test, others' stereotype perceptions, and criterion composition" (Hough et al., 2001, p. 177). A meta-analytic review, reported by McKay and McDaniel (2006), was said to be the biggest meta-analysis yet of black–white group differences in work performance. A base finding of $d = .27$ was lower than previous estimates—far lower than the value of .5 once widely accepted, but still favoring whites. The analysis investigated five kinds of moderator. Criterion type (i.e., such diverse criteria as task performance, work samples, success in training, job knowledge, turnover, etc.) was the most influential of these. Neither of these reviews, however, seemed to demand evidence of measurement invariance in reaching its conclusions.

Distributional Similarity

If mean differences are to be interpretable at all, the groups must have similar distributions. If the mean difference is zero, there can still be large and important differences between groups in those who reach some desired score level if the distribution in one group is tall and in the other is flat. In an entertaining paper, Baumeister (2007) pointed out that the fact that there are more men than women in high-level jobs, despite the absence of mean differences, comes from the fact that there is a large proportion of men in the high end of their distributions—and also in the low end. That may be just a statistical artifact, but it may also, Baumeister argued, be an important difference in the kinds of motivation driving men and women.

What do we know about group mean differences? They exist, they are descriptive, and they identify potential for adverse impact. We know many correlates of such differences, but not so many causes. We know that persistent research flaws have obfuscated knowledge of their magnitudes. We know that, by themselves, they do not offer a useful indication of bias in assessment methods.

DIFFERENTIAL FUNCTIONING OF ITEMS OR TESTS

Differential Item Functioning (DIF)

Some litigation has centered on a concept of bias in individual items. Traditional item statistics, such as the proportion in each subgroup giving a correct answer, or group mean differences in frequencies of correct responses, are inappropriate for studies of DIF because they depend on trait distributions in the groups studied. If group mean differences in correct responses reflect group differences in the trait, these statistics cannot disentangle actual trait differences from bias, and any question of statistical significance is a useless distraction. Psychometricians generally refer to *differential item functioning (DIF)* as a more descriptive and less emotional term than *item bias* (Embretson & Reise, 2000; Holland & Wainer, 1993). Item response parameters, in either classical or modern test theory, should be essentially the same across groups at all levels of the measured trait, even in groups with different distributions of the trait being measured. If they are not, the item functions differently in the groups compared, and critical thinking is required in searching for explanations. Research often finds inexplicable differences; they are less compelling than those that make sense.

In litigation, some litigants have called tests biased merely because of group differences in item pass rates. Drasgow (1987) described out-of-court settlements of two court cases based on this simple-minded statistic. In one case, *Golden Rule Insurance Company et al. v. Washburn et al.* (1984), the settlement stipulated that, on future tests, group item difficulties should differ by no more than .15. The second, *Allen v. Alabama State Board of Education* (1985) was more restrictive, specifying a maximum difference of .05. Item difficulty differences on a widely used test exceeded the .15 maximum of the *Golden Rule* agreement on 90% of the items when responses of black males and black females were compared to those of white males (Drasgow, 1987)—one of those apparently interesting but basically ambiguous bits of information. DIF analysis, however, identified less than half of the items as biased—and inconsistent in direction of effect; the numbers of items harder for minorities nearly equal the numbers of items easier for them. In short, the cancelling effect of these differing directions made the cumulative effect on total test scores very low. With similar findings for other subgroups, Drasgow concluded that no measurement bias existed in total test scores in the six groups studied. This is not an unusual finding.

Expert Judgment and Sensitivity Review

Not all comparisons of differential group response tendencies invoke measurement theory. In early research on potential subgroup response differences, focal group representatives were asked to read items and identify those biased against their group. Problems arose: judgments were unreliable, very large numbers of items were called biased, and reasons for calling them biased were often labored or not given at all. Nevertheless, such judgments may be important. A test, like Caesar's wife, not only must be above reproach but must appear to be above approach—not only must be unbiased but must be perceived as unbiased. A person who thinks an item is biased or offensive may respond to it differently from others; if enough people in a group see it similarly, the effect can be group-related. If members of a focal group think an item perpetuates negative stereotypes about their group, if they interpret items differently, or if they have different habits in taking tests, they may respond differently. The possibility causes many commercial test developers to establish sensitivity review guidelines and systematic procedures for evaluating possible group differences in answering proposed items, often using people deemed to be especially aware of subgroup attitudes that are potentially biasing. Members of review panels are sometimes required to answer yes or no to questions about bias in individual items, write reasons for their answers, and be prepared to discuss the reasons with other panel members to try to achieve consensus. The following half-dozen questions have been reported, but only the first two are common.[3]

1. Does the item include content that may be deemed offensive to most members of identifiable sexual, racial, cultural, ethnic, disability, religious, or age groups?
2. Does the item perpetuate sexual, racial, cultural, ethnic, disability, religious, or age stereotypes?
3. Will words or phrases used in the item have different meanings for members of those different groups?

---

[3] Once again, the realities of litigation arguments, not always sensible from a technical point of view, require me to emphasize that this is simply a listing of sometimes *useful considerations*—not a checklist of answers to be demanded. Some of these simply cannot be answered in many situations.

4. Will vocabulary level or complex sentence structure pose problems, not related to the purpose of the test, for some groups?
5. If the item alludes to experiences members of some subgroups are more likely than others to have had, would the experience or lack of it contribute to different probabilities in responding correctly?
6. Is the item format unusual and more likely to be unfamiliar to examinees in some groups?

Such questions can be important. Reliable, rational answers to them can help test developers. However, they cannot reasonably be expected to reduce bias. Panel members are unlikely to have a good technical grasp of the nature of psychometric bias, and more importantly, they are expected to make judgments without factual data not yet developed. Although I question the general value of these panels, a test developer who considers them necessary should establish judgment procedures that encourage rationality and permit estimation of the reliabilities of the resulting judgments.

Transformed Difficulty Statistics

Using the classical concept of item difficulty (p), Angoff (1972, 1982) offered a simple procedure for identifying potentially biased items when responses are scored dichotomously, as follows.

1. Within each subgroup, compute item difficulty levels for all items on a test and express them as probabilities of a correct answer, p.
2. Using tables of areas under the normal curve, transform all values of p to z-scores.
3. Transform z-scores to deltas using the equation $\Delta = 4z + 13$; thereby eliminating negative values. With two subgroups, a pair of delta values exists for each item.
4. Plot the pairs of delta values, as in Figure 9.1, and compute the correlation. It should be quite high.
5. Identify items where deltas are out of line, measuring location vertically from the regression line.

Figure 9.1 is hypothetical, but it shows the effect in an easily visible exaggeration. The correlation of delta values in the two groups is .90, somewhat lower than typically found; correlations of .98 or even .99 are not unusual. Three correlation-reducing outliers are identified as items 13, 21, and 28. Note that the method of analysis offers no clue why these items are more difficult in one group than in the other—only that they are. They might as well be removed from the test (or at least from the scoring key) because they reduce internal consistency. A more serious threat to psychometric validity is that they may even be measuring different constructs in the two groups. Equally damaging and equally plausible, for tests designed to measure content domains that are not homogeneous, is the threat that removal of items could destroy adequacy of content sampling.

The method is easy to use, has frequently been useful, and has been popular. However, delta values are not uniformly reliable. Another problem is that results can be misleading if the discrimination indices are not fairly uniform. High-discrimination items might be identified as biased only because they discriminate trait levels better, and items with relatively low discrimination indices may mask bias (Holland & Wainer, 1993). And the entire house of cards is built on the confounded item difficulty statistic.

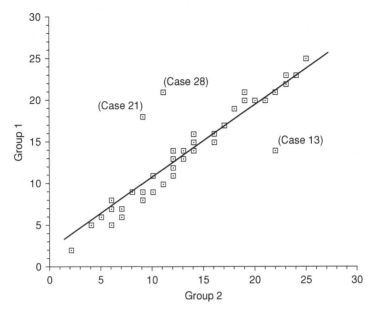

FIG. 9.1 A plot of transformed item difficulty statistics for the detection of biased items.

Contingency Methods

Methods based on contingency tables require groups matched on ability; the matching may reduce the confounding of DIF measures and group trait differences. Different methods of matching are used. Angoff (1982) suggested matching on an external variable. With IRT, matching may be based on theta, the estimated latent trait. Some methods match on total test scores; this is less risky than it may seem because total test scores seem relatively free from bias even when many items appear to be biased in one direction or the other (Stark, Chernyshenko, & Drasgow, 2004).

Contingency methods compare item functioning in groups of people who, depending on the effectiveness of the matching procedure, are similar regarding the trait measured. The basic data matrix for investigating DIF is shown in Figure 9.2. With two groups to compare, a reference group (i) and a focal group (j), and responses that may be keyed either correct (c) or not (w), the basic contingency table is the familiar 2×2 matrix. Comparisons may be made in each of several (k) trait levels within which the focal and reference groups are more or less matched. Cell entries may be either frequencies or proportions.

Early research on bias based on contingency models used ordinary chi square (χ^2) analysis of an $a \times b$ table for each item. The number of categories for one variable was the number of groups to be compared (usually two, focal and reference). The other variable was divided into the number of response categories (two for dichotomous responses but more with polytomous responses such as levels on rating scales or action options in a situation). From the simple 2×2 contingency matrix, as shown in Figure 9.2b and 9.2c, practice gravitated to models with more complex matching schemes. A simple extension is shown in Figure 9.2a, in which the 2×2 matrix is expanded by matching groups at five different trait levels (k), providing a $2 \times 2 \times 5$ ($a \times b \times k$) contingency table for each item. The resulting value of χ^2, with its accompanying degrees of freedom, can be checked in a table of

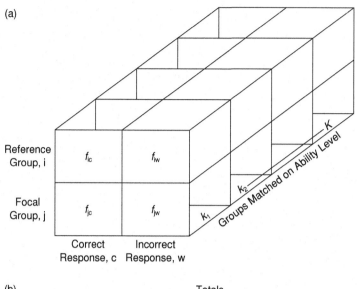

FIG. 9.2   Contingency tables for investigating differential item functioning: (a) a basic data matrix; (b) 2 × 2 frequency matrix for each of k matched groups.

chi-square values for statistical significance. A biased item, according to the various chi-square models, is one in which the group differences in cell frequencies or classical item difficulties are statistically significant. This definition, however, confounds the bias measure with sampling error.

A *full* chi square can be tested for statistical significance. Scheuneman (1979) proposed a *modified chi-square* approach. Her modification is intended to be analogous to an item characteristic curve, so it includes only the terms for correct responses. Many researchers, however, prefer the full chi-square because the distribution of the modified chi square is unknown, preventing the determination of significance.

The *Mantel–Haenszel* method (Mantel & Haenszel, 1959), another chi-square procedure for studying differences in matched groups, has been a widely used method of studying DIF. Holland and Thayer (1988) recommended it as a natural extension of chi-square procedures because it provides both a powerful test of significance and a measure of the degree of differential item functioning. The Mantel–Haenszel statement of the null hypothesis differs somewhat from the usual expression. Instead of stating it as the hypothesis of no difference between obtained frequencies and those expected from marginal totals, the Mantel–Haenszel null hypothesis (in DIF) is expressed as an equal ratio in each of the matched groups of the proportion of correct answers to the proportion of incorrect responses. With no examinee omitting a response, $p_c + p_w = 1$, and the basic null hypothesis is that $p_{ic}/p_{iw} = p_{jc}/p_{jw}$ in each of k matching categories. The test of the null hypothesis is

$$p_{ic}/p_{iw} = \alpha(p_{jc}/p_{jw}) \tag{9.1}$$

where α is identified as a common odds ratio across all of the k matching categories; the null hypothesis is that $\alpha = 1$. Alpha in this equation is the odds ratio $p_{ic}p_{jw}/p_{jc}p_{iw}$ for each of the k categories, and it provides a measure of the degree of differential item functioning. Holland and Thayer (1988) proposed a logarithmic scale, comparable to Angoff's delta scale, which is symmetrical around an estimated alpha of zero:

$$\Delta_{MH} = -(2.35)\ln(\alpha_{MH}) \tag{9.2}$$

The interpretation of these values is not difficult. α_{MH} is the average factor by which the odds that a reference group member will get the item correct exceeds the odds for a member of the focal group. If the value is greater than 1.0, the reference group generally did better on the item; if it is less than 1.0, the focal group was correct more frequently. Likewise, positive values of delta indicate how much more difficult the item was for the reference group, and negative values indicate how much more difficult it was for the focal group. At the Educational Testing Service, using three categories of MH DIF levels, an item was assigned to Category A (negligible DIF) if Δ_{MH} from Equation 9.2 was not significantly different from zero, $p < .05$, or in absolute terms was less than one delta unit (Dorans & Holland, 1993). It was assigned to Category C if $\Delta_{MH} > 1.5$ and was significantly, at $p < .05$, greater than 1.0 in absolute value. All others were in an intermediate category B.

I've given more attention to the Mantel–Haenszel method because it works with moderate-size groups: "moderate" may be defined as 100–300 cases. That is a small, maybe moderate, sample size in educational testing but larger than available for most personnel research; it is substantially less than required for IRT analyses. Even more attractively, it is the only method offering both a significance test and, more importantly, a measure of effect size, and it gives relatively stable results (Hills, 1989). Among the disadvantages: it might not do well with small groups having large mean score differences, and it is influenced by the manner of grouping score categories.

IRT Methods

Using IRT, a measure of DIF can be determined by measuring the area between item characteristic curves when item parameters are estimated independently in focal and referent groups. As with total scores, some limits must be set (e.g., ±3.0 on the Θ scale). For discussion of related computational procedures, see Hambleton and Swaminathan (1985).

If the area between the curves is zero, the probabilities of correct responses in focal and reference groups are the same at all levels of Θ, and all IRC parameters are equal, so the item functions similarly in the compared groups. An alternative analysis tests the significance of the difference between parameter estimates in the focal and reference groups. Would these tests be less likely to confound effect size and sampling error than other DIF significance tests? I think so. Sample sizes adequate for IRT analysis are fairly large, so sampling error would be relatively small. Nevertheless, I would be more interested in the area between the curves as a measure of effect size.

Confirmatory Factor Analysis (CFA)

DIF may occur if an item taps different constructs in the compared groups. That can happen when members of the groups have had different life experiences leading to group differences in item understanding or interpretation. CFA can test a hypothesis of measurement equivalence or invariance of items across groups. Measurement invariance in CFA takes various forms (Stark et al., 2006). *Configural invariance* exists if the same factors, with the same patterns of factor loadings, occur in both groups (i.e., the typical two-group comparison). If it is established, then *metric invariance* (equality of factor loadings) and, if it is established, *scalar invariance* (equality of intercepts for regression of items on the latent variable) can be examined. Lack of any form of invariance in that sequence suggests differential functioning, whether analyzing items or overall test scores.

CFA and IRT have some common features but different terminology, so it has been generally assumed that they are truly different. Using a common likelihood ratio procedure, Stark et al. (2006) compared CFA and IRT in a large simulation study under a variety of circumstances and found the two to be very much in agreement on DIF detection. As the recognition has grown of the common bases and purposes of CFA and IRT, research now often pushes the boundaries of either by combining them.

Worth noting for further study is that methods have been developed for special DIF problems. This discussion has been limited to dichotomous item responses in unidimensional measures, but many tests and inventories call for graded responses, such as rating scales, and other polytomous responses—most but not all of them assuming unidimensionality. Although CFA has more commonly been used with polytomous item responses, a method named DFIT (for *D*ifferential *F*unctioning of *I*tems and *T*ests), combining DIF and differential test functioning (DTF) analysis was introduced by Raju, van der Linden, and Fleer (1995). The method is broad enough to apply to either unidimensional or multidimensional assumptions and to either dichotomous or polytomous measures, and it distinguishes compensatory items from those that are noncompensatory. A Monte Carlo investigation of the unidimensional-polytomous situation supported the use of the DFIT model despite some concern about the balancing of the items differing in compensatory directions (Flowers, Oshima, & Raju, 1999). Oshima, Raju, and Flowers (1997) also extended DFIT for dichotomous responses to multidimensional testing. Meade, Lautenschlager, and Johnson (2007) pointed out IRT advantages for the method and conducted another Monte Carlo investigation of its use. Another special use is for the relatively rare case of crossed regression lines; Finch and French (2007) combined CFA and IRT to offer a "unified strategy" for this problem.

An Evaluation of DIF Research for Personnel Decisions

Although much abbreviated from the earlier edition, I give here perhaps unwarranted space to methods of DIF analysis. I have done so because the idea of bias is so ubiquitous that litigation is often based on charges that test bias is due to "bad" items. However, most methods of DIF analysis offer no standard measure of effect size, and worse, most of them ignore effect size in favor of significance tests heavily influenced by sample size. Burrill (1982) reviewed several studies comparing methods. Informed by her review and others, but with some personal license, I offer the following generalizations about DIF.

1. All of the methods give relative statements of DIF. Even where there are measures of the degree of DIF, the measures cannot be safely interpreted in absolute terms as effect sizes. DIF, determined by whatever method, may depend quite a bit on the item pool in which the item is studied; an item looking good when embedded in one set of items may be considered biased in another.

2. DIF analysis seems to be based on the primitive idea that "*the very notion of differential item functioning by groups implies a homogeneous set of life experiences on the part of the focal group* that are qualitatively different from the reference group and that affect verbal and mathematical reasoning" (Bond, 1993, p. 278; emphasis added). The implication is silly.

3. It is almost impossible to control for confounding trait differences when assessing DIF. IRT models do better at this than do other methods, but not always successfully, and the numbers of cases needed for IRT analysis make it infeasible for most on-site personnel research. Linn (1993) clearly showed that DIF values are associated with basic item statistics and do not succeed in controlling for trait differences. Certainly, a method that relies on observed variables alone, without modeling the latent variables underlying them, is insufficient and quite possibly a misuse of statistics for the study of measurement equivalence or bias (Meredith & Millsap, 1992).

4. Correlated results of the several procedures suggest only moderate convergence. If two methods are compared for a 50-item test, the correlation is based on 50 pairs of item difference statistics; at least some of them will probably suggest little or no DIF. The other items, those showing some DIF, will show differences in opposite directions. Such results verge on being uninterpretable; they are based on severely skewed distributions with low variance, so the correlations are low. The problem of poor method convergence may be one reason why DIF literature has dwindled in recent years. Many of us remain unconvinced that these diverse methods do in fact give useful or consistent information about group differences in responses at the item level.

5. DIF statistics are not acceptably reliable. The best correlation between DIF results in repeated test administrations, for any method, was .69 for the Mantel–Haenszel delta; the correlations were as low as .18 for a nondirectional chi-square based on a three-parameter IRT model. The correlations "are by any standards quite low and raise serious doubts about the ability of the indexes to identify biased items with any degree of consistency" (Skaggs & Lissitz, 1992, p. 233). I have no reason to think reliabilities have become any better.

6. There is little guidance to tell a test developer or user what to do when DIF is declared. Automatically eliminating the item from the test or scoring key is silly, especially when its removal also reduces test validity. When DIF is found, explanations are usually sought, but analysis methods rarely give useful explanations. This theme is repeated in many of the Holland and Wainer (1993) chapters. Attempts to dream up explanations to support an attribution of bias too often "explain" an observation because it is rewarding to do so.

7. Personnel decisions are not based on items; they may be based on total scores. Biased test scores should be avoided, of course, but such bias is unlikely to be identified by DIF analysis. The number of possible reasons for DIF is great, and the list probably

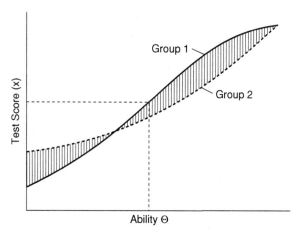

FIG. 9.3 Test characteristic curves with parameters estimated for two groups; the shaded area between the groups represents differential test functioning.

includes bias with its pop-culture connotation of prejudice. But we simply do not know. In my view, DIF analysis is important only when it raises answerable questions about the implications of retaining or eliminating an item, or when it is done as a precursor to or pairing with differential *test* functioning. These include implications for psychometric validity, for job-relatedness, or for attitudes of test takers.

Differential Test Functioning (DTF)

Stark et al. (2004) pointed out that, in practical terms, DTF is more important to organizations than DIF, if only because hiring is not based on individual item responses. The practical question, "Are tests biased?" began this chapter. To answer the question, they propose two different conceptions of invariance or equivalence: *relational equivalence* as well as *measurement equivalence*. The opposites of these terms are *relational bias* (more commonly known as differential prediction, or predictive bias) and *measurement bias.* Many investigations of possible differential prediction have contributed to a consensus that relational bias is rather uncommon. Where it is found, regression intercepts often differ but different slopes are rare. Measurement bias seems to be more common; it can be defined in terms of a poor match between observed score distributions and the underlying trait distributions.

IRT can be used to examine measurement bias for items or for total test sores. Groups with different ability distributions should provide (within a linear transformation) the same item parameters in a test of that ability and the same test characteristic curves. Figure 9.3 depicts test characteristic curves for two subgroups, suggesting that test performance interacts with group membership to a degree proportional to the area between the curves. The total area is infinite if the lower asymptotes differ—as they typically do—so the area measured typically has a restricted definition, for example, between Θ values of –3 and +3.

Two mathematical approaches to developing effect sizes (as opposed to significance tests) in test bias studies were suggested by Stark et al. (2004). One of them is based on test characteristic curves and is related to the logic of Figure 9.3. There, the two curves represent different functions, and the shaded area between them indicates effect size. For any given level of ability, vertical differences between the curves show differences in test scores expected at that level; scores in the groups differ by varying amounts at the different ability levels. A precisely zero difference in observed scores occurs only where the two TCCs cross. For any given observed score, people in each group differ in estimated ability, indicated by measuring the horizontal distance between the curves. The second method begins with the Guidelines concept of adverse impact and is termed the *selection ratio index*. Both of these measures of the practical importance of DTF are complex and require computer use; appropriate software is referenced in the article. Noteworthy is that these methods yield values that do not depend on sample size and are therefore more interpretable and more usefully informative than results of significance tests. Both of them explicitly indicate the degree to which one group is favored over another *at and above particular scores*. Therefore, they are explicitly relevant to selection procedures using cut scores, whether literally observed or *de facto*.

ADVERSE IMPACT

Adverse impact exists when members of a protected group are less likely to be hired than members of a favored group. Under the Uniform Guidelines, it is signaled when the adverse impact ratio (AIR), or $SR_h/SR_l < .80$, where SR is the selection ratio in a higher and lower group respectively. Another signal is the significance of the difference between the SRs. Over time, the signals—the operational definitions—became confused with the basic concept. Other signals (e.g., differences in group means, or difference in the IRT functions), share the confusion.

In Chapter 4, adverse impact was discussed primarily as part of the legal context for personnel decisions. Its importance goes beyond legal issues and its role as a trigger for regulatory actions. Adverse impact has social effects that are vitally important to communities and to the individuals affected. It may be, in fact, important enough to avoid being confused with measurement bias, which is socially important primarily as a source of predictive bias and then, perhaps, as a contributing factor in the perpetuation of poverty among disadvantaged ethnic groups.

In the context of a book on assessment, however, the main importance of adverse impact (the operating effect) may well be psychometric; operating adverse impact may have a reciprocal impact on assessment validity. In their organization of a broad theory of adverse impact, Outtz and Newman (2010) focused attention on sources of test score variance related to racial subgroups (and logically to other subgroups) that have no relevance to performance. According to the Standards (American Educational Research Association et al., 1999), validity refers to how well a test works to assure correctness of intended interpretations of or inferences from test scores. To whatever extent adverse impact can be explained by the effect of a different construct contributing to test score variance in one group but not in the other, and if that variance is not relevant to the intended performance-related interpretations, it can seriously reduce validity. Or, if the intended interpretation or inference is a descriptive statement of trait characteristics of people who have been assessed, variance irrelevant to that trait reduces the validity of the description.

Outtz and Newman gave three levels of detail in describing their theory of adverse impact. The basic level (they call it the first generation) is a description of core pathways from "genetic range" to job performance and test performance, with job knowledge and skill mediating the relationship between cognitive ability and job performance. It requires their

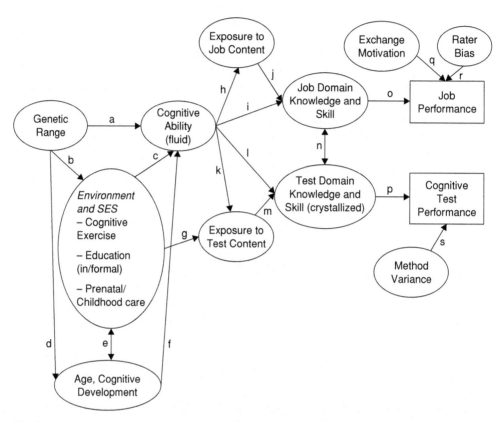

FIG. 9.4   Second-level model of adverse impact (without theory of race). Reprinted from Outtz, J. L. and Newman, D. A. (2010), A theory of adverse impact, in Outtz, J. L. (Ed.), *Adverse Impact: Implications for Organizational Staffing and High Stakes Selection*. New York: Routledge. © Taylor & Francis Group, LLC. Reprinted with permission.

second generation (Figure 9.4) to see comparable mediators in test performance, largely because their basic level doesn't consider the difference between fluid and crystallized intelligence. In their second generation, they add further environmental and experiential constructs and assign cognitive ability (the construct) to the fluid intelligence general factor; test knowledge and skill is added as a crystallized intelligence general factor. The third level of description adds theoretical constructs related to racial identification. My discussion centers on the second generation.

Consider first the paths leading to test performance. After recognizing a foundation in genetic endowment and personal development (how refreshing it is to recognize that personal development has a place in thinking about employment testing), a wide array of personal experiences influences exposure to the kind of content included in a cognitive test as well as the influence of cognitive ability. I wish Outtz and Newman had drawn a connection between test performance and job performance; it would be interesting to see if other components of the model would have been identified as moderators of that relationship. It would have been particularly interesting in the third-level model when variables in their theory of race are included.

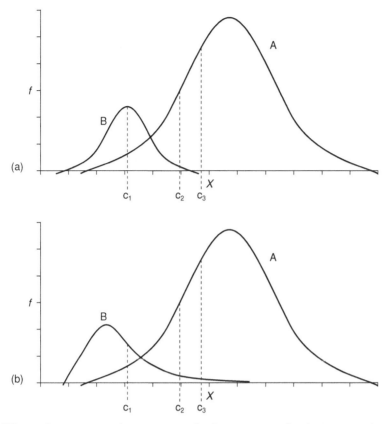

FIG. 9.5 Effects of cut scores, subgroup size, and subgroup score distributions on adverse impact ratios.

Some intellectual cobwebs need to be brushed aside. First, we must stop talking about adverse impact as if it were a fixed quantity. The AIR, for example, depends on many things. In Figure 9.5a, a cut score, explicit or *de facto*, just below the mean of group A would totally rule out selection from the smaller group B—and would at a still higher cut score *even if the two groups had precisely the same mean score* (i.e., $d = 0$), due partly to differences in variance but also to the disparity in sample sizes. Clearly, $d = 0$ does not necessarily indicate absence of adverse impact. In Figure 9.5b, with the smaller subgroup distribution substantially skewed, a few minority candidates would be selected with cut score c_3. The higher the cut score, the greater is the adverse impact. Adverse impact depends more on distribution sizes, relative positions in the score range, distribution shapes, and cut scores than on mean differences alone.

Second, group mean differences say nothing about adverse impact beyond the fact that the *potential* for it *may* (but not necessarily *will*) be greater with larger mean differences (cf. Potosky et al., 2005). Third, adverse impact is a social or legal concept, not a statistical or psychometric one, although the adverse impact *ratio* is a statistic—and not a particularly reliable one. Finally, whenever there are subgroups to be compared, some degree of adverse impact is virtually certain—even if the degree is too trivial to have any implications; an adverse impact ratio of precisely 1.0 is as unlikely a finding as precisely zero in testing a null hypothesis for any other statistic. Is the level of impact, as statistically signaled, severe enough to be a potential basis for litigation? Is the level of impact (especially with explicit cut scores) severe enough to suggest a risk of losing particularly promising employees? These are among the more serious questions about adverse impact.

Group Mean Differences and Adverse Impact

The jump from mean differences to assumptions of adverse impact, or even to statements of *potential* for adverse impact, needs to be tempered. Clearly, a large effect size d signals the potential, but many influences can account for it. Referring again to Table 9.1, it is clear that the effect size d varies according to both the construct being assessed and the groups being compared. It is not clear that values of d would correlate well with values of AIR. Suppose that the data in all of the studies summarized by Hough et al. (2001) had been transformed to z scores. It would be possible, then, to compare all studies holding the cut score constant in z score terms.[4] If both ds and AIRs were arranged in rank order, a rank difference coefficient of correlation could be computed, and I doubt that it would be very large. Another coefficient could be computed for a cut score at a lower value of z. Would it be higher or lower? I can't answer without more information or assumptions, but we can be fairly sure that it would be different from the first one. In short, a large value of d suggests the potential for adverse impact, but it does not specify its potential size.

Moreover, working from Table 9.1 does not necessarily give us a good start on predicting an AIR. One of the fascinating bits in the Hough et al. (2001) survey deals with adverse impact, women, and spatial ability—one of Thurstone's original seven primary mental abilities and one often invoked in predictive hypotheses. On tests identified generally as tests of spatial ability, the mean score for women was significantly lower than that for men—a suggestion of potential adverse impact. However, on tests of spatial visualization—a somewhat narrower construct but still typically considered a test of spatial ability—women had mean scores about the same as those for men. "Thus the test user's choice of spatial ability test affects the extent of adverse impact against women" (Hough et al., 2001, p. 160). Construct names are often convenient categories for classifying constructs that are different facets of the same general idea; some facets may be more relevant to a particular job than to others, and the job relevance of the construct, and certainly relational validity, can be another determinant of the level of adverse impact.

De Corte and Lievens (2005) were interested in estimating AIR as a function of d. Most such studies make a variety of assumptions, such as normal distributions, equal variances, top-down selection, and the use of a single predictor; De Corte and Lievens properly questioned the wisdom of these restrictive assumptions, rarely met in actual employment settings. In addition, I would urge questioning the wisdom of accepting the effect size found as a basis for predicting or estimating probable adverse impact. Relatively few reports of d indicate whether measures in the subgroups compared are equivalent; the question has simply not been salient to most personnel researchers. There have been several summaries and meta-analyses of research on group mean differences. Most of them seem to have ignored the question of measurement equivalence. My personal conclusion is that population estimates

---

[4] We'll overlook the problems in computing the z scores. What distribution would be used to compute them? The distribution in the reference group? The distribution in the total, undivided group? These questions matter, and so do several others, but I ignore them to make a different point.

of d from these analyses are therefore questionable and do not provide a solid basis for estimates of adverse impact, even when the defining circumstances are explicitly stated in the primary studies. Reports of studies that will become primary studies in a future meta-analysis should routinely report these circumstances as well as possible. When considering potential influences on the relationship of d and AIR, information should be available for all four of the traditionally considered distributional characteristics (i.e., mean, variance, skewness, and kurtosis), relative group sizes, selection ratios and cut scores, construct identification, equivalence of the measurement of the construct, and its logical relevance to the work to be done and the performance to be predicted. Modern multivariate analysis will take care of the question of relative importance.

Much of the research on mean differences, their antecedents, and their consequences has, of necessity, studied circumstances in Monte Carlo simulations. Simulations can be especially helpful in studies of successive hurdles in selection. Two examples were reported by Roth et al. (2006) in which the 80% rule for defining adverse impact in regulatory agencies might falsely suggest a more fundamental kind of adverse impact. The first of these investigated the possibility that the rule "falsely" indicated adverse impact under conditions where the population value of d was zero, i.e., no difference between the means of the two populations. They were particularly interested in assessment with *multiple-hurdle* selection systems, e.g., systems requiring a candidate to pass one test to qualify to take a second one. In both single-hurdle and two-hurdle simulations, "false positives"—showing adverse impact by the 80% rule even where d should be zero—were especially frequent with small selection ratios. Their second study simulated more realistic conditions with similar results. Whether adverse impact is defined in terms of d and its statistical significance or in terms of violations of the 80% rule seems less important to me than the fact that d does not necessarily predict, estimate, or foreshadow AIR, my main concern in this section.

Referring to *multistage selection* as a terminological alternative to *multiple hurdles*, De Corte et al. (2007) chose an analytic alternative to the Monte Carlo approach. They start from the realistic position that those planning a selection system, especially a multistage system, have in mind some predetermined results they want to achieve. For example, they may determine that they want the system to improve the overall level of performance in the work being done, the stability of the work force, or its demographic (or other) diversity and, at the same time, reduce the likelihood of adverse impact defined by the 80% rule. Without attempting to summarize a complex appendix detailing their method, I think it is important to recognize that these authors have actually approached what has previously been advocated but rarely achieved, the simultaneous consideration of multiple criteria, and doing it in multiple stage assessment systems. Nevertheless, their approach stems from a consideration of standardized mean differences. An alternative to this statistic is needed. Personally, I question the value of the mean difference approach to understanding and controlling adverse impact. We need serious consideration of some approaches to statistical or psychometric methods for defining adverse impact as a construct.

A Psychometric Approach to Adverse Impact

The need for a mechanism for triggering enforcement machinery is clear, but it is not clear that the Guidelines definitions offer the right kind of mechanism. There must be a better way to conceptualize adverse impact. In a widely unread article, Ironson et al. (1982) proposed "that the concept of adverse impact be redefined in terms of the degree of distortion of underlying differences in ability at the ability level where decisions are made" (p. 430).

The basis for their argument lies in the test characteristic curve relating expected test scores to theta (Θ), the level of the underlying latent trait.

I think I have shown that measurement bias ("Are tests biased?") requires modern measurement theory if it is to be unambiguously defined. So does the concept of adverse impact. Item response theory suggested a psychometric definition of it, without recourse to d (Ironson et al., 1982). That definition was offered more than a quarter of a century ago, when IRT was quite new in personnel research; perhaps a more precise definition could be developed with the growth of IRT models. An emphasis on measurement equivalence implies a concept of adverse impact based on the distortion—the overstatement or understatement—of latent subgroup trait differences. If there were no measurement bias (i.e., if measurement in the groups were equivalent), the TCC in one group would have the same parameters as the TCC in the other group. When the measurement procedure used in the two groups stays the same, a difference in TCCs, as in Figure 9.3, suggests nonequivalent or biased measurement, and the overall size of the effect is proportional to the shaded area between the curves.

A TCC is typically monotonic, so top-down selection is consistent with trait- or construct-based selection. In circumstances calling for hiring more than a few people, top-down selection offers no difficult selection decisions for those with very high scores indicating high levels of the estimated trait. The difficult decisions are faced when lower test scores are deemed in some sense acceptable (i.e., low enough to hire enough people to do the work, but high enough to assure an acceptable level of competence in performance).

At some point in an overall distribution, a *de facto* cut score can be identified—perhaps the low edge of an interval in which some candidates are deemed successful and get job offers and others are not. Figure 9.3 could be modified to illustrate a major difference between a psychometric definition of measurement bias and a psychometric definition of adverse impact. The difference is that only an area between curves starting with an "ability level where decisions are made" (as in the Ironson et al. definition) would be shaded. I suggest defining adverse impact psychometrically *as the area between the group TCCs at or above a* de facto *cut score.* (An alternative, and perhaps better, definition could be based on a specified value of theta.) This definition recognizes the possibility of true group differences in the distributions of the underlying construct in the groups compared. It also accepts as fact that a subgroup score difference at a given level of theta may exaggerate a true difference, understate it, hide it, or even go in the opposite direction. Of course, following Outtz and Newman (2010), we would then need to look at personal and social histories to explain why true differences exist.

The definition could be based on the total distributions of observed scores and traits, as shaded in Figure 9.3. However, if adverse impact is to be discussed in psychometric terms, the discussion should not deviate from conventional discussions so far as to become unrecognizable. The conventional regulatory view of adverse impact varies with differences in cut scores; by defining adverse impact psychometrically, the definition continues to recognize that the effects differ at or above different scores. Note that any discussion of subgroup mean differences is irrelevant to either the legal or the psychometric definition. Adverse impact depends on the level of scores where decisions are made. If one is trying very hard to maintain or improve workforce quality, the region of decision is likely to be in the above average ability range. If one is trying to fill as many positions as possible while maintaining some minimal sense of standards, the region of decision is lower. In either case, it is the distortion of proportional differences at a specific ability or score level that defines adverse impact, not the distortion at the level of group means.

ATTEMPTS TO REDUCE ADVERSE IMPACT

Group Disparities in Backgrounds as Potential Causes

An awful lot of potential causes of adverse impact have been suggested over the years. Figure 9.4 (Outtz & Newman, 2010) described a variety of background factors in which group disparity in those factors can lead to group disparity in performance and, at least by implication, to adverse impact. It would seem that reducing the background disparities, or taking them into account (e.g., as potential moderators), would also reduce adverse impact. Unfortunately, attempts to address these suspected causes have not been noted for their success. We'll consider a couple of examples.

One is the notion of stereotype threat, the idea that some minorities—maybe especially blacks—or females are somewhat threatened in situations in which a general stereotype about their abilities may be salient and therefore affect test scores in situations where the consequences of testing are important (Steele & Aronson, 1995). A survey of the extensive literature stimulated by this hypothesis (Evers et al., 2005) reported that roughly 100 laboratory studies of stereotype threat showed it to be supported in such research. Moving to field studies, however, they found little support for it. A correlational study of academic assessments and later job performance, in which a priori predictions were based on stereotype-threat theory, were not supported (Cullen, Hardison, & Sackett, 2004). Existing research has been limited mainly to looking for the existence of stereotype threat as having an effect on cognitive test performance; little (if any) has approached the very difficult task of proposing and testing a way to reduce or eliminate the effect on test performance and, again by implication, adverse impact.

A further example suggests that a test that is outside of the boundaries of one's experience with tests—test familiarity or unfamiliarity—can produce a form of test anxiety, and it can be reflected in spuriously low scores and resulting adverse impact, and also in perceptions that the test is unfair. If the degree of familiarity varies over different subgroups of applicants, some groups may be more affected and adverse impact may be expected. Truxillo, Bauer, Campion, and Paronto (2002) described a possible problem in using a video test for police candidates in a multistage selection system. By giving information about the test to candidates in the early stage they were able to increase perceptions of fairness, but it had no appreciable effect on the rate of quitting the program or on advancement to the next stage. I suspect that the increasing diversity of test media will eventually stimulate more research in this area, especially if protected groups differ from others in familiarity with the new media.

The first example illustrates programmatic research on subjective background variables on test performance. The second illustrates good research, not yet programmatic, on dropping out of a multistage process. Neither directly addresses adverse impact. In short, not many different personal causes of adverse impact, and not many associated remedies, have been hypothesized. Moreover, those that have been put forth have not been well supported by empirical data (Evers et al., 2005).

Procedural Causes and Remedies

Test Choices

The Guidelines urge employers who find adverse effect of the test being used, or proposed, to look for alternative tests with less adverse impact as the Guidelines define it (i.e., the 80% rule). "Alternative" is not clearly defined; are acceptable alternatives limited to tests measuring the same construct? Are they open to any kinds of measure? It has often been suggested (by regulators, researchers, and practitioners) that certain kinds of noncognitive tests have low adverse impact and should be used instead of the highly adverse cognitive tests. An example is the use of personality measures, either as replacements for cognitive ability or as additions to it in multiple assessment programs. Another suggestion calls for the use of more objective rather than less objective measurement. Still another calls for more careful matching of predictor and criterion constructs.

Of these suggestions, research has focused most on the use of alternative constructs (inherent in the first of these), especially in combination with cognitive ability. Results have not supported the idea very well, and at least one simulation study has found virtually no evidence of predictive bias in a fully specified model (Sackett et al., 2003). All of these suggestions overlook important considerations, identifiable in the language of modern test theory.

To illustrate, four examples of test scores distorting true mean ability differences are shown in Figure 9.6.[5] One distorting characteristic is the slope of the TCC. Figure 9.6a compares two tests with identical subgroup mean scores but different TCC slopes. Test A, with the steeper midrange slope, exaggerates true ability differences; Test B, with a relatively slight slope, constant throughout the ability range, minimizes those differences. Figure 9.6b shows that difficulty levels also influence adverse impact. The slopes of the two curves are the same, and subgroups have mean ability differences like those in the upper half, but Test C is easier than Test D. That is, the ability level required to achieve a given score on Test C is lower than the ability needed for Test D. The easy test masks true differences; the hard test exaggerates them. So far, there is no better way to compare alternative tests for adverse effect than comparing their test characteristic curve parameters.

I have not yet seen examples of such comparisons presented in the journals of personnel research. I'm not sure of the implications if they were. Would serious TCC differences lead to modifications of tests or items? Would the modifications be strong enough to eliminate or reduce substantially the distortion of underlying ability? In the present stage of research-based and theoretical knowledge, it appears that the idea of dropping one test and choosing another with apparently lower adverse impact does not work; it might even exacerbate the problem (Hough et al., 2001).

Criterion Bias

In criterion-related validation, the criterion should be reliable, valid, and free from third-variable biases. It is amazing how easy that sentence is to write and how difficult it is to accomplish. Reliability is often exceedingly difficult to ascertain for criterion measures; sometimes nothing short of generalizability analysis will do it, and often such analyses are not feasible in working organizations. A serious attempt to assess criterion validity may in itself be a way of assessing criterion bias. Evidence of valid measurement of the intended criterion construct is the sort of evidence most appropriate; a major question in construct validation is whether extraneous sources of variance influence the measures. If so, and if the numbers of cases allow, it should be possible to determine if the extraneous sources are related to subgroup composition. To what extent, however, does criterion bias signal adverse impact? I don't know.

It is common to suggest that objective criteria are less biased than subjective criteria. A meta-analysis of *d* values questions this conventional wisdom (Roth, Huffcutt, & Bobko, 2003). It found that mean values of *d* were much the same, or even larger, for objective

---

[5] This was also presented as Figure 6.11. It bears repeating.

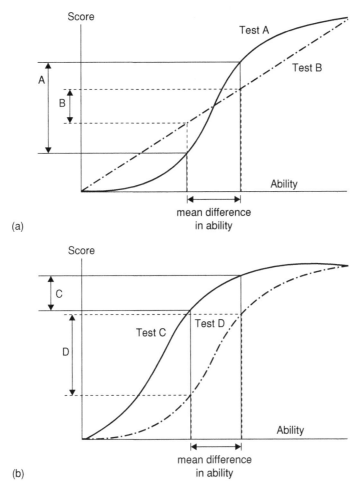

FIG. 9.6   Distorted reflections of true ability differences between groups using different tests when (a) tests are equated for ability but differ in slopes of their test characteristic curves, and (b) tests are of unequal ability but have test characteristic curves with identical slopes. Reprinted from Ironson, G. H., Guion, R. M., and Ostrander, M. (1982). *Journal of Applied Psychology, 67,* 419–432. Copyright 1982 by American Psychological Association. Reprinted with permission.

criteria, and that work samples and job knowledge tests used as criteria have bigger standardized mean differences than performance ratings. Because the standardized mean difference has been criticized as having too many confounds, it is hard to say whether the results would be similar for a meta-analysis comparing TCCs, but these findings should have a chilling effect (as lawyers would say) on enthusiasms for objective rather than subjective criteria—an enthusiasm that I have often expressed in my own opinions.

CONCLUDING NOTE

This chapter began with the question, "Are tests biased?" Even to move toward an answer, it was necessary to get a clearer idea of what we meant by *bias.* Defining bias in terms of the match between test score distributions and distributions of ability estimates makes good sense linguistically and psychometrically, but the definition does not answer the question. An answer will require meta-analyses of one, or probably more, sets of studies of such matches—studies that, frankly, are not being done.

A different question, implied if not explicit: How can adverse impact be determined in a psychological rather than a legal sense? Or can it? It can. A definition was easy within the logic of item response theory; psychological adverse impact exists when there is a disparity in test characteristic curves as measured by the area between them at or above a specified point on the scale of observed scores. However, the definition begs the questions of how large that disparity needs to be to suggest a nontrivial management or social problem, or what can be done about such disparities.

And that leaves us pretty much where we were at the beginning of the chapter. We have the definitions, and we suspect that at least sometimes the tests are biased. We do not fully understand, however, the reasons why measurements may be biased, how generally measurement bias exists, or what basically causes adverse impact.

In this chapter on bias, I have briefly reviewed some literature on fairness; fairness debates have pretty much disappeared with no recorded improvement in assessment or personnel decisions. I have considered group mean differences (considered by some to be measures of bias, if standardized) and found, among other things, that they are mainly uninterpretable because they confound measurement and ability. I have considered developments on differential item functioning and found that we do not know precisely how to account for it or how it relates, if at all, to bias. On questions of test bias, I have found ways to define it but not much else. I have reviewed notions of adverse impact and have found the 80% rule essentially silly, ambiguous, and unreliable—even though it is taken with deadly seriousness. All of this has reminded me once again of Wherry's words: "We don't know what we're doing, but we are doing it very carefully, and hope you are pleased with our unintelligent diligence" (Wherry, 1957, p. 1). Much very careful, diligent, sophisticated work has been done, and it can hardly be called unintelligent. Yet after reviewing reams of old and new material on the subject of bias in assessment, I find the concept ever more elusive.

So why have I given so much attention to these attempts to identify bias? One reason is that the concept of bias is ubiquitous and cannot be ignored. It is central to much litigation, social critics focus on it, minority communities are greatly concerned about it, and the literature about it in psychological and educational measurement and research is extensive. Another reason is that various approaches to bias have articulate, insistent advocates. A more important reason is that only those who are aware of the pitfalls of these methods can dispassionately make judgments about their usefulness in specific situations. However, the major reason is that bias, in its technical sense, is a real problem, socially and psychometrically. Fortunately, modern measurement theory seems to hold promise for helping us out of the existing mess. Without it, rampant and enthusiastic acceptance of assertions of bias with inadequate methods of evaluating them will continue to cause mischief, of which the *Golden Rule* decision is only one example.

This chapter concludes the theoretical, technical, and contextual considerations basic to assessment, especially testing, for personnel decisions. Next we look at the implications of all this for choosing and using testing principles in employment. Part III begins with some topics visited earlier—topics that need much more research work and maybe new paradigms before going on to those implications.

III
ASSESSMENT METHODS: PRACTICE AND RESEARCH

Chapters in Part III focus on assessment practices and decisions. Chapter 10 offers challenges to traditions and habits, suggesting other directions research and practice might take. Chapter 11 describes the development and use of standardized tests and inventories, whether traditional or new. Chapter 12 considers the less recognized (but no less common) role of subjective judgment in assessments and decisions, and Chapter 13 specifically considers subjective ratings as assessments. Chapter 14 goes on to recognize the relatively unstandardized assessment methods of interviewing and assessing other background information. Finally, Chapter 15 pulls together tests, ratings, interviews, and a variety of assessment exercises in multiple assessments, some standardized and statistically combined and others less so, used either in individual or group settings.

Personnel assessment has come a long way from the bivariate predictive hypotheses of Chapter 3 or the bivariate data analyses in Chapter 7. Methods and models described as traditional have given way to more comprehensive assessments and analyses. A different, and potentially more dramatic, change is the beginning of a transition in the concept of individual differences. In traditional, bivariate regression, individuals differed only on basic scale values of the two variables. Increasingly, attention is suggested to alternative assessments and prediction models, many of them more individualized, to replace occasionally the traditional, one-size-fits-all regression line.

10
Challenges to Traditional Ways

The traditional view is that decisions about who is to receive rewards or opportunities should be based on valid assessments of relevant characteristics. Judgments of the relevance of the characteristics to organizational objectives and other values, and of the validity of the assessments, should be based on competent research. I will not depart from that tradition. Do not confuse tradition with a stultifying habit of resisting change. Change happens. Hardly anything in personnel research is done now the way it was done in the middle of the twentieth century. No longer are we limited to two basic validation designs (present-employee and follow-up); instead, we now refer to a variety of validation designs. Among them, concurrent and predictive validation designs have replaced the older pair of terms. We often fail to recognize that the change in terms was also a change in the designs. We no longer score test responses with a red pencil. Multiple-choice items were common in "olden times," but so were many other item types rarely used now. The birth of the IBM answer sheet and, later, optical scanners pushed use of multiple-choice items far ahead of completion items or ranking optional responses. Technology not only changed scoring procedures; it began to change the nature of cognitive testing, too, and that change goes on as laboratory research and psychometric concerns begin to make common use of the relevant technology.

Change begets further change. Technological change, specifically computers and their software, turned an exotic test theory of latent traits (Lord, 1952) into a practical tool, which in turn led to computer adaptive testing (which, incidentally, shows that useful traditions can survive change—adaptive testing was a hallmark of Binet's approach to intelligence testing). Changes have a way of challenging existing ways of thinking. Situational specificity was the dominant idea of validity for most of the twentieth century; challenge to the idea led to meta-analysis (Schmidt & Hunter, 1977), and less happily to validity generalization now used by some with the same unthinking habit that situational specificity formerly enjoyed. Computer-instigated change has led to new statistical tools. Some of them (e.g., IRT and LISREL) have become more widely used; some have waned or even disappeared (generalizability and utility theories are much less often invoked, and the BCTRY computer package for cluster and factor analysis didn't even make it to desktop computers). New challenges still come along, and it is foolhardy to try confidently to predict which ones will be important or beget important further changes in assessment and prediction. Some of them will. This chapter describes challenges in four areas that may be among them.

CHALLENGES OF COMPUTERIZATION

I've been around longer than computers. The arithmetic for iteratively solving a large set of simultaneous equations for my dissertation was done on a card-programmed calculator; it

TABLE 10.1

Trends in Organizational Change and Corresponding Changes in Assessment and Selection

Organizational and work changes	*Assessment and decision changes*
1. Difficulty in predicting changes in job duties or functions in less stable work	More assessment of traits needed across a variety of functions, not necessarily in the present assignment alone
2. Increasing demand for knowledge and information	More assessment on potential for learning, less on more specific abilities
3. Increasing demand for speed	More efficient and faster assessment such as computerized assessment
4. More recognition of change as an enduring fact of organizational life	Assessment of dynamic criteria, whether as performance or outcome
5. Upgrading of work functions	More need for individual worker to use abstract thinking and self-assessment
6. Increased horizontal interfacing	Assessment of ability to discern and react to situational differences
7. Relatively more stress on output than on behavior	More stress on usefulness in the evaluation of assessment and decision procedures

Adapted from Jansen (1997), p. 132.

did what a desk calculator could do, but faster and without the mistakes (Guion, 1954). My first experience with an actual computer a few years later came when Raymond Cattell put our data in the ILLIAC for the Bourassa and Guion (1959) factor analysis. I acquired my first desktop computer in the early 1980s. I do not have any of the newer electronic gadgets (I still think of blackberries as being good in pies), but such things are available if I need them. Computers are not new, nor are their smaller digital spin-offs, but some of the challenges from computerization offer new (and often better) possibilities for psychometric assessment and research.

Work has changed and so have the organizations where work is done. Jansen (1997) identified seven kinds of changes stemming from information technology and listed them along with implications for selection and assessment in a summarizing table. His table is the basis for Table 10.1, although the somewhat longer terms are my own. People often called for many of the right-side changes before computers came along. For example, calls for measurement of more complex constructs, such as adaptability or the ability to think in abstractions, have been heard for decades, especially by critics of standardized testing. It would have been a good idea even if tasks had not changed, but computerization challenges us to transform ideas about necessary constructs into standard practices. Changing work, however, is a major stimulus for the suggestion that assessment should focus on traits that might someday be needed but aren't now, even when it conflicts with the Uniform Guidelines. I called for *dynamic criteria* (Guion, 1965a), along with others, when Ghiselli (1956) introduced the term. In those days, of course, we called for consideration of criteria that changed "on the average." Computers challenge us to consider individual differences in criterion change and, through that, to improve prediction based on paths of individual development.

The term *horizontal interfacing* reflects the resurgence of approval for flatter organizational structure and the accompanying requirement for people to work with more organizational work units, and more of them at one's own organizational level, than in a taller, hierarchical organization. (I refer to "resurgence" of approval and advocacy of the flatter organizational structure, admired as the Sears model in the 1940s.) Jansen considered the implication of this trend to be a call for "situational assessment" (Jansen, 1997, p. 132). He may have been referring to the trait assessed by a situational judgment test, but he may have meant something more complex, sometimes requiring negotiations and other times requiring accommodation. It is neither routine nor straightforward to suggest effective ways to test for abilities to discern differences in two similar situations, let alone to test for abilities to choose effective courses of action. Can computerized assessment provide effective ways? Possibly.

The changes reflected in Table 10.1 are not themselves changes in technology, but they influence, and are influenced by, the technological environment in which work is done—and which challenges all aspects of measurement, assessment, prediction, and personnel decisions. Computerization of job analysis, the linking of job characteristics and KSAs, recruitment, and computer-based or adaptive testing have bloomed prolifically in recent years. Investigations of measurement equivalence and psychometric properties of new testing media are being addressed more effectively. "Technological impact on performance evaluation systems, needs assessment, and training design are yet largely unexplored [but] The promise of optimal aptitude by instruction interactions can at last be realized with the new technologies" (Viswesvaran, 2003, p. 107).

The possibilities seem limitless, especially if users stretch the potential limits beyond treating computers as little more than another medium for presenting the same old tests. Even managers disappointed by their own use of technology reported intentions to increase it (Chapman & Webster, 2003). Too often, organizations invest heavily in high-tech computerized assessments without empirical evidence of their value. New technology is used as a child uses a new hammer—on everything—a general propensity that "humans never seem to outgrow" (Wainer, 2002, p. 287). New technology does not always replace the old; the old and the new "in some way, shall coexist" (Prieto & Simon, 1997, p. 121).

Computers in Assessment

An Idiographic Challenge

The terms *nomothetic* and *idiographic* are commonly applied to research design and objectives. *Nomothetic research* seeks principles that apply to people in general, "on the average." *Idiographic research* seeks generalizations or understandings that apply explicitly to the behavior of specific people. Personnel research is traditionally nomothetic, seeking general statements applicable to candidates "on the average." Idiographic approaches can move away from reliance on the statistical average to consider individual strengths and weaknesses—an approach that may be especially useful in situations of limited choice. They may move us away from a study of group differences back to the study of individual differences.

The candidate at hand is rarely average, and personnel predictions are rarely precisely accurate. Individual errors in nomothetic prediction vary from very slight to conspicuous outliers. Individual uniqueness is not often invoked as a reason for them, even though Thorndike (1949) included lasting and temporary characteristics of the person among things that can influence an individual's consistency over a population of assessment situations. Computers offer the potential, not yet explored, for studying individual differences in test-taking strategies—a topic often discussed with dismaying absence of data. Does an examinee skip hard items and return to them after responding to easy ones, or obsess over them so that time runs out? Do some people use a form of satisficing, settling for the first plausible response option? Would individual differences in willingness to guess account for some of the individual differences in accuracy of predictions from multiple-choice tests? I can imagine a scenario in which computerized assessment includes not only a score but a nomothetic prediction and some idiographic information that might help modify predictions and score interpretations.

Raw test scores have very little meaning unless transformed into something else—such as centiles or z-scores. Such transformation provides *normative scoring*, in which a person's score is interpreted relative to the scores of others. Alternatively, *ipsative scoring* interprets a person's score relative to the scores of that person on other scales; it permits an idiographic interpretation that normative scores cannot match. Many personality inventories—those with several constructs scored on the same basic scale—use ipsative scoring, but it has not been used widely for other constructs. One problem is that the appeal of idiographic assessment is dogged by the practical necessity for nomothetic prediction of criteria. Combining the two creates a lot of numbers to crunch, so computerization may make it more practical for researchers interested in the possibilities of the combination.

New Response Options

A test item presents a stimulus to which the examinee responds. The response, in a multiple-choice test, is both an evaluation of the options and a choice of one of them. The choice is recorded, perhaps on computers but traditionally on paper answer sheets or test forms. Computers expand overt response options: a click of the mouse, a finger touch on the monitor screen, a vocal indication of the choice, using the mouse to drag something from one location to another, and many others. Beyond right or wrong categories, new categories such as response latency may be feasible (Bartram, 2005a; Drasgow & Mattern, 2006). Drasgow and Mattern also reported active research on computer scoring of constructed responses. New response alternatives may be paired with new stimulus components such as moving graphics or multimedia sound and picture items. The growing options may make it possible to measure—not merely to wish to measure—constructs previously tested only in our dreams.

New Constructs

Dragging a mouse as a response method might identify a new psychomotor construct (eye–hand–mouse dexterity?), but more important constructs may become measurable, drawn from modern theories and experimentation in cognitive or physiological psychology. A book edited by Sternberg and Pretz (2004) is filled with provocative articles merging biology, cognitive constructs, and psychometric concepts of intelligence, a merger sought long ago by Cronbach (1957) and more recently by Kozhevnokov (2007).

Messick (1996) pointed out that Spearman's (1927) concept of g had two components; one quantitative, the other qualitative. Most subsequent mental measurement has concentrated, as a good scale of measurement must, on the quantitative question of "how much?" with little or no attention to qualitative questions. Indeed, *attention* is a key term in Messick's view of cognitive ability. Various modes of attention seem to illustrate Spearman's qualitative concept, the tendency or ability to create knowledge from prior sensory or mental experience, now typically called *working memory* (e.g., Hunt, 2004). Messick referred to modes of attention as *cognitive styles*, including narrow versus broad focus, field dependence versus field independence, and reflection versus impulsivity, among many others (Kagan, 1966; Lohman & Bosma, 2002). Such constructs, "new" to psychometrics, may predict effectiveness in meeting the cognitive demands of work. The reflective–impulsive dimension is assessed in lab studies by *response latency*, which can surely be measured better with a computer than with a stop-watch. Some stylistic constructs identified in the Kozhevnokov (2007) integrative theory call for advanced magnetic resonance imaging (MRI) technology. Technology challenges!

Cognitive styles are often considered forms of *cognitive control*; those "with early perceptual attention control may be less prone to distraction by irrelevant information than those who do not exhibit such a level of control" (Lohman & Bosma, 2002, p. 134). This sort of distraction-proneness seems important for explaining individual differences in job performance among people with the same level of general mental ability scores and is surely worth exploring in personnel research—despite an alternative view that "attempts to make strong predictions about behavior in a particular context on the basis of a style will generally not succeed" (Lohman & Bosma, 2002, p. 143).

I think development of measurement models for these stylistic constructs would not be wasted effort. Why isn't such measurement part of our tradition? One reason, perhaps, is that constructs such as breadth or scope of attention are not readily amenable to assessment by traditional methods. If so, computers may be more useful than traditional media for assessing the more cognitively complex processes likely to be needed in modern work. Such constructs, not really new but new in personnel assessment, can be hypothesized predictors. *Complex problem solving*, much studied in cognitive science, may be a process related to the acquisition of professional or technical expertise (Wenke, Frensch, & Funke, 2004). The process has been studied extensively in Germany with computer-simulated scenarios of complex management tasks. Such scenarios take a lot of assessee time and are very expensive to develop. Results so far are, at best, not consistently pleasing. Reliabilities reported by Kleinmann and Strauss (1998) are rather poor, and efforts to report something about construct validity were also frustrating because construct labels and definitions tend to be vague. Complex problem-solving skill can be assessed by computer, but not yet very well, and the computer makes possible a degree of complexity that even baffles the scenario developer (Funke, 1998). Kleinmann and Strauss (1998) found available information on criterion-related validity sparse and, so far, no better than validities traditionally obtained.

Computer-administered tests with graphics, with or without interactive capabilities, have clear advantages over paper-and-pencil tests for measuring job knowledge, especially when the knowledge is about things that move or change, such as moving parts of machinery or changing weather fronts. They also make possible, through interactive graphics and simulations, tests of job skills. Drasgow and Mattern (2006) described computerized simulations in professional certification and licensing examinations. One was for medical examiners. The test-taker is first shown a brief description of a patient's symptoms; the candidate (who is a physician) can request the patient's medical history and call for laboratory tests. While this is going on, the patient's condition changes and continues to change. For example, if a lab test requires two hours for results, the examinee sets a clock forward two hours to discover not only the results of the lab test but the patient's condition following that period of waiting. As treatment is prescribed, further patient changes occur. Another example is a relatively new version of the licensing examination for certified public accountants. After seeing portrayal of a client's needs, the examinee must work through several simulated steps, including literature searches, completing spread sheets, doing appropriate calculations, and making recommendations to the virtual client. Throughout the Drasgow and Mattern chapter, and throughout the book in which it appears (Bartram & Hambleton, 2006), fascinating ideas are presented for kinds of assessment not currently done and perhaps not possible with a paper-and-pencil medium or with simple testing equipment.

Virtual Reality

"Virtual reality . . . is a computer technology that enables users to view or 'immerse' themselves in an alternate world . . . users experience a computer-generated environment as if it is real and they are a part of it. Thus, users can walk on the surface of Mars, fly an aircraft, or stroll through the Sistine Chapel without really being there" (Aguinis, Henle, & Beaty, 2001, p. 70). Rarely does the literal reality of a job require one to walk on Mars, or even the moon, and a thorough search "found practically no indication that virtual reality is used for personnel selection purposes" (Aguinis et al., 2001, p. 77). At this point, it only offers challenges—and hopes.

One potential use of virtual reality (VR) is in presenting realistic job previews (RJPs), long known to be valuable, especially for employee retention. RJPs are traditionally offered in pamphlets, interviews, or discussions with incumbents; they might better be offered in real-time videos of people who actually do the job.

Performance Assessment

In concept if not always in fact, criteria are measures of individual contributions to the achievement of organizational goals. With computers, the same technology can simultaneously monitor the performance of automated processes and the performance of human operators. The difference in contributions of persons and technology are blurry, as it was before computers. The contributions of the old-time carpenter and his saw are similarly blurred. When the saw is sharp and otherwise appropriate, the worker looks good. When the saw is dull and not appropriate to the task, the worker looks bad. But the carpenter is responsible for choosing the right saw and keeping it sharp, so the saw and its condition are clearly relevant to the carpenter's performance. Technology may influence performance either by enhancing it or interfering, even if it is handsaw technology. I agree "that it is not appropriate to restrict the definition of performance to behavior that is completely under the control of the individual" (Hesketh & Neal, 1999, p. 25), but the reason for measuring performance must be considered. If the purpose is to provide the criterion for validation, the emphasis should, as much as possible, be on predicting the contribution the individual person might make to performance of the system. If a seemingly confounding variable is an integral part of circumstances at work, the predictive hypotheses should not be limited to traits as predictors; they should include attributes of the technology and people–technology interactions. If the purpose is to evaluate the system (e.g., if the subsequent decision is whether to transport the technology to other organizational units), then only a multilevel evaluation of people main effects, technology main effects, and interaction effects will help.

Performance on many jobs can be monitored by modern technology. Computerized monitoring of individual performance can "record, store, retrieve, and present information about attendance, speed, errors, and completion rates" (Hesketh & Neal, 1999, p. 41). It might increase objectivity in performance assessment, but at a risk of increasing negative attitudes among those whose performance is so impersonally monitored. Organizational leaders must be watchful to avoid unintended results of such monitoring. It might lead to changes in the way people approach their tasks if they are rewarded for the wrong things (e.g., customer service telephone workers who cut short troublesome calls to have time for more calls showing up in their counts of customers served).

The notion of adaptive performance (review in Chapter 3) seems to have increased salience in the context of technological influence on work. As technology changes, forcing new learning and coping, "one is no longer assessing absolute performance; rather, the focus is on responsiveness to changing job demands. In a sense, one is assessing the extent to which an employee is able to keep relatively close to a moving trajectory or target" (Hesketh & Neal, 1999, p. 47). That responsiveness may determine a person's ability to take advantage of technology to improve his or her own personal effectiveness, and measures of that ability can be developed.

Computer-Based Research

New technology challenges researchers to seek new understanding of human psychology—and of staffing processes from recruiting to decisions and beyond. A simple hypothesis is inadequate if it fails to consider the many factors influencing criteria and the effects of such influences. Reliance on such simplicity should be thrown away, like an apple too long on the ground. Personnel research must study, understand, and evaluate the interlocking and interdependent influences on success or failure of staffing decisions (whether about people or processes). In short, the challenge is to develop and support—or refute and abandon—nomothetic scientific generalizations; that is, to develop and test coherent theory. Meeting that challenge is as important to personnel decisions as the decisions themselves are important to the organization.

Monte Carlo studies are common ways to answer good questions, the kind that begin with "What if . . . ?" They can help considerably in understanding possibilities, but they do not by themselves support scientific generalization. They are great for trying out ideas, but researchers should not come to believe that simulations alone give the same results they would find in a real-world setting. Gathering real-world, real-time data and analyzing them can be even more complex than the simulation program, with results not so cleanly interpretable. If the simulation findings and their implications are supported empirically, perhaps even replicating findings, the results can contribute to a valid generalization—although a safe bet is that new questions will emerge. That is how scientific foundations grow.

The Internet

The internet is always on. The internet, unlike an office, is accessible all the time, any hour of the day, any day of the week, from any place in the world. Among its other challenges is the challenge to restrain oneself from excessive and unwarranted enthusiasm about what can be done on the web without waiting to evaluate how well it is done or what unintended consequences go along with doing it.

Recruiting

Recruiting is a lot of things, all intended to find and attract people the organization needs—and ultimately to hire and keep selected ones. In many organizations, employees are considered dispensable; retention is not an objective (Saks, 2005). This view is short-sighted. It used to be said that organizations and the people they hire enter into a mutual agreement—a psychological contract—that extends beyond the next paycheck or the next quarterly report. If there is such a contract, even implicitly, it is a two-way street. The organization looks for the people it needs, and recruits look for the kinds and levels of opportunities they seek. Recruiting is part of the selection process. "Can one recruit 'innovative staff' if the subsequent selection process assesses only ability to follow directions?" asked Higgs et al. (2000, p. 79).

The question is equally appropriate if management rewards only obedient behavior. Recruiting is part of a much bigger system, and applicants are more likely to be serious candidates if they see the opportunities they seek in the organization. Applicant reactions to recruiting and selection practices are being studied now much more than in the past; Chan and Schmitt (2004) offered directions for research on the nature of those reactions.

Computers and the internet now play major roles in recruiting. People seeking jobs can look for worldwide opportunities on websites whenever they have time; they do not need to ask a boss for time off to look for another job. Some sites offer RJPs providing candidates "with a realistic portrait of the job and the company . . . satisfaction and retention of those hired are improved" (Schneider, Kristof-Brown, Goldstein, & Smith, 1997, p. 404). Practices that oversell the job and company do not share these benefits. RJPs, being realistic, help recruits evaluate person–job or person–organization fit. The role of P–O fit in recruiting, as in other areas, is complicated. It seems to promote satisfaction, but if it has a dominant role in recruiting, it can lead to organizational homogeneity with a resulting lack of "diversity of perspectives required for effectiveness" (Schneider et al., 1997, p. 404).

Much remains to be learned about internet recruiting. It's nice to know (and we do) that an up-to-date website, one that is easy to use and looks good, is helpful, but there are more important things to know. What are the really critical features of a website in recruiting *qualified* candidates? What differences in the make-up of the resulting applicant pool, and in applicant choices, do organizational websites offer? What results do they get (e.g., in turnover or job satisfaction or performance) relative to other recruiting activity? How do different applicant subgroups react to websites; are reactions uniform or widely varied? "We simply do not know much about these questions" (Ployhart, 2006b, p. 875).

Computerization can take over initial screening. Software programs can sort résumés according to information categories such as educational level, types (or years) of work experience, average duration of previous jobs. Determining desirable résumé content should, of course, precede software choice; too often, the choices made by the software are based on standards that are not particularly useful for the recruiting organization. Much computer use would be better spent in validating the kinds of information the software pulls out of the résumés.

Interviewing

Interviews are typically conversations between two people seeking information from each other—hardly an idea invoking computers. As the wide use of chat rooms, technical support routines, and other interactive tools testifies, people do exchange ideas on the internet very much as they would in person. A structured interview can often seem too stilted to seem conversational, even if conducted face to face, so it is not likely to suffer much when done by computer—and structured interviews are better at eliciting useful information than unstructured conversations. I suspect, but do not know, that computerized interviews, even interactive ones, could reduce the likelihood of some irrelevant cues based on appearance or so-called body language.

In a field experiment, Chapman and Rowe (2002) studied variables related to the level of interview structure. Some applicants were interviewed by video conferencing, others in face-to-face settings. Those in face-to-face settings were more satisfied with the interview experience, and were more attracted to organizations, when interviews were less structured. Those in the video conference group preferred organizations using more structured interviewing, and they found more structured interviews more satisfying. Video conferencing may be hard to schedule and perhaps unavailable at times convenient for the candidate. Even so, it can cast a larger recruiting net, at much lower cost in candidate time and organizational expense, than flying candidates halfway around the world for face-to-face interviews, although the urge for personal contact will probably give traditional interviews a continuing place (Bartram, 2006b).

Online Testing

It is one thing to administer tests by computer where the network is pretty well limited to the software administering the test in the computer used by the examinee. It is quite a different matter if the examinee's computer is connected to the worldwide web. Candidates generally seem to react positively to online testing (Breithaupt, Mills, & Melican, 2006; Konradt, Hertel, & Joder, 2003; Sitzmann et al., 2006), but any highly publicized incident in which a testing program results in newsworthy mistakes can cancel the positive reaction, and problems pile up. Breithaupt et al. (2006, p. 242) said:

> Internet testing is not a mature technology . . . Server availability, delays caused by Internet traffic, and other variations in 'standard' installations sometimes led to slow screen refresh rates, and even termination of the field test for events for a given student. However, the technologists working in this area have made good progress. Secure Internet testing is becoming a reality and we continue to rely on this important resource to maintain our testing program into the future.

Despite the problems, web-based testing is happening, and "all of the personality inventories that are widely used in occupational assessment have become available in web-based versions" (Bartram & Brown, 2004, p. 278).

Web-based tests are typically given without proctors. Bartram and Brown therefore set out to discover whether supervision matters by comparing unsupervised scores on a 32-scale form of the Occupational Personality Questionnaire (OPQ), designed to inhibit faking and other sorts of response distortion, with scores in otherwise matched groups on a paper version of the test. The two versions differed in response format but were otherwise pretty much the same. Results (small values of d and other conventional statistics) led the authors to conclude that the two forms were, psychometrically, much the same if not equivalent and that the lack of supervision had no practical effect.

I have some doubts. If the design of the OPQ successfully inhibits faking, the results may not be typical. Beyond that, it seems to me that the challenge of unproctored online testing is not whether it affects means or other distributional characteristics, but whether unscrupulous or desperate candidates can cheat the system. Having a unique log-on for an individual does not satisfy the challenge; the designated examinee can log on, be approved, and slide out of the chair so that another more able or cleverer collaborator can complete the test or inventory. My doubts include questions of validity beyond the hardware and software problems. Panelists in the Tippins et al.'s (2006) discussion referred to unproctored tests as alternative forms for validated, proctored tests. They are alternatives, but unless they have been independently validated, users dare not confuse alternative with equivalent or parallel forms. Most of the panelists reserved serious consideration of unproctored, web-based testing to biodata, situational judgment tests (which I would not include), and some screening tests; the problems posed by the web environment are so important that the panel did not recommend such testing for high-stakes purposes—like getting a good enough score to be hired for a desired job. I strongly recommend detailed study of the Tippins panel before engaging in any important, web-based, unsupervised testing.

Talent Management

Talent management is another immature and challenging topic. Computerization is likely to be essential to the full scope of its development, but it won't be enough without a change in the traditional mindsets of those specializing in its various pieces: recruiting, justice, selection, placement, training and development, performance evaluation, reward systems, and other tools for finding and retaining talent. These are not independent activities; they need to fit into an integrated system. A challenging discussion of talent management is in a brief article by Frank and Taylor (2004), who described trends that have shaped present practices and will have further influence in the future.

First among these is the increasing use of technology in recruiting, worth repeating in this broader context. A second topic is training and development. Workplace learning, according to Frank and Taylor, has been boosted by the notion of the "learning organization" (Senge, 1990). The emphasis is shifting from developing individuals to developing collaborative work groups. Such groups need not be physically proximate; their development can be accomplished by interactive software and various forms of instant communication.

Fair treatment is a critical aspect of managing talent. In this century's first decade, more attention has been given to applicant reactions to recruiting, interviewing, and assessment tools than ever before. Fairness is increasingly necessary both for motivating people and for keeping them. Employment litigation has increased worldwide, encouraging fair employment practices. Affirmative action policies have been adopted in many countries, and Frank and Taylor (2004) reported that Japan has mandated quotas for hiring the disabled. Fair treatment, however, is not just a legal issue or even a social one; it is a matter of procedural justice, and the trend is, or needs to be, toward greater assurance that talent is treated justly from recruitment to retirement.

Frank and Taylor asserted that another trend is *retention* of talent, that the coming years will see employee retention as the dominant issue in talent management. Retention is more than avoidance of turnover. Harris and Brannick (1999, pp. 13–15) referred to "core cultures" (customer service, innovation, operational excellence, and "spirit"), and to the need to "align" selection and retention practices to one or more of these cores. Those seeking to retain staff need to remember that "what gets rewarded gets done" (Harris & Brannick, 1999, p. 157), and the rewards are not only, or even necessarily, financial. A retention plan recognizes the importance of participation, autonomy, and personal decision-making opportunities inherent in a job and the way it is managed.

Maintaining a full talent management *system* requires modern technology. A system so encompassing and complex cannot be handled well by old-fashioned log books and records. Talent management, well conceived, is a perpetually changing system and needs systematic organization, monitoring, and evaluation. Many decisions and much assessment of people, processes, and things must be among the components of such a system. Modern technology provides both the challenge and the means to manage talent well.

The skeptic in me is disturbed by the possibility that talent management might become just a new term for early identification of management potential. This poses several problems; I'll mention just two. First of all, *talent* means much more than managerial leadership. Skilled people are important in all functions and all levels in all kinds of organizations; some are more skilled than others and are considered talented. Some of their skills are occupation-specific (e.g., engineering or craft skills; bookkeeping knowledge and skill) and some very general (e.g., skill in juggling different tasks that need to be done, skill in troubleshooting whether the trouble is with a piece of equipment or planning a wedding, or skill in scheduling time). Extend these observations to those who work with customers, or design systems, or mop floors, and you will find many kinds of talents—all of which need nurturing, development, and recognition. It is narcissistic arrogance for managers and executives to think that managerial talent is the only talent that needs managing, planning, and development.

Second, there is no reason to limit talent management to "early" identification. Talent, wherever and whenever it is found, should be nurtured—managed if nurturance seems too wimpy. A practical problem with "early" identification is its inevitable association with "young" and the invitation to age discrimination suits.[1] Moreover, it ignores individual differences in personal growth rates; more on this below.

The Challenge to Users of Technology

Technological changes, especially those driven by computer-based testing (CBT), challenge researchers and practitioners alike to go beyond the limitations of traditional testing. The challenge can be reversed. Test developers and users tend to view computers as faster, more cost-effective, and better for measuring complex constructs. "However, the reality is that implementing CBT tends to dramatically increase costs and raise many new operational challenges and concerns" (Luecht, 2006, p. 91). I'll name a few challenges to users; more can be found in the references cited.

Concentrate on Constructs

Developers of computerized tests, no less than other test developers, need to define with some precision the construct to be measured—their "theory of the attribute." Figure 10.1 suggests a large-scale test development program consisting of five systems each with at least three subsystems—all requiring several pages of detailed amplification (Luecht, 2006). The program is detailed, but it fails to say what is to be measured or predicted. From his chapter content, I'm sure Luecht would agree (and assume that all readers would know) that measurement purpose must be clear before developing a program—but I'm less sure that it is routinely done.

Howard Wainer, with wry humor, pointed out that test users and others in psychometrics often use computers because *they are there*, just as a kid with a hammer thinks "everything looks like it could use a good whack. Clearly a reaction to the possibility of whacking precedes a deep analysis of what requires such a response. Humans never seem to outgrow this propensity" (Wainer, 2002, p. 287). And Bartram said that Googling *psychological tests* yields "hundreds of so-called 'tests,' most of which provide no indication of who produced them, *what they measure* or what their psychometric properties are" (Bartram, 2006a, p. 137; emphasis added).

Standardize Testing Mechanisms

CAT may be unstandardized in the traditional sense (e.g., the same items for everyone), but the computer–examinee interface needs standardization, even in adaptive testing

---

[1] Thanks to Frank Landy for pointing this out to me; he has been involved in several such cases.

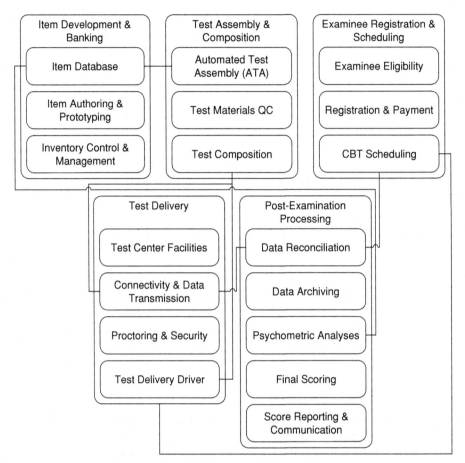

FIG. 10.1   Conceptual architecture of a computer-based testing program. Reprinted from Luecht, R. M. (2006). Operational issues in computer-based testing. In Bartram, D., and Hambleton, R. K. (Eds.), *Computer-based testing and the internet: Issues and advances*. Chichester, UK: Wiley. © 2006 by John Wiley & Sons; reprinted with permission.

(Booth, 1998). Standardization is necessary to make sure that some examinees do not enjoy a privilege that others do not. In part, these are hardware issues, often discussed though less often solved. Traditional discussion of psychometric assessment rarely examined the physical properties of the paper, ink, and pencils and their use by examinees (although I recall asking whether visual acuity contributed to the variance of a test printed in a step-down booklet with decreasing font sizes on brownish paper with brown ink (Guion, 1965a, p. 245). With CBT, however, characteristics of the medium and their influence on response reliability and construct validity are often discussed. A frequent worry is the speed of obsolescence; by the time the test is constructed and validated, computer processing speeds, monitor clarity, and response modes have changed, perhaps enough that either the original hardware for presenting the test or the software for responses is no longer supported. Moreover, scores depend on a combination of computer characteristics, including response methods (e.g., keyboard, mouse, touch screen, or voice activation). To put the complexity in perspective, consider that one mouse is *not* the equivalent of another one, or that the control panel settings for the mouse considered optimal by one user differ from those preferred by someone else. (Would Gertrude Stein say that a mouse is a mouse is a mouse?) Moreover, Irvine (2002) said that choice of response options can influence *what* a CBT measures, wreaking havoc with intended interpretations of scores. User interface requires a lot of research; Booth (1998) suggested several dependent variables for it, including the time to learn about the testing system, the speed of user input, number of input errors, retention of system knowledge, and user satisfaction.

Standardize Internet Characteristics

If ordinary CBT on a local personal computer poses serious issues, the internet exacerbates them. Bartram (2006b) listed four major topics for concern. The first is the inconsistency of internet performance. Internet and the local computer may operate at different speeds; for testing, the technology needs to control the timing of delivery of tests and items, and it should be dependable, not quitting somewhere in the middle of the test. That kind of consistency is not yet certain. Second is a set of security issues. One issue is the traditional concern for test security—keeping tests and items away from unauthorized eyes and use, tight control over rules for scoring, and being sure the responder is the person who is supposed to be taking the test. Another is security for the examinee—identity protection and security of results, keeping scores away from prying eyes. Third is the matter of privacy, particularly in data storage. Fourth is concern about the "digital divide" between those with prior access to computer technology and those without. Bartram's chapter describes several approaches to these four problems; many of them seem promising, but, in my opinion, none of them yet offers general solutions.

Influence of Software Change

Software, in particular, changes in ways that influence responses and, perhaps, in ways that change the constructs being measured. As Version 1.1 of a software program evolves into Version 3.5, it may be that the test must also evolve into a measure of something substantially different. In such cases, Bartram seemed to call for immediate test updating, but this strikes me as creating an unevaluated loss of psychometric validity. I have not seen a convincing case for asserting that validity is unaffected by frequent updates in hardware or software, or by slower changes in adapting to them, or other frequent changes.

Validity Issues

I am somewhat taken aback by the absence of the word *validity* in the index of the Bartram and Hambleton book or, indeed, in much of the CBT literature. Luecht (2006) does include the concepts of validity under the broader heading of *psychometric analysis*, and the Guidelines adopted by the International Test Commission (2005) do require that test developers and publishers consider psychometric qualities (including reliability and validity) and adhere to current standards. The psychometric requirements seem more cursory, however, than the requirements for technological competence. In the new CBT as well as old methods, predictive hypotheses and the component constructs must be identified. A major challenge to CBT is to attend more faithfully and comprehensively to questions of validity, both relational and psychometric.

Investment Issues

An organization's investment in CBT is substantial and varied. The most obvious investment is in equipment and programs, but other investments in time and personnel are also substantial. Organizational leaders buying impressive hardware must also be willing to invest in a long-range commitment to the program it makes possible.

CHALLENGE TO TESTING: ITEM GENERATION THEORY

Galton, whose work bridged the nineteenth and twentieth centuries, may be considered the first of the mental testers. His work was heavily influenced by nineteenth-century emphasis on the so-called law of the normal distribution with its distinctly statistical flavor. Boring (1961) complained accurately that the idea "that the normal law applies to biological and psychological variables . . . has continued well into the present century. The scaling of mental tests in terms of standard deviations . . . in some ways preserves this ancient fallacy" (p. 123). Mental testing pioneers after Galton built a mainly statistical tradition (see Boring, 1961; Guilford, 1936). They sometimes reached into existing theories, but by mid-century mental testing (more particularly, personnel testing) was largely atheoretical, although traditional test development typically starts with at least a vague idea of something to be measured, a rudimentary "theory of the attribute." Test items are created to fit that attribute to a degree, but even that level of theorizing evaporates when one is evaluating test scores (reliability and criterion-related validity) by purely statistical means. It is strange that people so interested in cognitive ability testing, so important in personnel selection, have paid so little attention to research in cognition. A relatively new and fascinating challenge to traditional test construction is *item generation theory*, usually (so far) based on cognition and cognitive theories. Despite some historical precedents and avant-garde articles, it did not develop a circle of proponents until the 1990s (and then mostly in educational measurement), and it remains a rather esoteric promise of things to come. Its main promise, and challenge, is not just to develop tests but to develop many parallel forms of them by using algorithms to create items with known psychometric properties without traditional item analysis. Reliability in traditional test theory emphasized the *idea* of parallel or equivalent test forms; item generation emphasizes making it happen.

The most exciting promise of item generation theory is that it will someday make possible on-the-spot creation of a new, parallel form of a test—with a new and different set of items—for each new examinee. Some approximations of the promise have been reported (e.g., in Irvine & Kyllonen, 2002), but the promise has not yet been realized. As with other innovative ideas, different authors have different ideas about implementing this one. However, they agree fervently on one point: an insistence that item generation requires a solid definition of the construct, in detail—much more than a vague, perfunctory theory of the attribute.

The item-generation challenge to tradition begins with that first step. It requires a well-defined construct, based on a thoroughly developed theory. (For a test used for credentialing, the "construct" may be a well-defined body of knowledge or skill.) The theory might stem originally from basic laboratory research but, because such research is often more interested in comparing theories than in comparing people, the theory usually requires expansion to become a fully specified theory of a differentiating attribute or construct continuum. When fully defined, operations or tasks (i.e., items) can be chosen to fit the definition. Sets of items and their characteristics are identified, varying substantially in difficulty and in other psychometric properties as well. "To be useful for item generation, a primary dependent measure for performance must be item difficulty . . . and, of course, it must be empirically supported" (Embretson, 2005, p. 253).

Some item characteristics influence item difficulty, but others do not. The influential ones are called "controlling factors" (Dennis, Handley, Bradon, Evans, & Newstead, 2002) or "radicals" (Irvine, 2002); item characteristics that do not influence difficulty are "non-controlling factors" or "incidentals." (I will use the terms "controlling" and "non-controlling.") When these influential characteristics are identified (often in the theory itself but sometimes requiring new research), they can be used to generate models of items that will indeed vary in difficulty along the continuum specified by the defined construct. For any given model, i.e., at a specified level of difficulty, a variety of items can be generated with identical controlling properties but appearing to be different because of differences in non-controlling characteristics. The result is, necessarily, a set of parallel items (which Bejar, 1993, called "clones" or "isomorphs"). This makes possible the generation of a large set of parallel forms for measuring the defined construct.

Item generation theory is still "in its infancy" (Kyllonen, 2002, p. 273). Its long-term objective—to generate a new form of a test every time the test is to be used, with all forms being valid and interchangeable measures of the construct—will be met when test developers have "a set of generating principles, with known relationships to item performance" (Embretson, 1998, p. 395).

The Promise of Item Generation

Item generation—with its insistence on detailed construct definition—promises to improve, or at least make easier, the interpretation of test scores. Anastasi (1986) said that validity, or its impairment, depends in part on properties built into a test during its development. If the construct to be measured is clearly defined, and if items that make up the test are explicitly designed to fit that construct, then the search for inferences of good construct validity have a leg up at the outset. Item generation encourages thinking of psychometric validity as a structure bringing together item development, response model fitting, and more traditional aspects of validation. In this perspective, items stem from a focus on the psychology of the intended test domain, and simultaneously specifying psychometric parameters as the items are generated. "Then every time a test is administered the psychology of the domain is tested, by contrasting the theoretical psychometric description with the performance of examinees, thus perennially assessing the validity of the scores" (Bejar, 1993, p. 329). Embretson (1998) went further to suggest that, although cognitive theory had so far contributed little to inferences of validity, the cognitive design system approach would "manipulate construct validity by the cognitive complexity of items" (p. 381).

A problem in traditional test development is the growing difficulty in finding suitable samples for pretesting test items. To the extent that item generation procedures work, pretesting will become less important and, it is hoped, will someday be supplanted altogether by more fundamental research efforts.

A perennial psychometric problem is the choice between multiple-choice and free-response items. Psychometrics has thrived on multiple-choice items, and the use of these items has generally been successful. Sometimes, however, free-response items make better sense. Finding controlling item features is not appreciably different for the two kinds, and IRT models for scaled responses or multivariate models make parameter estimation possible for open-ended items.

In several situations, a candidate may be assessed more than once for the same attributes. Many civil service jurisdictions and some private organizations, by statute or policy, allow retaking a test to improve one's score. Assessment for promotion may use the same tests previously used for the lower level job. If only one form of the test exists, or even two forms, the risk of retesting is that specific items may be remembered, and memory, learning, or practice effects can lead to overestimation of the measured trait. Multiple parallel forms can eliminate that problem, especially if records are kept that identify items the candidate has seen before; they should be avoided in retesting. Again, computer software can meet this challenge.

In some extreme situations—such as working in extreme weather conditions, for very long or unusual hours, or working in such unearthly environments as high altitudes or space or ocean depths—a person's performance may be repeatedly assessed throughout a work period because the effect of the situational stress needs to be monitored frequently. If the same performance tests are presented for all assessments in the series, without variation, score-enhancing practice effects can cancel negative effects of the stress, leaving it undetected. Multiple parallel forms, and lots of them, ease this problem; Goeters and Lorenz (2002) offer several examples of performance tests developed by item generation that have worked in such circumstances.

Coaching is another occasionally serious problem. Commercial test coaching services for various tests have grown substantially in Europe as well as in the United States. In German aviation, the growth of available coaching for its tests "created an urgent demand for tests that could be changed in short periods of time" (Goeters & Lorenz, 2002, p. 341). Item generation responded to that demand.

The growth of web-based assessment offers another example of the value of multiple parallel forms. If only a single form is available, or even a limited, small number of alternatives, memorization of items by examinees or by coaches can enhance scores as artificially as steroids enhance athletic performance. Multiple parallel forms may eliminate this problem too.

Even if item generation is in its infancy, it will grow up to be invaluable in such circumstances if its promise of genuine multiple parallel forms can be realized. Helping it along will help eliminate some assessment error.

Approaches to Item Generation

Item Generation Using Classical Test Theory

Most research on automated item generation has been based on IRT, but Gibson and Weiner (1998) reported a procedure, based on classical test theory, for developing equivalent forms of a content-oriented test for a national licensing program. As with licensing generally, the test was not intended to assess performance on a single construct (as typical item generation research has done) but on the diverse content of a profession. Items from a 639-item pool were grouped into relatively homogeneous sets called *item sampling groups*. Random sampling of items from each group provided test forms of 100 items, from which item difficulty and discrimination indices were determined and used to develop estimates of means, standard deviations, and reliabilities of tests drawn from calibrated pool items. After item calibration, 10,000 preliminary tests were generated, analyzed statistically, and screened for compliance with predetermined targets. Most were discarded, mainly for failure to come close enough to the target mean, many for standard deviations outside the target limits, but none because of failure to be within reliability limits. Even with tight targets, 2271 test forms survived to be considered equivalent forms.

Direct Prediction of Difficulty

Carroll, Meade, and Johnson (1991) developed a precursor of item generation research with classical item analysis and an IRT adaptation, a PCF, or Person Characteristic Function. They identified item characteristics in each of several diverse tests; I limit this report of it to tests of musical pitch, block counting, and spatial rotation. Item characteristics for musical pitch were, (a) the logarithm of an item's musical pitch, in Hertz, and (b) a measure of response bias. For block counting, they were (a) the proportion of blocks in a stack not seen in the drawing, and (b) a rating of symmetry. For spatial rotations of long strings blocks, more item characteristics were used: (a) whether the dichotomous answer to the item was same or different, (b) the number of 30° rotations, (c) whether the ends of the strings were or were not parallel, (d) product of characteristics a and c, and (e) product of characteristics b and c. These characteristics were used to predict empirical values of p, classical item difficulty. Multiple correlations for these three tests were .9951, .828, and .896, respectively; correlations were similar for three other kinds of tests studied, with the lowest being .715. In short, item difficulties can be predicted from item characteristics.

About a decade later, Irvine (2002) summarized a variety of other studies that had used more theoretically oriented approaches (such as cognitive decomposition of the tasks) to identifying controlling characteristics of items, with generally higher multiple correlation coefficients than many reported by Carroll et al. (1991). Predicting IRT b parameters seems more fruitful yet, although assurance of that will wait for studies actually comparing the two forms of the dependent variable in these predictions. In any case, it is clear that determining which item characteristics are controlling and which are not is an empirical question; answers are not yet readily available.

Dennis et al. (2002) reported research to predict difficulty parameters. In a study of tests for Britain's Royal Navy, based on a sample not as large as military samples often are, they reported a correlation between predicted and observed difficulty levels of .72. Dennis et al. called this a first approach; they also used a second approach because they would not recommend the first one without extensive research to evaluate the parallelism of forms intended to be parallel. Their second approach was a more cognitive one—which may end up taking more research effort than the first approach.

Cognitive modeling

Calling item generation theory "one of the most recent advances in large-scale assessment" with numerous benefits, Gorin and Embretson cautioned that test developers using the method must have firm knowledge of the processes guiding item responses: "This requires two types of knowledge: (a) knowledge of the relevant processes guiding the item solution and (b) knowledge of the manipulable task features corresponding to cognitive processing" (Gorin & Embretson, 2006, p. 394). Embretson has, for some time, been using a cognitive design system to generate test items (Embretson, 1985, 1998) and, recently, artificial intelligence, to make it possible to design adaptive tests while the examinee is taking them (Embretson, 2005) and to use item generation in the relatively intractable task of cognitively modeling reading comprehension paragraphs (Gorin & Embretson, 2006). Clearly, as item generation theory develops, it will take psychometrics a long way from the classical p and r_{bis} values still used by most test developers.

The cognitive design system requires a cognitive model for successfully processing the kind of items that measure the intended construct. The design system goes beyond specified cognitive theory in that it is based on an information-processing approach to item types. The information processing appropriate to tasks in the measurement of musical pitch is surely quite different from that required in matrix completion or object rotation items, so the task models must be substantially different. With some distortions of her views (some unintended, by superimposing my own views on hers, or stemming from my focus on employment testing), I offer the following abbreviated outline for cognitive design.

1. *Specify in advance the testing goals* (the KSA or competency—the construct—to be assessed and the nature of the subsequent performance to which the assessment is to be related). Specify the design features of the test (whether a fixed set of items or adaptive; the amount of time required from the examinee; the general difficulty level). If this seems unsurprising, it should also be obviously necessary.

2. *Develop the cognitive model.* Do a cognitive component analysis of the item types likely to be used in the test (or intended test—item generation is not just for parallel forms of existing tests but for test development at the outset). Specify the processes that lead to item solutions, the influence of the processes on level or quality of item performance, and features of tasks or items that influence those processes. The model may be developed from existing theory, from intuition, or from empirical research, but whatever its source, empirical verification of the components of the model is ultimately required. (No one ever said this would be easy!) In developing the model, the difference between cognitive experiments and cognitive measurement of individual differences needs to be clear. Cognitive experiments compare competing theories; cognitive measurement needs a theory of individual differences in performance on the kinds of tasks or items to be used. The task domain for measurement is broader than that for experimentation, so the model must allow for a broad range of difficulties.

3. *Specify processing features that apply to every item.* Item specifications must include distributions of complexity or difficulty and of item features.

4. *Revise or develop the test domain specifying both its cognitive and psychometric properties* (i.e., generate items according to the model). Embretson (1998) moved in this direction with her cognitive IRT model combining theta and a cognitive model of item difficulty.

5. *Evaluate how well the construct is measured by the new or revised test*, i.e., "do" construct validation. Most construct validation work involves relatively weak hypotheses, but Embretson's approach called for stronger ones; tests for them are more stringent but also more precisely interpretable. It included data to assure both construct representation and a meaningful nomothetic span (the nomothetic span being the major sort of evidence traditionally sought for construct validity). Note that cognitive design is far from a dreamy, purely verbal description of a psychometric castle-in-the-sky; it requires a rigorous and extensive empirical research base at several stages.

Problems, Caveats, and Implications

In a simple linguistic sense, any approach to item development is item generation; test developers have "generated" (created) items by thinking about them, taking them from other sources, or by hiring professional item writers. As used here, the term refers to something new, an approach to analyzing descriptive components of test items or tasks and relating them by algorithm to psychometric properties. The very word *algorithm* conjures up computers and computer use; most item generation work in this new sense does in fact use computers, but computerization is not essential to the basic idea. With or without computers, the basic idea must be recognized as still unfulfilled, even though it has been "promising" for nearly two decades. The promises, at least for personnel assessment, may be limited, even though fascinating and exciting. I hope the limits, problems, and caveats, along with some of my excitement, will be clear, so I will pass them along hopefully, by enumerating yet another list.

1. The promise of on-demand, equivalent forms, if realized, can simplify many practical testing issues, ranging from retesting candidates to web-based testing. Fears about unproctored internet testing would not disappear, but they would be dissipated a bit if every candidate were given a unique set of items that would, statistically and interpretatively, be equivalent to the set given to any other candidate. The warning is that the promise is limited to large-scale testing programs, such as national licensing examinations, or to industry-wide consortium testing programs, or to very large private or government organizations. It takes a lot of data, whether using CTT or IRT.

2. The entire promise is based on the notion that item difficulty, and perhaps the discriminability parameter as well, can be matched by the corresponding parameters of a generated item. When predicted and empirical difficulty parameters correlate .99, that notion seems trustworthy. The trust is shakier when that correlation is .66. Do we have a clear idea of the probable distribution of such correlations? Do we know the difference between the kinds of test items for which that promise can soon be fulfilled and those for which it is not likely—and therefore the situations where item generation works and those where (so far) it does not? I have not yet run across the answers, but I suggest that answers can be forthcoming as more research, on more kinds of tasks and items, gets done and reported. In the meantime, be aware that existing evidence is insufficient.

3. It follows that there is insufficient evidence of the parallelism of the generated items and the tests they inhabit. They hope to have multiple parallel forms that really are parallel, and the corresponding hope for an individually developed test form for each examinee, equivalent to the individually developed test form for all other examinees, is still just a hope. In commenting on three of the papers in the item-generation symposium (Irvine & Kyllonen, 2002), Morgan (2002, p. 389) said, "A major task for the future is to determine if the item parameters of cloned items are stable enough to support fungibility in test administration."

4. As pointed out earlier, any use of computers for test administration should stimulate worry about the interface of computer and examinee. The long-range hope for item generation is a new, equivalent test form for every examinee. In practice, this long-range hope will not be realized without computers. Item generation research must include research on that interface, explicitly on the interactions of the characteristics of the computer and its software and those of the person being tested.

CHALLENGE TO RESEARCH MODELS: MULTILEVEL RESEARCH

For years, personnel researcher have validated assessments of individual candidates against their performance as individual employees; for years, writers on matters related to personnel selection have said or implied that characteristics of various organizational levels influence, and may be influenced by, actions and relationships at the individual level. "Quality of hires," a frequent phrase in much of the print and internet discussions of recruiting and selection, is an organizational level criterion influenced, according to that common assumption, by individual-level decisions. In what may have been the first formal discussion of multilevel theory in the personnel selection literature, Schneider et al. (2000) said that those of us in IO psychology, especially in selection, "are experiencing a paradigm shift of which they may not be fully aware [from individualistic models] to a newer focus on the organizational implications of personnel selection practices" (p. 91).

Employees usually work in units (groups, departments, physical locations). Tasks are done within broader job or work categories. Performance may be measured at different time intervals. Performance can be measured at individual or work unit levels, at task or job levels, or after short or long time durations. Ployhart (2004) described different levels studied in organizational science, shown as Figure 10.2. Methods of multilevel analysis challenge researchers to test, not merely to assume, the truth of hypotheses cutting across such levels in selection research.

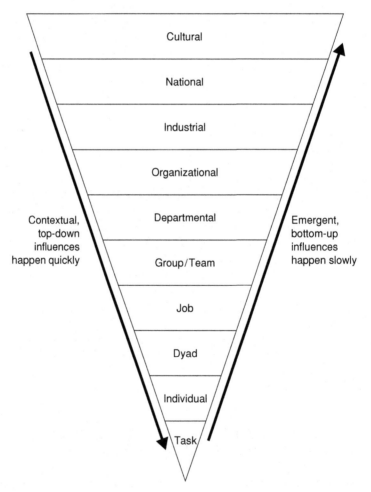

FIG. 10.2 Hierarchical levels studied in organizational science. Reprinted from Ployhart, R. E. (2004). Organizational staffing: A multilevel review, synthesis, and model. *Research in Personnel and Human Resource Management, 23,* 123–179. © Emerald Group Publishing Limited, all rights reserved. Reprinted with permission.

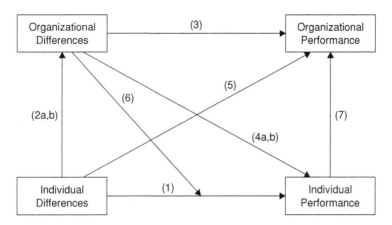

FIG. 10.3   A multilevel model of linkages. Reprinted from Schneider, B., Smith, D. B., and Sipe, W. P. (2000), Personnel selection psychology: Multilevel considerations. In Klein, K. J., and Kozlowski, S. W. J. (Eds.) *Multilevel Theory, Research, and Methods in Organizations.* San Francisco: Jossey-Bass (pp. 91 – 120). © 2000 by Wiley. Reprinted with permission.

"The days of data analysis being limited to a single level are dwindling. Multilevel analysis has dramatically burst upon the scene" (editor's note by David Kenny in Bickel, 2007, p. ix). Multilevel analysis is not as complicated as many people seem to think, nor does it require unusual knowledge or computer software. "It's just regression" as Bickel said in the subtitle of his book. Moreover, it is commonplace in other areas of social science research: education, business, political science, sociology among others. It has some strong advocates in IO psychology, but only a few.

Multilevel Models in Selection

Figure 10.3 (from Schneider et al., 2000) is a chart, somewhat like that of Binning and Barrett (1989, Figure 3.1 in this volume), that summarizes hypotheses and inferences related to seven linkages within two levels of analysis, the individual (Level 1) and the organization-as-a-whole level (Level 2). Linkage 1 is the traditional, individual-level validation practice. Linkage 2 refers to the validation of traits measured at Level 1 against varying criteria (across organizations) measured at Level 2. Of the many paths through which individual traits may affect organization-level criteria, Schneider et al. described two. Linkage 2a refers to the contextual or work environments that distinguish organizations, created or fostered by organizational leaders. Linkage 2b refers to the effect on work environments of aggregate characteristics of people in the organization, related to Schneider's (1987) ASA model. Aggregation assumes similarity of the aggregated individual traits and organizational characteristics.

Linkage 3 suggests that organizational characteristics (organizational traits, if you will), if clearly identified, can be linked to organizational performance. Rarely studied, and not routinely confirmed when it is, it is partly the organizational level counterpart to individual-level validation. Linkage 4 in Figure 10.3 goes downward, suggesting that individual performance, in aggregate or alone, is influenced not only by employee traits and experiences but by characteristics of the organizational context as well. Schneider et al. insisted that "it is absolutely imperative" to give more attention to the relative effect of individual and organizational differences on individual performance; I strongly agree.

Linkage 5 reverses the suggestion of Linkage 4; it suggests that aggregated individual attributes can influence organizational performance. This has been a common assumption through the years: that if you hire good people, they will perform well and the organization will therefore prosper—somehow. "Individual differences in the aggregate that might result from the application of validated personnel selection strategies could be reflected in differences in organizational performance, but the research on this possibility simply does not exist" (Schneider et al., 2000, p. 113). This in itself, to the extent it is still true, is a major but feasible challenge to traditional practice. The later discussion said that "impressive relationships" had been found (Ployhart & Schneider, 2002, p. 110), at least if internal criteria at the organizational level are taken as organizational characteristics.

Linkage 6 considers the possibility that organizational differences may act as moderators of the traditional individual level link of traits to performance. Conceivably, this could revive the now-discarded doctrine of situational specificity—with the important difference that the substantive situational characteristics would be defined more explicitly than the old doctrine ever considered. Linkage 7 considers the possibility that aggregated, individual performance levels influence organizational performance. I suspect that this linkage is not so simple as Figure 10.3 suggests.

A later version of the model, partially shown as Figure 10.4 (Ployhart & Schneider, 2002), is more precise and more detailed. It suggests consideration of three levels. It also

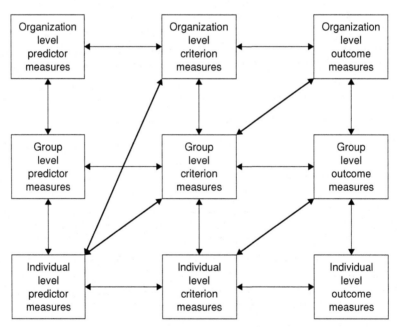

FIG. 10.4   Advanced multilevel selection model. Adapted, omitting mediating linkages and inference codes, from Ployhart, R. E., and Schneider, B. (2002). A multi-level perspective on personnel selection research and practice: Implications for selection system design, assessment, and construct validation. In Yammarino, F. J., and Danserau, F. (Eds.), *Research in Multi-level Issues, Vol. I: The Many Faces of Multi-level Issues.* Amsterdam: JAI Press. © Emerald Group Publishing Ltd, all rights reserved. Adapted by permission.

distinguishes internal organizational level criteria, such as aggregated climate perceptions, from organizational effectiveness as assessed by such external referents as market share or return on investment. Path models across organizational levels could be developed.

The two figures (10.3 and 10.4) were presented early in multilevel theorizing; they are not the final word, and since 2002 more has been said (e.g., Ployhart, 2004, 2006b; Ployhart & Schneider, 2005). Still more remains to be said before specific models or theories can be developed to answer questions currently unanswered. For example, consider the concept of human capital emergence. "Emergence" in this context refers to effects that start at a lower level of individual traits and, through interactions with others, "filter up" to unit or to higher levels to show up (emerge) even if in different form (Klein & Kozlowski, 2000). Such emergence is known to have individual-level consequences, but does it have unit or organizational level consequences as well, or are different types of human capital necessary for different kinds of employee groups? If different kinds are needed, how can they be combined to affect organizational performance or effectiveness (Ployhart, 2006b)? Can a poor individual-level predictor be aggregated to predict well a higher level criterion? Results of one laboratory study suggest that it can (LePine, 2003). Openness to experience has not fared well in meta-analyses of validation studies, at least relative to other Big 5 personality dimensions. Nevertheless, it was hypothesized to correlate well with a team performance measure after an unexpected task change. Using an additive form of aggregation, the multiple regression coefficient was not quite as strong for openness as for the achievement and dependability aspects of conscientiousness, but the aggregate score did not do badly at all for a dimension that has had relatively poor validity at the individual level.

Multilevel Analysis

Ordinary multiple linear regression (MLR) is well known and often used, and in Chapter 8 I used that term in preference to the alternative term, ordinary least squares (OLS). The initials MLR can also be used to refer to multilevel regression. Multiple linear regression (aka OLS) is essentially a single-level analysis, typically but not necessarily the individual level. To keep the distinction between single-level and multilevel regression obvious, I will use OLS in this chapter for single level regression and MLR for multilevel regression; this, I hope, will make comparisons more obvious.

MLR is "just regression under specific circumstances" (Bickel, 2007, p. 8). OLS generally is used to develop a monolevel model for predicting a criterion of organizational value. MLR, in contrast, "entails a procedure entirely foreign to OLS regression: using intercepts and slopes as *outcomes*!" (Bickel, 2007, p. 150; emphasis in original). OLS requires a hypothesis, whether bivariate or multivariate. MLR requires a theory with multiple, perhaps interlocking, hypotheses. Like structural equation modeling, the theory should be fully specified. Citing Rousseau (1985), Ployhart (2004, p. 131) named three kinds of errors, or fallacies: *misspecification*, assigning the wrong level to a construct or failure to match the construct and level of measurement; *cross-level fallacy*, incorrect generalization across different levels; and *contextual fallacy*, neglecting or wrongly interpreting effects of the context created at higher levels on lower ones. Establishing a theory and a plan of analysis for MLR is clearly more thought-demanding than the simple OLS hypotheses. It requires a strong reservoir of substantive knowledge to specify a model correctly.

OLS is ordinarily appropriate for only a single level of analysis; by definition, MLR cuts across the various levels in a hierarchy. OLS variables are assumed to be reasonably independent; MLR variables, by definition, are *nested* within levels. OLS intercepts and slopes (regression coefficients or parameters) are fixed within components of the level chosen; MLR regression coefficients may vary from group to group within a level, reflecting varying mean performance levels. Stated differently, MRL variables may be either fixed or random (random in this case meaning variables with probability distributions rather than fixed-point distributions).

"To ignore the nested nature of selection is to ignore the very basis of organizational science. We might select individuals, but who we select and how we select and how they will actually perform on the job are based on processes that evolve within a multilevel organizational system" (Ployhart & Schneider, 2005, p. 513). To ignore the system is to ignore possibilities for improving prediction. Look again at the idea of trait activation (Tett & Guterman, 2000). The idea is that situations relevant to a trait are likely to stimulate expression of the trait. But what creates the trait-activating situation? We don't know for sure, but it seems plausible to assume it is in the context created at higher organizational levels—a context deserving a place in the predictive hypothesis.

A consequence of nesting is that higher levels provide a context for hypotheses and relationships at lower levels. Not only does this reflect the sixth linkage in the Schneider et al. (2000) model, but it specifies cross-level interactions that can boost the regression slopes of lower level predictors. This was shown by Bickel (2007), who predicted math achievement in high schools from student-level SES scores. A multilevel analysis added just one contextual variable, the percentage of students taking an academic curriculum. OLS and MLR gave slopes and intercepts for the SES measure that were not especially different. The contextual variable in the MLR analysis, however, had a slope nearly four times as large as the SES slope. "Clearly, if the contextual factor had not been included, we would have missed an important predictor of math achievement" (Bickel, 2007, p. 54). Traditional personnel testers might be somewhat miffed if they found a contextual variable that much better than the variable to be validated, but we could tolerate the miff if the finding encouraged them to think more about the accuracy of prediction than about the validity coefficient of the principal assessment.

Another strong reason to use MLR instead of OLS is that OLS typically gives deflated estimates of the standard errors of regression parameters. This can lead to serious misinterpretation of comparisons of groups. Intercepts and slopes in traditional OLS are assumed to be fixed, but they may vary across groups in MLR. The standard error therefore permits identifying a range within which a specified proportion of group slopes will fit. Bickel (2007) gave an example in which family income was regressed on race of the head of the household. At the lower end of the 95% confidence interval the slope indicated a dramatically lower family income in households headed by a black person (compared to those headed by someone other than a black person), but family income was markedly better for black households at the upper end of the interval. Of course, such a difference makes generalizing difficult, but it reminds us once again that the slope in a fixed regression model is an *average* of the slopes that might be found in a random model (Bickel, 2007, pp. 128–129).

Person–Environment Fit: Challenge to Predictors

An old idea is that people who "fit in" to their environments generally do well. The idea was held in popular culture for a long time, and it was sometimes used as a surrogate for prejudice in hiring. However, the idea that person–environment fit (P–E fit) influences behavior has been a prominent construct in social psychology for a few decades. It is presenting a new challenge in recruiting and selecting employees, especially for collaborative groups. The concept has as many component facets as the facets of a person's environment, including subordinate forms such as person–job fit (P–J fit), which is what selection research has been about all along, P–G fit when a group defines the environment, P–U fit when the group is an organizational work unit, P–O fit to indicate the broader organization as the environment, and even P–C fit of the person in the community at large (Sacco & Schmitt, 2005). In their *Annual Review* chapter, Borman, Hanson, and Hedge (1997, p. 300) noted "increasing activity in person–organization (P–O) fit research, in part, we believe, as a reaction to emerging organizational realities" including growing emphasis on teams, globalization, and downsizing.

By its very nature, fit is a multilevel idea. P–O, P–G, P–J fit are not redundant terms; they refer to quite different organizational levels. The worker and the job may fit quite well even if the fit to the group or organization, or the dyadic fit to the supervisor, is not so good (cf. Kristof-Brown, 2000; Kristof-Brown, Zimmerman, & Johnson, 2005).

P-E fit at any level may change because of either change in the people or change in the environment. Do people who fit well at some level show less resistance to change than those who fit poorly? Is the answer dependent on environmental level of fit? The answer is elusive, but resistance to change is a genuine problem in organizations when change is not gradual; resistance to change, burnout, and other dysfunctional effects on organizational variables "seem to be far more prevalent than accounts of people readily embracing change" (Caldwell, Herold, & Fedor, 2004, p. 868). On the basis of their data, Caldwell et al. went on to say that understanding fit is necessary to a full understanding of the consequences of change.

Diverse Consequences of Fit

Good fit is generally considered a good thing for the person and for the organization—but that is not necessarily so. Good fit, at any level, seems positively related to job satisfaction and organizational commitment and negatively to intentions to quit, or positively to intention to stay (Kristof-Brown et al., 2005). The attraction–selection–attrition (ASA) model does, however, suggest negative consequences of good fit. If people are attracted to an organization or job on the basis of probable fit, and are selected because they are expected to fit well, the result may be that those not fitting so well will leave (the attrition part) and the remaining employees will tend to be homogeneous (Schneider, 1987; Schneider et al., 1995). The homogeneity may be pleasant, but Schneider et al. summarized some negative consequences found in the research literature. A highly competitive multitasker may face burnout and heart disease in a competitive, stressful work environment. Too many close fits rob the organization of the diversity of perspective needed for recognizing and understanding the implications of relevant information, or for coping with change in the organization and its environment. Shifting the focus to poor fit instead of good, it could happen that poor fit, although unpleasant, "*might* lead to development, self-awareness, better performance, or attention from others" if the misfit is not so extreme that it makes "the person withdraw or seek other employment" (Ryan & Kristof-Brown, 2003; emphasis in original). It might, but the uncertainty underscores the challenge to find out.

If excessive homogeneity is a bad thing for organizations, is its opposite, heterogeneity or diversity, necessarily a good thing? Increasing diversity—demographic diversity at least—is a fact of American and European societies, so such diversity in work environments is inevitable. The question may now be moot, according to Sacco and Schmitt (2005). In their example, the initial level of racial or ethnic diversity in a restaurant chain was related to declining profitability; that is, racial diversity may have a negative impact on the bottom line. Note that this finding refers to racial *diversity*, not to any particular racial group. "If this finding can be replicated in other settings, it presents a serious quandary for organizations that seek to become more racially diverse" (Sacco & Schmitt, 2005, p. 220). However, for turnover, the effect of misfit in sex, race, and age weakened over time.

Diversity, to Harrison and Klein (2007), means three things, not just one. *Separation* refers to horizontal differences in position (or opinion) among work unit members. *Variety* refers to differences of kind—differences in experience, knowledge, or information, somewhat like having an engineer, a psychologist, and a financial expert forming a collaborative work group. *Disparity* refers to vertical differences in valued resources such as pay or status. Each of these exists on a continuum from a little bit to a lot, but they differ in important ways, as shown in Table 10.2 and including appropriate design differences. I consider this article a major contribution to a vexing topic. Although it, like so many others, "highlights" (according to the abstract) demographic diversity, it is a far more general introduction to a theory of the meaning of the word *diversity*.

Fit as a Selection Tool

Mean corrected correlations in the meta-analyses of fit in four levels, reported by Kristof-Brown et al. (2005), were poor for predictions of job performance; for P–J fit, $\rho = .20$, and for P–O fit, $\rho = .07$, and in both cases the 80% credibility values included zero. With such dismal evidence about the predictive value of fit, I am also "somewhat wary of its migration into personnel selection" as Arthur, Bell, Villado, and Doverspike (2006, p. 787) put it; they also concluded from their meta-analysis that P–O fit is not a good predictor of performance, although they held out hope that it might prove to predict turnover.

Clarification of Fit

Just as Harrison and Klein (2007) clarified the construct of diversity, Harrison (2007) clarified the meaning of fit. A meaningful concept of fit cannot be derived from an ordinary conversational use of the word; it must "have recognizable borders and a coherent definition that distinguishes it from other conceptions" and if those borders are too broad and porous, "fit would come close to spanning most of the known universe of organizational research" (Harrison, 2007, p. 390). He defined fit as "a state of the compatibility of *joint* values of one or more attribute, $a, b, c, \ldots j$, of a focal entity (P), and a *commensurate* set of attribute values, $a, b, c, \ldots j$, of the entity's environment (E). In algebraic terms, fit is about $[(P_a, P_b, P_c, \ldots P) \cap (E_a, E_b, E_c, \ldots E_j)]$" (Harrison, 2007, p. 391). To think of fit under this definition, the attributes must have the same content for both P and E, and this may not always be the case in fit research.

Harrison identified six interrelated steps that are needed in planning fit research: (a) decide on the number of attributes to be included, (b) decide on their content—the same on both sides of the equation, (c) decide where the data will come from—preferably from separate observers or occupants of the realms, (d) define what would constitute perfect fit (in the simplest sense, perfect is the maximum when the values for P and E are equal—but life is rarely simple, and this step requires the next one), (e) define the metric by which the as, bs, cs, and js can be measured, and (f) choose the dependent constructs.

This is an appalling abridgment and simplification of Harrison's article, so I strongly recommend consulting it before doing research on P–E fit.

TABLE 10.2
Meanings and Properties of Within-Unit Diversity Types

Diversity Type	Meaning and Synonyms	Attribute Examples	Predicted Outcomes[a]	Foundational Theories
Separation (attribute S)	Composition of differences in lateral position or opinion among unit members . . .	Opinions, beliefs, values, attitudes, esp. about team goals and processes	Reduced cohesiveness, more interpersonal conflict, distrust, decreased task performance	Similarity-attraction; social categorization; attraction–selection–attrition (ASA)
Variety (attribute V)	Composition of differences in kind . . . relevant knowledge or experience . . . unique or distinctive information	Content expertise, functional background, network ties, industry experience	Creativity, more innovation, higher decision quality; task conflict, unit flexibility	Information processing; law of requisite variety; variation, selection, and retention (VSR)
Disparity (attribute D)	Composition of vertical differences in proportion of socially valued assets/ resources held by unit members . . .	Pay, income, status, decision-making authority, social power	Within-unit competition, resentful deviance, withdrawal	Distributive (in)justice . . . status hierarchy, social stratification

[a] Generally, but not in all conceptualizations or studies. *Note:* column describing shape of distribution at maximum diversity has been omitted. Entries are abbreviated; for more precise descriptions, see original article. Adapted and abridged from "Meanings and Properties of Within-Unit Diversity Types" by D. A. Harrison and K. J. Klein (2007), Table 1, p. 1203, *Academy of Management Review, 32,* 1199–1228. © 2007, Academy of Management. Adapted by permission of Academy of Management.

CHALLENGES OF GLOBALIZATION: WORLDWIDE STAFFING ASSIGNMENTS

Thomas Friedman said, "The World is Flat" (Friedman, 2006, title). The phrase, "flat earth," conjures up an image of Luddites who refuse to see the reality of a world more modern than they would like, but Friedman's metaphor of the flat earth is an apt symbol of the leveling of the world's economic "playing field." Globalism is a fact of life, affecting large corporations and small ones, employees and managers, customers and families. It promises opportunity, but it also threatens habit and security. In brief, globalization offers many kinds of challenge. For multinational corporations, the challenge is to improve staffing when work is to be done in a context that may be poorly understood. The challenge comes in part from cultural difference, but it includes differences in laws, accepted rules and regulations, and general expectations in different countries (Gaur, Delios, & Singh, 2007).

I'll limit this discussion to two challenges. One is assigning people to work in a country away from their home country; differences vary from minor inconveniences to major conflicts in values and habits of thought and behavior. The other is recruiting and hiring people from other cultural backgrounds, perhaps to immigrate, or transferring people from foreign units to positions in organization's home base. Both of these are multilevel challenges in that expatriates work within two cultures, one at home and one away from the home culture (van de Vijver, van Hemert, & Poortinga, 2008).

The Multinational Context

"It is no longer possible for any country, regardless of size, to exist without economic connections with other countries" (Landy & Conte, 2007, p. 30). Connections occur at many levels. A company headquartered in one of the so-called developed countries is increasingly likely to invest heavily in other countries, to send its own people to work in locations in other countries, and to bring in people from those other countries to work in locations in the headquarters country. Individuals and families cross national borders in growing numbers to pursue perceived economic opportunities and individually present themselves as candidates for employment. At all work levels, connections are influenced by a growing variety of free trade agreements and common markets. If no man is an island, no employing organization is either.

According to Caligiuri (2006), multinational companies further differ in geographic dispersion (the degree to which the organization operates across national boundaries) and multiculturalism (the extent to which employees, customers, and others relevant to organizational operations reflect disparate cultural backgrounds). They may also differ in how they balance the contradictory values of centralization (tight control from headquarters) and decentralization (local control). Benefits of strong central control include standardization of processes, products, and performance standards. Benefits of local control include better fit to local needs of employees and customers and to shades of difference in local cultures.

An often-cited theory of cultural differences is that of Hofstede (2001). He identified five dimensions of national culture, as follows.

1. *Individualism vs. collectivism* is probably the most common dimension studied and discussed in theories of cultural differences (see especially Triandis, 1994, 1997). People in cultures considered individualist tend to focus more on themselves (and their families) than on their communities; the pattern is reversed at the collectivist pole. At work this may be reflected in differences between individual- and group-level training.

2. *Power distance*, the equalization of power in national communities of interest, "rank-ing from relative equality (like Denmark) to very unequal (like the Philippines)" (Hofstede, 1997, p. 53). The work place where power distance is low may allow decentralized decision making or a relatively large supervisory span of control.

3. *Uncertainty avoidance* reflects national tendencies to accept uncertainty and to "take one day at a time" (Landy & Conte, 2007, p. 35) as opposed to tendencies to covet stability and certainty at work. One sign of the difference is the degree to which innovation may be hindered by following rules.

4. *Masculinity–femininity* is a dimension name that has been "criticized a lot" (Hofstede, 1997, p. 53), but it is the only dimension for which country scores depend largely on the sex of the respondent. In masculine cultures, men are more likely to describe themselves as competitive; in feminine cultures, it is the women who do so.

5. *Long-term vs. short-term orientation*, the degree to which people within a national culture expect immediate rather than delayed gratification of their needs and desires. Differences at work may be reflected in different concerns with thrift and honor of tradition.

A first step in facing multiculturalism is to recognize that the cultural differences a multi-national company encounters are not simply a matter of *our culture versus everyone else's*—that cultural differences across countries are real and sometimes dramatic. A company working across many borders is likely to find that it faces very large cultural differences. In multinational organizations, many company operations can be carried out with very differ-ent national profiles on Hofstede's five dimensions. Operations in Japan are within a culture strongly emphasizing uncertainty avoidance and long-term orientation but with relatively little emphasis on individualism; that is contrasted with the Netherlands, strongly indi-vidualistic but scoring low on masculinity (Hofstede, 1993). Do international differences in long-term or short-term orientation, or those in power distance, or in any of the others have any implications for assessments of candidates for assignment to (or from) any of the dif-fering countries? I do not know, but I'm fairly sure that assessment and personnel decisions will continue to focus on individuals, even within collectivist cultures. Culture influences behavior, as do many other contextual attributes: "individual skills and motivation, mana-gerial skills, leadership behaviors, HRM practices, and other individual and group variables" (Landy & Conte, 2007, p. 38).

The individualism–collectivism classification was reconsidered by Oyserman, Coon, and Kemmelmeier (2002), who preferred defining the terms as categories. They suggested that, in a collectivist society, status determines obligations and expectations, organizations are highly centralized, and social units share common fates, values, and goals. Individualist societies see responsibility as individually defined and carried out, including the responsib-ility to set one's goals and establish one's values. Although they found wide individual differences within either cultural category, they found little consensus in defining either term. That fact "contributes to an emerging tower of Babel in which cultural psychologists are quick to declare any cross-national difference to be 'cultural' and any cultural difference to be within the purview of IND–COL theory" (Oyserman et al., 2002, p. 44). Despite the undeniable Babel, the construct should not yet be abandoned.

Expatriate Performance

Those assigned away from their home countries, *expatriates*, are usually managers or tech-nical staff. To the extent that profiles of cultural variables differ in the home country and the assigned country, reactions to the change may be substantial. That does not imply that they will also involve "culture shock"; the differences may, for some people, make the assignment more interesting.

Reasons for expatriate assignments vary. They may be intended to fill positions where qualified candidates in the country of assignment are considered unlikely, or as a factor in management or organizational development (Collings, Scullion, & Morley, 2007). Despite cultural differences, performance assessment is similar to performance assessment anywhere (Caligiuri, 2006). Performance constructs must be identified and defined, whether in terms of corporate values or country-specific or position-specific behaviors. The equivalence of the constructs across national locations—the similarities if not precise equivalence in construct meaning—must be established. Defensible and procedurally fair operations for assessing the constructs must be developed. Construct equivalence is probably the most difficult of these three steps. For example, organizational commitment in Japan may mean "years of service," but in Singapore it might mean "expending effort at work." The construct is not equivalent in those two countries, but in both of them, "'hardworking' may be defined as coming in 1 hour before you are expected—and staying 2 hours past the time you are scheduled" (Caligiuri, 2006, p. 233). Whether the construct is commitment to the organization or working hard, the assessment operation is likely to be a rating—and likely to be influenced by the similarities of the national backgrounds of the rated manager and the boss doing the rating; Caligiuri suggested that frame of reference training might be helpful (see Chapter 13).

The most common criteria for evaluating expatriates on assignment are completion of the global assignment, cultural adjustment, and task performance. These are not entirely different from ordinary criteria, often variants on themes of staying on the job, eschewing counterproductive work behaviors, and core task performance (Van Vianen, De Pater, & Caligiuri, 2005). Nevertheless, the entire staffing process for expatriate assignment—recruiting, assessing, selecting, placing (assigning), and retaining—has created problems and challenges not encountered in purely domestic staffing.

Expatriate assignments are generally for a specified project or time period, commonly three to five years. The performance issue most commonly studied seems to be failure to complete the assignment. Ryan and Tippins (2009) estimated that about 20% of expatriate assignments end prematurely. Early departure seems not to be related to the work itself; in fact, the tendency to consider it may be moderated by perceptions of procedural fairness (Garonzik, Brockner, & Siegel, 2000). It seems to be a matter of adjusting to the different cultural context of the work, not only by the expatriate manager but by members of the family, particularly the spouse. Shaffer and Harrison (2001) reintroduced an old dilemma: If the performance of a prospective employee is likely to be influenced by the spouse, should characteristics of the spouse be considered in considering the candidate? They developed a theoretical model of spouse adjustment including some individual characteristics (such as varieties of self-efficacy), family and social networks, the candidate's probable work environment, and the environment of the assigned country. The theory is interesting, but it may not be practical—especially in the United States and countries with similar modal attitudes toward equality of men and women, or toward treating employees or candidates as individuals without tying them to others.

Much research has been done on expatriates wanting to terminate their assignments; it is a familiar turnover issue. Much less has been said or done about employees who explicitly seek opportunities to leave—for a wide variety of reasons—their home-country culture to experience a different one, or about expatriates who do not want to come home. This tendency raises questions that, as far as I know, are not answered. Should companies actively seek those people, or are those people seeking an escape from unpleasant features of the home country environment and, if so, does that imply something negative, such as lack of personal stability?

Performance, especially managerial performance, is always difficult to assess, even in purely domestic settings. It is influenced by variables beyond the control of individual managers or of the organization as a whole; the problem is exacerbated when performance occurs in a country far from the home country. Many factors, such as exchange rate fluctuations, affect external indicators of performance whether at home or abroad, but they often have a stronger impact on work done away from the home country (Collings et al., 2007). Economic ups and downs that follow different cycles at home and away, internal conflicts in the host country, business legislation that is inconsistent with that in the home country—all of these things have an impact on performance, and many of them are not realized at home where the performance assessment is done. More than in a home-country setting, international connections require clear statements of home office expectations of expatriate performance and the expatriate's own expectations. Both need to be explicit. Ikea, in Sweden, tells new managers that they should not accept an offer if they are not enthusiastic about working in three different countries in their first 10 years with the company.[2] International connections also require a clear system of performance appraisal that explicitly acknowledges that the expatriate is expected to adapt to the host country, its mores, and its conventional ways of functioning. Assessment principles may not be standard across assignments to different countries; standardization of expectations based on home country conventions is simply too limited.

Incoming Expatriates

Much research assumes that the expatriate manager leaves a Western cultural heritage to go somewhere else assumed to be culturally different. The process also operates in reverse, with citizens of Asian, African, or South American countries being assigned to work in, or immigrating to, English-speaking North America or Europe. Kim and Slocum (2008) reported a survey of Korean expatriates based in the United States. In general, their results were consistent with prior studies in the other direction, although with some predictors less commonly used. One was a measure of a self-monitoring personality, a tendency to be sensitive to social situations and institutions and to shape one's own behavior accordingly. Others included prior experience in the host country and local language fluency; it is strange that these have not been studied more often.

One finding seemed unique. Although some of their findings extended and supported previous findings on expatriate performance, one of them—the relationship of adjustment to intention to return home prematurely—was not. Several explanations were offered. For one thing, Korea is characterized as a "tight" culture, one with clear norms and commonly shared understanding of both expected and deviant behavior, and one in which organizations select new hires who will obedient to superiors and good organizational citizens. The result of a tight cultural background inhibits consideration of premature return to Korea "as a viable alternative" (Kim & Slocum, 2008, p. 114); that is, early leaving would be seen as being disloyal, less than a good corporate citizen. Other possible reasons include the desire to educate their children in the US, and the likelihood that expatriate spouses would be more likely to support the expatriate manager than would spouses from cultures with a more

[2] Thanks to Frank Landy for this example.

egalitarian family tradition. Korean wives (most of the managers were men) traditionally consider the husband's career to have high priority in their lives. More expatriate research in this direction, and more on immigration, needs to be reported.

Alternatives to Expatriate Assignments

Collings et al. (2007) suggested several alternatives to conventional expatriate assignments that could alleviate many of the problems. Short-term assignments, lasting longer than an ordinary business trip but under a year, might be more restricted in scope; for example, a short-term expatriate might be assigned to do no more than train people in the local workforce, or manage a special short-term project. Many of the control and management development purposes served in long-term expatriate assignments could be realized in short-term assignments at much lower costs, especially costs related to relocating entire families.

Another alternative they called "frequent flyer assignments" (p. 205); these involve business travel as a defining component of a person's work (apparently more often associated with technical or professional work than managerial). This alternative provides face-to-face contact with those in the foreign setting without relocation. (Does that mean not enough exposure to understand the cultural differences?) Commuter assignments are similar but last a bit longer, such as a couple of weeks away from home base. Rotational assignments involve a slightly longer period away followed by something akin to vacation time upon return. An alternative relying on modern technology is the use of virtual teams of geographically scattered members, coordinating their work electronically or by telecommunication; team leaders do not relocate but manage the team from their home base. Not nearly enough empirical information has been acquired or published on the effectiveness of these alternatives or of the long-term assignments they can replace.

A different alternative to expatriate assignment is to staff with nationals of the host country. Gaur et al. (2007) studied nearly 13,000 foreign subsidiaries of Japanese firms operating in 48 countries to investigate staffing and subsidiary performance, specifically comparing use of parent country nationals and host country nationals as general managers and as proportions of the subsidiary workforce. The investigation was concerned with differences (*institutional distances*) between parent and host countries in cultures and in established regulations and norms, that is, "factors such as a country's political systems, its laws and regulations, and its societal attributes" (Gaur et al., 2007, p. 633). They found that the likelihood of sending expatriates as subsidiary general managers increased along with these differences (although the effects of cultural differences were inconsistent). The greater the proportion of parent country nationals (Japanese) in the subsidiary workforce, the more subsidiary labor productivity was reduced by the effect of regulatory and normative distance. Surprisingly, these effects were diminished in older subsidiaries (the ones that had existed for longer). A balance needs to be struck between the legitimacy of a subsidiary in its own country and the control and profitability of the parent country organization.

Expatriate Assessment

Hough and Oswald (2000) identified interpersonal skill and adaptability as important factors in expatriate success, and family situations as the most commonly cited reason for failure. Much of the reported research on assessments for predicting adjustment to different cultural settings has concentrated on personality variables, especially the ever-popular Big Five. To these, Harvey and Novicevic (2002) added Jungian concepts of intuition and creativity (as kinds of intelligence). *Intuition* meant looking for possibilities in situations more than for facts or detailed information. Intuitive solutions to operating problems or opportunities seem to emerge without awareness or articulated intent or origin, but they are probably based on a substantial store of relatable knowledge acquired over long periods of experience and retrieved in working memory. *Creativity* tends to have a somewhat intuitive base, but it is more than that, according to Harvey and Novicevic. They thought of it as including experience-based expertise and basic cognitive ability and, beyond usual ideas of cognition, a preference for being different, in their thinking and in other respects (cf. Guilford, 1959)— and for working in an environment that supports change and diversity of thought. The effective expatriate has a need "to generate intelligent solutions to situations that have not been faced by the organization and expatriate managers in the past" (Harvey & Novicevic, 2002, p. 135). Another set of writers looking to intelligence with a specialized adjective is Earley, Ang, and Tan (2006). They recognize the reality of globalization, the increasing interconnectedness of people who would have been considered far-away and different before computers, telecommunication, and jet planes made the concept of a "global village" a fact. They also saw that it requires managers to adapt to a variety of social environments and to cope with cultural differences whether they work in their home country or some other. To explain individual differences in adapting to or coping with these realities, they proposed a concept of *cultural intelligence*, an ability they defined as "a person's capability for successful adaptation to new cultural settings, that is, for unfamiliar settings attributable to cultural context" (Earley et al., 2006, p. 5).

Some researchers have focused on competencies, often combining aspects of personality and ability. Shaffer, Harrison, Gregersen, Black, and Ferzandi (2006) reported three studies where they had assessed "stable dispositions" (specifically, the Big Five) and four "dynamic competencies" termed cultural flexibility, task orientation, people orientation, and ethnocentrism. They explicitly identified the competencies as characteristics or traits, although dynamic in the sense that they can be developing through training. Results, though modest, led them to conclude that selection of expatriates should be based less on technical competence than on the four competencies and the five personality variables (perhaps excepting conscientiousness, for which no hypothesized prediction was supported).

The notion of competencies also was strong in the recommendations of Cunningham-Snell and Wigfield (2005). They described linkages between eight behaviors global leaders must show and 11 competencies. The linkages did not seem very clear or clean, however; I shall not try to present them because they are less important to me in the present context than the idea that the requisite trait constructs can be defined as acquired competence in carrying out some more or less generic tasks. The challenge inherent in such lists of competencies is to move beyond traditional trait assessment to the assessment of more complex but nevertheless differentially characteristic skills at getting things done.

It seems that many writers in this field are seeking simpler ways to choose expatriates. Variants on the theme, "It all depends . . ." are not uncommon. The choice of a person to leave country X and locate in country Y surely involves a lot of judgment, and rigorous psychometric aids to such judgment are often unavailable or not very relevant. One interesting possibility is the development of decision models through policy capturing, described in Chapter 12. Tye and Chen (2005) obtained judgments from 33 professional human resources people, working in a variety of companies and in a variety of roles, about profiles of hypothetical candidates for expatriate assignments. (Some details of the study will be described further in the policy-capturing section in Chapter 12.) Each expert made four judgments in evaluating each profile: (a) the likelihood of sending the candidate abroad, (b) the candidate's likely adjustment in a foreign culture, (c) the likelihood of adequate job performance on the assignment, and (d) the likelihood of early return from the assignment. Candidate stress tolerance was the main contributor to all of these judgments, but previous international experience and the Big Five extraversion factor were also contributors. Domestic job performance and candidate sex made little contribution to any of the judgments. The models could have been determined individually (idiographically) for each expert, but these authors provided a consolidated policy. Individual judgments seem to be common and obvious bases for decisions like these, but the use of policy models, whether individual or aggregated, can provide more systematic judgments.

The challenge to traditional approaches to personnel assessment and decision making stemming from the growth of multinational organizations is to consider more kinds of information, not only candidate traits but background and contextual information. In short, the challenge is to go beyond traditional methods (which may not even be feasible to try) and to look for more inclusive ways to assess candidates for atypical assignments like those to other countries and cultures. Policy capturing, although rarely used even for domestic assignments, may well prove to be an effective response to the challenge.

The Challenge of Globalization: A Comment

Globalization presents many challenges to staffing, in assessment, in decision processes, and in performance evaluation. The published literature in psychology and business journals has much discussion of the challenges, some approaches to theory development, and many anecdotes. It includes some research reports, but not a coherent, comprehensive research literature. It is needed.

CHALLENGES TO PREDICTION MODELS: INDIVIDUAL PATTERNS OF GROWTH

Even in the face of change, people and the work they do stay somewhat the same over time. That stability is fundamental to the traditional prediction paradigm and to nomothetic generalization of principles of change. Nevertheless, change occurs in normal human development, and it is not likely to be linear. Chapters in the book edited by Cohen (2008) reported research in such developmental topics as childhood aggression, family contact in emerging adulthood, substance abuse, and age-related changes in maturing role adoption. Others included economic issues, and basic studies in cognitive lifespan development. All of them identified growth curves with specifically identified "turning points" where the curves changed direction. Moreover, despite aggregation for nomothetic purposes, they reported noteworthy individual differences in shapes of curves, position in time of the turning points, and even the direction of the regressions after the turning points.

The fact is that people and behavior do change, and not necessarily according to a common pattern; individual differences seem to exist in the direction, extent, and patterns of changes, and even in the latent structures of the behaviors studied (Cohen, Gordon, Kasen, & Chen, 2008). Until recently, these differences have been denied or ignored in personnel research. Two hypothetical versions of growth curves, each showing lifespan growth in cognition, are shown in Figure 10.5a and 10.5b. For simplicity, results of two curves for only four people are shown.

The pattern (sharp growth from infancy into the teens and becoming somewhat level after that) was supported by McArdle and Wang (2008), shown in Figure 10.6. It involves

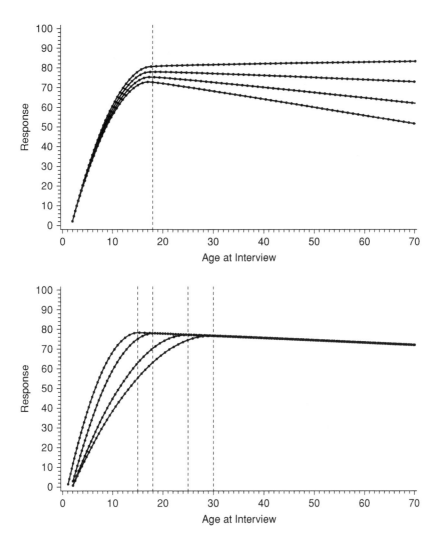

FIG. 10.5   Depiction of two alternative theoretical turning point processes. Reprinted from McArdle, J. J., and Wang, L. (2008). Modeling age-based turning points in longitudinal life-span growth curves of cognition. In Cohen, P., *Applied Data Analytic Techniques for Turning Point Research* (pp. 105–127). New York: Routledge, Taylor & Francis Group. © 2008, Taylor & Francis. Used by permission.

standard individual tests measuring crystallized intelligence. Data from prior longitudinal research on life span development were collected at intervals of ten calendar years or more, culminating in 1992. The figure plots the regression of crystallized intelligence on age at time of interviews. No data points exist for age zero, of course, but many of those tested and "interviewed" were preschool children. Counting this group as the first "wave" of data, and those interviewed and tested at approximate age decades at 10 through 70 as seven subsequent waves, individual growth curves show a somewhat consistent pattern: rapid growth during the years up to age 15 or so followed by a general leveling off. However, although the identification of individual curves with from 51 to 231 data points in the various years is very difficult, Figure 10.6 shows two things. First, there is a general trend applicable across the board so that aggregating the individual curves into one general summary would make

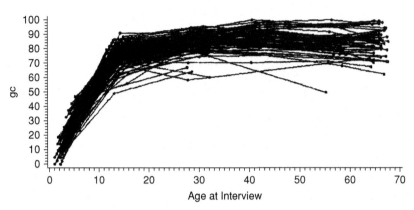

FIG. 10.6 Graphic presentation of raw data on individual growth curved in crystallized intelligence, based on the Bradway–McArdle longitudinal lifespan data. Reprinted from McArdle, J. J., and Wang, L. (2008). Modeling age-based turning points in longitudinal life-span growth curves of cognition. In Cohen, P., *Applied Data Analytic Techniques for Turning Point Research* (pp. 105–127). New York: Routledge, Taylor & Francis Group. © 2008, Taylor & Francis. Used by permission.

a valid, nomothetic statement about cognitive growth. Second, despite the generalization, there are individual differences after the teens; the "leveling off" segment drops sharply and soon—and continues—for one person and a similar, less dramatic drop occurs later for several people. For some, in fact, the curve tends to rise slightly until the interviews in the mid-50s, and even then little drop can be discerned. The challenge is to understand and consider these differences in individual growth rates.

None of these turning point studies involves work, but the concept is a challenge worth following.

The effect of the passage of time has long interested philosophers and developmental psychologists interested in individual differences in patterns of growth and decline. Theorists and laboratory researchers have begun to focus on time and change in newer patterns. McGrath and Tschan (2004) identified four psychological processes influencing behavioral change: (a) developmental processes occurring commonly but at different rates in different people, (b) learning, either formally or through experiences, (c) adaptation to changes in the context in which a person functions, and (d) "operational" processes that occur in the ways people carry out goal-directed activities.

With performance defined as behavior (Campbell et al., 1993), these behavioral-change processes must be recognized as influencing performance and its measurement in work settings. I suspect that the recognition of these time-related behavioral changes in personnel research has been inhibited by excessive faith in linearity and in stability of relative performance over time. Some assessment researchers, however, have noted changes associated with the passage of time. Examples date back at least to Humphreys (1960) and his interpretation of the simplex matrix and the time-related deterioration of validity coefficients in such a matrix. Helmreich et al. (1986) may have started another line of thought when they found that achievement motivation was related to performance after a job was well learned but not to performance in workers' first few months; they dubbed it a "honeymoon effect." Ackerman (1988), in a widely cited article, argued that skills are acquired in three phases: (a) a cognitive or controlled performance phase requiring close attention, making task performance slow and inaccurate, (b) an associative phase allowing procedures to be developed through stronger associations between stimulus and response, and (c) an autonomous or automatic performance phase in which responses are faster and less prone to error. Murphy (1989) combined Ackerman's three stages into two: (a) a *transition* or initial job learning stage, a period requiring general abilities including learning ability, and (b) a *maintenance* stage in which well-learned job skills are performed with little mental effort and performance is affected more by motivational characteristics than by differences in mental ability. He further suggested that the speed of movement from transition to maintenance depends on personal as well as job characteristics. This all suggests the plausibility of turning points in behavior at work, and it is time the personnel researchers turned attention to various forms of growth modeling.

Research Models

New statistical regression models challenge the traditional prediction paradigm; a useful introduction to various forms of growth curve modeling was offered by Duncan, Duncan, and Strycker (2006). Their examples include linear models, but those who question the ubiquitous linearity assumption form a growing chorus. Catastrophe theory was the model adopted by Keil and Cortina (2001). For low-ability workers, they found that performance increases smoothly if not linearly. For very bright workers, they found a discontinuity in performance, a point of sudden insight they dubbed the "Eureka effect." A cubic regression function fit data in both groups, but it was discontinuous (at the Eureka insight) for those with more mental ability. Discontinuity can be modeled using catastrophe theory analysis. (Obviously, it does not require a catastrophic event.) Discontinuity can also be modeled by neural network analysis (Hanges, Lord, Godfrey, & Raver, 2002). Hanges et al. considered neural network analysis along with catastrophe theory in their chapter.

Structural equation modeling is following other fields in looking toward growth and development, not ordinarily linear over time, as a potential alternative to a stable, linear regression allowing the study of change in individuals over time. Analysis of variance with repeated measures has also been used to study change, but it is limited; it describes average change in groups. Meredith and Tisak (1990) offered a latent trait theory for growth curves with individual parameters, and, later, Tisak and Tisak (2000) described two different structural equation approaches and provided a unified model combining them to compare changes in individuals over time. The model is based partly on the distinction between *traits* and *states*, a latent state–trait model (LST); traits are stable over time, and states are temporary, "an ephemeral effect that manifests itself at each measurement period but exhibits no carryover influence" (Tisak & Tisak, 2000, p. 177). It is also based partly on the concept of a *latent trajectory*, a regression form representing change in an attribute, as measured, primarily in the trait component. Three possible forms of regression are shown in Figure 10.7. One is a straight, horizontal regression, indicating absence of change. Another is a linear trajectory, with differing intercepts and slopes for different people, suggesting that each person has a constant rate of change, even though slopes and intercepts may differ from one person to another—truly a finding of individual differences. Still another is a curved trajectory, with more parameters to be estimated. A fourth possibility expects no "standard functional form" relating the trait to time. LST models allow decomposition of variance into three components: (a) a stable trait component, (b) a relatively temporary or "ephemeral" state component, and (c) the inevitable measurement error. Latent growth curve (LC) models depict change in an observed measure of an attribute, at an individual level. The Tisaks' unified model (acronym LC-LSTM) maintains the state–trait distinction while developing latent individual growth curves or trajectories.

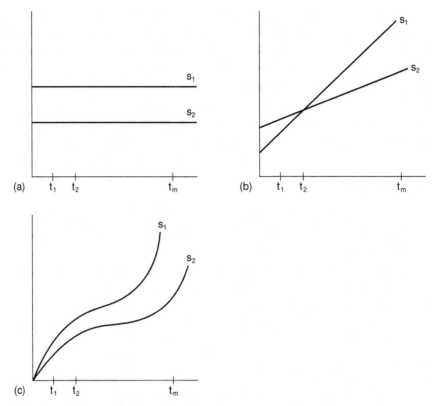

FIG. 10.7   Latent growth trajectories for two people, s_1 and s_2: (a) no growth; (b) linear growth in both but differences in regression parameters; (c) unspecified but nonlinear trajectories. Adapted from Tisak, J., and Tisak, M. S. (2000). Permanency and ephemerality of psychological measures with application to organizational commitment. *Psychological Methods*, 5, 175–198. © American Psychological Association. Adapted with permission.

A criterion measure may change across successive time periods; such changes might occur, during training, in level of skill achieved in successive periods, or at an organizational level in performance quality, market share in sales positions, or observer ratings of commitment to customer service. A measured characteristic of individuals has at least two systematic components, a trait component and a state component. They presented a set of algebraic equations to define the parameters of a structural model and, not incidentally, to guide one through a structural equation modeling program on local computers.

LC-LSTM is a combination of rather new ideas and some that have been around a long time, like the distinction between long-term traits and short-term states, often considered limited to emotional states. Traits, however, are broader characteristics, not limited to personality, temperament, or emotional traits. They are, in general, traits or characteristics of behavior, operationalized by measuring specified aspects of behavior. As a rule, measures of behavior do contain both the stable, long-lasting, habitual components and the fleeting, short-duration, ephemeral components, but the classical components of measurement have been preoccupied with the systematic-error variance dichotomy and have failed to recognize that some sources of systematic variance may be due to sources that are fleeting, occurring at one time of measurement but not necessarily at some other time. Such recognition seems especially important in measuring criterion variables—the variables to be predicted.

Thoresen et al. (2004) referred in their title to "individual job performance growth trajectories." They rejected the notion that performance is a stable, unchanging construct, citing "longstanding evidence that performance is dynamic" (p. 835). They defined performance trajectories "as idiosyncratic patterns of systematic performance growth across a specified period of time or a series of performance observations" (p. 836). Comparing the relationship of time (data collected for four quarters of the year) to the performance of pharmaceutical sales representatives, one group in the transitional stage and another in the maintenance stage, they found a cubic relationship between sales volume and time across the four quarters of the year. They were mainly interested in personality factors as predictors; conscientiousness and extraversion predicted performance in the maintenance group but not in the transitional group (similar to the Helmreich et al., 1986 findings for achievement motivation).

For personnel researchers, the issue comes under the heading of *dynamic criteria* (Ghiselli, 1956). Ghiselli suggested that criteria very often are static and linearly predictable, just as tradition has it, but that many situations make more sense with data analysis methods that permit nonlinear regression and changing rank order in performance. It was an idea whose time had not yet come, and some still think it is a mistaken idea. A brief review of the literature on dynamic criteria reported research generalizations based more on laboratory work than on field studies (Steele-Johnson, Osburn, & Pieper, 2000). Among the conclusions: (a) the pattern of intercorrelations formed a simplex matrix (Humphreys, 1960), (b) predictive validities of ability measures generally decline with practice (or experience), (c) the validities of some psychometric skills increase with practice on the task. Change does not necessarily speak to the issue of linearity—change can be linearly positive, linearly flat, or linearly negative within a given population. It does speak to the issue of the stability of rank orders—the core of the dynamic criterion concept—that the passage of time, for reasons not fully known, disrupts the relative rank orders of individual task performance and, in turn, results in changes in validity over time.

The model of dynamic criteria proposed by Steele-Johnson et al. (2000) suggests and thoroughly discusses many mediating variables influencing the relationship of an ability to performance: (a) job variables (consistency, complexity, and task interdependence), (b) task variables (consistency, complexity, and degree of structure in task definition), (c) organizational variables (changes in technology and work processes, situational strength), and (d) variables related to learning (skill acquisition and experience).

CONCLUDING NOTE

Much of the content of this chapter is not new, but it considers concepts and methods that seem to be overlooked in most personnel research. The section above on dynamic criteria suggests a resurgence and elaboration of Ghiselli's half-century-old idea that at least some regression is neither linear nor static. Therein is the challenge to tradition. It is not now and has never been a challenge to argue whether the stable criteria or dynamic criteria offer better prediction; that is an empirical task. The challenge is to seek generalizable principles of personal and job variables related, not to individual differences in performance, but to individual differences in changes in performance. The more general challenge is to raise and to investigate the possibility of alternative ways of doing things. What is new is the development of enabling technology to collect and analyze data to investigate change in general and, simultaneously, change at the individual level. The technology will enable nothing at all in personnel research if the questions remain unasked.

Tradition is habit. The challenges mentioned in this chapter, from computer use to the possibilities of new models that technology has released, is a challenge to relinquish habit as driving force in research design and in employment practices. The chapter might be seen as a segue from the methodological and contextual emphasis on research to greater emphasis on assessment and prediction in practice. The next two chapters, on standardized testing and judgment, consider both and therefore continue the segue. The remaining chapters emphasize assessment methods: what they are, how they may be used, and what research has shown about their development and use; in short, they complete the segue to the necessary symbiotic relationship of research and practice.

11
Assessments by Tests and Inventories

A *test* is an objective and standardized procedure for measuring a psychological construct using a sample of behavior. *Inventories* are also objective in scoring and standardized, so this chapter includes both types of assessment as *standardized tests* subject to the same principles for development and evaluation. Defining a test as a *sample of behavior* means that the examinee is not passive, but actively responds to the test items by writing answers, choosing among options, recognizing or matching things, making or creating something to fit specified requirements, ordering objects or ideas—among other kinds of response. A test is *objective* in that responses can be evaluated against external standards of truth or of quality—correct or incorrect, or better or poorer than a standard. Responses may be *selected* (choosing an option in a multiple-choice test or selecting a category in a scaled or graded response form) or *constructed* (e.g., creating an answer to a question, writing an essay, or, perhaps, performing a task). Constructed responses may be used in standardized tests if the key for evaluating responses is clear enough to apply reliably. *Measuring* implies quantification; tests are scored, with measurable precision, on numerical scales representing levels of the intended construct or content.

Standardized is harder to define. It implies a key of correct or preferred responses and matching an examinee's responses to the key—responses either fit the key or not, so part of the definition is objectivity in scoring. It implies something like experimental control in that circumstances of test administration that might influence scores are kept constant; the test is administered to all examinees under the same conditions, and using the same procedures and medium (paper, video, oral presentation, etc.) unless evidence of equivalence of differences is provided. The effort to minimize extraneous reasons for inconsistency, more than anything else, distinguishes standardized testing from other forms of assessment. Most of all, standardization implies a standard way to interpret scores, such as norm groups in classical testing or, in modern testing, estimates of latent traits.

Standardized testing is not an either–or proposition; there is a smooth continuum between highly standardized (one might say rigidly standardized) tests and inventories and more flexible assessment procedures. This chapter presents the more standardized end of the continuum—those with standard development and presentation procedures, scoring procedures using a fixed key, and standard bases for interpreting scores.

Standardized testing has a long history of research, measurement theory, and evaluation standards. In the middle half of the twentieth century, most tests, mainly tests of knowledge and abilities, were empirically developed and evaluated, inviting the pejorative term, "dustbowl empiricism." Some, to be sure, were informed by psychological theories, especially some personality assessments, but standardized inventories of interests or traits of personality or temperament have been common nearly as long. Less standardized assessment methods may be preferred for some purposes, or perhaps inevitable for some constructs, but the development and use of standardized tests and inventories provides a prototype for the development, use, and evaluation of assessment in other forms.

TEST DEVELOPMENT

This section focuses on the development of cognitive ability tests, but the procedures described apply just as much to developing other kinds of tests and inventories. Many different kinds of standardized tests and inventories are common assessment tools for selection, training, evaluation, or certification, and they are as common in educational or governmental programs as in employment use.

Those responsible for assessments in organizations need to understand how tests are developed, even if they do not become test developers. Those who (a) pass judgment on proposed testing programs, (b) administer testing programs, (c) develop assessment procedures, or (d) make decisions based on test results need to understand how tests are and should be developed. External consultants and in-house psychologists alike must accept responsibility for assuring such understanding where it is needed. Locally developed assessment procedures, even if not fully standardized, can be useful; they will have a better chance to be useful if based on solid test-development principles.

Scores on a standardized test fall on a scale with reliably fine gradations. Not all assessment programs describe traits with such fine precision, but any assessment procedure deserves careful development—even if it seeks no more than assignment of assessees to a few ordinal categories. The degree of precision in making fine distinctions between examinees is greater for tests than for many other assessment methods, but virtually all assessment is intended to make similar distinctions even if lumping examinees together in just a few ordinal categories. Both ends of the continuum are traditional assessment procedures and need the application of basic measurement principles in their development. Don't equate "traditional" with old or obsolete, and don't equate "modern" with better or preferable. Traditional testing has proved to be effective in a wide variety of circumstances, and most of its bugs have been fixed. Modern testing is promising but still developing; it is often interesting but just as often offers less guidance to many local testing programs.

Commercially Available versus Homemade Tests

It is almost always cheaper to buy a test than to develop one; moreover, commercial publishers and large consulting firms have more opportunity to do large-scale research and therefore to do a better job of writing, calibrating, and evaluating items and empirically evaluating the resulting test. Commercial tests have clear advantages over local development. However, a commercial test may have less face validity, and therefore be accepted less by candidates, than a locally developed test explicitly relevant to the work in question. Job-specific local tests developed by people well-trained in psychometrics can be as reliable and valid as commercially available ones. Hattrup, Schmitt, and Landis (1992) paired three subtests of the *Differential Aptitude Test Battery* (DAT) with related job specific tests. For example, the DAT Verbal Reasoning test, a measure of the verbal comprehension factor, was paired with a technical reading test based on manuals used on the job. Confirmatory factor analysis showed that the same constructs were measured in each of the three pairs of tests. Hattrup et al. concluded that test users do not gain much, psychometrically, by building homemade, job-specific tests, even good ones, but that they do not lose anything either, and may gain considerably in testing program acceptance.

Tests may have to be developed by local people to serve local purposes. I am not as skeptical of homemade tests as I was before validating a test of electronics knowledge developed by an inspection supervisor. The company, fearful of litigation but unwilling to challenge the supervisor, called for an outside evaluation of the test. It met every reasonable expectation. I have since seen other examples of psychometrically good homemade tests (and others that are not). Good job experts can make good tests, especially if helped by testing experts.

Traditional Item Types

Responses to questions on the earliest tests, such as oral trade tests (Osborne, 1940), were the examinee's own, not chosen from a limited set. These are *constructed responses*, and they have been around a long time. Generally, they are not included in "traditional tests." Except for simple sentence completion items, they are rarely scored objectively. They are regaining some popularity, and useful scoring keys have been developed for scoring them. Objectively (i.e., reliably) scored items, including some I would call *selected responses*, are illustrated in Figure 11.1. Most of these were written as if for tests of knowledge or ability, but the same types (and others) appear in interest or personality inventories and biodata forms.

Multiple-choice (MC) items are versatile, prototypical traditional items; an examinee selects one response from a set of options. They can test for knowledge of factual information (either at abstract or at simple levels). They can show abilities to reason from given premises; to calculate; to evaluate optional courses of action; to identify causes or effects or associations; to detect errors, to infer operating principles; or to comprehend principles, sequences, or arguments. They are common for good reason: they provide a variety of reliable, valid tests at relatively low cost.

MC testing has many advantages. It permits testing at different levels of cognitive functioning, from simple recognition to problem solving and solution evaluation. It permits better coverage of content domains than is possible with constructed responses. Compared to other types, it reduces scoring subjectivity and has higher reliability. It is often criticized as superficial, but superficiality is not inherent in the format; it depends on one's purpose. Figure 11.1 shows two multiple-choice items. One demands only recognition, often deemed trivial; the other calls for theoretical knowledge and its application; it is less likely to be called trivial.

Multiple-choice items are also criticized as discouraging creativity. Discouraging creativity is not a good idea, and it is a bad idea if one needs to assess creativity. For example, it is surely unwise to select managers who show no originality (although it happens); potential managers should be able to think unconventionally, to produce ideas readily and in volume, and to change ways of looking at things—all part of creativity and hard (but not impossible) to assess with traditional item types. However, managers should also be able to do arithmetic in their heads (to spot substantially wrong computations), choose words to convey special meanings, or perceive details quickly and accurately—all of which may be assessed very well with multiple-choice tests. Choosing a method of assessment should be based on the suitability of its purpose, not on an overgeneralized preference for one sort of test item over another.

Multiple choice is a kind of forced-choice item if the examinee is limited to a single option. A more common sort of forced-choice item is at the end of Figure 11.1. Such items

Sentence Completion

General assumptions about sources of random error variance in a set of test scores are made in the estimation of _____ .

Short Answer

Which correlational statistic is used to describe a discrimination index in traditional item analysis? _____ .

True-False or *Yes-No*

T F In a speech to the state legislature, Alexander Hamilton shouted "Give me liberty or give me death."
Y N Do you get seriously nervous when speaking to a large audience?

Scaled (Graded) Response

Do you get seriously nervous when speaking to a large audience?

Yes, Indeed	Sometimes	It Depends	Not Often	No, Not At All

Multiple Choice

Where is Mount Whitney located?   A ___ Alaska
                                    B ___ British Columbia
                                    C ___ Colorado
                                    D ___ Delaware

Multiple Choice

Several assessment methods are used in a day-long assessment process: a 50-item multiple-choice test of job knowledge, a performance exercise rated by observers, a brief essay test with 5 questions, and one large essay. Standard scores on the parts of the process are added to provide an overall composite score. Considering both reliability theory and reported experience with estimation methods, which of the following estimates of reliability do you consider most appropriate in evaluating overall scores?

A. __ Internal consistency within total assessment procedure
B. __ Performance stability from time to time during a day
C. __ Equivalence of components within the overall score
D. __ Level of agreement of observers and scorers

Forced Choice

Which one of the following statements is **most** likely to be used to describe you (M)? Which one is **least** likely to be used to describe you (L)? (Circle one M and one L.)

M L I can be depended on to do what I said I would do
M L I am very easy to get along with
M L I enjoy being in a large group of other people
M L I like to learn new things

FIG. 11.1   Examples of objectively scorable item types used in tests and inventories.

have been used in ability and knowledge testing, but they are more common in personality and interest inventories or in inventories assessing individual preferences.

The Basic Construct and Content Domain

Conceptual Definition of Purpose of Measurement

The first step in test development is to specify what is to be measured and how the scores are intended to be interpreted, and to do so with reasonable specificity of the content or construct that defines the intended meaning of scores. When the definitions are missing or vague, no one can adequately infer psychometric validity. The definition of a construct or content domain need not be daunting, but at least a rudimentary theory of the attribute to be measured is needed. The history of employment testing has many examples of useful predictors with not even a rudimentary theory of any attribute, where the test "items" were chosen purely empirically because the more successful job incumbents responded to them differently than the less successful incumbents. An outstanding example is the early Aptitude Index, developed for the selection of insurance agents (Goldsmith, 1922; Kurtz, 1941).

I use a broader notion of constructs than many colleagues do; I consider any idea or concept of an attribute of people, jobs, behavior, environments, or other entities to be a construct. Clarification of the idea constructed distinguishes it from other ideas and relates it to still others. A clear idea is more than a construct name; it is an idea defined in some detail, with defined boundaries. The definition should specify what the construct is and what it is not, and there should be some unity of concept within its boundaries. When defined, with boundaries and distinctions, it is a theory of the attribute to be measured—essential for understanding the scores used for decisions. To be useful, the construct must imply important differences among people, be subject to empirical quantification and evaluation, and remain reasonably stable over a substantial time period.

A construct is not necessarily unidimensional. Many important, clearly described constructs define multidimensional attributes with some basic functional unity. Many others are heterogeneous combinations of different kinds of content having unity only in the sense of being included in a specific content domain, and such a domain can be treated as providing a theory of an attribute, the "construct" of interest. Examples include work sample tests, occupational certification tests, and certain tests that straddle the boundaries usually dividing cognitive from personality measurement. How broadly, or how narrowly, the construct or content is defined is less important than its clarity.

Test Specifications

Construct boundaries enclose a *universe of admissible observations* (Cronbach et al., 1972, p. 20). Boiled down, that phrase means that a test developer identifies kinds of observations that fit the construct and some conditions or circumstances appropriate for making them. As the aphorism about skinning cats has it, most constructs can be measured by more than one kind of observation or circumstance. However admissible observations are defined, the following specifications should be part of test planning and clarification of the construct and its assessment.

1. *Specify the kinds of behavior to be observed and the kinds of stimulus materials to elicit that behavior*—in short, specify or define a test content domain. Test content is not limited to items; it includes all stimulus characteristics (instructions, form, time limits, etc.) consistent with the universe of admissible observations. Some content fits the construct better than other; good choices require thought, based on psychometric experience, practical considerations, likely attitudes of examinees, and social or legal consequences.

2. *Specify the nature of intended inferences from scores.* Most test scores are interpreted normatively, relative to the distribution of scores in a specific group, with z-scores or centile units, hence the term *norm-referenced* testing. Such interpretations answer the question, "How well did the candidate do relative to other people?" How well

Raw Score	Percentile Rank in		
	Group A	Group B	Group C
24			
23	99.9		
22	99.4	99.9	
21	97.7	99.6	
20	94.3	98.5	
19	88.4	96.4	
18	79.9	93.0	
17	70.2	88.6	
16	60.0	83.1	
15	50.0	76.9	
14	40.8	69.9	
13	32.3	62.1	99.9
12	24.6	54.0	99.2
11	18.1	45.5	97.2
10	12.7	36.7	94.1
9	8.5	28.2	89.3
8	5.4	23.9	82.6
7	3.1	16.7	73.9
6	1.7	10.6	63.2
5	.8	5.7	51.0
4	.3	2.5	37.5
3		.7	23.7
2		.2	11.9
1			4.0
0			.4

FIG. 11.2   Different inferences from a given test score in different norm groups with different score distributions.

depends on the comparison group. In Figure 11.2 (made up but illustrative), a candidate with a score of 12 did poorly relative to Group A but was excellent relative to Group C.

This is why *domain-referenced inferences* should be used for personnel decisions more often than they are. They answer an alternative question, "How well did the candidate do relative to a standard of excellence?"[1] The basic idea of domain-referenced interpretation is that a content domain of accomplishment is identified and defined. It should be defined clearly enough that people, even those who disagree about the definition, can generally agree on whether a specified fact or achievement is in the domain or not. Measures of the domain should sample all components of the defined content domain, and scores should be explicitly interpretable in terms of that content. Tests for credentialing—the awarding of a license or certificate or place in a register affirming an examinee's competence to practice a profession or trade—are important examples of domain referencing. They are widely used in

---

[1] Norm- and domain-referenced inferences are not as distinct as this introduction might imply. A test built to be norm-referenced, if found to be satisfactorily valid for distinction of levels excellence, can answer the question equally well. The distinction refers more to intention in test development than to rigid categorization.

governmental jurisdictions (nation, county, or state); by professional organizations, and by businesses certifying competence of, for example, employees who provide specialized repair service. Such tests are rarely homogeneous; internal consistency is not their intent. This allows domain-referenced interpretations to be diagnostic. A score of 12 on a 24-item test may mean knowledge of half of the content, but a better, fuller interpretation can identify the half not known.

The two approaches are not mutually exclusive. A job knowledge test, for example, might serve as a predictor in the usual norm-referenced hypothesis ("How much of this content does this candidate know compared to other candidates?") but it could also show where the candidate (or employee) could profit from special training. For norm-referenced testing, item statistics are particularly important. If domain-referenced interpretations are intended, domain sampling rules are more important.

3. *Specify test components and their intended psychometric characteristics.* Test components can be items or sets of items (testlets).[2] Characteristics such as difficulty or discriminability can be targeted in advance. For normative interpretations, classical psychometric theory suggests an average difficulty of 0.5. The score range where discrimination between high- and low-trait people is most important might be specified in advance. In item response theory (IRT) this might be best accomplished by specifying the points where item information functions should peak.

4. *Specify the medium of presentation.* Oral, paper, audiotape or videotape, and computer monitor are common presentation options. Alternatives should be carefully considered, and the choice should make sense for the construct to be measured. Much computer-based testing is traditional, linear testing where the computer is an "electronic page turner" (Olson-Buchanan, 2002, p. 46), as traditional psychometrically as paper and pencil.

5. *Specify the medium of response.* Written questions can be answered orally; responses to videotaped situations can be entered on machine-scored answer sheets. There is no compelling reason for the medium of presentation to be the medium of response, although keeping them the same is typical and more convenient. Whatever the choice, the response should fit the construct.

6. *Specify constraints on responses.* Should responses be constrained or relatively free? The answer should depend on the theory of the attribute, not on the convenience of testers or managers.

7. *Specify appropriate population characteristics.* Some reasons are obvious. Verbal items should be written to be understood by people in the intended population. A test item for tool and die makers may ask about the properties of metals—but maybe not in the jargon of metallurgical engineers. A less obvious but more important reason is that pilot studies should be done with samples sharing the defining population characteristics.

8. *Specify content allocations.* Domain boundaries, even for norm-referenced tests, may include several content topics. Boundary judgments imply desired content contributions (proportion of items, testing time, or points given to each) in the final test. Intentions may be hard to achieve. Items for some topics may not have the specified properties, judgments of the content relevance for some topics may be less consistent

---

[2] Testlets were introduced as homogeneous item sets used in computer adaptive testing (Wainer & Kiely, 1987); I use the term more broadly, meaning any internally consistent and scorable subset of items within the larger set that is the test.

than planned, and whole component topics can be lost if this specification is not met. It cannot be assumed that the first round of items will meet all specifications; second and even third rounds are not unusual.

9. *Specify any intended time limits.* Practicalities may impose some time limits; a test given during a training class, for example, may have to be completed, with time for instructions and retrieval of papers, within a 50-minute class period. Time limits may be set to recognize that speed is part of the construct. *Speeded* tests differ from *power* tests, the latter show what examinees can do without the constraints of imposed time limits. If the intended construct is defined by power, but administrative considerations impose a time limit, the specified time should allow nearly all examinees to complete the test—effectively limiting test length.

10. *Specify other standard circumstances of testing.* Specifying instructions, offering sample items, limiting explanation, arranging the items in sequence, sizing the type, adjusting the video display resolution or color-coding materials for assembly, establishing scoring procedures, and the required qualifications for test administrators, among others, may need standardization. Some specifications may require pilot studies; if so, the test development plan should include their design.

The above 10 points are not exhaustive, but they describe the variety of considerations in test development—the statements, decisions, and clarifications needed for a workable plan. A test plan, like a house plan, can be changed as the work moves along; a particular specification may prove too costly, ambiguous, esthetically poor, time-consuming, or otherwise flawed. Houses and tests are constructed according to prior plans, but deviations can be anticipated. Nevertheless, test plans should include procedures for recording deviations and the reasoning behind them. Such records are useful, often essential, in evaluating psychometric validity.

Developing Items or Other Components

Good professional judgment and experience are required to develop items. Because most employment tests have multiple-choice items, I concentrate on them. A multiple-choice item has three parts: a stem, a correct response, and a set of distracters. One way to write a multiple choice item is to (a) write a true statement, (b) delete a word or phrase as one would in writing a completion item, (c) write some words or phrases that would be unacceptable but plausible answers in a completion item, and (d) list them and the correct one as a set of options. These items assume that people who know the correct answer will choose it and that there is no widespread *mis*information on the item's topic (Horst, 1966). The first assumption is fairly safe in most employment settings. The second assumption is less safe, especially with some job knowledge items; not often, but often enough to merit concern, people will talk about experiences, build on them, and build on the comments of others so much that they "know" things that simply are not true. Items influenced by widespread misinformation can often be identified in item analysis.

Over the years rules or principles have evolved for writing good multiple-choice items (cf. Ebel, 1972; Millman & Greene, 1989; Thorndike & Hagen, 1955). Examples include the following.

1. Give each item some "face validity." Make items clearly relevant to the announced purpose of the test; use word choices and reading levels appropriate for the intended examinees.

2. Be sure the item content is suitable for the purpose of the test and for the examinee population intended.

3. Write in clear and simple language and style; keep vocabulary as simple and unobtrusive as the content allows.

4. Avoid negative words or words that exclude something (e.g., *not*, or *except*); if they cannot be avoided, emphasize them with capital letters *and* italics or boldface type.

5. Be sure that there is just one correct (or best) answer; be sure that options are false (or, if all are partly true, that there is a clear principle for declaring one better than the others). If the item involves controversial matters, ask for the position held by a specified authority (or, better, ask about the nature of the controversy).

6. Be sure the problem for the examinee is clear in the stem. Phrasing the stem first as a question may help the test developer clarify the task to be set for examinees; then edit the question to say in a different item form (e.g., a true but incomplete sentence); edit again to multiple-choice with the completing phrase being the correct answer.

7. Put as much of the item as possible in the stem, avoiding repeated use of a phrase in each response option (unless repetition provides more clarity); options should be as brief as possible. The stem should be as brief as consistent with clarity.

8. Avoid *specific determiners*—cues within items giving away the correct answer. An example is a stem ending with the article "an." If only one option begins with a vowel, that option is most likely to be chosen by an examinee who lacks the necessary knowledge. Other specific determiners include variations in length or grammatical structure of the options, use of the same word in the stem and an option, implausible conditions such as *never* or *always*, or consistent placement of correct options among items.

9. Keep the number of options constant. If this cannot be done, vary the number of options early in the test to avoid establishing spatial sets.

10. Be sure distracters are plausible. Good distracters can come from a pilot study giving stems as questions calling for constructed, written responses.

11. Keep distracter content similar. Otherwise, each option becomes a true–false item, and answers depend more on cleverness in eliminating options than on knowledge or understanding of the test material.

12. Keep options independent of each other; if two options are merely different ways to say the same thing, they can both be discarded quickly by an alert examinee.

13. Avoid "none of the above" or "all of the above" as options, especially when examinees are to choose the best rather than the correct answer.

14. Keep items independent; do not let information in one item provide a cue to the answer to another one.

Some psychometrics text books give similar rules for other item types, but some types are used so rarely that there has not been enough experience to form general rules. If a rare item form is needed, developers need to set—and test— their own rules in advance to make item development more systematic.

Pilot Studies

Pilot studies should be routine. Choices are made at nearly every step in test development. Some can be made rationally, considering one's options and the relevant arguments for or against them. Other choices need data, and sometimes data must be developed locally.

Choices need to be informed by answers to one or both of two kinds of questions: *Is this working?* and *What if . . . ?*

Preliminary Studies

Pilot studies need not be elaborate or sophisticated; they may be simple trials of procedural ideas or choices. Simple trials often show whether time allowances are too restrictive for a power test, or whether instructions are clear. Structural glitches may be suspected and lead to "is it working?" questions. The more novel the test, the more important such questions are. Some of them may require full-scale experiments, but many of them can be answered by trying out the instructions, or the time limits, or purely physical aspects of the test to see if they work or cause trouble. A useful trial might ask a few people to think out loud as they take the test; the listening test developer can learn where instructions go awry, or which distracters do not distract. Interviews after a trial can be helpful.[3] The trials should, of course, use appropriate samples, but the samples need not be large. Such trials are easy, but should not be dismissed as trivial luxuries. It is terribly arrogant, and self-defeating, to assume that one's expertise assures a good, workable plan.

Conventional Item Analyses

Likewise, it is terribly arrogant and surely self-defeating to assume that items work as intended; item analysis is necessary. Where possible, samples should be large enough to provide reliable item statistics, they should be similar to the population for whom the test is intended, and the trait measured should be distributed somewhat as it is in that population. These are tall orders, unlikely to be fully satisfied, but they provide goals to be approximated as well as reality permits. Doing the best one can, even if imperfectly, is preferable to doing nothing.

Two kinds of item statistics are traditional. The easier of these is item difficulty, computed as the proportion of those tested who give the keyed response (OK, it's really easiness but it reflects difficulty). Conventionally, 0.50 is considered an optimal proportion, but other target levels may be better for some uses. Conventional wisdom also suggests that item difficulties should be essentially equal and that item responses should be highly correlated (to produce an internally consistent test).

Such "wisdom" needs to be tempered with good judgment. If all items are perfectly correlated, and if all items have difficulty indices of 0.50, then the test yields a two-point distribution where half of the scores are zero and the other half are perfect. The result is classification, not measurement. To develop a fairly internally consistent, homogeneous test with scores distributed along a scale, item difficulties must vary. If the intended examinees define a general population, perhaps the average around which that variation occurs should be .50. For homemade tests, however, the intended use may require that distinctions be most reliable at higher or lower levels of the trait, and the average item difficulty around which specific item difficulties are distributed may therefore be higher or lower.

The other traditional item statistic is a discrimination index. For dichotomously scored items, a preferred index is a biserial correlation coefficient. The criterion in computing this coefficient is usually the total score (excluding the item being analyzed); sometimes an external criterion is used. Both were used in developing the *Purdue Mechanical Adaptability*

---

[3] Thanks to Jason Adams for reminding me of this simple tool.

Test. Internal consistency was one goal, so one item analysis pitted item responses against total scores. Another goal was to have a test that measured mechanical knowledge, not general intelligence; therefore, a second item analysis pitted item responses against scores on a test of general mental ability. To be retained, an item had to correlate well with total score but not with general mental ability. I do not know why this excellent example has not been more widely followed.

Item Analyses for Construct Relevance

Further pilot studies provide data for the preliminary evaluation of tests. Some of these might be major undertakings; for example, a full-scale generalizability analysis requires large samples and careful planning. Construct validation requires reliable testing of several confirmatory, disconfirmatory, and competing hypotheses. Even if big studies are not feasible, they can be outlined conceptually; doing so can suggest plausible sources of contaminating error.

Attitudes of Candidates

Too often overlooked is the effect a test may have on candidate attitudes. A test that seems irrelevant, trivial, or excessively demanding can impair test-taking motivation, and motivation to do well is a key ingredient for validity in ability testing. A nine-scale *Test Attitude Scale* (TAS), developed and used by Arvey, Strickland, Drauden, and Martin (1990), accounted significantly for variance on other tests; mean attitudes differed significantly for job applicants (as in predictive or follow-up validation designs) and incumbents (as in concurrent designs) on seven of the scales. Scores on some scales correlated significantly (but not highly) with race, sex, or age. A TAS composite score (reflecting positive test-taking dispositions) moderated predictions of college grades by both ability and personality tests—but in different directions (Schmit & Ryan, 1992). Positive motivation was associated with higher validity for the ability test; a negative motivation composite was associated with higher personality test validity.

Test anxiety is especially likely in selection testing, especially for coveted or "high-stakes" opportunities. In a simulation study, McCarthy and Goffin (2005) found it lowered scores on a cognitive test and that highly anxious applicants may be disadvantaged. If these are also potentially high performers on a job, the cost of ignoring anxiety may be more than a loss of validity; it could also be a loss of some excellence on the job.

Test content and the medium in which it is presented can influence attitudes, although it is not easy to separate these two sources (Chan & Schmitt, 2004). A burgeoning literature has examined reactions to new technology in all aspects of the employment process; the general finding seems to be more favorable for the newer technology than for old in a variety of technological media (Anderson, 2003). Is the preference for the new technology due to its relative novelty, its absence from the old-hat list of media, or some intrinsic attractiveness independent of novelty? Stay tuned, but enjoy that attitude while, and however long, it lasts.

Computerized Adaptive Testing (CAT)

Conventional testing is *linear testing*. Items in many linear tests are arranged in order of difficulty and all items are presented in that order to all examinees. A high-ability person flies through the easy items; only harder items near the end show just how able that person is. A low-ability person struggles through the easy items and merely guesses by the end of the set. Linear testing is clearly not efficient. In contrast, *adaptive testing* uses a branching algorithm and, therefore, fewer items. It begins with one item of moderate difficulty. The next item depends on the response a person has given to the first one—and so on until a predetermined criterion for stopping the test has been reached. Adaptive testing has a century-long history, but it required the combination of modern computers and the development of item response theory to bring it to its current level of sophistication.

Considering how long adaptive testing has been used and discussed in psychological testing, it is amazing that it has not been a central topic, even yet, in employment testing. Binet used it in his intelligence test for children, continued in the Terman revisions (Stanford–Binet). Other examples appeared in an apparently unavailable ETS technical report by Angoff and Huddleston in 1958 (cited in Thissen & Mislevy, 1990), and the Cronbach and Gleser (1965) proposal for a two-stage testing system for decision making. Adaptive testing has predated the "computerized" adjective, but has until very recently been rarely considered by employment and HR testers. These days, adaptive testing is widespread in education, health sciences, and other professions. We need to catch up.

The basic patterns are shown in Figure 11.3. If items in the linear set are in fact arranged according to difficulty, the first items are very easy and the last few are very difficult. The adaptive version omits items that are not needed to establish a stable estimate of ability. It is faster, offers less susceptibility to random error, and has better user acceptance.

Generating and Calibrating Items

In one sense, an adaptive test is developed on the spot, while in use. The items constituting the test are selected by the adaptive choices of successive items. In another sense, an adaptive test requires much more background research than does a traditional linear test. For simplification, assume multiple-choice items and don't worry about item generation theory. *Generating* items requires thinking them up and then writing and editing them. *Calibrating* items requires the choice of an IRT model, the collection of large amounts of data, and the estimation of the item response curve (IRC) parameters for the model chosen.

In an adaptive form, an item somewhere in the middle of the difficulty range (taking care to avoid using the same one over and over) is presented to an examinee as the first item (item 11 in Figure 11.3). A correct response to it is followed by a more difficult one (item 14); this first part of the test pathway is indicated by the solid arrow. A wrong response to the first item would lead to an easier one (item 8), but that is hypothetical—item 8 never appears in the adaptive version for this examinee (hence the dashed arrow and shading); the solid arrows show this person's path through the test from the first item to the final one. The path ends when a criterion rule for termination is satisfied, for example, when estimates of Θ after items 20 and 19 agree within previously set limits. Thus a five-item adaptive test replaces the 25-item linear form, and it yields a far more precise estimate of true ability.

Let's take a slightly more detailed, but necessarily over-simplified, trip through the CAT development process. It assumes unidimensionality, although multidimensional IRT exists, because "the application of MIRT is still in its infancy" (Thissen, Reeve, Bjorner, & Chang, 2007, p. 111). It assumes dichotomous response (polytomous response models are available and commonly used in educational, biological, and sociological research). It makes no assumptions about item types, whether multiple choice or graded response. Even though it overlooks many important considerations, it may provide enough CAT flavor to make the coming section on multistage adaptive testing easier to follow.

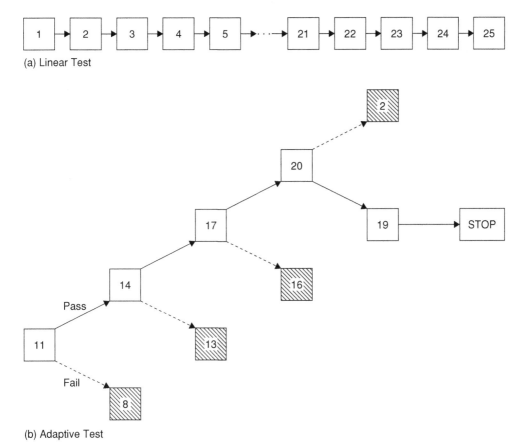

(a) Linear Test

(b) Adaptive Test

FIG. 11.3 A 25-item test administered (a) in linear form (all 25 items) and (b) in adaptive form (only five items administered).

Item Banks

Some authors use the terms *item bank* and *item pool* interchangeably. Both terms are a bit ambiguous, but distinguishing them is useful. I like the distinction implied by Belov and Armstrong (2005) in which an item pool is a set of items (or potential items) available for CAT, and an item bank may include several different item pools and other items not in any pool. Far more than the 25 items assumed in Figure 11.3 should be in the pool; developers of tests for "high-stakes" assessment need substantial item pools from which to choose good items for adaptive testing—without overexposing any of them. For relatively simple dichotomously scored items, in unidimensional tests, the pool of calibrated items available for the test should contain about 100 items or more (Embretson & Reise, 2000).[4] In general, all items in the pool should have been shown in prior calibration to have high discrimination

---

[4] That target may not be feasible, and sometimes it may not be necessary. Polytomously scored items do not need so many, and "it is difficult to conceive of a large number of discriminating items with a wide range of difficulty values being written to assess some personality constructs (e.g., aggression, paranoia)" (Embretson & Reise, 2000, p. 264).

parameters (steep IRC slopes) and difficulty parameters spread over a wide range of trait levels. To require a wide range of difficulty parameters is central to CAT development in education and some other applications requiring precision in measurement at all levels. The requirement may be less important in selection or certification testing, where precision in measurement is important mainly in those regions of score distributions where hard decisions—those where the candidate is neither well qualified nor poorly qualified, but somewhere between—must be made.

Numerical values of item parameters are, strictly speaking, invariant only with linear transformation to a common scale; moreover, IRT does not assume invariance across different populations. Therefore, building an item pool for a specified CAT requires specification of the population in which the test will be used. Samples used in estimating item parameters should be samples of that population. In employment testing, the target population is not likely to be "people in general," but will the population assessed by the proposed test be all people who apply, or will it be limited by something more specific, such as those passing a preliminary screening test?

Items for the item pool must, if unidimensionality is sought, tap the intended dimension without serious contamination from other dimensions. Where another dimension is frequently associated with the one intended and the two dimensions jointly contribute to the variance in responses to many of the items, it might be worthwhile to include relatively pure items, testlets, or even to create a companion item pool. Item dimensionality is hard to determine, but item factor analysis, structural equations, or comparisons of slopes of IRCs obtained with different items in different subgroups can offer evidence (Thissen et al., 2007). A rigid demand for unidimensionality is not needed; items with multiple sources of variance can be combined into a meaningful and useful index score with at least reasonable functional unity.

In some test development organizations, very large item banks are developed from which item pools for specific tests may be extracted. Such an item bank may include items calibrated in different populations for different dimensions. To develop a specific test from such a heterogeneous group of possible items, a more specific set of appropriate items needs to be identified. Appropriate items measure the intended construct or content, they have been calibrated on one or more samples from the target population, the discrimination parameters imply steep IRC slopes, and the difficulty parameters are widely scattered throughout the expected range of ability (even if concentrated in a specific critical range).

Information from prior calibration of items in the bank needs careful evaluation. Many computer-based tests (CBTs) are mere translations of paper-and-pencil versions; parameter estimates garnered in these different media may be different from those found in CAT. Prior calibration should have been done with the IRT model to be used in selecting and using an item pool. Another consideration is user interface (Booth, 1998). I have not seen enough research on the effect of different aspects of the user interface on parameter estimates in CBTs. It may be prudent to ignore prior parameters in a large item bank and to collect data for new ones that consider effects of person–computer friendliness. If the number of items is very large, more manageable, smaller groups of items can be administered to several samples from the appropriate target population; the resulting parameter estimates can be placed on a common scale by using linkage procedures (Embretson & Reise, 2000).

The End of the Test

Rules need to be established for deciding when to stop selecting and presenting further items; the process is not eternal, and the computer needs to be told when it has done enough.

Common stopping points are established by setting rules based on consistency of trait estimates, minimal change in information levels (from TIFs of successive scores), or standard errors of measurement. Sometimes rules simply set the number of items to be presented (fixed-length adaptive testing). IRT-based rules seem to make more sense.

PERFORMANCE TESTS

Tests are often developed for use across a variety of situations. A test of general mental ability, for example, may be useful at many different job levels, in jobs defined with different tasks to be performed, or in combination with other traits varying from personality to sensorimotor. Many tests, however, are developed for more specific use, such as work samples, occupational certification tests, civil service tests, or tests to measure hard-to-define constructs that seem important, such as situational judgment tests.

Multistage adaptive testing (MSAT) is in the last of these categories, used mainly in certification of specific educational and occupational achievement and performance. Similar certification, although on a narrower scale, is done in the assessment of special competencies or through work sample tests, and these will be briefly discussed first to set the stage for discussing MSAT development. The first three examples all assess people to certify some sort of competence: competence in performing jobs, competence in carrying out aspects of jobs, and competence in meeting occupational responsibilities.

Work Samples

Flight testing of a candidate for a pilot's license uses a standard checklist of required maneuvers and the check pilot evaluates how well each one of them is performed. A candidate for an office job may be tested on how well they edit mangled text in a word processor. These are work samples; both are standardized abstractions of work actually done on a job. There are degrees of abstraction. A work sample might faithfully simulate actual assignments or critical work components. Simulations imitate actual work but omit its trivial, time-consuming, dangerous, or expensive aspects. *High-fidelity* simulations imitate a task almost exactly, as in some simulations of aircraft cockpits. *Low-fidelity* simulations simply abstract—pull out of context—elements of key tasks (Motowidlo, Dunnette, & Carter, 1990). A common assumption is that more faithful simulations predict performance better, but the assumption deserves questioning. Actually, prediction may be better when the sample focuses more explicitly on the crucial, enduring essence of a job. Low-fidelity simulations, if they emphasize that basic core, have predicted as well or better than more faithful alternatives (Motowidlo et al., 1990; Motowidlo & Tippins, 1993).

Work samples also serve as criteria. An example in police work is writing incident reports. Jackson, Harris, Ashton, McCarthy, and Tremblay (2000) developed a standardized incident-reporting sample and validated predictors of it; along the way, they also noted several advantages of work sample use.

Developing Work Samples

Work samples begin with job or work analysis to identify and select tasks and knowledge to be included—the test content domain. A work sample may sample performance, job knowledge, or both so long as it conforms to the defined content domain. Equipment or material used in task samples should match those actually used on the job rather than using stuff not yet thrown away. With repeated use, equipment can show wear; it should be monitored to assure that conditions nevertheless stay standard. Pilot studies should evaluate clarity of instructions, scoring procedures, and effects of time limits, even if these aspects of testing fall outside of the work content domain.

Work Sample Scoring

Performance in work samples is usually scored by rating; instructions to the rater should be clear and detailed, and raters should demonstrate understanding of the rating task. A score might be obtained by matching a work sample product to one of a set of samples previously scaled from very poor to excellent (Millman & Greene, 1989); the score is the scale value of the standard sample it most closely matches. More objective measures can be used. A score on machine set-up might be the completion time or, on a word processing task, the number of corrections needed.

Situational Judgment Tests

Many objective assessments—objective in the sense of reliable scoring—have no "demonstrably correct answer" (Bergman, Drasgow, Donovan, Henning, & Juraska, 2006, p. 223). Situational judgment tests (SJTs), along with many biodata forms, interviews, or assessment center exercises, are among those requiring the test-taker to judge the relative goodness of available responses. Assessments somewhat like SJTs have been around since about the 1920s, but those we now call SJTs are relatively new and growing in practical use. A typical one presents an applicant with a set of situations, varying in content and complexity, actually or potentially encountered on the job. Constructed responses may be required, but SJTs usually offer a set of optional ways a job incumbent might handle the situation. Response might call for choosing the best and least effective options, rating anticipated effectiveness of options, or choosing a best option fitting a given definition of "best." SJTs may be administered orally or on paper; video procedures have also been used (e.g., Lievens, Buyse, & Sackett, 2005).

Development of SJTs

An SJT item has a situation description, a response procedure, and a scoring method. Situations may be gleaned from job analytic methods, theory, or informed imagination; Weekley and Ployhart (2006) advocated critical incidents reported by job incumbents or their supervisors. A situation derived from actual incidents is understood more completely by the one who reported it than by a test-taker reading an abstract of the situation in an item stem. As an abstraction, it is likely to be ambiguous, making the SJT item something like a projective test, in which the assessee projects his or her own experiences and values to the test stimulus, whether it be a situation, an ink blot, or an incomplete sentence. Stem abstractness led Gessner and Klimoski (2006) to suggest that a "theory of the test taker" can be explored to see how those with different kinds of stakes make sense of the situations in an SJT.

Different response forms may evoke different constructs, perhaps depending on the way responses are scored. Bergman et al. (2006) identified six different scoring strategies: (a) empirically developed keys that relate well to a criterion, (b) keys reflecting theoretical positions, (c) hybrid scoring, using two keys, one theoretical and one empirical according to specified algorithms for combining them to reach item scores, (d) scoring based on expert judgments, (e) factorial scoring, and (f) subgrouping (used more in biodata than in SJTs). Their study created 11 scoring keys from the first five of these general methods. Criterion-related validities varied widely with scoring methods; only the empirical, expert judgment, and hybrid keys correlated significantly with their criterion. They drew no general conclusion about the relative merits of the keys (after all, one study does not a generalization make, as they acknowledged), but they did conclude firmly that validity depends partly on the scoring procedure chosen—and that a poor choice can lead to incorrect conclusions about the usefulness of the test.

What Do SJTs Measure?

Construct identification has often been identified in this book as the first step in the development of assessment procedures. I hope readers noted and objected to its absence in the description of SJT development. It is missing because SJTs are rarely developed to fit a clearly defined construct. SJTs are multidimensional, often an unexplored mishmash, because on-the-job problem situations are widely varied. A rudimentary theory concept is probably common, but perhaps only as a vague idea that job incumbents need to make good judgments in difficult circumstances. Researchers seem more likely to try to discover constructs measured than to define constructs in creating SJTs.

I'll mention three kinds of answers to the question. Brooks and Highhouse (2006) advocated the notion of *quasi-rationality judgment* (to be revisited in Chapter 12), combining analytic and intuitive judgment processes; they attributed the pleasing validities of SJTs to the intuitive component, although they recognized some limitations to judgment quality. Chan and Schmitt (2005) proposed multidimensional situational *judgment competencies*, such as interpersonal sensitivity, conflict resolution, or moral courage, each a specific combination of individual KSAOs. The third has appeared as several terms, largely under theories of intelligence offered by Sternberg; specifically, *practical intelligence* (Stemler & Sternberg, 2006) or *successful intelligence* (Sternberg, 1999). The frequent finding of predictive validity from SJT scores was attributed to the Sternberg concept of *tacit knowledge* by McDaniel et al. (2001). This was placed by Motowidlo, Hooper, & Jackson (2006) under the rubric of *procedural knowledge* (described by Campbell et al., 1993 as knowing not only what to do but how to do it).

Although various kinds of judgment tests or practical intelligence tests have been around a long time, they have been described more often as promising than as promise fulfilled. In about the past 15 years, however, reports of replicable predictive validity have appeared more often, even for incremental validities. Now that the question of what they measure is being seriously discussed, the hope of promise fulfilled seems stronger than ever.

Multistage Adaptive Tests

Multistage adaptive testing (MSAT) uses two or three "stages" of testing and a modification of adaptive item choices within stages by using testlets or sets of items. MSAT program development has mainly been the province of large test publishers, governments, trade or professional associations, or major consulting firms. MSAT has been used in occupational licensing and certification, education (e.g., state proficiency exams), and advocated for studies of patient outcomes in medical research (which seems a model for studies of decision outcomes in employment testing). It is relatively new, but it offers a sensible approach that seems applicable to employment testing. These tests will be available for purchase from test development organizations and big consulting firms. Some of them will offer better products and services than others; those who buy them need to be informed consumers.

Distinctions between CAT and MSAT

Educational achievement, patient outcomes, and occupational competence are certainly not homogeneous constructs. One distinction between CAT and MSAT is that CAT requires tighter definitions of construct dimensions and MSAT requires mixed, more heterogeneous item content domains. A second distinction is that, instead of individual items, the basic unit in MSAT is a *set* of items, a *testlet*; the examinee's path through MSAT calls for choices of testlets, not individual items. Each testlet is calibrated for difficulty and test information functions, as are items in CAT, and each testlet is assembled in accordance with pre-specified constraints. A third distinction is that, in MSAT, all examinees complete all stages of the program (usually two or three but sometimes more) instead of being stopped when a termination rule is satisfied.

Figure 11.4 illustrates a pattern for a three-stage MSAT. The numbered squares represent links in the pathway an examinee takes from initial testlet to test completion. Four different paths exist: links 1,2,4; 1,2,5; 1,3,5; and 1,3,6. Each link (1, 2, and 3; not the final one in Stage 3) is a point where the program or administrator decides how difficult the next stage testlet will be and, for that level of difficulty, which testlet will be presented. Circles represent testlets; for convenience, Figure 11.4 puts three at each link. Testlets and difficulty level at each link are intended to be equivalent, with the test information functions virtually the same. However, values of Θ associated with peak TIF should vary across stages.

A further distinction between CAT and MSAT is that all items presented to the examinee in CAT are chosen during the testing process; the test form is different for each examinee.

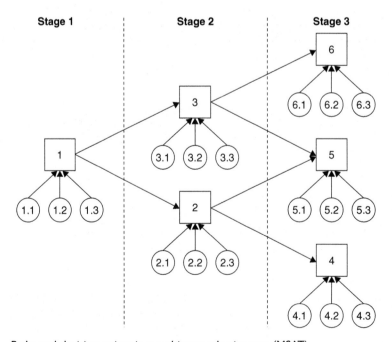

FIG. 11.4   Paths and decision points in s multistage adaptive test (MSAT).

Therefore, subject matter experts and other interested parties have no opportunity to examine and evaluate the specific set of items before the examinee sees them. For a unidimensional trait measure this is not a technical problem; statistical analysis trumps expert judgment. For a test of complex knowledge, typical of MSAT, different topics or aspects of that knowledge must be sampled, fitting domain specifications, and the boundaries of those aspects are blurry. Judging the adequacy of content coverage may be as important as estimating testlet parameters; in any case, prior judgments about the content of individual testlets is often necessary and happens with MSAT.

Different MSAT programs differ in purpose and content. Some maximize measurement precision, especially near critical levels of competence in performance or knowledge. Some emphasize abstract constructs; others emphasize observable behaviors, knowledge, or skill. Some individualize assessment as much as possible while maintaining the ideal of standardization; others standardize assessment materials and procedures as thoroughly as possible while adapting to individual differences. Some build in many stages; others think two stages is plenty. Clearly, detailed general rules for test assembly do not exist and probably never will. Nevertheless, Luecht and Nungester (1998) recommended three fundamental steps: (a) establish psychometric targets for testlets (they called them *modules*) across stages, (b) designate and allocate content specifications and constraints across stages, and (c) create different versions of the *panels* that define each stage; a panel in Figure 11.4, in their terms, would be the specification of a link and the testlets associated with it, that is, all the possibilities at a stage. Each of these steps requires detailed planning and evaluation of prior data.

Item Banks and Pools

In MSAT, an item *pool* is a set of items meeting specified content and parameter constraints, from which selected items may be assembled into a testlet. An item *bank* is a larger, less constrained set of items, typically much larger and still more heterogeneous, and it can be searched for items for specific item pools.

Content Constraints

Constraints impose limits on the freedom to assign items to testlets (Belov & Armstrong, 2005, 2008). Whether content is intellectual, physical, or attitudinal, choosing among alternatives, ordering objects or ideas, creating free responses, or other kinds of responses nearly always have cognitive aspects. At least so far, MSAT assessments are primarily cognitive. Identification of specific cognitive skills to be required in a testlet specifies a constraint; tapping some skills but not others is a stronger constraint. Other constraints might, in a given case, include topic limitations, rules about content diversity, and rules limiting item exposure (e.g., see Breithaupt & Hare, 2007). Testlet length may be set at a constant number of items. Relative positions of different items or kinds of items may be specified, and item "enemies" are to be avoided (enemies are pairs of items that must not appear together because they offer clues to the keyed responses for each other).

Commentary

Many articles illustrating possibilities in computer automated test development for MSAT have appeared without describing actual testing programs. Some use Monte Carlo procedures with simulated data; some use items from actual examinations (Luecht & Nungester, 1998;

van der Linden & Adema, 1998) or compare different testlet models (Li, Bolt, & Fu, 2006). Articles like these report theory and research evaluating theoretically sound procedures, but they do not report on operational testing programs or their evaluations. One exception is the description of the licensing examination of the American Institute of Certified Public Accountants, but even here the emphasis of the article is methodological; it focuses on automated assembly of multistage testlets (Breithaupt & Hare, 2007).

To retrieve an old cliché, MSAT is an idea whose time has not yet come. More accurately, its time is here but neither the technology nor HR personnel are quite ready for it, even in large organizations. Nevertheless, the basic ideas can be put to work in employment testing, even in moderate-size organizations. The results may not be as positive as those anticipated in the reports of methodological MSAT studies, but they can, and I think would if tried, be better in many ways than purely linear testing. For one example, job knowledge testing for trades or professions could be based on classical item statistics, but IRT parameters, along with content constraints, would probably develop better testlets to use in assessing candidate readiness for an advanced training program or special assignment, and they can be tailored to be explicitly relevant to the roles played by these occupations within an organization or industry. Testlets can be approximately matched at specific average difficulty levels, they can be matched for content, and they can consist of items with useful discrimination indices. The prerequisite for doing so is a clear definition of a content domain (which should be available before developing a linear version anyway), and a clear specification of that part of the domain sampled by the testlet. Are these requirements so new? About the only thing genuinely new would be arranging the testlets in order of difficulty, starting testing at a middle level, establishing two or three stages. The resulting assessment could reduce the boredom associated with a string of exceedingly easy items, or the stress of too many very hard items, and therefore reduce careless errors and reliability-reducing random guessing on hard items. Why not try it?

Establishing Cut Scores and Standards

Licensing or certification testing implies cut scores. Setting cut scores, or standards, is an old topic and a difficult one. In previous chapters, I have expressed opposition to cut scores for selection tests. Dichotomization reduces validity and is costly, rarely appropriate, basically silly, and otherwise repugnant (in my opinion!). I rail against cut scores because too often they are set only for convenience. They let managers avoid making judgments more taxing than whether a candidate's test score exceeds the cut point or not—and they make it unnecessary to try to explain more valid decision processes. It would not be worth mentioning were it not so common, so unnecessary, and so damaging to assessment usefulness. Especially frustrating is the reason I most often hear for setting cut scores: "My managers just can't handle anything more complicated than a pass-or-fail score." I don't know why so many testers assume that decision makers lack the brains to evaluate test scores sensibly.

On the other hand, some situations do justify and even require cut scores. Among them are the following.

1. *Licensing and certification.* The question here is not a candidate's level of competence but whether the examinee meets a predetermined standard of competence—the cut score. In testing to certify adequate proficiency or knowledge, one does not ask

about the slope of a continuous regression line; the important question is whether those who meet or exceed the standard are actually more competent than those who do not.

2. *Civil service eligibility lists.* Jurisdictions may give a test to many candidates at one time and not test any others for the next year or two. Candidates are listed in an "eligibility list" for top-down selection, ordered from those with the highest score to a minimally acceptable score below which no one will be hired. The cut score provides one of many bases for deciding when to develop a new exam. Indeed, for reasons unrelated to psychometric issues, an eligibility list may be declared "exhausted" before the minimum score is reached.

3. *Cyclical hiring.* For example, a large company in a small community may have a policy of hiring new graduates from high schools or colleges to work as trainees during the spring graduation season. They first work as trainees, later placed in regular positions as openings arise through the year. By forecasting the number of likely openings before the next hiring season, and with a fairly good idea of the probable score distribution, one can establish a cut score likely to provide enough people in the trainee pool to fill positions that become available.

4. S*equential assessment.* An initial assessment may be scored on a pass–fail dichotomy to decide who gets to the next step. Where many candidates compete for one or a few positions, preliminary screening may be used for all candidates, saving complete or costly assessments (e.g., assessment centers or complex simulations) for the most promising ones. For some jobs, the preliminary assessment may look for intrinsically disqualifying considerations (e.g., proofreader candidates who catch few misspellings).

Setting Cut Scores: Early Methods

A brief history of methods for setting cut scores offers background for more recent approaches. In old or new methods, setting a cut score or standard of proficiency is the end point in a long process beginning with job, work, or occupational analysis. It might start from cumulated qualitative, even anecdotal, information permitting judgments of what a certifiably proficient worker should be able to do.

The *predicted yield method* (Thorndike, 1949) was not intended for certification; its purpose was to set cut scores high enough to get good employees and low enough to get enough of them—illustrated above under cyclical hiring. It relies on forecasts of openings, probable applicant score distributions, planned retirements, transfers, promotions, and maybe prior data on natural turnover (i.e., that due to sickness, death, or changed family circumstances). Expected organizational and community changes also help. Cut scores based on such data need not be firm; as time goes by, an original cut score may be too high or too low to provide the predicted yield, or the predicted number of openings is too high or low, and adjustments may be needed.

Regression functions can provide cut scores empirically related to predicted criterion performance—logically, performance at or better than a level deemed acceptable, and usually better than minimally acceptable. Figure 11.5 shows once again four kinds of regression; unlike earlier figures, it shows their implications for cut scores. Panel (a) shows positive linear regression, and panel (b) shows positive logistic regression. Both are monotonic, and in either case, top-down selection is appropriate though the asymptotic logistic curve does

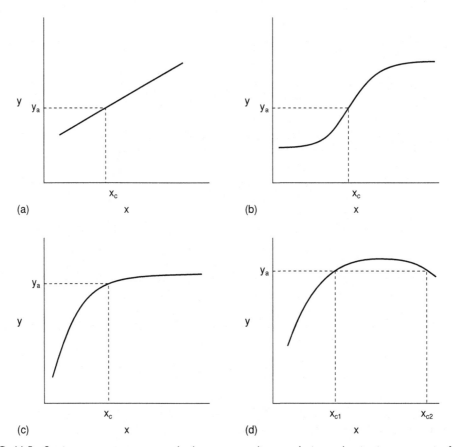

FIG. 11.5 Setting cut scores or standards corresponding to designated criterion scores in four different forms of regression.

not differentiate well at the highest score levels. Both permit easy fitting of a critical score or cut score corresponding to a designated criterion level deemed acceptable or desirable.[5]

Panel (c) is a positive monotone up to a point, after which the curve levels off and differences in X imply no differences in Y. Top-down selection makes no sense for scores above that point because there are no appreciable differences in Y. The leveling point on the regression curve could serve as a cut score if enough people scored above it to fill the positions. If that is too restrictive, a lower regression-based cut score could be developed as in panel (b).

Panel (d) (relatively rare) is nonmonotonic. The curve is positive up to a point, after which increases in X are associated with *decreases* in criterion performance. The acceptable level of criterion performance may have corresponding high level scores as well as low level; both low and high critical scores might be appropriate. It seems that such patterns are more likely with personality inventories or attitudes than with measures of cognitive skill.

[5] A critical score optimally distinguishes those whose predicted level of criterion performance is satisfactory (or acceptable, or superior) from those whose predicted performance is not (Society for Industrial and Organizational Psychology, 1987). A cut score is a decision point that may or may not be based on predicted performance.

In educational proficiency testing, early standards (cut scores with a nicer connotation) were typically based on *expert judgment* methods. Test performance is domain-referenced, and tests are used to certify prior achievement, not to predict future performance. Two major sources—a special issue of the *Journal of Educational Measurement* (Shepard, 1978) and a comprehensive chapter by Jaeger (1989)—provide much background information about educational standard setting. The two most common judgment methods are the *Nedelsky* and the *Angoff* procedures, two variations on a common theme. As described by Jaeger (1989), they require judgments by subject matter experts. With minor differences, the two methods lead to judgments, for each item in a test, of the probability that a *minimally competent* person will answer the item correctly. Both methods lead to score estimates for minimally competent people, and the mean of estimates from several judges can be the operational cut score.

Current Methods of Standard Setting

Many standard-setting procedures in large-scale educational proficiency testing incorporate IRT procedures. (For more, see Beretvas, 2004; Cisek, 2001; Mitzel et al., 2001; Plake & Hambleton, 2001; Wang, 2003). At least one approach is firmly attached to classical test theory (MacCann, 2008). I offer only a highly abbreviated preview of some newer methods in contemporary use.

The *bookmarking* method seems to be the most commonly used; Beretvas (2004), citing a paper presented by K. L. Egan, said that well over half of the states in the United States used the procedure to set standards for their state-wide exams. The method was described in detail by Mitzel et al. (2001), and my abbreviated description generally follows theirs—with some amendments for workplace instead of academic assessment.

The first step estimates item difficulty parameters of the IRCs and assembles a special booklet arranging items, one per page, in order of difficulty (perhaps in several relatively homogeneous content categories). Small groups of panelists then discuss KSAs needed to respond correctly and why the item under discussion is more difficult than the previous one. Panelists avoid discussing content, concentrating instead on requirements for item mastery. Individually, panelists put marks (*bookmarks*) between successive items to mark the difficulty level that, in their individual judgments, they consider a good line to draw between items requiring mastery and the easier items. Additional steps culminate in the total group of panelists (15–20 or more) discussing the bookmarks and finally setting the standard. Figure 11.6 illustrates the end point, a consensus placing the dividing line between the shaded items, group B, where mastery is expected, and the remaining unshaded items, group A, where mastery may be shown but is not uniformly expected. This procedure differs from the original Angoff method and its modifications in that difficulty is not judged but computed; and it uses expert judgments, but less cognitively complex, to indicate mastery as opposed to minimal competence.

For many certification assessments, assuming unidimensionality is not warranted; moreover, test developers increasingly call for constructed responses that can be constructed only after making some complex judgments. Although IRT methods continue to be developed for such responses, they are not yet ready for the prime time of mandated licensing and certification assessment.

A method not using IRT, the *analytic judgment procedure*, was discussed explicitly for complex constructed responses by Plake and Hambleton (2001). Before considering it, look at Figure 11.7; it shows score distributions on an old oral trade test for expert bricklayers,

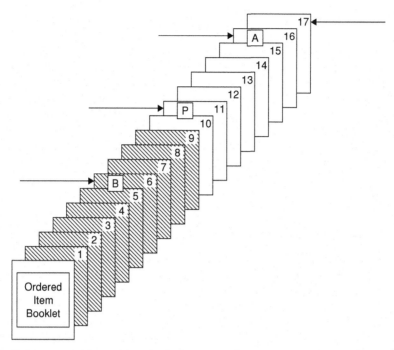

FIG. 11.6 Illustration of order item booklet for bookmark procedure in setting standards or cut scores. Reprinted from Mitzel, H. C., Lewis, D. M., Patz, R. J., and Green, D. R. (2001), The bookmark procedure: Psychological perspectives. In Cizek, G. J. (Ed.), *Setting Performance Standards* (pp. 249–281). Mahwah, NJ: Lawrence Erlbaum Associates. © 2001 by Taylor and Francis Group; reprinted by permission.

apprentices and helpers, and people who do related work (Osborne, 1940). So far as I know, systematic oral trade tests have not been used for years; I mention them because they were evaluated by comparing distributions in three columns representing different levels of competence (i.e., knowledge gained in different competence levels). So it is with proficiency testing as described by Plake and Hambleton. Proficiency is not a simple dichotomy. Some people are competent enough for routine work, others have a level of proficiency clearly above minimal requirements, and some are such genuine experts that they are especially admired by those with enough proficiency to recognize their superiority.

The analytic judgment method they advocated is both an expanded concept of proficiency and a different way to get and to use expert judgment. First, for a given item (a question or task), a set of responses is chosen, pretty well sampling the entire range of quality. Working independently, subject matter experts judge each response and rate it on an a priori scale. In one field test, the scale levels were *novice*, *apprentice*, *proficient*, and *advanced*. Another rated responses as *below basic*, *basic*, *proficient*, and *advanced*. For each category, one of two or three levels could be chosen, making a scale of perhaps 12 graded judgment categories. After individual experts have made their judgments, small panels are convened to discuss them—not to achieve consensus but to compare reasons for the judgments, to analyze them as a group and perhaps to change perspectives in looking for the cues that will influence judgments on other items. As with bookmarking, much more can be said, but this may be enough to round out a view of the possibilities in setting sensible cut scores matching or defining proficiency standards.

FORM I

Score	Expert Bricklayers (n = 65)	Apprentices and Helpers (n = 25)	Related Workers (n = 35)
15	xx		
14	xxxxxxx		
13	xxxxxxxxxxxxxxx		
12	xxxxxxxxxxxxxxxxxxxx*		
11	xxxxxxxx	x	
10	xxxxx	xx	
9	xx		x
8	xx	x	
7		xx	
6		x	x
5		xxxxxx*	
4		xxxxx	x
3		xx	xxx
2		xx	xx
1		xxx	xxxxxxxxxxx*
0			xxxxxxxxxxxxxx

FIG. 11.7 Distributions of scores on one form of an oral trade test. Reprinted from Osborne, S. J. (1940). Oral trade questions. In Stead, W. H., and Shartle, C. L. (Eds.), *Occupational Counseling Techniques: Their Development and Application* (pp. 30–48). New York: American Book Company.

Competency Assessment

Much is said about competencies; many experts view complex competencies of one sort or another as more important than unitary traits; indeed, competencies are best described as mutually contributing *combinations* of KSAs with none overwhelming others (Landy & Conte, 2007, p. 109). Much less is said about methods for assessing them, although Funke and Schuler (1998) developed interactive, computer-aided videos for assessing social competence. Bartram (2005b) and other authors have emphasized competencies more as job performance or job analysis components than as predictors. That may be wise, but it leaves open the competency assessment problem. My personal view is that competency assessment is a certification procedure. The certification could be a dichotomy (the person does or does not achieve a standard or acceptable level of competency), but I think some graded categories are often preferable (e.g., highly competent, competent, or marginally competent). Either way, assessment of competency could be considered a specific form of credentialing, and MSAT might give competency assessment more precision and greater examinee acceptance than alternative procedures.

Sensory and Psychomotor Testing

Physical Abilities and Fitness

Performance may not be exclusively or primarily cognitive. Performance of some tasks, especially over extended time periods, may call for strength, muscular flexibility, stamina, or general fitness. Testing them may require standardized equipment and individual testing. Equipment needs may be simple, as described by Fleishman and Reilly (1992b), such as a simple step test to assess stamina. At the other extreme, stamina might be assessed using an electronically monitored treadmill with an accompanying electrocardiograph.

At many occupational levels, task performance, physical fitness, and health may be related. Task performance may be supported by physical abilities (e.g., stamina). Abilities may be supported by physiological systems (e.g., cardiorespiratory systems), but these may be impaired by poor health. For example, a person with emphysema suffers cardiorespiratory impairment, resulting loss of stamina, and difficulty in performing tasks requiring climbing stairs. Poor physical fitness can be a problem for both the person and the employer.

Testing for medical and physical problems should have higher priority than it gets, if for no other reason than protection from litigation. Under negligent hiring, an organization may be liable for hiring unhealthy or physically inept employees. It can be liable under ADA. Employees who hurt themselves in physically demanding jobs add to workers' compensation costs. Fatigue or clumsiness may cause errors or accidents and legal action from fellow employees, customers, or the general public. Rejected applicants may sue under civil rights laws and, of course, the testing must be carefully done to avoid applicant injury and legal action.

In considering the physical demands of a job, some perennial questions must be faced. A physically demanding task may not be performed often but, when it is, injury might result. Should employment decisions be based on the ability to perform that task? Workers may have little chance on the job to develop or maintain the necessary physical skill for infrequent tasks, but infrequency may give time for rest and recovery between occasions. Should the job be redesigned, with the rare but risky task assigned to another physically demanding job, or should such tasks be spread around? Perhaps there is no option. In police work, sometimes defined as boredom occasionally interrupted by panic, the need to meet unusual or unexpected physical demands is always present. Should physical fitness testing look at the job as a whole or at its maximum requirements? Should it be assessed periodically? How much loss of musculoskeletal flexibility, cardiovascular impairment, or hearing loss must be experienced before job performance or quality of life deteriorates? In medical examinations, answers to such questions are usually left to the judgment of the individual physician—but they are rarely validated. Fleishman (1988) offered a promising approach to systematizing such judgments. A guide to impairment evaluation published by the American Medical Association (1977) was tied to his scales for analyzing physical job demands; guides were developed for physicians' use to judge whether a candidate's impairment would prevent effective performance of specific tasks.

In many jobs, recurring personnel decisions about employees' here-and-now readiness to work are needed almost daily; for example, is this pilot fit to fly today? Is there an impairment that would make this construction worker's job especially dangerous today? Temporary proficiency impairments may be due to medication or drugs (including alcohol), fatigue, illness, or preoccupation with stress—whether work-related or not. Drug testing is widely used, but drug tests or tests for blood alcohol level or body temperature do not assess impairment. It may be more useful to use performance tests of the specific proficiencies required, or perhaps physiological measures of performance impairment.

Olian (1984) offered a unique suggestion to reduce health hazards: genetic testing for people expected to work in environments where they risk disorders stemming from specific hazards (e.g., hazardous chemicals); some people, genetically, may be at higher risk than others. Her suggestion deserves consideration; as Murphy's Law says, where something can go wrong, some day it will, and the possibility of harm to people especially sensitive to a given hazard is real. Maybe one reason why the suggestion is still unique, despite progress in genetic testing, is the justifiable paranoia felt in employing organizations when trying something not yet tested in court.

Sensory and Psychomotor Proficiencies

Work combines cognitive, muscular, sensory, and attitudinal components; a useful work sample might focus on the sensory component. Requisite here-and-now job performance may include sensory proficiency such as correct identification or distinctions of distant shapes, colors, musical pitch, or unseen but touched objects. Except for some classic studies (e.g., occupational vision; see Guion, 1965a; Tiffin, 1942), little research has addressed the assessment of sensory skill for personnel decisions. Fleishman and Reilly (1992b) identified assessment methods for a few sensory abilities; more importantly, perhaps, they identified some important skills (e.g., night vision) for which no existing measures had then been identified.

Psychomotor skills, especially dexterity and coordination, are more widely tested. Commercial psychomotor tests are available, but sometimes manipulations imitating those required on a job predict better. High skill levels in some sensory or psychomotor areas may compensate for deficiencies in others. Rehabilitation counselors tell about people lacking certain sensory (or motor) skills performing well on jobs many employers would have denied them. Hope for finding compensatory skills is based more on anecdotes than on research. General propositions about genuinely compensatory patterns are not available.

STANDARDIZED INVENTORIES

Inventories are usually self-report measures of interests, motivation, personality, or values. Developing standardized inventories uses the same principles used in test construction; like tests, inventories are scored by summing item scores, 0 or 1 for dichotomous response options. Dichotomous responses may be true or false, yes or no, agree or disagree, keyed or not keyed, or some other pair of opposites. Unlike tests, responses are based on opinions or attitudes, and these responses are neither right nor wrong. Standardized inventories therefore may spread out response options using rating scales of three or more levels (e.g., agree, uncertain, disagree, or maybe a numerical rating scale anchored at the ends by the polar opposites). Item scores for these responses may start at zero for one end of the scale and be higher at each succeeding scale level.

Inventories often provide scores for several constructs; items for different constructs may be mixed throughout a total set to make assessment of the different traits less obvious. Test and inventory scores are typically interpreted *normatively* as a standard score or percentile rank within a norm group. *Ipsatively*, a person's score on one dimension is compared to that person's scores on other dimensions (Cattell, 1944). In ability testing, ipsative interpretations identify relative strengths and weaknesses; the interpretation in inventories is analogous. It may not be optimal in predicting turnover, for example, to identify an applicant's strong need for security; the strength of that need relative to the applicant's other needs (e.g., for prestige or self-actualization) may be more useful.

A classic article by Hughes and Dodd (1961) reported a case where ipsative scoring was valid and normative scoring was not. Normative scoring reflected a stereotyped view of sales people as highly sociable. However, these people sold computer systems; to make a sale, they had to learn a customer's problem and devise a computer system to fit it. Ipsative scoring showed the sociability scale on the Gordon Personal Profile to be negatively related to job performance.

Ipsative scoring is rare, partly because of statistical problems in using it. Most statistical analyses require variables to be independent; ipsative scales are not independent, so they don't meet the assumptions of multiple regression. Moreover, scores to be compared must be on a common scale. If all scales in an inventory are based on the same measurement specifications, ipsative scores are comparable. Scales from different instruments, developed at different times with different people and different specifications, can have a common metric only using a normative standard score scale, a procedure that confounds normative and ipsative measurement.

Basic Item Types

Item types listed in Figure 11.1 are also useful in standardized inventories. One type common in inventories but not in tests (and not in Figure 11.1) is the checklist. Candidates may be asked to check words or phrases in a list (items) that are self-descriptive, and items may tap several traits, interspersed to avoid making the categories obvious.

Scaled, or *graded*, responses with three or more categories in an ordinal sequence are also common. The Minnesota Multiphasic Personality Inventory (MMPI)—with response options of "true," "false," and "cannot say"—may be the oldest still in use. Such a scale is essentially a dichotomy with an escape clause. A middle category such as *cannot say* or *no opinion* "functions differently for different groups of people" (Hernandez, Drasgow, & Gonzales-Roma, 2004, p. 697). Most response scales have five or seven scale points, such as the five-point scale shown in Figure 11.1. However, an even number of scale points avoids the ambiguous middle-of-the-scale problems.

Forced-choice instruments: Multidimensional inventories may group multiple response options, each reflecting a different construct. A common form assembles a group of four phrases (or words or sentences); the examinee may choose one of them as the most (and another as least) like him or her. These are ipsative in that they force the respondent to compare traits for self description.

Problems in Inventory Measurement or Assessment

The accuracy of self descriptions can be questioned. When applying for a job, people like to make a good impression. Sometimes they are not very truthful in describing themselves, deliberately faking to make a favorable impression. Sometimes more general habits cause unintended distortions in self descriptions. Sometimes people lack real insight into their own behavior—or repress it. It is a perennial topic in personnel testing, but its importance may not match the ink, time, and space devoted to it.

Faking and Other Response Distortions

A response set (also called *response style* or *response bias*) is a tendency to follow a particular habit in responding to inventory items. A relevant example is known as a *social desirability response set*, the tendency to say things one thinks others want to hear, or to describe oneself in positive terms—in short, the tendency to try to look good to other people. Candidates for a job usually want the job; they are motivated to present themselves favorably during interviews, when taking tests, or when completing inventories. That tendency can slip into intentionally false responses deemed desirable, and is known as *faking*.

Faking has been a special concern in assessing job candidate personality traits. An applicant for a position requiring alertness, even someone with distinct Walter Mitty tendencies, is likely to say "no" if asked, "Do you daydream frequently?" An applicant for a sales position is unlikely to say "yes" to the question "Do you dislike talking to other people?" These are *response distortions*, not necessarily deliberate. Related terms include *image enhancement* and *self-deceptive enhancement*. A nicer term, and one with much broader organizational implications, is *impression management* (cf. Smith & Robie, 2004). These terms, along with social desirability and faking, are different conceptually but hard to distinguish empirically; that may be why they are often all grouped together as *faking*.

Faking deserves its own definition: "We define faking as a deliberate attempt to match one's own personality profile to one's perception of what management sees as the ideal personality for a specific job" (Martin, Bowen, & Hunt, 2002, p. 248). Many researchers try to determine inventory fakability but use an approach that violates that definition. The familiar method uses two groups of research subjects; one group is told to answer honestly and the other group is to give answers that make them look good. Often, but not uniformly, the mean scores are different in the groups. This procedure does not reflect a specific job or a perception of a personality ideal for incumbents in that job. Martin et al. designed research to fit their definition better: (a) to fake for a specific job (junior manager), (b) to specify the research participant's (a student's) ideal personality profile for that job, (c) to compare that ideal profile to the profile of importance ratings provided by managers actually supervising junior managers, and (d) to compare normative and ipsative versions of the questionnaire for response distortion. Substantial agreement was found between the students' and the managers' profiles of personality requirements for the job. Results showed that the students could change self descriptions to come closer to their perceptions of the ideal personality for the job—but only when using the normative form of the questionnaire, not when using the ipsative form. The Martin et al. findings follow others in showing that ipsative formats tend to reduce faking.

A meta-analysis of 33 studies compared scores of people applying for jobs and scores of non-applicants on Big Five traits (Birkeland, Manson, Kisamore, Brannick, & Smith, 2006). Except for agreeableness, the mean score of applicants was significantly higher than that of nonapplicants, especially on conscientiousness and emotional stability. Rank orders of mean differences varied across jobs, leading these researchers to the unsurprising conclusion that response distortion is more likely or greater on personality dimensions seen as especially relevant to the job sought.

Some inventories have special scales to try to detect faking. The MMPI has a "Lie Scale." Hough (1998) and Hough and Tippins (1994) developed a detection scale they called "Unlikely Virtues." With high scores on a faking scale, and maybe very low ones as well, one loses confidence in inferences drawn from personality scores, so such distortion detection scales may identify examinees who make questionable responses. Such faking scales sometimes are said to call for score adjustments on the trait scales, but these adjustments rarely improve prediction of job performance. However, a simple warning that faking can be identified, and that consequences follow, may be enough to reduce distortion in responding (Dwight & Donovan, 2003).

If a candidate understands the demands of a job well enough to fake appropriately, on-the-job behavior may be appropriate, even if behavior away from work is different. I am more concerned about the people who conscientiously avoid faking their responses and can be penalized for honesty (see, e.g., Rothe, 1950, and arguments by Dwight & Donovan, 2003). Faking is, after all, only one of several kinds of social desirability response set; nine social desirability factors were identified among the 42 Edwards Personal Preference Schedule items (Messick, 1960). At least some of these, unlike intentional faking, are probably inadvertent.

Acquiescence

The tendency to accept or agree with an item regardless of what it says, the *acquiescent response set*, has been well documented (e.g. Jackson & Messick, 1958). Suppose a set of positively stated inventory items were rewritten in a second form as negatively worded statements. Responses to the positive and negative forms should logically be negatively correlated. Agreement with any positively worded item should ordinarily predict disagreement when the item is reversed and worded negatively; for example, when the positively worded item is "I like my job" and its negatively worded counterpart is "I do not like my job." A person who says yes to the first statement is generally expected to say no to the second. However, for many inventories, such reversals of item content often result in the same responses for both and, over several items and several people, the correlation of scores is positive, not negative. That is, no matter whether the item is worded in one direction or its opposite, people tend to respond in the same way—to acquiesce, however it is worded. This response set is not deliberate distortion, but it can lower the psychometric validity of the resulting scores.

Response Set and Predictive Validity

If response sets distort scores of enough people, the contaminating variance lowers psychometric validity, but may not affect prediction. Ruch and Ruch (1967) offered two explanations for the moderate predictive validities of self-report inventories: they work either *despite* their fakability or *because* of it. Their research supported the latter; uncorrected MMPI scores valid for predicting sales success were less valid when the K scale for detecting faking was applied. The widely-used Gordon Personal Inventory (GPI), ordinarily measuring four personality traits in a forced-choice format, was used by Kreidt and Dawson (1961) and scored as simply the number of favorable self descriptions regardless of the trait scale. It correlated .47 with performance ratings; trait scales did not predict ratings, even when the total score (used as a measure of social desirability) was partialed out. These findings did not say that the GPI is not a useful predictor; it may be useful precisely *because* it measures recognition of the most desirable choices, or perhaps because it functioned as a measure of self-esteem.

We tend to think of response sets as psychometric nuisances. A more appropriate view may consider them characteristic "styles" or modes of behavior with wide influence—behavioral consistencies that integrate and control other behavior. Understanding such stylistic tendencies, in work as well as in tests and inventories, should be a high research priority. Unfortunately, interest in such research seems to have waned without having reached clear conclusions.

Advances in Assessment Methods

In addition to various forms of printed inventory, personality assessment has included structured interviews (Van Iddekinge, Raymark, & Roth, 2005), reference checks (Taylor,

Pajo, Cheung, & Stringfield, 2004), and a variety of tools from modern technology. The variety of constructs beyond the Big Five is burgeoning (e.g., Berry, Ones, & Sackett, 2007). Even more changes are on the way. I've chosen to describe briefly three new forms of assessment, each chosen for a different reason, to illustrate opportunities for change.

Conditional Reasoning in Indirect Assessment

Indirect assessment is inferring an intended construct from an apparent measure of something else. My all-time favorite example is the Michigan Vocabulary Profile test, measuring vocabulary levels in eight relatively independent kinds of activities. It was used, however, as an interest inventory, based on the assumption that people acquire better vocabularies in the fields in which they have special interest. Considering the many response distortions plausible in self-reports, indirect measurement seems actually to be more objective, but it has a history of unfulfilled promise.

James (1998), James, McIntyre, Glisson, Bowler, and Mitchell (2004), and James et al. (2005) developed another indirect method for measuring personality constructs (first for achievement motivation and later for aggressive tendencies) called the conditional reasoning approach—conditional in that the solution to a reasoning problem may depend on one's motives or biases. The 2004 and 2005 articles reported a *Conditional Reasoning Test for Aggression* (CRT-A). Test development was based in part on six justification mechanisms, or biases, abbreviated in Table 11.1, and the variety of rationalizations they support. These mechanisms were derived from research and theory on aggression; the source literature is more fully described and referenced in James et al. (2005). Multiple-choice items were developed, each with a two-part stem and four response options. The stem first describes a situation or state of affairs and then asks a question about it (e.g., *how can this be explained?*, or *what is an appropriate action?*). One of the four options is reasonable only if one or more of the six biases contributes to it, and it is scored +1. A different option is reasonable

TABLE 11.1
Aggression Justification Biases

1. *Hostile attribution bias:* A strong tendency to attribute behavior of others to malevolence and harmful intent, central to rationalizing one's own hostile verbal or physical behaviors as acts of self-defense.

2. *Potency bias:* The perception that interpersonal interactions are contests to determine dominance and submissiveness, reasoning that aggressive dominance acts show virtues like strength, daring, or fearlessness and that nonaggressive behavior shows weakness, cowardice, or impotence.

3. *Retribution bias:* A tendency to consider retaliation as more rational than reconciliation, stimulated by disrespect, challenges to self-esteem, or loss of pride.

4. *Victimization by powerful others bias:* A view based on the assumption that powerful people will do things that harm those less powerful.

5. *Derogation of target bias:* An implicit tendency to attribute bad or untrustworthy characteristics to an intended target of aggression.

6. *Social discounting bias:* Cynical reasoning about social events based on disdain for tradition or convention such that aggressive behavior can be justified as a release from the stifling effects of social custom.

Abridged from Table 1 in James, L. R., McIntyre, M. D., Glisson, C. A., Green, P. D., Patton, T. W., LeBreton, J. M., et al. (2005), A conditional reasoning measure for aggression, *Organizational Research Methods, 8*, 69–99. © 2005 Sage, abridged by permission of SAGE publications.

without a justifying bias, scored −1; the other two are illogical and scored 0. Just as the Michigan test measured actual vocabulary level from which interest level could be inferred, so the CRTs actually must measure logical reasoning; the division of two logical and two illogical response items is therefore necessary. If one logical option (but not the other) depends on a justifying bias, and if an examinee chooses a lot of +1 options and has a high score, it is sensible to infer that biases justifying aggression "are instrumental in shaping their reasoning" (James et al., 2005, p. 78).

The fakability of the CRT-A was examined in three studies reported by LeBreton, Barksdale, Robin, and James (2007). The first of these demonstrated the value of indirect assessment by showing an effect on group mean differences when the intended inferences were disclosed. The other two studies were more traditional (although well designed), using both student samples and job applicants or job incumbents. No significant group mean differences occurred under standard instructions (i.e., without disclosure of the intended inferences).

In its history, indirect measurement has been charged as being deceitful. Maybe an element of deceit exists in the CRT-A. In my own view, the failure to disclose purpose fully is trumped by the growing need to curb workplace violence. I cannot say, at this time, that CRT is the best way to go, but it certainly deserves attention.

Scale Development for International Personality Assessment

Globalization requires assessment systems that cross cultural and national boundaries. The challenge of personality assessment, even within a single country, seems far more daunting than the challenge of mental ability assessment. It seems overwhelmingly more daunting if the assessment is international in scope.

Yet it is done. Most often, it is done by translating a test or inventory that works well in a home country into the language of a different country. The practice is beset by a host of psychometric problems, not the least of which is translating a key word into a language that has no word with precisely the same connotations. Nevertheless, several widely used English-language personality inventories have been translated successfully into a variety of other languages. These successes were acknowledged by Schmit, Kihm, and Robie (2000, p. 154), who also argued that such translations, done one language at a time, often result in scores with no clear interpretation. Schmit et al. developed the Global Personality Inventory,[6] with international collaboration in the various stages of inventory development. Perhaps personality assessment for international use is less daunting if done globally from the outset.

Personnel Decisions International (PDI), with which the Schmit et al. were identified, wanted a personality assessment procedure for use in its offices around the world, both for individual comparisons and cross-cultural research. It was to measure a common set of constructs in different venues world-wide. The procedure was intended for use at middle management and executive levels. Development of the inventory began with the assembly of an international group of 10 development teams, each consisting of PDI psychologists and some university researchers; team members represented 14 different home countries.

---

[6] "Global" as in "worldwide," not as the word is used to imply generality of content, as in "global intelligence tests."

At the outset, each team searched relevant literature, drew inferences, discussed those inferences, and reached agreement on two principles. First, the five-factor model would be the organizing theory for lower order (i.e., more narrowly specific) facets of the five more inclusive personality traits. Second, the job performance model would consist of core performance factors (cf. Campbell et al., 1993). Team members were then instructed to create items in their own languages, translate them into English, and go through several checks of the translations. After several rounds of discussion and item development, an initial (alpha) form of the inventory consisted of 32 trait scales (facets of the Big Five) and seven syndrome scales as trait composites (i.e., combinations of two or more facet traits), with 13 items for each scale.

Data for evaluation (validation and more) were collected in worldwide samples; within cultures, people were tested at as many different work levels as possible, with over-representation at middle management and executive levels. Major analyses were conducted with samples from the United States, Spain, and China because these were the largest samples. Classical item analysis first dropped three items from each scale so that all had 10 items. For the remainder, an IRT graded response model provided item parameter estimates and test information functions. DIF and DTF analyses gave evidence supporting the use of the same GPI items and scales across cultures. Other analyses were done, but this is enough to show that (a) organizations with the resources to do so can in fact develop instruments for personality assessment to use in diverse countries and cultures, (b) modern psychometric theory, explicitly IRT, is important to the evaluation of these instruments, and (c) such an instrument can be versatile enough to use for a variety of performance criteria in work at a variety of organizational levels.

Computerized Adaptive Personality Assessment

CAT is not limited to cognitive assessment. Walter Borman and his associates have applied it to performance rating (discussed in Chapter 13) and to personality assessment for the United States Navy, described here. The *Navy Computer Adaptive Personality Scales* (NCAPS) were developed to augment, potentially, the cognitive *Armed Services Vocational Aptitude Battery* (ASVAB). The computerized NCAPS measure the following traits: Achievement, Social Orientation, Stress Tolerance, Adaptability/Flexibility, Attention to Detail, Dependability, Dutifulness/Integrity, Self-Reliance, Willingness to Learn, Vigilance, Leadership Orientation, Perceptiveness/Depth of Thought, and Self-Control/Impulsivity (Schneider et al., 2006). These are more specific than the Big Five (e.g., Hofstee et al., 1992) and are intended to predict relatively specific performance criteria.

The NCAPS approach is unusual, assessing personality traits rather than cognitive traits, usually the focus of CAT methods. It is unusual as a personality inventory in being multidimensional as a whole with independent, essentially unidimensional scales. Most of all, it is unusual in its eclectic combination of judgment, traditional statistical tools, and modern measurement methods. For example, trait levels tapped by individual items were determined by expert judgment, not by IRCs or confirmatory factor analysis (CFA). Traditional analyses were done, including conventional reliability estimates, factor analysis, and correlational studies, for evidence of construct validities, but test information functions were maximized in pairs of statements presented for forced-choice responses.

The latter needs some explanation. The broad outline of the plan was to develop independent trait assessments using self-report items tapping different levels of the traits, pairing items, and instructing examinees to pick the one statement (item) considered the better self-description. To carry out the plan, trial items were written, independently, by research team members, each writing items targeted for high, medium, and low levels of the traits. When the initial items (the unpaired statements) were written, 25 experts in personality research rated the level of the trait represented if the statement were reported to be self-descriptive. Even experts can go astray, so both correlational and Euclidean distance statistics were used to compare ratings of each individual expert with the mean ratings of the rest of the group. Three raters gave substantially different patterns and levels of ratings, so their data were dropped from further analyses.

Using pre-planned statistical criteria, analysis of the remaining ratings flagged nearly a quarter of the pool for further judgment. Some of these were kept "as is," some were rewritten to be used in a second round of item writing and evaluation, and some were discarded, all on the basis of the judgments of research team members. First-round analysis had shown that more items were needed at the middle trait levels (virtually always true); these were written and included in the second round. Both judgmental and statistical data led to a set of items for pilot studies, which included factor analysis, to assure that items fit the intended traits, and correlations with marker items as a first approach to evaluating construct validities.

The computerized version, intended for operational use, used forced-choice pairs of statements. A traditional, paper-and-pencil format was developed for comparison. For this version, each statement was an independent item; responses to these items were made on a five-point scale ranging from *strongly agree* to *strongly disagree*; scoring considered both the rated trait level of the statement and the level of the response option chosen.

As said before, this is a work in progress. Results so far with the computer adaptive version were deemed promising. Some statistical analyses suggested that the traditional version and the CAT version had similar reliabilities and correlations with selected marker variables, but the CAT version, with only 10 item pairs per scale, is much faster to administer and, in a small sample ($N = 95$), validities against supervisor ratings were in the mid to high .30s, twice as large as the validities of the traditional format. Also, standard errors of measurement were low, test information was high, and both were consistent throughout the trait ranges. Again, this is research deserving to be replicated and extended.

CONCLUDING NOTE

Standardized testing, including standardized inventories, has worked well over the years, but efforts continue to be made to improve it—as shown in this chapter and in much of the previous one. Like Chapter 10, and Chapter 12 to follow, this chapter is part of a transition from the emphasis in the early chapters on research methods, contexts, and theories for assessment and assessment-based decisions. In these transitional chapters, the emphasis moves a bit toward in-house or local assessment practices while still noting the advances researchers are making in large-scale applications. For example, test development was described, not as a process accessible only to researchers armed with the latest theory and statistical methodology, but as a practical tool for those in organizations where they must sometimes develop their own tests for their own special purposes.

By this time, I hope it is clear that valid assessment and its use on personnel decision making does not need to be a mechanistic, robotic procedure driven by the numbers. Judgment is involved throughout the process, starting with forming an understanding of the work to be done through job analysis. It is involved in developing a predictive hypothesis considering both the organizationally needed behavior or outcome worth predicting and the personal attributes that might predict it. It is involved in choosing or developing an assessment method. It is certainly involved in making actual personnel decisions. An emphasis on judgment and decision making, both as research areas and as components of professional practice, continues the transition in the next chapter. Further chapters describe approaches to assessment that rely especially heavily on human judgment, such as ratings of performance or products, interviewing, and group and individual multiple assessment procedures.

12

Judgment in Assessment and Prediction

Judgment is always a necessary part of a personnel decision. Judgments begin to form, even in the most casual decision procedure, in the first moments of reading applications from candidates or seeing them face to face. More formally, judgments are made, perhaps with a checklist as an aid, at the end of an interview—although usually earlier. Judgments are involved in job analyses, in forming predictive hypotheses (whether impulsively or systematically), in evaluating research information and the inferences based on it, and on every other part of the process leading to a decision. Some judgments are in fact the predictors, often recorded as ratings; they are as subject to evaluation (validation) as tests or any other sort of assessment.

Predictions, even those statistically based, are judgments. Procedural decisions about the research for a statistical basis are based on professional judgments, such as how desired qualifications might be assessed or how to evaluate and use the assessments, and ideally these decisions are made by researchers. Actual personnel decisions, however, are usually made by managers in less than ideal circumstances. For example, nothing is ideal when considering unique candidates. Statistical models for prediction are very useful—"on the average," or "as a rule"—but unique candidates are neither average nor good fits to a general rule. Traditional models for evaluating assessments or predictions statistical are nomothetic, applicable to people in general. A unique candidate (e.g., think of accommodation under ADA) may not fit a particular nomothetic generalization, even a well-supported one, and judgment is important in deciding what to do. Judgments themselves may be predictors, presenting special problems for validation; different people making judgments can reach different, even conflicting, conclusions from the same data. Are judgments of some people more valid, as measures of traits or as predictors, than those of others? Can reasons for differences be identified?

Cognitive psychology has long been interested in the way people make judgments, in how wisely the judgments are made, and how they can be integrated in choices or decisions. Personnel psychology has been slow to adopt the resulting judgment and decision theory. It is happening, and it needs to acquire a more nearly central place in thinking about personnel decisions. Judgments and decisions are rarely as rational as people think they are or wish they were. Many kinds of flaws in reaching them have been found experimentally. Nevertheless, judgment aids, good information, and experience in decision making can improve them.

Collaboration by managers and researchers can lead to better bases for judgment, better judgment processes, and wiser decisions. The meaning of "wise" decisions can be clarified by a useful heuristic treating four words as forming a hierarchical continuum.[1] At its base

---

[1] Thanks to Frank Landy (personal communication, February 16, 1996) for this continuum.

is *data*, such as scores or correlation coefficients. A step higher is *information*, an integration and interpretation of data. Another step is *knowledge*, an integration of the information at hand with other information stored from prior experience. At the top is *wisdom*, where perhaps disparate sorts of data, information, and knowledge—and experience—are integrated in making decisions. Researchers and HR specialists should not merely pump data—assessment scores —to decision-making managers; they should make sure that the assessments are informative and fit into a broader scheme of managerial knowledge about people, jobs, the organization, and the position at hand—a point also made by Schneider (1996).

JUDGMENT AND DECISION MAKING

These two terms, judgment and decision making, often appear together. *Judgment* is the cognitive portion of the process culminating in *decisions*, choices between options. Under this joint heading, we will briefly consider some of the research findings under either heading. Some of it is field research, but most of it has been done in the labs of cognitive psychologists. A major distinction between the two is that laboratory research, being better controlled, can give insight into what is possible. Much research was initially devoted to studying decision theory as developed by economists, whose view of a good decision was that it maximized gains and minimized losses—in short, that it was the decision that would be made by a rational person. Psychological research rather quickly cast doubt on the degree to which people were rational in making decisions.

Beach and Connolly (2005) said that psychological decision theorists and organizational theorists see the world differently. The latter see the organization as the unit of interest, as if the organization makes decisions. The former emphasizes individuals, often ignoring the context, and treating the organization's decisions as collaboration by individuals. We need to recognize both individual and collaborative decision making in making major decisions.

The Pioneering Work of Herbert Simon

Herbert Simon, a psychologist who was a Nobel laureate in economics, saw early that people do *not* try to maximize gains and minimize losses when they make decisions. Particularly for personnel decisions, his writings have contributed two still-influential ideas (e.g., Simon, 1979). *Bounded rationality* continued focus on the "rational person" but added that rationality in decision making has boundaries, reducing information by limiting it to factors that represent "only the most salient information" and basing decisions on these "representations" (Beach & Connolly, 2005, p. 10).

Satisficing, the better known of the two, assumes that a decision maker has an idea, whether fully articulated or not, of a set of standards to be met by any option the decider might choose—standards that must be met if the option is to be minimally satisfactory. The first option considered that meets these standards is chosen. This is not a fully rational decision; other options not yet considered might be much better; rationally, the "satisficing" option may not be the best possible option. Rationality is "bounded" in part by the fullness and clarity of the standards and by the sequence in which options are considered.

Simon was describing in these terms what decision makers do, not prescribing what they should do, in reaching their decisions. Unfortunately, however, many people tend to think of them as prescriptive. Satisficing may describe—and may prescribe—what leaders should do in an emergency, but most decisions should be made before organizational issues become emergencies. Critical non-emergency situations usually deserve the time it takes to consider, if not all possible options, at least an array of possibilities and choose the best among those considered. For some kinds of personnel decisions, such as choosing one candidate among several for a very responsible position, satisficing seems a poor approach to decision making.

Some Generalizations from Cognitive Research

Largely because of Simon's work, but also because of psychology's increased interest in cognition, research on judgment and decision making jumped during the last third of the twentieth century. A few of the generalizations that can be drawn from that research are as follows.

1. People facing many options tend to use decision strategies that differ from those used with only a few options. For example, they are likely to use noncompensatory strategies if there are many but compensatory strategies if options are few.
2. Rank orders given to the options change as situational contexts change, that is, preference reversals can occur because of things other than attributes of the alternatives. Highhouse (1997) illustrated this change in the rank order of job finalists when the context included those he called "decoys" (candidates with little or no likelihood of being chosen) or those called "phantoms"—the fish that got away—who change the reference points for considering those who remain.
3. If a choice entails some kind of loss for the organization or decision maker, that loss looms larger in the judgments made than do the gains the same choice implies.
4. When one option is better than the others in all considered attributes, the choice is easy. Otherwise, cognitive conflicts arise. The effect of such conflict is to delay choice even if settling for poorer overall quality of the choices actually made. Deferring the choice is more likely with a lot of conflict than with mild conflict.
5. People tend to see a combination of specific statements, events, or outcomes as more likely than any one of them alone; that is, decision makers (whether experts or novices in a professional field) are more likely to choose options that include a lot of detail over those that appear to be less informative. "Decision makers are seemingly compelled to choose options that provide more specific detail" (Highhouse, 1997, p. 457).
6. Decisions, rationally, should be based only on relevant information, but in fact decision makers often fail to ignore irrelevant information and allow it to influence decisions.

Heuristics and Biases

Heuristics are simplifications, or rules of thumb, offering paths to decision that may save time but often cause serious errors in judgment. Such paths may be deliberately chosen or used with full awareness of what one is doing, but deciders may be unaware that they determine the path of the decisions being made. Bazerman (2006) identified three major categories of heuristics. One is *cognitive availability*. What is easily remembered, or imagined, and fairly specific is most likely to influence judgments of the probability or frequency of encountering a particular instance of it. The salience and ease of a memory or image, even if irrelevant to the judgment to be made, can cause judgment error. Some writers refer to this as a *recognition* heuristic, emphasizing that it relies "on an extensive knowledge base to make judgments about situations and decide how to act" (Phillips, Klein, & Sieck, 2004, p. 303). *Representativeness*, another heuristic category, refers to the degree to which a person to be judged in terms of likely performance is thought to be representative of a broader group of people who have been generally good, marginal, or poor performers. This can sometimes be helpful, but it can lead to serious error, even actionable discrimination, if the person is assumed to be representative of the wrong group or a group improperly perceived as performing poorly. Finally, the *affect* heuristic means that judgments and decisions are often based substantially on emotional reactions or biases that preclude cognitive sorting of information (as in "I don't like this guy, so he can't be any good on this job").

Continued use of these heuristics can lead to mindsets that systematically bias judgments across situations. Bazerman (2006, pp. 18–40) offered a list of 13 such biases (others could have been named) that are commonly encountered sources of judgment error. Examples include presumptions of stereotypical associations of events occurring together, failure to consider base rates for events occurring, the "conjunction fallacy" (example 5 in the list of generalizations above), anchoring (e.g., letting a first impression of someone influence judgments about that person at some later time), and "the confirmation trap" in which judges tend to note information that fits a preconceived notion of a rule or potential outcome—and to ignore information that does not. Another bias, self-perceived objectivity, is a mindset—a belief in one's own objectivity in observation—that leads one to believe that "I think it, therefore it's true" (Uhlmann & Cohen, 2007, title).

RATIONALITY, INTUITION, AND COMMON SENSE

The obstacles to good decisions discovered in decision theory research seem pretty grim; more ways seem to be used to make irrational judgments, choices, or decisions than to make rational ones. But cheer up. Irrationality does not have to be the norm.

> For reasons yet to be discovered by historians, the normative models (usually some form of expected utility theory) acquired the status of standards of rationality, and deviations from what was prescribed by these models was seen as evidence that man was an irrational decision maker. While there is no dearth of examples of less-than-perfect decisions even in high places where experienced decision makers operate, the state of the world nevertheless does not seem to be quite as bad as one would expect from the hypothesis that people are incompetent and irrational decision makers. (Brehmer, 1999, p. 9)

Consider also the words of Doherty and Balzer, who joined with others who have

> decried the tendency of psychologists to study what might be called 'Man the Intuitive Barbarian.' That is, in spite of the fact that human beings are tool-users *par excellence*, cognitive psychologists typically study people in situations in which they are not permitted to use those tools for thought normally used in everyday commerce with the environment. (Doherty & Balzer, 1988, p. 164)

They went on to decry, albeit more grimly, the "nomothetic bias" of much judgment research—a bias for seeking generalizations applicable to "people in general"; they called for a more idiographic approach; that is, more attention to individual differences.

In short, the situation in judgment and decision research is not currently as bleak as it was a few years ago. Gigerenzer (2004) considered heuristics to be essential to rational judgment—rationality with boundaries, to be sure, but rational nevertheless.

The Cognitive Continuum

If a rational decision is one that maximizes gain and minimizes loss, it is true that rational decisions are hard to come by. Some decisions (I think many of those made by responsible leaders of organizations) are at least somewhat rational—one might say *quasirational*. In fact, that is precisely what Hammond (1996), borrowing a Brunswikian term, called them in articles and reports dating back to the 1970s describing a *cognitive continuum theory*. It is a unified theory based on five premises which, taking liberty, I describe pretty much in my own terms as follows.

1. Treating rational or (a better term) analytic and intuitional thought as two sides of a dichotomy is false; it should be replaced by treating them as opposite ends of a continuum.
2. Between the extremes of the continuum lie varying mixtures of analysis and intuition that permit research on common sense, known also as quasirational thought.
3. Properties of a cognitive task induce matching cognitive activity. That is, to the extent task properties induce analysis, analytic reasoning will be applied and the cognitive judgments or decisions will approach the analytic end of the cognitive continuum; tasks that induce imagination and intuition lead to cognitive activity closer to the intuitive end. Figure 12.1 is based on these first three premises. The task and cognitive continua will ordinarily be less precisely matched, but different cognitive tasks seem to call for different mixtures of the two varieties of cognitive action.
4. Cognitive activity is changing, not static, so over time it will change its location on the cognitive continuum. Acknowledging that little is known about specific changes and their sources, "The theory asserts . . . that successful cognition inhibits movement; failure stimulates it. The theory also asserts that when movement occurs, cognition oscillates between analysis and intuition" (Hammond, 1996, p. 201 in his summary,

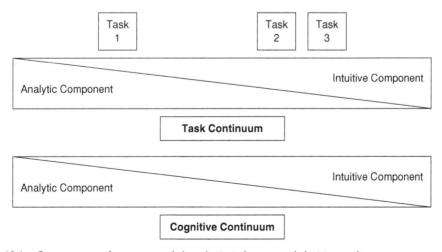

FIG. 12.1   Components of quasirational thought in judgment and decision tasks.

but see also pp. 195–196 for hypotheses about the role of time in a theory of judgment and decision making).

5. Human cognition can recognize patterns and use functional relations. This premise is a foundation for social judgment theory and the use of the lens model (described below), and it signifies some acceptance of the generally ignored concepts of Gestalt psychology.

Resist the temptation to assume that analytic processes are necessarily superior to intuitive ones. In their study of judgments of highway engineers, conducted to test the implications of the cognitive continuum theory, Hammond, Hamm, Grassia, and Pearson (1987) found that analytical cognition did not form a ceiling that achievement based on intuitive or quasirational processes could not exceed. Moreover, errors in judgment, as assessed by r_a, an achievement index, were far more variable in analytical cognition; that is, both the highest and lowest values of the achievement index occurred under analytical processing. The biggest errors are likely to occur with analytic processes. To me, the most important finding is that when task characteristics and cognitive characteristics are congruent (i.e., both the nature of the task and the person's approach favor either analytic or intuitive processes—the third premise in the list above), achievement is maximized. Adaptation to task demands seems to promote the best judgment.

Expert Judgment

Some decision tasks allow no time for analysis. Typically, these are emergency situations. Examples at work include those faced by people trained as emergency workers, but they happen in ordinary life as well: emergency actions while driving or when a family member is hurt. Decisions in such settings are not made by inert hand-wringing or by contemplation and evaluation of alternatives, nor are they purely intuitive. Successful actions often stem from the recognition of similarities in different situations. Recognition is one of the judgment heuristics and often has negative connotations, but it can lead to sensible decisions and actions, especially in the hands of experts. Experts tend to rely on their knowledge and ability to recognize situational similarities in a present situation and one encountered before so that they make *recognition-primed decisions* (Phillips et al., 2004). These are characteristic of emergency leaders such as captains of fire-fighting squads, who may have no time to consider all options. If a situation is seen as a common one, appropriate action decisions come from accumulated experience; if it is seen as somehow unique, the leader can quickly try to clarify the situation and draw diagnostic inferences triggering recognition of aspects of the situation.

In the fire-fighter example, among others, the expertise of the captain is not only professional expertise but decision-making expertise growing out of experience in making professional judgments. With this distinction in mind, Phillips et al. (2004) suggested some hypotheses about recognition-primed decisions. (a) Recognition strategies are more likely than analytical comparisons of options among expert decision makers regardless of the field of work. (b) The proportional use of recognition strategies increases with relevant decision-making experience. (c) For even moderately experienced decision makers, the first option for action developed is typically satisfactory—in both the decider's view of it and in the success of the action taken. (d) Options are more likely to evaluated by "mental simulation" (Phillips et al., 2004, p. 303) than by some received criteria of alternative options. (e) With experience, decision makers spend more of their decision time studying situations than comparing options.

These are still essentially untested hypotheses, and they do not permit quick or easy testing. It takes time to acquire the knowledge and experience needed to qualify as an expert in any field—far longer than typical laboratory studies—so longitudinal field research may be necessary. The mark of the expert is that their recognition-primed decisions typically work quite well and, typically, are shrugged off as "just common sense"—even if uncommon.

Judgments of Validity

Where data for statistical analysis are unavailable and unlikely to become available, expert quasirational judgment of *expected* validity coefficients is a feasible alternative. Validity, whether psychometric or relational, is always a matter of inference. Validity is always a judgment, inferred only if the preponderance of evidence supports the intended interpretation. A computed validity coefficient is accepted as evidence of valid prediction only if the data, the data collection, and the data analysis are judged adequate.

If local validation is not feasible, and no relevant meta-analysis exists, job-relatedness can be based on two sequential judgments in an option emphasizing psychometric validity. First, a trait must be judged prerequisite (or at least helpful) to performance of important aspects of the job—the predictive hypothesis. Second, assessment of that construct must be judged a valid measure of it (see American Educational Research Association, American Psychological Association, & National Council on Measurement in Education, 1999, Standard 14.12, p. 161). If logic and data support both judgments, the assessment is judged a valid predictor of performance of those job aspects; it is arguably a valid measure of a job-related trait. A brief reprise of the distinction between job-relatedness and psychometric validity, and slightly rephrased questions for evaluating them, may highlight the role of judgment. The first six items are from Chapter 5; the rest are from Chapters 1, 3, and 7 and Guion (1991):[2]

1. Did the developer of the procedure seem to have a clear idea of the attribute (construct) to be measured—at least a rudimentary theory of the attribute? Were the assessment methods consistent with that idea?
2. Is the stimulus content appropriate? Is the content domain unambiguous and relevant to the purpose? Was it properly sampled? Can responses be scored, observed, or evaluated reliably?
3. Was the assessment instrument developed carefully and skillfully? Were pilot studies and item analyses done, and done well?
4. Does the assessment domain reflect just one attribute, or is it heterogeneous? If the former, are items internally consistent? If the latter, was it well defined and sampled, with at least some internal consistency?
5. Are scores stable over time?
6. Are their relationships to other variables consistent with those expected from the theory of the attribute? Can alternative hypotheses about the meaning of the scores be ruled out?
7. Does the predictive hypothesis sensibly relate the attribute to job performance? Do job experts consider the attribute relevant? Does prior research suggest or demonstrate its relevance?

[2] The list is presented as a guide to serious thought, not as a checklist for routine use. I have presented such lists in several places, with the number of listed items deliberately varied (from 4 to 18!) in an attempt to discourage the checklist mentality.

8. Does a well-formed predictive hypothesis require other attributes of equal or nearly equal importance? If so, can the job relatedness of the attribute at hand be evaluated on its own?

9. Is there any reason to suspect a nonmonotonic relationship? If so, does any evidence suggest the points in the assessment distribution where the relationship changes from positive to zero to negative?

10. In prior research, have criteria been measured validly and predicted reliably? The question applies to both job-related and construct-related criteria; answers require judgments about the psychometric validity of the criterion, any possible contaminants, adequacy of research design, sample size and composition, and other considerations.

Some answers can be found in manuals or reports of local research. Some questions can be answered with data, if the data are judged adequate. If an overall judgment of job-relatedness is based on good reasons for favorable responses to most of the first nine questions, it is probably better than evidence based on a single, local, unreplicated, criterion-related validity study—unless the research implied in the tenth is based on favorable responses to the first nine.

Estimates of Criterion-Related Validity Coefficients

Criterion-related validity coefficients can be estimated by informed, expert judgments. Schmidt, Hunter, Croll, and McKenzie (1983) asked eminent personnel psychologists, chosen for experience and expertise in personnel selection, to make such judgments. The pooled judgments of such experts estimated population correlations nearly as accurately as validation studies with fairly large sample sizes. The experts were acknowledged leaders in the field of personnel selection. Not everyone with appropriate credentials has a similar level of expertise. Hirsh, Schmidt, and Hunter (1986) replicated the study using recent PhDs in industrial and organizational psychology. Compared to the more established experts, these judges substantially overestimated the coefficients, with a larger mean error, but their pooled estimates were about as accurate as those obtained from typical small-sample empirical studies.

These are important findings. They offer an alternative way to judge job-relatedness. I once called on experts to estimate criterion-related validity of a test that had been challenged in litigation. The case sort of dwindled away with no conclusion; although these estimates were never entered as evidence, they were shared and I like to think they may have been influential in the dwindling. We used two methods of estimation, one a direct estimate much like that in Schmidt et al. (1983), the other based on estimates of factor loadings. The latter method still has had no scientific test, but I think it can be useful when an estimated validity coefficient is needed and experts with the necessary qualifications are available.

To start, a panel of 15 experts was convened. All were highly experienced in personnel selection and as carefully chosen as those in the Schmidt et al. (1983) study. They examined detailed job descriptions, test items, and item analysis results. They then linked categories of KSAs to major job duties; linked test items both to job duties and to the KSAs; evaluated test content, scoring key, and probable psychometric properties of the items; and estimated the criterion-related validity coefficient. At each step, each panelist made and recorded his or her independent judgments; when all had done so, group discussion of them followed. In the final step of a detailed process, the panelists estimated the probable correlation coefficient that would have been obtained in a competent validation study if it had been feasible. The median of these direct estimates was .40.

Overall Job Performance	KSA Factor Category	Total Test Score
.30	A. Verbal Comprehension	.65 × .3 = .19
.30	B. Number Fluency	.30 × .3 = .09
.35	C. Perceptual Speed and Accuracy	.20 × .35 = .07
.20	D. General Reasoning, Judgment	.45 × .2 = .09
.30	E. Interpersonal Sensitivity	.05 × .3 = .02
		.46
0	F. Systematic Test Score Variance Unrelated to Criterion	.14
.47	G. Systematic Criterion Variance Unrelated to Test Scores	0

FIG. 12.2 A form for estimating validity coefficients by first estimating factor loadings.

A second estimate was based on the logic of factor analysis. A product–moment correlation coefficient is the sum of the products of the orthogonal common factor loadings in the two variables. If only one common factor contributes to variance on both variables, and it has a factor loading of .5 on one variable and .6 on the other, the product of the two loadings is .3, and so is the coefficient of correlation between them. Quantitative judgments about factors with loadings on both test and criterion can therefore give indirect estimates of validity coefficients.

Figure 12.2 shows a form for recording estimates of factor loadings and thus to obtain an indirect estimate of the validity coefficient.[3] It has been filled in as if by one of the expert judges. This hypothetical judge believed that performance on the overall job would tap all of the test factors to similar degrees and would systematically tap a set of other variance sources, none major, not included in the test (e.g., contextual criteria such as helpfulness to coworkers). The judge considered test variance to be due primarily to verbal comprehension and to judgment or general reasoning, with almost no variance due to interpersonal sensitivity. The arithmetic is shown in the margin; cross-products of factor loadings sum to .46, the judge's estimate of the criterion-related validity coefficient that might have been obtained had such a study been feasible.

Would this procedure add anything to the direct estimation procedure of Schmidt et al. (1983)? Perhaps not, when the experts are so carefully chosen. I suspect, however, that guesses about factor loadings may be more on the mark than guesses about validities when the experts know the factor analytic literature well but have less direct experience with employment test validation. If so, the pool of useful experts could be expanded.

Making Wise, or At Least Sensible, Decisions

People can usually take time to make their choices and decisions somewhat analytically. I'm not referring to obsessing interminably about them, but to taking time to consider one's

---

[3] Actually, this differs from what was done; it shows what *should* have been done in the panel's meeting. The form actually used omitted the estimates of unique variance in the criterion and in the test. Because these people were indeed expert, this omission resulted in their taking unique variance into account in different ways. The form given here is more like the one recommended by the panel after discussion.

options for a few hours or days or even longer. Problem situations, especially in organizational life, take time to develop, so it's often reasonable to allow a bit of time to decide what to do about them—to collect information, to organize one's ideas, or perhaps "to sleep on it." That time is well spent if the resulting decision is reasonably rational, realistic, and effective in outcome—in short, wise. "Choosing wisely is a *skill*, which like any other skill can be improved with experience" (Hastie & Dawes, 2001, p. 2, emphasis in original). Perhaps this is why Phillips et al. (2004), in their fifth hypothesis, suggested that experienced decision makers spend more time analyzing situations than looking for associations.

Hastie and Dawes (2001) described two main types of thought processes: *automatic* and *controlled*, not quite the same as the intuitive–analytic continuum. Automatic thought is illustrated by habits of thought or simple associations that lead at best to overgeneralization and at worst to superstitious behavior. Automatic thought is not necessarily negative; a student driver or student pilot, for example, has not really learned to drive or fly until several motor and cognitive processes become automatic. In this sense, the controlled thought of the novice becomes the automatic thought of the expert; choosing wisely is a skill stemming from experience, much of it repetitive.

Controlled thought is illustrated by clarity of perception, imagination, generation of ideas, or scenario building—the "what if?" game. If a desired outcome is getting accepted by a college of one's choice, the controlled thinker asks, "What if I do get accepted there?" and then considers possible outcomes. The controlled thinker is also realistic enough to ask, "What if I do *not* get accepted there? What other options do I have, and how do I expand the list and prepare for them?" He or she then actively seeks answers and takes actions appropriate to them, perhaps applying to other schools with different likely outcomes.

"Rational choice," according to Hastie & Dawes (2001, p. 18), meets four criteria: (a) it takes advantage of one's current strengths—physiological, psychological, social, and emotional —which may require realistic assessment of personal weaknesses; (b) it is based on recognition of various likely consequences of choices; (c) it evaluates uncertain consequences in probabilistic terms; and (d) it is adaptive and modifiable within the patterns of probabilities and within the values and satisfactions concomitant with possible consequences. "Don't we make all our decisions like that?" asked Hastie and Dawes, and they answered, "Decidedly not . . . We are affected not only by our present state but by *how we got to it*. The past is over and cannot be changed, but we often let it influence our future in an irrational manner" (Hastie & Dawes, 2001, p. 18, emphasis in original). Examples included (a) habit in choosing the same things repeatedly, (b) conforming to the choices of others, real or perceived, and (c) following religious or cultural mandates and choosing to do as our parents or other authorities have taught us.

"The past is over" in judgment research so far as heuristics and biases are concerned, but the past has been re-examined and the present view is that they can, if controlled, lead to rational or at least quasirational judgments (Gigerenzer, 2004).

Franklin's Advice

In the eighteenth century, Benjamin Franklin advised Joseph Priestly, as current jargon would put it, to use a "linear, additive model" to make a "quasirational choice." He did not advise his friend on *what* the decision should be, but on *how* to reach it; his advice went something like this (with apologies to Mr Franklin, I'm abbreviating and paraphrasing it in a more current style):

The reasons pro and con an action do not come to mind all at once, so we are perplexed by uncertainty. To get over the perplexity, I divide a sheet of paper by drawing a line to make two columns, one headed Pro, the other Con. Then, for three or four days, I put down the "motives" or values or arguments pro or con as they occur to me. When I have them all in one view, I try to estimate how I should weight them. Where I find two, one on each side, that seem equal, I strike them out. If I find that two con reasons are equal in weight to three pro reasons, I strike out all five. In this way I find whether the balance favors the pro or the con side. After another day or two, if nothing new and important occurs for either side, I decide accordingly. (For the original wording, see Hastie & Dawes, 2001, pp. 236–237)

His advice requires that one be explicit about what is valued or considered important. It is also seen as the forerunner of modern decision theory: to break down a complex problem into simpler ones, deal with them with clarified thought, and then logically fit the small solutions into the big, complex problem (Larrick, 2004).

PERSONNEL DECISIONS

Managers—not researchers, staff psychologists, or human resources specialists—make personnel decisions. Most managers have no training in psychometrics or test theory and no knowledge of cognitive theory; they may not understand the constructs assessed, and they may hold unwarranted views about tests, but they know they want to make decisions quickly. To help them (or to help their programs), some staff psychologists establish rules or standard procedures for using and interpreting assessments. The rules might specify preferred score levels or patterns, circumstances to justify overlooking poor scores, or further information to consider along with test scores or other systematic assessments. They might be theoretically developed judgment or decision aids designed to overcome obstacles to effectiveness in analytic or intuitive or quasirational judgment. Some managers may decide for themselves whether to use test information and, if so, how to use it, but that seems an odd policy. Developing and validating systematic assessment programs requires much investment; it is strange if individual whims determine how or whether the results of the investment will be used. Strange it may be, but it happens—often. Those responsible for the assessment programs should also be responsible for assuring that decision-making managers know how to use the assessment results meaningfully.

Judgment Aids

To reiterate: making selection decisions is a reasonable prototype for other kinds of personnel decisions; aids to judgments for selection decisions—whom to choose for something desirable—not as well-established, research-based generalities, but as ideas (or even hunches) that may be useful. Development of such aids requires some preliminary planning. The first step is to clarify the judgments to be made. Those who make selection judgments need a clear idea of the major responsibilities of the position to be filled and the qualifications required for it. The clarification serves to define and document the judgments required and the expected sequence in making them.

Detailed plans for assessment and other procedures make the judgment process more systematic and therefore more reliable. Completed plans can identify the sequence of judgments to be made and the steps to follow in making them. For each candidate, at each step, the decision may be to move the candidate to the next step—which may call for new information or new assessments—or to drop the candidate from further consideration. The plan should clearly state the qualifications to be assessed at each step and the assessment procedures to be used. Procedural justice argues for a plan followed as consistently as possible across candidates at each step.

Assessment Scales

Test scores are assessments; so are judgments in the form of ratings based on observations in interviews or assessment centers or on information in résumés or personnel files. Information (including observations) may be assessed on more than one dimension. Prior responsibilities, for example, might be assessed in terms of the cost of error, the scope of the responsibility accepted, or the quality of the achievement in fulfilling it—or something else. If judgment dimensions are not specified, raters may appear to disagree only because they rate the information on different dimensions. Clear definitions of the attributes to be judged are essential aids, and carefully developed and explained rating scales can clarify definitions.

To assure procedural justice and reliability, the information to be used should be specified as unambiguously as possible. Graphic depictions of relevant information and information that is extraneous to intended judgment can be very helpful, and may also aid the development of the measurement (rating) scales to be used. Some people want to have all assessments made on the same scale, whether based on test scores, interviews, or information in files or credentials, but such uniformity disregards the differences in possible precision of measurement. For judgments, I tend to use nine-point scales, such as that shown in Figure 12.3, for no better reason than the unsupported idea that it encourages raters to make two sequential ratings on easy three-point scales: first, choosing the high, middle, or low third of the scale and, second, choosing the specific high, middle, or low point within that range as a rating. In Figure 12.3, a rater may have seen no record of accomplishment deemed worthy of being designated "major" or "important" and choose the bottom third of the scale; however, the ratee may have a fairly persistent record of getting things done, even if not noteworthy things, and the rater may therefore use the highest value within that lower third as the assessment of accomplishment.

At some point, at least some candidates are likely to be interviewed. Interviewer judgments are notoriously lacking in evidence of validity—unless the interviews are well structured (Arvey, Campion, & Gialluca, 1982). Predeveloped assessment scales help specify and standardize the nature of the judgments to be made. What kinds of information are sought? Why is such information appropriate or relevant to the position to be filled? What construct

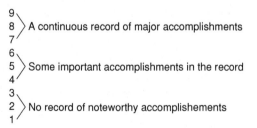

FIG. 12.3   A nine-point scale for rating a history of achievements using data from interviews, references, and résumés.

is reflected by the information? How should it be evaluated? What relative weight should it have? Advance preparation for rating can answer such questions and assure a degree of systematic, procedural justice in evaluating file information or interview performance, in comparing ratings from one evaluator to another.

Expectancy Charts

For assessments not empirically validated, theoretical expectancy charts can be developed from estimated correlation coefficients, and they can be invaluable aids to judgment. They can be developed based on correlation estimates (a) computed in local validation research, (b) reported in a manual or other research report based on a comparable situation, (c) based on an appropriate meta-analysis, (d) culled informally from prior research fitting parts of the local situation, or (e) made by panels of experts.

Consider a situation where the assessment plan for a specialized sales position includes assessment by tests of two traits, general intelligence and surgency. Suppose that, for both psychometric and theoretical reasons, the scores on the Watson-Glaser *Critical Thinking Appraisal* (*CTA*; Total Score) and the *Hogan Personality Inventory* (*HPI*; Sociability Score) are the chosen assessment tools. Assume that no relevant validity coefficient was found for the CTA, but that an expert panel linked component scores to job duties and concluded that a total score validity coefficient, appropriately corrected, would not be less than .35. A validity coefficient of .51 reported in the Hogan Manual (Hogan & Hogan, 1992) for advertising sales, a position making interpersonal demands similar to those in the position at hand, was rounded down to .50. These estimates permit theoretical expectancy charts for these two tests, shown in Figure 12.4. Score intervals on the CTA were derived from the full norms for upper division college students (Watson & Glaser, 1980); those for the HPI are based on total sample norms (Hogan & Hogan, 1992).

One might assume, reasonably in this case, that the two tests are uncorrelated. One might also assume, although less reasonably, that neither is correlated with ratings of information obtained from interviews, letters of endorsement, work histories, and accomplishments. Assuming orthogonal information may simplify judgments, but if the assumption is unwarranted, it is likely to reduce their validity. Figure 12.4 gives two different charts, assuming orthogonality. The charts allow the decision maker to make two different judgments of expected success; if these are disparate expectations, the judgment will need to be based, perhaps, on other information or perhaps on weighting the relative importance of the two attributes.

Helping Managers Learn to Make Selection Decisions

New managers, and old-timers who have given little attention in the past to assessments for selection decisions beyond comparing a candidate's score to a cut score, or merely deciding whether they like a candidate, are both novices in making selection decisions. Both groups need training in using the tools available to them.

Expectancy Charts as Training Aids

The relationship of test scores to a performance criterion can be expressed in many ways. One might use actual regression lines with Cartesian coordinates, with scatterplots super-imposed; managers can quickly learn to understand them without learning about the

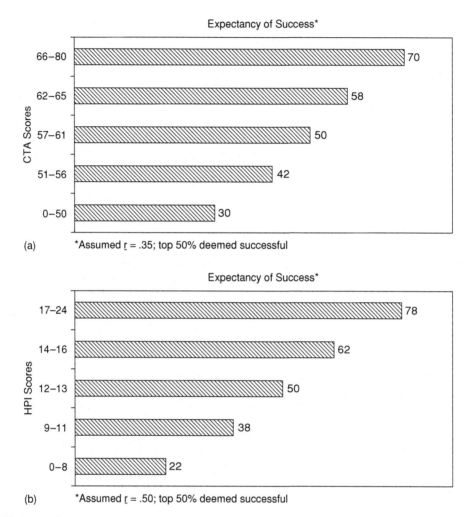

FIG. 12.4 Theoretical expectancy charts for two tests for a hypothetical sales position.

statistical procedures that developed them. It usually seems easier, however, to explain the same principles with expectancy charts. In either case, careful and systematic training is needed. The most important objective is to develop a habit of thinking in terms of probabilities instead of certainties—and of gradual changes in those probabilities rather than sudden discontinuities. Expectancy charts can serve as tools for teaching these things. If 85% of those scoring in the upper fifth of a score distribution turned out to be good workers, 15% did not. The odds are 85:15, or 17:3, or 5.67:1, and many managers know enough about odds in gambling about horses, ball clubs, or political candidates to recognize that probabilities dilute certainty.

I think a staff psychologist's or researcher's responsibility includes assuring that decision makers are trained in (a) the nature of the constructs being assessed, (b) why they are important, (c) the fundamental principles by which their assessment was evaluated, (d) the nature of defensible and indefensible inferences from scores, and (e) acceptable limits of individual judgments to override ordinarily defensible inferences in individual cases. All of these can be helped by using expectancy charts. Not only do they help get across the idea that prediction of success or failure is uncertain and probabilistic, but they can show that the probability of success is greater in higher score levels, or in higher scores within levels. Good training would also teach the limits of predictions such as those imposed by the criterion chosen; an expectancy of a superior level of production gives no clue about probable performance on a criterion the decision maker might have wished, such as a dependability or ingenuity.

Probabilities annoy managers who want definite answers; their annoyance is enhanced when two or more probabilistic statements are incompatible—when the probability of being satisfactory on one criterion is high but is accompanied by a low probability of being satisfactory on another one equally valued. Training should stress that people may not function at the same level in all aspects of work-related performance. For example, people who work carefully and make no errors may not get much done. Incompatible predictions require reconciling them, not denunciation of the assessments. Where research permits predictions of independent criteria, managers should be trained to expect incompatibility and given guidance for dealing with it in selection decisions.

Training wears off. Personnel decisions such as selection, promotion, or transfer are not everyday events for individual managers, and the training may be old when test scores are reported to them for pending decisions. Human resources (HR) specialists, if competently trained themselves, can work with the manager, refreshing the principles of expectancy chart use, when decisions are to be made.

Score Bands as Training Aids

Banding establishes a score interval of indifference, a band of scores in which some score differences are considered too trivial to use for decisions. Decisions within the band are therefore based on information other than the test score. Using additional information about people within a band can be used in a policy-capturing exercise (policy capturing is discussed later in this chapter) to demonstrate differences in individual policies, the differences between relevant and irrelevant information, and the effects irrelevant information can have in biasing the judgments about the candidates within a band to be selected.

Resistance might be expected if managers dislike the available bases for choice within bands, such as random choice or choice based on demographic variables. To gain acceptance, managers should get training in the meaning of bands and in the variety of work-relevant considerations that might drive their decisions. Making decisions collaboratively with (or monitored by) HR specialists seems useful and often necessary. Managers, trainers, and testers should recognize that letting work-relevant factors influence choices among people whose test scores differ only trivially might enhance, not reduce, the usefulness of assessment. As Kriska (1995, p. 94) pointed out, banding offers no guarantee of better decisions, "but it does provide a rational, cost effective way of considering additional information." In general, however, researchers and specialists also have much to learn before they can offer much help for managers to make better judgments within bands.

Teaching Rating Techniques

Ratings, whether as criteria or predictors, are records of judgments made. Training managers to make ratings is an important part of teaching judgment techniques. Before considering training issues, we need to consider much more about ratings and research on different aspects of the total rating process. This is done in Chapter 13. Rating is a major, even ubiquitous, form of judgment, and several different ways to train raters have been used.

Judgments as Predictions and Decisions

Personnel decisions are judgments that imply prediction. They often have no research foundation and follow no known plan. Typically, they are not seriously evaluated beyond vague statements like, "Joe really knows how to size people up." We can do better.

Statistical versus Judgmental Prediction

Many judgments are not even recognized as predictors, although prediction of something is usually implied. One might formally frame and test a hypothesis that a firm handshake, looking one squarely in the eye, or some other body language indicates that the candidate will work hard or be conscientious. More often, I think, such cues are not even recognized as the basis for judging that "this person is a good bet."

Clinical and counseling psychologists make "clinical predictions"—judgments—of likely future behavior. In evaluating a convict being considered for parole, a psychologist may predict whether the person, if paroled, will be a repeat offender. Such predictions are not made lightly; the psychologist gathers much data about the person, considers much data about recidivism in general, and gives these data much thought before making the prediction. Decision theory suggests that the judgment based on such an over-abundance of information is likely to be flawed, especially when much of it is irrelevant to the purpose of decision.

A decision maker may make informed judgments about candidates and their expected performance. Candidates might be tested, interviewed, and evaluated in assessment centers; their backgrounds might be checked, and people who have known them in various contexts might be interviewed for still more data. Much of the data about a candidate might be useless, and the decision maker may not know the value of specific pieces of information. Yet a decision must be made, it can be based on a lot of information—and, in this case, too, the over-abundance of information of doubtful relevance can lead to flawed judgments and decisions.

Statistical analysis can also be misleading, particularly if data are poor or greatly violate statistical assumptions. Nevertheless, Meehl (1954) long ago demonstrated the consistent superiority of statistical predication over clinical (judgmental) prediction. Among his suggestions for improving judgmental prediction was that optimal prediction might be based more on patterns of relationships among predictors than on the linear, additive relationships (Meehl, 1967). People making judgments might be using information in a "configural" way (i.e., using algorithms that may be nonlinear, nonadditive, or even noncontinuous). It was an interesting idea, but in subsequent research, it did not pan out. It has been a well-accepted view that statistical prediction is almost always, some even say necessarily, better than prediction by human judgment (see, e.g., Goldberg, 1991).

That view needs to be qualified a bit. In general, research does show that statistical prediction works better than judgments, but I think this is not *necessarily* so. The persistent finding may be explained by conventions in the design of judgment research that favor linear, additive models for predicting judgments, a topic discussed in a later section on judges' insight into their judgment policies. For now, I consider Meehl's original position to be plausible still: where judgments are substantially and consistently configural—a condition not addressed in most of the research—statistical prediction may not necessarily be better. This condition, however, may be exceptional; where there is not substantial configurality, statistical prediction is probably still superior.

At least it works nicely for candidates who fit neatly to the research samples from which the statistics spring. Exceptions to the rule are statistically anomalous and even may be obvious, such as a disabled person needing accommodation in test procedures, or the average-scoring person who has an outstanding record of continuous achievement relevant to the opportunities at hand. Some anomalous candidates, however, must be detected by alert observers, whose judgments may assure that a statistical rule "does not blindly commit injustices or do stupid things" (Beach & Connolly, 2005, p. 39), such as willfully ignoring highly important information simply because of the uniqueness of a candidate for whom it is a new kind of information.

When there is a choice, statistical prediction is surely superior to prediction based on judgment. When hiring a great number of new employees from an even larger number of candidates, establishing a general predictive hypothesis, choosing or developing standard operational definitions of the predictor and criterion constructs, collecting and analyzing data that will either support or fail to support the hypothesis—all of this is reasonable, good professional practice, and only the adoption of stupid decision rules will spoil it. More and more, however, these reasonable practices are not feasible, and judgmental procedures must take over from the infeasible statistical approach. Even with a major selection program, it may be fiscally and operationally necessary to start with a great number of candidates and use some form of successive hurdles to whittle the number of those to be seriously considered down to a few finalists, an even smaller number of whom will be chosen judgmentally (Highhouse, 1997).

Prediction and Decision without Statistics

Many decisions must be made without the luxury of research data. For unusual jobs, many high-level jobs, or lower level jobs in small organizations, many candidates may be assessed but only one (or very few) may be chosen. The cost of error in these cases, and the reward for being right, may be greater than in those where statistical predictions are feasible. If only one person is chosen, that person's performance is the crucial evaluation of the decision. In the higher organizational levels of responsibility, few are hired. Even with dozens of keepers of accounts, there is but one comptroller. When that comptroller retires, moves to a different organization, gets fired, or dies, another person—only one—must be chosen to fill the position; perhaps a dozen people or more may be considered. There is no choice between judgmental and statistical prediction; judgment is the only option.

That judgment may be made by one person or collaboratively by a selection or screening committee. Each committee member should make an independent judgment, as if he or she were the only person making it; the group, meeting as a whole, can then reconcile differences. Despite the old saw about a camel being a horse assembled by committee, group judgments tend to be more reliable than individual judgments, and it usually seems appropriate to use committees composed of members of various constituencies. But it is well to remember that better reliability does not necessarily translate to better validity, relatively unresearched in evaluating committee judgments.

Some circumstances permit candidate comparisons; others do not. Perhaps a candidate must be assessed and either accepted or rejected without further ado. Examples may occur under the Americans with Disabilities Act (ADA). Suppose a candidate protected under ADA applies for a job for which a test and an expectancy table are ordinarily used; suppose further that the candidate has a history of epilepsy (or cardiac arrhythmia, or whatever) and that the condition has for some time been controlled by appropriate medication. The disability is not likely to interfere with either job performance or assessment. The expectancy chart can be used (even if with slight misgivings); accommodation is not needed.

Suppose instead that the candidate's condition is a form of learning disability, and that accommodation in assessment requires someone to write down the candidate's answers to orally administered test questions. Or perhaps the candidate requires a test form in large print. In either case, validities may differ in unknown ways from those based on standard conditions. One can only hope that judgments about scores, other information, and associated probabilities may provide rational grounds for adjusting expectancy chart probabilities subjectively. A rating or a subjectively adjusted probability is surely less valid than an appropriate score on a valid, standardized test, but it is not necessarily any less valid than an inappropriate test score. When standard testing procedures are changed, validity information is no longer applicable; some degree of error, direction and extent unknown and unknowable, has probably contaminated the resulting scores. A disabled candidate's score might be nudged up or down a bit, depending on a psychometric judgment of the validity retained in the accommodation, but so far, no clear principles for making such adjustments are available.

Combining Information for Overall Assessment

Decisions in low-frequency judgment situations seem usually to be inconsistent in procedure, unreliable in result, and difficult to explain by the people who make them. They have unknown validity, and they may not even be recognized as predictive decisions. Careful planning of procedures for them can help, and methods of consolidating information can be part of the planning.

Conventional Models

With common scales, the several assessments of a candidate can simply be averaged, with or without differential weights. I recommend the mean assessment, rather than the sum, to ease the problem of missing data—often severe with interviews or credential files. Disjunctive, conjunctive, and other noncompensatory combinations described in Chapter 8 may also make sense, but they need to be clearly developed and explained, probably frequently, to the decision makers.

Use of Empirical and Subjective Probabilities

An expectancy chart gives empirically based probabilities of meeting a performance standard in different categories of information. The probability is the proportion of people in the score interval, X, meeting a specified standard or event, Y. It is written formally as $P(Y \mid X)$, the probability of Y given X. Probability statements may help make judges more careful.

At the opposite extreme is the joker who thinks he knows it all and utters such nonsense as "Nine times out of ten a man who can't look you in the eye spells trouble." Set aside the silliness of the statement; examine it for what it illustrates. Two features merit attention. First, it is imprecise. "Spells trouble" has no clear meaning; neither the nature nor the level of trouble is specified. Equally imprecise is the complaint: "can't look you in the eye." Eye contact can vary between none at all to unwavering; either extreme can be disconcerting.

Second, it is merely a verbal habit, uttered with neither data nor logic, based on simple prejudice or stereotype or common notions. If written formally, it is a statement that $P(Y \mid X)$ = .9, a probability pulled from thin air. It may sound like a probability statement, and it may influence decisions of the one who utters it, but it is not the mark of a person whose judgments are carefully considered.

In Figure 12.4 the top score interval on the CTA is between 65.5 and 80.5. Would anyone seriously believe that the success expectancy is precisely .70 for scores of both 68 and 78? Even a person with no statistical training might expect a higher probability of success for the higher score, perhaps guessing that the probability is .64 or .65 at the lower score and .77 at the higher one. These guesses do not rely on a table of areas under the normal curve; they simply illustrate that subjective probabilities *can* be based on available information and empirical data.

Consider an applicant whose CTA score is 63 and whose HPI score is 15. Assume that this applicant is a paroled felon and that company policy is to give employment to deserving ex-convicts. From test scores alone, remembering that the two sets of scores are probably nearly uncorrelated, the success probability must be greater than .62; my guess is about .68. A different probability to consider is the likelihood of the candidate committing another crime. That estimate might be derived from literature on recidivism, particularly where prior research considers the type of crime, socioeconomic variables, and other relevant data. If that probability is estimated to be nonzero to an important degree, the subjectively estimated probability of success on *both* criteria may be lower than that based on test scores alone. If the selection ratio is about .50, and the resulting estimate of the probability of success is more than .5, the decision maker may decide to hire the candidate, despite the prison record.

Technically, there are two different questions. First, what is the probability of success, defined as being in the top half, given the scores on the CTA and the HPI? Let $P(Y)$ be the probability of being in the top 50%. With no prior information, $P(Y) = .5$. If the score on the CTA is 63, then $P(Y \mid CTA) = .58$ from Figure 12.4. With an HPI score of 15, $P(Y \mid HPI)$ = .62. Both of these values exceed $P(Y)$, so $P(Y)$ must be greater than .62—but I have not made up enough information to say how much greater. To assert subjectively that $P(Y \mid CTA,HPI)$ ≈ .68 is a pure guess, albeit an informed one. The second question is easier: What is the probability of avoiding further criminal behavior? Given the subjective probability of $P(Y \mid CTA,HPI)$ ≈ .68 and if it is empirically derived in the research literature that $P(S \mid D) = .85$ (where S is being free of further crime and D is the accumulated information on recidivism), the probability of being both in the top half of the performance distribution and free of further criminality is a multiplicative function, about equal to .68 × .85, or about .58. It is not necessary, however, to be so precise; it *is* necessary to provide heuristics that can keep decision makers thinking in probabilistic terms without requiring training in probability theory.

In short, it is possible to combine empirical probabilities and informed guesses in making probabilistic predictions about the outcomes of personnel decisions. That is, the cardinal rule of psychometrics—standardization—may be set aside; different information for different candidates can be combined when it can be expressed probabilistically, with a firmer basis than routine verbal habit.

Dangers are inherent in the use of personal or subjective probabilities; in general, they are subject to many sources of bias. Little is known about procedures that can be fairly sure of reducing bias and enhancing the accuracy of such probability statements. Therefore, I can advocate subjective "nudging" of empirical probabilities or expectancies, but when the empirical data are available, and the decisions are critical, I cannot advocate much reliance on purely subjective probabilities.

SOCIAL JUDGMENT THEORY AND
LENS MODEL RESEARCH

Social judgment theory provides a framework for research. Its characteristics are remarkably apt for applied research, and it is relatively free of the nomothetic bias decried by Doherty and Balzer (1988). It stems from Brunswikian research on perception (Brunswik, 1956), later extended to research on clinical judgments, then to learning, "and subsequently to human judgment in social circumstances" (Brehmer, 1988, p. 18). A common feature in all of these applications is the use of the *lens model*, Brunswik's metaphor for studying the cues people use in understanding, responding to, or functioning in their environments.

The Lens Model

Many research paradigms are used to study judgment and decision making; the lens model (Brunswik, 1956; Hammond, 1966, 1993) is particularly well suited to personnel decisions.[4] The metaphor is that a designated set of variables, or cues, serves somewhat like a lens through which an object (or person) in the environment may be perceived and judgments made about it. Basic to lens model research is the principle of representative design, differing from the experimental research ideal of manipulating one variable, observing another, and allowing nothing else to vary. Representative design recognizes both the multivariate nature and the uncertainty of the perceived environment and of the judgments people make about things in it. Failure to present cues reasonably realistically poses threats to the external validity of the research.

A diagrammatic description of the lens model, stripped to essentials, is shown in Figure 12.5a. On the left is a criterion, the dependent variable of interest, something to be evaluated or predicted. On the right is a judgment about the criterion. In the center is a set of k variables thought to be related either to the criterion or to judgments about it—"cues" that make up the metaphorical "lens" through which events or conditions are perceived. They may be predictors of the criterion, and they may influence or predict people's judgments about it. If the criterion is, for example, job performance, the judgments may be non-statistical, even intuitive, predictions of performance. They could be overall assessments of job candidates intended as predictors of performance. Profiles of the lens variables are accumulated for many candidates, actual or hypothetical; the "judge" makes predictions or assessments of each candidate based on the cues in the lens.

The lens model is usually used to study the judgments of individuals. For each one, each cue variable is correlated with judgments across profiles, yielding $r_{j1}, r_{j2}, r_{j3}, \ldots r_{jk}$, or with the criterion itself, yielding $r_{c1}, r_{c2}, r_{c3}, \ldots r_{ck}$. Cues can be combined in any of the ways described in Chapter 8; multiple regression is typical (but not necessarily the best or most descriptive model). The judgment side represents the judge's judgment policy, and the environmental side is, in effect, the policy of the real world. A judge's policy can be evaluated by comparing it to the real-world policy.[5]

---

[4] I do not discuss the lens model in the detail it deserves, and I do not mention other approaches at all. Instead, I recommend reading the more comprehensive presentation by Hammond (1996) or Stevenson, Busemeyer, and Naylor (1990).

[5] Calling this a real-world policy may stretch credulity; for example, the criterion might be simply another judgment, perhaps pooled, or a very imperfect approximation of some sort of empirical reality. But this language provides a quick taste of policy capturing.

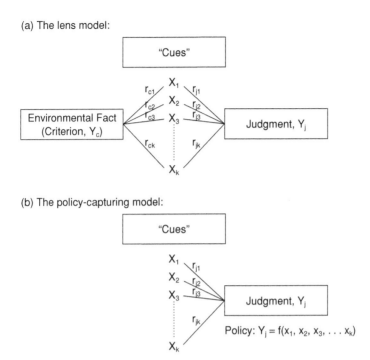

FIG. 12.5 A simplified description of the lens model and of policy capturing.

Policy Capturing

Different people with the same information make judgments differently. One may consider some information and ignore other, giving implicit weights to some pieces of information but no consideration or weight to others. Another may use all of the information provided but treat some of it as more important than other, implicitly using differential weights. Another might treat it all as equally important. Still another may consider one piece of information so crucial that, if it is missing or inadequate, no other information will compensate for its lack. An *if–then* approach might first analyze or decompose one sort of information into component parts, each component suggesting a different judgment or course of action. Even if these various patterns of judgment are not conscious or deliberate, they can be captured by a mathematical model, most commonly multiple regression. Policy capturing is depicted in Figure 12.5(b), the right-hand side of the full lens model.

Policy-capturing research can be used to identify differences among decision makers, such as interviewers. If two or more distinctly different policies are found, it may be possible in conference to consolidate them into a single organizational policy that the judges can learn to use. It is, however, useful to think of different policies as requiring independent evaluation (or validation).

The Lens Model Equation

A more complete depiction of the lens model is shown in Figure 12.6. Actual judgments, Y_j, can be correlated with those predicted from the policy, Y_j'. In effect, this is done in computing the multiple coefficient of correlation between cues and judgments, so we denote

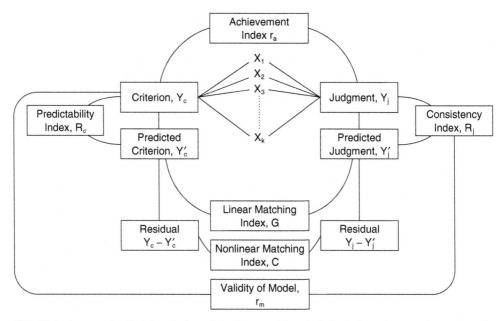

FIG. 12.6   A more detailed description of the lens model and of the indices that may be computed.

it simply as R_j, identified in Figure 12.6 as the *consistency index*. On the environmental side, the corresponding index is the criterion predictability index, R_c.

The correlation of actual judgments across the profiles, Y_j, with the criterion, Y_c, is the *achievement index*, r_a, a criterion-related validity coefficient for the judgments; judgments made by different people may differ in r_a. Judgments predicted by the policy equation can also be correlated with the criterion; this correlation, which I designate r_m, is the validity of the judgment model or policy equation. It is typically larger than r_a.

A general equation integrates the lens model (Tucker, 1964):

$$r_a = GR_cR_j + C\sqrt{(1 - R_c^2)}\sqrt{(1 - R_j^2)} \tag{12.1}$$

where G is a linear matching index, the correlation between predicted criterion values and judgments predicted from the policy. C is the correlation between residuals; if it is substantial relative to G, a linear additive model is unlikely to be optimal; it can be checked by the Brannick and Brannick (1989) equations (Chapter 8, Equations 13 and 14).

Cognitive Control

In introducing the concept of cognitive control, Hammond and Summers (1972) distinguished knowledge from the ability to use the knowledge. The consistency index, R_j, is considered a measure of the cognitive skill, or cognitive control, one has in using knowledge. Within the lens model equation, G was taken to represent the judge's knowledge of the relationships of cues to the criterion. If a least squares prediction of the criterion from the cues, and the least squares prediction of the judgments from those cues, match closely, then the subject has substantial knowledge or understanding of the environment about which judgments are to be made. It does not necessarily follow that the judgments will be very consistent, or controlled, as measured by R_j, because consistency depends on G and the judge's understanding of the criterion predictability (Brehmer, 1976).

Cognitive Feedback

Learning a cognitive skill requires knowledge of results, or feedback, but effectiveness depends on the kinds of results or feedback received. *Outcome feedback* tells how well a judgment matched the criterion value. *Cognitive feedback* gives information about the judgment process being used and the relationships among the components of the process, such as the environmental validities and intercorrelations of cues, differential cue weights, functional relationships of cues to criteria, and so on. There is consistent evidence that outcome feedback offers little if any improvement in either judgment or policy validity—that it may even hinder skill development in making judgments (Doherty & Balzer, 1988); Hammond (1993) characterized the result of outcome feedback as "slow, 'stupid' learning" (p. 213). Cognitive feedback is a far superior aid to learning to make consistent judgments from the available cues.

Some Questions to Consider

The following three questions seem important for a coherent organizational policy.

1. What form should a policy model take? The most common is multiple regression. Nonlinear or nonadditive models are sometimes proposed, but Dawes and Corrigan (1974) argued that complex models account for little or no more variance than simpler ones. Practical researchers, however, may be less interested in variance than in recognizable judgment policies and the accuracy of predictions to be made from them.

    Another practical consideration is that additive, compensatory models do not always make sense. Suppose one must hire a company physician. The judgment in a typical design might be an HR specialist's rating of a candidate's acceptability by the current dispensary staff. Cues might include age, years of experience, perhaps an index of medical school quality, classification of internship or practice experience, and maybe a couple more. A lot of profiles would be developed. Judgment policies would be modeled by multiple regression to use the profile cues to predict the ratings. Note that all profiles make the ordinarily valid assumption that each candidate has a legal license to practice medicine, so possession of a license would not be included; it would have little or no variance and therefore could not account for variance in ratings. But suppose that one or more of the actual candidates did not have, for whatever reason, a valid license. None of the other variables would matter, the unlicensed candidates would be rejected, and a compensatory model of judgment policy would not fit that judgment. A less fanciful alternative example substitutes the practice category. The company physician is necessarily a generalist; one who has specialized in one area, especially an esoteric one, might be passed over regardless of other virtues. Both examples are configural judgments, one based on a variable not included in the research because it seems unlikely, the other included but inappropriately modeled.

2. *Do judges understand their own policies?* The level of insight people have about their judgments is questionable. It has long been known, for example, that interviewers

tend to make up their minds about interviewees within the first few minutes of the interview (Webster, 1964), but they continue on for extended periods gathering new information, apparently unaware that they have already made up their minds. Moreover, the subjective weights that judges assign to the variables bear little resemblance to the beta weights of a multiple regression equation. Efforts to get people to talk through their reasons for a judgment or decision often provide only unreliable data. A study suggesting insight into configural policies is described below.

3. *Are judgment policies so idiosyncratic and compelling that people will continue to use their policy even under contrary instructions; can people learn to use an alternative policy?* From an organizational point of view, the question is extremely important. If procedural justice is to be perceived in selection, for example, judgments made by interviewers after the collection of several kinds of data (e.g., test scores, biodata forms, background checks, references, and information gathered in the interview itself) should be consistent; the decision about a candidate should not depend on which interviewer was seen. A uniform organizational policy should be reflected in the judgments of the several interviewers.

Lens Model Research Design

Cue Profiles

A common approach to lens model research gives the judge a booklet containing the set of profiles of variables (cues). Many profiles are needed; many researchers want at least a 10:1 ratio of profiles to cues. Judgment research has usually shown that the number of variables to consider (cues) should be kept small; large numbers of cues can be confusing, may be more likely to include irrelevant information, and will surely be counterproductive. Profiles may describe real or hypothetical people, perhaps combining situational and personal characteristics. Tasks vary. For each profile, the judge may predict the criterion level expected for people with such a profile (e.g., whether such a person will or will not quit within six months, or an expected level of performance), indicate an appropriate decision (e.g., to hire or not), or provide a more global evaluation (e.g., skill level, readiness for promotion). "Paper people" profiles in booklets may not be representative (Gorman, Clover, & Doherty, 1978)—unless profiles come from actual files and operational decisions are also based on those or similar files.

Cue Weights in a Policy Equation

The achievement index, r_a, offers one evaluation of the judgments. Another is the correlation between the criterion and the judgments predicted by the captured policy, r_m, in which validity depends on the judgment model assumed. In the linear, additive model most often assumed, validity may depend on the weights for the various cues.

Subjective weights might be used; that is, judges may be asked to estimate subjectively the weights they have used (or intend to use) in making their judgments. Empirical weights are more often developed to optimize the correlation between cues and judgments or criteria. These weights are optimal only in that they maximize (within the profiles sampled) the correlation between the composite and the criterion. One might pursue simplicity and simply add cue values together; if so, all cues should be oriented to have a positive correlation with the criterion and be expressed in a common metric.

Policies captured by multiple regression are generally more valid than the judgments they predict (Dawes, 1979; Dawes & Corrigan, 1974). When the most valid policy of a group of decision makers is found, the implication is that the equation of that policy should be used instead of the actual, relatively unreliable judgments of individual decision makers. It is an easy implication, supported by a lot of evidence, but it is hard to put into practice in an organization. Pride in our abilities to size up people makes few of us willing to be replaced by an equation.

Lens Model Applications

An Early Demonstration

So far as I know, the first use of the lens model for personnel decisions was by Roose and Doherty (1976). They developed profiles of 360 life insurance agents from company records. Of these, 160 were held back for cross-validation; the rest were presented to 16 agency managers who predicted whether the person described would survive the first year. The profiles included 64 variables, combining listed variables and narrative statements as shown in Figure 12.7. A confidence scale incorporated with the dichotomous predictions placed the judgment on a 10-point scale. Multiple regression was used throughout. Results included the following.

1. The survival criterion was clearly predictable from cues in the profiles. Estimating aggregate R_c by two methods gave values of .32 and .43, validity coefficients typical of more standardized predictors.
2. Judges' policies consistently overused the Aptitude Index Battery (AIB), specially developed for the life insurance industry. Its regression weights were consistently greater across judges than merited by the test's validity coefficient in this sample, for an interesting reason: some judges treated it as a nonlinear relationship. Given that managerial training had emphasized the historic nonlinearity of AIB validity, the finding that at least some of them remember it is hardly surprising. The more sobering finding is that most judges treated it as linearly related to survival and therefore inflated the importance of the AIB.
3. The judges did not agree much. Differences in judgments (on the 10-point scale) may have been partly due to differences in base rates of hiring decisions; they ranged from 12% to 71%.
4. Unit weights provided more valid predictions of the criterion than did the judgments themselves or the models of the managers' policies. As the researchers pointed out, however, the variables chosen for unit weighting were picked by using traditional multiple regression procedures.

The wide variability in decisions led the researchers to look at those profiles on which there *was* agreement to hire or reject among 13 of the 16 managers. Treating these managers as a single group making dichotomized judgments about this limited set of profiles, a consensus policy equation was derived. The consensus policy is not necessarily an organizational policy, but it provides useful information for a policy development conference. For example, the consensus equation, like most individual ones, overemphasized the AIB relative to its empirical validity for these profiles. The managers were clearly influenced by the amount of deviation of an individual score from an established cut score, and this influence is grist for the group discussion mill.

Applicant # *116*

Age	*26*
Source	*Employment Agency*
Marital Status	*Married*
Wife's Activities	*Working at a permanent job*
Number of Children and Ages	*None*
Housing	*Rents a house*
Face Amount of Life Insurance on Self (Not Including Group)	*$45,000*
Annual Premium Paid for Above	*$444*
Present Monthly Needs	*$798*
Savings	*$4800*
Equity in Home if Owned	*N/A*
Net Worth	*$9300*
Occupational Classification	*Proprietor, executive, or official*
Number of Full Time Jobs Held	*2*
Number of Years Had Full Time Job	*3*
Presently Employed — Full Time	*No*
Aptitude Index Battery Score	*16*
Recommended Starting Salary	*$800*

The applicant has been married for 1 year and has lived in the local area for 1½ years. He and his wife are in good health. He is serving in the Marine Reserves and will be discharged in 1973. He enjoys lake activities and spectator sports and belongs to the Elks. He and his wife entertain in their home about 2 times per month and are entertained by others approximately 2 times a month.

The applicant maintained a B average in high school and served as Class Vice-President. He attended college and received his B. A. degree in 1970. He paid all his college expenses by working. He majored in Finance in which his grade point average was 2.0–3.0; his overall average was 1.6. He received his worst grades in English. While in college he pledged a social fraternity but eventually dropped out because of his heavy work load.

The applicant worked for the State Highway Department 2 years before beginning college. While in school he held several part-time jobs—a boat rigger, oil field roustabout, and ambulance driver. After graduating from college he became a partner in a landscape company and earned $10,000. He recently sold out to his partner because he wanted a career more in line with his college training. It is thought he has an upper-middle class market.

☐ Yes, I think this applicant will still be employed as an SRT at the end of his first year in business.

☐ No, I don't think this applicant will still be working as an SRT at the end of his first year.

How confident are you of this decision?

I could be easily swayed by other field supervisors					If my manager disagreed, I would argue my position strenuously
1	2	3	4	5	

FIG. 12.7 A sample profile for judgmental prediction of success in life insurance work. Reprinted from Roose, J. E., and Doherty, M. E. (1976). Judgment theory applied to the selection of life Insurance salesmen. *Organizational Behavior and Human Performance, 16*, 231–249.

Overall Job Performance Ratings

How do raters determine the relative importance of disparate kinds of information in reaching judgments of overall job performance? Rotundo and Sackett (2002) used policy capturing to answer the question. The disparate information included task, citizenship, and counterproductive performance. Judgments are heavily influenced by context, so raters judged performance profiles set in five different occupations. Different raters held different supervisory occupations (six in all) from 15 different organizations.

The profiles were paper people. Each profile had three sentences, one for each performance component. The sentences were scaled *a priori* "to ensure that they varied over equivalent standard deviation units in their respective populations in an attempt to avoid making an unfair comparison about the relative importance of the three performance components" (Rotundo & Sackett, 2002, p. 70)—a procedure that ought to become standard where paper people profiles are created. Altogether, they have 504 judges, and a policy equation was determined for each one. For most judges, all three components influenced overall ratings, although citizenship behavior was generally given less weight than the other two. Regression coefficients for each of the five occupations varied widely (even wildly!), but there were no significant context differences across the 15 organizations.

Ethnically Diverse Police Candidates in The Netherlands

Judgment research finds that inexperienced judges consider more of the available information, including more of the irrelevant information, than experienced ones do. Arguing that ethnic majority judges are more "experienced" in making judgments about members of their own group and less experienced in judging or knowing members of ethnic minorities, a plausible hypothesis is that judgment policies of judges in ethnic majorities will consider more information, with more of it irrelevant, in making judgments about minority candidates compared to those about majority candidates (DeMeijer, Born, van Zielst, & van der Molen, 2007).

Profiles included measures of the Big Five personality factors, ratings from an assessment center, and interview ratings on 12 dimensions, analyzed with linear models. The findings were precisely as hypothesized.

Decision Policies for Expatriate Assignment

Tye and Chen (2005) used policy capturing to discover how human relations professionals viewed some previously suggested predictors related to expatriate assignments: domestic job performance, previous international experience, extraversion, stress tolerance, and gender. Each of these was presented in vignettes representing hypothetical candidates in one of two levels, expressed qualitatively rather than numerically. In an overall policy aggregating all 33 HR professionals, weights assigned to the five variables were noticeably different, but they formed a consistent pattern for four different judgments: (a) the likelihood of deciding to send a candidate abroad, (b) the likelihood that the candidate will adjust well to the expatriate assignment, (c) the likelihood that the candidate will perform well, and (d) the likelihood of premature return from the assignment. This study is more a demonstration of what might be done than a prescription for decisions, but the demonstrated procedure is worth following; it shows promise.

Insight into Policies

The absence of self-insight is often inferred from the discrepancies between modeled and subjectively stated weights. Reilly and Doherty (1989, 1992) found, however, that many students judging the desirability of potential job offers or of potential roommates could indeed recognize their own policies. Why did these results differ from the common view that insight is rare? One reason might be that the judgment tasks were genuinely relevant to the ordinary concerns of the student subjects.

One plausible reason for apparent lack of insight is that an additive policy model does not recognizably represent the way a person thinks in reaching judgments. That possibility was illustrated by Ikomi (1989; Ikomi & Guion, 2000). Ikomi was a commercial pilot and flight instructor as well as a psychologist, who wondered whether instructors in a flight school had similar policies for sending student pilots for their first solo flights. Before solo flight, student pilots must have learned to do preflight checks of the airplane, use the rudder in taxiing, take off properly, stall and recover, turn or climb or descend smoothly, do simple maneuvers, handle radio communications, and above all land the airplane safely without stressing it with bounces, excessive speed and braking, or going off the runway. A compensatory decision model seems inappropriate. A flight instructor would not say, "this student can't be counted on to land the plane safely but traces beautiful figure eights over a road intersection, so I might as well send him or her on a solo flight."

Ikomi's research used actual file data for student pilots who had or had not flown solo. Deleting the information on whether the instructor had or had not sent the student on solo flight, the rest of the information was placed in a form similar to that in the files. Traditional linear modeling was used. Both the C index of nonlinear matching and Brannick's equation (Equation 14 in Chapter 8) were used in a pilot study to test for nonadditive judgment policies, and both suggested substantial nonlinear, nonadditive components. In a further study, flight instructors declared the policies they had used, mostly noncompensatory algorithms. In general, declared policies predicted judgments as well as or better than regression policies. It seems safe to say that judges can have some degree of insight into their judgment policies, particularly where making such judgments is a realistic, important, and essentially daily task.

To suggest that people making judgments understand how they arrive at their judgments flies in the face of a lot of contrary evidence. However, methodological problems may account for much of that evidence. One potential problem is that the booklets of profiles may not be genuinely representative; the profiles gleaned from files (e.g, Ikomi, 1989; Roose & Doherty, 1976) or real-life decisions (e.g., DeMeijer et al., 2007) fit the demands of representative design much better. Inconsistency in individual judgments may be deliberate. In a specific case, a particular fact may stand out as more important than usual, and get more weight in reaching the judgment than it would in other cases. This is inconsistency, but it is not necessarily error, although the inconsistency reduces the correlation based on the more reliable averages. That does not mean that the judge does not understand how he or she considers data in arriving at a judgment—only that the judge is not as rigidly consistent as the equation.

Moreover, there is no good psychological reason (as opposed to a statistical one) for judgment research to assume automatically that a regression model is a good model of the judgment process. If a person has a judgment policy, can express it in words, equations, or algorithms, then that policy can be modeled, the model can be validated, and the stated model may have greater reliability and validity than the person's raw judgments.

Training in Policy Use

Different people, making the same kinds of judgments, are likely to have different policies. Whether the people judged are employees in cubicles, assessment center assessees, students being recruited, walk-in job candidates, or click-in web-based recruits, procedural justice seem to require a degree of uniformity in policies. At the very least, those making the judgments should all look for the same behavioral cues and weight them in pretty much the same way. Can judges be trained to follow consistently the same judgment policies?

Galbraith (1985) presented the desired judgment policy to each of a group of experienced assessors, giving them in rank order the importance of the cues (task information). Half of the subjects received the same information at a session the next day; the other half received cognitive feedback. People in *both* groups learned to use the policy; cognitive feedback did not show the expected superiority. In a related study for judgments in job evaluation, Stang (1985) gave cognitive feedback with an interactive computer program. She found that (a) judges developed and used a consistent policy, (b) they learned to use consistently a policy other than their own, and (c) they remembered either policy well enough to use it consistently without further feedback. In this case, cognitive feedback helped. Some of these judges were highly consistent from the outset, but most of them began with ample room for improvement.

Training interviewers can change interviewing policies. Dougherty, Ebert, and Callender (1986), in a field study of judgments of three full-time interviewers, did so successfully. The three taped their interviews over a period of several months, and these tapes provided the profiles. Midway through the study, they were given special training. This was not training in the use of a weighted policy. Rather it was training in how to interview to assess three different applicant characteristics: compatibility, attitude toward the job, and responsibility. These were three of eight dimensions on which each judge rated each applicant based on the taped interview. Using only these three dimensions, policy equations (with differential weights) were computed for the period before training and for the period after training. All three interviewers benefited from training; in policy equations predicting 10 criteria, post-training equations generally did better than pre-training equations, and judgments were more consistent.

In short, through lens model research, managers' judgment policies can be identified, evaluated, discussed, and even argued over, and the managers can be trained to use a modified policy. If based on the full lens model, the new policy could consider cue validities; broader organizational concerns may also influence the policy, for example, workforce homogeneity or diversity, or responsibilities of the organization within the larger community in which it operates. The decision makers can be trained to use a new policy consistently. More important, the policy can say what the judgment should be in *most* cases like one at hand, and users who understand it well can more effectively consider additional information in modifying that judgment in unusual cases.

AN INTEGRATED PROGRAM FOR PERSONNEL DECISIONS

What follows is imaginary, not a report of an actual program. I write as if it were a description, but it is really only a hope. A system like this would take much conferring, writing, and research, even for a pilot effort. I cannot put all I have imagined in just a few pages, but I can illustrate what an integrated system might be like—the judgments it would involve, the research needed, how assessments can be used, and evaluative procedures. Because the system is a product of my imagination (prodded by actual experiences with organizations that do some of the things my imagination suggests), I invite readers to add to it from their own imaginations. There are signs in various recent reports that some researchers are in fact approaching at least some parts of such a system.

An Overview

The program is for all salaried personnel, except the top-tier executive level, in a large corporation with several thousand employees and multiple locations. It is decentralized in many ways, but the ever-present possibilities of litigation led to a strong central office influence on the system. Many people helped develop it, but details were worked out in the headquarters office. The program calls for decisions to be made locally, not centrally. A supervisor or manager in any location initiates the process and makes decisions within his or her realm. Individual employees, whether salaried or hourly, permanent or temporary, can start the program by applying for new opportunities.

Program Objectives

The overarching objective is to improve unit performance throughout the corporation through a systematic and persistent improvement in workforce and individual qualifications. To reach that goal, more detailed objectives include the following.

1. To stabilize the workforce by maximizing both employee retention and job security. This objective is met, in part, by personnel transfer and personnel development. Temporary employees are occasionally used (and included in a personnel inventory), but a long-term permanent workforce has been shown, at least in this organization, to have more lasting advantages.
2. To base decisions on valid predictions (empirically or implied) of outcomes. This objective is met, and meeting it is documented, by an initial and continuing program of research.
3. To minimize the time required to fill vacancies. This objective is met by a computerized, corporation-wide human resources inventory system that can identify people, both within the organization and outside of it, who are qualified for specific opportunities. The people so identified may be *invited* to apply, even though they did not know of the opening.
4. To help employees increase the scope of opportunities for which they are qualified and to strengthen their existing qualifications. This objective is met through diagnostic performance evaluation, by providing opportunities for specialized training or for more general personal development and career planning, and through information systems that publicize them.
5. To assure procedural justice—that all internal and external candidates for opportunities have equal treatment and equal opportunity. This objective is met by unambiguously spelling out procedures, including procedures for making judgments, and monitoring to assure compliance.

System Requirements

In a work unit, a vacancy occurs or is anticipated by the unit's supervisor. It can be filled by a lateral transfer of someone currently working at about the same level somewhere (anywhere) else in the corporation, by promotion, or from outside the organization. The supervisor and a local HR representative work together to find suitable candidates, but the final decision is the supervisor's responsibility. Several general resources are needed, including:

A Standard Work Activity Thesaurus

The thesaurus lists and defines the terms to be used in a job analysis or a detailed job plan, describing the critical components or key elements of the work to be done and the components to be considered in evaluating performance. It has been developed by prior job analyses and is regularly updated by further research.

A Personnel Requisition Form

An example of a requisition form is shown as Figure 12.8. It is completed on the basis of job analysis or detailed planning, describing the position with the standard vocabulary, and specifying the qualifications for the position. Some supervisors, unchecked, would build empires. Some, excessively cost-conscious, would add mercilessly to the workloads of present employees rather than bring in someone new. Some would not fully understand, even after extensive and periodically updated training, the materials, terms, and procedures of the system. Therefore, the requisition is completed with the advice, assistance, and consent of the supervisor's own supervisor, and it is approved or rejected by still higher authority in both the unit's organizational line and HR functions.

A Master List of Qualifications

Research has established, and the master list identifies, the qualifications required for standard key elements and methods for assessing them. Some listed qualifications are based on collaborative judgments, others on empirical research. Qualifications are also specified for several common combinations of job components. Qualifications listed are the attributes (traits, training, or specific kinds of relevant experience) needed to do the work. Methods of assessment are the tools to be used in assessing individual qualifications. The matching of attributes and assessment methods is based, as much as possible, on the relevant research literature; meta-analyses and transportable validation studies are the preferred bases for matching, but theoretical works often provide indirect but related information that can be used. A *personnel research system specialist* is responsible for continually updating the list and its recommendations. No matter how carefully the master list is updated, unusual task elements (or unusual combinations of them) and personal hypotheses of individual managers will require deviations from it; these are acceptable in this system.

A Personnel Inventory

This inventory record includes current and recent performance evaluations and the assessed attributes (qualifications) of employees in the corporation at, or aspiring to be at, the salaried

Personnel Requisition

Plant: 7	Dept: 15	Date Issued: *10/1/95*	Date Needed: *1/2/96 or before*	Req. No.:

Issued By: *B. V. Helmquist*

Reason for Need: *Planned retirement of present incumbent*

Position Title and Description: *Technical Report Production Editor.*
Enters draft reports in personal computer from hard copy or disk: edits
reports for format, grammar, spelling, style, and content consistency.
Creates graphics as needed. Prepares final file for production.

Critical Job Components	Code	Qualifications	Code
Uses personal computer to edit documents.	*8D143*	*Level 3 knowledge of major programs for:*	
		word processing	*AC614*
		spreadsheets	*AC615*
		graphics	*AC617*
		desktop publishing	*AC619*
Edits executive level documents	*87519*	*Memory for verbal content*	*MC127*
		Memory for numerical content	*MC128*
		Level 5 knowledge of English usage	*VE210*
Maintains confidences	*2A116*	*General trustworthiness*	*PC001*

FIG. 12.8   A personnel requisition form that might be used in the hypothetical integrated program for personnel decisions. Only the most critical components and qualifications are listed. Code numbers refer to entries in the system thesaurus giving full definitions of job components and preferred methods of assessment. Requisitions may contain additional information (salary levels, EEO constraint, etc.).

level. Searching it is the first step in filling the vacancy. As many vacancies as possible are to be filled from within the organization, but the inventory also includes people who have applied for work in the corporation and have wanted to be included. Some qualifications (e.g., licenses, academic degrees, specialized training completed) are matters of record in the personnel inventory; the inventory may also record results of other forms of personal assessment. It should be examined regularly to purge data too old to be currently useful, but success in doing so proves elusive, so getting current assessment data before making decisions is often required. Assessment is the mutual responsibility of the supervisor and a personnel specialist or HR representative in the local unit. Tests or assessment centers are primarily the responsibilities of professional personnel specialists or HR staff, and the structure and content of interviews or rating systems may be primarily the responsibilities of the managerial staff. In either case, managers and professionals in assessment have face-to-face meetings to plan, discuss, and evaluate the results.

System Operation

A system like this can be detailed on paper, bound in a handsome notebook, given a prominent place on the supervisor's desk and in general be very impressive—and utterly useless. It is useless if critical components of positions are defined idiosyncratically by each individual supervisor, each time a vacancy occurs. It is useless if qualifications are specified by hunch or unverified, totally intuitive "common sense." It is useless if qualifications are assessed by *ad hoc* methods letting principles of validity and validation be completely foreign, or by exotic ideas relegated only to university-based research. However, a system such as this can be very useful indeed if vacancies can be described in well-understood, standard terms also understood by other supervisors who contribute to or search the personnel inventory records; if qualifications are linked to position requirements systematically, reliably, and validly; and if the assessment of those qualifications is demonstrably job-relevant and psychometrically valid. These are tall orders, and even the best programs meet them only partially. Explicitly stating and operationally encouraging the ideal, however, is a start toward meeting them more fully.

Position Analysis

When a need for a new employee is recognized, the supervisor analyzes or otherwise determines the task components of the position to be filled, using a corporate-wide task-oriented checklist. Then the personnel requisition form is completed and entered in the system with terms from the standardized thesaurus. If the new position is unusual, the thesaurus may not mention it, but a critical component of it may be part of any other job in the corporation. Departures from the standard list of positions are inevitable reasons for and topics of conversation between the supervisor and the personnel specialist.

Thesaurus job component definitions include required or desired qualifications: the abilities, skills, training, experience, or other qualifications required (or helpful) for excellent performance, and these are elaborated in the qualification master list. Panels of experts (primarily psychologists specializing in the study of individual differences) developed these statements. For components where prior research was unavailable or inadequate, panels of psychologists and panels of job experts worked together to develop appropriate predictive hypotheses. They also specified ways to assess qualifications in the standard list. The assessment methods were diverse, including tests, personality inventories, specially developed biodata forms, elements of qualifying training or experience, performance ratings, behavioral exercises, and structured interviews.

The Personnel Inventory

Information is not included in the inventory merely because it is available or because someone thinks it might be nice to have. It does include the following.

1. *Identification data:* This includes each person's name and identification code; location and identification of the person's operating unit; whether he or she is employed full-time, part-time, share-time, etc.; birth date; date of initial employment; and EEO codes.
2. *Prehire employment history:* Here are recorded job and occupation codes, type of industry, tenure on previous jobs, and employment status (e.g., was a prior job held full-time or as part-time student employment?).
3. *Company employment history:* Employment history includes dates of changes in employment status or jobs or locations, salaries and salary changes and reasons for them, summary evaluation of performance data at the time of each job change, and recent performance evaluations.
4. *General qualifications:* These include scores on tests or results of other systematic assessments; educational background, including specific kinds of courses taken and grades received; and special abilities, such as language skills or skills associated with active hobbies or avocations.
5. *Job-related qualifications:* These entries include qualifications associated with critical components of jobs held and satisfactorily performed, knowledge or skills acquired in specialized training and development programs, results of job-specific testing or other assessment programs, qualifications in the standardized list known but not required in the employment history, and rated characteristics related to outstanding contextual work behavior.
6. *Disabilities:* Basically, this includes only identification of any special accommodations requested under ADA and full information about accommodations withdrawn at the employee's request.
7. *Preferences:* The person's preferences for fields of work, locations preferred in the event of transfer, special family-related accommodations.
8. *Career path data:* Career suggestions designated by management (e.g., potential sequence of and rated readiness to begin career-path promotions) or by the individual (transfer or promotion preferences, training and development opportunities wanted, etc.).

Recruiting

The principal recruiting source is the personnel inventory, but only in the sense of providing a list of potential candidates. Turning a potential candidate into an actual candidate who wants serious consideration for the position may require more. The personnel requisition should provide basic information for a realistic job preview (Rynes, 1991; Wanous, 1980). Recruiters in the corporation's ongoing program of college recruiting have current vacancy lists, but they know that many vacancies are filled from within. Therefore, they seek candidates willing to be placed on a list if not on a job. The corporate website includes recruiting functions.

Employee-Initiated Procedures

An employee—even a well-satisfied and productive one—may seek a transfer for the sake of more money, more responsibility, more interesting work, less commuting time, or something else. For whatever reason, employees are encouraged to request a local or corporate-wide search of the personnel inventory for vacancies, either current or anticipated, for which that employee is or can become qualified. This includes vacancies in in-house training programs or training or educational opportunities through a related company-sponsored tuition refund program.

Decisions

Decisions are made jointly by several people. For the organization, the ultimate decision responsibility within the organization lies in the hands of a hiring supervisor or the head of a training program. If the opportunity is offered, however, the truly ultimate decision is made when the employee or trainee decides to accept or to reject it. These are the central decision roles, but others are usually involved. The supervisor's own supervisor and other officials in the operating unit play advisory roles, as do personnel or HR specialists. They do not have veto power; the supervisor may hire someone others think less than the best. Supervisors who consistently ignore the judgments of others, however, are not wise. To minimize controversial conflicting judgments, the program offers guidance in the form of a policy model emphasizing categories of variables to be considered and appropriate sequences or weights to use in considering them. These models have been developed through prior policy-capturing research and subsequent policy conferences.

Evaluating the System

This program is fiction, but it is not implausible. It incorporates most of the procedures so far described in this book, and it does so as a system rather than as a set of isolated functions. It incorporates a solid empirical foundation, it is necessarily multilevel in scope, and its use entails many kinds of judgments. If it were an actual program, how well would it work? And how would one find out?

Overall Evaluation

Quasi-experimental research seems appropriate. Traditional validation research would be irrelevant. Because the system was envisioned for a corporation with units in many geographical areas, and because it takes time in even one location to get it operational, the research design might build on the one designated Design 1 in Chapter 8 (see "Three Generally Interpretable Designs" in that chapter). It might consider three groups of locations. Some of the corporate locations could be more or less matched, providing two corporate groups somewhat similar in function, size, or some other characteristic. Unmatched locations could form a third group.

Observations at location level would be dictated by the program objectives. They call for a unit level of analysis and might include the following.

1. *Mean unit productivity:* Different things are produced at different locations or in different operating units, so a common measure of unit productivity may be hard to develop. Some cost/benefit ratio might be feasible. Maybe an engineering or financial standard could be computed and the productivity assessed as a percentage of that standard. Whatever it is, a productivity construct must be defined and operationalized to take differences into account and provide valid assessment of productivity across locations.

2. *Work force characteristics:* These might include several things: work force stability (turnover), mean level of job satisfaction or other employee attitude (company identification, intention to stay or quit, perceptions of procedural justice, etc.), diversity, or a measure of work force quality.
3. *Mean time of unfilled vacancies:* This is a straightforward, direct measure of the achievement of one of the program objectives.
4. *Growth in employee initiatives:* Perhaps a measure such as the number of requests for transfer, training, or personal development opportunities per hundred employees would serve. The construct here is the degree to which employees seize the opportunities the system can provide.

Some people would urge the development of a composite measure of all these outcomes—the development of which would be an exercise in group judgment or policy. One necessary judgment is whether a particular outcome is sufficiently under company control; that is, can any company-initiated program influence it directly? The answer would differ for different outcomes. My own judgment, however, is that each measure should be treated individually as an observation and the design used to test, diagnostically, any pattern of strengths or weaknesses in program outcomes (similar to principles of test use in Guion, 1961).

For each outcome measure, then, the modified design would have five periods of observation—the length of the observation period depends on several things such as criterion stability, seasonal variations, or the patience of management. The first one would be before work began on program development, providing a baseline set of observations. The second would be a period of program development in the first set of locations. The third would be the time of program introduction in that set, a period of debugging. Fourth would be a period after the program is declared fully operational. The fifth period would come after the program is fully operational in both matched groups. In each period, observations might be recorded for the group of locations with the system, the matched group without it until the fourth period, and the third group which did not match the others. Diagrammed, the design would be:

$$
\begin{array}{ccccc}
O_1 & O_2 & X,O_3 & O_4 & O_5 \\
O_1 & O_2 & O_3 & X,O_4 & O_5 \\
O_1 & O_2 & O_3 & O_4 & X,O_5
\end{array}
$$

Process Evaluation

A practical problem with this research design is that it would take a long time. Observation periods as brief as three months (probably too short) would require 15 months to collect data for this design. However, before trying to design an evaluation of the overall system, evaluation should consider how well component resources (the thesaurus, personnel requisitions, qualifications master list, and personnel inventory) are developed and how well they are accepted by the supervisors.

Many of the system components are amenable to evaluation by expert judgment, preferably pooled judgments. The evaluation of this judgmental integrated system is itself judgmental, and evaluation must ask whether the judgments are or are not generally good ones. Does wisdom reign, or is the system only superficially integrated and thoughtful? Make no mistake: in most organizations, even those where validation and personnel research are routinely done, actual personnel decisions are reached in an undeclared model somewhat like this one—at least as judgmental as this but less systematic, less well-informed by research, and not evaluated as a total program.

CONCLUDING NOTE

Research in psychology has, for several decades, made immense leaps forward in teaching us lessons about the role of judgment in decision making. The research has been digested by only a relatively small set of industrial–organizational psychologists—and still fewer specialists in individual differences, assessment, and employee selection. So far, it has had little impact on daily practice or on scientific discourse in these fields. Yet decisions are made; judgment is involved in them.

In a real sense, the latter parts of this chapter extend the previous chapter on testing. Judgments are often, like tests, cast in the role of predictors: judgments made by interviewers, or by assessors in assessment centers, are the most obvious examples. Even for these, however, personnel research has shown less interest in evaluative validation research than it has shown in tests and inventories used as predictors. It is time to remedy the situation in practice and in research.

The chapters to follow describe some very common selection practices based (at least in part, even when unacknowledged) on human judgment. Chapter 13 focuses on ratings, whether used as the criteria to be predicted or as scores for predictors in rating credentials, interview performance, performance on exercises or work samples among other subjectively evaluated data. Chapter 14 describes procedures in interviewing and other procedures for gathering background information from or about candidates and often scored with some kind of rating. The final chapter returns in part to testing procedures and the applications of the principles of combining tests to individual and group assessment programs—inherently programs of applied judgments.

13

Assessment by Ratings

Ratings and rating forms are everywhere. Guests in hotels rate the service. Patients in a rheumatologist's office rate their pain on a 10-point scale. Chocolate, wine, or movies are rated by their enthusiasts on a variety of exotic attributes. Instructors are rated by students, usually on less exotic dimensions.

Ratings are ubiquitous in the workplace, too. Attitude scales are often self-ratings. Work products may be rated for various sorts of judgments, written material rated for clarity, work samples for quality or speed, ideas for innovativeness. Job performance ratings, overall or component dimension, are common. Raters may be peers, superiors, subordinates; or outsiders (e.g., customers or vendors). Ratings may be done by one person or several, working independently or as a panel. Ratings may be criteria, predictors, or performance feedback.

Ratings as methods of assessment, especially performance ratings, are often held in low esteem. They are victim to many forms of error, both systematic and random. Kane (1987) said the field of personnel psychology was stagnant because of inadequate measurement of its major dependent variable, performance at work. Concerned about the use of ratings in validation, Wallace complained that observed reliability too often "stems not from consistency in performance but from criterion contamination . . . We can do a better job of predicting what people will say about an individual's performance than the performance itself" (Wallace, 1974, p. 403). However, Campbell et al. (1993, p. 55) said, "Although ratings generally have bad press, the overall picture is not as bleak as might be expected," and that work ratings are more likely to be explained by ratee performance than by contaminants. While regretting that the criterion problem in general is still "subservient to the predictor," Austin and Crespin (2006, p. 10) said their chapter is "optimistic," although I'm not sure why. Many problems remain. Most attempts to overcome them fit in three categories: (a) to improve rating formats, (b) to train raters, and (c) to influence the rating process.

Rating is a cognitive process, requiring at least three kinds of cognitive activity: (a) receiving and perceiving information, usually from observation or records, (b) organizing and remembering the information in preparation for rating, and (c) quantitatively evaluating what was remembered according to some rule. Remembering observations is central, but the demands on memory vary. In rating a product, for example, the time from observation to evaluation is a few minutes; for annual job performance ratings, it is up to a year.

RATING METHODS

Rating is more than making a mark on a form; it is an evaluation at the conclusion of a process that is both cognitive and psychometric. Right now we concentrate mainly on options for the form and on evaluating procedures for developing such forms and evaluating the ratings—evaluations—indicated by the marks raters put on them. The form is important insofar as it provides a way to organize the cognitive components of the process or offers a procedure less vulnerable than other options to psychometric problems. The classic Landy and Farr (1980) review of research on ratings called for a moratorium on rating format research. In fact, little has been reported that is really new since their article (noteworthy exceptions are articles, discussed below, by Borman and his associates and by Kane and his). Nevertheless, if ratings are used—and they will be—some method for organizing, recording, and quantifying them is necessary. Developers of rating systems should seek the best methods available for their purposes.

Graphic Rating Scales

Graphic rating scales are the most common of all rating methods and are used for many purposes requiring rating things, ideas, items, and performance of all kinds. They may be overall ratings or ratings of components. Variants of graphic rating scales are shown in Figure 13.1. The basic form is (a), with (b) showing how ratings become numbers. Some users prefer to anchor scale points with descriptive verbal phrases instead of numbers, as in (c).

The number of scale divisions varies; it is usually an odd number with "average" occupying a central position in the scale. More discrimination may be needed at the "above average" levels, so scales like (d) can put average somewhat off center. Eliminating the basic line, as in (e), eliminates problems of wondering where a rater meant to put a sometimes hasty check mark, as does scale (f), which includes verbal anchors and more definition of the performance trait being rated. Numerical and verbal anchors are combined in (g), which also uses more and finer gradations from the low to the high end of the scale. How many response categories are needed? Two or three is probably not enough, and it's absurd to ask raters to make distinctions along a 25-point range (although scale (g) simplifies the task by asking, in effect, for sequential judgments). The five-point scale is so widely used that it seems ordained on tablets of stone. Some writers put the limit at nine scale points (Landy & Farr, 1980), but the number is arbitrary. The number seems not to matter much; the choice boils down to the users' preferences.

Some scales (e.g., (h)) can change the numerical values of response choices according to the relative importance of the dimension being rated. In the example, "quality" has been prejudged to be worth a maximum of 15 points; other dimensions might have different maximum values for a differential weighting scheme. If, for example, "cooperation" is deemed worth 25 points, the scale would have different numerical values, but still placed in eight response positions. Scale (i) offers no visual scale; it does, however, put more structure in the task by defining more clearly what is to be rated.

The developer of a graphic rating scale should try to reduce ambiguity; beyond that, the research literature gives little help in choosing one format over another. But format can influence ratings. Using a nine-point scale, Madden and Bourdon (1964) asked groups of raters to rate 15 occupations on seven dimensions. Each group worked with a different scale format, but format differences were not dramatic. The biggest main effect was not for dimension; it was for scale format despite the apparently trivial differences.

Employee Comparisons

Method of Rank Order

Ratees may be ranked from highest to lowest on some dimension (e.g., conscientiousness, or overall job performance). Their names, in random order, might be listed on a sheet of

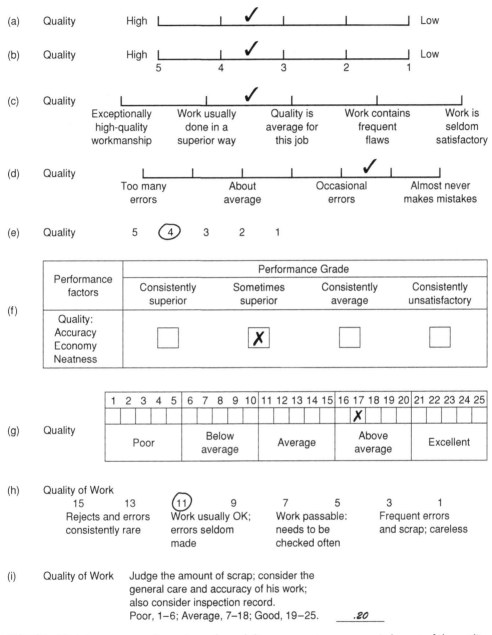

FIG. 13.1 Variations on a graphic rating scale; each line represents one way a judgment of the quality of a person's work may be recorded. From Guion, 1965a.

paper, and raters may place the number 1 by the name of the best of the lot, 2 by the next best, and so on through the list. It is probably better to put names on cards, presented in random order, to be rearranged in rank order on the dimension. Alternation ranking is recommended; it asks the rater to identify first the highest ranking person and put the card with that name face down on the desk. Then the rater finds the card for the one who will be at the bottom of the list and places it, name up, as the start of a second stack of cards. The process continues with the remaining cards, alternating from best to worst, until all have been ranked. The task gets progressively harder; extreme judgments are easy, but differences nearer the center of the distribution are harder to identify.

Ranking provides only an *ordinal* scale; it gives no information about the extent of differences. The difference between the person or object ranked 1 and the one ranked 2 may be large or trivial; there is no way to know. Guilford (1954) transformed ordinal rankings into an *interval* scale, showing a degree of separation between cases, by assuming a normal distribution of the rated attribute. Ranks can be converted to an interval scale with the standard deviation (in *z* scores or any preferred standard scale) as the assumed (but questionable) unit of measurement.

Ranking is a weak method. It offers only the relative goodness or effectiveness of the objects of measurement, not how good or how effective they might be. The poorest member of a very good work unit may be above average in another; the method ignores or even hides such differences. The method is too often used only for negative personnel decisions, deciding who shall be fired—Murphy (2008a, p. 151) called it a "rank-and-yank" system to weed out "perennially weak performers"—which is, considering the non-equivalence of the rankings, thoroughly unfair. Other employee comparison systems are open to the same criticisms, being merely different ways to achieve rank order.

Method of Forced Distribution

With many people to be rated and fine distinctions unnecessary, a forced distribution offers a crude ranking. Each person is placed in a category in frequencies that mimic the assumption of a normal distribution. Some number of categories is chosen, and proportions of a distribution (translated into frequencies) to be placed in each category are specified. A five-category example is shown in Figure 13.2. A rater with 38 names to rank writes the names of the four top people in column A, the names of the next best eight people in column B, and so on. It's still a kind of rank order, subject to the same problems, but easier.

Method of Paired Comparisons

Based on the "law of comparative judgment" (Thurstone, 1927), sensory experiences, attitudes, and traits can be scaled by pairing objects of measurement (i.e., people in this context) and calling for judgments as to which one in each pair is considered to have more of a specified attribute. In judgments of core work competence, each ratee can be compared in pairs to each of the other ratees. For each pair of names, the rater indicates the more competent one; the one chosen most frequently is the one ranked at the top of the list. (Yes, it's still a way to put people in rank order—but a more reliable one.) Common conventions for presenting the pairs have developed. The same name should not appear in two consecutive pairs. Each person should be listed first and second equally often. Pairs should be presented in roughly random order—"roughly" to follow the first two constraints. There might be a lot of pairs; if five people are to be compared, there are 10 pairs of names. Ten people require 45 pairs, 190 pairs for 20 people. (These numbers assume that each pair is compared only once; the number of pairs is $n(n - 1)/2$; each pair could be listed twice, using both orders, doubling these numbers!) Lawshe and Balma (1966) provided tables for setting up such pairs. The number of times a given name is preferred can be transformed into a standard score scale, often with a mean of 50 and standard deviation of 10. If the assumption of normality is troublesome, the score (rating) can be simply the number of times a ratee is chosen.

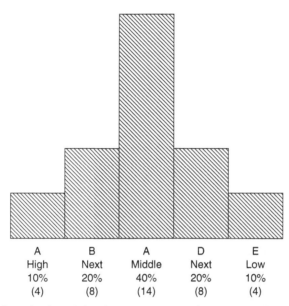

A	B	A	D	E
High	Next	Middle	Next	Low
10%	20%	40%	20%	10%
(4)	(8)	(14)	(8)	(4)

FIG. 13.2   A sample form for forced distribution ratings; numbers in parentheses show how a rater with 38 people to evaluate should distribute them across these five segments. From Guion, 1965a.

With a long list of people to be compared, the amount of time required can get out of hand. Reasonable people disagree about how long is too long. Guilford (1954) put the limit at about 15 objects or people, but Lawshe, Kephart, and McCormick (1949) reported that a list of 24 names (276 pairs) was rated reliably in 30 minutes—not an excessively wearying task. However, the required number of pairs can be reduced (see, e.g., McCormick & Bachus, 1952; McCormick & Roberts, 1952).

Scaling Methods

Ratings can be based on attitude scaling methods; the two most widely used are the method of equal-appearing intervals (Thurstone, 1928) and the method of summated ratings (Likert, 1932). They both apply psychometric methods to ratings, although the Thurstone method has a firmer, less purely intuitive foundation in measurement theory.

Method of Equal-Appearing Intervals

A checklist can be given to a rater who simply checks those statements that describe the person being rated. The items are previously scaled on the theoretical assumption that equally often noticed differences are equal (Thurstone, 1928), an assumption first made for psychophysical scaling by Fechner (Boring, 1950). In this procedure, a judge sorts statements into piles representing steps judged to be equal on, say, an 11-point scale.[1] A very favorable statement may be placed in pile 10 or 11; a very unfavorable one belongs in pile 1. When

---

[1] The sorting procedure described here is traditional but not really necessary. Scales are often smaller, and judgments can be obtained equally well by listing the statements, following each with the number series from 1 to 7 (or whatever range of values is being used); the judge simply circles the desired number (Prien & Campbell, 1957; Seigel & Seigel, 1962). Many other variations have been used.

Item	Scale value	Variance
___ Makes costly errors of judgment in the work	*1.4*	*.33*
✓ Does as little as possible...	*1.9 −4.1*	*1.39*
✓ Plays favorites	*2.6 −3.4*	*1.45*
___ Makes unreasonable requests.	*3.0*	*1.60*
✓ Sizes up people poorly.	*3.4 −2.6*	*.93*
___ Conduct borders on insubordination..	*3.6*	*5.35*
✓ Is inclined to be impatient with others...	*4.2 −1.8*	*.66*
___ Is self-conscious in the presence of superiors	*5.0*	*2.15*
___ Is very outspoken..	*5.7*	*3.01*
___ Conceals own weaknesses very effectively	*6.4*	*3.14*
✓ Is almost never late for work..	*6.8 +.8*	*2.86*
___ Can stand criticism without feeling hurt..	*7.4*	*1.94*
___ Keeps a firm hold without becoming unreasonable	*7.8*	*2.19*
___ Praises good work without becoming flattering	*8.4*	*2.04*
✓ Understands the problems of other departments well	*9.0 +3.0*	*2.10*
___ Shows remarkable clarity in thinking a problem through	*9.4*	*1.64*
___ Is a "born leader"...	*10.0*	*1.65*
___ Is destined for a brilliant future..	*10.6*	*.94*

Total score   __−8.1__

FIG. 13.3   Checklist statements scaled by the method of equal appearing intervals. Drawn from Uhrbrock, R. S. (1950), Standardization of 724 rating scale statements. *Personnel Psychology, 14,* 285–316. The author and publisher intended this set of scaled items to be used as a pool from which to draw in developing local rating forms. © John Wiley & Sons. Reproduced with permission.

all judges in a group have recorded their judgments, the mean and standard deviation of judged scale values (or median and semi-interquartile range) are computed for each statement. The item's scale value is the mean (or median); the standard deviation (or semi-interquartile range) indicates the item's ambiguity. The least ambiguous statements throughout the scale are assembled into a checklist, as shown in Figure 13.3. The rater would see the statements within the frame of Figure 13.3, not the scale values or variances; an operational checklist should omit the high-variance item, "conduct borders on insubordination."

After descriptions have been checked, a final score (rating) is computed. The recommended scoring procedure requires the neutral value (6 in the 11-point case) to be subtracted from the scale value of each item checked; the score may be the algebraic sum of these positive and negative values. The numerical rating is determined by someone with a scoring key, someone other than the rater.

Measuring item ambiguity is a key feature of the method. If a word means different things to different people, it is a source of unreliability. For example, the statement, "conduct borders on insubordination," may mean troublemaker behavior to one rater and to another a commendable independence that does not cross the border. In contrast, the statement, "does as little as possible," means about the same to everyone.

Method of Summated Ratings

Just as several test items all reflecting the same construct are used to develop a test, several detailed statements, based on a common construct, can form a rating scale. Instead of

Performance Rating Form
for
Patrol Officers

Officer's Name _____   Badge No. _____

Rater's Name _____   District _____

(Job Competence Scale)

1. This officer's reports are clear and to the point.

     Strongly Agree   Agree   Unsure   Disagree   Strongly Disagree

2. This officer gives court testimony completely and precisely, with good recall.

     Strongly Agree   Agree   Unsure   Disagree   Strongly Disagree

3. When confronted with a set of completely new circumstances, this officer grasps the situation very quickly.

     Strongly Agree   Agree   Unsure   Disagree   Strongly Disagree

4. This officer knows how and when to search a suspect in making an arrest.

     Strongly Agree   Agree   Unsure   Disagree   Strongly Disagree

5. This officer has a firm working knowledge of police procedures as outlined in general orders, special orders, etc.

     Strongly Agree   Agree   Unsure   Disagree   Strongly Disagree

FIG. 13.4   Sample items for a rating procedure based on the method of summated ratings.

dichotomous items, Likert (1932) used items for which responses could fall on a graphic rating scale with three to perhaps nine or more scale values. Individual scales are typically simple ones like the first five in Figure 13.1, and response options show how strongly the rater agrees or disagrees with the statement as a description of the ratee, as in Figure 13.4. All of the statements in Figure 13.4 describe good or desirable behavior, and the responses range from 5 (*strongly agree*) to 1 (*strongly disagree*). Other rating forms might use more or fewer scale points, and the verbal anchors might reflect different kinds of dimensions; responses for frequency of occurrence of something might, for example, range from *always* to *never*, although less extreme words would be better. Some items might describe something unfavorable, such as poor performance or the occurrence of counterproductive behavior; values for these would be reversed, with 5 assigned to *strongly disagree* or *never*. Neutral items give no hint of the appropriate direction for scoring, so items must clearly be either favorable or unfavorable; Pedhazur and Schmelkin (1991) recommended equal numbers of favorable and unfavorable items. The final rating is the sum of the values of the response categories chosen by the rater, that is, summated ratings.[2]

Item analysis is required, usually item-total correlations and means and standard deviations of item responses. Poor items, those with large variances or none at all, or poor item-total

---

[2] In measuring attitudes, the item response scale is often given as ranging from "Strongly Agree" through "Undecided" to "Strongly Disagree"; the abbreviations for a five-response scale are typically SA, A, U, D, SD. Many people refer to a single item using the SA to SD response scale as a "Likert-type scale." This is a betrayal of ignorance; such scales were used long before Likert reported his method in 1932. A Likert-type scale is a multiple-item, summated-response scale. It is better simply to call it a summated response scale, as he did.

correlations, are deleted before the scale is used operationally. A dubious advantage of the method is that it can be used without prior pilot studies; the item analysis can use the same data.

Items for performance ratings should be based on job analysis defining a content domain to be assessed. Items written to fit aspects of a job content domain can be interpreted with reference to the defined domain, that is, domain-referenced interpretations are feasible. Ranking or scaling by equal-appearing intervals leads generally to norm-referenced inferences.

Behaviorally Anchored Rating Scales (BARS)

Smith and Kendall (1963) described the use of relatively unambiguous behavioral anchors for graphic rating scales. As a system of rating, Borman et al. (2001) rightly declared it "fundamentally different from other rating instruments" (p. 965). Their method, however, is more than just another format; it is a system of domain sampling, of engaging raters in the development process, and of developing anchors for rating scales that are likely to be meaningful and clear to the raters who use them. Their approach was unique because it was thoroughly embedded in a larger system, to which I will return later. For now, I discuss it simply as a rating method.

Principles for Developing BARS

Smith and Kendall (1963) described a logical basis and a procedure for developing a performance rating system. Many scales have been said to follow the Smith and Kendall approach, but they do not often follow it completely. The attractiveness of behaviorally oriented scale anchors has resulted in the generic term *behaviorally anchored rating scales* or *BARS*. The many rating methods called BARS, and some criticisms of BARS not relevant to the Smith–Kendall procedures, called forth a clarification by Bernardin and Smith (1981). They pointed out that the Smith–Kendall approach was a sequence beginning with observation followed in order by inference, scaling, recording, and summary rating.[3] Developing and using the rating process is itself a complex system, but it is only part of the system envisioned by Smith and Kendall.

The Smith–Kendall procedure assumes that raters are fairly bright people, who know the demands of the jobs involved, who can define those demands in terms of performance characteristics or dimensions, who have watched people meet or fail to meet the performance demands, and who know how workers functioning at different performance levels behave at work. The procedure assumes that these bright people can approach consensus on interpretations of performance behaviors without having them imposed by an outside researcher. This implies the assumption and acceptance of the idea that potential raters may have valid implicit theories of performance. The procedure therefore calls for groups of potential raters to make implicit theories explicit by expressing, in their own terms, the kinds of behavior representing different levels or kinds of performance.

Smith and Kendall rejected several kinds of rating formats. Graphic scales like those in Figure 13.1, with ratings limited to specific points on five- or seven- or nine-point scales, were rejected as too confining. They preferred a continuous scale, where raters could assign

---

[3] Some say that the method has evolved, and that evolution accounts for the variety. It can be said more accurately that it has been distorted by treating it merely as another rating format, without treating the form as part of a larger, comprehensive system.

values between the anchored scale points. Scaling of critical incidents was rejected because incidents identified as critical do not often occur, and because critical incidents tend toward extremes rather than being in the ordinary range where most people do their work. Forced choice, a procedure interesting many researchers at the time, was rejected largely because of user resistance.

For supervisory ratings of nurses, they chose vertical graphic rating scales with anticipated kinds of behavior (anchors expressed as *behavioral expectations*) placed at different heights to indicate differing levels of the performance characteristic being rated. Performance characteristics (the dimensions to be rated) and the behavioral descriptions related to them were to be developed, not by the researchers, but by supervisors. Smith and Kendall (1963) did not use the term, "behaviorally anchored rating scales"; the title of their article referred to reducing anchor ambiguity and to "retranslation of expectations," identifying key provisions of their method.

The first key provision was the use of behavioral expectations, rather than actually observed behavior, as anchor points on the scale. The behavioral anchors were descriptions of behavior that could be anticipated or "expected" of people working at different levels of performance—examples that might be "expected" of people working at any of these levels, even if the ratee had not actually shown the behavior. They were "expectations" in the sense of, "That's just the sort of thing you come to expect from Joe."[4] Raters were asked to decide whether behavior of a nurse being rated, behavior actually observed, would lead them to expect (or not be surprised by) behavior from that nurse like the behavior described in a scale anchor. Anchors were not glittering generalities such as "shows interest in patients' description of symptoms"; the anchors consisted of things real nurses might do, such as, *If this nurse were admitting a patient who talks rapidly and continuously of her symptoms and past medical history, could be expected to look interested and listen.* Calling for the rater to make such predictions implies that he or she is willing to infer from observations of behavior, has at least an implicit belief about the intercorrelation of behaviors. "The present procedure gambles that among a relatively homogeneous group of judges such as head nurses, these beliefs will be reasonably well standardized" (Smith & Kendall, 1963, p. 151).

The second key provision is *retranslation*—a procedure to assure that behavioral statements originally written by one group to describe potential behavior for a given dimension are seen by others as fitting that dimension. The analogy is to translating a passage from one language into another. A first group of judges writes behavioral expectations to fit each dimension. A second, independent, group of judges (a) reads statements for all dimensions, mixed together in random order, (b) discusses definitions of dimensions for a common understanding, and then (c) independently allocates each statement to a dimension. A "good" item is generally allocated to the dimension for which it was developed. If there is no modal agreement about where it belongs, the statement is dropped. An entire dimension may be dropped if items written for it are not generally assigned to it.

The third key provision minimizes ambiguity of scale value by using the method of equal-appearing intervals. The variance of judgments is a measure of the ambiguity of the statement; high-variance statements are eliminated.

---

[4] I've experienced some difficulty with an ambiguity in the term "expect." Raters have told me that they *expect* every ratee to perform at the top of every scale; the implication is that they expect this even from ratees who are unlikely to perform that well. Expectations, in the Smith–Kendall sense, are anticipations of reality more than idealistic dreams of job demands or obligations.

A fourth feature of the Smith–Kendall procedure is usually ignored by other BARS developers. It permits, and I think should require, raters to give at least one example of ratee behavior actually observed for each dimension rated, inserted at the point on the scale that appropriately identifies its position relative to the defining anchors. With this feature, it is clear that the Smith–Kendall procedure is more than just another rating format; it is a system of stimulus material (the form) being developed from the informed observations and inferences of potential raters and used with records of continued real-time observations by actual raters.

The Procedure

Smith–Kendall principles may be applied, in the following steps, for nearly all kinds of work.

1. *Convene one or more groups of potential raters.* These may be some immediate supervisors who will ultimately use the rating system and who represent various organizational locations or functions.

2. In conference, *develop a list of the performance characteristics (dimensions) to be evaluated.* Reduce the list to those believed most important, retaining terms used by the potential raters.

3. In each group, *develop definitions of high, acceptable, and low performance for each dimension.*

4. In each group, for each dimension, *develop lists of actual behavioral examples of high, acceptable, and low performance.* A brief account of the situation in which the behavior occurred may be necessary for clarity. Edit the behavioral examples into the behavioral expectations form. (Some editing can be done later by the researchers if the key words of potential raters are retained.)

5. *Give the lists of behavioral expectations and the dimension definitions to one or more new groups of potential raters not included in the first groups.* These groups may meet physically to discuss definitions, but each person should work independently to allocate behavior statements to dimensions (the retranslation). Statements should be randomized, and a specified level of agreement (e.g., 80%) should be set in advance. Also, a prior criterion can be set to identify the proportion of behavioral examples written for a dimension that must be allocated to that dimension; dimensions that fail to meet the criterion may be eliminated. This process should not be excessively mechanical; judgment is useful. Dimensions may be combined, definitions may be edited, and some intermediate data collection may be needed—but always with the involvement of potential raters.

6. For each dimension, *have individuals rate an outstanding worker, and one who is unsatisfactory, for each behavioral statement* to get a statistical index of item discrimination power.

7. *Give surviving statements to those in another group of potential raters to be scaled by the method of equal appearing intervals.* Provide the scale definition and definitions of high, low, and acceptable levels of performance; a nine-point scale is convenient. It is useful to offer distinctions between the dimension at hand and other dimensions with which it might be confused. Items with relatively large variances are eliminated as ambiguous. Items retained should have minimal overlap in the dispersions of scale value judgments.

8. *Develop and distribute a final rating form to raters before ratings are due.* This provides time for familiarization with the dimensions, for observing behavior among the workers to be rated, and for recording observations. The form typically uses a vertical scale with limiting values (in the Smith–Kendall report) of 0 and 2.0, marked off in increments of .25. This is a nine-point scale, but the decimal notation seems to encourage the use of intermediate values not explicitly identified or anchored by scaled expectations on the printed form. The form should give definitions (definition of the dimension generally and of high, low, and acceptable performance), the array of scaled expectations, space to write in some actual observations, and space to record the rating.

Clearly, the procedure takes time. An ordinary graphic rating scale can be developed by one person in a matter of minutes, so the time required for all these steps, plus data analysis, may seem excessive. Perhaps it is. But if the resulting set of performance ratings is more reliable, more valid, more easily interpreted, and more likely to survive as a tool for performance management, it may well be worth the extra effort—and the avoidance of shortcuts.

Figure 13.5 is an example of a rating form developed by part of the Smith–Kendall method. It is a bad example because it is based on some procedural shortcuts and because it used only those parts of the system that lead to a rating form, not the system as a whole. For example, it has no provision for recording actual behavior fitting between anchors. It was designed for peer ratings of work motivation among engineers. In calling it a bad example; I am not disclaiming the research—indeed, it is a good example of a behaviorally anchored rating scale. It is a bad example only because it does not follow the overall system of the Smith–Kendall approach.

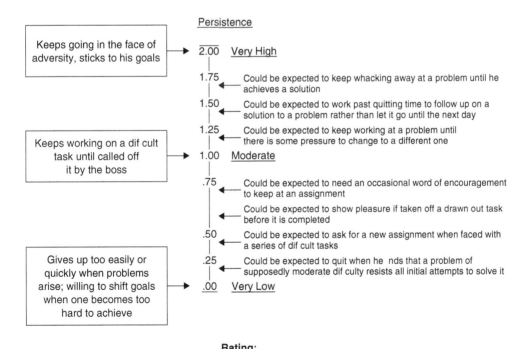

FIG. 13.5 An example of a behaviorally anchored rating scale (BARS) to assess work persistence (an aspect of work motivation) among engineers.

This is not contradictory. The term BARS has come to refer to a rating scale using some Smith–Kendall procedures, perhaps for scale definitions and for generating, retranslating, and scaling behavioral statements, but not necessarily expressing statements as likely behavior or providing for raters recording actual observations on the scale. We must not overemphasize the form over the system. Pat Smith and I developed a performance evaluation system for a local police department. Our system, and a ten-year follow-up, are described below in the performance management section.

Behavioral Observation Scales (BOS)

Instead of largely unobserved behavioral expectations, Latham and Wexley (1981) rated actually required job behaviors, grouped for specific job dimensions. Their scales are called *Behavioral Observation Scales* (BOS). Smith and Kendall (1963) used Thurstone's method of equal-appearing intervals for scaling behavior expectations; the BOS approach used Likert's method of summated ratings. The response scale is frequency of observation, a five-point scale ranging from 1 (*almost never*) to 5 (*almost always*). The five points are defined in terms of the percent of the time the behavior is observed. Latham and Wexley suggested percentages of 0–64% for (*almost never*) through 65–74%, 75–84%, 85–94%, and 95–100% (*almost always*); they have also reported using a straightforward 20% increment for each scale point. The obvious problem for scale development, for BOS and other methods, is that a highly favorable behavior could also be rarely seen; rare behavior should be avoided when writing items. The response scale does not have to be a frequency scale. In skilled trades, for example, it might refer to the cost of errors attributed to not carrying out the behavior or carrying it out poorly. For customer service personnel, it might call for a judgment of impact on customer relations.

BOS can be developed in less time than BARS because prior item scaling is not needed. If job analysis is well done and well organized, behavioral statements should be prepared with minimal effort and time. Job analysis surveys may be too elemental; if so, job experts may consolidate elementary items into broader, more comprehensive statements. Items are usually equally weighted, but differential weights could be assigned by expert judgment. The job relevance of the ratings is obvious, making them easily defensible in litigation.

When ratings have been collected, item analysis (variability and item-total correlations) can identify poorly functioning items (e.g., high variance, excessively skewed, or unreliable means). Removal of these can result in spreading out the range of actual ratings (Latham & Wexley, 1981). The method is generally norm-referenced; its purpose is to differentiate between people who perform at different levels. If the ratings form a criterion measure for validation, norm-referencing is fully appropriate. If, however, the purpose is to determine adequacy of individual performance or to serve as a reference in developing standards (for hiring, for promotion, for tenure, etc.), then a domain-referenced interpretation seems better; in such cases, item analysis results should not eliminate important items that nearly everyone does frequently or well.

Computerized Adaptive Rating System (CARS)

Computerized adaptive testing has become commonplace. Computerized adaptive rating has not—yet. Borman et al. (2001) introduced CARS, an adaptive rating model different from other rating procedures. For the introductory study, they chose three dimensions of citizenship behavior to be rated: *personal support*, *organizational support*, and *conscientious initiative*.

To evaluate the CARS procedure, it was decided that each dimension would have three different rating forms, the CARS, seven-point graphic scales, and BARS developed in the Smith–Kendall tradition.

The researchers generated behavioral statements for the three dimensions and had them retranslated in two stages. First, Air Force NCOs allocated statements to the three dimensions and rated the effectiveness of the behaviors described. Many items were edited or revised on the basis of information from the first step. In the second stage, staff members of Personnel Decisions Research Institute, not previously involved in the work, reallocated and re-rated item effectiveness. Results of the two stages satisfied the researchers that the retained items fit the intended dimensions well. The statements were to be presented in a paired comparisons form; this use required a new computer algorithm to develop item response curves as well as a new program for the adaptive presentation (cf. Stark & Drasgow, 1998, for details).

In this initial trial, 112 participants (students and local employees, many of whom in both groups had supervisory experience) viewed videotaped performance of six ratees, performances scripted to provide targeted levels on the three contextual criteria. All participants used the CARS approach and either the graphic or the BARS for comparison. Considering the detailed results, "it seems there is some feature of the CARS format that creates more reliable and valid differentiation between ratees" (p. 970).

A subsequent study of CARS for assessing competence of managers (Schneider et al., 2003) was done to (a) find out whether the earlier work on citizenship dimensions would be applicable for task performance and (b) check a modification of the earlier procedure to see if fewer item pairs could be used without loss in precision of estimating performance parameters.

A conceptual model of management performance was developed for a client organization; it included at least 10 dimensions. Five of these are task dimensions, shown with sample statements in Table 13.1. For each statement the effectiveness level is the mean of the four-point ratings assigned by a group of consultants. Statements in item pairs differed somewhat in effectiveness level. In simulations, at least (and the authors acknowledge the need to go beyond simulations), a change in the stopping rule allowed for fewer pairs to be rated without loss of precision. CARS seems to be a method to consider further in a variety of situations.

Distributional Rating Method

Performance is not uniform from week to week, or day to day, or even hour to hour. It varies over time, even short times, on all performance dimensions. Most rating procedures seem based on assumptions of stability from one moment, day, or week to another. In her title, Fisher (2008) asked, "What if we took within-person performance variability seriously?" She has done so (Fisher, 2008; Fisher & Noble, 2004).

So did Kane (1996). Viewing performance evaluation from that perspective, he developed *performance distribution assessment*. He emphasized outcomes, not behavior, as Campbell et al. (1993) and others have, saying "performance on any aspect of a job can be conceived and assessed as a distribution of occurrences over a continuum of outcomes or behaviors" (Kane, 1996, p. 123), and defined performance as "the record of outcomes achieved in carrying out a specific job aspect during a specified period" (p. 125), or "the *record* of the person's accomplishments" (p. 124; emphasis in original). He acknowledges that jobs have different "aspects" or dimensions, but he seems to prefer assessing overall job performance with a distributional index termed *total performance effectiveness.* "Distributional assessment

TABLE 13.1

Task Dimensions, Sample Items, and Effectiveness Levels for CARS

Performance Dimension	Abbreviated Definition	Sample Behavior Statement	Effectiveness Level
Focus on the customer	Deliver fast response to meet customer needs. Build strong relationships with customers based on trust and respect	Proactively identifies and rectifies potential customer concerns before they surface as complaints	3.81
Understand the business	Know in depth customers, competitors, and associates. Keep current on matters affecting us. Maintain expertise	Makes decisions for his/her work group that are not consistent with the company's strategic priorities	1.20
Take action	Seek creative solutions, add value. Analyze info quickly, make timely decisions. Show bias for action that matters	Achieves closure or significant progress on most key issues in meetings he/she conducts	3.00
Take responsibility	Be accountable. Relentlessly pursue goals. Take responsibility for mistakes and failures. Step in to help clients even if not your job	Offers to assume responsibility for addressing difficult problems and issues that others seek to avoid	3.77
Communicate	Share information. Listen carefully and be open to others' views. Build opinion-sharing environment	Leads the way in creating a climate in which candid dialog is valued and encouraged	3.89

Adapted from Schneider, R. J., Goff, M., Anderson, S., & Borman, W. C. (2003). Computerized adaptive rating scales for measuring managerial performance. *International Journal of Selection and Assessment, 11*, 237–246. © John Wiley & Sons. Adapted by permission.

stands as an alternative to *judgmental assessment*, which is employed in all conventional performance rating methods" (Kane, 1996, p. 127; emphasis in original).

Procedures for arriving at this index differ from traditional rating methods where, even if a performance distribution over time period is assumed, the rater is assumed to report a judgment of either the mean of that distribution or the maximum point on it. Kane's method not only assumes a distribution but wants to see it—to be able to draw it. Once performance (or its component dimensions) is defined, "a frequency distribution is then generated for each factor from the reported frequencies reflecting each individual's record of performance" (Kane & Woehr, 2006, p. 78). Graphically, frequency of occurrence is the ordinate; level of effectiveness is the abscissa. With the distribution available, the method can consider other descriptive distributional characteristics: standard deviations, skewness, kurtosis, and their interactions. The distribution can be shown graphically as a percentage of all outcomes in a specified time period, and for a specified job aspect or dimension, at each of several levels of effectiveness, as in the examples in Figure 13.6. A record of outcomes might be retrieved from company records or, for less readily observable outcomes, from memory, diary, or whatever. Fisher (2008) explicitly recommended an old idea of keeping diaries in which to record observations as they occur. That can be a daunting expenditure of time, so some shortcuts can be used. She recommended a plan for sampling times to record observations; in my own work, I have asked supervisors (of small numbers of ratees) to record near the end of the work period the most and least effective things each ratee did that day (or that week).

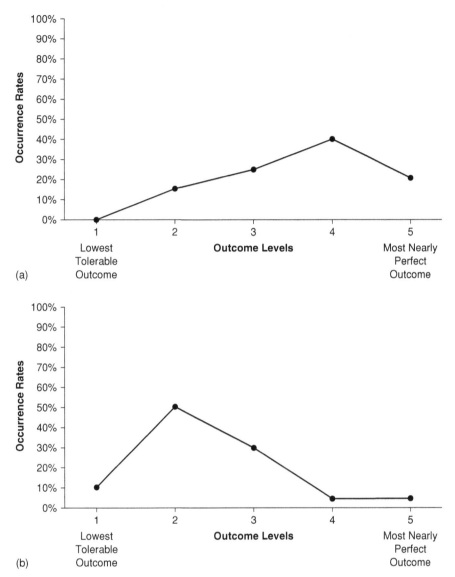

FIG. 13.6   Distribution of performance data for two people. Part (a) is reprinted from Kane, J. S. (1996),
The conceptualization and representation of total performance effectiveness. *Human Resource Management
Review*, 6, 123–145, © 1996 by Elsevier Science & Technology Journals; used by permission. Part (b) has
been drawn to represent the opposite form of skewness.

The curves in Figure 13.6 are hypothetical performance distributions that "contain
all the information there is to know about that particular performance, except for its trend
over time" (Kane, 1996, p. 125). That exception is not trivial. Trend information, even if
available, is usually ignored in other assessments of performance (but refer to the growth
curve trajectories discussed in Chapter 10). Moreover, performance trends markedly affect
ratings, and they differentially affect ratings for developmental and administrative purposes
(Reb & Greguras, 2010).

The negatively skewed distribution, (a), from Kane's article, was said to represent performance of one who avoids unfavorable outcomes. The positively skewed distribution, (b), was added to represent someone with a motivation problem, one who *can* do very well but does so in fact only when closely monitored. Such inferences are possible but not really part of the ordinary performance rating procedure. The distributions, without spurious inferences, provide more information about performance than can be gleaned from averages or peaks of effectiveness. An effectiveness index can be determined for the distributions of all job aspects, and these can be combined according to Kane's formula (Kane, 1996, p. 133) for the total performance effectiveness rating. The proposition that recalled frequencies correlate well with actual frequencies have been supported by laboratory studies; the Kane and Woehr (2006) report of that support is generally favorable, but it also emphasizes unknowns that call for new research.

Will the concept improve efforts to use ratings as performance assessments? Fox, Bizman, and Garti (2005) applied ratings of recalled (not recorded) performance distributions on eight dimensions. They also compared these distributional ratings with conventional graphic ratings on the eight dimensions, using average ratings as surrogates for true scores. The distributional system provided substantially more agreement with those averages than for the traditional scales. Fisher and Noble (2004) also found a place for ratings, keeping records of self-report ratings of performance at each of five time periods per day. Studies like these try to avoid sudden departure from traditional ratings, and more of them could be useful. Where it is really feasible, however, I would prefer more research on Kane's departure, based on real performance records.

Comment: Methods and Moratoria

At this point, a proper textbook author would offer lists of relative advantages and disadvantages of the several methods and, perhaps, recommend some over others, at least for some purposes. I cannot do so. Few comparative studies have been done, and those few have not consistently shown certain methods superior to others. Studies that did find one method better than another generally do not say why. Conventional wisdom is that the choice of method does not matter. Conventional wisdom endorsed a Landy and Farr (1980) proposal for a moratorium on rating format research. I still agree, but conventional wisdom too often studies trivial characteristics of ratings (e.g., vertical versus horizontal graphic scales) and therefore finds only trivial differences.

A series of studies directed by E. K. Taylor began with one by Taylor and Manson (1951). They built graphic scales using every available suggestion for improvements, supervised the ratings, and insisted on following prescribed procedures. Results pleased them: no sign of classical rating errors. Further research refined the structure of the format, and then, in a grand finale study, all of the good results of that structure faded; the research team expressed disenchantment with graphic rating scales (Taylor, Parker, & Ford, 1959). In commenting on the series (Guion, 1965a), I pointed out that most of the successes in the series—the studies where format mattered—were done with relatively inexperienced and unmotivated raters. The final set of raters consisted of highly experienced raters who had long considered performance rating an important component of their jobs. For them, and for similarly experienced raters in an earlier study (Taylor & Hastman, 1956), format choice was trivial. For inexperienced samples, format mattered. A moratorium is less important than the choice of research samples.

Rating methods that work well for one purpose may not fit a different one. Ratings based on performance in an audition or interview differ from ratings of performance over a year or so. Rating objects, such as portfolios or work sample products, differs from rating people. Ratings may differ in time span of observations or of memory, in dimension complexity, in data organization, in opportunity to reconsider, and in many other details. Effects of such differences have not been studied. The *de facto* but unintentional moratorium on them should disappear.

One area of needed research would consider the meaningful differences between domain-referenced and norm-referenced assessment. Prescaled checklists and behaviorally anchored rating scales tend to be domain-referenced in construction and can be in interpretation. On the other hand, employee comparison is strictly norm-referenced. The distinction is not trivial. Norm referencing ratings are valuable in selection, but, especially for those used as criteria, greater attention should be given to the concept of domain-referencing. If validation does no more than determine the variance in a predictor associated with variance in a criterion, a common aim, norm-referenced rating is fine. For demanding jobs, ratings (whether of performance or qualifications), research on psychometric properties of the methods should not be abandoned but should move toward explicitly domain-referenced assessments of performance.

PSYCHOMETRIC ISSUES

Questions and issues in the psychometric evaluation of tests apply as well to ratings. Measurement implies individual differences in the trait rated; that implies variance and the need to identify likely sources of variance. To be valid, variance in ratings should be mainly associated with variance in the actual trait level (e.g., performance) of ratees. Variance in the ratings may also be due to influences of the measurement procedure, its purposes, irrelevant worker characteristics, characteristics of the situation in which performance is measured, and characteristics of the raters. In short, the usual psychometric problems are exacerbated in measurement by ratings.

Questions of Validity

Through most of the history of personnel testing, ratings have been the criteria against which tests are validated. As such, ratings are criterion *measures*, and should be evaluated as such. Validation of criteria is now considered sensible, but it has not always been considered so. In the mid-twentieth century, when validation meant computing a correlation between scores on the test and criterion, it was said that efforts to validate criteria would just lead to an infinite regress. Criteria, it was thought, needed evaluation only in terms of reliabilities. By the end of the twentieth century, of course, construct validity (psychometric validity) was advocated in criterion validation. In this newer century, many psychologists retain that psychometric emphasis.

Referring to those ratings called performance appraisals, Murphy (2008b, p. 198) said, "The recognition that raters in organizations are not simply passive measurement instruments . . . is critically important for understanding the potential sources for both systematic variance and error variance in performance ratings." Perhaps I project my own attitudes, but I think Murphy meant that performance appraisal, for broad management purposes, must be concerned with more than the adequacy of the quantification, which (despite my admitted quantitative bias) seems eminently reasonable. From this perspective, arguing that appraisal is distinct from measurement is much ado about nothing much. There is always some relevance of psychometric issues, so I'll just get on with it!

"Accuracy"

Some psychometric literature confuses accuracy with reliability, but the literature on ratings often seems to confuse accuracy and validity. In Chapter 5, I defined accuracy as the degree to which the identity, $Y = X$, describes the relationship between a measure, X, and a standard, Y. Discussions of rating accuracy, however, typically stem from a validity perspective: Does variance in a set of job performance ratings really correspond to variance in actual job performance? It is impossible to know "true" performance with which rated performance can be compared, or to compare true distributions of performance with rating distributions (Woehr, 2008), but that has not stopped authors from using either "true performance" or "accuracy" in describing either the problems or their proposed solutions. Indeed, these terms *are* semantic "misnomers" (Woehr, 2008, p. 162). Typically, researchers simply declare something to be a standard set of ratings, such as a set of experts' ratings. "Yet, what evidence do we have that the 'expert ratings' actually reflect 'true performance' or are 'better' than some other set of ratings? None, and thus we come full circle and all we can definitely conclude is how one set of ratings compare with another" (Woehr, 2008, p. 162).

Much research on so-called rating accuracy has been done in laboratory settings in which a target rating is developed to be used as the standard, Y. Targets are usually set by panels of experts with virtually unlimited opportunity to study materials to be rated (e.g., videotapes of people doing things, or "paper people" vignettes). Alternatives include using an average of all the ratings in a set as the target using average ratings for prescaled items (Sulsky & Balzer, 1988). Such averages are surrogates for the psychometric "true score" notion, used by Cronbach (1955) in identifying four aspects of accuracy in subjective judgment. I have found this approach underwhelming and therefore merely mention it. However, much of the laboratory research on ratings has used these aspects of accuracy as a dependent variable. These experiments have often used short-term periods of observation and evaluation, such as in rating work products, interview behavior, or performance in assessment center exercises. I have serious reservations about their generalizability to long-term performance rating.

Constructs Rated

Whether the intent of assessment is to predict or to describe, evidence of fulfilling the intention is needed. If the evidence is a validity coefficient, it needs replication. Even if replicated, it should be evaluated for irrelevant but systematic sources of error that may either enhance or limit the persuasiveness of a validity argument. An inferred description needs (a) clarity in defining the attribute to be described by the measure, and, (b) data concerning irrelevant but systematic sources of error that may either support or question the use of the measure as a trait description. Effective assessment requires identifying and defining the construct to be rated and evidence that the ratings do in fact assess it—in short, evidence of construct validity (Austin & Crespin, 2006)—and it is needed for ratings as well as for other assessments. It is rarely provided; in general, ratings are used on faith, and despite several recent attempts to be analytic, that still seems the dominant practice.

One issue is that hardy perennial question: should the construct be narrow or broad? Some researchers argue that job performance is mainly general and that aspects of performance others describe are either sources of error or trivial lower factors (cf. Viswesvaran et al., 2005). Others overlook the issue, considering components of overall performance, despite nagging worries about their independence, as more important to organizational functioning.

A second issue is whether performance constructs are stable or dynamic. The notion of dynamic criteria is now well developed, but it seems to have been studied more as changes in predictability than as changes in the nature of constructs. The latter focus seems too recent (although it isn't) and, so far, insufficiently explored, to be dogmatic about it, but maybe dynamic changes in performance do in fact involve changes in constructs, that is, changes in the nature of the performance rated. A number of influences on the dynamics have been reported even without going so far as to argue for construct change over time (e.g., Becker, 2000; Dierdorff & Surface, 2007; Sturman, Cheramie, & Cashen, 2005).

Questions of validity differ depending on whether the ratings are used as predictors or as criteria. As predictors, ratings may be validated just as other predictors are. For example, validity coefficients may be computed—but preferably not using other ratings as criteria, and certainly not with the same raters. As criteria, descriptive construct validity is essential. As both—when ratings serve both predictor and criterion functions—a dandy correlation just might be due to shared method variance, especially when both sides of the equation share the same raters.

MTMM for Construct Validity

Constructs rated are rarely as well defined as those measured by standardized tests. Without definitions, investigation of construct validity is difficult.[5] One approach uses *multitrait–multimethod matrices (MTMM)* (see Chapter 6). If measures of a trait are correlated fairly well when measured by the different methods, the measures are said to show *convergent validity*. If the measures of the different traits show convergent validity, but do not correlate much with measures of other traits, even when measured by common methods, the measures are said to show *discriminant validity*. It takes both to support inferences of construct or psychometric validity. At best, however, the MTMM approach is fraught with questions about whether differences in methods are really "maximally" different, and this may be especially true when the different "methods" are all ratings. Is a graphic rating scale "maximally" (or even sufficiently) different from the method of equal appearing intervals? Do raters drawn from different organizational levels (e.g., supervisors, peers, or subordinates) constitute different methods of measurement (Pedhazur & Schmelkin, 1991)? The implication in this last question, unstated and often unrecognized, is that a named performance dimension is the same construct at all three levels of relationships. Some support for the implication has been reported (Facteau & Craig, 2001; Woehr, Sheehan, & Bennett, 2005), but it is still worth asking whether raters at different levels are rating different things. They may have different ideas about what is important in performance or have different definitions or different weights for the various rating dimensions; they may work from different samples of ratee behavior. The potential differences in construct can be illustrated by questions raters at the three levels might ask about a ratee. The supervisor might ask, "How much of my time must be spent with this ratee giving instructions or correcting errors?" A peer might ask, "Does this ratee carry his share of the workload?" A subordinate might ask, "Does this ratee treat me fairly?" A general caveat is that evidence of convergent validity, or of interrater

---

[5] I began using the term "psychometric validity" in Chapter 5, hoping that it would disassociate itself from the older trinitarian doctrine of validity, and hoping also that it would imply a broader approach to validity. Here I revert to "construct validity" to give more attention to the need to clarify constructs when seeking ratings.

reliability for that matter, may be little more than evidence of converging biases.[6] MTMM can help, but it alone is not enough.

Bias as Invalidity

Any investigation of construct validity, including the validity of ratings, must consider the possibility that systematic error biases the ratings. Ratee characteristics not being rated are validity-reducing sources of bias if they influence ratings. One possible source of bias in performance rating is the simple matter of how well rater and ratee (e.g., supervisor and subordinate) get along and work with each other (Duarte, Goodson, & Klich, 1993). Somewhat different is the "same as me" effect. Although similarity of ratee to rater may be a source of bias, bias should not be automatically assumed. In one study, ratings of interviewees apparently had a small but significant "same-as-me" effect for race (Lin, Dobbins, & Farh, 1992). The researchers' alternative interpretation was that minority candidates may have been more comfortable in a same-race setting and therefore gave more information to the interviewer. If so, the resulting ratings are not necessarily biased.

A widely cited meta-analysis by Kraiger and Ford (1985) found that raters gave higher ratings to ratees of their own race. A possible moderator was the "salience" of race; as the percentage of blacks among ratees increased, the race effect was less pronounced. Sackett, DuBois, and Noe (1991) found a similar salience effect when comparing ratings of men and women. Sackett and DuBois (1991) compared the Kraiger and Ford findings with those in gigantic USES and Project A databases. In the USES data, and in the Army technical proficiency and personal discipline ratings, both white and black raters gave higher mean ratings to whites. For military bearing, blacks received higher ratings from both black and white raters. Why do the findings of these big studies differ from those of Kraiger and Ford? Sackett and DuBois wondered and looked again at the studies in the Kraiger–Ford meta-analysis. Two were lab studies, four used peer ratings; of the eight supervisory ratings studies, four were done before 1970. The four post-1970 entries had a +.03 effect size (corrected) compared to −.23 in the pre-1970 items. The largest effect differences were in the peer rating studies (−.80) and the lab studies (−.60). They concluded that white and black raters differed very little in their ratings of white ratees but differed much more in their ratings of black ratees, and that the conclusion that raters rate people of their own racial group higher than others was "premature" (Sackett & DuBois, 1991, p. 876). Conclusions from other studies of racial mix in rater–ratee pairs were similar (e.g., Pulakos, White, Oppler, & Borman, 1989).

However, in interview panels for police promotions, Prewett-Livingston, Feild, Veres, and Lewis (1996) found the same-race effect reported by Kraiger and Ford; moreover, they found a similar effect for the majority race on the panel, that is, candidates of the same race as the majority of those on the interview panel had higher ratings. Will some future meta-analysis, either of police interviews or of panels generally, support the finding? I do not know, but I am sure the interaction question will not soon go away.

The Sackett and DuBois comparison of pre- and post-1970 studies suggests that research findings, particularly when major social issues are involved, are specific to the times, to the *Zeitgeist*, in which they are obtained—as Cronbach (1975) had warned. Perhaps this presumed interaction is another example where social change—greater acceptance of diversity—has resulted in a change in what is scientifically demonstrable.

---

[6] Thanks to Wally Borman for these observations.

Validity of Ratings as Predictors

Ratings as predictors are incorporated in interviews, assessment centers, work samples, portfolios of past achievements, auditions, free-response tests, and more. Note that the predictor in these assessment methods is not the interview, assessment center, etc.; it is the rating summarizing someone's judgment based on observations.

Borman's Models

Look again, in Chapter 8, at Hunter's path model (Figure 8.8) as expanded by Schmidt et al. (1986). Hunter's original model had four components. Using Project A data, Borman, White, Pulakos, and Oppler (1991) replicated Hunter's original path analysis, modified into a linear path model of the four components: ability to job knowledge to proficiency, and ultimately to rated performance. Further work expanded the model to that shown in Figure 13.7, including that linear core plus achievement motivation and dependability as ratee characteristics, along with awards and disciplinary actions. The expanded model accounted for more than twice the variance accounted for by Hunter's original model (for these data, $R^2 = .31$ versus Hunter's .14) and reinforced the view that ratings are indeed more valid than once thought. Continuing the search for inclusive models, Borman, White, and Dorsey (1995) omitted

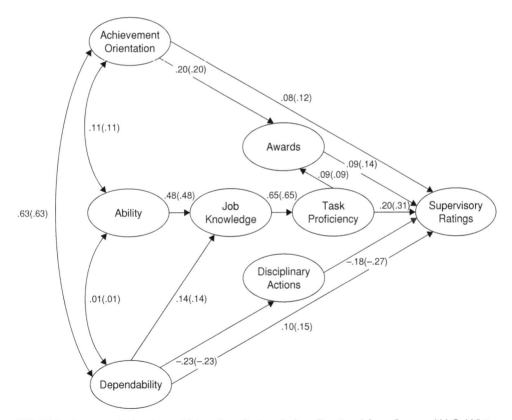

FIG. 13.7 An expanded path model based on Project A data. Reprinted from Borman, W. C., White, L. A., Pulakos, E. D., & Oppler, S. H. (1991), Models of supervisory job performance ratings. *Journal of Applied Psychology*, 76, 863–872. Reprinted by permission.

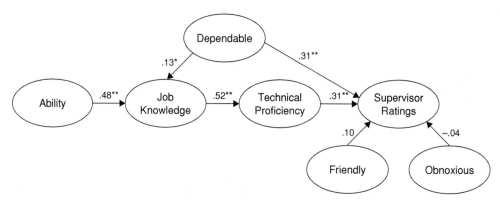

FIG. 13.8 An expanded path model of supervisory ratings including interpersonal factors. Reprinted from Borman, W. C., White, L. A., & Dorsey, D. W. (1995), Effects of ratee task performance and interpersonal factors on supervisory and peer performance ratings. *Journal of Applied Psychology, 80,* 168–177. Reprinted by permission.

achievement motivation, awards, and disciplinary actions but included dependability and some interpersonal variables, as shown in Figure 13.8. The four-component linear model, with job knowledge and task proficiency mediating supervisory ratings, was still central in the expanded models. Dependability had a direct influence on rated performance, plus an indirect influence through job knowledge; dependability is important to organizations, so these results add further credence to the validity of overall performance ratings.

Because of their reliance only on military samples, these studies do not suggest that performance ratings have high and generalized validity, but they do increase confidence that performance appraisal systems, designed and conducted well, can be valid.

These studies go beyond explaining supervisory ratings; they explain *why* ratings worked. Look again at Figure 13.8. It is simple in appearance but profound in that it points again to the plausibility of using path analysis for a multivariate validation of predictors in these data from Project A. Accept, at least momentarily, my view that job knowledge and technical proficiency (as indicated in work samples for Army MOS jobs) are more important criteria in a predictive hypothesis than the supervisory ratings. Judging from the path coefficients (measures of effect size in the causal model, analogous to standardized regression weights in ordinary multiple regression), predictors measuring ability not only influenced but were valid predictors of job knowledge, and job knowledge may also be considered a valid predictor of proficiency in a work sample. Similar path coefficients in other situations would suggest a reasonable "if–then" approach to selection: "If the candidate is not experienced on the job, then use ability testing as a basis for personnel selection decisions; if the candidate has relevant job experience, use a test of job knowledge."

A second implication of Figure 13.8 for validation comes when one looks at the other three traits measured. If path coefficients show influences that can support predictions, then the validity of early information (as in the employment process) can be evaluated as part of a subsequent chain of events. Dependability influenced supervisory ratings, but did not have so much influence on job knowledge and had no influence at all on work sample proficiency. Friendliness and obnoxiousness influenced ratings but not the intermediate links in the chain. Traits that influence ratings but do not influence job knowledge or technical proficiency do not strike me as valid tools for selection decisions. The path analysis offers a new perspective on validation; validity is not limited to the proposition that one variable has a quantifiable influence on another, but that the influence is either direct or mediated as part of a causal chain leading to the criterion.

The Classical Psychometric Errors

Different raters have different personal habits or styles in rating, a source of systematic error, and therefore of reduced validity. Some of these habits have been matters of concern for nearly a century, and the concerns have not yet been set to rest. The best advice I can offer someone setting up a rating system is to be aware of these habitual errors and to do the best you can to minimize their influence.

Central Tendency

Some raters cluster all ratings around a central point on the scale, a mean, a midpoint, or a subjective average. The result is low variance and therefore low correlations with anything else. Central tendency seems to indicate raters who avoid unpleasant consequences by avoiding extreme ratings.

Leniency or Severity

Some raters are easy, some hard; some lenient, others severe. Early discussions of the leniency error (e.g., Guilford, 1936) described it as giving higher ratings to people the rater knows; the more general idea of habitual tendencies toward leniency or severity in rating soon became part of the definition (e.g., Guilford, 1954) and is now dominant. Raters with very high mean ratings are considered systematically lenient; those with low means, systematically severe. Again, the effect is low variance.

Halo

Halo error has created more talk and research—and, I think, less change—than any other. E. L. Thorndike defined it as a "marked tendency to think of the person in general as rather good or rather inferior and to color the judgments of the [specific performance dimensions] by this general feeling" (E. L. Thorndike, 1920, p. 25), as quoted by Balzer and Sulsky (1992, p. 975). According to Balzer and Sulsky, Thorndike had contradictory definitions of halo: (a) correlations of ratings on specific scales with overall ratings, and (b) intercorrelations among dimension scales. The one operational definition assumes that a general impression influences ratings on dimensions; the other assumes that raters simply fail to distinguish dimensions. Both assumptions of halo lead to spurious intercorrelations and loss of discriminant validity. This classical error, halo, is not easily dismissed in a few sentences.

Dimensions to be rated are ordinarily not orthogonal, so observed correlation is not error by itself. Decades of research have "provided documentation that the phenomenon is ubiquitous. More recently, a great deal of effort has been expended on reducing halo, a modest amount on articulating the sources of halo, and surprisingly little on whether haloed ratings are inaccurate" (Cooper, 1981, p. 219). Intercorrelations may be influenced by reality or by the rater's implicit theory of personality or performance; they may also be due to rater habits of ignoring differences between dimensions; that is, rater error.

Balzer and Sulsky found a variety of recent operational definitions of halo, but none consistent with either of the Thorndike concepts. They questioned whether halo is helpful in evaluating rating quality. The disturbing sense of ambiguity must be tempered by the results of a series of studies by Lance, Fisicaro, and others. Fisicaro and Lance (1990) identified three possible causal models for halo error: a general impression model, a salient dimension model, and an inadequate discrimination model. A comparison of the three models found that the general impression model fit observed halo better than either of the others, even in contexts specifically designed to induce different concepts of halo (Lance, LaPointe, & Fisicaro, 1994).

Halo has been considered important enough to use up a lot of research hours. What should be done about it? Most answers fall under headings of training raters and increasing their experience and motivation. Effective training is expected to assure that ratings of the dimensions are meaningfully distinguished, at least as well as the raters think they need to be. Experience can augment training. Most of all, I think, raters must be convinced that the differences between dimensions, and the differences between ratees, are important enough to acknowledge. This may be one excellent reason for asking potential raters to define the dimensions they think are important rather than imposing dimensions from academic theory (cf. Smith & Kendall, 1963).

Individual Differences in Ability to Rate

Some raters are more qualified to rate than others. Whether rating candidates or incumbents, the main qualification is relevant knowledge, including knowledge of work demands and understanding of ratee behavior. It may include knowledge of the work process and of both desirable and flawed product characteristics. In rating performance, rater qualifications may differ in effectiveness of cognitive processes, such as differences in the ability to remember observed behavior or to distinguish conceptually different dimensions of performance.

Qualifying knowledge comes from observation or experience, not from hearsay, prejudice, or stereotypes. Typically, although not always, immediate supervisors are more qualified to rate job performance than second-level supervisors who are more removed from the person and the work being rated (Landy & Farr, 1980). For some work samples, the most qualified raters may be people who have demonstrated a high level of skill at the work, although highly skilled people may use the skills too automatically to notice clearly when a ratee fails to carry out certain steps.

Relevant Trait Differences

Research on trait differences among raters has waned. It would be nice to think it has because all questions have been answered, but it's more likely because answers are elusive. Questions and potential answers still appear; Bernardin and Villanova (2005), suggested that the tendency to give inflated ratings is in part due to low perceived self-efficacy; their work suggests that experience and special self-efficacy training can improve ratings. Further exploration of this path was reviewed by Tziner, Murphy, and Cleveland (2005). Their review points to studies that show personality, especially conscientiousness, as a factor in quality of performance appraisal. General intelligence of the rater seems pretty well established as a factor in ratings, but Smither and Reilly (1987) said its relationship to rating accuracy may be nonmonotonic. Implicit theories about occupations may interact with intelligence; Hauenstein and Alexander (1991) found a nonlinear relationship of intelligence to accuracy, moderated by raters' implicit theories. Other traits have been proposed as influences on skill in rating and have seemed obvious and convincing until a research literature developed and failed to support individual propositions. Individual differences in field independence seem related to the ability to distinguish individuals from the groups they work in, or to distinguish dimensions, and that seems important. Closely related are differences in selective attention (Cardy & Kehoe, 1984).

Cognitive complexity as a trait has been suggested as important in rating, especially where multiple dimensions are rated (e.g., Dunnette & Borman, 1979; Feldman, 1981; Guion, 1983b; Jacobs, Kafry, & Zedeck, 1980; Landy & Farr, 1980). Schneier (1977) found that raters with cognitive complexity levels "compatible" with the cognitive demands of the rating scale gave psychometrically superior ratings. Perhaps because the idea is intuitively appealing, several attempts to replicate these findings have been reported—and have failed. Why? Reasons might lie in the difficulty of measuring the construct; or perhaps a lack of clarity in the construct itself. Whatever the reason, I would not join those who would simply drop the idea; its logical sense makes it worth pursuing—by anyone with a better idea of how to define it or measure it. My reluctance might be due to the challenge of computerization in measuring formerly elusive traits. Return to Chapter 10 for a moment and note again elusive constructs, such as cognitive styles, that seem potentially measurable with computer presentations of stimulus material.

Rater Motivation

Poor, invalid ratings may be expected from a rater who lacks confidence in the purpose of the ratings (not to be confused with lack of confidence in one's own skill), distrusts the researcher, or simply "has other fish to fry." Understanding and accepting purpose is crucial; a supervisor who sees the request for ratings as "still more paperwork" is likely to see the request more as an infringement on his or her time than as a way to achieve personal or organizational goals. Motivation might differ for different rating purposes. A rater might be more highly motivated to be careful where ratings may determine who gets merit pay or special recognition, or other rewards (Williams, DeNisi, Blencoe, & Cafferty, 1985).

Training

Minimal rater training should clarify the purpose of rating, the meaning of words and phrases on the rating form, the procedure to follow in rating, and aspects of the judgment process such as avoidance of rating errors. Much can be and needs to be added. Bernardin and Buckley (1981) advocated training that emphasizes observation of behavior, such as the following.

1. Diary keeping, in a formal system, with top support assuring that supervisors are themselves evaluated on how well they keep diaries of subordinates' performance and other behavior.
2. Frame of reference (FOR) training to help raters develop a common understanding of the dimensions to be rated and of the observations that support different levels of ratings.
3. Teach raters how to be honestly critical. Many raters hate giving negative ratings. Training may increase ability to handle encounters resulting from negative appraisals. Its value could be tested in both field and laboratory research, but it has not had much evaluation in either.

Different people may observe a worker's performance from different perspectives, or frames of reference. A dominant, modal frame of reference may develop in an organization, maybe not deliberately. Different people view work, performance, and performance evaluation differently, perhaps with personal implicit theories. A cluster of potential raters may share a frame of reference; it may be better than the organizational mode. Either of these can differ from the frame of reference from which the rating system was developed. If raters have, or can acquire, a common frame of reference, they can define levels of performance effectiveness for different performance dimensions with a common language. Frame of reference training (FOR) has become one of the most widely studied approaches to rater training (Day & Sulsky, 1995; Lievens & Thornton, 2005).

One procedure gives raters a list of critical behaviors and, for each behavior described, asks them to rate the effectiveness of the behavior and how well it fits a specified dimension. In the FOR tradition, raters who do not agree with most other raters are considered idiosyncratic and "idiosyncracy is negatively related to performance rating accuracy" (Uggerslev & Sulsky, 2008, p. 717); those defined as idiosyncratic are targeted for FOR training and brought together to consider the job description, to discuss the important performance dimensions, and to understand the differences between "correct" (usually modal) evaluations and various idiosyncratic ones. Such training uses a conference method of group problem-solving techniques to arrive at a consensus about how rating should be done. Two studies using FOR training cited by Bernardin and Beatty (1984) found increased interrater agreement and accuracy, both with paper-people vignettes and with ratings of the performance of real people.

I question training only the idiosyncratic raters. I would have those with a common view and those with uncommon views included in training together. Both groups can contribute to the discussions, and the common or modal view can be questioned and defended or modified.

Organizational Level

People at different organizational levels may have different qualifications to rate. Oppler, Peterson, and McCloy (1994) found that peer and supervisory ratings were predicted by different things and were not interchangeable. They attributed the differences to the greater exposure of peers to fellow trainees, especially in army settings.

Research on qualifications to rate work performance may not apply to other rating problems, such as rating assessment center exercise performance. Peers may be better able to rate traits such as work motivation. For some purposes, self ratings may be more valuable, such as self ratings of confidence. For other purposes, outsiders may be better raters: customers can rate service; experts can rate work sample results; or professional people can rate readiness for something (such as readiness to return to work or to fly a plane with passengers).

Agreement, Reliability, and Generalizability

Interrater Reliability and Interrater Agreement

Interrater agreement is often treated as a form of reliability, but agreement and reliability are different (see, e.g., Lawlis & Lu, 1972; Tinsley & Weiss, 1975). Judges agree if they make the same ratings; they are reliable if they put ratees in roughly the same relative order. The

TABLE 13.2

Hypothetical Ratings Illustrating Different Levels of Interrater Agreement and Interrater
Reliability for Interval; Scaled Data

	Case 1: High interrater agreement, high interrater reliability			Case 2: Low interrater agreement, high interrater reliability			Case 3: High interrater agreement, low interrater reliability		
	Rater			Rater			Rater		
Rater	1	2	3	1	2	3	1	2	3
A	1	1	1	1	3	5	5	4	4
B	2	2	2	1	3	5	5	4	3
C	3	3	3	2	4	6	5	4	5
D	3	3	3	2	4	6	4	4	5
E	4	4	4	3	5	7	5	4	3
F	5	5	5	3	5	7	5	5	4
G	6	6	6	4	6	8	4	4	5
H	7	7	7	4	6	8	5	5	4
I	8	8	8	5	7	9	4	5	3
J	9	9	9	5	7	9	5	5	5
M	4.8	4.8	4.8	3.0	5.0	7.0	4.7	4.4	4.1
SD	2.7	2.7	2.7	1.5	1.5	1.5	.5	.5	.9

Reprinted from Tinsley, H. E. A., & Weiss, D. J. (1975), Interrater reliability and agreement of subjective judgments. *Journal of Counseling Psychology*, *22*, 358–376. © by the American Psychological Association. Reprinted with permission.

distinction is clear in Table 13.2. Reliability can be high without agreement about the degree to which the characteristic being judged describes the ratees (Case 2). It can be low without necessarily meaning much disagreement among raters (Case 3). Both agreement and reliability give useful information about a set of ratings, but the choice depends on the intended use. As predictors or criteria, interrater reliability (or "rate–rerate" reliability) is more important because reliability limits validity. For decisions based on proficiency, agreement is more important.

Suppose that the manager and assistant manager of a restaurant independently classify every candidate for entry-level work; a candidate might be considered further for kitchen work, dining area work, or neither. Assume the pattern of agreements and disagreements in Table 13.3. Summing actual proportions in the diagonal cells shows 46% agreement. Is 46% substantial, reasonable, or poor agreement? To answer, consider the expected (chance) proportion of agreement. The corresponding sum based on marginal proportions is 38%. Is 46% agreement enough greater than chance (38%) to justify this way to assess candidates? The answer to this, too, is a judgment call, but several indices of rater agreement have built-in consideration of chance agreement. An early index was *kappa* (Cohen, 1960), appropriate for the case with two raters and nominal ratings:

$$kappa = (p_a - p_c)/(1 - p_c) \tag{13.1}$$

where p_a = actual proportion of agreements, and p_c = expected or chance proportion of agreements. (*Kappa* can also be computed directly from frequencies, substituting the

TABLE 13.3

A Matrix of Agreements Expressed as Proportions

		Manager			
		K[a]	D	N	Marginal Total
Assistant Manager	K	.06 (.02)[b]	.10 (.08)	.04 (.10)	.20
	D	.04 (.04)	.15 (.16)	.21 (.20)	.40
	N	.00 (.04)	.15 (.16)	.25 (.20)	.40
Marginal Total		.10	.40	.50	1.00

[a] Raters indicated that a candidate should (a) be considered further for kitchen work (K), (b) be considered further for dining area work (D), or (c) not be considered further (N). [b] Actual proportions of assignments to a cell are given first; proportions in parentheses are expected proportions based on the marginal totals.

corresponding frequencies for proportions, and using the number of ratees, *N*, instead of 1.) For Table 13.3, *kappa* = .13. For perfect agreement, *kappa* = 1.00, so this is not a pleasing level of agreement, quite apart from questions of statistical significance.

Kappa works well with a few nominal categories, but it is less satisfactory for an array of scaled categories (as in a rating scale). On a nine-point scale, such as in Table 13.2, a constant difference between two raters prevents any literal agreements at all; all ratees are placed in the same rank order by both raters, but one rater uses scale values of 1–8 and the other uses 2–9. No ratee is rated at the same scale point by both raters, yet it makes no sense to say the raters are not agreeing at all. Options exist. By policy, some discrepancies are trivial and can be ignored. If two or more raters use adjacent scale values for the same ratee, for example, they might be considered in essential agreement. Such definitions of agreement are, of course, wholly arbitrary; they might be bolstered by arguments based on scale length, on the portion actually used by raters, and on clear reasons why small discrepancies can be considered unimportant. Agreement statistics other than kappa have been proposed; several of them were described and compared by Lindell and Brandt (1999).

Kenny (1991) offered a general mathematical model of agreement, or consensus, among raters. Six parameters of the model are postulated as determining the level of agreement: (a) the amount of information available to the judges, (b) the extent to which the two judges have seen the same behaviors, (c) the degree to which the various judges view an observation as meaning the same thing, (d) consistency of the ratee's behavior, (e) the degree to which ratings are based on irrelevant information, and (f) communication of the impressions each rater has gathered. Most agreement research focuses on the number of available observations and on ratee consistency. Kenny sees two others as at least equally important: overlap and similarity of meaning of observations.

Agreement and reliability have much in common. If a set of ratings is rather reliable, systematic disagreements like those in cases 2 and 3 in Table 13.2 are necessarily relatively small. In fact, James and his colleagues, in defining interrater reliability, explicitly identified it as "the extent to which judges 'agree' on a set of judgments" (James, Demaree, & Wolf, 1984, p. 86)—or would were it not for systematic variance due to response biases. Nevertheless, the distinction is useful if for no reason beyond forcing researchers to investigate ratings to see if systematic differences in judgment occur.

Estimates of Interrater Reliability

If the ratings can be considered to fit an interval scale reasonably well, reliability can be estimated by ordinary methods (i.e., correlation, analysis of variance). For multiple raters, interrater reliability is often estimated by intraclass correlation. Some warnings of potential misuse of the statistic have been issued. For example, "There are numerous versions of the intraclass correlation coefficient (ICC) that can give quite different results when applied to the same data. Unfortunately, many researchers are not aware of the differences between the forms" (Shrout & Fleiss, 1979, p. 420). Similar warnings were issued by Fagot (1991), so I recommend that ICCs be used rarely and only by those who are thoroughly familar with the variety of intraclass coefficients and the requirements for specific ones.

Fairly wide use has been made of the within-group statistic, $r_{WG(J)}$, proposed by James et al. (1984) and computed by

$$r_{WG(J)} = 1 - (s_{xj}^2/\sigma_{EU}^2) \tag{13.2}$$

where s_{xj}^2 is the variance within a set of judges and σ_{EU}^2 is the variance of expected error from a uniform or rectangular distribution of judgments. This definition has been the foundation of many variants, most of them stemming from criticism of the assumption of a uniform distribution as null (see, e.g., Brown & Hauenstein, 2005; Cohen, Doveh, & Eick, 2001; Lindell, Brandt, & Whitney, 1999).

Reliability can be increased by pooling raters, using the Spearman–Brown equation. "If the reliability of a single rating is .50, then the reliability of two, four, or six parallel ratings will be approximately .67, .80, and .86, respectively" (Houston, Raymond, & Svec, 1991, p. 409). I like this quotation because the word *approximately* recognizes that statistical estimates are "on the average" statements of what might be expected if all goes as assumed. Beyond that, the operative word is *parallel.* Averaging ratings (or using Spearman–Brown) if one rater is, for example, systematically lenient, simply does not fit the assumption. If essays are each rated by two raters, one more lenient than the other, the problem is like that of using two multiple choice tests of unequal difficulty (nonparallel forms). Scores based on different (unequated) test forms are not comparable. So it is with mixing lenient and difficult raters; the reliability of the pooled ratings is incorrectly estimated by the Spearman–Brown equation of classical test theory. Matters are worse if each judge defines a construct a bit differently.

Agreement to some extent, and reliability to a greater extent, are psychometric issues, clarified by Putka, Ingerick, and McCloy (2008), who pointed out two quite different perspectives in studies of rating errors. One is reliability-based, accepting early classical reliability assumptions that random error (at least) is not correlated with anything else. The other is validity-based and sees some measurement error as essentially random but other errors as systematic—as I do. Putka et al. have put the two together in a mixture including generalizability theory notions along with some generalized statistical models called "linear mixed models." Their model does not aggregate ratings; in fact, it disaggregates them so that each rater–ratee pair is properly treated as a separate observation. The analysis permits estimating the amount and classification of systematic errors while continuing to recognize random (i.e., inexplicable) error. It is an approach worth watching as the literature on inter-rater reliability and agreement grows.

Generalizability Studies

A path model, as in Figure 13.8 suggests classes of variables that might affect ratings generally. The ratee trait or performance is the construct that provides the intended meaning of the ratings. Settings include those in which ratings are made or ratees are observed, circumstances in which rating is done, or the purposes of rating. Some of these variables may have an influence on the trait being rated. Others may have an influence but should not; they are systematic errors that Wherry (see Wherry & Bartlett, 1982) called *bias*; for example, situations in which ratee behavior was observed, time of observation, instructions to raters, and impressions formed in observations unrelated to the behavior being rated.

When many potential sources of error variance are likely, beyond random error, I think the logic of generalizability analysis is required. With two or more raters, a rater facet can enter such an analysis. Frequently, raters are not independent (Wallace, 1965); generalizability across raters can be an artifact of common information about ratees, whether relevant or not. In diagnostic ratings, overall variance should be associated with variance across dimensions. If so, generalizability analyses should be done within dimensions or groups of correlated dimensions. In short, Figure 13.8, despite being a path model, may be at least as useful in choosing facets for generalizability studies. The facets chosen depend in large part on their threats as unwanted sources of variance.

In the Job Performance Measurement Project in the military services of the United States, Kraiger (1990) studied experimental performance ratings in each of four Air Force specialties. Generalizability analyses were basically three-facet designs: rating forms (with individual items nested within forms), rating sources (self, peer, or supervisor), and ratees. The major source of variance in all four specialties was not ratees but the interaction of ratees with rating sources.

COGNITIVE PROCESSES IN PERFORMANCE RATINGS

Context Effects

This should be a chapter on ratings in general, but much of it so far has included, even emphasized, performance ratings. Throwing off all pretense, I now enter this topic with unabashed limitation to performance rating, although most of it applies to other ratings as well, because organizational constraints, actual or not, are part of the perceived context, as reviewed by Tziner et al. (2005).

Actual versus Simulated Settings

My reservations about laboratory and other simulations were expressed well by Landy and Farr (1983): "Rather than throwing the baby out with the bath water, they [paper-people experiments] ultimately drown the baby with experimental control" (p. 95). They also said that, over perhaps a year, a "supervisor and the subordinate have interacted frequently and probably know each other reasonably well . . . we are dealing with the appraisal of a long string of actions rather than a single one; in addition, we are dealing with a constellation of activities rather than with single physical or mental operations in isolation" (Landy & Farr, 1980, p. 74). The comment identifies several context variables that may influence ratings, a major one being the time span. Rating performance for a year is different from rating performance in a 15-minute exercise. Frequency of interaction is another. In a work setting, interactions of supervisors and subordinates may occur several times a day, but some people in sales or skilled trades may work anywhere over a large area. If the boss sees them only occasionally, their ratings may be based on very small samples of observed worker behavior. Such things are *boundary variables*—variables that define the conditions to which research must generalize. Experimental research is usually done at some remove from the conditions it simulates; some boundary variables can be represented among the controlled conditions, but rarely can experiments include the long time span and the possibly critical consequences of an annual performance appraisal.

Problems addressed by researchers differ from those that raters or ratees think important. Researchers train to reduce rating errors; ratees think raters should be trained to understand the nature of the performance they are rating and to recognize work factors beyond the individual worker's control. Researchers study rater motivation in terms of the purpose of rating; raters point to deliberate distortion of ratings as a greater problem in rater motivation (Bernardin & Villanova, 1986). I recall a personnel manager who told me that his selection and placement decisions were 96% accurate because 96% of those hired were later rated 3 on a five-point scale. Supervisors told me that 3 was the only safe rating; those with ratings of 4 or 5 were likely to be promoted out from under them, and they would not be able to get rid of anyone rated 1 or 2.

It should be remembered, however, that most experiments on ratings have been done within boundary conditions that match reasonably well the conditions of short-term ratings such as those for assessment centers, work samples, or interviews. Even for these, however, the problem of validity remains. The absence of serious consequences in a research setting can cast doubt on the applicability of the findings for administrative actions.

Administrative versus Research Context

Ratings often have administrative consequences, even if not on purpose. Raters seem to be more lenient in "for real" ratings than in rating people for research use only (Landy & Farr, 1980). In research, a constant leniency effect may not matter much. The problem matters with differential leniency in administrative ratings. Although lacking convincing evidence, I think that administrative ratings may often be lenient for those who have been loyal employees for a long time, or maybe for employees with special family or health problems— and severe at the other end of a leniency–harshness scale for those who annoy the rater. Such factors seem less likely to influence ratings to be used for research only. They lead one to expect a relatively low correlation between ratings where administrative consequences are expected and the research ratings where honesty hurts no one.[7]

Aids to Observation and Memory

Records

In many settings, daily production records are kept. Review of such records can jar the rater's memory and point out aspects of performance such as level and consistency of production,

---

[7] I was proposing research under court supervision. The client informed me, with reasonably compelling arguments, that the judge was biased against testing. In testimony about what we might do, I received support from that judge when I said that we would not consider administrative ratings as criteria but would, thank you, develop our own! He had never clearly articulated his objection to validation research with administrative ratings as criteria, but it turned out to be the source of his anti-testing bias.

recorded errors, and related facts. If the problem is to assess performance quality, and if such factual information is available, why rate? A part of the answer is that information in the files may be uneven in quality and relevance. A simple thing like the number of widgets produced each day may be tempered by a rater's knowledge of the specific equipment a ratee uses; some pieces of equipment are more prone to breakdown, slower in function, and so on. The best assessment may still be a subjective judgment—but an informed judgment reached by considering an array of factual information.

Incident Files or Diaries

Some appraisal forms list job duties on one side of the page and require the rater to write an anecdote or critical incident illustrating a ratee's performance of each duty. The principle is like the Smith–Kendall BARS approach of assigning ratee behavior examples to appropriate scale points in the scale: supporting ratings with specific behavioral or outcome evidence. A problem is that the evidence recalled while rating may not be a good summary description of the ratee or ratee behavior. The rater is more likely to remember the dramatic, salient example of a single brilliant achievement or major blunder than more typical incidents. Recent events are more likely to be recalled than those long ago.

I once suggested that supervisors keep an incident file—records of observations of effective and less effective behavior. Remembering is easier if the rater has regularly kept such a file. I asked supervisors to schedule time to record, each week at least, one or two of the best things each subordinate has done that week and one or two of the worst. The best may not necessarily be very good, the worst may be satisfactory; with 52 weeks of such incidents, the range of subordinate behavior will be documented and helpful in rating. If trained to strive for descriptive objectivity, supervisors can learn to replace glittering generalities such as "is a good leader" with behavioral evidence of leadership such as "delegated authority to subordinate" (Guion, 1965a, pp. 110, 468). At the time, I didn't think supervisors would ever keep such records, but the idea (described as keeping a "diary") actually has been used and accepted.

Bernardin and Buckley (1981) recommended diary keeping as a training method if it is done systematically and has support from the top of the organization. Top support for diaries implies that supervisors themselves are evaluated on how well they keep diaries; I think it would also imply that their bosses keep records of *supervisors'* behavior—including diary keeping. Raters, they said, will find other things to do if diary keeping is not viewed as important.

Diaries offer no panacea. In an experiment, Balzer (1986) found that a diary system can slip badly for those who have good impressions of the ratee but do not see the rating task as very important; it will work best for those who have good impressions *and* see the task as central to their jobs. This is a field-testable hypothesis; it deserves testing.

Bernardin and Beatty (1984) offered recommendations for training people to maintain such records. Among them: (a) Tie training in recording observations to scale familiarization training so that observations are recorded relative to the behavioral dimensions to be rated. (b) Record objectively, not evaluatively. (c) Record a predesignated minimum number of observations per scale. (d) Make the diary-keeping system a formal part of organizational policy and practice. (e) Require the rater's supervisor to monitor the diary keeping.

The Promise of Cognitive Research

Feldman (1981) proposed a cognitive model of the performance appraisal process. That process, he said, requires attention to and categorization of information, recalling it, and integrating it, either through automatic or controlled cognitive processing. He described research in cognitive psychology and its potential importance for understanding what happens when one person rates the performance of another. The article made sense and was a watershed contribution to research on ratings. It begat a large body of experimental research intended more to promote understanding of the process than to generalize to operational ratings. Some of it has already been cited and described; the following list offers a summary.

1. Observations tend to be selective. It is not clear whether the observational set can be influenced by training.
2. Impressions, especially early ones, strongly affect ratings and may have more influence than actual observations.
3. Impressions are as likely to stem from stereotypes as from observations; implicit theories of performance may explain some apparent demographic biases. Direction of effects is not always clear or as expected.
4. Implicit performance theories influence rater observations and the factor structure of the resultant ratings.
5. Different implicit theories produce different patterns of predictor validities when ratings are the criteria.

That's probably enough, at this time. In the 1998 edition of this book, I pointed to growing skepticism about the value of much of the cognitive research. It has grown further. Effect sizes were usually small, showing (like Figure 13.8) the influence of many sources. Moreover, the research led to remarkably little advice on improving ratings. Recommendations based on the research differ little from the advice that would have been given prior to 1980: know the job, the standards of performance, and the reason for rating; observe often; and focus on the purpose so that extraneous considerations have minimal effect on ratings.

Ilgen and Favero (1985) surveyed three basic kinds of theory (attribution, implicit personality theory, and social cognition) and concluded that none of them generalized well. In a later article (Ilgen, Barnes-Farrell, & McKellin, 1993) it was said that the cognitive process research had "reached a point of diminishing returns" (p. 362). They were right; relatively few new researches have been reported. In fact, when a search of reference lists and recent journals located a couple of new studies, they brought us back to the future by stressing attribution theory again. Homsma, Van Dyck, De Gildere, Koopman, and Elfring (2007) did not study ratings but the work was clearly relevant to them, and Taggar and Neubert (2008) explicitly focused on "free-riders" on teams. Controlled research on cognitive processes has provided, and can continue to provide, impetus to theory building, but it seems unlikely to help raters with long-term administrative purposes.

RATINGS AND PERFORMANCE MANAGEMENT SYSTEMS

Ratings are based on relatively brief observation such as rating characteristics of work samples, impressions during interviews, or performance on assessment center exercises. The kinds of ratings that cause the most concern and invoke the most interest are the ratings called performance appraisals. Typically, performance appraisals are ratings made by a direct supervisor, annually or quarterly, and evaluating performance since the prior appraisal.

Performance appraisals seem to be disliked by almost everyone involved. Raters often view them as wasteful paper work, ratees view them with apprehension, researchers view them as psychometrically unsound, and management scholars view them somewhere between useless and dangerous. W. Edwards Deming is reported to have said that performance appraisal is a "deadly disease" that "nourishes short-term performance, annihilates long-term planning, builds fear, demolishes teamwork" (quoted by Shields, 2007, p. 22). Coens and Jenkins (2000) entitled their book *Abolishing Performance Appraisals*—and not just for fun. The book devoted much space to reasons why performance appraisals fail.

In my opinion, when performance appraisals fail, it is because the rating process has become an end in itself. The kinds of decisions that should rest, at least on part, on ratings fade into background because of the emphasis on form, whether the rating form itself or form in a bureaucratic sense.

This book, and this chapter in it, is about assessment of individual people so that decisions about them can be somewhat objective and consistent with organizational values. It is a book on measurement and its use, not a treatise on management practices—not even on performance management. Nevertheless, I find that some management scholars would disagree with Coens and Jenkins. For example, appraisal "is a necessary part of the plan-do-check-act cycle" (Williams, 1998, p. 2). It seems to be seen, as some of us see computers, as a necessary evil we can no longer function without. Performance appraisal (or simply rating of performance) may be a basis for individual personnel decisions, but they ought to be used in the context of a larger system. Let's consider the police example mentioned in the discussion of a full application of the Smith–Kendall approach to BARS.

Behaviorally Based Management of Police Performance

The Original Scales and System

Our town, and its police division, are small. A citizens' committee, of which I was a member, was appointed to evaluate performance evaluation practices for police patrol officers. The procedures formerly in use had created a series of grievances filed by the officers' union. A union member and a command sergeant also served on the committee. Eventually I suggested scrapping a rating procedure that was heavy on counting things such as traffic stops and replacing it with behaviorally anchored rating scales. The committee was favorable; we added Pat Smith (my colleague, and the Smith in Smith–Kendall) to be sure we followed the Smith–Kendall approach. BARS were developed for each of four "intangible" dimensions. A fifth scale, without behavioral anchors, was developed for evaluating those activity statistics.

BARS were developed with the full participation of all sergeants supervising patrol officers (plus some on other assignments who had previously been patrol supervisors) and several patrol officers. Iterative trials were used in helping sergeants learn to write behavioral (as opposed to evaluative) statements. Items were "retranslated" and scaled. Those with relatively small variances and spreading as far as possible through the range of scale values were chosen as anchors for the scales of "intangibles" (their term for considerations that did not involve counting something). For each dimension, the rating scale was one part of a page devoted to that dimension. The group-developed definition of the dimension was included, and space was provided to write in behaviors actually observed during the rating period, the date when the behavior was observed, and the scale value the rater assigned to that behavioral example relative to the anchors on the rating scale itself. The rating scale was headed: "This officer is the sort of person who could be expected to:" and below the scale, in asking for an overall rating, appropriately worded for the dimension, "Considering the observations you have recorded, and the kinds of things you have come to expect from this officer, give your overall rating of this officer's [**attention to safety**] during this period." The phrase bracketed was the dimension name, always in boldface.

Each sergeant was expected to carry a small notebook in which to record observations for each officer under his or her supervision. Each lieutenant was expected to check the notebooks for clarity of recorded observations and for adherence to behavioral description at least twice during the rating period, and the higher command (chief and assistant chief) committed themselves to assuring that the procedure was followed.

Ratings were to be done at the end of each 28-day period, according to the union contract. Quarterly ratings were done after three 28-day cycles. The quarterly ratings were somewhat different. Comments rather than observations were to be recorded. Supervisors changed, at least on some days and shifts, during the three cycles, but one was nominally "the" supervisor of a given officer. According to the system developed, that sergeant conferred with other sergeants who had observed the officer's work and then wrote a summary comment about performance during the quarter. The sergeant's overall rating of the officer for the quarter was to be recorded, considering observations, ratings, and discussions with other supervisors. The system was approved by city and by union officials in 1996. One committee recommendation was not approved. We had recommended that the committee stay active and review the procedures annually. This was not done, and its rejection was not explained. Procedural monitoring was done only within the police division command structure.

Ten Years Later

During the subsequent decade, many changes occurred. New technology had invaded the patrol service, with computers and other technology in all cars. Substantial changes had occurred in the community. Two chiefs of police had retired and been replaced. Some patrol officers were questioning the relevance of some of the behavioral anchors after all these changes. The surprising fact was that the system was still in use, and basically accepted, after a 10-year period, unmonitored by the original committee or the system developers.

In response to change and questions, a new citizens' committee was appointed, with some overlap with the original committee. Pat Smith and I looked at documents from current practices, and recommended that "retraining" be done because of personnel at the different levels who had not participated earlier. Because we were unable to take part ourselves, we recommended retaining qualified people to do the follow-up work. Staff in the Institute for Psychological Research and Application (IPRA) at Bowling Green State University were retained, and I was able to meet with them frequently. The general consensus within the division was that original dimensions should be retained, but item generation, allocation, scaling, and related activities were repeated (although this time items could be taken from existing rating forms to add to those generated by group meetings. IPRA, under the leadership of Dr Jennifer Gillespie, developed standard forms, similar but not identical to the originals, for 28-day, quarterly, and annual evaluations (Gillespie, Guion, Colatat, Nolan, & Wolford, 2007).

Note that the system, original and revised, involves all patrol-related personnel. Note also that it is a training and development procedure—training not merely in using the rating forms, but in considering and discussing incidents that improve or deviate from desired police behavior; in a goal-setting sense, officers can themselves set goals of remaining calm and polite when questioning distraught crime victims, or considering ways to approach intoxicated people so they might be handcuffed without incident.

Use of Ratings in Larger Systems

The police program was not devised to be just a system of performance appraisal, nor was it intended to be a comprehensive system of performance management, even though it approached one. It is far from the comprehensive personnel system described in Chapter 12. Few systems reported in the management literature have included all the components that they might have. But consider now the sort of system one might envision as a target and see how the performance rating component might fit into the system as a whole.

A thorough system of performance management is multi-level and recognizes a variety of interrelated performances at different levels: performance of individual duties at any organizational level, unit performance in achieving unit objectives set for it, and, at the most inclusive levels, organizational performance perhaps involving market shares, profitability, or some measure of a mix between stability and moving forward to greater things. Williams (1998) summarized several performance management theories. Different theories emphasize performance at different organizational levels, but nearly all of them recognize the complex interrelatedness of performance at the various levels.

From my perspective, the first requirement of a good performance management system is an organization where leaders actually believe, not merely giving lip-service to the idea, that people are important and deserve respect (Rucci, 2008) and that people really are the most important resource the organization can have. It follows that a good performance management system would be "employee-centered" (Williams, 1998, p. 33), recognizing both the intrinsic value of people and their value as the organization's human capital, to be chosen wisely, to be nurtured well, and to be rewarded as deserved.

Focusing explicitly on individual performance, Figure 13.9 provides a graphic approach to a discussion of the idea of performance appraisal within a more general performance management system. The figure follows fairly well one presented by Shields (2007, p. 23), with only a few differences in the wording to fit terms earlier in this book. My discussion is influenced not only by Shields but by several other authors writing from other points of view.

First of all, it shows performance management as cyclical, "a continuous, future-oriented, and participative system" (Shields, 2007, p. 22). It is not a linear process, with a clear beginning and ending (Bacal, 1999), nor are the components of the cycle (the outer ring) as neat and discrete as the figure might suggest. One component might shade slightly into another or even leap-frog across one of them. One might occur rarely (e.g., annually for a formal performance appraisal) and another virtually continuously (e.g., monitoring and informal feedback). The system, and component aspects of it, relate also to other systems: staffing, training and development, and especially to reward systems. The virtue of the figure is that it shows that performance appraisal cannot occur or be effective in isolation from other considerations. It is, whether planned or not, part of a system.

CONCLUDING NOTE

People—researchers, practicing psychologists, HR specialists, regulatory officials, lawyers, judges—speak generically of employment tests. Sometimes *test* is the appropriate word. As described in the next chapter, some very highly structured interviews use standard questions for which keyed responses can be scored—essentially oral tests. Most interviews, however, do not have such structure. Interviewees may be evaluated with a vague, idiosyncratic statement

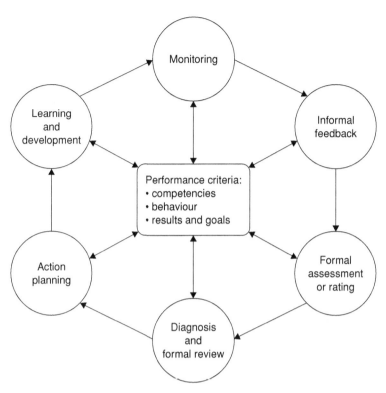

FIG. 13.9 The performance management cycle. Adapted from Shields, J. (2007), *Managing Employee Performance and Reward*. Cambridge, UK: Cambridge University Press. © Cambridge University Press. Adapted by permission.

or with a set of more or less standard scales for rating interview information. Either way, the assessment is a subjective rating. Other employment procedures such as résumés or letters of recommendation are also rated, whether formally or not.

Ratings have bad press, and it is often deserved. Too often neither the raters nor the people who ask for them know what the ratings are supposed to mean. I hope this chapter has stressed, even if *ad nauseam*, that a rating should be a quantification of something, it should be interpretable to raters and recipients alike in terms of that something, and that the something is a construct which needs clear and detailed definition to be kept in mind during the entire rating process—from its development through to the actual ratings of individuals. Well-trained raters have clear ideas of the construct they are rating (i.e., measuring with a rating) and how it differs from other constructs that could have been rated. It is from this perspective that we move on to other methods of assessment that are not tests but can, if rated well, be helpful indicators of intended predictive attributes.

14

Assessment by Résumés, Interviews, and Personal History

Testing and scaling are two basic psychometric procedures, each with its own theoretical foundations. Most standardized tests and inventories are based on test theory, classical or modern, although some inventories, and some rating methods, are based on scaling theories. Many widely used assessment methods have no basis in either measurement theory or procedural standardization, relying instead on subjective judgment. Interviewing may be the most common of these. Throughout its long history, "it has been heralded, criticized, challenged, studied, and remade" according to Huffcutt and Youngcourt (2006, p. 181), a state of affairs that led them to offer delightful pairs of references giving diametrically opposed bits of information, suggesting a verbal pattern (for which they are not to blame) of saying: *A first review found this, but a second review found no such thing.*

This chapter focuses mainly on interviews, with enough history to show why they are often held in disrepute, and the persistent attempts to improve them. The focus then shifts, briefly, to judgments made from candidates' backgrounds. All of these, from interviews to biodata, share the use of self reports from applicants as the content of the assessment and the use of judgment (ratings) in "scoring" that information. The trend seems to be a move away from haphazard procedures toward systematically planned and structured judgmental assessments. That's the good news. Unfortunately, research and practice seem to focus more on procedure than on assessment of candidate characteristics. What is to be assessed by these methods? Do interviewers and judges of background information try to assess very global, holistic appraisals of concepts such as work ethic, narrower concepts such as fit or work-relevant competencies, or more nearly unitary constructs such as agreeableness? Such questions are being asked, but not often enough or insistently enough.

INTERVIEWING: RESEARCH AND PRACTICE

Judgments made during interviews include assessments, predictions, and decisions. They are often intuitive and disorganized. Assessment may be no more than "sizing up" an interviewee. Prediction may be no more than a vague hunch that the person, as sized up—and if hired, retained, promoted, or assigned to special training—will be great, or will not be bad, or just won't do. Assessments are often secondary to decision; some interviewers want only to reach a decision and then get on with other matters. Herriot (1993) criticized psychometric orientations in interview research; he said that the purpose is to make a decision and that evaluating decisions through statistical prediction is of more interest to academics than to managers. I agree; that is the usual purpose, but I argue that good decisions require both competent assessment and explicit prediction. Predictions merely implied are rarely articulated or evaluated.

My view is that interviews intended for personnel decisions *are* psychometric devices, *are* assessments, and *should be* evaluated by the principles applied to other psychometric devices. Decision making without concern for validities of assessments and predictions is irresponsible.

Conventional Practice

No single approach to interviewing is a tradition; interviewing practices are too idiosyncratic. Nevertheless, some procedures are too common to consider them *un*conventional. So perhaps it will be useful to refer to conventional, but not necessarily traditional, interviews.

Conventionally, an interview is a face-to-face conversation. A conventional interviewer might look at an applicant's file and plan some questions to be inserted during the course of the conversation, but a different conventional interviewer might not. Some interviewers might see the interview as an opportunity to evaluate candidate qualifications, and others (or the same interviewer with a different candidate) might see the purpose as selling the organization or job. Most of them start with vague, and stereotypic, implicit theories of an ideal applicant. Those who take interviewing seriously may read a variety of "how-to-interview" books and try to follow every suggestion, including those they think are dumb, using their own personal twists on them. The results may at worst be illegal, or at best merely bias the conduct of the interview. "As a consequence, the candidate's performance in the interview may reflect more of the interviewer's conduct of the session than the actual qualifications of the candidate" (Dipboye, Wooten, & Halverson, 2004, p. 298). In short, conventional practice can be dominated by wide individual differences among interviewers.

Nevertheless, the number of article titles (in research journals or in the pop management press) with the phrase "the interview" is appalling. The term seems rooted in an unmerited assumption that all interviews are alike. Different interviewers look for different things and often use different methods. Some interviews are entirely unplanned; others are as tightly structured and standardized as any printed test. Assessment is the avowed purpose of some; it is a hidden purpose in others and a denied purpose in still others. Some are short; some seem interminable. Some use one interviewer; others use panels. Some interviewers are highly skilled (or highly experienced, which may not be the same); others do not have a clue as to useful procedures. Some interviewers encourage the interviewee to talk; others dominate the conversation. Interview content consists partly of the questions or tasks posed and partly of the characteristics of individual interviewers. Interviewers are not as standardized as questions; the same questions can be asked in different ways by different interviewers. The evaluation of the interviews of one interviewer may not apply at all to those of another. In short, "conventional wisdom" (Judge, Higgins, & Cable, 2000, p. 384) starts by asserting that interviews are unreliable and subject to various sources of bias.

Influences on Interviewer Judgments

Interviewer Experience and Habit

Experience is usually a good thing, but sometimes we learn things from experience that are not so, including bad habits. Gehrlein, Dipboye, and Shahani (1993) demonstrated that experience may not be helpful. College admissions officers in their study were experienced interviewers of college applicants; their work was supplemented by alumni, faculty, and others in an "inexperienced" group interviewing other applicants. No one in the experienced group made significantly valid judgments for predicting GPA; inexperienced interviewers did much better. The authors suggested that experience tends to breed unwarranted confidence. Less experienced people may compensate for lower confidence by carefully planning their interview strategies. A comprehensive survey of research on the effect of experience on interviewer judgments found very little reason to suggest that experience is helpful (Dipboye & Jackson, 1999).

Some interviewers habitually talk too much. The classic study by Daniels and Otis (1950) found that interviewers generally do most of the talking, sometimes two or three times as much as the interviewees, perhaps depending on first impressions. If preliminary study of application materials is favorable, the interviewer is likely to talk more and listen less. In interviews conducted to assess candidate characteristics, the interviewer's contributions may be relatively brief, encouraging the candidate to speak freely. If the purpose is to persuade the candidate to accept an offer, perhaps the interviewer should in fact talk more. In general, however, the interviewer is more likely to create a good organizational image by listening than by talking. First impression effects have raised other questions about the validity of interviewer judgments (Dougherty, Turban, & Callender, 1994).

Nonverbal Cues

Much has been written about the influence of nonverbal communication on interviewers (Anderson, 1991). Interviewers should know that they can be unduly influenced by such behavior, but many of them base judgments on it, anyway. Experienced (not necessarily good) interviewers have told me that they rely on a variety of nonverbal candidate behaviors: leaning back after making a statement (reason for distrust), firm handshake (strong character), catching one's breath (sign of lying), clean clothes (sign of neat work habits). They have not, however, given me validity evidence. Neither has research. At present, at least, interviewer reliance on interviewee nonverbal behavior, including reliance on eye-contact or general pleasantness, must be considered a potential source of error. The influence of nonverbal behavior does not happen just because interviewers rely on it. Based on their review of relevant literature, DeGroot and Motowidlo (1999) identified five visual cues, and five more vocal cues, considered likely to impress interviewers favorably. Although their research provided some support, they were not willing to recommend explicit use of these cues before substantial replication. Later, Dipboye (2005) identified research showing, for example, that some desirable nonverbal behavior leads to better ratings in interviews, whether contributing to validity or not.

Stereotypes, Prototypes, and Biases

Van Vianen & Willemsen (1992) asked 307 technical workers in university scientific and technical jobs in the Netherlands to check adjectives describing attributes identified in job advertisements. One group of subjects filled out the checklist from the point of view of evaluating a future colleague. The other half responded to the items as generally associated with men, with women, or with both. Items were classed as "masculine" or "feminine" or "sex neutral." The final, abbreviated list was dubbed the "Sex Stereotype Attribute List." Its scoring key, applied to future colleague evaluations, showed gender stereotypes for ideal applicants for various jobs, and interviewer judgments were consistent with them.

Stereotypes bias interviewers' judgments, but prototypes of an ideal applicant can be different. A stereotype is a widely accepted belief, usually oversimplified without confirming evidence, about nearly all members of a definable group. A prototypical ideal candidate can be based on job analysis and defined by a set of attributes that distinctively define desired candidates and distinguish them from those less desired. I have long thought "that work on the idea of a prototype as a planned ideal will be more fruitful than work on more or less generally accepted stereotypes of what is" (Guion, 1987b, p. 202).

"Similar-to-me" may also bias judgment. A candidate like the interviewer (especially demographically) is more likely to be judged favorably. The effect has also been found where interviewer–interviewee similarity was in level of conscientiousness, but only for high-conscientiousness interviewers (Sears & Rowe, 2003). Other findings also suggest that raters use an "ideal candidate" concept in rating candidates. "Similar-to-ideal candidate" seems a useful match to an ideal prototype; if the prototype is valid, matching it should imply valid assessment as well (cf. Dalessio & Imada, 1984).

Interviewers' similarity biases potentially include demographic variables such as sex, race, ethnicity, or age, but research generally reports few or nonsignificant differences in interviewers' ratings of men and women, or of different ethnic groups. However, a more general "similar-to-me" bias could inflate tendencies toward bias. In one study, racial similarity effects were stronger in conventional than in structured interviews, although mixed-race panels of interviewers avoided the effect (Lin et al., 1992). Similarity effects were not found for age. Another study of panels of interviewers showed a similar racial effect, giving higher ratings to candidates of the same racial identity as the majority of the panel (Prewett-Livingston et al., 1996).

Interviewee Characteristics

Some characteristics, including qualifications, of the person interviewed should influence decisions, but others can be sources of error. One is memory. Interviews generally consist of questions requiring the interviewee to respond with a recalled event, state, or behavior, but personal recall may not be accurate (Pearson, Ross, & Dawes, 1992)—perhaps because people have implicit theories of their own personalities that emphasize stability (e.g., *This is how I think now, so I must have thought similarly then*). Other people, or the same people responding to other questions, have implicit theories that lead them to exaggerate changes that have occurred, attributing change to external events or sources. If they emphasize personal stability, and they recognize change, their implicit views of self say that something external must have happened. If a person recalls behavior (e.g., leaving a job) associated with an attitude, and if the attitude has changed, the response would ordinarily describe behavior more in line with the present attitude than with the earlier reality. If the attitude is greatly changed, the behavior (or the stimulus for it) may be exaggerated to account for it.

Personality variables seem likely to influence interviewers' judgments, particularly with the mediating effect of efforts to make a good impression (Van Iddekinge, McFarland, & Raymark, 2007). Candidates try, deliberately or not, to manage the impression being made on the interviewer, and there are individual differences in how well they do it and in the tactics they use. *Impression management (IM)* is the attempt to influence the impression made on others; it is somewhat like faking in personality assessment, but it is a broader, more socially oriented behavior. Individuals surely differ in self-presentation skills, but there is little information about kinds of job performance these skills may predict or the kinds of assessments they may contaminate (Fletcher, 1990). A comprehensive review of IM in interviews (Gilmore, Stevens, Harrell-Cook & Ferris, 1999) surveyed theory and research but could offer few unambiguous generalizations. Does behavior successfully creating the desired impressions with one interviewer work as well with another? Can interviewers learn to detect the deceptions the term "impression management" implies? If so, can they successfully ignore it in making job-relevant assessments or decisions? It seems so. In a widely cited article, Kinicki, Lockwood, Hom, and Griffeth (1990) found that two factors described interviewer ratings on six dimensions. One they labeled "interview impression," the other was called "relevant qualifications." The terms are adequately descriptive; only the relevant qualifications factor validly predicted independent job performance ratings.

Do some kinds of interview questions induce more (or different kinds) of impression management? Different IM tactics were used in responding to situational judgment and to experience-based questions (Ellis, West, Ryan, and DeShon, 2002), results repeated by Peeters and Lievens (2006). Both studies gave explicit IM instructions to the interviewees; would the results be the same if the "instructions" consisted of advice from friends or counselors? In a different experiment, Van Iddekinge et al. (2007) created strong and weak interview situations, following the trait-activation concept (Tett & Burnett, 2003; Tett & Guterman, 2000), and found situational strength to moderate relationships between antecedent variables (personality and format) and interview effectiveness. Would they have found a similar moderating effect between such variables and job effectiveness?

Candidates do tend to distort responses to questions in ways that seem desirable given the demands of the jobs they seek (Levashina & Campion, 2007). Perhaps interviewers can distinguish impressions from real qualifications (Kinicki et al., 1990). Lievens and Peeters (2008) also found importance of IM tactics to be small compared to considerations more relevant to performance. Both studies were conducted in realistic work environments. The suggestion from both is that biasing factors, instead of being studied in isolation, should often be studied in comparison to more relevant variables.

Research and Reviews on Conventional Interviews

Early Reviews

Interviews have been considered too unreliable to be valid since Hollingworth (1923) reported rank orders assigned to 57 candidates by each of 12 sales managers—with virtually no agreement. A series of narrative reviews from Wagner (1949) to Wright (1969) consistently identified unreliability as a major problem. Not until Schmitt (1976) did reviews comment on the problem of lumping together data from interviewers varying in skill, although earlier reviewers also lamented the lack of standardization in interviewing. Precursors of *structured interviews* (those with pre-planned procedures and sets of questions to be asked) included *standardized interviews* (Hovland & Wonderlic, 1939) and McMurry's (1947) *patterned interview*. Accepting Bingham and Moore's definition of an interview as "a conversation with a purpose," Uhrbrock (1948, p. 275) argued that the conversation needed planning—structuring, as we would now say. His argument was reflected in later reviews by Arvey and Campion (1982), Harris (1989), and Judge et al. (2000).

It would be nice to conclude from the chronology that interviews in employment practice have improved. I am not so sure. Early research pretty much accepted interviews as they were—haphazard, idiosyncratic, spur-of-the-moment events—and pretty much limited to prediction of performance. It rarely tried to specify what was being assessed in making the prediction; in fact, Uhrbrock (1948) said flatly that interviewers' ratings were not measures of applicant traits but of interviewers' opinions—essentially, opinions about probable future job performance. That is still true enough, but most researchers now think of these opinions as measures of traits, even if imperfect. The imperfection now is seen as a reason for insisting that interviewers' judgments (opinions, if you like) are as subject to construct validation as to criterion-related validation.

In most organizations, I suspect, the insistence makes little difference in interviewing by decision-making supervisors and managers. Those who wrote early reviews about "the" interview were reviewing studies of actual employment interviewers, most of them having neither training nor information from books on the subject (Uhrbrock, 1948). Authors of more recent reviews on "the" interview are more likely to review hypothesis-driven research. A review of actual practice describes and evaluates what *is* done. A review of research generated by hypotheses is likely to describe and evaluate what *can* be done. Developments over the years have probably influenced researchers without having much influence on the way most operational interviews were and are conducted—haphazard, idiosyncratic, and spur of the moment. My hunch is that interviews in general are no better than they were when Uhrbrock wrote his piece, even though the literature available for reviewers to summarize, integrate, or meta-analyze has improved a great deal. If I'm right, we probably know a lot more about assessment by interviewing, how to use interviewers' judgments to make predictions, and in general to make valid, interview-based decisions than we have communicated to the world at large—where (I suspect) poor interviews remain the rule.

Pioneering Research

Serious research on interviewing began with a series of experiments at McGill University on variables influencing interviewers' decisions (Webster, 1964). The following were among the reported conclusions.

1. Interviewers sharing similar backgrounds develop a stereotype of a good candidate and try to match interviewees and stereotypes.
2. A favorable or unfavorable bias appears early in the interview, and decisions are generally consistent with it. (One finding was that most decisions are actually made within the first four minutes of the interview, even if the interview continues well beyond that time.)
3. Interviewers are more impressed by unfavorable information than by favorable information. It is more likely that an early favorable impression will turn into an unfavorable decision than the reverse. Interviewers are "not prepared to take a chance" (Webster, 1964, p. 87).
4. Interviewers seek information to support or refute hypotheses (or hunches) about candidates. When satisfied, they attend to something else.

The McGill studies, well replicated, were experiments intended to describe the process of reaching a decision, not to evaluate the decision or the reasons for it. However, a decision is an assessment; a favorable decision implies a more qualified candidate than does an unfavorable decision. Validation of that, as of any assessment, is necessary.

Meta-Analyses

Beginning with Hunter and Hunter (1984), a series of meta-analyses have augmented the narrative reviews and provided explicit generalizations about the validity of (generally) aggregated interviews as predictors of job performance and other criteria. Mean validity coefficients reported in early studies were low but positive; in later analyses, mean coefficients were higher as the literature grew and, perhaps, reported research with better interviews. A reasonable figure is a coefficient (corrected for criterion unreliability and range restriction) of about .36 or .37 (Huffcutt & Arthur, 1994; McDaniel, Whetzel, Schmidt, & Maurer, 1994). Further attention to meta-analyses comes later, but getting the historical sequence a bit up to date requires attention to an important set of meta-analytic findings.

Six possible moderators were studied by Marchese and Muchinsky (1993); the most significant was structure, structured interviews being more valid. Others were length of interview (longer interviews were less valid) and sex (better validities in pools with mostly female applicants). The authors also found year of publication an important moderator. More recent articles were more likely to report relatively good validity coefficients, to be based on structured interviews, to be primarily female samples, to be blue collar samples, and to use just one interviewer.

A dramatic difference in mean coefficients (corrected for criterion unreliability and restriction of range) was reported by Wiesner and Cronshaw (1988): $r_c = .20$ for unstructured and $r_c = .63$ for structured interviews. McDaniel et al. (1994) reported a mean corrected validity coefficient of .51 for job-related, structured interviews for research (versus administrative) criteria, but removing structure reduced the mean coefficient in that category to .00. Huffcutt and Arthur (1994) considered structure a probable moderator, dividing it into four levels: (Level 1) wholly unstructured, (Level 2) constraints limited (typically) to topic standardization, (Level 3) prespecifiction of questions (with varying probes allowed), and (Level 4) all applicants asked precisely the same questions without deviations or follow-up questions— essentially an oral test. The four levels of structure, respectively, had mean validities of .20, .35, .56, and .57, all corrected for criterion unreliability and range restriction. The close coefficients at Levels 3 and 4 suggest a possible point of diminishing returns from structure, but it is clear that structuring interviews, removing their haphazard quality, can produce good predictions of performance. Worth pointing out is that, by the very fact that the interviews were part of the employment process, predictive, not concurrent, validity was reviewed.

Meta-analytic conclusions generally evaluate interview validity more favorably than did the narrative reviews. That may be an artifact of the demands of meta-analytic research; the ability to compute a correlation coefficient to serve as a data point implies some degree of structure. If validity coefficients for judgments made in the casual conversations called interviews could be computed, they would probably be lower on average than those with correlation coefficients computed but still called unstructured (McDaniel et al., 1994). My admittedly cynical conclusion is that, although well-structured interviews are likely to provide quite valid prediction, operational interviews are too often neither structured nor valid.

Structure in Interviews

What is meant when calling an interview structured is not always clear; interviews can vary widely in the kind, degree, or rigidity of the intended structure. Structured versus unstructured is a dichotomy only rhetorically; descriptively the terms are relative. For a generic definition, consider: A *structured interview, relative to unstructured, substantially reduces variability in questions asked, the kinds of responses sought, and their evaluation from one interviewer to another, or from one interview to another conducted by the same interviewer* (cf. Huffcutt & Youngcourt, 2006, p. 183). This definition sounds familiar, as if defining standardization.

Standardization and Structure

Wagner (1949) did not call for *structured* interviews; he called for *standardized* interviews. *Structure* and *standardization* are similar in meaning, but they are not synonyms; a structured interview is usually standardized, but not always. By the time meta-analyses were examining moderators of interview validity, Wagner's term had almost disappeared, although some authors still use both terms interchangeably. A distinction is worth keeping. *Structured* typically refers to interviews tailored to fit the work to be done. *Standardization* refers to maintaining standard procedures (structure) across all interviews for a given classification. Standardized interviews are necessarily structured, but not all structured interviews are standardized (individualized structured interviews are described below). Structuring begins with the job description (or description of work done in a work unit or job family), pay classification, promotion patterns, and related data. From such information, qualifications or traits needed for effective performance may be inferred, and relevant questions or tasks can be identified.

Different people have different ideas of how interviews should be structured. The next four headings, levels of structure, describe most of the variety. The first requires minimal structure, retaining a great deal of interviewer discretion during an interview; it provides guidance, not dictation, for interview procedures. The second provides questions to be asked but permits interviewers enough discretion that different candidates might be asked some different questions. The other two are more firmly structured, allowing little or no deviation.

Individualized Structured Interviews

In a conventional, unstructured interview, the interviewer may get on with it without knowing anything about the applicant, although an application form might be consulted during the interview. A job candidate may have submitted a file folder full of credentials such as an application form, résumé, transcripts of academic records, letters of recommendation, or portfolios of prior achievements. Many interviewers examine these before the interview takes place and then plan (i.e., structure) the topics to be discussed. More structure might be formed if the application materials highlight concerns worth exploring; the interviewer can decide ahead of time what questions will be asked and their sequence, what kinds of judgments will be made, and how they will be recorded. The structure in such a case is unique for each candidate. It is not standardized, but it is structured, specifically for that person. Structure, in this approach, means careful planning before conducting an interview, and the plans may differ for individual interviewees if preliminary information suggests different concerns.

Patterned, Behavior Description Interviews

McMurry (1947) developed patterned interviews, anticipating slightly structured procedures. It required stating clear, acceptable bases for selection—such as desired traits, background experiences, or training. An interviewer's guide listed kinds of questions that might be asked for each of these; special training was supposed to assure understanding of the questions and the selection standards. Appropriate rating scales were provided for recording summary evaluations.

A more complex modification, somewhat more structured, was originally called the *Patterned Behavior Description Interview* (Janz, 1989), although most writers now omit the word *patterned*. Janz, Hellervik, and Gilmore (1986) gave examples of the interview patterns of questions for 16 jobs. Their method is based on the aphorism that the best predictor of

TABLE 14.1
Examples of Behavior Description Interview Questions

Content Area	Examples
Credentials, achievements, biographical facts	What level of education have you completed? What was your GPA? How large is the budget you managed?
Technical knowledge	What statistical packages have you used? What does the router do in a computer system?
Experience; activities	What have you done in previous jobs that require working with outside people? What has been your biggest project?
Self-evaluation	What are your major strengths and weaknesses? What kinds of tasks have you most enjoyed?
Behavior descriptions	Tell me about a situation where you had to handle a dispute between two subordinates. What did you do to resolve it?

future behavior is past behavior. Because all questions ask about past behavior, it may be seen as an oral personal history inventory. Question development started by seeking critical incidents, and Janz et al. classified the resulting information into five content areas, not unlike those in Table 14.1, which also gives examples of possible initial questions. Some of these were questions I have used, and some were suggested from my reading of Janz et al. and of Salgado and Moscoso (2002), who seem to reach beyond broad content areas to consider more targeted constructs assessable through behavior description interviews. Questions (both initial and follow-up questions) may be written for each topic area unless an alternative to an interview (e.g., tests, biodata, credentials) would assess it better. Questions need not be limited to a single content area; the same initial question can, with appropriate follow-up probes, provide information for more than one category. Note the term, "*appropriate* follow-up probes."

Probes are within the discretion of the interviewer. For example, a critical incident for an employment test specialist might have been "Developed a valid hands-on performance test to measure problem-solving skills when informed under court order that written tests would not be permitted." The initial question might be, "Tell me about a time when you solved a measurement problem that precluded conventional testing procedures." Follow-up questions might include, "What was unusual about your solution?" and "How did you get others to accept your solution?" If the job dimensions included creative problem solving and persuasiveness, this question and its probes can tap both. After the interview, the candidate is rated on each job dimension on a simple five-point graphic rating scale. The sum of the dimension ratings provides a total score.

Situational Interviews

Situational interviews are based on a goal-setting theory that behavior depends more on goals or intentions than on past behavior. Theoretically, if people are asked to say how they would respond to critical situations others have faced on a job, their answers reveal behavioral intentions. Responses can be systematically scored using a scale anchored by behavioral responses.

Steps required to develop a situational interview, as described by Latham (1989), include job analysis using a critical incident technique, selecting those fitting the performance criteria

You are in charge of truck drivers in Philadelphia. Your colleague is in charge of truck drivers 800 miles away in Atlanta. Both of you report to the same person. Your salary and bonus are affected 100% by your costs. Your buddy is in desperate need of one of your trucks. If you say no, your costs will remain low and your group will probably win the Golden Flyer award for the quarter. If you say yes, the Atlanta group will probably win this prestigious award because they will make a significant profit for the company. Your boss is preaching costs, costs, costs as well as cooperation with one's peers. Your boss has no control over accounting who are the score keepers. Your boss is highly competitive, he or she rewards winners. You are just as competitive, you are a real winner!

Explain what you would do?

Record answer:

_____

_____

_____

_____

Scoring Guide
(1) I would go for the award. I would explain the circumstances to my buddy and get his or her understanding.
(3) I would get my boss' advice.
(5) I would loan the truck to my buddy. I'd get recognition from my boss and my buddy that I had sacrificed my rear-end for theirs. Then I'd explain the logic to my people.

FIG. 14.1   An example of a question and scoring guide for a situational interview. Reprinted from Latham, G. P. (1989), The reliability, validity, and practicality of the situational interview. In Eder, R. W., and Ferris, G. R. (Eds.), *The Employment Interview: Theory, Research, and Practice.* (pp. 169–182). Newbury Park, CA: Sage Publications. © Sage Publications. Reprinted by STM permission.

(e.g., cost-conscious behavior) to be predicted. Each incident becomes a "what would you do if . . . ?" question. Further steps include developing, for example, five-point scales for recording judgments of responses to each question and providing a scoring guide to facilitate agreement among interviewers on what constitutes a good (5), acceptable (3), or unacceptable (1) response to each question. An example of a question and scoring guide is shown in Figure 14.1. Pilot studies are recommended to eliminate questions where applicants all give the same answers, or where interviewers cannot agree on the scoring.

Noteworthy in this sequence is the early focus on performance appraisal, calling for developing criteria first—good advice for any approach. Equally noteworthy is the explicit provision for pilot research. It is noteworthy because people who would never dream of developing written tests without pilot studies often do not hesitate to develop interview guides without them. Building a psychometric device without pilot studies displays unwarranted arrogance—or ignorance of the many things that can go wrong. Among things that can go wrong with this method is anchoring the ends of the five-point rating scales with examples that do not get used because they are too ridiculous or idealistic. Pilot studies can identify such scales.

Comprehensive Structured Interviews

This term (Harris, 1989), distinguishes a generic structured interview from very highly structured procedures, for example, the Campion, Pursell, and Brown (1988) procedure (described below) where everything is structured—comprehensively. Comprehensive structuring begins with job analysis to identify KSAs from which interview questions can be developed. Many kinds of questions or tasks are acceptable, including behavior descriptions or situational questions, job knowledge questions, simulations, or walk-throughs, and "willingness" questions presenting aspects of realistic job previews. If job requirements differ in importance, the difference is supposed to be reflected by the relative number of questions asked. Responses are to be rated, typically on five-point scales, anchored at extremes and the midpoint. The interview score is a simple sum of the ratings.

A comprehensive interview offers the developer more freedom, and the interviewer less, than do other levels. For standardization, all candidates are asked precisely the same questions, and no prompting or follow-up questions are permitted. Scores of all candidates should be available before any decision is made, so the comprehensive interview is explicitly norm-referenced. If interviewer panels are used; the same panel is convened and the same process is followed for every candidate. A specified panel member is to conduct all interviews and ask all questions; all other panel members are to take extensive notes. Questions, answers, and candidates are not to be discussed between interviews, but, after all candidates have been interviewed, large discrepancies in ratings may be discussed and changes made if appropriate. Candidates may not ask questions during the interview, although the procedure calls for a later nonevaluative interview with a personnel representative in which questions are permitted.

The procedure is certainly structured, and comprehensively so, but its feasibility seems (to me) very limited. For example, I don't recall ever working with an organization willing to wait long enough to fill most positions to have every candidate interviewed by the same panel—or, for that matter, to concentrate decision-making panel members for a great enough portion of their time to maintain evaluative consistency. The method would be feasible, perhaps, for choosing employees to be sent to a particular short-term project or training program. Perhaps the scheduling would be feasible in considering candidates for unique positions such as CEO or many professional positions, but I would expect such candidates to be quite negative about the detail-oriented nature of the questions.

The examples above describe the variety of approaches to structuring; they are not offered as prototypes to be precisely matched. Perhaps they never are. Campion, Palmer, and Campion (1997) identified the following 15 components of comprehensive structured interviews. With comments on some of them, they are as follows.

1. All questions should be based on job analysis.
2. Every candidate is to be asked the same questions, exactly worded. (If the management purpose of the interview is to learn the special strengths and weaknesses of individual candidates, this requirement may interfere.)
3. When the question has been asked, and answered, go on to the next one without prompting, follow-up, or elaborating questions. (This one denies the older concept of interviews as conversations.)
4. Use better types of questions. (Campion et al. (1997) listed four types—situational, past behavior, background, and job knowledge questions—but no definitive reason to consider one type superior to another.)
5. Increase the number of questions. (This seems based on the Spearman–Brown effort to increase reliability, but it does not satisfy the Spearman–Brown concept of equivalence.)
6. Control ancillary information; that is, don't permit the candidate to ramble or volunteer information not directly answering the question.

7. Do not allow questions from the candidate until the interview is finished.
8. Evaluate each answer as soon as it is given.
9. Rate on the pre-planned rating scale.
10. Take detailed notes. (There has been some controversy about note taking during interviews. The Campion approach seems to demand it, although it is not clear why.)
11. Use more interviewers. (Campion et al. (1997) seem to prefer panels, but separate multiple interviews are optional.)
12. Use the same interviewer(s) for all candidates. (As commented above, how many organizations, other than governmental, have hiring practices and policies that permit getting all interviewing done all at once?)
13. Do not discuss candidates or answers between interviews.
14. Provide extensive interviewing training (a good idea for any level of structure or conversation).
15. Use statistical, not judgmental or clinical, prediction.

Levels of Structure

Conway, Jako, and Goodman (1995) listed five levels of interview structure, dividing them somewhat differently the four above. They range from virtually no structure to the most highly comprehensively structured, as in Table 14.2. I'm not sure it matters very much what level of structuring is used so long as the interviews are structured to some degree. Structured interviews all seem, on the basis of meta-analyses, to lead to judgments with reasonable psychometric properties, and all have been defended as practical. There are, however, unanswered questions. How much structure is necessary? Does the level of structure reach some point of diminishing returns (cf. Huffcutt & Arthur, 1994). Answers lead to more questions. The most comprehensively structured interviews are essentially oral tests whether with constrained or constructed responses. What is the essential, distinguishing feature of structured interview that makes it different from a test? After all, the same questions could be asked and answered in written form, and the responses could be scored by readers, with no face-to-face component at all. The presence of a person asking the questions might be no more than an alternative mode of presentation. Would oral and written versions of the same list of questions be alike in reliability and validity? Would one form or the other be more susceptible to contaminating sources of variance? Would examinee reaction be the same? We do not know; it is worth investigation, but my best guess is that the two modes of presentation will have different effects. We can ask, as Hakel (1989) did, why structured interviews are superior to unstructured interviews, or as useful as other structured forms of assessment. We still cannot answer definitively, but the evidence of their superiority is compelling. Would similar evidence be found comparing comprehensively structured interviews with paper-and-pencil counterparts?

Performance Interviews

Conventional interviewing asks questions and listens to answers, a verbal exercise for both the interviewer and interviewee. In the title of their article introducing performance interviews, Morgeson, Campion, and Levashina (2009), asked instead, "Why don't you just show me?" Much that has been said about work samples and their varying levels of fidelity to actual work can be applied to interviewing situations where the interviewer poses key tasks for particular skills. Morgeson et al. were interested in skill-based promotional systems. They

TABLE 14.2
Interrater Reliabilities at Varying Levels of Structured Questioning

Statistic at Levels	Panel Interviews	Separate Interviews
Level 1: No formal constraints (unstructured)		
Mean	.69	.37
Variance	.007	.029
n	1,725	766
Number of studies	14	14
Level 2: Topics specified, perhaps with sample questions		
Mean	.72	.61
Variance	.020	.056
n	915	245
Number of studies	5	4
Level 3: Pool of primary questions provided and interviewer choice permitted		
Mean	.75	.56
Variance	.026	.031
n	1,572	1,798
Number of studies	9	12
Level 4: Primary questions specified; follow-up probing permitted		
Mean	.75	.66
Variance	.013	.003
n	3,428	281
Number of studies	33	4
Level 5: Primary questions specified; no follow-up probing allowed		
Mean	.92	.59
Variance	.004	.021
n	1,724	95
Number of studies	14	2

Table adapted from Tables 1 and 4 in Conway, J. M., Jako, R. A., & Goodman, D. F. (1995). A meta-analysis of interrater and internal consistency reliability of selection interviews. *Journal of Applied Psychology, 80*, 565–579. © by the American Psychological Association. Used by STM permission.

chose to call their approach a *performance interview* because they used the format of a comprehensive structured interview and it uses a performance test on the job site. The concept can be broader, however, than for promotions alone when applied to job candidates claiming a specified skill.

Morgeson et al. suggested, with useful detail, some principles and procedures for developing these interviews. They also applied these suggestions to employees in a manufacturing setting and found psychometric evidence of high reliability, an uncorrected validity coefficient of .47, and maybe more to the special point, a high level of employee acceptance of the assessment procedure. It will be interesting to see whether the article stimulates broader investigation of performance interviews for the kinds of skills called competencies. It should.

Evaluation of Interview-Based Decisions

Interviews are not cloned. To speak of evaluating "the" interview is silly. It is usually equally silly to speak of "evaluating" any interview unless we specify the aspect of it being evaluated.

When referring to the reliability or validity of interviews, we refer not to the interview process but to the judgments or decisions reached in it. If the purpose is to predict, then the judgments must be reliable and valid predictors. If the purpose is to describe one or more attributes of the persons being interviewed, the judgments must describe them reliably and with psychometric validity. If the purpose is to augment other recruiting activities, or to let an unsuccessful candidate down easily, then the evaluation is not as concerned with psychometric concerns as with interviewee attitudes toward the process. For most personnel decisions, however, psychometric considerations are the major kinds of evaluations of the decisions or of the judgments on which they are based.

Individual Differences among Interviewers

For a field based in large part on the fact of individual differences, the lack of attention to differences from one interviewer to another is disappointing. For conventional interviews, individual differences among interviewers probably account for substantial sources of unreliability when all interviewers are lumped together in a data pool, whether in a primary analysis or a meta-analysis. Such differences can be seen in differences in early impressions, in ways of gaining rapport, general friendliness, or sensitivity to the interviewee's reactions to questions. It is often asserted that such differences cancel each other in meta-analyses, but I find these assertions unconvincing, especially in view of paucity of relevant data. One reason for structuring interviews is that it may lead to a reduction in the influence of the individual interviewer characteristics on decisions reached. Even for structured interviews (except, perhaps, for the most test-like), individual differences exist. Information that can be classified into several categories may allow differences in weighting information that lead to substantially different judgments, and some of these judgments are more or less valid, predictively or descriptively. Dipboye (2005) has pointed to individual differences in processing information relevant to candidate qualifications. Graves and Karren (1999) concluded that interviewers differ in validity of predictions based on their judgments and in the patterns of information utilization. Research has not always found such differences. Again, it is an area where researchers should check the similarity of validities of different interviewers; without the check, potentially important differences will go unnoticed. A general shortage of solid research needs to be remedied by showing how real-life interviewers, working with different levels of structure, differ from each other in background information, approach to the interview and to the interviewee, in cognitive and social processes during the interview and in evaluation of information gleaned—and then by showing how, if at all, such differences affect resultant judgments and decisions.

Reliability of Judgments

Early reviews of interview research focused on their apparently severely limited reliability, especially interrater reliability—precisely the complaints of Hollingworth (1923) and Webster (1964). A meta-analysis of interrater reliability and internal consistency reported by Conway et al. (1995) has been considered "the classic work in this area" (Huffcutt & Youngcourt, 2006, p. 186). Findings concerning reliability are summarized in Table 14.2; note that the levels of structure in this table are limited to structure of questions; structure also varies according to response evaluations, procedures for combining ratings, and others, but the principal characteristic of most structured interviewing is the standardization of questioning across interviews. Table 14.2 notes varying levels of question standardization, drawn from the levels suggested in Huffcutt and Arthur (1994) but with the addition of one more level, Level 3 in Table 14.2. For individual (separate) interviews, dividing the data according to prior levels results in very few studies summarized for Levels 2, 4, and 5, but comparing Level 1 (unstructured interviews) with the midpoint of the four structured levels (.61) makes the point clearly that the old fuss about unreliable interviews must fade when the interviews are structured to at least some extent, even though these data do not show important reliability differences with different degrees of structure.

Also worth noting again is the reinforcement of the principle that reliability improves with additional observations (the Spearman–Brown principle, even without measurement equivalence); panel interviews show substantially better reliability at all five levels, including the totally unstructured level. In other words, the Conway et al. meta-analysis shows well that the application of sound psychometric principles can turn interviewing from disreputable to effective assessment.

Criterion-Related Validity Coefficients

Recall that reliability establishes limits to criterion-related validity (and, with less numerical precision, any other description of validity). Conway et al. (1995) computed the upper limits of validity at three levels of structure based on the limits set by interrater reliability. "Estimates of upper limits . . . were .67 for highly structured interviews, .56 for moderately structured interviews, and only .343 for interviews with low structure" (Conway et al., 1995, pp. 573–574). Structure pays. In their "85-year" summary, Schmidt and Hunter (1998, p. 265) reported that structured interviews were tied with general mental ability tests as second only to work samples in predicting job performance and contributed 24% additional variance when combined with general ability. Unstructured interviews were also good predictors, although clearly not as good.

Interview validity is typically described in terms of predicting job-related criteria; in meta-analyses, current mean validity coefficients are higher than those reported earlier, possibly because some of the more recent analyses have been limited to structured interviews (Moscoso, 2000). Nevertheless, the studies within a meta-analysis may underestimate validity by pooling data across interviewers who differ in individual validity and whose judgments are not independent (Dreher, Ash, & Hancock, 1988). Van Iddekinge, Sager, Burnfield, and Heffner (2006) reported that, of the six published studies since the Dreher et al. results, five report individual differences among interviewers' validities; the only exception used highly structured interviews. For most interviews, the remedy seems obvious: the data points in meta-analyses should be validity coefficients for individual interviewers. It seems obvious to me, but Van Iddekinge et al., with military interviewers using structured interviews, were less sure. They looked for individual differences among those using structured interviews, and they found them, although statistical artifacts accounted for most differences. The results were about the same for individual panels of raters. Similar results had been found among supervisors in a large government agency by Pulakos, Schmitt, Whitney, and Smith (1996). Their work needs to be repeated in diverse situations several times, particularly in smaller or less centralized organizations, before concluding that individual differences do not matter, even for structured interviews.

The use of data-points for individual interviewers will not be a feasible remedy until more researchers recognize individual differences among interviewers in designing their research. Some people think that meta-analysis cures all ailments and point as evidence to analyses of validities of various cognitive tests combined in a single meta-analysis. Including in a single analysis interviews conducted by people whose qualifications are limited to "knowing how to size people up" along with those done by people who know the interviewing literature well is like throwing cognitive tests developed by psychometric professionals in the mix with those appearing in pop culture magazines.

Incremental Validity

Incremental validity, the increase in variance accounted for when a new predictor is added to those already accounting for some of it, is ordinarily determined by stepwise multiple regression analysis (see Chapter 15). Tests and inventories are entered first to determine their validity; interview data are entered in the next step to see how much validity is added by interview judgments (if any). This order of entry arose because tests were more likely to be valid than interviews. As time went by, and structured interviews gave evidence of predictive validity, questions of their incremental validity became important.

Interviews *will* be used, in most organizations, for most jobs; in most organizations, conventional interviews are the assessment method of choice. Unless the word gets out about the virtues of structure, many of them will be psychometrically poor. Properly pretested, well-structured interviews usually predict job performance. Are they good enough predictors to add validity when used with other assessments?

Maybe not. Walters, Miller, and Ree (1993) developed a structured interview for pilot trainees. It led to seven ratings with, individually, validity coefficients that were modest but comparable to validities for scores on written tests. Equations for written tests with or without the interview ratings did not give significantly different coefficients, perhaps because traits influencing interviewers were also measured by the written tests. Shahani, Dipboye, and Gehrlein (1991) also found no incremental validity for interview assessments. On the other hand, criteria such as client relations and cooperation were predicted better when interviews were added to the equation reported by Day and Silverman (1989), and interviews provided incremental validity in predicting criteria of leadership, military bearing, and personal discipline (McHenry, Lough, Toquam, Hanson, & Ashworth, 1990).

Sometimes the order can or should be reversed. If interviews are as valid as recent meta-analyses suggest, and if most organizational leaders insist on them, why not ask whether testing programs would add incrementally to the validity of the interviews. Campion, Campion, and Hudson (1994) did it both ways. They combined a 30-item structured interview and a nine-test battery and found that interview scores added 8% to the criterion variance accounted for by tests; in reversing the order, tests accounted for only 4% more than interviews alone! Remember, however, that this sort of structured interview is more like an oral test than a traditional interview; maybe it was simply a better test. Where does such disparate information take us? To the conclusion we already knew: We do not know enough about the incremental validities even of well-structured interviews. At this point we can do no better than to say that low correlations of interviewer judgments with cognitive or personality tests suggested "considerable potential" for incremental validity (Huffcutt & Youngcourt, 2006, p. 188).

Interviews for Trait Assessment

Most research on construct validity in interviews is more interested in constructs the interviewers try to assess than in how well they assess specified constructs. Construct validity is a two-question notion: one asks whether the judgments do in fact assess the construct, and the other asks whether unintended constructs contaminate the assessments. The answers, if based on data carefully collected and analyzed, and if asked about a reasonably well-defined construct, describe the inferences that can be validly drawn about interviewees from interviewers' judgments. Stated differently, understanding the meaning or defensible interpretation of an interviewer's judgment requires identification of a theoretical, or a plausible, construct and data to confirm or disconfirm it as an explanation of the ratings.

Research must identify variables best assessed by interviews (Landy, Shankster, & Kohler, 1994; Schmitt, 1976). It has not yet happened, although several studies, while sparse, have appeared. The first task is to identify traits most associated with interviewer judgments, that is, traits that account for variance in the judgments. Work by Huffcutt, Conway, Roth, and Stone (2001) is a good beginning. To prepare for their meta-analysis, they sorted 338 rating scales from interview studies to match an a priori taxonomy of seven construct categories relevant to employment interviews. A report of the classification is shown in Table 14.3—greatly abridged, but enough to show the variety of constructs and terms used as rating

TABLE 14.3

Interview constructs and dimension labels

Category	Construct	Common Dimension Labels
Mental Capability	General intelligence	Intelligence, mental ability, ability to learn, analytical ability, mental alertness, ability to think quickly
	Creativity and innovation	Creativity, creativeness, innovation
Knowledge & Skills	Job knowledge and skills	Technical knowledge, product knowledge, use of tools, budgeting
	Education & training	Education, academic achievement, grades in school
Basic Personality Tendencies	Conscientiousness	Dependability, responsibility, reliability, willingness to work hard, initiative, persistence, integrity, professionalism
	Emotional stability	Stress tolerance, poise, social adjustment, self-control, self-confidence, ego strength
Applied Social Skills	Communication skills	Oral communication, expression, ability to present ideas, conversation ability, voice & speech, listening
	Interpersonal skills	Social skills, social sensitivity, working with others, adapting to people, teamwork, cooperation, team building
Interests & Preferences	Occupational interests	Job interest, investment, commitment to a career
	Hobbies & general interests	Hobbies
Organizational Fit	Values & moral standards	Quality orientation, safety orientation, customer service, customer focus, pride in the organization
Physical Attributes	General physical attributes	Health, appearance, attractiveness
	Job-related physical skills	Physical ability, stamina, agility

Abridged from Table 1 in Huffcutt, A. I., Conway, J. M., Roth, P. L., & Stone, N. J. (2001). Identification and meta-analytic assessment of psychological constructs measured in employment interviews. *Journal of Applied Psychology*, 86, 897–913. © American Psychological Association. Used by permission.

TABLE 14.4

Meta-analyses of Conventional and Structured Interview Ratings and Related Variables

Variable	Conventional		Structured (behavioral)	
	K	r_c	K	r_c
General Mental Ability	53	.41	22	.28
Job Experience	5	.29	5	.71
Job Knowledge	–		8	.53
Situational Judgment	–		6	.46
Grade Point Average	28	.13	5	.17
Emotional Stability	16	.38	10	.08
Extraversion	19	.34	7	.21
Openness to Experience	16	.30	6	.09
Agreeableness	18	.26	6	.12
Conscientiousness	18	.28	13	.17
Social Skills	6	.46	5	.65

Adapted from Tables 3 and 4 in Salgado, J. F., & Moscoso, S. (2002). Comprehensive meta-analysis of the construct validity of the employment interview. *European Journal of Work and Organizational Psychology*, *117*, 299–324. © 2002 by Taylor & Francis Group; used by permission. K = number of correlations; r_c = average correlation corrected for sampling error, unreliability in both variables, and range restriction in interview scores.

scale labels presumed to fit the categories.[1] The remaining question is whether the ratings made under the various labels do reflect the constructs associated with them—their construct validity.

Salgado and Moscoso (2002) distinguished conventional interviews and structured behavioral interviews. Table 14.4 reports the corrected mean validity coefficients for judgments reported in each type of interview for each variable named in the left column. Two constructs (job knowledge and situational judgment) were found in the analysis of behavioral interviewers' judgments but not in judgments by conventional interviews. Results for conventional interviews were quite diffuse, ranging from .13 to .46. For structured interviews, the correlated variables were with job experience, social skills, job knowledge, and situational judgment. These studies, like many other trailblazers, have limitations, but they suggest that even conventional interviewer judgments have more systematic foundation than previously thought.

A methodologically different study was reported by van Dam (2003). Eight experienced interviewers in a consulting organization had interviewed many candidates for a wide variety of jobs at widely different job levels. In these interviews, which were classed as conventional, the interviewers (while interviewing) wrote down terms deemed descriptive of the person interviewed, and these stayed in the interview record, along with a dichotomous recommendation (hirable vs. not hirable). Terms were identified that fit terms found in the circumplex models of the Big Five personality factors (Hofstee et al., 1992). Biserial correlations were computed for each individual interviewer for each of the Big Five terms. For five of the eight interviews, recommendations were significantly correlated with factor scores on three

---

[1] The actual meta-analysis examined criterion-related validity coefficients for the full set of ratings, for ratings from low structure, and ratings from high structure interviews. Overall, the ratings had validities about equal to those of relevant standardized tests, and the validities found from high structure interviews were substantially better than those from interviews low in structure. I mention the study here to focus on construct identification.

factors: conscientiousness, emotional stability, and openness to experience. Worth considering is an experiment with the unsurprising showing that interviewers' judgments of personality were better in face-to-face interviews than in telephone interviews (Blackman, 2002).

Correlational studies lack the causal support needed to identify constructs that drive interviewer judgments. They are suggestive, but clear causal answers are likely to stay elusive. Roth, Van Iddekinge, Huffcutt, Eidson, and Schmit (2005) agreed that the question is important, but they pointed out that, unlike determining the constructs basic to other assessments, interviews rely largely on individual information processing—with all that implies about human judgment and the variety of influential constructs. Judgments by people in general, and interviewers and managers explicitly, are marred by overlooking or denying the probabilistic nature of prediction and relying instead on their obvious expertise because of their great experience (Highhouse, 2008; the sarcasm is mine). Moreover, individual differences among those interviewed include differences in the constructs accounting for answers to questions or in response sets. Do not expect the near future to yield clear answers to the question, "what constructs are assessed in interviewers?" and do not assume those answers lead to answers about construct validities of interviewer judgments. The constructs that *should* be used should be identified in job and need analyses, not in serendipitous exploring. Then the question becomes, "how validly do interviewers assess those constructs?"

Although interviewer ratings are made in a context different from many other ratings, they are, after all, subject to the problems of other ratings. We will not clearly understand what interviewers can assess until the research enterprise starts to (a) develop theoretical statements of constructs appropriate for interview assessment, (b) train interviewers in their meanings and manifestations, (c) appropriately structure interviews, (d) collect data, and (e) conduct the confirmatory and disconfirmatory research needed to determine whether interviewers' ratings on these constructs lead to valid inferences about them.

Arthur and Villado (2008) emphasized the importance of the distinction between a predictor construct and a predictor method used in assessing it. A *predictor construct* is a behavioral domain, observable or latent, to be sampled in some way. That "way," a *predictor method*, is a technique chosen to sample that domain and eventually to make inferences about it and its relevance for potential use. The distinction was, of course, basic to the MTMM (Campbell & Fiske, 1959), but Arthur and Villado expanded the discussion and explicitly applied it to employment assessment important to three problems in comparing predictors: criterion-related validity, reduction of subgroup mean differences, and applicant reactions to assessments. For a given construct, a variety of assessment methods is plausible (e.g., interviewing, rating background data, paper-and-pencil testing, or computer-based tests). Their plea in making the distinction more sharply is for research to fill in more definitively the cells of a comprehensive MTMM for employment purposes.

We simply do not know, despite some good speculation, what is assessed in an interview; general answers are unavailable, so no general principles can be offered for improving the meaningfulness of interviews as assessments. Does it matter? Can the decisions be valid even in ignorance of the constructs used in reaching them? Of course. But at this point in the history of employment psychology we should be getting tired of not knowing what we are doing, even when we do it with commendable care.

Content-Oriented Considerations

Interview guides, rating scales, and general structure of interviews are often content-related, relying on job analysis in their development. Considering content and content representativeness may prove more meaningful than searching for elusive theoretical constructs. Lawshe's content validity ratio (CVR; Lawshe, 1975) was computed for items in each of three structured interview guides developed by Carrier, Dalessio, and Brown (1990). One of the guides was for use with experienced applicants, the other two for inexperienced ones. For experienced candidates, the approach worked quite well; the highest CVR items combined to form the best criterion-related validity. Not so for the inexperienced ones. Is content sampling, then, a useful approach to structuring interviews only for experienced candidates?

I think so. Content samples, like work samples and the old oral trade tests, are drawn from job analysis leading to questions and ratings appropriate for those claiming experience and capable of distinguishing truly experienced candidates from those who merely claim the experience. Assessment of applicants who lack experience, and claim none, should focus on aptitude for the work they have yet to learn; aptitude is surely assessed better by tests than by interviewers' ratings. This view follows the concept of alternative assessments for somewhat individualized selection strategies, described in Chapter 2, with different assessments for people with different experience.

The Case for Policy-Capturing

The comments on evaluating interviews have repeatedly stressed the need to individualize them to some extent. In part, this is necessary because of differences among candidates (e.g., differences in experience). In part, it is necessary because of differences among interviewers: some are better at it than others, some perceive things in candidates that others do not, some prepare for conventional interviews (and maybe for structured ones) more carefully than others. Neither candidates nor those who interview them come pressed in a common mold. Interviewing, if it is to be different from an oral test, is the sensible place to see job candidates as individuals.

I admit to a predilection for seeing the world and the people in it as forming a complex environment. The road to understanding individualization of interviewer practices is through some form of policy capturing, described in Chapter 12 mainly by the lens model. Policy-capturing research, the little that has been done, has in fact shown individual differences in the ways interviewers use information to reach overall judgments and in the criterion-related validity of those judgments; treating different interviewers as mere replications of each other (as in pooling data across interviewers) is unwise. Three studies, not new, have dominated citations in this area.

1. Zedeck, Tziner, and Middlestadt (1983) reported overall validity coefficients of "the" interview (aggregated over 10 interviewers) at barely greater than zero. Data were too sparse for individual interviewers to compute individual coefficients, but Zedeck et al. showed that individual interviewers had distinctly different decision policies and concluded that aggregating data (lumping different interviewers together) is inadvisable.

2. Three interviewers audiotaped interviews used in initial screening for entry clerical and technical jobs (Dougherty et al., 1986). Each of the three interviewed some applicants and rated them on eight job-related dimensions and on an overall rating scale. All three interviewers rated all applicants from the tapes. Those hired were subsequently rated by their supervisors on 10 dimensions, including overall performance. Validity coefficients are shown in Table 14.5. ("Live" judgments are those of the actual interviewer at the time of the interview; other columns refer to judgments

TABLE 14.5

Validity Coefficients for "Live" Overall Judgments, Mean of Overall Judgments, and Individual Interviewer Judgments

			Interviewer		
Criterion Dimension	Live[a] Judgments (n = 57)	Mean of[b] Judgments (n = 57)	Judge 1 (n = 56)	Judge 2 (n = 54)	Judge 3 (n = 56)
Learning tasks	.10	.17	.09	.07	.24
Minimal supervision	.05	.32	.19	.09	.41
Organizing	.09	.18	.13	−.05	.26
Judgment	−.05	.24	.23	.07	.26
Job knowledge	−.09	.12	.07	−.11	.23
Cooperation	−.04	.09	.13	−.01	.08
Productivity	.03	.19	.12	−.05	.32
Accuracy	.18	.28	.25	.19	.27
Involvement	.06	.28	.27	.04	.34
Overall performance:					
Actual	.06	.21	.15	.02	.26
Predicted[c]			.23	.19	.26

[a]Overall judgments made by interviewers in the actual, live interviews; all other columns are correlations based on judgments from the tape recordings. [b]Mean of the judgments based on tapes by the three interviewers. [c]Using judgments predicted from the interviewer's own policy equation. Adapted from Dougherty, T. W., Ebert, R. J., & Callender, J. C. (1986). Policy capturing in the employment interview. *Journal of Applied Psychology, 71,* 9–15. © The American Psychological Association. Adapted with permission.

based on the tapes.) Again, aggregated interviewer overall judgments were not significantly correlated with supervisory ratings of overall job performance; neither were ratings from two of the interviewers. The third, however, significantly and substantially predicted all supervisory ratings but one. The study went beyond demonstrating individual differences in interviewer validity; it also suggested that interviewers can be trained to use more effective policies.

3. The situation seemed reversed in a study by Kinicki et al. (1990). They found significant validity for aggregated data but not for individuals. Again, only a couple of their interviewers had enough cases for appreciable statistical power, and correlations for these disappeared under cross-validation.

What conclusion can be drawn? I conclude that important individual differences exist in interviewing skill and judgment validities. Further, I conclude that lumping together interviewers who differ in policies and in effectiveness has not provided much useful information. Against my predilection, however, are three caveats.

1. The best of these three studies used only three interviewers, and very few data from individual interviewers were presented in the others.

2. Clustering techniques find some interviewers quite similar in the information they consider in making their judgments. Moreover, the similarities can be enhanced by training interviewers to use designated policies.

3. Meta-analyses have provided no reason to assume serious individual differences, even while making it clear that structure is extremely important. The importance of

individual differences among interviewers may be greatly reduced with well but not rigidly structured interviews.

INTERVIEWING: GENERAL CONCLUSIONS

A large body of research on interviewing has, in my opinion, given too little practical information about how to structure an interview, how to conduct it, and how to use it as an assessment device. I think I know from the research that (a) interviews can be valid, (b) for validity they require some degree of structuring and standardization, (c) structure, like many other things, can be carried too far, (d) without carefully planned structure (and maybe even with it) interviewers talk too much, and (e) the interviews made routinely in nearly every organization could be vastly improved if interviewers were aware of and used these conclusions. There is, however, much more to be learned and applied.

Sometimes the sophistication of current research interferes with learning important things about interviewing. Research has been, during the periods of both conventional and well-structured interviewing, preoccupied with the validity of interviewers' judgments as predictors of future job behavior. That research is important. Nevertheless, it is also important to recognize other purposes for interviewing; for example, recruiting, building identification with and commitment to the organization, public relations, and more generally changing attitudes—and, most of all, assessment of defined qualifications. Despite some reports of studies on how well such purposes are met, they have in fact been relatively neglected. Even for prediction, it is important to keep in mind that structuring takes many, varied forms. Is it possible that the different purposes require different forms of structure?

As this is written, psychological research on employment practice is, in general, almost exclusively nomothetic. I am biased toward the belief that individual differences require more effort to search for the ways in which different people reach different judgments from the same information. We should be learning more about the individual differences in the processes and policies that lead to differential validities. A great deal more attention should focus on differences among interviewers in such cognitive activities as knowing and interpreting cues to applicant characteristics, combining oral information, and perceiving conclusions not necessarily intended at the start. Policy-capturing research is one way among others to focus on these matters that rely heavily on human judgment.

ASSESSMENT OF CANDIDATES' BACKGROUNDS

Early in the twentieth century, a common hiring practice for factory jobs was to line up early morning applicants, let a supervisor look at them and point to some who looked promising, and send the rest away. As personnel procedures became somewhat more sophisticated, procedures came to be based less on muscular appearance than on the aphorism that the best predictor of future behavior is past behavior—a cliché, to be sure, but often true and encapsulated in the term *behavioral consistency*. A candidate who performed well on a job in the past is likely to perform well on a similar job in the future; one who has behaved responsibly in the past is likely to be responsible in the future. Interviews sought, and still seek, background information about candidates, among other things, but assessment procedures like printed application forms and reference checks often focused more exclusively on background history. The general purpose of a background investigation is to determine whether a candidate has actually demonstrated the competencies and KSAs needed for the work for which he or she is being considered (McGonigle & Curnow, 2007), but until recently the determination has usually been pretty casual.

Assessment by interviewer judgment is a common method for learning about candidates' backgrounds. Interviews have changed from haphazard and generally unreliable events to structured plans for getting and evaluating information reliably. Interviewing has changed from a spur-of-the-moment conversation to a well-planned question-and-answer period intended to systematize interviewer judgments. Interviewer judgments have concomitantly changed from being often invalid to having validities comparable to those of general mental ability tests (Schmidt & Hunter, 1998). Twelve of the 19 methods of assessment classified by Schmidt and Hunter rely heavily, like interviews, on judgments as assessments—and some of them are directly focused on assessing aspects of candidates' backgrounds. For such assessment, the change from haphazard to structured lags only slightly behind that for interviewing. It is still subject to the interviewing problems already described, especially that of defining what aspect of a person's background, or of the things that might be learned from it, is to be assessed.

Use of many of the traditional methods of getting information for identifying behavioral consistencies has not yet evolved into more structured and clearly defined procedures. Many, indeed, have become virtually illegal. Former procedures might have called for credit checks, or for extensive conversations with listed references or former employers, in so-called reference checks. Privacy principles now preclude many such checks. The Americans with Disabilities Act precludes background checks entirely before a conditional job offer is made (conditional on a satisfactory outcome). In an earlier, less litigious era, one could learn much about an outsider's past behavior from reference checks; these days, such queries often produce little more than verification of dates of enrollment or employment. Getting information that is neither distorted nor unreliable is the first problem. The second is to turn the information into a useful assessment. Reference checks were once pretty useful; Schmidt and Hunter (1998) reported a mean corrected meta-analytic result of .23 and, importantly, an incremental ability (over general mental ability test scores alone) of .12.

Nevertheless, I think they are no longer useful given the fear of litigation if information is given about prior employees. Although Schmidt and Hunter thought a change in the legal environment in the United States and elsewhere might restore their early value as an added predictor, I am more pessimistic.

Application Forms

As personnel departments developed, personnel managers (and staffs) created application forms for each company. It's unfair to say they were truly haphazard, but they seemed so. A common practice was to collect forms used in other companies, pick out apparently useful components, modify them for local settings, and print a coherent set of requests for information. Typical forms included identification information and past work history (subject to verifying results of reference checks). As they grew in popularity and size, some forms asked about hobbies, aspirations, family matters, financial status, or organizational memberships; sometimes the developers of these forms would have a hard time explaining why some questions were asked but many of them were based on theories—folk theories more than psychological theories.

In applying for a job, one wants to emphasize his or her qualifications and perhaps to minimize deficiencies in them. It is no wonder, then, that job applicants often exaggerate or otherwise misrepresent those qualifications—especially in describing educational or job experience backgrounds. Wood, Schmidtke, and Decker (2007) mentioned studies that had estimated from 30% to as much as 70% (for résumés) of the applicants had exaggerated or misrepresented qualifications in some way. It is not a trivial problem, and it is exacerbated by the open-ended nature of résumés and traditional application forms.

Evaluative judgments of qualifications based on relevant work experience, education, and training are often based on completed application forms, résumés, interviews, examination of credentials, or questionnaires. In the Schmidt-Hunter meta-analysis of 1998, none of these showed much validity when traditionally assessed. When work experience was assessed with carefully-constructed measures and scored in terms of behavioral consistency, they were found essentially as valid ($r_c = .45$) as the far more costly and rarely used procedure of hiring people and assessing their performance over perhaps a several-month period before deciding whether to keep them or let them go ($r_c = .44$)—and they seem likely to be less controversial than standardized tests of KSAs. Unfortunately, a behavioral consistency approach is as expensive in cost and time as ability test or personality inventory construction. It is nevertheless a thoroughly structured assessment procedure that needs further attention, particularly in the light of a theoretical analysis of its possibilities by Levine, Ash, and Levine (2004).

Weighted Application Forms

With increasingly widespread use, many application forms came to be developed and evaluated like tests. Precedent was well established. An early example of assigning point values to response categories was reported for nine personal history items by Goldsmith (1922). The response categories must, of course, be classified somehow; Goldsmith classified prior occupations as social or unsocial in nature and her work had been preceded by the insurance industry's Aptitude Index, which had its beginning in 1919 as a weighted application blank in one company. Subsequently, application blank information came to be scored for such traits as energy level, persistence, specific job skills, or relevance of prior experience. This led to including some stylistic categories such as using initials instead of full given names, or number of misspelled words (Scollay, 1956).

Weights were generally determined statistically, essentially correlating responses to later performance. Many different methods for weighting were developed, summarized long ago in Guion (1965a). Not only were the earliest examples clearly predictive (rather than concurrent), they were also statistically proper. That is, weights were developed on one sample of applicants, but validated on another sample, avoiding the "baloney" coefficient, as Cureton (1950a) dubbed so-called validity coefficients in which the data used in getting the weights were also used to get the validity coefficient. Sometimes, weighting was subjective, based loosely on perceptions of company policy (before policy capturing research was developed).

Résumés

An application form is employer-generated. It asks for information that the employer wants to know (within legal constraints). Applicants tend to provide similar information in applicant-generated forms, introducing themselves to an employer by providing a résumé giving their personal background information. A résumé routinely includes identification information for contact purposes and, minimally, prior work and educational history. It probably also presents information to emphasize things the applicant wants the employer to know about them and things they think the employer wants to know: special accomplishments, awards and honors received, and perhaps special skills which, even if not precisely job-relevant point out that the applicant has a history of note-worthy achievement. It may include personal information about interests or community activities (e.g., volunteer work), and it may offer a glimpse of the future in the form of career or personal goals. Sometimes a résumé gives too much information. Listing hobbies and nonwork activities may be seen as cluttering up the application with information that is not really work-relevant. It may simply be too long and detailed. More importantly, some information (e.g., family matters, ethnicity) might be included that is better for the employer not to know under existing employment law (Catano et al., 1997).

Increased use of résumés may be attributable to the internet and associated software. Candidates may choose from many software packages one that will help them prepare an attractive and informative résumé, and employers have similar choices. The literature is full of advice to candidates, some of it probably good, but relatively little guidance appears for employers. One major difference between candidates' résumés and employers' personal history forms is the lack of uniformity in the résumés. The employers' materials tend to be more standardized, at least in form, and therefore more likely to be scorable. Whereas application forms can be given numerical scores to reflect specific background characteristics or constructs of interest, great variation across résumés can be expected. The variation means that any assessment of even vaguely defined constructs is strictly judgmental and probably idiosyncratic. My own view is that résumé use is overrated and that organizations should develop and validate their own personal history forms.

Biodata Forms

The principle of basing decisions on biographical information dates back to 1894 (Stokes, 1994), or perhaps to 1884 (Schoenfeldt & Mendoza, 1994). Apparently its value was observed long before those years. Levine et al. (2004) cited as an example the advice Polonius gives Laertes in *Hamlet*. The use of biographical data was prominent in the 1920s, again in the military during the Second World War, and then in and since the 1980s—largely because of the persistent research of William Owens and his students and colleagues. Application blanks traditionally included biographical questions about educational and work experiences, but modern biodata forms "bear only slight resemblance" (Stokes, 1994, p. xv) to earlier application forms. Many of them seem much more like personality inventories and are often designed to assess personality constructs. Early forms were called Biographical Information Blanks (BIBs), a term replaced by *biodata*, and scored less like weighted application blanks and more like standardized inventories.

The Boundaries of Biodata

Are biodata forms different from personality inventories? Biodata include items about prior events or behaviors; some of them may ask about prior feelings or attitudes. An item such as "How did you feel when ... ?" may be found in either kind of inventory. Is there a genuine difference between items that tap the personality domain and those of biodata? Does it matter?

The kinds of constructs measured with biodata overlap substantially with those measured by personality inventories, but there are differences too. Both reflect personality attributes, but biodata tap a larger domain, reflecting interests, attitude, skills, and abilities in a single set of questions. Even with overlapping content, the difference in approach probably matters little for predictive validity. It matters more when trying to explain or to understand validity coefficients. What makes biodata predictive? What constructs do these assessment tools measure? Answers to such questions are more elusive for biodata, maybe because boundaries of biodata content are more often sought.

A guide to the boundaries was provided by Mael (1991), summarized in Table 14.6 as a guide to information that may be considered biographical. Briefly, the limiting boundaries of biodata include the following.

TABLE 14.6
A Taxonomy of Biodata Items

Historical	*Future or Hypothetical*
How old were you when you got your first paying job?	What position do you think you will be holding in 10 years?
	What would you do if another person screamed at you in public?
External	*Internal*
Did you ever get fired from a job?	What is your attitude toward friends who smoke marijuana?
Objective	*Subjective*
How many hours did you study for your real-estate license test?	Would you describe yourself as shy?
	How adventurous are you compared to your coworkers?
First-hand	*Second-hand*
How punctual are you about coming to work?	How would your teachers describe your punctuality?
Discrete	*Summative*
At what age did you get your driver's license?	How many hours do you study during an average week?
Verifiable	*Nonverifiable*
What was your grade point average in college?	How many servings of fresh vegetables do you eat every day?
Were you ever suspended from your Little League team?	
Controllable	*Noncontrollable*
How many tries did it take you to pass the CPA exam?	How many brothers and sisters do you have?
Equal access	*Nonequal access*
Were you ever class president?	Were you captain of the football team?
Job-relevant	*Not job-relevant*
How many units of cereal did you sell during the last calendar year?	Are you proficient at crossword puzzles?
Noninvasive	*Invasive*
Were you on the tennis team in college?	How many young children do you have at home?

1. Biodata must be *historical*, the items referring to events or experiences that have occurred in the past. Intentions, or presumed behavior in hypothetical circumstances, do not fit within the boundary.
2. Biodata items are *external* actions. They can be observed by others; they are not events solely within one's own head. Many biodata forms ask questions of the "how did you feel?" variety. I think such questions are outside the biodata domain.
3. The biodata domain is *objective* in the sense that responses are basically factual, not interpretations of events. Biographical information should be first-hand, not attributions to others. The item "I thought my parents were disappointed in me" is not within the boundaries.
4. *Discrete* actions or events have beginnings and endings; a driver's license was in fact obtained (or not) at a specified age. An item calling for a summary of an entire flock of events typically does not clearly fit a single domain; it requires consideration of too much information. Market researchers have long noted that questions answerable with explicit information are better than those that ask the respondent to compute something; "how many bags of potato chips did you buy last month?" is a better, more explicitly biographical, question than, "On the average, how many bags of potato chips do you buy each month?" Discrete information seems more likely to carry the possibility, even if remote, that someone might know or can find out whether the answer given is correct. The common-sense view that *verifiable* answers, even if no one is likely to take the trouble to verify them, seem less likely to be faked was not supported (or not well) in some studies (e.g., Harold, McFarland, and Weekley, 2006).
5. Ordinarily, asking people about things over which they had no *control* is pointless. However, past experiences that shaped and influenced present behavior are within the boundaries because of their influence on the person. Even if the experiences were beyond the person's control, reactions to them (e.g., learning from them) were possibly controllable. If *equal access* to means of control is unlikely, the experience is outside the appropriate boundaries for biodata. Concepts of fairness must be considered, and I do not refer to psychometric or statistical models. Fairness excludes items where different people have had different opportunities to experience relevant controls. Items with specific historical inequalities in accessibility seem inherently discriminatory, such as opportunities to gain experience previously closed to girls and women or to certain ethnic minorities.
6. Items should be *relevant to the job* sought; they should have face validity. Items appearing irrelevant to the job are not likely to be very effective even if otherwise within biodata boundaries.
7. Items should be *noninvasive*. As a matter of ethics, empathy, or good sense, the boundaries should draw the line excluding background actions or events people are likely to consider none of an employer's business. Invasion of privacy seems increasingly unacceptable.

Developing Biodata Forms

Biodata items (or ideas for creating them) can be found (inadvisably) by plundering forms used by others.[2] Imagination will add a few more, the whole set can be given an empirical

---

[2] Or, more nicely, using "archival item generation" (Mumford, Whetzel, Murphy & Eubanks, 2006, p. 220).

trial, and those with "good" item statistics can form the "new" questionnaire. Such biodata forms are criticized as excessively empirical, with no clear understanding of what is measured or why it might be working. The alternative is to specify one or more constructs to be assessed, to develop its theory or rationale, and to generate systematically the kinds of items believed to tap it.

Item Generation

I think I have said in every chapter that efforts to enhance prediction and understanding begin by clarifying the measurement purpose. I hope so. For selection, transfer, or promotion, job or work analysis begins the process toward clarification. For training and development, it starts with a diagnostic analysis of problems through analysis of work. Russell (1994) offered further points of departure based on personality and vocational choice theories and suggested procedures for generating items for the constructs identified as likely to be predictive. Mumford et al. (2006) offered a broader array of potential item content, summarized in Table 14.7 with illustrative items for two of the Big Five personality

TABLE 14.7

Eight Types of Background Data Item Content

Item Type	Openness to Experience	Achievement Motivation
Situational exposure	How many times did your family move while you were in grade school and high school?	How much encouragement did your parents give you when you were trying to do something new?
Situational choice	How often have you taken a class simply to learn something new?	How many difficult classes did you take in high school?
Behavior in situation	How often have your looked for a new way to complete an assignment?	How often have you put aside other tasks to complete a difficult assignment?
Reactions to a situation	How much have you enjoyed meeting new people at parties?	To what extent have you felt proud after completing a difficult assignment?
Others' reactions to a situation	How often have people described your approach to problems as different or unusual?	How often has your supervisor thanked you for putting in extra time on a project?
Outcomes associated with situational exposure	How many times has a project you worked on resulted in a patent or publication?	How often have you been asked to step in when someone else was having difficulty finishing a piece of work?
Life narratives (turning point events)	How often has your work role significantly changed?	How many times have you had a dramatic increase in work responsibility?
Negative life experiences	How many times have you been involved in a merger, acquisition, or downsizing?	How many times have you fallen short of your goals?

Reprinted from Table 8.2 in Mumford, M. D., Whetzel, D. L., Murphy, S. T., & Eubanks, D. L., Background data. In Whetzel, D. L. & Wheaton, G. R. (Eds.) *Applied Measurement: Industrial Psychology in Human Resources Management* (pp. 2201–2233). Mahwah, NJ: Lawrence Erlbaum Associates. Reprinted by permission.

constructs. As they also pointed out, events in life situations differ for people in different age cohorts or backgrounds. Perhaps different items (or even different scoring keys) are needed for candidates in different age cohorts or organizational levels (Mumford et al., 2006, p. 207).

How should items be generated? Russell (1994) pointed out that researchers themselves may be poor sources; he said he was in the "thirty-something generation," and he had trouble generating life history events as item content for those who were recently teenagers. He suggested life history interviews with job incumbents, who have the twin advantages of knowing the job and of being closer in relevant background experiences. Incumbents, of course, can be anywhere between new entries and those close to retirement; those interviewed should probably be recently hired. Interviewing incumbents is particularly useful for developing job-specific biodata forms.

Interviewing should not, however, lead to a collection of anecdotes, unconnected to each other or to anything else. It should lead the interviewer, first, to identify likely constructs hypothesized to predict the anticipated criterion performance, and later, to developing hypotheses about reasons why particular kinds of life experiences might reflect one or more of these constructs (Mumford et al., 2006, pp. 214–215). Construct-based biodata forms (the approach preferred by Russell, 1994, and Hough & Paullin, 1994) are standardized assessments, like tests, and are similarly developed and require multiple items for each construct. No single item is likely to be an adequate measure of a given construct, but one item augmented by several others intended to measure the construct might prove useful and generalizable.

Items for construct-related biodata forms may be generated by expert panels in which each expert is a psychologist familiar with biodata research and with research on the constructs for which items are to be developed. Panels usually have multiple meetings, working on not more than two or three constructs in each session. A fairly typical procedure calls for panelists to work independently for a few minutes to write potential items, then to read their items to the group and explaining the hypothesis that structured it. The group considers each item for appropriateness, both for the biodata boundaries and the construct, and for technical issues such as feasible responses and their scoring or problems such as inducing a social desirability response set.

Behavioral consistency, usually implicitly but inherently fundamentally, is the keystone of all biodata use; some biodata forms are explicitly based on it (Mumford et al., 2006). Expert panels can be quite useful for these as well. Unlike panels for purely construct-based forms, panel members for job-relevant behavioral consistency forms need knowledge of the work to be done, usually defined by job or work analysis, in addition to experience with biodata. In the work to be done, some activities are typical, and the hypotheses formed about life experiences with that kind of activity are fundamental to item development. The behavioral consistency approach is obviously useful for assessing the background experience of people experienced at the targeted kinds of work, but Mumford et al. showed that the principle is also applicable to more general life experiences.

Scale Construction

Items generated, whether by archival search, construct definition, or behavioral patterns, must be organized and responded to before the biodata provide a scale of measurement. Then, like test items, they can be analyzed for psychometric properties. Early approaches, like those for weighted application blanks, were purely empirical. Items were chosen from a pool by comparing responses to an external criterion, such as attendance or ratings of performance. Items that correlated well with the criterion, or more typically, items with significantly different response frequencies in high and low criterion groups, were chosen for the scoring key. Many sources have provided procedures for this sort of analysis (e.g., Divlin, Abrahams, & Edwards, 1992; Guion, 1965a). Obviously, validities of the resulting scales require cross-validation.[3]

Once items have been written and used, useful theory might be derived. Some of the item-producing panels develop the scales from theories; theory for more empirically developed scales may stem from a combination of exploratory and subsequent confirmatory analyses, such as factor analysis. Biographical scales can be developed to represent certain factors (Russell, 1994). Hough and Paullin (1994) argued, however, that factor scales lose important information and that factor analytic taxonomies are inadequate. I agree and would add that the factor analysis probably does little more than identify constructs one could use if starting over with construct-oriented item development. Schoenfeldt and Mendoza (1994), however, preferred factor analytic approaches, at least partly because they can reduce the number of items in the form.

Rainforest empiricism was the descriptive term used by Mael and Hirsch (1993) for one of two biodata forms developed for military academy leadership research. The "rainforest" approach (so called to isolate it from the pejoratively termed "dustbowl" empiricism) required items clearly relevant to an intended construct, with cumulative empirical data across studies, consistent patterns of item relationships, and multifaceted profiles of criterion performance. The other form, they said, was developed by a *quasirational* approach, that is, a construct-oriented approach. It specified a personality construct, the development of objective personal history items believed relevant to that construct, and items keyed directly to an external personality inventory validly measuring the construct. In short, the quasirational method did not lack empirical data, nor did the empirical aspect lack rational thought. Both biodata forms added incremental predictive validity to existing assessments, although the rainforest approach added more validity with less contamination from social desirability. Whether called construct-oriented or rainforest empiricism, a combination of data and thought is surely superior to either thoughtless empiricism or naive theorizing.

No matter how items are conceived or generated, responses to them must be scored in some way. Any of the types of item response used in tests or inventories can be used with biodata, but Mumford et al. (2006) expressed a firm preference for the ordinary five-point rating scale, largely because they considered such scales more reliable than other options and because of requiring smaller samples than required for purely categorical responses.

As in tests or personality inventories, decisions have to be made about sequence of item presentation. Should all items intended for a specific construct or a specific behavioral pattern be grouped together, or should they be mixed together in a random or spiral omnibus pattern? My personal preference (it is no more than that) is for mixing them to avoid producing spurious response sets—but I do not know whether it really makes any difference.

The "Individual Achievement Record"

The development of a biodata form for use in selection for the United States federal government, as described by Gandy, Dye, and MacLane (1994), offers a prototype for an empirical

---

[3] At least it should be obvious since the publication of the wryly funny, memorable address by Ted Cureton, "Validity, reliability, and baloney" (Cureton, 1950a). It was precisely this procedure that led him to insist that independent cross-validation evidence is essential.

method that emphasizes prior achievements without being atheoretical. Steps in the development and validation of the form included the following.

1. Reviewed information from job analysis of federal nonsupervisory professional and administrative positions and available biodata taxonomies.
2. Established criteria for acceptable biodata items, essentially consistent with Table 14.6 with added concern for use in the public sector (although they permitted items with attributions to others).
3. Wrote multiple-choice items with five response options; in most cases, the options represented a quantitative continuum, but many had the appearance of multiple-choice test items. No preliminary list of constructs guided item development; rather, items reflected "loosely formed hypotheses" (Gandy et al., 1994, p. 277) that the experiences were related to job performance. Experiences in school, work, and interpersonal areas were included in the pool and believed to tap a variety of constructs.
4. Designated a criterion (supervisory performance ratings) and subjects (entry-level professional and administrative people hired over a four-year period) and collected data.
5. Selected items and developed a scoring key based on double cross-validation.
6. Validated scores empirically and analyzed for fairness (using the Cleary method) with data from more than 6,000 employees.
7. Did exploratory and confirmatory factor analyses, identifying four factors among the scored items (also evaluated construct validity by analyzing relationships to reference tests).

Other evaluative studies were done with the completed form, including some designed to promote greater understanding of the factor scores. The project shows the sort of work that can be done with a large sample.

The "Accomplishment Record"

Professional people dislike being tested, believing that personnel decisions about them should be based on their records. Lawyers in a federal regulatory agency might also have objected to a test look-alike; for example, a biodata inventory. For them, Hough (1984) developed what she called an *accomplishment record* form and scales.

The critical incident approach to job analysis was used to generate examples of effective and ineffective job behavior; these were sorted by psychologists into dimensions of job performance. An open-ended form was developed for attorneys to use in describing their major accomplishments in each dimension. An example of part of the form is shown in Figure 14.2.

Responses were scored using a BARS format. The retranslation procedure was used to assign accomplishment descriptions to the eight dimensions. (Two dimensions seemed confused in the retranslation and were consolidated.) Sixty accomplishments were scaled for each of the resulting seven dimensions by expert judges; descriptions were chosen from those scaled to anchor points on a rating scale.

The method is time-consuming for researchers, administrators, and examinees, but it is unarguably job-related, it does not rely on statistical subtleties, it is a reasonably valid promotion tool, and it seems not to have different effects for men and women or for people of different ethnic groups. In short, it is well worth the time it takes. And it, like many of the

USING KNOWLEDGE

Interpreting and synthesizing information to form legal strategies, approaches, lines of argument, etc., developing new configurations of knowledge, innovative approaches, solutions, strategies, etc., selecting the proper legal theory, using appropriate lines of argument, weighing alternatives and drawing sound conclusions

Time Period *1974–75*

General statement of what you accomplished

I was given the task of transferring our anti-trust investigation
of   into a coherent set of pleadings presentable
to   and the Commission for review and approval within the
context of the Commission's involvement in shopping centers nationwide

Description of exactly what you did

I drafted the complaint and proposed order and wrote the underlying legal memo justifying all charges and proposed remedies. I wrote the memo to the Commission recommending approval of the consent agreement. For the first time, we applied anti-trust principles to this novel factual situation

Awards or formal recognition

         none

The information verified by *John   , Compliance*

FIG. 14.2   One dimension of the Accomplishment Record Inventory and an example of a response. Reprinted from Hough, L. M. (1984), Development and evaluation of the "accomplishment record" method of selecting and promoting professionals. *Journal of Applied Psychology, 69,* 135–146. © The American Psychological Association. Reprinted by permission.

procedures described here, is a far more structured approach to the use of biographical information than was the early, weighted application form which was a wholly empirical method, often without coherent interpretations.

CONCLUDING NOTE

Subjective judgment is probably the most common tool for selecting employees, and it is one that assessment research has considered often enough. Tests and inventories can be expected in large corporations and certainly in most governmental jurisdictions. Subjective judgment alone is probably more common in smaller organizations or even in large ones selecting for unique or uncommon positions. Unfortunately, judgments are too often based on whim (perhaps momentary). Managers may rely more on judgment than on tests because of unsupportable beliefs that virtually perfect prediction (as opposed to probabilistic estimates) of performance is possible by those who are experienced in selecting new workers (Highhouse, 2008).

Assessment research on the use of judgment has grown, at least for commonly used procedures such as interviews and résumés and related methods for personal history consideration. It has moved rather steadily toward greater standardization and, therefore, greater structure—and therefore to greater predictive accuracy and greater understanding of the judgments. Research has moved toward test-like procedures for obtaining and evaluating subjective judgments. I expect very little controversy about these statements.

I expect a lot of disagreement with my emphasis on individual differences among the people who make the judgments. Commonly, personnel research relies heavily on means, and that is appropriate; the mean of a distribution of nearly anything is the most reliable value in the distribution. However, being firmly rooted in the tradition of individual differences, I think variance is too often treated simply as an inconvenient source of error, not as a potentially useful fact. An emphasis on individual differences applies both to those who are making the judgments and judgment-based decisions and to those about whom the judgments are made. I have argued here, as in Chapter 12, that judgment and decision *processes* must be studied with a genuine concern for individual differences. I have reiterated the importance I perceive in Dunnette's (1963a) individualistic model for selection research and the practical importance of idiographic models for capturing policies of individual judges. I think I have offered enough support for this view, here and in earlier chapters, and I offer no apology for it.

The next chapter recognizes the need to base decisions on more than one sort of assessment. It begins with multiple regression, a very conventional statistical approach. But much of it will again use ratings as the expression of judgments, and the emphasis on individual differences (and how they might be overcome when inconvenient) will be continued and familiar. For example, with interviews, the value of pooling of interviewers in the *process* of making judgments (rather than simply aggregating individual interviewers' ratings) leads easily to asking whether similar value can be found in pooling the judgments of observers in an assessment center.

15

Multiple Assessment Procedures

A single predictor is rarely optimal. Most personnel decisions are based on the assessments of several applicant traits considered relevant to important criteria. For some jobs, formal assessment of one truly critical trait (e.g., a physical skill or general mental ability) may be enough, but even that assessment is likely to be augmented by others, especially for more complex jobs or positions. This chapter describes three systematic approaches to multiple assessments: (a) administration of tests in batteries, with an emphasis here on sequential testing; (b) multiple assessments of individuals, and (c) group assessment centers.

USE OF TEST BATTERIES

Let's start with a condensed reprise of multiple regression principles from Chapter 8. These principles form a background for both individual and group multiple assessment procedures. These are typically described collectively as a *battery* of tests or other procedures.

Compensatory Models

A prototype for multiple assessments is a battery of tests, used in combination at about the same time, to predict a single criterion. Scores of individual tests in the battery are added (prototypically) using a compensatory, additive combination of scores. Simply put, scores on the several tests are added (with or without different weights) to form a composite score which, by itself, has no meaning beyond its prediction of criterion level. That is, although the individual predictors are measures of more or less clearly defined constructs, the composite cannot ordinarily be interpreted as a definable construct. Prediction based on the composite is enhanced when scores on every test in the battery predict the criterion but have low correlations with other tests in the battery. Three basic principles should guide all multiple assessments: (a) each predictor should validly predict the criterion variable (although batteries may include mediators or moderators), (b) predictors should not correlate appreciably with each other (should be independent rather than redundant), and (c) each predictor should be highly reliable.

Theory, at least rudimentary theory, is important, but it does not necessarily influence the prototype; that is, one *can* compute sums of scores and even regression weights without invoking theoretical constructs at all. However, as in Chapter 3, battery developers should identify constructs when they develop predictive hypotheses for each variable.

Using more than one measure for each predictor construct may be redundant, but it can also increase reliability of measurement of each basic, latent construct. A battery of 10 cognitive tests used for enlistments in Sweden used CAT measurement to assess three constructs in a theoretical hierarchy: a general factor, a verbal factor, and somewhat tentatively, a spatial factor (Mårdberg & Carlestedt, 1998). Latent scores on the three factors can be combined, with more reliability, more assured independence, and less statistical error than the combination of ten sets of raw scores. Another way to accomplish such an increase in measurement precision is to use multidimensional IRT models; unidimensional IRT is commonly used to analyze item responses in a battery, one test at a time. Wang, Chen, and Cheng (2004) pointed out that unidimensional approaches ignore correlation between latent traits, whereas multiple models capitalize on them to improve measurement precision of individual traits with fewer items per test.

The use of additive, compensatory models has been effective for many decades; it is well established and not to be abandoned capriciously. However, a different concept of compensatory batteries, different from the prototype, might be helpful. Essentially, the additive model is described with the word *and*: the decision is based on a composite consisting of test A *and* test B *and* test C, and so on. What is often needed is compensation by allowing alternative assessments where the operative word is *or*. This is implied in the Dunnette selection model depicted in Figures 2.9 and 2.10. It seems especially necessary under the accommodation provisions of ADA. Moreover, it is feasible in algorithms for judgmental policies.

Individual and group assessment programs typically combine multiple assessments judgmentally, not statistically. One advantage they may have is that they can facilitate compensatory processes by compensating for prior conditions (e.g., experienced versus inexperienced candidates)—*or* rather than *and*. If classifying prior conditions calls for judgments about them (and sometimes it may do so), what we know of judgmental versus statistical prediction raises the possibility that such efforts might have the serious disadvantage of being less valid.

Statistical models for prediction are usually multivariate only on the predictor side of the equation; typically, a single criterion is predicted, although it may be global and complex. Consider, however, a circumstance in which different criteria are predicted, and perhaps even one in which the different predictions suggest different decisions. Such a situation might arise if the predicted criteria are actual job production (in some dollar amount per unit of cost) and a contextual criterion such as dependability or integrity. These may be predicted by different tests. If both criteria are placed on a standard scale ($M = 50$; $SD = 10$), what should a manager do with a candidate whose predicted level is 70 on one of these criteria (calling for a favorable decision) and 30 on the other (calling for rejection)?

This is a common enough problem, evaded rather than solved by insisting that all validation research use a single, global criterion. Different predictions cannot be expected to have universally consistent implications for decisions unless the different criteria correlate highly enough to justify combining them. I see three possible, nonevasive solutions to the problem: one can (a) average predictions, perhaps weighting them by the judged importance of the different criteria; (b) set minimum acceptable criterion levels on each one (a multiple cut-score approach for predictions); and (c) use managerial judgment of the relative importance of the different criteria in view of current organizational needs. I consider (c) best. Long ago I argued that the different predictions should be made and that decisions should be based on the criteria most important when the decision must be made (Guion, 1961).

The opportunity to exercise such judgment can be useful in organizational diagnostics. I once found that the same scores predicted good performance and early quitting. Top-down selection would create a highly capable but unstable work force. Good management judgment would ask why the best people were most likely to leave; the problem of selection decisions should be secondary to the organizational question.

Sequential Models

Multiple regression generally requires that all predictor variables be available at the time of analysis. This requirement becomes impractical if the assessment of major interest costs too much to be used for all candidates. Costly assessments include highly complex simulations, individual assessment programs, or assessment centers. In such cases a preliminary assessment (interview, test, or credentials check) may help choose those who go on to further assessment. Consider college recruiting; preliminary assessments (e.g., interviews, checks of grades and references) occur on campus; recruits evaluated most highly are then invited to go to the organization's home or regional office for further assessments. Another frequent example is the use of a preliminary interview to determine which candidates will be sent to an assessment center (Dayan, Fox, & Kasten, 2008). (In setting up programs of sequential assessment, organizations might find themselves in court for violating the 1982 ruling in *Connecticut v. Teal*.)

Preliminary screening tests that are computer-based, online, and unproctored may lead to subsequent proctored exams for those who score relatively well on the preliminary test, often with concern. The score-enhancing possibility of cheating in unproctored situations (with or without computers) was addressed by Nye, Do, Drasgow, and Fine (2008). In their study, 856 job applicants in nine European countries successfully completed an unproctored, preliminary online screening battery; it included one form of a speeded perception test. A second step included a telephone interview and two more online tests, also unproctored. Survivors of these preliminary steps were asked to go the agency's local office for proctored tests, including the parallel form of the perceptual speed test. Results indicted that the concern over possible cheating was not warranted, at least for this test. The Nye et al. study, with two parallel forms of a test at two points in a sequence, does not represent most sequential models. More typically in such models, different assessments at different stages or steps of the sequence assess different constructs. But it is a frequently recommended way to handle the issues with unproctored online exams.

When should the different assessments occur in a sequence? Roe (2005) offered suggestions for simultaneous consideration. First, choices of cut scores, based on selection ratios at the different stages can manipulate the candidate flow (he recommended low cut-offs at the earlier stages to compensate for possibly falsely indicating low performance on the next step in the sequence). Second, more costly procedures should ordinarily be postponed for later stages. Third, the logistics of time, location, and space present bothersome considerations when numbers of candidates are large. Internet testing can handle large numbers of candidates, anywhere, at their convenience, but individually administered assessments should be at the end. Fourth, steps with very good predictive validity should ordinarily come early in the sequence. I would add a fifth, very important in the United States: the potential for adverse impact. Since the US Supreme Court's decision in *Connecticut v. Teal*, each step in the sequence must have minimal adverse impact and maximal validity (*Connecticut v. Teal*, 1982).

In sequences with several stages, validation can become a serious problem at the later stages because of the increasing restriction of range. The first stage includes everyone, so no restriction occurs—but no criterion is available, either. Is going on to stage 2 a sufficient criterion? Or should criteria in all stages assess job-related behavior? The second stage poses the same questions; variance is restricted, and will be restricted further if the criterion must wait for candidates to be hired and accumulate job performance data. Each stage assesses fewer candidates with increasing restriction of assessment variance; severe restriction can occur by the final stage of the sequence. Criterion-related validation is not feasible, nor particularly desirable. Instead, the designer of the assessment program must diligently design it—with carefully developed predictive hypotheses and effectively measured predictors—so that each component has demonstrable job relevance and psychometric validity (i.e., a strong validity argument).

INDIVIDUAL ASSESSMENT PROGRAMS

In the broadest sense, individual assessment occurs when one person, an assessor, evaluates (with at least rough quantification) one or more characteristics of another person, the assessee. More focused individual assessment occurs when an assessor quantifies or evaluates an assessee's qualifications to do something, and perhaps the assessee's relative strengths or weaknesses among qualifying characteristics—clearly *multiple* assessments.

Individual assessment occurs in many different contexts. It occurs in counseling centers and in psychological clinics to help people with personal problems. It occurs in schools to evaluate and provide remedies for learning problems. It occurs in religious centers to help parishioners and others with spiritual growth, preparation for marriage, etc. Many of these assessments are done by people with credentials appropriate to their own professions. Some assessments happen without special credentials, especially spontaneous assessments made when people get together—we continually assess those with whom we come in contact. However, individual assessment as an organizational tool needs well-trained, experienced assessors because it must be purposeful, comprehensive, and carefully planned. Most purposes fit within two major categories: (a) to provide a basis for personnel decisions (selection, promotion, etc.) or (b) to provide a basis for systematic programs of personal development. The discussion here, as in the rest of this book, focuses on decisions and on assessments for guidance in decision making.

The basic purpose of individual assessment is to produce insights into the person's work-relevant skills, knowledge, ideas, motivation, and habits or styles of working with others (Frisch, 1998; Jeanneret & Silzer, 1998a) and to use those insights in making predictive judgments about future behavior on the job and in the organization. Its comprehensiveness implies assessment of an array of psychological characteristics deemed relevant to a desired outcome: cognitive, physical, or social skills and knowledge, traits of temperament and personality, or that hybrid category known as competencies. (In fact, individual assessment more properly assesses complex competencies rather than simpler, more internally consistent traits.) Jeanneret and Silzer (1998b) entitled their book *Individual Psychological Assessment* to distinguish the formal, planned assessment process for organizational use from other sorts of individual assessment. I continue to use the shorter term, but it should be understood as implying assessment of all sorts of traits, attributes, and characteristics such as those described in Chapter 3 for forming predictive hypotheses.

Individual assessment rarely follows standard (traditional?) "textbook procedures" (Ryan & Sackett, 1998, p. 58). The differences define the method. Standard practice emphasizes cognitive skill; individual assessment tends to emphasize personality. Standard practice emphasizes the prediction of performance; individual assessment is more likely to emphasize organizational fit. Standard practice emphasizes statistical prediction; individual assessment necessarily emphasizes inferential judgments. Standard practice increasingly uses well-structured interviews; individual assessment is more likely to use no more than moderate structure. Standard practice is more highly standardized in that all candidates are assessed by a standard set of tools; individual assessment may adapt the assessment tools to fit individual candidates. Standard practice is rooted in a research model; individual assessment is more comfortable approaching a clinical model. The one-on-one nature of individual assessment makes some departures from standard practice necessary, but common preferences in individual assessment can be found.

The Design of Individual Assessment

In a survey of members of the Society for Industrial and Organizational Psychology (SIOP), Ryan and Sackett (1987) found that those doing individual assessments are likely to be external, licensed consultants, members of consulting firms where others also did such assessments. Respondents reported many purposes; selection and promotion (including planning for succession) and outplacement were the major ones. They also reported that assessment typically required at least a half day; some were shorter, and some required two full days. Assessment tools included personal history data, ability tests, personality and interest inventories, and interviews; the repertoire has since expanded to include evaluations of work samples, portfolios of prior accomplishments, and tools made possible by modern information technology (Goodstein & Prien, 2006). In general, conclusions depended mainly on professional judgment; assessors generally rejected statistical or other relatively rigid techniques for setting specific composite or overall scores as cutoffs for recommendations. A few respondents reported using the same assessment procedures regardless of the position to be filled (a practice not inconsistent with seeking global appraisals), but most of them varied the content of their assessments to fit the position. Information about organizations and positions was typically gathered more in conversations and interviews than from more systematic organizational and job analyses. Information sought included the usual emphasis on tasks and responsibilities, conventional KSAs, and critical incidents involving prior successes and failures. Respondents said they needed a wider variety of information than conventional job analysis supplies: interpersonal relationships, supervisory expectations, and broad statements of functions were commonly mentioned, and some mentioned such considerations as organizational climate, opportunities for advancement, subordinate characteristics, and the criteria used in evaluating work performance in the position. If the survey were repeated now, I think that more respondents would endorse these as reported practice.

Frisch (1998) and Goodstein and Prien (2006) identified steps necessary for the design of a successful program for the assessment of individual candidates. Although differing in presentation, the two were not very different. I put my own spin on them in the sections below, intending to emphasize that much of the design work must be done explicitly for each new assessment assignment.

Knowing the Organizational Context

The assessor must understand the organization, the context in which it functions, and the context or climate in which the chosen candidate will work. The assessor is likely to be an external consultant, and maybe he or she has worked often for the organization. If so, much of this information will seem redundant, but a clear understanding of the role the chosen candidate will have, and of the situation in which it will be played out, is necessary. When the client–consultant relationship is new, more formal organizational analysis may be needed. "Designing an assessment process is akin to menu planning for a formal dinner . . . The menu planner draws from a palette of options, each representing a category that must be included if the meal is to feel complete" (Frisch, 1998, p. 135). I suspect that Frisch would not object to continuing the metaphor by including the layout and equipment in the kitchen, the butler's pantry, and the dining room as categories on that palette.

It is helpful, even necessary, to be aware of the organizational history, especially regarding assessment practices, that may have influenced the current climate. Has the organization known, and are current members aware of, noteworthy achievements credited to assessment practices—or noteworthy frustrations attributable to assessment blunders? Do people in the organization generally favor systematic assessment practices or oppose them? Are such practices seen as unnecessarily time-consuming or as good investments of time? The answers may influence choice of assessment instruments and whether the schedule will be restricted to one day or allowed to use two.

Organizational characteristics not obviously related to assessment *per se* may also be important. Is the climate likely to foster collaborative work between organizational levels, or does it favor a chain of command? Who will make the decisions—where will the buck stop—based on assessor recommendations? Who, and at what organizational level, provided the impetus for seeking a consultant to assess candidates? Knowing the organization includes knowing its goals and objectives, especially those closely related to the function for which an assessed candidate will be considered. Whether the organization makes cars or sells a service, it needs to clarify its intentions; does it, for example, intend to serve an up-scale or a mass market? Assessors need such information to judge, for example, the importance of a trait such as meticulous attention to detail.

Individual assessment focuses mainly on managerial, executive, or sales jobs, and occasionally on high-level technical positions—positions often defined by their incumbents. Tasks, responsibilities, and ways of doing things may only define the position as it was handled by the previous incumbent; they may not be the tasks, responsibilities, and procedures defining it for the new person. Typical task analysis may be less appropriate than gaining a broad understanding of the situation. Understanding may require answers to questions such as these: (a) Will the person fill essentially the same functions filled by a predecessor, or will functions be shifted around? (b) Is the vacancy created or influenced by organizational change, by new technology, or by division of existing duties? (c) How is the position defined relative to others? (d) What must be done right away, and what can wait for training or learning on the job? (e) Which specific qualifications are essential, and which merely nice to have? (f) How much freedom (or constraint) does the position offer? What will be permitted, encouraged, or frowned upon by superiors and coworkers? Such questions arise from concern not only about future performance but about how well the assessee "fits" the organization.

Assessor Qualifications

Goodstein and Prien (2006) identified three levels of assessor competence, which I shall dub the novice, the well-trained, and the highly experienced expert levels. Novices may do individual assessments for relatively routine jobs, under supervision; they may administer some of the assessment procedures. However, most responsibility for system design and planning requires someone at a higher level. The well-trained assessor has at least the equivalent of a master's degree in industrial and organizational psychology, with the knowledge of psychological theory and psychometrics the degree implies, and supervised experience outside of academia. The highly experienced expert is likely to have a doctorate, probably in psychology, strong knowledge of psychometrics, and much experience in individual assessment. He or she has probably moved into the role of supervising others with less experience.

Assessor qualifications should be specified—and met. In most states, psychologists qualified to be assessors beyond the novice level, and especially at the expert level, are licensed. Licensure is often considered the first level of qualifying credentials. Being an outsider may be an important qualification; most organizations use external consultants even when capable in-house consultants are at hand. One reason is that outsiders are less likely to have had prior contact, even indirectly, with persons being assessed and are therefore likely to do the assessment with less prejudicial (or in-house political) baggage. Another is that, as consultants, outsiders are likely to have broader experience across organizations in the industry with which to compare individual performance on assessment instruments (Frisch, 1998, p. 138).

Internal or external, essential qualifications include the ability to analyze work, to see the implications of that analysis for future work activity, and to write an intelligible, coherent description of the results. A broad knowledge of the psychology of individual differences and of psychometrics, both theory and methods, makes optimal choices of constructs and instruments more likely, as opposed to persistent (or perseverating) return to the same old familiar ideas and tools used before.

Knowledge of the organization has already been mentioned as an essential qualification. Another is general knowledge of the ethical responsibilities of psychologists, particularly as the published standards relate to the equal protection of clients and assessees (Goodstein & Prien, 2006; International Task Force on Assessment Center Guidelines, 2009).

Job Analysis for Individual Assessment

Chapter 2 outlined several methods for analyzing work; it offers many options for Frisch's metaphorical palette. For individual assessment, assessors should concentrate more on the broader concept of analyzing the work to be done and its implications than on task analysis. Traditional job analysis contemplates assessment of many people for essentially the same work, but individual assessment calls for broad understanding of the work to be done by people in positions not closely replicated in other positions. Because the assessee may be considered for a position not quite like that of any other, and because the position is likely to change over time and experience, work analysis needs to give more attention than usual to general work habits, to flexibility in thought, and to likely future demands on the incumbent.

Planning the Assessment Activity

Planning is partly logistic and partly theoretical. The theoretical part leads to (a) choices of constructs deemed relevant to the role to be taken, (b) choice of assessment methods, and (c) perhaps the rejection of some constructs that would seem useful in more conventional assessment programs. Choices require psychometric consideration of reliability evidence, content relevance, psychometric validity, availability of relevant norms, and available and relevant prior studies or meta-analyses. Essentially, planning calls for multiple predictive hypotheses fitting inference 1 in the Binning and Barrett model (Figure 3.1), the inferred judgments of relationships between the constructs describing a person and the constructs describing desired performance or outcomes.

The logistic part leads to schedules of events, persons, and places. Interviews will probably be conducted by the expert assessor, although others may participate in panels or conduct special purpose interviews. Subordinates may be trained to administer specific assessment tools such as tests or job samples. Some procedures may require special facilities. It may be that several individual candidates, perhaps for different positions or even different organizations, will be assessed in the same general facility at the same time. All such considerations turn the mere scheduling of rooms and people into a big logistic problem to be solved in the advance planning.

Many methods offer data from which levels of the characteristics of people can be assessed on a one-at-a-time basis. The variety of possible assessment tools include traditional résumés and interviews (usually not very highly structured, if at all); formal tests and inventories; work samples, simulations, or portfolios of accomplishments; ratings of various candidate or work product characteristics by peers, supervisors, and assessors; and direct observations of candidate behavior. Within each of these broad categories, many operational choices are on the palette. Some of them may be less valid than others—maybe not valid at all— but many assessors use the whole range from purely narrative information, unique to the individual, to standardized measurement—all in the apparent hope that something useful will turn up.

Redundancy in individual assessment is usually desirable; it provides a defense against deficiencies of well-established measurement or psychometric habits. Those habits call for selecting one instrument to measure each trait, but individual assessment often uses two or three ways to assess a trait. For example, a personality inventory and a simulation exercise can both tap the same basic construct. A test of ability might well be accompanied by a competing publisher's test of the same ability, or a personality inventory purporting to assess the first Big Five factor as *surgency* might be augmented by another inventory purporting to measure it as *extraversion.* Agreement in redundant assessments may increase confidence in inferences about the person assessed; disagreements can sharpen distinctions in permissible inferences.

Matching Person and Work Analyses

Actual assessments evaluate documents and credentials, administer and score tests and exercises, conduct interviews and complete ratings based on them, and integrate assessment data with information about the organization, the organizational substratum, and the work to be done. Assessors make judgments and inferences, perhaps drawing conclusions, about the fit of the candidate to the organization and to the work role anticipated. The matching of assessment results to work demands can be organized somewhat like the chart in Figure 15.1. It shows needed competencies, derived from work analysis, and assessment methods, each tapping some of those competencies. I created the chart, but I don't know exactly what it means, and I certainly could not use it to judge the quality of the assessment plan without a lot more information. The phrases describing competencies are utterly meaningless without a record of work done collaboratively by the assessor (or team) and organizational executives; they should have developed detailed definitions of those competencies, not mere labels. More standard procedures would have been more likely to list well-established psychological constructs. Terms such as *verbal comprehension*, or *perceptual speed and accuracy*, or even relatively complex traits such as *spatial ability* or *creativity* would be intelligible to virtually any expert assessor. Interpretation of a phrase such as *general knowledge of technical aspects of subordinates' projects* requires much knowledge of and insight into the nature of the work done by those subordinates. Likewise, the methods of assessment become comprehensible, and the shading of relevant cells reflects sensible inferences only with explicit knowledge of the tests, inventories, exercises, and ratings used. These things must be stated clearly in

Competencies	Methods of Assessments						
	KSA Tests	Personality Inventories	In-Basket Exercise	Employment History	Simulation Exercise	Peer Ratings	Interview
Planning and prioritizing events							
Ability to work with subordinates with higher education levels							
General knowledge of technical aspects of subordinates' projects							
In uencing and mentoring subordinates and colleagues							
Developing good personal relations with subordinates							
Maintaining open dialogues between others with different views							
Maintaining high personal standards and integrity							

FIG. 15.1   A plan for a specially designed individual assessment. Interpretation of the chart requires knowledge of the planning that preceded its development (and is not provided for this figure).

the planning phase, and they require much collaboration. The shading of the cells in such planning should reflect a judgment shared (at least accepted) by assessors and by organization sponsors.

Reporting Assessment Results

The assessor is neither a decision maker nor one whose career is at risk, but one who reports both to organizational authorities and to the assessee. Some experts insist that it is an ethical obligation to give feedback reports to candidates (Hogan & Hogan, 1998). These may be oral, but written reports may be both prudent and helpful for the candidate's career development.

The assessor is usually required (by contract and by common sense) to prepare a report for the client organization describing assessee characteristics as plainly and unambiguously as the data and the assessor's own communication skills allow. Detailed written reports should go into organizational files, if only for protection in possible litigation, but condensed reports, written or oral, to individuals or management groups, may be more useful for making decisions. The detailed report should specify the reasoning in planning the assessment, clearly report candidate assessments, and be forthright in identifying characteristics that might be important but that, for whatever reason, were not assessed.

The Ryan and Sackett (1987) survey described two facets of reporting that have sometimes been controversial. One is whether a written report is sufficient; the other is whether reports should include explicit recommendations for action. They found that written reports were usually followed by telephone or face-to-face discussions with the client. Reports rarely included actual test scores—and should not.

Parenthetically, my "should not" comment needs to be considered with reference to the age of the person who made it—me. In my professional formative years, in the 1940s and 1950s, telling a person his or her test score was considered absolutely unethical, especially if that person had not been appropriately trained in tests and measurements. By the time the 1974 *Standards* was published (American Psychological Association (APA), American Educational Research Association (AERA), & National Council on Measurement in Education (NCME), 1974), some ambivalence was evident, brought on largely by the emphasis on personal and civil rights during the 1960s. For example, Standard J2 said that scores should "ordinarily be reported only to people who are qualified to interpret them," but it went on to say that if they are reported to people not so qualified, the report should be accompanied by a lot of explanation. The very next Standard, J2.1, said that a person tested (or that person's agent) "has the right to know his score and the interpretations made"— even to the extent of knowing "scores" on individual items. Standard J2.1 was identified as an ethical rather than a technical standard, and the conflicts between it and standards of test security were recognized; the comment went on to say that it was preferable to have a qualified intermediary sympathetic to the interests of the person tested get and interpret the score. By the 1985 version (AERA, APA, & NCME, 1985), no fewer than 13 standards referred to reporting actual scores, all based on the "right to know" rather than on technical arguments. From a technical point of view, I still adhere to the view that reporting actual test scores, especially to clients who are representatives of organizations rather than the individual tested, should not be done in individual assessment; interpretations are far more important and far less likely to lead to bizarre and idiosyncratic misinterpretations.

Returning to the Ryan and Sackett review: Strengths and weaknesses, and suggestions for personal development, were usually included in assessment reports. Reports did not necessarily include recommendations; about a third of the respondents reported making ratings on specific traits or expected performance dimensions. (In my own work, I explicitly refuse to make recommendations, preferring to end appraisal reports with a series of questions suggested by my conclusions about the candidate. These questions were intended to force the person ultimately responsible for a hiring decision to get independent information, e.g., through telephone calls to candidates, to earlier employers or to other references and to form his or her own conclusions without abdicating responsibility to an outsider.)

The central body of a report should be the description of the person from inferences based on the assessments. This does not mean reporting scores on tests or specific ratings, although these might be useful to have for future reference in the back-up detailed report; it does mean integrating the information received, reaching conclusions from it about the relative standing of the person—relative meaning either normative, relative to groups in similar positions or to other candidates, or ipsative, relative to other strengths and weaknesses of the assessee. Where standardized tests are used, relative standing may be described visually with norms from the test manual, but it is likely to be more useful if the assessor gives final judgments, considering all assessment activity, on the candidate's standing on the characteristics agreed upon as important during the assessment planning.

In one chart, Frisch (1998) proposed reporting three levels of characteristics—*clear strength, on par, or needs development*—for each of several candidates assessed individually. The result is at once both a normative and an ipsative interpretation. Assignment to one of these levels represents the assessor's conclusions. Recommendations are usually made, and often required in planning, on the basis of those conclusions. Recommendations are often dichotomous (hire or do not hire), but sometimes with an intermediate level of uncertainty. Whether the client organization goes along with the recommendations is often more a matter of employment activity at the time than a reflection of confidence in the consultant.

Follow-up and Evaluation

Assessors should have in place a plan for following those they have assessed to learn the outcomes. An immediate outcome, of course, is whether the candidate was successful or not in getting the position toward which the assessment was aimed. Subsequent level of success in the position (if hired or promoted to it) should be determined, as should the person's level of satisfaction with it. For those who did not get the position, follow-up should try to find out how they fared in subsequent work and how consistent the subsequent performance and satisfaction were with the conclusions from the assessments. Follow-up can serve at least two purposes: to help assessors hone their skills, and to provide data for evaluating (validating) the program at large. Unfortunately, both individual follow-up and program validation are uncommon.

Varieties of Individual Assessment Programs

Individual assessment programs differ. Descriptions of them in the criterion-related validation literature are old, generally dating to the 1950s and 1960s; Ryan and Sackett (1998) found none more recent than 1970. Legal uncertainties of the EEO era may have inhibited publication of such programs. Legal uncertainty remains; Ryan and Sackett (1987) reported that nearly 30% of their respondents were not sure that their practices were consistent with the *Uniform Guidelines*. They were not likely to be, because the *Guidelines* was already more than 15 years out of date when the survey was done. Moreover, their survey found that newer programs had introduced few innovations (other than frequently dropping criterion-related research).

A Psychometric Emphasis

In the 1950s, a research and consulting group at Western Reserve University (now Case-Western Reserve) developed an assessment program for higher level sales and managerial personnel. The program description is still the most complete in easily accessible literature (e.g., Campbell, 1962; Campbell, Otis, Liske, & Prien, 1962; Huse, 1962; Otis, Campbell, & Prien, 1962). The seven-article series is a prototype for assessment and assessment research, and I highly recommend careful study of it beyond this brief synopsis. The basic program included the following.

1. A staff member visited clients to learn about the job to be filled, the organization, and the social environment. Information gained was used to tailor the assessment program.
2. Two psychologists together interviewed candidates, independently rating them on several scales. They did not have access to test data.
3. Projective test responses were analyzed by a clinical psychologist who rated the candidate on the same scales without seeing the candidate personally and without knowledge of other test results.
4. A test battery was developed specifically for each job in question. At a minimum, the battery included two personality inventories, an interest inventory, and tests of abilities hypothesized as important.
5. One psychologist–interviewer wrote a report describing social skills, intellectual functioning, drive and ambition, personal adjustment, and a judgment of probable effectiveness.

The program and its components were validated by the traditional criterion-related methods aggregating data across candidates and organizations. The batteries of psychometric tests were the most valid components of the program.

A Clinically Oriented Program

An assessment procedure was developed for district marketing managers of a national firm. The core feature of the program was an intensive two-hour interview by a clinically oriented consulting psychologist. Other components included a personal history form, two traditional mental ability tests, a sentence completion test, and a human relations problems test (Albrecht, Glaser, & Marks, 1964). The interviewer prepared the report with final ratings. The consultants, high-level managers, and peers provided criterion ratings on four dimensions. Multitrait–multimethod convergent validities provided rather good evidence of construct validity. High validity coefficients were reported for consultant recommendations for all four criteria.

A Content-Oriented Approach

Robinson (1981) reported an approach beginning with detailed job analysis, identifying important job objectives or dimensions, the behaviors required to meet them, and critical tasks. Critical tasks were seen as content samples from a broader job universe. Major assessment procedures were work sample tests specifically sampling job content, but a structured interview was also part of the procedure. Candidates recruited through advertising were assessed, and one of them was hired. The evaluation consisted of a report that he was considered to be doing well a year later.

Criticisms of Individual Assessment

Individual assessment programs are not rare, but they are rarely discussed, described, or evaluated systematically. Too many of them invite serious criticisms; I list some of them here.

1. Individual assessment is rarely subjected to serious validation efforts, except for the Western Reserve program and some unpublished ones for proprietary programs. Traditional validation is often not possible, but validation by quasi-experimental program evaluation would make sense, at least in firms doing a lot of assessment. Evaluation could follow Binning and Barrett (1989) and Figure 3.1; that is, job-related constructs could be identified and evidence could be acquired to evaluate the validity of inferences drawn for inference 3 (predictor psychometric validity) and inference 5 (the logical relationship of the predictor and criterion constructs).
2. Assessment conclusions are often unreliable. Different assessors evaluate candidates differently, perhaps because they rely on different information and perhaps because they lack a standard basis for consistency.
3. One or two parts of an assessment program, parts that could have been the whole of the assessment, too often influence assessment summaries. This is not surprising; assessment summaries are judgments of the report writer, and judgment research shows that judgments are typically based on only a few of the available cues.
4. Individual assessments, being individual, cannot assess interpersonal skills from actual interpersonal behavior. Most individual assessment is done with candidates for

managerial or sales work, work that requires interaction with others; assessment without such interaction may be deficient; this may be one reason why group assessment center approaches have dominated the assessment literature in recent years.

5. It may be ethically and legally questionable to seek information not explicitly relevant to the work to be done, yet individual assessments typically include intellectual and personality exploration, gathering general and diverse data about a person. Many people think collecting information without direct job relevance is an unwarranted invasion of privacy. Other people consider it unfair or unethical or incompetent to base decisions on one or two traits without a complete picture of the individual.

6. Individual assessment too often falls in the category of art with little scientific component, especially when the assessment depends heavily on clinical intuition for the assessment of "whole persons" rather than isolated traits. Highhouse (2002) provided a detailed and extensive discussion of this criticism. As those who have read the previous chapters here already know, I argue strongly for considering an individualistic approach to personnel decisions. My argument sits firmly on the fence between old-fashioned individual differences based on variances and the holistic notions of individual differences based on patterns. As Highhouse pointed out, we sorely lack the empirical evidence needed to support my view (or, for that matter, to refute it). It is time for serious researchers to consider these alternative positions more frequently and more carefully so that, eventually, we will acquire a historical database to provide supported empirical generalizations to guide the art of individual assessment. Are variances and patterns, in fact, mutually exclusive alternatives? Is it not possible to validate patterns with a rigor comparable to that used in evaluating contributions to criterion variance? My personal criticism is that much that is done in individual assessment abandons the evaluative process because traditional evaluations are not feasible (e.g., in selection for unique or for very uncommon positions). Effort expended to develop procedures to gather competent evidence of the practical value of such programs is sorely lacking.

The Future for Individual Assessment

Despite criticism, individual assessment will continue to be done, some by well-trained personnel psychologists and some by outsiders. One fundamental reason is that it is about the only option in filling a growing proportion of the positions to be filled in a worldwide economy—at least the only assessment-based approach to personnel decisions. Procedures for assessing groups of candidates, from which enough will be hired to make predictive validation possible, simply do not fit the problems of assessing candidates for executive or high-level professional jobs. In the summarizing chapter of their edited book, *Individual Psychological Assessment*, Silzer and Jeanneret (1998) presented a number of directions they foresaw or hoped would occur in the evolving process of individual assessment. In closing this section, I will concentrate on a half-dozen that seem especially provocative or promising.

1. They anticipated more collaborative involvement of assessment psychologists and senior executives. The assessment psychologist, in their view, will be more of an organizational psychologist (in the broadest sense) than one known only for giving tests and interpreting scores. Instead, he or she will "take responsibility for knowing the organization and its business strategies" (p. 448); failure to do so will be seen as failure to serve clients fully and to improve decisions.

2. As a business partner working collaboratively with senior executives, the assessor will help clients know and use multiple purposes of individual assessment, not just for selection (or promotion), but for personal development and behavior change.

3. When assessors and executives agree that individual assessments are necessary for personnel decisions (they won't always be deemed so), the assessors will analyze total situations in determining the requirements, success factors, competencies, or performance expectations traditionally called criteria. They will also understand and follow measurement principles, whether assessing competencies, cognitive and other abilities, personality traits, relevant skills, knowledge, or behavior samples. This analysis goes beyond conventional work analysis, bivariate predictive hypotheses (as in Chapter 3), and psychometric theory; it anticipates understanding the interrelatedness of job competencies, predictors, measurement principles, and performance outcomes. This, they said, requires knowing much more than is now known about any situational variables and psychological constructs expected to influence the effectiveness of assessment. This all requires seriously developing validity arguments.

4. The range of assessment tools will be broadened (and, in fact, it has happened). That means continuing to validate and standardize the instruments of assessment, including those not conventionally used in individual assessment—for example, simulations more likely to be used in group assessment centers. Silzer and Jeanneret also anticipated the broader use of computers and other aspects of information technology, but with somewhat less enthusiasm for computerized interviews.

5. They anticipated—more accurately, advocated—efforts to combine "mechanical" (i.e., "statistical") and clinical or judgmental approaches to data integration. They have stressed that assessments must not be so rigidly planned that the process leaves no room for serendipitous discovery of unique expertise or experience uniquely helpful in anticipated work assignments. Advocacy, or even awareness, of uniqueness seems to preclude "mechanical" processes of data integration or data analysis.

6. They anticipated clearer understanding of effective behavioral change agents and of the possibilities for change through individual assessment. This referred not only to changing the behavior of the person assessed but to the broader concept of organizational change. "The question will be whether assessment psychologists dealing with individual cases and psychological data can learn how to leverage assessment data for broader organizational uses" (Silzer & Jeanneret, 1998, p. 461).

I'm not sure I share their anticipations, but I join them in advocating changes in these directions.

ASSESSMENT CENTERS

Assessment centers (ACs) may be defined as programs of assessment, lasting from several hours to several days. They are "multiple" in several respects. They combine multiple exercises and other component procedures, they assess multiple assessees, usually in multiple small groups, on multiple dimensions by multiple assessors (Collins et al., 2003; Hoeft & Schuler, 2001; Thornton & Rupp, 2006). They are programs, not the places where the programs happen. Most of them are organization-specific, and most of them are developed and run by external consultants rather than by experts within the organization. Guidelines for the definition, design, and conduct of assessment centers were developed by an International Task Force on Assessment (International Test Commission, 2005).

Table 15.1 illustrates multiple dimensions (four cognitive skills and two personality traits) and multiple methods of assessment (three exercises and three tests). A basic AC assumption is behavioral consistency (Wernimont & Campbell, 1968); specifically, that dimensions important to job performance are fairly long-lasting and generalizable among assessment situations and to the job itself. That is, a dimension measured by an exercise rating or a standardized test is expected also to be measured in certain other exercises or tests and generalizable to them and to performance on the job.

Table 15.2 considers the leaderless group discussion exercise and shows how each of two different assessors might be assigned to observe only two of the assessees among the six, and how each assessee in the group could be explicitly assigned to two different observers. Each observer might make notes or ratings only for the assigned assessees in that exercise, but all observers may make overall assessment ratings (OARs) at the end of the AC. The design of the AC program can determine whether the assessors make OARs for all assessees or for some limited subset of them. Consensus on OARs is important, both for dimension ratings and for the OAR. Discussions leading to consensus sometimes take longer than the assessment center itself.

Two broad purposes of ACs are to provide assessment-based data for (a) administrative decisions such as selection or promotion, or (b) employee-centered decisions providing special training or personal career development paths. These different objectives may require somewhat different designs with somewhat different dimensions and methods.

TABLE 15.1

Plausible Assessment Components and Dimensions Assessed

Dimension	Exercise or Test					
	LGD	*Role Play*	*Stress Interview*	*Test A*	*Test B*	*Test C*
Reasoning	X	X				X
Perceptual Skill				X	X	
Oral Communication	X	X	X			
Memory	X			X		X
Surgency	X	X				
Stress Tolerance		X	X			

TABLE 15.2

Observer Assignments for Leaderless Group Discussion

Candidate	Assessor/Observer					
	A	*B*	*C*	*D*	*E*	*F*
Adams	X		X			
Beaverson		X		X		
Collins		X			X	
Delius	X					X
Edwards			X			X
Franklin				X	X	

Attributes Assessed

Traits Identified in Job or Work Analysis

A well-designed assessment center requires a thorough, detailed job or work analysis as a basis for almost everything. Traditional job analysis focuses on tasks or on well-defined behaviors necessary for effective performance, but these approaches may not be adequate; work for which ACs are used is no longer defined by a simple, slowly changing set of tasks. A casually developed, quickly written job description won't do, nor will a carefully done, traditional analysis of how a job has been done in the past. The times are indeed changing, especially in the levels of work for which multiple assessments are used. Analysis for AC design necessarily focuses more on the interconnectedness of the work and the objectives and plans of the organization in which the work is done. I will not repeat here the content of Chapter 2 beyond an emphasis on careful, thoughtful, thorough, forward-looking, and competent analyses to undergird discussions leading to the development and definition of the dimensions to be rated in a well-planned AC.

Exercises or other AC components give candidates an opportunity to show evidence of the degree to which they show the behavioral characteristics or traits required for excellence (or at least competence) in performance of the anticipated work. "Degree" implies dimensionality; observers or assessors rate or score individual candidates on those dimensions. Dimensions may include trait constructs, competencies, or perhaps quality of exercise task performance. Whatever the category, the dimension itself is a construct, and the inferences from the ratings, as measures of that construct, are to be evaluated in terms of construct (psychometric) validity. The first and overriding problem is to define that construct, initially, perhaps, in very general terms but eventually with some precision, based on competent work analysis. Constructs as defined by the analysis may vary in generality or specificity, in terms of existing traits or the potential for developing desired ones, or by the firmness of any theoretical foundations. Definitions grounded in extensive empirical and theoretical literature can lead to superior ACs.

Broad, general, poorly defined terms are inherently ambiguous. The growing tendency to use competencies as the dimensions to be assessed carries this danger if competencies are defined so broadly that different raters focus independently on different facets of them. A very broad personality or motivational concept can become a complex amalgam of narrower, more traditional constructs. Examples given in one discussion include *customer service orientation* and *continuous quality improvement*; "'customer service orientation' and 'continuous quality improvement' are worthy organizational goals, but they need operationalization into behavioral dimensions" (Lievens & Thornton, 2005, p. 246). I agree. At least the broad, complex dimensions need operationalization into coherent, logical, consistent constructs reasonably expected to generalize to aspects of job performance.

Common Attribute Names

Constructs proposed for many ACs are simply labels, sometimes idiosyncratically provided without much definition at all. The labels may be terms commonly used in discussion or conversation, or may have been used in other ACs for similar purposes, so they may seem to offer a comfortable sense of familiarity. At least, they are easily found. The number of labels that have been used in various kinds of assessment is extravagant. In preparing to do a meta-analysis of criterion-related validities of dimensions, Arthur, Day, McNelly, and

Edens (2003) found 34 articles reporting dimension validities, with a grand total of 168 different dimension names in the primary studies. They were able to classify reliably nearly all of these into six broad categories. (A seventh category, not included in their meta-analysis because of its ambiguity is, ironically, named tolerance for stress or uncertainty.) A less restricted search (attributed to Rupp, Gibbons, Runnels, and Thornton, 2003, in Thornton and Rupp, 2006) found 1,095 named dimensions from 65 sources which they consolidated into 16 dimensions, shown in Table 15.3.

The difference between the list of six and the list of 16 is due not so much to differences in a priori constraints (i.e., constraining the Arthur et al. list of primary reports to those

TABLE 15.3

Common Assessment Center Dimensions Identified by Rupp et al. (2003)

Dimension	Definition
Problem solving	Identifies problems or issues, analyzing them for logical relationships; develops courses of action; makes and evaluates logical decisions
Information seeking	Gathers data; identifies and finds relevant and essential information needed to solve a problem and analyzes it effectively
Creativity	Generates and recognizes imaginative solutions and innovations in work-related situations; questions traditional assumptions
Planning & organizing	Systematically monitors tasks, activities, or responsibilities of self and subordinates to assure meeting specific objectives; sets priorities; uses time and resources well; makes plans; handles administrative detail
Adaptability	Modifies behavior to accept new tasks, responsibilities, values, attitudes, or people; shows resilience to constraints, frustrations, or adversity
Stress Tolerance	Maintains composure and performance under pressure, opposition, tight time-frames, and/or uncertainty while working for constructive outcomes
Conscientiousness	Works efficiently, consistently, and thoroughly to meet deadlines and expectations; shows attention to detail; thinks carefully before acting
Motivation	Initiates action rather than reacting; sustains effort to achieve desired objectives; seeks advancement through self-development
Oral communication	Expresses ideas by speaking clearly in a manner appropriate for an intended audience
Written communication	Expresses ideas clearly, succinctly, and appropriately grammatically in writing; adjusts word choices, tone, and writing style for audience
Listening	Gives active attention to comments and questions of others; asks questions when appropriate
Persuasiveness	Obtains agreement or acceptance of an idea, plan, activity, or product; gains support and commitment from others
Interpersonal skill	Maintains effective relationships by positive manners, even in conflict; responds to needs and opinions of others and uses relationships to achieve personal and organizational goals
Leadership	Guides and motivates subordinates; gives regular, constructive feedback; promotes positive change
Teamwork	Works well with others toward common goals; creates a sense of team spirit
Conflict management	Recognizes and addresses conflict appropriately while maintaining positive working relationships

Adapted from Table 5.2 in Thornton, G. C., III, & Rupp, D. E. (2006). *Assessment Centers in Human Resource Management.* Mahwah, NJ: Lawrence Erlbaum Associates. © Taylor & Francis Group. Adapted by permission.

reporting dimensional criterion-related validities) as to differences in the encompassing breadth of meaning given the labels and the a priori assumptions about the behavioral nuances to be emphasized in using them. Consider, for example, the single *communication* dimension in the Arthur et al. list. Rupp et al. identified four dimensions under that heading: oral communication, written communication, listening, and persuasiveness. The first three of these can be considered aspects of a more broadly defined sort of communication, but *persuasiveness* in the Rupp et al. list might be interpreted in more interpersonal terms such as *influencing others* in the shorter six-dimension list. Defining dimension labels in a few short phrases, or even fairly long ones, does not eliminate ambiguity.

Ambiguity in defining psychological constructs is not likely to be eliminated in any context, but if dimensions are developed by local experts, officials, and potential assessors for a local AC, the ambiguity may not be particularly threatening within their specific setting. It might even be reduced to a point of no concern if the constructs to be assessed locally have truly been collaboratively developed and defined after thorough work analysis and discussion by the local people (i.e., those in the same organization, even a multi-location one). Moreover, some of the serious debate about the validities of AC measures might be reduced to minor annoyances with greater attention to unambiguous, independent, and thorough (and thoroughly understood) definitions.

Research goes forward as researchers seek correlates of AC dimension ratings with individual differences on more traditional dimensions. The seven dimensions identified by Arthur et al. (2003) correlated significantly with the Big Five's extraversion factor, three of them were negatively correlated with neuroticism, and none of them correlated with two cognitive factors (Furnham, Jensen, & Crump, 2008). Dilchert and Ones (2009), on the other hand, found that the same seven AC ratings correlated with both cognitive and personality factors.

Sharpening Dimension Definition

AC dimensions assessed in assessment centers may be defined narrowly as KSAOs, but they may also be broader attributes of the person or of trait–situation interactions. Jackson, Stillman, and Atkins (2005) assessed 199 applicants for retail sales and customer service jobs, comparing trait-based and situationally task specific dimensions.[1] They had reviewed several efforts to improve the construct validities of assessment center ratings, concluding that the efforts had "failed." Briefly, they asserted that rating task performance (i.e., task-specific dimensions) rather than traits might offer more improvement, and they asserted that their research supported that view. As pointed out by Thornton and Rupp (2006), however, not enough research has been done to demonstrate special value for task-based ratings; they recommended that person-centered attributes continue to be the dimensions rated in an assessment center.

I believe that the distinction between task-based and trait-based dimensions will create a lot of debate in the coming years, but I also believe the debate will be unnecessary and even counterproductive. Trait-based and task-based dimensions seem much less orthogonal than the debate would suggest. Too much attention to the distinction may obscure more important ways to create more useful, more valid ratings such as combining trait and exercise concepts to increase the focus on trait-activating situations (cf. Tett & Burnett, 2003). Another way to blur the distinction might focus more strongly on quality of task performance as a

---

[1] Note that these are nonmanagerial jobs, which may matter.

trait potentially generalizable to many work settings. That way, however, may also blur the distinction between constructs and methods (cf. Arthur & Villado, 2008), a distinction needing sharpening. Dimensions with sharper definitions may emerge from more and possibly more spirited discussions among those chosen to do the observation and evaluation of behavior asking what, precisely, they expect to see done by a candidate well qualified for the work at hand.

Exercises and Other Components

There is no such thing as a "typical" or "traditional" assessment center. Each one is designed to fit the purposes of the organization using it; component assessment methods vary widely. They are alike, however, in two essential ways. Assessment centers nearly always include performance exercises that are intended to simulate some aspect of the work for which the assessment is done, and they nearly always use more than one assessment method for each designated dimension. Within these similarities, assessment tools offer a virtual buffet of choices (mostly scored by observer or peer ratings) including simulations, work samples, interviews, and tests and inventories.

Simulation Exercises

Assessment center exercises often consist of work samples or simulations of aspects of work to be done; in fact, simulation exercises, whether abstract or high fidelity, are defining features of most ACs. Simulations vary widely in fidelity and level of abstraction. Work samples have high fidelity if they duplicate actual work conditions closely and sample all major aspects of the work: the use of a high-fidelity job simulation assumes that the level of future job performance can be predicted best by having candidates perform its tasks under conditions very similar to the actual job (Tsacoumis, 2007). Simulations are typically less comprehensive, but those of relatively high fidelity reflect several job tasks requiring important KSAOs. Of course, the conditions of being assessed by observers and those of actual job activity under daily conditions are inherently different, so some fidelity is immediately lost. Lower fidelity simulations include tests or job-related exercises resembling traditional tests in that they are administered on paper with questions for which there may be keyed answers etc. (cf. Motowidlo et al., 1990; Motowidlo & Tippins, 1993). The question is whether essential characteristics of the exercise are similar enough to job characteristics to allow generalization from performance on one to performance on the other. Computer-based simulations, of either high or low fidelity, are rapidly growing in use; the question applies as much to them as to more traditional ones.

One of the oldest types of exercise is the leaderless group discussion (LGD) (Bass, 1950). In these, small groups, with no designated leader, are asked to do something: devise a plan, solve a problem, choose a course of action, etc. Assessees may or may not be assigned roles to play in the discussion, but not the role of leader. A time limit is usually imposed, including time for candidates to read material describing the background of the situation and perhaps time to write a report of conclusions reached. Observers watch, without intervening; each observer–assessor records events associated with one or two specific assessees, planned so that each assessee is by assignment observed by at least two assessors (a characteristic of virtually all assessment center exercises).

Probably the most ubiquitous exercise is some form of an in-basket, in which the candidate is handed materials presumably drawn from a real life in-basket or in-file. Working alone, as if having come back in the evening when others are not present to distract or to help, that candidate disposes in some way of each item. An item might be held back for further information, or an action might be designated immediately. In some cases, the candidate is expected to write an explanation for the way each item was disposed.[2] Again, the behavior shown, the choices made, and explanations offered are reviewed and evaluated by at least two assessors, usually independently.

Other examples can include various types of presentation (if making presentations is relevant to the job), role-playing, analysis of documents related to a specified situation (including perhaps interviews with persons playing the role of someone involved in it), written or oral presentations of the analysis and conclusions reached, and perhaps answers to questions the assessors may ask.

Other Components

The breadth of other possible components may be seen by looking at a couple of examples. In the Management Progress Study at AT&T, component assessments included cognitive tests of general mental ability, creative thinking, and general knowledge; two personality inventories and two projective tests; an in-basket; group exercises, including a business game for groups of six assessees and a group discussion with assigned roles (a variant on the leaderless group discussion exercise), and extensive interviewing (Bray, Campbell & Grant, 1974).

A second example is in an early assessment center for police officers (described by Guion, 1998, and briefly in the discussion of BARS in Chapter 13) included those described in Table 15.4 along with various standardized tests and inventories.

The dominant component, whether called a test or an exercise, was the *Test of Perceptual Skill*, a movie. It was both unusual and archaic. "Early" in describing this movie means "before video tape" and a long time before DVD, which have been used in other programs. Because it illustrates fashioning an exercise to fit the job, because the job is generally if vaguely known, and because it was by far the most valid part of the assessment center, it deserves a fuller description than given in Table 15.4.

Perceptual skill is extremely important for patrol officers, but their skill differs from the typical perceptual speed and accuracy test where examinees compare objects. An officer may look for something specific, such as a license number, which must be perceived quickly and accurately, but more often the officer must simply be alert to things that merit curiosity. An officer on patrol or on investigative work must attend to detail without knowing which details in a visual scan might be important. Perception must be accurate, it must be quick, and it must be remembered to be retrieved if later events make it important.

The first section of the film gave instructions and some illustrative but very brief scenes, narrated by an off-screen voice. A later memory test was based on these scenes. Following them were several brief episodes, each followed by some multiple-choice questions about it. Some scenes had a story line and were played by actors. Others were just camera shots (e.g., people wandering through a park on a summer day). The medium, of course, presented behavioral information that could not have been included in traditional perception tests.

If faced again with the same problem, I would use the largest screen available, requiring scanning in fairly large arc. Computer-augmented tape or DVD imaging could, of course, be projected on large screens, probably with better resolution than films, but an ordinary

---

[2] That probably departs from most real-life work, but it may be a useful assessment addition.

TABLE 15.4
Components of an Early Assessment Center for Police Candidates

Exercise	Description
Test of Perceptual Skill	A motion picture consisting of vignettes and multiple-choice questions measuring perceptual alertness without specific things to be watching for; also two memory components.
Situations Test	Booklet with three situations, each followed by witness statements. Open questions asked for differences between statements, further information desired, judgments of relative witness credibility.
Training Bulletin Test	At end of day, recruits had to read (without taking notes) a stack of training bulletins over which tests would be taken the next day. The test was given to assess memory, but various interruptions, including being called out for interviews twice, were intended to induce mild stress.
Analysis Interview	Recruit read a brief description of a crime and met with two observers, one of whom played role of witness while recruit played role of investigative officer. Recruit wrote a report on conclusions from the interview.
Stress Interview	Recruit met with two observers, one a uniformed officer who posed a police problem (for which recruit was not yet trained) and asked how it should be handled. No satisfactory answer was likely for the problem at hand, even for experienced officers. The first answer was criticized, at first kindly and then with increasing hostility.
Leaderless Group Discussion	In groups of six, recruits met twice, once with, and once without, assigned roles. In each, one observer read instructions and presented a problem. The group was to reach consensus and prepare a written report within 30 minutes.
Competitive Exercise	Groups of six recruits were divided into two teams of three. Each team worked at a table on which were three sets of colored blocks, differing in size and shape and in point value. Each recruit chose a color and the team built a structure according to a plan provided. Individual scores summed the point values of the blocks in the structure for that individual, a bonus for highest or next highest points, and a further bonus if the team won, providing some conflict between cooperative team work and individual goals.

For further description of the assessment center, see Guion (1998).

computer monitor or TV screen would not command the breadth of visual exploration required of officers on patrol.

Assessors

Assessor Functions

Zedeck (1986) identified three assessor functions. A major function is simply to observe and record behavior in the exercises. Behavior is commonly recorded in descriptive (and perhaps evaluative) reports of the observers. Fulfillment of this function requires careful and reasonably extensive training (Thornton & Rupp, 2006). Ratings for a given dimension may be made by different pairs of assessors in different exercises, although assessors may specialize. Differences in dimensional inferences and in ratings are necessarily attributable in part to the differences in exercises, but they should not be attributable to different assessors having different understandings of the nature of the dimension; training should assure common understanding. A related problem is that the observers may also be part of the stimulus, and different observers may stimulate different reactions. Videotaped exercise performance may help with this; the assessors can observe tapes, even with "instant replay" if needed (Ryan et al., 1995).

An assessor may serve the second function, a role player who is an active participant in an exercise. In many exercises, assessors are interviewers, usually with another assessor in place simply as an observer and rater. In role playing, a participant–assessor serves usually to provide a stimulus to which the assessee responds. One problem for this function is lack of standardization. Role players may change their own behavior during the sequence of interviews. In a stress interview, for example, some may get harsher over a sequence of interviews whereas others may say, in effect, "to heck with it"—and cause less stress. If different assessors play the same role, standardization is even less likely. In my opinion, assessors should not be role players. Trying to be an actor and an observer simultaneously is cognitively hard. Also, assessors are unlikely to be good actors; standardization would be more likely using professional actors, especially those experienced in improvisation. Moreover, assessors (in my judgment) should be as unobtrusive as possible.

Zedeck's third function is as a predictor. Assessors may make explicit predictions, or prediction may be based on the ratings, whether dimensional ratings or OARs. In any case, predictions of assessors need validation.

Assessor Qualifications

Qualifications for AC assessors are much like those in individual assessment, but practices in selecting them seem different. In either setting, assessors may be psychologists, but most writers on individual assessment consider a degree in psychology an essential credential. Many AC advocates prefer HR staff, job experts, or managers given a week or two or three of training specifically focused on the AC at hand. Whatever the background, training should be intensive, with frequent refreshers, on the details of the assessment center components; training is essential if assessors are to be fully familiar with the exercises and the kinds of behavior they might observe. They should fully understand the terms and concepts related to the ratings they are to make.

Managers' practical knowledge of the organization and its policies and climate makes them useful assessors. The benefit of their special knowledge must be weighed against the cost of taking them from their jobs for periods of training and actual assessing. Training may take two weeks. An assessment center may take a week at a time with consensus meetings at the end, and it may be conducted six times in a year; altogether, eight weeks of high-level management time can be taken from their principal jobs. Many organizations find the cost acceptable for the benefits accrued, but others find it excessive. External professional assessors offer an alternative. Tsacoumis (2007), for example, considered it a sensible one, not only because their use avoids pulling internal people away from their jobs, but also because the externals understand the assessment center processes better, because they avoid the problem of prior knowledge of assessees, and finally, because their use "enhances the credibility and perceived objectivity of the assessment center process" (Tsacoumis, 2007, p. 278). Whether managers or traveling assessors, they should be good observers, objective in temperament, intelligent, and articulate in conference and report writing.

Other questions emerge. Should assessors be specialists in the kinds of behavior they observe? Should one assessor be a specialist in the leaderless group discussion and another a specialist in personal history interviews? Should an assessor be a specialist on evaluating people on certain dimensions? In group exercises, should each assessor try to observe and rate all candidates in the group or be assigned to observe and rate no more than one or two? These questions stem from efforts to maximize reliability and validity of the assessments provided. I do not know the answers and call again for more research.

VALIDITY ISSUES

If a given dimension or trait—a construct—is generalizable and is validly measured, measures of it should correlate reasonably well across all test and exercise situations evoking it. This assertion has been taken in discussions over the last few decades as referring to psychometric validity, more commonly termed construct validity.[3] Discussion of construct validity as a special problem in assessment centers probably began with the Sackett and Dreher (1982) article. It showed that the correlations between ratings on the same dimension across different exercises were lower than the correlations across different dimensions within the same exercise—and thus the dimension ratings lacked or were weak in construct validity.[4]

This empirical finding has often been repeated. Woehr and Arthur (2003) called it the validity paradox. Sackett and Tuzinski (2001) called it a dilemma. Paradox or dilemma, a gap exists between the basic AC generalizability assumption and the evidence. If validity is a unitary concept (AERA et al., 1999, p. 11), then this pair of findings is contradictory. The unitary notion implies that different aspects of validity evidence are necessarily somewhat consistent with each other, but Woehr and Arthur said that evidence of content-related validity and of criterion-related validity are accepted in assessment centers even when evidence of the construct-related validity of AC ratings is sorely lacking. Much in this line of reasoning makes me uncomfortable, particularly its resurrection of psychometric trinitarianism (Guion, 1980) and its uncritical acceptance of criterion-related validity as if universally sensible. Nevertheless, it cannot be denied that research fails to support the conventional idea of generalizable validity of inferences or interpretations based on assessment center dimension ratings.

Criterion-Related Validity of Assessment Center Ratings

"The validity of assessment centers" typically refers to a correlation between OARs and external criteria representing some form of job performance. Most reviews of such research, including meta-analyses, suggest that criterion-related evidence of validity of overall AC judgments is so well established that it need not be questioned—although I do question it. The most widely cited meta-analysis (Gaugler, Rosenthal, Thornton, & Benson, 1987) presented a mean corrected validity coefficient of .37, which is not at all trivial. A meta-analysis of studies published after the Gaugler et al. review found a lower corrected validity coefficient, .28 (Hermelin, Lievens, & Robertson, 2007). Accepting the value of .37 reported by Gaugler et al., and a mean validity of .51 for general mental ability tests, Schmidt and Hunter (1998)

---

[3] In this discussion, I will use the term *construct validity*, somewhat reluctantly, to follow the bulk of the literature (AERA, APA, & NCME, 1999, p. 174).

[4] Never mind for now that this does not correctly state the Sackett and Dreher conclusions; it states a view often attributed to them. Let's live with the misstatement long enough to illustrate the dilemma. A better statement is that they "assert that evidence is lacking . . . that the constructs measured are those intended by their designers" (Sackett & Tuzinski, 2001, p. 117).

reported that combining GMA tests and assessment center OARs offered only a .02 incremental validity for the AC ratings.

Krause, Kersting, Heggestrad, and Thornton (2006) reported incremental validities beyond cognitive tests. A two-day AC assessed managerial candidates for a training academy for executive positions in German police departments. A composite cognitive test score became a measure of GMA. AC components assessed eight dimensions rated by assessors; the OAR was an average of consensus dimension ratings. The final examination score at the end of academy training served as criterion. When the composite GMA was entered first in hierarchical multiple regression, its validity was .53; adding the OAR composite accounted for an incremental 5% of the criterion variance in academy learning performance. When individual ability scores were entered as a first step in the multiple regression analysis, followed in the second step by the various AC ratings on the same dimensions, and the OAR as well, the resulting correlation with Academy learning was somewhat higher than found with the composites. It provided slightly less incremental criterion variance, 4%, but either way, the dimension ratings provided a useful increase in predicting learning.

A meta-analysis of incremental dimension contributions, reported by Meriac, Hoffman, Woehr, and Fleisher (2008), started with the sensible proposition that GMA is the best predictor. Hierarchical analysis followed GMA with a block of personality factors. The question was whether AC dimensions add anything substantial to the validities provided by these starting points. The six AC dimensions earlier reported by Arthur et al. (2003), plus the seventh dimension they deleted from their analysis, provided an AC block of dimension ratings. In their regression analysis, GMA was entered first, with $R = .32$ (much lower than that reported by Schmidt & Hunter, 1998). Adding in the personality block raised it to $R = .44$ (with $\Delta R^2 = .095$). Adding in the block of seven AC dimensions raised it further to $R = .543$ (with $\Delta R^2 = .097$). Examining dimension ratings independently made important differences. Ratings of *organizing and planning* provided the best incremental validity.

Jansen and Stoop (2001) reported a study, unusual in that the criterion was salary growth over time (reported for from one through seven years elapsing between predictor data collection and criterion measurement) with starting salary partialed out. The assessment center itself consisted of just two exercises, a group discussion and an analysis presentation. OARs were made by consensus during an end-session discussing ratings made during the two exercises. Data also came from other predictors (interviews and tests) that could have been considered in making final OARs but were not. Participants were college recruits hired during 1987–1997 for a Dutch postal and telecommunications company. Results showed a partial validity coefficient for the OAR based on the two exercises, corrected for range restriction, of .39 for those still employed after seven years, but very low and mostly nonsignificant partial correlations for shorter time differences—quite different from the usual simplex pattern over time. Tenure alone predicted the salary growth criterion nearly as well as the AC did.

In sum, overall ratings based on assessment center components are generally valid predictors, but the criterion-related validity they provide by themselves can be exceeded by that from GMA tests alone; ratings of assessment center dimensions can, however, provide some useful incremental validity.

Construct-Related Evidence of Dimension Validity

The heading here reflects the term used by Woehr and Arthur (2003). They retained the three sources of validity evidence of earlier *Standards* while following the assertion that the unity of validity stems from multiple sources of evidence.[5] They therefore used *construct-related validity* to refer to specifiable evidence from which to infer the adequacy of the *construct validity* of AC dimension ratings.

Failure to support construct validities of assessment dimension ratings has been consistently reported for more than a quarter-century, based primarily on multitrait–multimethod matrix analysis, considering different tests or exercises to be different methods of assessment. The basic AC logic argues a need for convergent validity; assessments of a given construct should agree in exercises intended in part to evoke that construct, and they should agree with (generalize to) evaluations of subsequent job performance—by argument if not empirically. Correlations of assessments of a single construct in two different exercises should be substantial but not necessarily high. (Exercises are not designed as parallel measures, so the intercorrelations could not reach the levels of reliability coefficients.) The basic AC logic also argues for divergence; too much correlation between ratings of separately identified dimensions suggests redundancy.

Factor analytic evidence suggests that neither convergent nor divergent validities match the basic AC logic. Tables 15.5, 15.6, and 15.7 illustrate the problem. Table 15.5 suggests an AC with five components (exercises) rated on some subset of dimensions from a larger set of seven; no two exercises are thought to evoke precisely the same set of dimensions. In all, 23 dimension ratings (composites such as averages across multiple raters) are depicted; their intercorrelations could be factor analyzed. The ideal result, according to the basic AC logic, is depicted in Table 15.6; ideally, all ratings on a dimension would load heavily on a single factor, regardless of the exercise in which the rated behavior occurred. That is, each of the seven dimensions would define its own factor.

Typically, however, that ideal pattern is not found. A more typical pattern is shown in Table 15.7, in which each exercise, regardless of the dimension rated in it, defines a factor. The difference between the findings depicted by these two tables of significant factor loadings defines the dilemma, or paradox, of the construct validity of the dimensional ratings. The problem, which has dominated the AC literature for more than 25 years without resolution, is unlikely to be resolved here.

TABLE 15.5
Seven Rated Dimensions in Five Exercises

Dimension Rated	Exercise				
	A	B	C	D	E
Dimension 1	X	X	X		X
Dimension 2	X		X		X
Dimension 3	X	X	X		
Dimension 4	X		X	X	X
Dimension 5	X	X		X	
Dimension 6			X	X	X
Dimension 7		X		X	X

[5] Acceptance of the terminological distinction implies no judgment about validity arguments. I use it to imply that clarity of the distinction between evidence and the inferences drawn from it is essential in thinking about the problem created by persistently reported data challenging the construct validity of ACs.

TABLE 15.6

Idealized Significant Factor Loadings for Dimensions Rated in Exercises

Dimensions Rated in Exercises	Factors						
	1	*2*	*3*	*4*	*5*	*6*	*7*
Dimension 1 in A	X						
Dimension 1 in B	X						
Dimension 1 in C	X						
Dimension 1 in E	X						
Dimension 2 in A		X					
Dimension 2 in C		X					
Dimension 2 in E		X					
Dimension 3 in A			X				
Dimension 3 in B			X				
Dimension 3 in C			X				
Dimension 4 in A				X			
Dimension 4 in C				X			
Dimension 4 in E				X			
Dimension 5 in A					X		
Dimension 5 in B					X		
Dimension 5 in D					X		
Dimension 5 in E					X		
Dimension 6 in C						X	
Dimension 6 in D						X	
Dimension 6 in E						X	
Dimension 7 in B							X
Dimension 7 in D							X
Dimension 7 in E							X

Some Suggested Solutions

One approach attempts to reduce cognitive demands on raters. Using behavioral checklists instead of more common ratings seemed to do so; it helped some, but exercise factors still dominated over dimension factors. Considering a large number of dimensions puts heavy cognitive demands on raters and interferes with discriminant validity. It seems reasonable to suppose that reducing the number of dimensions, like reducing potholes, would provide smoother roads to valid inferences; it may have diminishing returns, however, if the reduction blurs dimension definitions enough that raters do not distinguish well between them—perhaps perceiving them to be overlapping. Raters tend to reduce the number of dimensions on their own by using relatively few of them in making overall ratings. "Transparent" dimensions are also supposed to ease the cognitive load. I think the term usually means making sure dimensions are very well defined and understood by the raters so that observers can clearly identify dimension-relevant behaviors called forth by the exercises that reflect the dimensions. As Sackett and Tuzinski (2001) said, transparency seems to increase halo effects and to reduce discriminant validity.

Research aimed at understanding the cognitive *processes* at work in AC ratings may be more fruitful. Sackett and Tuzinski (2001) asserted that the problem is not the validity of measures of intended constructs but knowing the constructs observers actually use in rating

TABLE 15.7

Typical Pattern of Factor Loadings in Assessment Center Analyses

	Factors				
Exercise/Dimension	I	II	III	IV	V
Exercise A-1	X				
Exercise A-2	X				
Exercise A-3	X				
Exercise A-4	X				
Exercise A-5	X				
Exercise B-1		X			
Exercise B-3		X			
Exercise B-5		X			
Exercise B-7		X			
Exercise C-1			X		
Exercise C-2			X		
Exercise C-3			X		
Exercise C-4			X		
Exercise C-6			X		
Exercise D				X	
Exercise D				X	
Exercise D				X	
Exercise D				X	
Exercise E					X
Exercise E					X
Exercise E					X
Exercise E					X
Exercise E					X

dimensions. The point was stressed further by Jones and Born (2008), who suggested that the constructs in use might be the raters' own—personal constructs—not those intended by the AC developer. They also argued that the use of MTMM analyses, factor analyses, and related linear, additive models is inappropriate because (among other reasons) these assume independence among the dimensions instead of first determining how the dimensions might or theoretically should be related. To repeat: the problem might well reside in the failure to define dimensions thoroughly and thoughtfully. They suggested three considerations for an acceptable dimension definition: (a) its probable permanence or consistency over time, (b) the specificity of the behavior marking it, and (c) its interrelationships (especially nesting and interactions) with other dimensions.

Understanding the constructs actually used by assessors may lead to a change in the nature of designer-intended constructs. Perhaps instead of predicting job performance from personal attributes, instead of seeing exercise factors as contaminating method bias, assessment center dimensions should focus on behavior in specific exercises intended to simulate or otherwise reflect actual behavior relevant to specifiable aspects of overall job performance. A task-based performance dimension, compared to attribute-based dimensions, may be more stable, its behavioral components can be specified more clearly from job or work analysis, and it may be more likely to generalize to job performance. It may also be more difficult to achieve.

An Intended Comparison

A fortunate happenstance led to a widely cited study comparing attribute-based dimensions to task-based ratings of managerial functions (Joyce, Thayer, & Pond, 1994). A state government agency established a two-year management training program requiring two assessment centers, one at the time of entry into the program and the second at graduation from it. Both conventionally used attribute-based ratings. After more than 200 potential trainees had gone through the first one, many of them complained that they couldn't "translate" the attribute-based feedback they received to the workplace; they preferred to have their performance discussed in terms of what they had done in the AC. Responding, the designers of the program changed the second AC ratings (using the same exercises) "so that exercise performance was evaluated according to the functions performed in the exercises and . . . represented the structure of managerial work" (p. 110). Seven attribute dimensions were rated in the first AC; the second rated several managerial functions (i.e., tasks).

MTMM analyses in both ACs were consistent with the Sackett and Dreher findings. However, with the benefit of hindsight and an extensive subsequent literature, I consider this study suggestive but inadequate because the "managerial functions" did not inform the development of the exercises.

An Original: The AT&T Management Progress Study

In most of this book, I've tried to give some historical perspective to the topics at hand; but I have conspicuously overlooked the early history of assessment centers. It's time to remedy that, although I still overlook the development of ACs in the Second World War for the Office of Strategic Services. (For that history, see MacKinnon, 1977.) I mention it only because Douglas Bray, later a psychologist with AT&T and the creator of management ACs, was involved in the wartime OSS program research.

The AC designs so far described, all different in detail but fundamentally similar in general, seem to be the kind commonly reported in practice and research. The original management AC design, the AT&T Management Progress Study, was initiated under Bray's leadership during the 1950s (Bray et al., 1974). It was designed to track the careers of managerial personnel in AT&T, more a program for career development than for selection or promotion. In fact, during the research period, assessment data were withheld from decision makers so that its value could be empirically established. It was. Assessment data differentiated people in successful and unsuccessful careers for more than 20 years of follow-up data collection (Bray et al., 1974).

The design of this original assessment center differed in several ways from that I have presented so far. Exercises were developed to sample, not dimensions, but dimension domains (Howard, 1997). An exercise for an interpersonal domain might, for example, be expected to shed light on a set of dimensions in it, such as persuasiveness, leadership, agreeableness, or willingness to compromise. Unlike the ACs described in the tables and text of this chapter, however, the observer–assessors did not rate their assigned assessees on these dimensions (or the dimension domain) as soon as the exercise was over. Instead, they continued their observation functions until all exercises and tests were complete; only then would they write reports of their observations. They made no ratings until all reports were in and had been discussed. Although they might have made independent preliminary ratings on the dimensions being considered, the real dimension ratings, including the OAR, were determined by consensus after all exercises had been completed. This may be called an *across-exercise* approach as contrasted to the *within-exercise* approach described previously. We can think of these as two distinct AC models, but many ACs are mixtures of the two.

The Joyce et al. (1994) MTMM analysis was, virtually by definition, a within-exercise approach. According to Howard (1997), their in-basket sampled administrative skills, the case analysis sampled cognitive skills, and the coaching/counseling exercise sampled interpersonal skills—all of which represented skills important to managerial work. From this point of view, an OAR would be based on a combination of ratings of domains, not on ratings of dimensions never intended or expected to be wholly independent.

A Hesitant Look Ahead

I've been looking back. Looking forward may have more virtue. I do so hesitantly, with full awareness that the sentence beginning with "He who sticks his neck out . . ." has many different endings, most of them dire. But some endings imply seeing things further, higher, or more clearly. In that hope, I mention some things that I think, or hope, will happen.

First, I think the dimension–exercise dilemma will go away, replaced by the growing emphasis on competencies in describing jobs (e.g., Bartram, 2005b; Brannick et al., 2007; Schippmann, 1999). Competencies are compound constructs, analogous to dimension domains. I suggest that (a) attributes at some level are important in any AC design, and (b) the exercises and other components should be chosen to represent well the various *categories*, *competencies*, or *domains* the job requires, as revealed by job or work analysis, whether the emphasis is on tasks, traits, or compound constructs. Whatever dimensions are to be rated (assessed) should reflect different facets of these domains and therefore is not expected to be essentially independent, and, of course, the evaluation of the validities of the ratings would require asking and answering different questions in different ways for the models chosen.

Enough ink has flowed on the recurring construct validity "dilemma." It is time to rethink the nature of the variables to be assessed. Should we assess quality of task performance or the extent to which the performers demonstrate propensities for excellence in performance? What, precisely, do we seek to generalize from one AC component to another? If we find it, does it really generalize beyond the AC? What analytic methods can best answer these questions? Are we still arguing residues of the century-old disagreements between the systems of psychology—behaviorism on one hand and psychophysical or functionalist trait psychology on the other?

Recent discussions of competencies describe task- or work-based attributes, moving beyond that long-lasting, fruitless task-vs.-attribute debate. A detailed taxonomy of job-relevant competencies, defined perhaps, within those broad categories of work where assessment centers are used (e.g., managerial, scientific, educational, technical, or personal service). Brannick et al. (2007) said that named competencies are so often in proprietary sets that fitting them into a coherent taxonomy is unlikely. I understand their view, but I do not share their pessimism. I think, or hope, that serious, independent researchers will be able to fence in the domain of competencies so that they will successfully avoid the proprietary pitfalls. I anticipate results something like the lexical research on personality traits identifying a few very broad competencies subsuming smaller sets of narrower ones. At some level in taxonomic efforts, I think it is likely that competencies will come to define work-related attributes of people, probably acquired quite early in life but still modifiable when entering organizations, that can best be assessed within the boundaries of exercises developed explicitly to require them.[6]

With still less certainty, I anticipate seeing more assessment centers using doctoral-level professionals (psychologists, educators, HR researchers) as recurrent observer–assessors—a new professional specialty, perhaps. Professional observers of people and their behavior may be more cognizant of individual behavioral and trait differences, less focused on performance in small, even high-fidelity, simulations. However, I join the Thornton and Rupp (2006) call for more research on optimal assessor characteristics, perhaps differing for different assessor roles. In particular, a growing use of interpersonal or social contact seems to be characteristic of assessment centers and AC research; along with this, or so it seems likely, is a growing concern for social perception skills among assessors. Other specific changes in recommended assessor qualification seem likely as well.

Tentatively, I expect to see more serious considerations of the influence of different cultures on assessment center design and assessee performance. In one sense, this seems inevitable, given the increased awareness of globalism and of national differences in values and orientations. Perhaps I am not unreasonable when I expect more intercultural study on similarities across cultures in habits, attitudes, beliefs, and values. I also expect to see more consideration of a narrower cultural concept, something akin to the concept of organizational cultures. It can be important in ACs for promotion within an organization, but the idea might be extended to include the kind of work culture an outside candidate may have experienced before.

Much less tentatively, I anticipate many changes in assessment exercise design because of more technological options. I expect simulations to have ever increasing fidelity, and so do Thornton and Rupp (2006), who list three reasons to expect it: the speed of electronic developments, the current high cost of assessors (including travel costs), and increased pressure for objectivity. Not much observed in current ACs can be stored in a file cabinet, retrievable when necessary. Electronic simulations, and electronic scoring of performance in them, can be kept in ever-smaller storage systems for review in the event of challenges. Computerized scoring may not prove as helpful as potential exercise improvements. Too many of the computer assessment systems now in use are little more than electronic multiple-choice tests. If a managerial simulation, for example, calls for such responses, the fidelity of the exercise itself is lost; the managerial jobs are more likely to require managers to identify or create their own alternative responses to the situation and then to justify the option they choose (Lievens & Thornton, 2005).

I do not anticipate the demise of assessment centers. Few methods of assessment have comparable levels of acceptance from those assessed. Old-fashioned paper-and-pencil tests may predict performance better, or at least as well, but they are more likely to be feared and distrusted.

CONCLUDING NOTE

For many kinds of work, perhaps most, a major theme of this book has been that optimal prediction generally requires the assessment of more than one predictor. Bluntly, I argue

---

[6] Those who know of my earlier view that competencies were nothing more than newer and more ambiguous terms for traits may find that sentence surprising. OK. Old dogs *can* learn. And competency research *can* be creative and grow.

that bivariate prediction just doesn't suffice. Chapter 2 emphasized the search for multiple traits, including areas of knowledge and skill, required for effective performance on various criteria. Chapter 3, on the other hand, dealt essentially, but appropriately, with the development of bivariate predictive hypotheses, with one predictor and one criterion. I say "appropriately" because bivariate hypotheses converge to become multivariate hypotheses or theories of specified sorts of work, with multiple predictors, mediators, moderators, and even multiple criteria. The many limitations of bivariate analyses, described in Chapter 5, urged personnel research and practice to do more multivariate thinking. Multivariate thinking implies more than multiple regression (which is a bivariate model when the multiple assessments become a single composite). The theme reached its zenith in Chapter 12 with its hope for, someday, a truly comprehensive, organization-wide system of analysis, assessment, and decision making. It continued into this chapter describing multiple assessments in stages, individual assessments, and assessment centers which, even in the face of OARs, cannot logically be reduced to bivariate thinking. The theme has faced controversy, although I think less so as I write now (in 2010) than just a decade ago. A related assessment controversy, mentioned often from Chapter 1 onwards, expands the trait–situation debates into a much broader, and also probably unending, debate about the appropriate comprehensiveness of the candidate characteristics assessed. How broadly should potential predictors, and perhaps the mediating or moderating variables, be defined? Should situations, whether for assessment or for work, be considered sources of error, deflating the scientific integrity of the generalizations offered? Or should they be considered systematic, generalizable influences on the assessments themselves, or perhaps potential predictors in their own right?

Starting with g or GMA, job-relevant characteristics become more numerous and narrower as the naming of them moves along a continuum of terms such as group factors, competencies or complex attributes, down to first-order factors, themselves divisible even to the extreme of the structure of intellect theory. If one believes that GMA is the only cognitive level needed in predicting performance at work, and that all that needs to be predicted is overall job performance, the life of a validation researcher may seem relatively simple; bivariate prediction is as sufficient as it seemed in the middle of the twentieth century. The simplicity can be spoiled by considering more things: moderators and suppressors, mediators, the shape of regression patterns, multiple and maybe independent criteria, or the number of cases needed to achieve stable generalizations, but fundamental bivariate oversimplification would remain.

More intense controversy surrounds a further major theme in this book, definitely central to and culminating in this chapter. That theme expands the distinctions between clinical and statistical prediction. Legitimate, arguable differences of opinion exist about the role of subjective judgment (beyond ratings) in personnel research and decision-making. My personal opinion, I hope, has been clear: research needs to consider the possibility that judgment can be effective in some forms and circumstances, that judgment may be necessary because of departures in the decision-making situation from the standard situation in which research is done (think ADA!), that we will not learn to identify effective forms of judgment, or to handle the unexpected or uncommon candidate situations, unless we stop sweeping away the possibilities and problems of systematic judgments and start giving them extensive consideration.

If one believes that GMA is a sufficient predictor, but accepts the proposition that it is the third level of a three-level hierarchical factor structure, it can be tested by a relatively simple bivariate analysis. But if one also accepts the view that another predictor has useful incremental predictive power, one has moved into multiple assessment. In view of the meta-analyses reported by Schmidt and Hunter (1998) and their finding that GMA plus work samples or integrity tests or structured interviews predicts overall job performance better than does GMA alone, endorsement of multiple assessment is a necessary choice—and a widely accepted one—even if the assessments must be done sequentially or with judgment—including those instruments of human judgment called ratings that we live with all the time. And of course, if one does not accept the view that GMA is enough, if one inches just a little toward the fractionated end of the continuum, the necessity for multiple assessment is a given. Why then has this chapter entitled "multiple assessment procedures" been devoted solely to the predictor side of the predictive hypothesis? Why does it not include a substantial section on multiple assessment of criteria? It's a good question. I'm sorry I don't have a good answer.

References

Abelson, R. P. (1995). *Statistics as principled argument.* Hillsdale, NJ: Lawrence Erlbaum Associates.

Ackerman, P. L. (1988). Determinants of individual differences during skill acquisition. *Journal of Experimental Psychology: General, 117,* 288–318.

Age Discrimination in Employment Act of 1967 29 U.S.C. 631 (1967).

Aguinis, H., Henle, C. A., & Beaty, J. C., Jr. (2001). Virtual reality technology: A new tool for personnel selection. *International Journal of Selection and Assessment, 9,* 70–83.

Aguinis, H., Mazurkiewicz, M. D., & Heggestad, E. D. (2009). Using web-based frame-of-reference training to decrease biases in personality-based job analysis: An experimental field study. *Personnel Psychology, 62,* 405–438.

Aguinis, H., & Pierce, C. A. (2006). Computation of effect size for moderating effects of categorical variables in multiple regression. *Applied Psychological Measurement, 30,* 440–442.

Aiken, L. S., & West, S. G. (1991). *Multiple regression: Testing and interpreting interactions.* Newbury Park, CA: Sage.

Albemarle v. Moody. (1975) (Vol. 422 U.S., p. 405).

Albrecht, P. A., Glaser, E. M., & Marks, J. (1964). Validation of a multiple-assessment procedure for managerial personnel. *Journal of Applied Psychology, 48,* 351–360.

Allen v. Alabama State Board of Education, No. 81-697-N (consent decree filed with the United States District Court for the Middle District of Alabama Northern Division, 1985).

Allison, P. D. (1984). *Event history analysis: Regression for longitudinal event data* (J. L. Sullivan & R. G. Niemi, Eds.) (Vols. 7–46). Beverly Hills, CA: Sage.

American Educational Research Association, American Psychological Association, & National Council on Measurement in Education. (1985). *Standards for educational and psychological testing.* Washington, DC: American Psychological Association.

American Educational Research Association, American Psychological Association, & National Council on Measurement in Education. (1999). *Standards for educational and psychological testing.* Washington, DC: American Educational Research Association.

American Medical Association. (1977). *Guide to the evaluation of permanent impairment.* Monroe, WI: American Medical Association.

American Psychological Association. (2001). *Publication manual of the American Psychological Association* (5th ed.). Washington, DC: American Psychological Association.

American Psychological Association, American Educational Research Association, & National Council on Measurement in Education. (1954). Technical recommendations for psychological tests and diagnostic techniques. *Psychological Bulletin, 51,* 201–238.

American Psychological Association, American Educational Research Association, & National Council on Measurement in Education. (1966). *Standards for educational and psychological tests and manuals.* Washington, DC: American Psychological Association.

American Psychological Association, American Educational Research Association, & National Council on Measurement in Education. (1974). *Standards for educational and psychological tests.* Washington, DC: American Psychological Association.

American Psychological Association, American Educational Research Association, & National Council on Measurement in Education. (1985). *Standards for educational and psychological testing.* Washington, DC: American Psychological Association.

Amrine, M. (1965). Special issue: Testing and public policy. *American Psychologist, 20,* 857–870.

Anastasi, A. (1986). Evolving concepts of test validation. *Annual Review of Psychology, 37,* 1–15.

Anastasi, A. (1988). *Psychological testing* (6th ed.). New York: Macmillan.

Anderson, N. (2003). Applicant and recruiter reactions to new technology in selection: A critical review and agenda for future research. *International Journal of Selection and Assessment, 11,* 121–136.

Anderson, N. (2005). Relationships between practice and research in personnel selection: Does the left hand know what the right is doing? In A. Evers, N. Anderson, & O. Voskuijl (Eds.), *The Blackwell handbook of personnel selection* (pp. 1–24). Malden, MA: Blackwell.

Anderson, N. R. (1991). Decision making in the graduate selection interview: An experimental investigation. *Human Relations, 44,* 403–417.

Angoff, W. H. (1972, September). *A technique for the investigation of cultural differences.* Presented at the American Psychological Association conference, Honolulu, HI.

Angoff, W. H. (1982). Use of difficulty and discrimination indices for detecting item bias. In R. A. Berk (Ed.), *Handbook of methods for detecting test bias* (pp. 96–116). Baltimore: Johns Hopkins University Press.

Angoff, W. H. (1988). Validity: An evolving concept. In H. Wainer & H. I. Braun (Eds.), *Test validity* (pp. 19–32). Hillsdale, NJ: Lawrence Erlbaum Associates.

Arnold, J. D., Rauschenberger, J. M., Soubel, W. G., & Guion, R. M. (1982). Validation and utility of a strength test for selecting steelworkers. *Journal of Applied Psychology, 67,* 588–604.

Arthur, W., Jr., Bell, S. T., Villado, A. J., & Doverspike, D. (2006). The use of person–organization fit in employment decision making: An assessment of its criterion-related validity. *Journal of Applied Psychology, 91,* 786–801.

Arthur, W., Jr., Day, E. A., McNelly, T. L., & Edens, P. S. (2003). A meta-analysis of the criterion-related validity of assessment center dimensions. *Personnel Psychology, 56,* 125–154.

Arthur, W., Jr., & Villado, A. J. (2008). The importance of distinguishing between constructs and methods when comparing predictors in personnel selection research and practice. *Journal of Applied Psychology, 93,* 435–442.

Arvey, R. D. (1979). *Fairness in selecting employees.* Reading, MA: Addison-Wesley.

Arvey, R. D., & Campion, J. E. (1982). The employment interview: A summary and review of recent research. *Personnel Psychology, 35,* 281–322.

Arvey, R. D., Salas, E., & Gialluca, K. A. (1992). Using task inventories to forecast skills and abilities. *Human Performance, 5,* 171–190.

Arvey, R. D., Strickland, W., Drauden, G., & Martin, C. (1990). Motivational components of test taking. *Personnel Psychology, 43*(166), 695–716.

Ash, R. A., Johnson, J. C., Levine, E. L., & McDaniel, M. A. (1989). Job applicant training and work experience evaluation in personnel selection. *Research in Personnel and Human Resource Management, 7,* 183–226.

Austin, J. T., & Crespin, T. R. (2006). Problems of criteria in industrial and organizational psychology: Progress, problems, and prospects. In W. Bennett, Jr., C. E. Lance, & D. J. Woehr (Eds.), *Performance measurement: Current perspectives and future challenges* (pp. 9–48). Mahwah, NJ: Lawrence Erlbaum Associates.

Austin, J. T., & Villanova, P. (1992). The criterion problem: 1917–1992. *Journal of Applied Psychology, 77*, 836–874.

Bacal, R. (1999). *Performance management.* New York: McGraw-Hill.

Baker v. Columbus Separate School District (329 F. Supp. 706, Trans.). (1971). DC Miss.

Baker v. Columbus Separate School District (462 F. 2d 1112, Trans.). (1972). Ca 5.

Baldridge, D. C., & Veiga, J. F. (2001). Toward a greater understanding of the willingness to request an accommodation: Can requesters' beliefs disable the Americans with Disabilities Act? *Academy of Management Review, 26*, 85–99.

Balma, M. J. (1959). The development of processes for indirect or synthetic validity (a symposium): 1. The concept of synthetic validity. *Personnel Psychology, 12*, 395–396.

Balzer, W. K. (1986). Biases in the recording of performance-related information: The effects of initial impression and centrality of the appraisal task. *Organizational Behavior and Human Decision Processes, 37*, 329–347.

Balzer, W. K., & Sulsky, L. M. (1992). Halo and performance appraisal research: A critical examination. *Journal of Applied Psychology, 77*, 975–985.

Barney, M. (2002). Macro, meso, micro: Six sigma. *Industrial–Organizational Psychologist, 39*, 104–107.

Barrick, M. R., Mitchell, T. R., & Stewart, G. L. (2003). Situational and motivational influences on trait–behavior relationships. In M. R. Barrick & A. M. Ryan (Eds.), *Personality and work: Reconsidering the role of personality in organizations* (pp. 60–82). San Francisco: Jossey-Bass.

Barrick, M. R., Mount, M. K., & Judge, T. A. (2001). Personality and performance at the beginning of the new millennium: What do we know and where do we go next? *International Journal of Selection and Assessment, 91*, 9–30.

Bartram, D. (2000). Internet recruitment and selection: Kissing frogs to find princes. *International Journal of Selection and Assessment, 8*, 261–274.

Bartram, D. (2005a). Computer-based testing and the internet. In A. Evers, N. Anderson, & O. Voskuijl (Eds.), *The Blackwell handbook of personnel selection* (pp. 399–418). Malden, MA: Blackwell.

Bartram, D. (2005b). The great eight competencies: A criterion-centric approach to validation. *Journal of Applied Psychology, 90*, 1185–1203.

Bartram, D. (2006a). The impact of technology on test manufacture, delivery and use and on the test taker. In D. Bartram & R. K. Hambleton (Eds.), *Computer-based testing and the internet: Issues and advances* (pp. 135–148). Chichester, UK: Wiley.

Bartram, D. (2006b). Testing on the internet: Issues, challenges and opportunities in the field of occupational assessment. In D. Bartram & R. K. Hambleton (Eds.), *Computer-based testing and the internet: Issues and advances* (pp. 13–37). Chichester, UK: Wiley.

Bartram, D., & Brown, A. (2004). Online testing: Mode of administration and the stability of OPQ 32i scores. *International Journal of Selection and Assessment, 12*, 278–284.

Bartram, D., & Hambleton, R. K. (2006). *Computer-based testiing and the internet: Issues and advances.* Chichester, UK: Wiley.

Bass, B. M. (1950). The leaderless group discussion. *Personnel Psychology, 3*, 17–32.

Bass, B. M. (1962). Further evidence on the dynamic character of criteria. *Personnel Psychology, 15*, 93–97.

Bauer, D. J., & Curran, P. J. (2004). The integration of continuous and discrete latent variable models: Potential problems and promising opportunities. *Psychological Methods, 9*, 3–29.

Baumeister, R. F. (2007). *Is there anything good about men?* Retrieved from www.psy.fsu. edu/~baumeistertice/goodaboutmen.htm

Bazerman, M. (2006). *Judgment in managerial decision making* (6th ed.). New York: Wiley.

Beach, L. R., & Connolly, T. (2005). *The psychology of decision making: People in organizations* (2nd ed.). Thousand Oaks, CA: Sage.

Becker, G. (2000). How important is transient error on estimating reliability? Going beyond simulation studies. *Psychological Methods, 57*, 370–379.

Beer, M., & Spector, B. (1993). Organizational diagnosis: Its role in organizational learning. *Journal of Counseling and Development, 71*, 642–650.

Bejar, I. I. (1993). A generative approach to psychological and educational measurement. In N. Frederiksen, R. J. Mislevy, & I. I. Bejar (Eds.), *Test theory for a new generation of tests* (pp. 323–357). Hillsdale, NJ: Lawrence Erlbaum Associates.

Bell, B. S., Wiechmann, D., & Ryan, A. M. (2006). Consequences of organizational justice expectations in a selection system. *Journal of Applied Psychology, 91*, 455–466.

Belov, D. I., & Armstrong, R. D. (2005). Monte Carlo test assembly for item pool analysis and extension. *Applied Psychological Measurement, 29*, 239–261.

Belov, D. I., & Armstrong, R. D. (2008). A Monte Carlo approach to the design, assembly, and evaluation of multistage adaptive tests. *Applied Psychological Measurement, 32*, 119–137.

Benson, M. J., & Campbell, J. P. (2007). To be, or not to be, linear: An expanded representation of personality and its relationship to leadership performance. *International Journal of Selection and Assessment, 15*, 232–249.

Beretvas, S. N. (2004). Comparison of bookmark difficulty locations under different item response models. *Applied Psychological Measurement, 28*, 25–47.

Bergeron, D. M. (2007). The potential paradox of organizational citizenship behavior: Good citizens at what cost? *Academy of Management Review, 32*, 1078–1095.

Bergman, M. E., Drasgow, F., Donovan, M. A., Henning, J. B., & Juraska, S. E. (2006). Scoring situational judgment tests: Once you get the data, your troubles begin. *International Journal of Selection and Assessment, 14*, 223–235.

Berk, R. A., & Rossi, P. H. (1990). *Thinking about program evaluation.* Newbury Park, CA: Sage.

Bernardin, H. J., & Beatty, R. W. (1984). *Performance appraisals: Assessing human behavior at work.* Boston: Kent.

Bernardin, H. J., & Buckley, M. R. (1981). Strategies in rater training. *Academy of Management Review, 6*, 205–212.

Bernardin, H. J., & Smith, P. C. (1981). A clarification of some issues regarding the developmeng and use of behaviorally anchored rating scales (BARS). *Journal of Applied Psychology, 66*, 458–463.

Bernardin, H. J., & Villanova, P. (1986). Performance appraisal. In E. A. Locke (Ed.), *Generalizing from laboratory to field settings* (pp. 43–62). Lexington, MA: Lexington Books.

Bernardin, H. J., & Villanova, P. (2005). Research streams in rater self-efficacy. *Group & Organization Management, 30*, 61–88.

Berry, C. M., Ones, D. S., & Sackett, P. R. (2007). Interpersonal deviance, organizational deviance, and their common correlates: A review and meta-analysis. *Journal of Applied Psychology, 92*, 410–424.

Berry, C. M., Page, R. C., & Sackett, P. R. (2007). Effects of self-deceptive enhancement on personality–job performance relationships. *International Journal of Selection and Assessment, 15*, 94–109.

Beyerlein, M. M., Freedman, S., McGee, C., & Moran, L. (2003). *Beyond teams: Building the collaborative organization.* San Francisco: Jossey-Bass.

Bickel, R. (2007). *Multilevel analysis for applied research: It's just regression!* (D. A. Kenny, Ed.). New York: Guilford Press.

Binning, J. F., & Barrett, G. V. (1989). Validity of personnel decisions: A conceptual analysis of the inferential and evidential bases. *Journal of Applied Psychology, 74*, 478–494.

Birkeland, S., Manson, T. M., Kisamore, J. L., Brannick, M. T., & Smith, M. A. (2006). A meta-analytic investigation of job applicant faking on personality measures. *International Journal of Selection and Assessment, 14*, 317–335.

Blackman, M. C. (2002). The employment interview via the telephone: Are we sacrificing accurate personality judgments for cost efficiency? *Journal of Research in Personality, 36*, 208–223.

Blancero, D., Boroski, J., & Dyer, L. (1996). Key competencies for a transformed human resource organization: Results of a field study. *Human Resource Management, 35*, 383–403.

Block, J. (1995). A contrarian view of the five-factor approach to personality description. *Psychological Bulletin, 117*, 187–215.

Bobko, P. (1983). An analysis of correlations corrected for attenuation and range restriction. *Journal of Applied Psychology, 68*, 584–589.

Bobko, P. (1990). Multivariate correlational analysis. In M. D. Dunnette & L. M. Hough (Eds.), *Handbook of industrial and organizational psychology* (2nd ed., pp. 637–686). Palo Alto, CA: Consulting Psychologists Press.

Bobko, P., & Roth, P. L. (2003). Meta-analysis and validity generalization as research tools: Issues of sample bias and degrees of misspecification. In K. R. Murphy (Ed.), *Validity generalization: A critical review.* Mahwah, NJ: Lawrence Erlbaum Associates.

Bond, L. (1993). Comments on the O'Neill & McPeek paper. In P. W. Holland & H. Wainer (Eds.), *Differential item functioning* (pp. 277–279). Hillsdale, NJ: Lawrence Erlbaum Associates.

Booth, J. F. (1998). The user interface in computer-based selection and assessment: Applied and theoretical problematics of an evolving technology. *International Journal of Selection and Assessment, 6*, 61–81.

Boring, E. G. (1919). Mathematical vs. scientific importance. *Psychological Bulletin, 16*, 335–338.

Boring, E. G. (1950). *A history of experimental psychology* (2nd ed.). New York: Appleton-Century-Crofts.

Boring, E. G. (1961). The beginning and growth of measurement in psychology. In H. Woolf (Ed.), *Quantification: A history of the meaning of measurement in the natural and social sciences* (pp. 108–127). Indianapolis, IN: Bobbs-Merrill.

Borman, W. C. (1987). Personal constructs, performance schemata, and "folk theories" of subordinate effectiveness: Explorations in an Army officer sample. *Organizational Behavior and Human Decision Processes, 40*, 307–322.

Borman, W. C. (2004). The concept of organizational citizenship. *Current Directions in Psychological Science, 13*, 238–241.

Borman, W. C., Buck, D. E., Hanson, M. A., Motowidlo, S. J., Stark, S., & Drasgow, F. (2001). An examination of the comparative reliability, validity, and accuracy of performance ratings made using computerized adaptive rating scales. *Journal of Applied Psychology, 86,* 965–973.

Borman, W. C., Hanson, M. A., & Hedge, J. W. (1997). Personnel selection. *Annual Review of Psychology, 48,* 299–337.

Borman, W. C., Kubisiak, U. C., & Schneider, R. J. (1999). Work styles. In N. G. Peterson et al. (Eds.), *An occupational information system for the 21st century: The development of O*NET* (pp. 213–226). Washington, DC: American Psychological Association.

Borman, W. C., & Motowidlo, S. J. (1993). Expanding the criterion domain to include elements of contextual performance. In N. Schmitt & W. C. Borman (Eds.), *Personnel selection in organizations* (pp. 71–98). San Francisco: Jossey-Bass.

Borman, W. C., White, L. A., & Dorsey, D. W. (1995). Effects of ratee task performance and interpersonal factors on supervisory and peer performance ratings. *Journal of Applied Psychology, 80,* 168–177.

Borman, W. C., White, L. A., Pulakos, E. D., & Oppler, S. H. (1991). Models of supervisory job performance ratings. *Journal of Applied Psychology, 76,* 863–872.

Born, M. P., & Jansen, P. G. W. (1997). Selection and assessment during organizational turnaround. In N. Anderson & P. Herriot (Eds.), *International handbook of selection and assessment* (pp. 247–265). Chichester, UK: Wiley.

Botwin, M. D., & Buss, D. M. (1989). Structure of act–report data: Is the five-factor model of personality recaptured? *Journal of Personality and Social Psychology, 56,* 988–1001.

Boudreau, J. W. (1983). Economic considerations in estimating the utility of human resource productivity improvement programs. *Personnel Psychology, 36,* 551–576.

Bourassa, G. L., & Guion, R. M. (1959). A factorial study of dexterity tests. *Journal of Applied Psychology, 43,* 199–204.

Brannick, M. T. (1986). The development and evaluation of some models for detecting the presence of noncompensatory combinations in phenomena of interest to industrial and organizational psychologists (Doctoral dissertation). *Dissertation Abstracts International, 47,* 3564B.

Brannick, M. T. (2001). Implications of empirical Bayes meta-analysis for test validation. *Journal of Applied Psychology, 86,* 468–480.

Brannick, M. T., & Brannick, J. P. (1989). Nonlinear and noncompensatory processes in performance evaluation. *Organizational Behavior and Human Decision Processes, 44,* 97–122.

Brannick, M. T., & Hall, S. M. (2003). Validity generalization from a Bayesian perspective. In K. R. Murphy (Ed.), *Validity generalization: A critical review* (pp. 339–364). Mahwah, NJ: Lawrence Erlbaum Associates.

Brannick, M. T., Levine, E. L., & Morgeson, F. P. (2007). *Job and work analysis* (2nd ed.). Los Angeles: Sage.

Braun, H. I., Jackson, D. N., & Wiley, D. E. (2002). *The role of constructs in psychological and educational measurement.* Mahwah, NJ: Lawrence Erlbaum Associates.

Bray, D. W., Campbell, R. J., & Grant, D. L. (1974). *Formative years in business: A long-term AT&T study of managerial lives.* New York: Wiley.

Brehmer, B. (1976). Note on clinical judgment and the formal characteristics of clinical tasks. *Psychological Bulletin, 83,* 778–782.

Brehmer, B. (1988). The development of social judgment theory. In B. Brehmer & C. R. B. Joyce (Eds.), *Human judgment: The SJT view* (pp. 13–39). North Holland: Elsevier Science Publishers.

Brehmer, B. (1999). Reasonable decision making in complex environments. In P. Juslin & H. Montgomery (Eds.), *Judgment and decision making: Neo-Brunswikian and process-tracing approaches* (pp. 9–21). Mahwah, NJ: Lawrence Erlbaum Associates.

Breithaupt, K., & Hare, D. R. (2007). Automated simultaneous assembly of multistage testlets for a high-stakes licensing examination. *Educational and Psychological Measurement, 67,* 5–20.

Breithaupt, K. J., Mills, C. N., & Melican, G. J. (2006). Facing the opportunities of the future. In D. Bartram & R. K. Hambleton (Eds.), *Computer-based testing and the internet: Issues and advances* (pp. 219–251). Chichester, UK: Wiley.

Brennan, R. L. (2001). *Generalizability theory.* New York: Springer.

Briggs, S. R. (1992). Assessing the five-factor model of personality description. *Journal of Personality, 60,* 253–293.

Brogden, H. E. (1946). On the interpretation of the correlation coefficient as a measure of predictive efficiency. *Journal of Educational Psychology, 35,* 65–76.

Brogden, H. E. (1949). When testing pays off. *Personnel Psychology, 2,* 171–183.

Brooks, M. E., & Highhouse, S. (2006). Can good judgment be measured? In J. A. Weekley & R. E. Ployhart (Eds.), *Situational judgment tests: Theory, measurement, and application* (pp. 39–55). Mahwah, NJ: Lawrence Erlbaum Associates.

Brown, R. D., & Hauenstein, N. M. A. (2005). Interrater agreement reconsidered: An alternative to the r_{wg} indices. *Organizational Research Methods, 87,* 165–184.

Brunswik, E. (1956). *Perception and the representative design of psychological experiments* (2nd ed.). Berkeley, CA: University of California Press.

Bureau of National Affairs. (1990). ADA: Americans With Disabilities Act: Text and analysis. *Labor Relations Reporter, 134*(11), S-3–S-47 (Supplement).

Burrill, L. E. (1982). Comparative studies of item bias methods. In R. A. Berk (Ed.), *Handbook of methods for detecting test bias* (pp. 161–179). Baltimore: Johns Hopkins University Press.

Caldwell, S. D., Herold, D. M., & Fedor, D. B. (2004). Toward an understanding of the relationships among organizational change, individual differences, and changes in person–environment fit: A cross-level study. *Journal of Applied Psychology, 89,* 868–882.

Caligiuri, P. M. (2006). Performance measurement in a cross-national context. In W. Bennett, Jr., C. E. Lance, & D. J. Woehr (Eds.), *Performance measurement: Current perspectives and future challenges* (pp. 227–243). Mahwah, NJ: Lawrence Erlbaum Associates.

Campbell, D. T. (1957). Factors relevant to the validity of experiments in social settings. *Psychological Bulletin, 54,* 297–312.

Campbell, D. T., & Fiske, D. W. (1959). Convergent and discriminant validation by the multitrait–multimethod matrix. *Psychological Bulletin, 56,* 81–105.

Campbell, J. P. (1999). *The changing nature of performance: Implications for staffing, motivation, and development* (D. Ilgen & E. D. Pulakos, Eds.) (pp. 399–429). San Francisco: Jossey-Bass.

Campbell, J. P., McCloy, R. A., Oppler, S. H., & Sager, C. E. (1993). A theory of performance. In N. Schmitt & W. C. Borman (Eds.), *Personnel selection in organizations* (pp. 35–70). San Francisco: Jossey-Bass.

Campbell, J. T. (1962). Assessments of higher level personnel. I. Background and scope of the research. *Personnel Psychology, 15,* 57–62.

Campbell, J. T., Otis, J. L., Liske, R. E., & Prien, E. P. (1962). Assessments of higher level personnel. II. Validity of the overall selection process. *Personnel Psychology, 15,* 63–74.

Campbell, W. J., & Reilly, M. E. (2000). Accommodations for persons with disabilities. In J. F. Kehoe (Ed.), *Managing selection in changing organizations: Human resource strategies* (pp. 319–367). San Francisco: Jossey-Bass.

Campion, M. A., Campion, J. E., & Hudson, J. P., Jr. (1994). Structured interviewing: A note on incremental validity and alternative question types. *Journal of Applied Psychology, 79,* 998–1002.

Campion, M. A., Palmer, D. K., & Campion, J. E. (1997). A review of structure in the selection interview. *Personnel Psychology, 50,* 655–702.

Campion, M. A., Pursell, E. D., & Brown, B. K. (1988). Structured interviewing: Raising the psychometric properties of the employment interview. *Personnel Psychology, 41,* 25–42.

Cardy, R. L., & Kehoe, J. F. (1984). Rater selective attention ability and appraisal effectiveness: The effect of cognitive styles on the accuracy of differentiation among ratees. *Journal of Applied Psychology, 69,* 589–594.

Carretta, T. R., & Ree, M. J. (2000). General and specific cognitive and psychomotor abilities in personnel selection: The prediction of training and job performance. *International Journal of Selection and Assessment, 8,* 227–236.

Carretta, T. R., & Ree, M. J. (2001). Pitfalls of ability research. *International Journal of Selection and Assessment, 9,* 325–335.

Carrier, M. R., Dalessio, A. T., & Brown, S. H. (1990). Correspondence between estimates of content and criterion-related validity values. *Personnel Psychology, 43,* 85–100.

Carroll, J. B. (1976). Psychometric tests as cognitive tasks: A new "structure of intellect." In L. B. Resnick (Ed.), *The nature of intelligence* (pp. 27–56). Hillsdale, NJ: Lawrence Erlbaum Associates.

Carroll, J. B. (1993). *Human cognitive abilities: A survey of factor-analytic studies.* New York: Cambridge University Press.

Carroll, J. B., Meade, A., & Johnson, E. S. (1991). Test analysis with the person characteristic function: Implications for defining abilities. In R. E. Snow & D. E. Wiley (Eds.), *Improving inquiry in social science: A volume in honor of Lee J. Cronbach* (pp. 109–143). Hillsdale, NJ: Lawrence Erlbaum Associates.

Cascio, W. F. (2003). *Managing human resources: Productivity, quality of work life, profits* (6th ed.). Boston: McGraw-Hill.

Cascio, W. F., Jacobs, R., & Silva, J. (2010). Validity, utility, and adverse impact: Practical implications from 30 years of data. In J. L. Outtz (Ed.), *Adverse impact: Implications for organizational staffing and high stakes selection* (pp. 271–288). New York: Routledge.

Catano, V. M., Cronshaw, S. F., Wiesner, W. H., Hackett, R. D., & Methot, L. L. (1997). *Recruitment and selection in Canada.* Toronto, Canada: ITP Nelson.

Cattell, J. M. (1890). Mental tests and measurements. *Mind, 15,* 373–380.

Cattell, R. B. (1944). Psychological measurement: Normative, ipsative, interactive. *Psychological Review, 51,* 292–303.

Cattell, R. B. (1949). r_p and other coefficients of pattern similarity. *Psychometrika, 14,* 279–298.

Cattell, R. B. (1963). Theory of fluid and crystallized intelligence: A critical experiment. *Journal of Educational Psychology, 54,* 1–22.

Cattell, R. B. (1986). The actual trait, state, and situational factors important in functional testing. In R. B. Cattell & R. C. Johnson (Eds.), *Functional psychological testing: Principles and instruments* (pp. 33–53). New York: Brunner/Mazel.

Cattin, P. (1978). A predictive-validity-based procedure for choosing between regression and equal weights. *Organizational Behavior and Human Performance, 22,* 93–102.

Chan, D. (2002). Longitudinal modeling. In S. G. Rogelberg (Ed.), *Handbook of research methods in industrial and organizational psychology* (pp. 412–430). Oxford, UK: Blackwell.

Chan, D., & Schmitt, N. (2004). An agenda for future research on applicant reactions to selection procedures: A construct-oriented approach. *International Journal of Selection and Assessment, 12,* 9–23.

Chan, D., & Schmitt, N. (2005). Situational judgment tests. In A. Evers, N. Anderson, & O. Voskuijl (Eds.), *The Blackwell handbook of personnel selection* (pp. 219–242). Malden, MA: Blackwell.

Chapman, D. S., & Rowe, P. M. (2002). The influence of videoconference technology and interview structure on the recruiting function of the employment interview. *International Journal of Selection and Assessment, 10,* 185–197.

Chapman, D. S., & Webster, J. (2003). The use of technologies in recruiting, screening, and selection processes for job candidates. *International Journal of Selection and Assessment, 11,* 113–120.

Christal, R. E., & Weissmuller, J. J. (1988). Job–task inventory analysis. In S. Gael (Ed.), *The job analysis handbook for business, industry, and government* (Vol. 2, pp. 1036–1050). New York: Wiley.

Cisek, G. J. (2001). *Setting performance standards.* Mahwah, NJ: Lawrence Erlbaum Associates.

Civil Rights Act (1964). 42 US Code. Pub.L. 88–352, 78 Stat. 241, enacted July 2, 1964.

Civil Rights Act of 1991 (1991). 42 U.S. Code 1981A. Pub.L. 102–166, 105 Stat. 1071.

Claudy, J. G. (1978). Multiple regression and validity estimation in one sample. *Applied Psychological Measurement, 2,* 595–607.

Cleary, T. A. (1968). Test bias: Prediction of grades of Negro and white students in integrated colleges. *Journal of Educational Measurement, 5,* 115–124.

Clegg, C. W., & Wall, T. D. (1981). A note on some new scales for measuring aspects of psychological well-being at work. *Journal of Occupational Psychology, 54,* 221–225.

Coch, L., & French, J. R. P., Jr. (1948). Overcoming resistance to change. *Human Relations, 1,* 512–532.

Coens, T., & Jenkins, M. (2000). *Abolishing performance appraisals: Why they backfire and what to do instead.* San Francisco: Berrett-Koehler.

Cohen, A., Doveh, E., & Eick, U. (2001). Statistical properties of the $r_{WG(J)}$ index of agreement. *Psychological Methods, 6,* 297–310.

Cohen, J. (1960). A coefficient of agreement for nominal scales. *Educational and Psychological Measurement, 20,* 37–46.

Cohen, J. (1983). The cost of dichotomization. *Applied Psychological Measurement, 7,* 249–253.

Cohen, J. (1988). *Statistical power analysis for the behavioral sciences* (2nd ed.). Hillsdale, NJ: Lawrence Erlbaum Associates.

Cohen, J. (1990). Things I have learned (so far). *American Psychologist, 45,* 1304–1312.

Cohen, P. (2008). *Applied data analytic techniques for turning points research.* New York: Routledge.

Cohen, P., Gordon, K., Kasen, S., & Chen, H. (2008). Developmental structural change in the maturity of role assumption. In P. Cohen (Ed.), *Applied data analytic techniques for turning points research* (pp. 195–214). New York: Routledge.

Cole, N. S. (1973). Bias in selection. *Journal of Educational Measurement, 10,* 237–255.

Coleman, V. I., & Borman, W. C. (2000). Investigating the underlying structure of the citizenship performance domain. *Human Resource Management Review, 10,* 25–44.

Collings, D. G., Scullion, H., & Morley, M. J. (2007). Changing patterns of global staffing in the multinational enterprise: Challenges to the conventional expatriate assignment and emerging alternatives. *Journal of World Business, 42*, 198–213.

Collins, J. M., Schmidt, F. L., Sanchez-Ku, M., Thomas, L., McDaniel, M. A., & Le, H. (2003). Can basic individual differences shed light on the construct meaning of assessment center evaluations? *International Journal of Selection and Assessment, 11*, 17–29.

Connecticut v. Teal. (1982) (Vol. 457 U.S., p. 440).

Conway, J. M., Jako, R. A., & Goodman, D. F. (1995). A meta-analysis of interrater and internal consistency reliability of selection interviews. *Journal of Applied Psychology, 80*, 565–579.

Cook, T. D., & Campbell, D. T. (1979). *Quasi-experimentation: Design and analysis for field settings.* Chicago: Rand-McNally.

Cook, T. D., Campbell, D. T., & Peracchio, L. (1990). Quasi-experimentation. In M. D. Dunnette & L. M. Hough (Eds.), *Handbook of industrial and organizational psychology* (2nd ed., Vol. 2). Palo Alto, CA: Consulting Psychologists Press.

Coombs, C. H., Dawes, R. H., & Tversky, A. (1970). *Mathematical psychology: An elementary introduction.* Englewood Cliffs, NJ: Prentice Hall.

Cooper, W. H. (1981). Ubiquitous halo. *Psychological Bulletin, 90*, 218–244.

Cortina, J. M. (1993). What is coefficient alpha? An examination of theory and applications. *Journal of Applied Psychology, 78*, 98–104.

Coward, W. M., & Sackett, P. R. (1990). Linearity of ability–performance relationships: A reconfirmation. *Journal of Applied Psychology, 75*, 297–300.

Crandall, L. G., White, D. L., Schuldheis, S., & Talerico, K. A. (2007). Initiating person-centered practices in long-term care facilities. *Journal of Gerontological Nursing, 33*(11), 47–56.

Cranny, C. J., & Doherty, M. E. (1988). Importance ratings in job analysis: Note on the misinterpretation of factor analyses. *Journal of Applied Psychology, 73*, 320–322.

Cronbach, L. J. (1951). Coefficient alpha and the internal structure of tests. *Psychometrika, 16*, 297–334.

Cronbach, L. J. (1955). Processes affecting scores on "understanding of others" and "assumed similarity." *Psychological Bulletin, 52*, 177–193.

Cronbach, L. J. (1957). The two disciplines of scientific psychology. *American Psychologist, 12*, 671–684.

Cronbach, L. J. (1970). *Essentials of psychological testing* (3rd ed.). New York: Harper and Row.

Cronbach, L. J. (1971). Test validation. In R. L. Thorndike (Ed.), *Educational measurement* (2nd ed., pp. 443–507). Washington, DC: American Council on Education.

Cronbach, L. J. (1975). Beyond the two disciplines of scientific psychology. *American Psychologist, 30*, 116–127.

Cronbach, L. J. (1980). Validity on parole: How can we go straight? *Proceeding of the ETS Invitation Conference, Measuring Achievement: Progress Over a Decade,* Vol. 5, pp. 99–108.

Cronbach, L. J. (1988). Five perspectives on validity argument. In H. Wainer & H. I. Braun (Eds.), *Test validity* (pp. 3–17). Hillsdale, NJ: Lawrence Erlbaum Associates.

Cronbach, L. J., & Gleser, G. C. (1957). *Psychological tests and personnel decisions.* Urbana, IL: University of Illinois Press.

Cronbach, L. J., & Gleser, G. C. (1965). *Psychological tests and personnel decisions* (2nd ed.). Urbana, IL: University of Illinois Press.

Cronbach, L. J., Gleser, G. C., Nanda, H., & Rajaratnam, N. (1972). *The dependability of behavioral measurements: Theory of generalizability for scores and profiles.* New York: Wiley.

Cronbach, L. J., & Meehl, P. E. (1955). Construct validity in psychological tests. *Psychological Bulletin, 52,* 281–302.

Cullen, M. J., Hardison, C. M., & Sackett, P. R. (2004). Using SAT-grade and ability–job performance relationships to test predictions derived from stereotype threat theory. *Journal of Applied Psychology, 89,* 220–230.

Cunningham-Snell, N., & Wigfield, D. (2005). Selection of leaders in global organizations. In A. Evers, N. Anderson, & O. Voskuijl (Eds.), *The Blackwell handbook of personnel selection* (pp. 440–457). Malden, MA: Blackwell.

Cureton, E. E. (1950a). Validity, reliability, and baloney. *Educational and Psychological Measurement, 10,* 94–96.

Cureton, E. E. (1950b). Validity. In E. F. Lindquist (Ed.), *Educational measurement* (pp. 621–694). Washington, DC: American Council on Education.

Cureton, E. E. (1958). The definition and estimation of test reliability. *Educational and Psychological Measurement, 18,* 715–738.

Daboud, A. J., Rasheed, A. M. A., Priem, R. L., & Gray, D. A. (1995). Top management team characteristics and corporate illegal activity. *Academy of Management Review, 20,* 138–170.

Dachler, H. P. (1989). Selection and the organizational context. In P. Herriot (Ed.), *Assessment and selection in organizations: Methods and practice for recruitment and appraisal* (pp. 45–69). Chichester, UK: Wiley.

Dalessio, A., & Imada, A. (1984). Relationships between interview selection decisions and perceptions of applicant similarity to an ideal employee and self: A field study. *Human Relations, 37*(1), 67–80.

Daniels, H. W., & Otis, J. L. (1950). A method for analyzing employment interviews. *Personnel Psychology, 3,* 425–444.

Dawes, R. M. (1979). The robust beauty of improper linear models in decision making. *American Psychologist, 34,* 571–582.

Dawes, R. M. (1991, June). *Discovering "human nature" versus discovering how people cope with the task of getting through college: An extension of Sears's argument.* Presented at the American Psychological Society, Washington, DC.

Dawes, R. M., & Corrigan, B. (1974). Linear models in decision making. *Psychological Bulletin, 81,* 95–106.

Day, D. V., & Silverman, S. B. (1989). Personality and job performance. *Personnel Psychology, 42,* 25–36.

Day, D. V., & Sulsky, L. M. (1995). Effects of frame-of-reference training and information configuration on memory organization and rating accuracy. *Journal of Applied Psychology, 80,* 158–167.

Day, V. B., Erwin, F., & Koral, A. M. (1981). *A professional and legal analysis of the Uniform Guidelines on employee selection procedures.* Berea, OH: American Society for Personnel Administration.

Dayan, K., Fox, S., & Kasten, R. (2008). The preliminary employment interview as a predictor of assessment center outcomes. *International Journal of Selection and Assessment, 16,* 102–111.

Dean, M. A., & Russell, C. J. (2005). An examination of biodata theory-based constructs in a field context. *International Journal of Selection and Assessment, 13,* 139–149.

De Corte, W., & Lievens, F. (2005). The risk of adverse impact in selection based on a test with known effect size. *Educational and Psychological Measurement, 65,* 737–758.

De Corte, W., Lievens, F., & Sackett, P. R. (2007). Combining predictors to achieve optimal trade-offs between selection quality and adverse impact. *Journal of Applied Psychology, 92,* 1380–1393.

De Corte, W., Van Iddekinge, F., & Sackett, P. R. (2006). Predicting adverse impact and mean criterion performance in multistage selection. *Journal of Applied Psychology, 91,* 523–537.

DeGroot, T., & Motowidlo, S. J. (1999). Why visual and vocal interview cues can affect interviewers' judgments and predict job performance. *Journal of Applied Psychology, 84,* 986–993.

DeMaris, A. (2004). *Regression with social data: Modeling continuous and limited response variables.* Hoboken, NJ: Wiley-Interscience.

de Meijer, L. A. L., Born, M. P., van Zielst, J., & van der Molen, H. T. (2007). Analyzing judgments of ethnically diverse applicants during personnel selection: A study at the Dutch police. *International Journal of Selection and Assessment, 15,* 139–152.

Dennis, I., Handley, S., Bradon, P., Evans, J., & Newstead, S. (2002). Approaches to modeling item-generative tests. In S. Irvine & H. Kyllonen (Eds.), *Item generation for test development* (pp. 53–71). Mahwah, NJ: Lawrence Erlbaum Associates.

De Pater, I. E., Van Vianen, A. E. M., Bechtoldt, M. N., & Klehe, U.-C. (2009). Employees' challenging job experiences and supervisors' evaluations of promotability. *Personnel Psychology, 62,* 297–325.

DeShon, R. P. (2002). Generalizability theory. In F. Drasgow & N. Schmitt (Eds.), *Measuring and analyzing behavior in organizations* (pp. 189–220). San Francisco: Jossey-Bass.

Dierdorff, E. C., & Surface, E. A. (2007). Placing peer ratings in context: Systematic influences beyond ratee performance. *Personnel Psychology, 60,* 93–126.

Digman, J. M. (1990). Personality structure: Emergence of the five-factor model. *Annual Review of Psychology, 41,* 417–440.

Dilchert, S., & Ones, D. S. (2009). Assessment center dimensions: Individual differences correlates and meta-analytical incremental validity. *International Journal of Selection and Assessment, 17,* 254–270.

Dipboye, R. L. (2005). The selection/recruitment interview: Core processes and contexts. In A. Evers, N. Anderson, & O. Voskuijl (Eds.), *The Blackwell handbook of personnel selection* (pp. 121–142). Malden, MA: Blackwell.

Dipboye, R. L., & Jackson, S. L. (1999). Interviewer experience and expertise effects. In R. W. Eder & M. M. Harris (Eds.), *The employment interview handbook* (pp. 259–278). Thousand Oaks, CA: Sage.

Dipboye, R. L., Wooten, K., & Halverson, S. K. (2004). Behavioral and situational interviews. In M. Hersen (Ed.), *Comprehensive handbook of psychological assessment* (Vol. 4, pp. 297–316). Hoboken, NJ: Wiley.

Divlin, S. E., Abrahams, N. M., & Edwards, J. E. (1992). Empirical keying of biographical data: Cross validity as a function of scaling procedure and sample size. *Military Psychology, 4,* 119–136.

Doering, P. F. (1992). Letter to the Editor. *Smithsonian (Washington, DC), 23*(3), 14.

Doherty, M. E., & Balzer, W. K. (1988). Cognitive feedback. In B. Brehmer & C. R. B. Joyce (Eds.), *Human judgment: The SJT view* (pp. 163–197). North Holland: Elsevier Science Publishers.

Dorans, N. J., & Holland, P. W. (1993). Dif detection and description: Mantel-Haenszel and standardization. In P. W. Holland & H. Wainer (Eds.), *Differential item functioning* (pp. 35–66). Hillsdale, NJ: Lawrence Erlbaum Associates.

Dorsey, D., Cortina, J., & Luchman, J. (2010). Adaptive and citizenship-related behaviors at work. In J. L. Farr & N. T. Tippins (Eds.), *Handbook of employee selection* (pp. 463–487). New York: Routledge.

Dothard v. Rawlinson. (1977) (Vol. 426 U.S., p. 321).

Dougherty, T. W., Ebert, R. J., & Callender, J. C. (1986). Policy capturing in the employment interview. *Journal of Applied Psychology, 71,* 9–15.

Dougherty, T. W., Turban, D. B., & Callender, J. C. (1994). Confirming first impressions in the employment interview. *Journal of Applied Psychology, 79,* 659–665.

Drasgow, F. (1982). Biased test items and differential validity. *Psychological Bulletin, 92,* 526–531.

Drasgow, F. (1984). Scrutinizing psychological tests: Measurement equivalence and equivalent relations with external variables are the central issues. *Psychological Bulletin, 95,* 134–135.

Drasgow, F. (1987). Study of the measurement bias of two standardized psychological tests. *Journal of Applied Psychology, 72,* 19–29.

Drasgow, F., & Hulin, C. L. (1990). Item response theory. In M. D. Dunnette & L. M. Hough (Eds.), *Handbook of industrial and organizational psychology* (2nd ed., pp. 577–636). Palo Alto, CA: Consulting Psychologists Press.

Drasgow, F., & Mattern, K. (2006). New tests and new items: Opportunities and issues. In D. Bartram & R. K. Hambleton (Eds.), *Computer-based testing and the internet: Issues and advances* (pp. 59–75). Chichester, UK: Wiley.

Drauden, G. M. (1988). Task inventory analysis in industry and the public sector. In S. Gael (Ed.), *The job analysis handbook for business, industry, and government* (Vol. 1, pp. 1051–1071). New York: Wiley.

Dreher, G. F., Ash, R. A., & Hancock, P. (1988). The role of the traditional research design in underestimating the validity of the employment interview. *Personnel Psychology, 41,* 315–327.

Drever, J. (1952). *A dictionary of psychology.* Baltimore: Penguin.

Duarte, N. T., Goodson, J. R., & Klich, N. R. (1993). How do I like thee? Let me appraise the ways. *Journal of Organizational Behavior, 14,* 239–249.

Dudley, N. M., Orvis, K. A., Lebiecki, J. E., & Cortina, J. M. (2006). A meta-analytic investigation of conscientiousness in the prediction of job performance: Examining the intercorrelations and the incremental validity of narrow traits. *Journal of Applied Psychology, 91,* 40–57.

Duncan, T. E., Duncan, S. C., & Strycker, L. A. (2006). *An introduction to latent variable growth curve modeling.* Mahwah, NJ: Lawrence Erlbaum Associates.

Dunnette, M. D. (1963a). A modified model for test validation and selection research. *Journal of Applied Psychology, 47,* 317–323.

Dunnette, M. D. (1963b). A note on the criterion. *Journal of Applied Psychology, 47,* 251–254.

Dunnette, M. D. (1992). It was nice to be there: Construct validity then and now. *Human Performance, 5,* 157–169.

Dunnette, M. D., & Borman, W. C. (1979). Personnel selection and classification systems. *Annual Review of Psycholgy, 30,* 477–525.

Dupper, O., & Strydom, E. M. L. (2004). *Essential employment discrimination law.* Lansdowne, South Africa: Juta Law.

Dwight, S. A., & Donovan, J. J. (2003). Do warnings not to fake reduce faking? *Human Performance, 16,* 1–23.

Earley, P. C., Ang, S., & Tan, J.-S. (2006). *CQ: Developing cultural intelligence at work.* Stanford, CA: Stanford University Press.

Ebel, R. L. (1972). *Essentials of educational measurement.* Englewood Cliffs, NJ: Prentice Hall.

Edwards, A. L. (1976). *An introduction to linear regression and correlation.* San Francisco: Freeman.

Edwards, J. E., Scott, J. C., & Raju, N. S. (2003). *The human resources program-evaluation handbook.* Thousand Oaks, CA: Sage.

Eels, R., & Walton, C. (1961). *Conceptual foundations of business.* Homewood, IL: Irwin.

Einhorn, H. J., & Hogarth, R. M. (1975). Unit weighting schemes for decision making. *Organizational Behavior and Human Performance, 13,* 171–192.

Einhorn, H. J. (1971). Use of nonlinear, noncompensatory models as a function of task and amount of information. *Organizational Behavior and Human Performance, 6,* 1–27.

Ellis, A. P. J., West, B. J., Ryan, A. M., & DeShon, R. P. (2002). The use of impression management tactics in structured interviews: A function of test type. *Journal of Applied Psychology, 87,* 1200–1208.

Ellis, B. B., & Mead, A. D. (2002). Item analysis: Theory and practice using classical and modern test theory. In S. G. Rogelberg (Ed.), *Handbook of research methods in industrial and organizational psychology* (pp. 325–343). Oxford, UK: Blackwell.

Embretson, S. E. (1985). *Test design: Developments in psychology and psychometrics.* Orlando, FL: Academic Press.

Embretson, S. E. (1998). A cognitive design system approach to generating valid tests: Application to abstract reasoning. *Psychological Methods, 3,* 380–396.

Embretson, S. E. (2005). Measuring human intelligence with artificial intelligence: Adaptive item generation. In R. J. Sternberg & J. E. Pretz (Eds.), *Cognition & intelligence: Identifying the mechanisms of the mind* (pp. 251–267). Cambridge, UK: Cambridge University Press.

Embretson, S. E., & Reise, S. P. (2000). *Item response theory for psychologists.* Mahwah, NJ: Lawrence Erlbaum Associates.

Employment Equity Act, Annual Report 2006. Gatineau, Canada: Ministry of Labour (2007).

English, H. B., & English, A. C. (1958). *A comprehensive dictionary of psychological and psychoanalytic terms.* New York: Longmans, Green and Co.

Equal Employment Opportunity Commission. (1966). *Guidelines on employment testing procedures.* Washington, DC: Equal Employment Opportunity Commission.

Equal Employment Opportunity Commission. (1970). Guidelines on employee selection procedures. *Federal Register, 35*(149), 12333–12336. Washington, DC: Equal Employment Opportunity Commission.

Equal Employment Opportunity Commission, Civil Service Commission, Department of Labor, & Department of Justice. (1978). *Uniform guidelines on employee selection procedures. Federal Register, 43*(166), 38290–38315. Washington, DC: Equal Employment Opportunity Commission.

Evers, A., te Nijenhuis, J., & van der Flier, H. (2005). Ethnic bias and fairness in personnel selection: Evidence and consequences. In A. Evers, N. Anderson, & O. Voskuijl (Eds.), *The Blackwell handbook of personnel selection* (pp. 306–328). Malden, MA: Blackwell.

Eysenck, H. J. (1991). Dimensions of personality: 16, 5, or 3? Criteria for a taxonomic paradigm. *Personality and Individual Differences, 12,* 773–790.

Ezekiel, M. (1941). *Methods of correlation analysis* (2nd ed.). New York: Wiley.

Facteau, J. D., & Craig, S. B. (2001). Are performance appraisal ratings from different rating sources comparable? *Journal of Applied Psychology, 86*, 215–227.

Fagot, R. F. (1991). Reliability of ratings for multiple judges: Intraclass correlation and metric scales. *Applied Psychological Measurement, 15*, 1–11.

Faley, R. H., Kleinman, L. S., & Lengnick-Hall, M. L. (1984). Age discrimination and personnel psychology: A review and synthesis of the legal literature with implications for future research. *Personnel Psychology, 37*, 327–350.

Feild, H. S., & Holley, W. H. (1982). The relationship of performance appraisal system characteristics to verdicts in selected employment discrimination cases. *Academy of Management Journal, 25*, 392–406.

Feldman, J. M. (1981). Beyond attribution theory: Cognitive processes in performance appraisal. *Journal of Applied Psychology, 66*, 127–148.

Ferris, G. R., Witt, L. A., & Hochwarter, W. A. (2001). Interaction of social skill and general mental ability on job performance and salary. *Journal of Applied Psychology, 86*, 1075–1082.

Finch, W. H., & French, B. F. (2007). Detection of crossing differential item functioning. *Educational and Psychological Measurement, 67*, 565–582.

Fine, S. A. (1955). Functional job analysis. *Journal of Personnel Administration and Industrial Relations, 2*(1), 1–16.

Fine, S. A. (1988). Functional job analysis. In S. Gael (Ed.), *The job analysis handbook for business, industry, and government* (Vol 2, pp. 1019–1035). New York: Wiley.

Fine, S. A., & Cronshaw, S. F. (1999). *Functional job analysis: A foundation for human resources management.* Mahwah, NJ: Lawrence Erlbaum Associates.

Fine, S. A., & Getkate, M. (1995). *Benchmark tasks for job analysis: A guide for functional job analysis (FJA) scales.* Mahwah, NJ: Lawrence Erlbaum Associates.

Fisher, C. D. (2008). What if we took within-person performance variability seriously? *Industrial and Organizational Psychology, 1*, 185–189.

Fisher, C. D., & Noble, C. S. (2004). A within-person examination of correlates of performance and emotion while working. *Human Performance, 17*, 145–168.

Fisher, R. (1935). *The design of experiments.* Edinburgh, UK: Oliver & Boyd.

Fisicaro, S. A., & Lance, C. E. (1990). Implications of three causal models for the measurement of halo error. *Applied Psychological Measurement, 14*, 419–429.

Fleishman, E. A. (1988). Some new frontiers in personnel selection research. *Personnel Psychology, 41*, 679–701.

Fleishman, E. A., & Quaintance, M. K. (1984). *Taxonomies of human performance: The description of human tasks.* Orlando, FL: Academic Press.

Fleishman, E. A., & Reilly, M. E. (1992a). *Administrator's guide: F-JAS, Fleishman Job Analysis Survey.* Bethesda, MD: Consulting Psychologists Press.

Fleishman, E. A., & Reilly, M. E. (1992b). *Handbook of human abilities: Definitions, measurements, and job task requirements.* Palo Alto, CA: Consulting Psychologists Press.

Fletcher, C. (1990). The relationships between candidate personality, self-presentation strategies, and interviewer assessment in selection interviews: An empirical study. *Human Relations, 43*, 739–749.

Flowers, C. P., Oshima, T. C., & Raju, N. S. (1999). A description and demonstration of the polytomous-DFIT framework. *Applied Psychological Measurement, 23*, 309–326.

Fox, S., Bizman, A., & Garti, A. (2005). Is distributional appraisal more effective than the traditional performance appraisal method? *European Journal of Psychological Assessment, 21*, 165–172.

Frank, F. D., & Taylor, C. R. (2004). Talent management: Trends that will shape the future. *Human Resource Planning, 27*, 33–41.

Frederiksen, N., & Melville, S. D. (1954). Differential predictability in the use of test scores. *Educational and Psychological Measurement, 14*, 647–656.

French, J. W. (1951). *The description of aptitude and achievement tests in terms of rotated factors.* Psychometric Monographs, No. 5. Iowa City, IA: The Psychometric Society.

Freyd, M. (1923). Measurement in vocational selection: An outline of research procedures. *Journal of Personnel Research, 20*, 215–249, 268–284, 377–385.

Friedman, T. L. (2006). *The world is flat: A brief history of the twenty-first century (updated and expanded).* New York: Farrar, Strauss and Giroux.

Frisch, M. H. (1998). Designing the individual assessment process. In R. Jeanneret & R. Silzer (Eds.), *Individual psychological assessment: Predicting behavior in organizational settings* (pp. 135–177). San Francisco: Jossey-Bass.

Funke, J. (1998). Computer-based testing and training with scenarios from complex problem-solving research: Advantages and disadvantages. *International Journal of Selection and Assessment, 6*, 90–96.

Funke, U., & Schuler, H. (1998). Validity of stimulus and response components in a video test of social competence. *International Journal of Selection and Assessment, 6*, 115–123.

Furnham, A., Jensen, T., & Crump, J. (2008). Personality, intelligence and assessment centre expert ratings. *International Journal of Selection and Assessment, 16*, 356–365.

Gael, S. (1988). *The job analysis handbook for business, industry, and government.* New York: Wiley.

Galbraith, J. T. (1985). Training assessment center assessors: Applying principles of human judgment (Doctoral dissertation, 1985). *Dissertation Abstracts, 45*, 3104-B.

Gandy, J. A., Dye, D. A., & MacLane, C. N. (1994). Federal government selection: The individual achievement record. In H. S. Stokes, M. D. Mumford, & W. A. Owens (Eds.), *Biodata handbook: Theory, research, and use of biographical information in selection and performance prediction* (pp. 275–309). Palo Alto, CA: CPP Books.

Garonzik, R., Brockner, J., & Siegel, P. A. (2000). International assignees at risk for premature departure: The interactive effect of outcome favorability and procedural fairness. *Journal of Applied Psychology, 85*, 13–20.

Gaugler, B. B., Rosenthal, D. B., Thornton, G. C., III, & Benson, C. (1987). Meta-analysis of assessment center validity. *Journal of Applied Psychology, 72*, 493–511.

Gaur, A. S., Delios, A., & Singh, K. (2007). Institutional environments, staffing strategies, and subsidiary performance. *Journal of Management, 33*, 611–636.

Gehrlein, T. M., Dipboye, R. L., & Shahani, C. (1993). Nontraditional validity calculations and differential interviewer experience: Implications for selection interviewers. *Educational and Psychological Measurement, 52*, 457–469.

Gelman, A., & Hill, J. (2007). *Data analysis using regression and multilevel/hierarchical models.* Cambridge, UK: Cambridge University Press.

Genaidy, A. M., & Karwowski, W. (2003). Human performance in lean production environment: Critical assessment and research framework. *Human Factors and Ergonomics in Manufacturing, 13*, 317–330.

George, J. M., & Zhou, J. (2001). When openness to experience and conscientiousness are related to creative behavior: An interactional approach. *Journal of Applied Psychology, 86*, 513–524.

Gessner, T. L., & Klimoski, R. J. (2006). Making sense of situations. In J. A. Weekley & R. E. Ployhart (Eds.), *Situational judgment tests: Theory, measurement, and application* (pp. 13–38). Mahwah, NJ: Lawrence Erlbaum Associates.

Ghiselli, E. E. (1956). Dimensional problems of criteria. *Journal of Applied Psychology, 40*, 1–4.

Ghiselli, E. E. (1960a). Differentiation of tests in terms of the accuracy with which they predict for a given individual. *Educational and Psychological Measurement, 20*, 675–684.

Ghiselli, E. E. (1960b). The prediction of predictability. *Educational and Psychological Measurement, 20*, 3–8.

Ghiselli, E. E. (1964). Dr. Ghiselli comments on Dr. Tupes' note. *Personnel Psychology, 17*, 61–63.

Ghiselli, E. E. (1966). *The validity of occupational aptitude tests.* New York: Wiley.

Ghiselli, E. E., & Brown, C. W. (1949). The prediction of accidents of taxicab drivers. *Journal of Applied Psychology, 33*, 540–546.

Ghiselli, E. E., Campbell, J. P., & Zedeck, S. (1981). *Measurement theory for the behavioral sciences.* San Francisco: Freeman.

Ghiselli, E. E., & Haire, M. (1960). The validation of selection tests in the light of the dynamic character of criteria. *Personnel Psychology, 13*, 225–231.

Gibson, J. W., & Prien, E. P. (1977). Validation of minimum qualifications. *Public Personnel Management, 6*, 447–451, 456.

Gibson, W. M., & Weiner, J. A. (1998). Generating random parallel test forms using CTT in a computer-based environment. *Journal of Educational Measurement, 35*, 297–310.

Gigerenzer, G. (2004). Fast and frugal heuristics: The tools of bounded rationality. In D. J. Koehler & N. Harvey (Eds.), *Blackwell handbook of judgment and decision making* (pp. 62–88). Malden, MA: Blackwell.

Gillespie, J. Z., Guion, R. M., Colatat, M. C., Nolan, K. P., & Wolford, K. (2007). *Updating the police officer performance appraisal system.* Bowling Green State University, Bowling Green, OH: The Institute for Psychological Research and Application.

Gilmore, D. C., Stevens, C. K., Harrell-Cook, G., & Ferris, G. R. (1999). Impression management tactics. In R. W. Eder & M. M. Harris (Eds.), *The employment interview handbook* (pp. 321–336). Thousand Oaks, CA: Sage.

Goeters, K.-M., & Lorenz, B. (2002). On the implementation of item-generation principles for the design of aptitude testing in aviation. In S. H. Irvine & P. C. Kyllonen (Eds.), *Item generation for test development* (pp. 339–360). Mahwah, NJ: Lawrence Erlbaum Associates.

Goldberg, L. R. (1991). Human mind versus regression equation: Five contrasts. In D. Cicchetti & W. M. Grove (Eds.), *Thinking clearly about psychology. Volume 1: Matters of public interest (Essays in honor of Paul E. Meehl)* (pp. 173–184). Minneapolis: University of Minnesota Press.

Goldberg, L. R. (1995). What the hell took so long? Donald Fiske and the big-five factor structure. In P. E. Shrout & S. T. Fiske (Eds.), *Advances in personality research, methods, and theory.* Hillsdale, NJ: Lawrence Erlbaum Associates.

Goldberg, L. R. (Ed.). (1999). *The development of five-factor domain scales from the IPIP item pool.* Unpublished manuscript. Retrieved from http://ipip.ori.org/ipip/memo.ht

Golden Rule Insurance Company et al. v. Washburn et al., No. 419-76 (Circuit Court of Seventh Judicial Circuit, Sangamon County, IL, Stipulation for dismissal and order dismissing cause 1984).

Goldman, B. M., Gutek, B. A., Stein, J. H., & Lewis, K. (2006). Employment discrimination in organizations: Antecedents and consequences. *Journal of Management, 32*, 786–830.

Goldsmith, D. B. (1922). The use of the personal history blank as a salesmanship test. *Journal of Applied Psychology, 6*, 149–155.

Goldstein, I. L., & Ford, J. K. (2004). *Training in organizations: Needs assessment, development, and evaluation.* Belmont, CA: Wadsworth.

Goodstein, L., & Prien, E. P. (2006). *Using individual assessments in the workplace: A practical guide for HR professionals, trainers, and managers.* San Francisco: Pfeiffer.

Gorin, J. S., & Embretson, S. E. (2006). Item difficulty modeling of paragraph comprehension items. *Applied Psychological Measurement, 30*, 394–411.

Gorman, C. D., Clover, W. H., & Doherty, M. E. (1978). Can we learn anything about real people from "interviews" of paper people? Two studies of the external validity of a paradigm. *Organizational Behavior and Human Performance, 22*, 165–192.

Gough, H. G. (1985). A work orientation scale for the California Psychological Inventory. *Journal of Applied Psychology, 70*, 505–513.

Gowing, M. K., Kraft, J. D., & Quick, J. C. (1998). *The new organizational reality: Downsizing, restructuring, and revitalization.* Washington, DC: American Psychological Association.

Graves, L. M., & Karren, R. J. (1999). Are some interviewers better than others? In R. W. Eder & M. M. Harris (Eds.), *The employment interview handbook* (pp. 243–258). Thousand Oaks, CA: Sage.

Green, B. F. (1950). A note on the calculation of weights for maximum battery reliability. *Psychometrika, 15*, 57–61.

Greener, J. M., & Osburn, H. G. (1980). Accuracy of corrections for restriction of range due to explicit selection in heteroscedastic and nonlinear distributions. *Educational and Psychological Measurement, 40*, 337–346.

Griffin, R. W., & Lopez, Y. (2005). "Bad behavior" in organizations: A review and typology for future research. *Journal of Management, 31*, 988–1005.

Griggs v. Duke Power Co. (1971) (Vol. 401 U.S., p. 424).

Gruys, M. L., & Sackett, P. R. (2003). Investigating the dimensionality of counterproductive work behavior. *International Journal of Selection and Assessment, 11*, 30–42.

Guilford, J. P. (1936). *Psychometric methods.* New York: McGraw-Hill.

Guilford, J. P. (1954). *Psychometric methods* (2nd ed.). New York: McGraw-Hill.

Guilford, J. P. (1956). The structure of intellect. *Psychological Bulletin, 53*, 267–293.

Guilford, J. P. (1959). *Personality.* New York: McGraw-Hill.

Guion, D. M. (1973). *Music and experimental science in sixteenth century Italy.* Unpublished Master's thesis, University of California, San Diego.

Guion, R. M. (1954). Regression analysis: Prediction from classified variables. *Psychological Bulletin, 51*, 505–510.

Guion, R. M. (1961). Criterion measurement and personnel judgments. *Personnel Psychology, 14*, 141–149.

Guion, R. M. (1965a). *Personnel testing.* New York: McGraw-Hill.

Guion, R. M. (1965b). Synthetic validity in a small company: A demonstration. *Personnel Psychology, 18*, 49–63.

Guion, R. M. (1974). Open a new window: Validities and values in psychological measurement. *American Psychologist, 29*, 287–296.

Guion, R. M. (1976). Recruitment, selection, and job placement. In M. D. Dunnette (Ed.), *Handbook of industrial and organizational psychology* (pp. 777–828). Chicago: Rand-McNally.

Guion, R. M. (1980). On trinitarian doctrines of validity. *Professional Psychology*, *117*, 385–398.

Guion, R. M. (1983a, August). *The ambiguity of validity: The growth of my discontent.* Presidential address to the Division of Evaluation and Measurement presented at the American Psychological Association, Anaheim, CA.

Guion, R. M. (1983b). Comments on Hunter. In F. Landy, S. Zedeck & J. Cleveland (Eds.), *Performance measurement and theory* (pp. 267–275). Hillsdale, NJ: Lawrence Erlbaum Associates.

Guion, R. M. (1987a). Actions, beliefs, and content: Some ABCs of validity. In C. J. Cranny (Ed.), *Content validity III: Proceedings* (pp. 1–12). Bowling Green, OH: Bowling Green State University.

Guion, R. M. (1987b). Changing views for personnel selection research. *Personnel Psychology*, *40*, 199–213.

Guion, R. M. (1991). Personnel assessment, selection, and placement. In M. D. Dunnette & L. M. Hough (Eds.), *The handbook of industrial and organizational psychology* (2nd ed., Vol. 2, pp. 327–397). Palo Alto, CA: Consulting Psychologists Press.

Guion, R. M. (1997). Criterion measures and the criterion dilemma. In N. Anderson & P. Herriot (Eds.), *International handbook of selection and assessment* (pp. 267–286). Chichester, UK: Wiley.

Guion, R. M. (1998). *Assessment, measurement, and prediction for personnel decisions.* Mahwah, NJ: Lawrence Erlbaum Associates.

Guion, R. M., & Gottier, R. F. (1965). Validity of personnel measures in personnel selection. *Personnel Psychology*, *40*, 135–164.

Guion, R. M., Highhouse, S., Reeve, C., & Zickar, M. J. (2005). *The self-descriptive index.* Bowling Green, OH: Sequential Employment Testing.

Gulliksen, H. (1950a). Intrinsic validity. *American Psychologist*, *5*, 511–517.

Gulliksen, H. (1950b). *Theory of mental tests.* New York: Wiley.

Gully, S. M., Incalaterra, K. A., Joshi, A., & Beaubien, J. M. (2002). A meta-analysis of team efficacy, potency, and performance: Interdependence and level of analysis as moderators of observed relationships. *Journal of Applied Psychology*, *87*, 819–832.

Gutenberg, R. L., Arvey, R. D., Osburn, H. D., & Jeanneret, P. R. (1983). Moderating effects of decision making/information-processing job dimensions on test validities. *Journal of Applied Psychology*, *68*, 602–608.

Gutman, A. (2000). *EEO law and personnel practices* (2nd ed.). Thousand Oaks, CA: Sage.

Gutman, A. (2010). *EEO law and personnel practices* (3rd ed.). New York: Taylor & Francis.

Gutman, A., & Dunleavy, E. M. (2009). On the legal front: The Supreme Court ruling in *Ricci* v. *Destefano*. *The Industrial-Organizational Psychologist*, *47*, 57–71.

Gutman, A., Koppes, L. I., & Vodanovich, S. J. (2010). *EEO law and personnel practices* (3rd ed.). New York: Routledge.

Guttman, L. (1945). A basis for analyzing test–retest reliability. *Psychometrika*, *10*, 255–282.

Guttman, L. (1955). A generalized simplex for factor analysis. *Psychometrika*, *20*, 173–192.

Hackett, R. D., Bycio, P., & Guion, R. M. (1989). Absenteeism among hospital nurses: An idiographic–longitudinal analysis. *Academy of Management Journal*, *32*, 424–453.

Hackman, J. R. (2009). The perils of positivity. *Journal of Organizational Behavior*, *30*, 309–319.

Hakel, M. D. (1989). The state of employment interview theory and research. In R. W. Eder & G. R. Ferris (Eds.), *The employment interview: Theory, research, and practice* (pp. 285–293). Newbury Park, CA: Sage.

Hambleton, R. K. (1989). Principles and selected applications of item response theory. In R. L. Linn (Ed.), *Educational measurement* (3rd ed., pp. 147–200). New York: American Council on Education/Macmillan.

Hambleton, R. K., & Swaminathan, H. (1985). *Item response theory: Principles and applications.* Boston: Klewer-Nijhoff.

Hammond, K. R. (1966). Probablistic functionalism: Egon Brunswik's integration of the history, theory, and method of psychology. In K. R. Hammond (Ed.), *The psychology of Egon Brunswik* (pp. 15–80). New York: Holt, Rinehart, & Winston.

Hammond, K. R. (1993). Naturalistic decision making from a Brunswikian viewpoint: Its past, present, and future. In G. A. Klein et al. (Eds.), *Decision making in action: Models and methods* (pp. 205–227). Norwood, NJ: Ablex.

Hammond, K. R. (1996). *Human judgment and social policy: Irreducible uncertainty, inevitable error, unavoidable injustice.* New York: Oxford University Press.

Hammond, K. R., Hamm, R. M., Grassia, J., & Pearson, T. (1987). Direct comparison of the efficacy of intuitive and analytical cognition in expert judgment. *IEEE Transactions on Systems, Man, and Cybernetics, 17,* 753–770.

Hammond, K. R., & Summers, D. A. (1972). Cognitive control. *Psychological Review, 79,* 58–67.

Hanges, P., Lord, R. E., Godfrey, E., & Raver, J. L. (2002). Modeling nonlinear relationships: Neural networks and catastrophe analysis. In S. G. Rogelberg (Ed.), *Handbook of research methods in industrial and organizational psychology* (pp. 431–455). Oxford: Blackwell.

Hanson, M. A., & Borman, W. A. (2006). Citizenship performance: An integrative review and motivational analysis. In W. Bennett, Jr., C. E. Lance, & D. J. Woehr (Eds.), *Performance measurement: Current perspectives and future challenges* (pp. 141–173). Mahwah, NJ: Lawrence Erlbaum Associates.

Harold, C. M., McFarland, L. A., & Weekley, J. A. (2006). The validity of verifiable and non-verifiable biodata items: An examination across applicants and incumbents. *International Journal of Selection and Assessment, 14,* 336–346.

Harris, J., & Brannick, J. (1999). *Finding and keeping great employees.* New York: AMACOM.

Harris, M. M. (1989). Reconsidering the employment interview: A review of recent literature and suggestions for future research. *Personnel Psychology, 42,* 691–726.

Harrison, D. A. (2002). Structure and timing in limited range dependent variables: Regression models for predictinig if and when. In F. Drasgow & N. Schmitt (Eds.), *Measuring and analyzing behavior in organizations* (pp. 446–497). San Francisco: Jossey-Bass.

Harrison, D. A. (2007). Pitching fits in applied psychological research. In C. Ostroff & T. A. Judge (Eds.), *Perspectives on organizational fit* (pp. 389–416). New York: Lawrence Erlbaum Associates.

Harrison, D. A., & Klein, K. J. (2007). What's the difference? Diversity constructs as separation, variety, or disparity in organizations. *Academy of Management Review, 32,* 1199–1228.

Hartigan, J. A., & Wigdor, A. K. (1989). *Fairness in employment testing: Validity generalization, minority issues, and the General Aptitude Test Battery.* Washington, DC: National Academy Press.

Hartman, E. A., Mumford, M. D., & Mueller, S. (1992). Validity of job classifications: An examination of alternative indicators. *Human Performance*, *5*, 191–211.

Harvey, M., & Novicevic, M. M. (2002). The hypercompetitive global marketplace: The importance of intuition amd creativity in expatriate managers. *Journal of World Business*, *37*, 127–138.

Harvey, R. J. (1986). Quantitative approaches to job classification: A review and critique. *Personnel Psychology*, *39*, 267–289.

Hastie, R., & Dawes, R. M. (2001). *Rational choice in an uncertain world: The psychology of judgment and decision making.* Thousand Oaks, CA: Sage.

Hattrup, K., Schmitt, N., & Landis, R. S. (1992). Equivalence of constructs measured by job-specific and commercially available aptitude tests. *Journal of Applied Psychology*, *77*, 298–308.

Hauenstein, N. M. A., & Alexander, R. A. (1991). Rating ability in performance judgments: The joint influence of implicit theories and intelligence. *Organizational Behavior and Human Decision Processes*, *50*, 300–323.

Hawk, J. A. (1970). Linearity of ability–performance relationships: A reconfirmation. *Measurement and Evaluation in Guidance*, *2*, 249–251.

Hedge, J. W., Teachout, M. S., & Laue, F. J. (1990). *Interview testing as a work sample measure of job proficiency* (Tech. Rep. No. AFHRL-TP-89-60). Brooks Air Force Base, TX: Air Force Systems Command.

Hedges, L. V. (1988). The meta-analysis of test validity studies: Some new approaches. In H. Wainer & H. W. Braun (Eds.), *Test validity* (pp. 191–212). Hillsdale, NJ: Lawrence Erlbaum Associates.

Helmreich, R. L., Sawin, L. L., & Carsrud, A. L. (1986). The honeymoon effect in job performance: Temporal increases in the predictive power of achievement motivation. *Journal of Applied Psychology*, *71*, 185–188.

Heneman, H. G., III, Huett, D. L., Lavigna, R. J., & Ogsten, D. (1995). Assessing managers' satisfaction with staffiing services. *Personnel Psychology*, *48*, 163–172.

Hermelin, E., Lievens, F., & Robertson, I. T. (2007). The validity of assessment centres for the prediction of supervisory performance ratings: A meta-analysis. *International Journal of Selection and Assessment*, *15*, 405–411.

Hernandez, A., Drasgow, F., & Gonzales-Roma, V. (2004). Investigating the functioning of a middle category by means of a mixed-measurement model. *Journal of Applied Psychology*, *89*, 687–699.

Herriot, P. (1993). Commentary: A paradigm bursting at the seams. *Journal of Organizational Behavior*, *14*, 371–375.

Herriot, P. (1997). Business change and psychological responses. In N. Anderson & P. Herriot (Eds.), *International handbook of selection and assessment* (pp. 215–218). Chichester, UK: Wiley.

Herriot, P., & Anderson, N. (1997). Selecting for change: How will personnel and selection psychology survive? In N. Anderson & P. Herriot (Eds.), *International handbook of selection and assessment*. Chichester, UK: Wiley.

Hesketh, B., & Neal, A. (1999). Technology and performance. In D. Ilgen & E. D. Pulakos (Eds.), *The changing nature of performance: Implications for staffing, motivation, and development* (pp. 21–55). San Francisco: Jossey-Bass.

Higgs, A. C., Papper, E. M., & Carr, L. S. (2000). Integrating selection with other organizational processes and systems. In J. F. Kehoe (Ed.), *Managing selection in changing organizations: Human resource strategies* (pp. 73–122). San Francisco: Jossey-Bass.

Highhouse, S. (1997). Understanding and improving job-finalist choice: The relevance of behavioral decision research. *Human Resource Management Review*, *74*, 449–470.

Highhouse, S. (2002). Assessing the candidate as a whole: A historical and critical analysis of individual psychological assessment for personnel decision making. *Personnel Psychology*, *55*, 363–396.

Highhouse, S. (2008). Stubborn reliance on intuition and subjectivity in employee selection. *Industrial and Organizational Psychology*, *1*, 333–342.

Hills, J. R. (1989). Screening for potentially biased items in testing programs. *Educational Measurement: Issues and Practice*, *8*(4), 5–11.

Hirsh, H. R., Schmidt, F. L., & Hunter, J. E. (1986). Estimation of employment validities by less experienced judges. *Personnel Psychology*, *39*, 337–344.

Hodge, R. W., & Lagersfeld, S. (1987). The politics of opportunity. *Wilson Quarterly*, *11*(5), 109–127.

Hoeft, S., & Schuler, H. (2001). The conceptual basis of assessment centre ratings. *International Journal of Selection and Assessment*, *9*, 114–123.

Hoffman, C. C., & McPhail, S. M. (1998). Exploring options for supporting test use in situations precluding local validation. *Personnel Psychology*, *51*, 987–1003.

Hofstede, G. (1993). Cultural constraints in management theories. *Academy of Management Executive*, *7*, 91.

Hofstede, G. (1997). The Archimedes effect. In M. H. Bond (Ed.), *Working at the interface of cultures: Eighteen lives in social sciences* (pp. 47–61). London: Routledge.

Hofstede, G. (2001). *Culture's consequences: Comparing values, behaviors, institutions, and organizations across nations.* Thousand Oaks, CA: Sage.

Hofstee, W. K. B., de Raad, B., & Goldberg, L. R. (1992). Integration of the big five and circumplex approaches to trait structure. *Journal of Personality and Social Psychology*, *63*, 146–163.

Hogan, J. (1991a). Physical abilities. In M. D. Dunnette & L. M. Hough (Eds.), *Handbook of industrial and organizational psychology (Vol. 2)* (pp. 753–831). Palo Alto, CA: Consulting Psychologists Press.

Hogan, J. (1991b). Structure of physical performance in occupational tasks. *Journal of Applied Psychology*, *76*, 495–507.

Hogan, J., & Hogan, R. (1998). Theortical frameworks for assessment. In R. Jeanneret & R. Silzer (Eds.), *Individual psychological assessment: Predicting behavior in organizational settings* (pp. 27–53). San Francisco: Jossey-Bass.

Hogan, J., Hogan, R., & Busch, C. M. (1984). How to measure service orientation. *Journal of Applied Psychology*, *69*, 167–173.

Hogan, J., & Quigley, A. M. (1986). Physical standards for employment and the courts. *American Psychologist*, *41*, 1193–1217.

Hogan, R., & Hogan, J. (1992). *Hogan Personality Inventory Manual.* Tulsa, OK: Hogan Assessment systems.

Hogan R., & Hogan, J. (2001). Assessing leadership: The view from the dark side. *International Journal of Selection and Assessment*, *9*, 40–51.

Holland, P. W., & Thayer, D. T. (1988). Differential item performance and the Mantel-Haenszel procedure. In H. Wainer & H. I. Braun (Eds.), *Test validity* (pp. 129–145). Hillsdale, NJ: Lawrence Erlbaum Associates.

Holland, P. W., & Wainer, H. (1993). *Differential item functioning.* Hillsdale, NJ: Lawrence Erlbaum Associates.

Hollenbeck, J. R., & Whitener, E. M. (1988). Criterion-related validation for small sample contexts: An integrated approach to synthetic validity. *Journal of Applied Psychology, 73*, 536–544.

Hollingworth, H. L. (1923). *Judging human character.* New York: Appleton.

Homsma, G. J., Van Dyck, C., De Gildere, D., Koopman, P. L., & Elfring, T. (2007). Overcoming errors: A closer look at the attributional mechanism. *Journal of Business and Psychology, 21*, 559–583.

Horn, J. L., & Cattell, R. B. (1966). Refinement and test of the theory of fluid and crystallized intelligence. *Journal of Educational Psychology, 57*, 253–270.

Horst, P. (1966). *Psychological measurement and prediction.* Belmont, CA: Wadsworth.

Hough, L. M. (1984). Development and evaluation of the "accomplishment record" method of selecting and promoting professionals. *Journal of Applied Psychology, 69*, 135–146.

Hough, L. M. (1992). The "big five" personality variables—construct confusion: Description versus prediction. *Human Performance, 5*, 139–155.

Hough, L. M. (1998). Effects of intentional distortion in personality measurement and evaluation of suggested palliatives. *Human Performance, 11*, 209–244.

Hough, L. M. (2003). Emerging trends and needs in personality research and practice beyond main effects. In M. R. Barrick & A. M. Ryan (Eds.), *Personality and work: Reconsidering the role of personality in organizations* (pp. 289–325). San Francisco: Jossey-Bass.

Hough, L. M., & Ones, D. (2001). The structure, measurement, validity, and use of personality variables in industrial, work, and organizational psychology. In N. Anderson, D. S. Ones, H. K. Sinangil, & C. Viswesvaran (Eds.), *Handbook of industrial, work, and organizational psychology* (pp. 233–277). Thousand Oaks, CA: Sage.

Hough, L. M., & Oswald, F. L. (2000). Personnel selection: Looking toward the future— remembering the past. *Annual Review of Psychology, 51*, 631–664.

Hough, L. M., Oswald, F. L., & Ployhart, R. E. (2001). Determinants, detection, and amelioration of adverse impact in personnel selection procedures. *International Journal of Selection and Assessment, 9*, 152–194.

Hough, L. M., & Paullin, C. (1994). Construct-oriented scale construction: The rational approach. In H. S. Stokes, M. D. Mumford, & W. A. Owens (Eds.), *Biodata handbook: Theory, research, and use of biographical information in selection and performance prediction* (pp. 109–145). Palo Alto, CA: CPP Books.

Hough, L. M., & Tippins, N. (1994, April). New designs for selection and placement systems: The Universal Test Battery. In N. Schmitt (Chair), *Cutting edge developments in selection.* Symposium conducted at the Society for Industrial and Organizational Psychology, Nashville, TN.

Houston, W. M., Raymond, M. R., & Svec, J. C. (1991). Adjustments for rater effects in performance assessment. *Applied Psychological Measurement, 15*, 409–421.

Hovland, C. I., & Wonderlic, E. F. (1939). Prediction of success from a standaradized interview. *Journal of Applied Psychology, 23*, 537–546.

Howard, A. (1997). A reassessment of assessment centers: Challenges for the 21st century. *Journal of Social Behavior and Personality, 12*(5), 13–52.

Howard, A. (1994). *Diagnosis for organizational change: Methods and models.* New York: Guilford Press.

Huffcutt, A. I., & Arthur, W. J. (1994). Hunter and Hunter revisited: Interview validity for entry-level jobs. *Journal of Applied Psychology, 79*, 184–190.

Huffcutt, A. I., Conway, J. M., Roth, P. L., & Stone, N. J. (2001). Identification and meta-analytic assessment of psychological constructs measured in employment interviews. *Journal of Applied Psychology*, *86*, 897–913.

Huffcutt, A. I., & Youngcourt, S. S. (2006). Employment interviews. In D. L. Whetzel & G. R. Wheaton (Eds.), *Applied measurement: Industrial psychology in human resources management* (pp. 181–199). Mahwah, NJ: Lawrence Erlbaum Associates.

Hughes, J. L. (1956). Expressed personality needs as predictors of sales success. *Personnel Psychology*, *9*, 347–357.

Hughes, J. L., & Dodd, W. E. (1961). Validity versus stereotype: Predicting sales performance by ipsative scoring of a personality test. *Personnel Psychology*, *14*, 343–355.

Hulin, C. L., & Glomb, T. M. (1999). Contingent employees: Individual and organizational considerations. In D. Ilgen & E. D. Pulakos (Eds.), *The changing nature of performance: Implications for staffing, motivation, and development* (pp. 87–118). San Francisco: Jossey-Bass.

Hull, C. L. (1928). *Aptitude testing.* Yonkers-on-Hudson, NY: World Book.

Humphreys, L. G. (1952). Individual differences. *Annual Review of Psychology*, *3*, 131–150.

Humphreys, L. G. (1960). Investigations of the simplex. *Psychometrika*, *25*, 313–323.

Humphreys, L. G. (1979). The construct of general intelligence. *Intelligence*, *3*, 105–120.

Hunt, E. (2004). Information processing and intelligence: Where we are and where we are going. In R. J. Sternberg & J. E. Pretz (Eds.), *Cognition & intelligence: Identifying the mechanisms of the mind* (pp. 1–25). Cambridge, UK: Cambridge University Press.

Hunter, J. E. (1983). A causal analysis of cognitive ability, job knowledge, job performance, and supervisor ratings. In F. J. Landy & S. Zedeck, & J. Cleveland (Eds.), *Performance measurement and theory* (pp. 257–266). Hillsdale, NJ: Lawrence Erlbaum Associates.

Hunter, J. E. (1997). Needed: A ban on the significance test. *Psychological Science*, *8*, 3–7.

Hunter, J. E., & Hunter, R. F. (1984). Validity and utility of alternative predictors of job performance. *Psychological Bulletin*, *96*, 72–98.

Hunter, J. E., & Schmidt, F. L. (1990). *Methods of meta-analysis.* Newbury Park, CA: Sage.

Hunter, J. E., & Schmidt, F. L. (2004). *Methods of meta-analysis: Correcting error and bias in research findings* (2nd ed.). Thousand Oaks, CA: Sage.

Huse, E. F. (1962). Assessments of higher level personnel. IV. The validity of assessment techniques based on systematically varied information. *Personnel Psychology*, *15*, 195–205.

Ikomi, P. (1989). *The prediction of judgement in realistic tasks: Do judges have self-iinsight?.* Unpublished doctoral dissertation, Bowling Green State University.

Ikomi, P., & Guion, R. M. (2000). The prediction of judgment in realistic tasks: An investigation of self-insight. *International Journal of Aviation Psychology*, *10*, 135–153.

Ilgen, D. R., Barnes-Farrell, J. L., & McKellin, D. B. (1993). Performance appraisal process research in the 1980s: What has it contributed to appraisal in use? *Organizational Behavior and Human Decision Processes*, *54*, 321–368.

Ilgen, D. R., & Favero, J. L. (1985). Limits in generalization from psychological research to performance appraisal processes. *Academy of Management Review*, *10*, 311–321.

Ilgen, D. R., & Pulakos, E. D. (1999). Introduction: Employee performance in today's organizations. In D. Ilgen & E. D. Pulakos (Eds.), *The changing nature of performance: Implications for staffing, motivation, and development* (pp. 1–18). San Francisco: Jossey-Bass.

Ilgen, D. R., & Schneider, J. (1991). Performance measurement: A multi-discipline view (Vol. 6). In C. L. Cooper & I. T. Robertson (Eds.), *International review of industrial and organizational psychology* (pp. 71–108). Chichster, UK: Wiley.

International Task Force on Assessment Center Guidelines. (2000). Guidelines and ethical considerations for assessment center operations. *Public Personnel Management, 29,* 315–331.

International Task Force on Assessment Center Guidelines (2009). Guidelines and ethical considerations for assessment center operations. *International Journal of Selection and Assessment, 17,* 243–253.

International Test Commission. (2005). *International guidelines on computer-based and internet-delivered testing.* Retrieved from www.intestcom.org/guidelines

Ironson, G. H., Guion, R. M., & Ostrander, M. (1982). Adverse impact from a psychometric perspective. *Journal of Applied Psychology, 67,* 419–432.

Irvine, S. H. (2002). The foundations of item generation for mass testing. In S. Irvine & H. Kyllonen (Eds.), *Item generation for test development* (pp. 3–34). Mahwah, NJ: Lawrence Erlbaum Associates.

Irvine, S. H., & Kyllonen, P. C. (2002). *Item generation for test development.* Mahwah, NJ: Lawrence Erlbaum Associates.

Jackson, D. J. R., Stillman, J. A., & Atkins, S. G. (2005). Rating tasks versus dimensions in assessment centers: A psychometric comparison. *Human Performance, 18,* 213–241.

Jackson, D. N., Harris, W. G., Ashton, M. C., McCarthy, J. M., & Tremblay, P. F. (2000). How useful are work samples in validational studies? *International Journal of Selection and Assessment, 8,* 29–33.

Jackson, D. N., & Messick, S. (1958). Content and style in personality assessment. *Psychological Bulletin, 55,* 243–252.

Jacobs, R., Hoffman, D. A., & Kriska, S. D. (1990). Performance and seniority. *Human Performance, 36,* 107–201.

Jacobs, R., Kafry, D., & Zedeck, S. (1980). Expectations of behaviorally-anchored rating scales. *Personnel Psychology, 33,* 595–640.

Jaeger, R. M. (1976). On bias in selection (Special issue). *Journal of Educational Measurement, 13,* 3–99.

Jaeger, R. M. (1989). Certification of student competence. In R. L. Linn (Ed.), *Educational measurement* (3rd ed.) (pp. 485–514). New York: American Council on Education/Macmillan.

James, L. R. (1998). Measurement of personality via conditional reasoning. *Organizational Research Methods, 1,* 131–163.

James, L. R., & Brett, J. M. (1984). Mediators, moderators, and tests for mediation. *Journal of Applied Psychology, 69,* 307–321.

James, L. R., Demaree, R. G., & Wolf, G. (1984). Estimating within-group interrater reliability with and without response bias. *Journal of Applied Psychology, 69,* 85–98.

James, L. R., McIntyre, M. D., Glisson, C. A., Bowler, J. L., & Mitchell, T. R. (2004). The Conditional Reasoning Measurement System for aggression: An overview. *Human Performance, 17,* 271–295.

James, L. R., McIntyre, M. D., Glisson, C. A., Green, P. D., Patton, T. W., LeBreton, J. M. et al. (2005). A conditional reasoning measure for aggression. *Organizational Research Methods, 8,* 69–99.

James, L. R., Mulaik, S. A., & Brett, J. M. (1982). *Causal analysis: Assumptions, models, and data.* Beverly Hills, CA: Sage.

Jansen, P. G. W. (1997). Assessment in a technological world. In N. Anderson & P. Herriot (Eds.), *International handbook of selection and assessment* (pp. 125–145). Chichester, UK: Wiley.

Jansen, P. G. W., & Stoop, B. A. M. (2001). The dynamics of assessment center validity: Results of a 7-year study. *Journal of Applied Psychology, 86,* 741–753.

Janz, T. (1989). The patterned behavior description interview: The best prophet of the future is the past. In R. W. Eder & G. R. Ferris (Eds.), *The employment interview: Theory, research, and practice* (pp. 158–168). Newbury Park, CA: Sage.

Janz, T., Hellervik, L., & Gilmore, D. C. (1986). *Behavior description interviewing: New, accurate, cost-effective.* Boston: Allyn and Bacon.

Jeanneret, P. R. (1990, August). The Position Analysis Questionnaire: Applications based on quantitative job profiles. In *Quantitative job description and classification: Nomothetic approaches and applications.* A symposium conducted at the American Psychological Association, Boston.

Jeanneret, P. R., & Strong, M. H. (2003). Linking O*NET job analysis information to job requirement predictors: An O*NET application. *Personnel Psychology, 56,* 465–492.

Jeanneret, P. R., & Zedeck, S. (2010). Professional guidelines/standards. In J. L. Farr & N. T. Tippins (Eds.), *Handbook of employee selection.* New York: Psychology Press.

Jeanneret, R., & Silzer, R. (1998a). An overview of individual psychological assessment. In R. Jeanneret & R. Silzer (Eds.), *Individual psychological assessment: Predicting behavior in organizational settings* (pp. 3–26). San Francisco: Jossey-Bass.

Jeanneret, R., & Silzer, R. (1998b). *Individual psychological assessment: Predicting behavior in organizational settings.* San Francisco: Jossey-Bass.

Jenkins, J. G. (1946). Validity for what? *Journal of Consulting Psychology, 10,* 93–98.

John, O. P., Hampson, S. E., & Goldberg, L. R. (1991). The basic level in personality-trait hierarchies: Studies of trait use and accessibility in different contexts. *Journal of Personality and Social Psychology, 60,* 348–361.

Johnson, J. W. (2007). Synthetic validity: A technique of use (finally). In S. M. McPhail (Ed.), *Alternative validation strategies: Developing new and leveraging existing validity evidence* (pp. 122–158). San Francisco: Jossey-Bass.

Johnson, J. W., Carter, G. W., & Tippins, N. T. (2001, April). A synthetic validation approach to the development of a selection system for multiple job families. In J. W. Johnson & G. W. Carter (Chair), *Advances in the application of synthetic validity.* 16th Annual Conference of the Society for Industrial and Organizational Psychology, San Diego.

Jones, M. B. (1966). Individual differences. In E. A. Bilodeau (Ed.), *Acquisition of skill* (pp. 109–146). New York: Academic Press.

Jones, R. G., & Born, M. P. (2008). Assessor constructs in use as the missing component in validation of assessment center dimensions: A critique and directions for research. *International Journal of Selection and Assessment, 16,* 229–238.

Jones, R. G., Stevens, M. J., & Fischer, D. L. (2000). Selection in team contexts. In J. F. Kehoe (Ed.), *Managing selection in changing organizations: Human resource strategies* (pp. 210–241). San Francisco: Jossey-Bass.

Jones, R. G., Stout, T., Harder, B., Levine, E., Levine, J., & Sanchez, J. I. (2008). Personnel psychology and nepotism: Should we support anti-nepotism policies? *The Industrial–Organizational Psychologist, 45*(3), 17–20.

Joyce, L. W., Thayer, P. W., & Pond, S. B., III. (1994). Managerial functions: An alternative to traditional assessment center dimensions? *Personnel Psychology, 47,* 109–121.

Judge, T. A., & Cable, D. M. (2004). The effect of physical height on workplace success and income. *Journal of Applied Psychology, 89*, 428–441.

Judge, T. A., Higgins, C. A., & Cable, D. M. (2000). The employment interview: A review of recent research and recommendations for future research. *Human Resource Management Review, 10*, 383–406.

Kagan, J. (1966). Reflection–impulsivity: The generality and dynamics of conceptual tempo. *Journal of Abnormal Psychology, 71*, 17–24.

Kane, J. S. (1987, April 22). *Wish I may, wish I might, wish I could do performance appraisal right.* Unpublished manuscript, School of Management, University of Massachusetts, Amherst, MA.

Kane, J. S. (1996). The conceptualization and representation of total performance effectiveness. *Human Resource Management Review, 6*, 123–145.

Kane, J. S., & Woehr, D. J. (2006). Performance measurement reconsidered: An examination of frequency estimation as a basis for assessment. In W. Bennett, Jr., C. E. Lance, & D. J. Woehr (Eds.), *Performance measurement: Current perspectives and future challenges* (pp. 77–110). Mahwah, NJ: Lawrence Erlbaum Associates.

Kane, M. T. (2001). Current concerns in validity theory. *Journal of Educational Measurement, 38*, 319–342.

Kanfer, R., Wanberg, C. R., & Kantrowitz, T. M. (2001). Job search and employment: A personality–motivational analysis and meta-analysis. *Journal of Applied Psychology, 86*, 837–855.

Kanter, R. M., Stein, B. A., & Jick, T. D. (1992). *The challenge of organizational change: How companies experience it and leaders guide it.* New York: Free Press.

Kehoe, J. F. (2002, July 1). *Generalizing validity from research to practice: The meaning of the measure matters.* Invited address, 26th Annual IPMAAC Conference on Personnel Assessment, New Orleans, LA.

Keil, C. T., & Cortina, J. M. (2001). Degradation of validity over time: A test and extension of Ackerman's model. *Psychological Bulletin, 127*, 673–697.

Kelly, G. A. (1955). *The psychology of personal constructs.* New York: Norton.

Kenny, D. A. (1991). A general model of consensus and accuracy in interpersonal perception. *Psychological Review, 98*, 155–163.

Khattree, R., & Naik, D. N. (2000). *Multivariate data reduction and discrimination with SAS software.* Cary, NC: SAS Institute.

Kim, K., & Slocum, J. W., Jr. (2008). Individual differences and expatriate assignment effectiveness: The case of U.S.-based Korean expatriates. *Journal of World Business, 43*, 109–126.

Kinicki, A. J., Lockwood, C. A., Hom, P., & Griffeth, R. W. (1990). Interviewer predictions of applicant qualifications and interviewer valildity. *Journal of Applied Psychology, 75*, 477–486.

Kirchner, W. K., & Dunnette, M. D. (1959). An industrial psychologist's lament: The problem of shrinking sample size. *American Psychologist, 14*, 299–300.

Kirk, R. E. (1996). Practical significance: A concept whose time has come. *Educational and Psychological Measurement, 56*, 746–759.

Kitchener, K. S., & Brenner, H. G. (1990). Wisdom and reflective judgment: Knowing in the face of uncertainty. In R. J. Sternberg (Ed.), *Wisdom: Its nature, origins, and development* (pp. 212–229). Cambridge, UK: Cambridge University Press.

Kleiman, L. S., & Faley, R. H. (1985). The implications of professional and legal guidelines for court decisions involving criterion-related validity: A review and analysis. *Personnel Psychology, 38*, 803–833.

Klein, K. J., & Kozlowski, S. W. J. (2000). *Multilevel theory, research, and methods in organizations: Foundations, extensions, and new directions.* San Francisco: Jossey-Bass.

Klein, K. J., & Zedeck, S. (2004). Theory in applied psychology: Lessons (re)learned. *Journal of Applied Psychology, 89,* 931–933.

Kleinmann, M., & Strauss, B. (1998). Validity and application of computer-simulated scenarios in personnel assessment. *International Journal of Selection and Assessment, 6,* 97–106.

Kline, R. B. (2004). *Beyond significance testing: Reforming data analysis methods in behavioral research.* Washington, DC: American Psychological Association.

Konradt, U., Hertel, G., & Joder, K. (2003). Web-based assessment of call center agents: Development and validation of a computerized instrument. *International Journal of Selection and Assessment, 11,* 184–193.

Kozhevnokov, M. (2007). Cognitive styles in the context of modern psychology: Toward an integrated framework of cognitive style. *Psychological Bulletin, 133,* 464–481.

Kraiger, K. (1990). *Generalizability of performance measures across four Air Force specialties* (Air Force Systems Command No. AFHRL-TP-89-60). Brooks AFB, TX: Air Force Systems Command.

Kraiger, K., & Ford, J. K. (1985). A meta-analysis of ratee race effects in performance ratings. *Journal of Applied Psychology, 70,* 56–65.

Krause, D. E., Kersting, M., Heggestrad, E. D., & Thornton, G. C., III. (2006). Incremental validity of assessment center ratings over cognitive ability tests: A study at the executive management level. *International Journal of Selection and Assessment, 14,* 360–371.

Kraut, A. I. (1996). *Organizational surveys: Tools for assessment and change.* San Francisco: Jossey-Bass.

Kreidt, P. H., & Dawson, R. I. (1961). Response set and the prediction of clerical job performance. *Journal of Applied Psychology, 45,* 175–178.

Kriska, S. D. (1995). Comments on banding. *The Industrial–Organizational Psychologist, 32*(2), 93–94.

Kristof-Brown, A. L. (2000). Perceived applicant fit: Distinguishing between recruiters' perceptions of person–job and person–organization fit. *Personnel Psychology, 53,* 643–671.

Kristof-Brown, A. L., Zimmerman, R. D., & Johnson, E. C. (2005). Consequences of individuals' fit at work: A meta-analysis of person–job, person–organization, person–group, and person–supervisor fit. *Personnel Psychology, 58,* 281–342.

Kuder, G. F., & Richardson, M. W. (1937). The theory of estimation of test reliability. *Psychometrika, 20,* 151–160.

Kurtz, A. K. (1941). Recent research in the selection of life insurance salesmen. *Journal of Applied Psychology, 25,* 11–17.

Kyllonen, P. C. (2002). Item generation for repeated testing of human performance. In S. H. Irvine & P. C. Kyllonen (Eds.), *Item generation for test development* (pp. 251–275). Mahwah, NJ: Lawrence Erlbaum Associates.

LaHuis, D. M., Martin, N. R., & Avis, J. M. (2005). Investigating nonlinear conscientious–job performance relations for clerical employees. *Human Performance, 18,* 199–212.

Lance, C. E., LaPointe, J. A., & Fisicaro, S. A. (1994). *Organizational Behavior and Human Decision Processes, 57,* 83–96.

Lance, C. E., & Vandenberg, R. J. (2002). Confirmatory factor analysis. In F. Drasgow & N. Schmitt (Eds.), *Measuring and analyzing behavior in organizations* (pp. 221–254). San Francisco: Jossey-Bass.

Lance, C. E., & Woehr, D. J. (Eds.), *Performance measurement: Current perspectives and future challenges* (pp. 77–110). Mahwah, NJ: Lawrence Erlbaum Associates.

Landy, F. J. (1986). Stamp collecting versus science: Validation as hypothesis testing. *American Psychologist, 41,* 1183–1192.

Landy, F. J. (2003). Validity generalization: Then and now. In K. R. Murphy (Ed.), *Validity generalization: A critical review* (pp. 155–195). Mahwah, NJ: Lawrence Erlbaum Associates.

Landy, F. J. (2007). The validation of personnel decisions in the twenty-first century: Back to the future. In S. M. McPhail (Ed.), *Alternative validation strategies: Developing new and leveraging existing validity evidence* (pp. 409–426). San Francisco: Jossey-Bass.

Landy, F. J., & Conte, J. M. (2007). *Work in the 21st century: An introduction to industrial and organizational psychology* (2nd ed.). Malden, MA: Blackwell.

Landy, F. J., & Farr, J. L. (1980). Performance rating. *Psychological Bulletin, 87,* 72–107.

Landy, F. J., & Farr, J. L. (1983). *The measurement of work performance: Methods, theory, and applications.* New York: Academic Press.

Landy, F. J., Shankster, L., & Kohler, S. S. (1994). Personnel selection and placement. *Annual Review of Psychology, 46,* 261–296.

LaPolice, C. C., Carter, G. W., & Johnson, J. W. (2008). Linking O*NET descriptors to occupational literacy using job component validation. *Personnel Psychology, 61,* 405–441.

Larrick, R. P. (2004). Debiasing. In D. J. Koehler & N. Harvey (Eds.), *Blackwell handbook of judgment and decision making* (pp. 316–337). Malden, MA: Blackwell.

Latham, G. P. (1989). The reliability, validity, and practicality of the situational interview. In R. W. Eder & G. R. Ferris (Eds.), *The employment interview: Theory, research, and practice* (pp. 169–182). Newbury Park, CA: Allyn and Bacon.

Latham, G. P., & Wexley, K. N. (1981). *Increasing productivity through performance appraisal.* Reading, MA: Addison-Wesley.

Lawlis, G. F., & Lu, E. (1972). Judgment of counseling process: Reliability, agreement, and error. *Psychological Bulletin, 78,* 17–20.

Lawshe, C. H. (1952). What can industrial psychology do for small business? (A symposium). 2. Employee selection. *Personnel Psychology, 5,* 31–34.

Lawshe, C. H. (1959). Of management and measurement. *American Psychologist, 14,* 290–294.

Lawshe, C. H. (1975). A quantitative approach to content validity. *Personnel Psychology, 28,* 563–575.

Lawshe, C. H. (1987). Adverse impact: Is it a viable concept? *Professional Psychology: Research and Practice, 18,* 492–497.

Lawshe, C. H., & Balma, M. (1966). *Principles of personnel testing* (2nd ed.). New York: McGraw-Hill.

Lawshe, C. H., Bolda, R. A., Brune, R. L., & Auclair, G. (1958). Expectancy charts. II. Their theoretical development. *Personnel Psychology, 11,* 545–560.

Lawshe, C. H., Kephart, N. C., & McCormick, E. J. (1949). The paired comparison technique for rating performance of industrial employees. *Journal of Applied Psychology, 33,* 69–77.

Lawshe, C. H., & Schucker, R. E. (1959). The relative efficiency of four test weighting methods in multiple prediction. *Educational and Psychological Measurement, 19,* 103–114.

LeBreton, J. M., Barksdale, C. D., Robin, J., & James, L. R. (2007). Measurement issues associated with conditional reasoning tests: Indirect measurement and test faking. *Journal of Applied Psychology, 92,* 1–16.

Lee, R., Miller, K. J., & Graham, W. K. (1982). Corrections for restriction of range and attenuation in criterion-related validation studies. *Journal of Applied Psychology, 67,* 637–639.

Lee, T. W. (1999). *Using qualitative methods in organizational research.* Thousand Oaks, CA: Sage.

Leibowitz, H. W. (1996). The symbiosis between basic and applied research. *American Psychologist, 51,* 366–370.

LePine, J. A. (2003). Team adaptation and postchange performance: Effects of team composition in terms of members' cognitive ability and personality. *Journal of Applied Psychology, 88,* 27–39.

Levashina, J., & Campion, M. A. (2007). Measuring faking in the employment interview: Development and validation of an interview faking behavior scale. *Journal of Applied Psychology, 92,* 1638–1656.

Levine, E. L., Ash, R. A., & Levine, J. D. (2004). Judgmental assessment of job-related experience, training, and education for use in human resource staffing. In M. Harsen (Ed.), *Comprehensive handbook of psychological assessment* (Vol. 4, pp. 269–296). Chichester, UK: Wiley.

Lewis, D. (1960). *Quantitative methods in psychology.* New York: McGraw-Hill.

Li, H., Rosenthal, R., & Rubin, D. B. (1996). Reliability of measurement in psychology: From Spearman-Brown to maximal reliability. *Psychological Methods, 1,* 98–107.

Li, Y., Bolt, D. M., & Fu, J. (2006). A comparison of alternative models for testlets. *Applied Psychological Measurement, 30,* 3–21.

Lievens, F., Buyse, T., & Sackett, P. R. (2005). The operational validity of a video-based situational judgment test for medical college admissions: Illustrating the importance of matching predictor and criterion construct domains. *Journal of Applied Psychology, 90,* 442–452.

Lievens, F., & Highhouse, S. (2003). The relation of instrumental and symbolic attributes to a company's attractiveness as an employer. *Personnel Psychology, 56,* 75–102.

Lievens, F., & Peeters, H. (2008). Interviewers' sensitivity to impression management tactics in structured interviews. *European Journal of Psychological Assessment, 24,* 174–180.

Lievens, F., & Thornton, G. C., III. (2005). Assessment centers: Recent developments in practice and research. In A. Evers, N. Anderson & O. Voskuijl (Eds.), *The Blackwell handbook of personnel selection* (pp. 243–264). Malden, MA: Blackwell.

Likert, R. (1932). A technique for the measurement of attitudes. *Archives of Psychology, 140,* 1–55.

Lin, T. R., Dobbins, G. H., & Farh, J. (1992). A field study of race and age similarity effects on interview ratings in conventional and situational interviews. *Journal of Applied Psychology, 77,* 367–371.

Lindahl, L. G. (1945). Movement analysis as an industrial training method. *Journal of Applied Psychology, 29,* 420–436.

Lindell, M. K., & Brandt, C. J. (1999). Assessing interrater agreement on the job relevance of a test: A comparison of the CVI, T, $r_{wg(j)}$, and $r^*_{wg(j)}$. *Journal of Applied Psychology, 84,* 640–647.

Lindell, M. K., Brandt, C. J., & Whitney, D. J. (1999). A revised index of interrater agreement for multi-item ratings of a single target. *Applied Psychological Measurement, 23,* 127–135.

Lindemann, B., & Grossman, P. (1996). *Employment discrimination law* (3rd ed.). Washington, DC: Bureau of National Affairs.

Linn, R. L. (1968). Range restriction problems in the use of self-selected groups for test validation. *Psychological Bulletin, 69*, 69–73.

Linn, R. L. (1993). The use of differential item functioning statistics: A discussion of current practice and future implications. In P. W. Holland & H. Wainer (Eds.), *Differential item functioning* (pp. 349–364). Hillsdale, NJ: Lawrence Erlbaum Associates.

Linn, R. L., & Dunbar, S. B. (1986). Validity generalization and predictive bias. In R. A. Berk (Ed.), *Performance assessment: Methods & applications* (pp. 203–236). Baltimore: Johns Hopkins University Press.

Linn, R. L., Harnisch, D. L., & Dunbar, S. B. (1981). Corrections for range restriction: An empirical investigation of conditions resulting in conservative corrections. *Journal of Applied Psychology, 66*, 655–663.

Lodahl, T. M., & Kejner, M. (1965). The definition and measurement of job involvement. *Journal of Applied Psychology, 49*, 24–33.

Loevinger, J. (1957). Objective tests as instruments of psychological theory. *Psychological Reports, 3*, 635–694.

Lohman, D. F., & Bosma, A. (2002). Using cognitive measurement models in the assessment of cognitive styles. In H. I. Braun, D. N. Jackson & D. E. Wiley (Eds.), *The role of constructs in psychological and educational meaurement* (pp. 127–146). Mahwah, NJ: Lawrence Erlbaum Associates.

London, M., & Mone, E. M. (1999). Continuous learning. In D. Ilgen & E. D. Pulakos (Eds.), *The changing nature of performance: Implications for staffing, motivation, and development* (pp. 119–153). San Francisco: Jossey-Bass.

Lord, F. M. (1952). *A theory of test scores.* Psychometric Monographs, No. 7. Iowa City, IA: The Psychometric Society.

Lord, F. M. (1962). Cutting scores and errors of measurement. *Psychometrika, 27*, 19–30.

Lord, F. M. (1963). Cutting scores and errors of measurement: A second case. *Educational and Psychological Measurement, 23*, 63–68.

Lord, F. M. (1980). *Applications of item response theory to practical testing problems.* Hillsdale, NJ: Lawrence Erlbaum Associates.

Lord, F. M., & Novick, M. R. (1968). *Statistical theories of mental test scores.* Reading, MA: Addison-Wesley.

Luecht, R. M. (2006). Operational issues in computer-based testing. In D. Bartram & R. K. Hambleton (Eds.), *Computer-based testing and the internet: Issues and advances* (pp. 91–114). Chichester, UK: Wiley.

Luecht, R. M., & Nungester, R. J. (1998). Some practical examples of computer-adaptive testing. *Journal of Educational Measurement, 35*, 229–249.

MacCann, R. G. (2008). A modification to Angoff and bookmarking cut scores to account for the imperfect reliability of test scores. *Educational and Psychological Measurement, 68*, 197–214.

MacKinnon, D. W. (1977). From selecting spies to selecting managers: The OSS assessment program. In J. L. Moses & W. C. Byham (Eds.), *Applying the assessment center method* (pp. 13–30). New York: Pergamon Press.

Madden, J. M., & Bourdon, R. D. (1964). Effects of variations in rating scale format on judgment. *Journal of Applied Psychology, 48*, 147–151.

Mael, F. A. (1991). A conceptual rationale for the domain and attributes of biodata items. *Personnel Psychology, 44*, 763–792.

Mael, F. A., & Hirsch, A. C. (1993). Rainforest empiricism and quasi-rationality: Two approaches to objective biodata. *Personnel Psychology, 46*, 719–738.

Mallamad, S. M., Levine, J. N., & Fleishman, E. A. (1980). Identifying ability requirements by decision flow diagrams. *Human Factors, 22*, 57–68.

Mantel, N., & Haenszel, W. (1959). Statistical aspect of the analysis of data from retrospective studies of disease. *Journal of the National Cancer Institute, 22*, 719–748.

Marchese, M. C., & Muchinsky, P. M. (1993). The validity of the employment interview: A meta-analysis. *International Journal of Selection and Assessment, 1*, 18–26.

Mårdberg, B., & Carlestedt, B. (1998). Swedish enlistment battery (SEB): Construct validity and latent variable estimation of cognitive abilities by the CAT-SEB. *International Journal of Selection and Assessment, 6*, 107–114.

Marquardt, L. D., & McCormick, E. J. (June, 1972). *Attribute ratings and profiles of the job elements of the Position Analysis Questionnaire (PAQ)*. Report No. 1. West Lafayette, IN: Department of Psychological Sciences, Purdue University.

Martin, B. A., Bowen, C.-C., & Hunt, S. T. (2002). How effective are people at faking on personality questionnaires? *Personality and Individual Differences, 32*, 247–256.

Maxwell, S. E. (2010). Introduction to the special section on Campbell's and Rubin's conceptualizations of causality. *Psychological Methods, 15*, 1–2.

McArdle, J. J., & Wang, L. (2008). Modeling age-based turning points in longitudinal life-span growth curves of cognition. In P. Cohen (Ed.), *Applied data analytic techniques for turning points research* (pp. 105–127). New York: Routledge.

McCall's Assembles. (1968, March). Life in the Year 2001. *McCall's, 95*(6), 84–89, 142–146.

McCarthy, J. M., & Goffin, R. D. (2005). Selection test anxiety: Exploring tension and fear of failure across the sexes in simulated selection scenarios. *International Journal of Selection and Assessment, 13*, 282–295.

McClelland, D. C. (1973). Testing for competence rather than for intelligence. *American Psychologist, 28*, 1–14.

McCormick, E. J. (1959). Application of job analysis to indirect validity. *Personnel Psychology, 12*, 402–413.

McCormick, E. J. (1979). *Job analysis.* New York: AMACOM.

McCormick, E. J., & Bachus, J. A. (1952). Paired comparison ratings: 1. The effect on ratings of reductions in the number of pairs. *Journal of Applied Psychology, 36*, 123–127.

McCormick, E. J., & Jeanneret, P. R. (1988). Position Analysis Questionnaire (PAQ). In S. Gael (Ed.), *The job analysis handbook for business, industry, and government* (Vol. 1, pp. 825–842). New York: Wiley.

McCormick, E. J., Jeanneret, P. R., & Mecham, R. C. (1972). A study of job characteristics and job dimensions as based on the Position Analysis Questionnaire (PAQ). *Journal of Applied Psychology, 56*, 347–368.

McCormick, E. J., Mecham, R. C., & Jeanneret, P. R. (1989). *Technical manual for the Position Analysis Questionnaire (PAQ)* (2nd ed.). West Lafayette, IN: Purdue Research Foundation.

McCormick, E. J., & Roberts, W. K. (1952). Paired comparison ratings: 2. The reliability of ratings based on partial pairings. *Journal of Applied Psychology, 36*, 188–192.

McDaniel, M. A., Morgeson, F. P., Finnegan, E. B., Campion, M. A., & Braverman, E. P. (2001). Use of situational judgment tests to predict job performance: A clarification of the literature. *Journal of Applied Psychology, 86*, 730–740.

McDaniel, M. A., Schmidt, F. L., & Hunter, J. E. (1988a). Job experience correlates of job performance. *Journal of Applied Psychology, 73*, 327–330.

McDaniel, M. A., Schmidt, F. L., & Hunter, J. E. (1988b). A meta-anaysis of the validity of methods for rating training and experience in personnel selection. *Personnel Psychology*, *41*, 283–314.

McDaniel, M. A., Whetzel, D. L., Schmidt, F. L., & Maurer, S. D. (1994). The validity of employment interviews: A comprehensive review and meta-analysis. *Journal of Applied Psychology*, *79*, 599–616.

McDermott, P. A. (1998). MEG: Megacluster analytic strategy for multistage hierarchical grouping with relocations and replications. *Educational and Psychological Measurement*, *58*, 677–686.

McDonald, R. P. (1999). *Test theory: A unified treatment.* Mahwah, NJ: Lawrence Erlbaum Associates.

McFarland, L. A., Ryan, A. M., & Kriska, S. D. (2002). Field study investigation of applicant use of influence tactics in a selection interview. *Journal of Psychology*, *136*, 393–398.

McGonigle, T. P., & Curnow, C. K. (2007). Measures of training and experience. In D. L. Whetzel & G. R. Wheaton (Eds.), *Applied Measurement: Industrial Psychology in Human Resources Management* (pp. 161–180). Mahwah, NJ: Lawrence Erlbaum Associates.

McGrath, J. E., & Tschan, F. (2004). *Temporal matters in social psychology: Examining the role of time in the lives of groups and individuals.* Washington, DC: American Psychological Association.

McHenry, J. J., Lough, L. M., Toquam, J. L., Hanson, M. A., & Ashworth, S. (1990). Project A validity results: The relationship between predictor and criterion domains. *Personnel Psychology*, *43*, 335–354.

McKay, P. F., & McDaniel, M. A. (2006). A re-examination of black–white mean differences in work performance: More data, more moderators. *Journal of Applied Psychology*, *91*, 538–554.

McMurry, R. N. (1947). Validating the patterned interview. *Personnel*, *23*, 263–272.

McQuitty, L. L. (1957). Elementary linkage analysis for isolating orthogonal and oblique types and typal relevancies. *Educational and Psychological Measurement*, *17*, 207–229.

Meacham et al. v. Knolls Atomic Power Laboratory, aka KAPL (2008). 103 FEP Cases (BNA) 908.

Meade, A. W., Johnson, E. C., Braddy, P. W. J., & Johnson, E. C. (2008). Power and sensitivity of alternative fit indices in tests of measurement invariance. *Journal of Applied Psychology*, *93*, 568–592.

Meade, A. W., Lautenschlager, G. J., & Johnson, E. C. (2007). A Monte Carlo examination of the sensitivity of the differential functioning of items and tests framework for tests of measurement invariance with Likert data. *Applied Psychological Measurement*, *31*, 430–455.

Meehl, P. E. (1954). *Clinical versus statistical prediction.* Minneapolis, MN: University of Minnesota Press.

Meehl, P. E. (1967). What can the clinician do well? In D. N. Jackson & S. Messick (Eds.), *Problems in human assessment* (pp. 594–599). New York: McGraw-Hill.

Meehl, P. E. (1991). Why summaries of research on psychological theories are often uninterpretable. In R. E. Snow & D. E. Wiley (Eds.), *Improving inquiry in social science* (pp. 13–59). Hillsdale, NJ: Lawrence Erlbaum Associates.

Meglino, B. M., & Korsgaard, M. A. (2007). The role of other orientation in reactions to job characteristics. *Journal of Management*, *33*, 57–83.

Meredith, W., & Millsap, R. E. (1992). On the misuse of manifest variables in the detection of measurement bias. *Psychometrika*, *57*, 289–311.

Meredith, W., & Tisak, J. (1990). Latent curve analysis. *Psychometrika*, *55*, 107–122.

Meriac, J. P., Hoffman, B. J., Woehr, D. J., & Fleisher, M. S. (2008). Further evidence for the validity of assessment center dimensions: A meta-analysis of the incremental criterion-related validity of dimension ratings. *Journal of Applied Psychology*, *93*, 1042–1052.

Mertz, W. H., & Doherty, M. E. (1974). The influence of task characteristics on strategies of cue combination. *Organizational Behavior and Human Performance*, *12*, 196–216.

Messick, S. (1960). Dimensions of social desirability. *Journal of Consulting Psychology*, *24*, 279–287.

Messick, S. (1989). Validity. In R. L. Linn (Ed.), *Educational measurement* (3rd ed.) (pp. 13–103). New York: American Council on Education/Macmillan.

Messick, S. (1996). Human abilities and modes of attention: The issue of stylistic consistencies in cognition. In I. Dennis & P. Tapsfield (Eds.), *Human abilities: Their nature and measurement* (pp. 77–96). Hillsdale, NJ: Lawrence Erlbaum Associates.

Meyer, H. H. (1959). A comparison of foreman and general foreman conceptions of the foreman's job responsibilities. *Personnel Psychology*, *124*, 445–452.

Miller, C. S., Kaspin, J. A., & Schuster, M. H. (1990). The impact of performance appraisal methods on Age Discrimination in Employment Act cases. *Personnel Psychology*, *43*, 555–578.

Millman, J., & Greene, J. (1989). The specification and development of tests of achievement and ability. In R. L. Linn (Ed.), *Educational measurement* (3rd ed., pp. 335–366). New York: American Council on Education/Macmillan.

Millsap, R. E. (2002). Structural equation modeling: A user's guide. In F. Drasgow & N. Schmitt (Eds.), *Measuring and analyzing behavior in organizations* (pp. 257–301). San Francisco: Jossey-Bass.

Miner, M. G., & Miner, J. B. (1978). *Employee selection within the law.* Washington, DC: Bureau of National Affairs.

Mischel, W. (1968). *Personality and assessment.* New York: Wiley.

Mischel, W. (1977). The interaction of person and situation. In D. Magnusson & N. S. Endler (Eds.), *Personality at the crossroads: Current issues in interactional psychology.* Hillsdale, NJ: Lawrence Erlbaum Associates.

Mitzel, H. C., Lewis, D. M., Patz, R. J., & Green, D. R. (2001). The bookmark procedure: Psychological perspectives. In G. J. Cizek (Ed.), *Setting performance standards* (pp. 249–281). Mahwah, NJ: Lawrence Erlbaum Associates.

Moeller, A., Schneider, B., Schoorman, F. D., & Berney, E. (1988). Development of the Work Facilitation Diagnostic. In F. Schoorman & B. Schneider (Eds.), *Facilitating work effectiveness* (pp. 79–103). Lexington, MA: Lexington Books.

Mohrman, S. A., & Cohen, S. G. (1995). When people get out of the box. In A. Howard (Ed.), *The changing nature of work* (pp. 365–410). San Francisco: Jossey-Bass.

Morgan, R. (2002). Discussant remarks. In S. H. Irvine & P. C. Kyllonen (Eds.), *Item generation for test development* (pp. 385–389). Mahwah, NJ: Lawrence Erlbaum Associates.

Morgeson, F. P., Campion, M. A., & Levashina, J. (2009). Why don't you just show me? Perfomance interviews for skill-based promotions. *International Journal of Selection and Assessment*, *17*, 203–218.

Morgeson, F. P., Delaney-Klinger, K., Mayfield, M. S., Ferrara, P., & Campion, M. A. (2004). Self-presentation processes in job analysis: A field experiment investigating inflation in abilities, tasks, and competencies. *Journal of Applied Psychology*, *89*, 674–686.

Morgeson, F. P., & Humphrey, S. E. (2006). The Work Design Questionnaire (WDQ): The Work Design Questionnaire (WDQ): Developing and validating a comprehensive measure for assessing job design and the nature of work. *Journal of Applied Psychology*, *91*, 1321–1339.

Morrison, D. E., & Henkel, R. E. (1970). *The significance test controversy: A reader.* Chicago: Aldine.

Moscoso, S. (2000). Selection interview: A review of validity evidence, adverse impact and applicant reactions. *International Journal of Selection and Assessment*, *8*, 237–247.

Mossholder, K. W., & Arvey, R. D. (1984). Synthetic validity: A conceptual and comparative review. *Journal of Applied Psychology*, *69*, 322–333.

Motowidlo, S. J., Dunnette, M. D., & Carter, G. W. (1990). An alternative selection procedure: The low-fidelity simulation. *Journal of Applied Psychology*, *75*, 640–647.

Motowidlo, S. J., Hooper, A. C., & Jackson, H. (2006). A theoretical basis for situational judgment tests. In J. A. Weekley & R. E. Ployhart (Eds.), *Situational judgment tests: Theory, measurement, and application* (pp. 57–81). Mahwah, NJ: Lawrence Erlbaum Associates.

Motowidlo, S. J., & Tippins, N. (1993). Further studies of the low-fidelity simulation in the form of a situational inventory. *Journal of Occupational and Organizational Psychology*, *66*, 337–344.

Mount, M., Ilies, R., & Johnson, E. (2006). Relationship of personality traits and counterproductive work behaviors: The mediating effects of job satisfaction. *Personnel Psychology*, *59*, 591–622.

Mumford, M. D., Peterson, N. G., & Childs, R. A. (1999). Basic and cross-functional skills. In N. G. Peterson, M. D. Mumford, W. C. Borman, P. R. Jeanneret & E. A. Fleishman (Eds.), *An occupational information system for the 21st century: The development of O*NET* (pp. 49–69). Washington, DC: American Psychological Association.

Mumford, M. D., Whetzel, D. L., Murphy, S. T., & Eubanks, D. L. (2006). Background data. In D. L. Whetzel & G. R. Wheaton (Eds.), *Applied measurement: Industrial psychology in human resources management* (pp. 201–233). Mahwah, NJ: Lawrence Erlbaum Associates.

Mun, E. Y., von Eye, A., Bates, M. E., & Vaschillo, E. G. (2008). Finding groups using model-based cluster analysis: Heterogeneous emotional self-regulatory processes and heavy alcohol use risk. *Developmental Psychology*, *44*, 481–495.

Murphy, K. R. (1983). Fooling yourself with cross-validation: Single sample designs. *Personnel Psychology*, *36*, 111–118.

Murphy, K. R. (1989). Is the relationship between cognitive ability and job performance stable over time? *Human Performance*, *2*, 183–200.

Murphy, K. R. (1999). The challenge of staffing a postindustrial workplace. In D. Ilgen & E. D. Pulakos (Eds.), *The changing nature of performance: Implications for staffing, motivation, and development* (pp. 295–324). San Francisco: Jossey-Bass.

Murphy, K. R. (2002). Using power analysis to evaluate and improve research. In S. G. Rogelberg (Ed.), *Handbook of research methods in industrial and organizational psychology* (pp. 119–137). Oxford: Blackwell.

Murphy, K. R. (2008a). Explaining the weak relationship between job performance and ratings of job performance. *Industrial and Organizational Psychology*, *1*, 148–160.

Murphy, K. R. (2008b). Perspectives on the relationship between job performance and ratings of job performance. *Industrial and Organizational Psychology*, *1*, 197–205.

Murphy, K. R., Cronin, B. E., & Tam, A. P. (2003). Controversy and consensus regarding the use of cognitive ability testing in organizations. *Journal of Applied Psychology*, *88*, 660–671.

Murphy, K. R., & Myors, B. (1999). Testing the hypothesis that treatments have negligible effects: Minimum-effect tests in the general linear model. *Journal of Applied Psychology*, *84*, 234–248.

Murphy, K. R., & Newman, D. A. (2003). The past, present, and future of validity generalization. In K. R. Murphy (Ed.), *Validity generalization: A critical review* (pp. 403–424). Mahwah, NJ: Lawrence Erlbaum Associates.

Murray, H. (1938). *Explorations in personality.* New York: Oxford University Press.

Myart v. Motorola. (1964). *Congressional Record, 110*, 5662.

Nagle, B. F. (1953). Criterion development. *Personnel Psychology, 6*, 271–289.

Newman, D. A., & Lyon, J. S. (2009). Recruitment efforts to reduce adverse impact: Targeted recruiting for personality, cognitive ability, and diversity. *Journal of Applied Psychology*, *94*, 298–317.

Ng, T. W. H., & Feldman, D. C. (2008). The relationship of age to ten dimensions of job performance. *Journal of Applied Psychology, 93*, 392–423.

Nickerson, R. S. (2000). Null hypothesis significance testing: A review of an old and continuing controversy. *Psychological Methods, 5*, 241–301.

Nye, C. D., Do, B.-R., Drasgow, F., & Fine, S. (2008). Two-step testing in employee selection: Is score inflation a problem? *International Journal of Selection and Assessment, 16*, 112–120.

Offerman, L. R., & Gowing, M. K. (1993). Personnel selection in the future: The impact of changing demographics and the nature of work. In N. Schmitt & W. C. Borman (Eds.), *Personnel selecton in organizations* (pp. 385–417). San Francisco: Jossey-Bass.

Office of Federal Contract Compliance. (1968). Validation of tests by contractors and subcontractors subject to the provisions of Executive Order 11246. *Federal Register, 33*(186), 14392–14394.

Office of Federal Contract Compliance. (1971). Employee testing and other selection procedures. *Federal Register, 36*(192), 19307–19310.

Olian, J. D. (1984). Genetic screening for employment purposes. *Personnel Psychology, 37*, 423–438.

Olson, D. M., & Borman, W. C. (1989). More evidence on relationships between the work environment and job performance. *Human Performance, 2*, 113–130.

Olson-Buchanan, J. B. (2002). Computer-based advances in assessment. In F. Drasgow & N. Schmitt (Eds.), *Measuring and analyzing behavior in organizations* (pp. 44–87). San Francisco: Jossey-Bass.

Omran, M. G. H., Engelbrecht, A. P., & Salman, A. (2007). An overview of clustering methods. *Intelligent Data Analysis, 11*, 583–605.

Ones, D. S., Viswesvaran, C., & Schmidt, F. L. (2008). No new terrain: Reliability and construct validity of job performance ratings. *Industrial and Organizational Psychology, 1*, 174–179.

Oppler, S. H., Peterson, N. G., & McCloy, R. A. (1994, April). *A comparison of peer and supervisory ratings as criteria for the validation of predictors.* Presented at the Society for Industrial and Organizational Psychology, Nashville, TN.

Oreg, S. (2003). Resistance to change: Developing an individual differences model. *Journal of Applied Psychology, 88*, 680–693.

Organ, D. W., Podsakoff, P. M., & MacKenzie, S. B. (2006). *Organizational citizenship behavior: Its nature, antecedents, and consequences.* Thousand Oaks, CA: Sage.

Orr, J. M., Sackett, P. R., & DuBois, C. L. Z. (1991). Outlier detection and treatmemt in I/O psychology: A survey of researcher beliefs and an empirical illustration. *Personnel Psychology, 44*, 473–486.

Osborne, S. J. (1940). Oral trade questions. In W. H. Stead & C. L. Shartle (Eds.), *Occupational counseling techniques: Their development and application* (pp. 30–48). New York: American Book Company.

Oshima, T. C., Raju, N. S., & Flowers, C. P. (1997). Development and demonstration of multidimensional IRT-based internal measures of differential functioning of items and tests. *Journal of Educational Measurement, 34*, 253–272.

Oswald, F. L., & McCloy, R. A. (2003). Meta-analysis and the art of the average. In K. R. Murphy (Ed.), *Validity generalization: A critical review* (pp. 311–338). Mahwah, NJ: Lawrence Erlbaum Associates.

Otis, J. L., Campbell, J. T., & Prien, E. P. (1962). Assessments of higher level personnel. VII. The nature of assessments. *Personnel Psychology, 15*, 441–446.

Outtz, J. L., & Newman, D. A. (2010). A theory of adverse impact. In J. L. Outtz (Ed.), *Adverse impact: Implications for organizational staffing and high stakes selection.* New York: Psychology Press.

Oyserman, D., Coon, H. M., & Kemmelmeier, M. (2002). Rethinking individualism and collectivism: Evaluation of theoretical assumptions and meta-analyses. *Psychological Bulletin, 128*, 3–72.

Paajanen, G. E. (1988). *The prediction of counterproductive behavior by individual and organizational variables.* Unpublished doctoral dissertation, University of Minnesota.

Pampel, F. C. (2000). *Logistic regression: A primer* (M. S. Lewis-Beck, Ed.). *Quantitative applications in the social sciences* (Vol. 132). Thousand Oaks, CA: Sage.

Parikh, S. (1997). *The politics of preference: Democratic institutions and affirmative action in the United States and India.* Ann Arbor, MI: University of Michigan Press.

Parker, S. K., Williams, H. M., & Turner, N. (2006). Modeling the antcedents of proactive behavior at work. *Journal of Applied Psychology, 91*, 636–652.

Paterson, D. G. (1957). The conservation of human talent. *American Psychologist, 12*, 134–144.

Peak, H. (1953). Problems of objective observation. In L. Festinger & D. Katz (Eds.), *Research methods in the behavioral sciences* (pp. 243–299). New York: Dryden.

Pearlman, K. (1980). Job families: A review and discussion of their implications for personnel selection. *Psychological Bulletin, 87*, 1–28.

Pearson, R. W., Ross, M., & Dawes, R. M. (1992). Personal recall and the limits of retrospective questions in surveys. In J. M. Tanaur (Ed.), *Questions about questions: Inquiries into the cognitive bases of surveys* (pp. 65–94). New York: Russell Sage Foundation.

Pedhazur, E. J., & Schmelkin, L. P. (1991). *Measurement, design, and analysis: An integrated approach.* Hillsdale, NJ: Lawrence Erlbaum Associates.

Peeters, H., & Lievens, F. (2006). Verbal and nonverbal impression management tactics in behavior description and situational interviews. *International Journal of Selection and Assessment, 14*, 206–222.

Peters, L. H., & O'Connor, E. J. (1988). Measuring work obstacles: Procedures, issues, and implications. In F. Schoorman & B. Schneider (Eds.), *Facilitating work effectiveness* (pp. 105–123). Lexington, MA: Lexington Books.

Petersen, N. S., & Novick, M. R. (1976). An evaluation of some models for culture-fair selection. *Journal of Educational Measurement, 13*, 3–29.

Peterson, C. (2009). Minimally sufficient research. *Perspectives on Psychological Science, 44*, 7–9.

Peterson, N. G., Mumford, M. D., Borman, W. C., Jeanneret, P. R., & Fleishman, E. A. (1999). *An occupational information system for the 21st century: The development of O*NET.* Washington, DC: American Psychological Association.

Peterson, N. G., Wise, L. L., Arabian, J., & Hoffman, R. G. (2001). Synthetic validation and validity generalization: When empirical validation is not possible. In J. P. Campbell & D. J. Knapp (Eds.), *Exploring the limits in personnel selection and classification* (pp. 411–451). Mahwah, NJ: Lawrence Erlbaum Associates.

Philips, S. E. (1993, June). Update on testing accommodations. *National Council of Measurement in Education Quarterly Newsletter, 20*(1), 2–3, 6.

Phillips, J. K., Klein, G., & Sieck, W. R. (2004). Expertise in judgment and decision making: A case for training intuitive decision skills. In D. J. Koehler & N. Harvey (Eds.), *Blackwell handbook of judgment and decision making* (pp. 297–315). Malden, MA: Blackwell.

Plake, B. S., & Hambleton, R. K. (2001). The analytic judgment method for setting standards on complex performance assessment. In G. J. Cizek (Ed.), *Setting performance standards* (pp. 283–312). Mahwah, NJ: Lawrence Erlbaum Associates.

Ployhart, R. E. (2004). Organizational staffing: A multilevel review, synthesis, and model. *Research in Personnel and Human Resource Management, 23*, 123–179.

Ployhart, R. E. (2006a). The predictor response process model. In J. A. Weekley & R. E. Ployhart (Eds.), *Situational judgment tests: Theory, measurement, and application* (pp. 83–105). Mahwah, NJ: Lawrence Erlbaum Associates.

Ployhart, R. E. (2006b). Staffing in the 21st century: New challenges and strategic opportunities. *Journal of Management, 32*, 868–897.

Ployhart, R. E., & Schneider, B. (2002). A multi-level perspective on personnel selection research and practice: Implications for selection, system design, assessment, and construct validation. In F. J. Yammarino & F. Dansereau (Eds.), *Research in multi-level issues, Volume I: The many faces of multi-level issues* (pp. 95–140). Amsterdam: JAI Press.

Ployhart, R. E., & Schneider, B. (2005). Multilevel selection and prediction: Theories, methods, and models. In A. Evers, N. Anderson & O. Voskuijl (Eds.), *The Blackwell handbook of personnel selection.* Malden, MA: Blackwell.

Potosky, D., Bobko, P., & Roth, P. L. (2005). Forming composites of cognitive ability and alternative measures to predict job performance and reduce adverse impact: Corrected estimates and realistic expectations. *International Journal of Selection and Assessment, 13*, 304–315.

Prewett-Livingston, A. J., Feild, H. S., Veres, J. G., III, & Lewis, P. M. (1996). Effects of race on interview ratings in a situational panel interview. *Journal of Applied Psychology, 81*, 178–186.

Prien, E. P., & Campbell, J. T. (1957). Stability of rating scale statements. *Personnel Psychology, 10*, 305–309.

Prieto, J. M., & Simon, C. (1997). Network and its implications for assessment. In N. Anderson & P. Herriot (Eds.), *International handbook of selection and assessment* (pp. 97–124). Chichester, UK: Wiley.

Primoff, E. S. (1953). *Test selection by job analysis: The J-Coefficient* (US Civil Service Commission, Test Development Section). Washington, DC: US Civil Service Commission.

Primoff, E. S. (1959). Empirical validation of the J-coefficient. *Personnel Psychology, 12*, 413–418.

Pulakos, E. D., Arad, S., Donovan, M. A., & Plamondon, K. E. (2000). Adaptability in the workplace: Development of a taxonomy of adaptive performance. *Journal of Applied Psychology, 85*, 612–624.

Pulakos, E. D., & O'Leary, R. S. (2010). Defining and measuring results of workplace behavior. In J. L. Farr & N. T. Tippins (Eds.), *Handbook of employee selection* (pp. 513–529). New York: Routledge.

Pulakos, E. D., Schmitt, N., Whitney, D., & Smith, M. (1996). Individual differences in interviewer ratings: The impact of standardization, consensus discussion, and sampling error on the validity of a structured interview. *Personnel Psychology*, *49*, 85–102.

Pulakos, E. D., White, L. A., Oppler, S. H., & Borman, W. C. (1989). Examination of race and sex effects on performance ratings. *Journal of Applied Psychology*, *74*, 770–780.

Putka, D. J., Ingerick, M., & McCloy, R. A. (2008). Integrating traditional perspectives on error in ratings: Capitalizing on advances in mixed-effects modeling. *Industrial and Organizational Psychology*, *1*, 167–173.

Putka, D. J., & Sackett, P. R. (2010). Reliability and validity. In J. L. Farr & N. T. Tippins (Eds.), *Handbook of employee selection* (pp. 9–49). New York: Routledge.

Raaheim, K. (1974). *Problem solving and intelligence*. Bergen, Norway: Universitetsforlaget.

Raftery, A. E., & Dean, N. (2006). Variable selection for model-based clustering. *Journal of the American Statistical Association*, *101*, 168–178.

Raju, N. S., & Burke, M. S. (1983). Two new procedures for studying validity generalization. *Journal of Applied Psychology*, *68*, 382–395.

Raju, N. S., & Ellis, B. B. (2002). Differential item and test functioning. In F. Drasgow & N. Schmitt (Eds.), *Measuring and analyzing behavior in organizations* (pp. 156–188). San Francisco: Jossey-Bass.

Raju, N. S., Laffitte, L. J., & Byrne, B. M. (2002). Measurement equivalence: A comparison of methods based confirmatory factor analysis and item response theory. *Journal of Applied Psychology*, *87*, 517–529.

Raju, N., Steinhaus, S. D., Edwards, J. E., & DeLessio, J. (1991). A logistic regression model for personnel selection. *Applied Psychological Measurement*, *15*, 139–152.

Raju, N. S., van der Linden, W. J., & Fleer, P. F. (1995). IRT-based internal measures of differential functioning of items and tests. *Applied Psychological Measurement*, *19*, 353–368.

Rasch, G. (1980). *Probabilistic models for some intelligence and attainment tests*. Chicago: University of Chicago Press.

Raykov, T., & Marcoulides, G. A. (2008). *An introduction to applied multivariate analysis*. New York: Routledge.

Raymark, P. H., Schmit, M. J., & Guion, R. M. (1997). Identifying potentially useful personality constructs for employee selection. *Personnel Psychology*, *50*, 723–736.

Reb, J., & Greguras, G. J. (2010). Understanding performance ratings: Dynamic performance, attributions, and rating purpose. *Journal of Applied Psychology*, *95*, 213–220.

Regents of University of California v. Bakke. (1978) (Vol. 438 U.S., p. 265).

Reilly, B. A., & Doherty, M. E. (1989). A note on the assessment of self-insight in judgment research. *Organizational Behavior and Human Decision Processes*, *44*, 123–131.

Reilly, B. A., & Doherty, M. E. (1992). The assessment of self-insight in judgment policies. *Organizational Behavior and Human Decision Processes*, *53*, 285–309.

Reise, S. P., & Waller, N. G. (2002). Item response theory for dichotomous assessment data. In F. Drasgow & N. Schmitt (Eds.), *Measuring and analyzing behavior in organizations* (pp. 88–122). San Francisco: Jossey-Bass.

Ricci v. DeStefano. (2009) (Vol. 557 U.S.).

Richardson, M. W. (1941). The combination of measures. In P. Horst (Ed.), *The prediction of personal adjustment* (pp. 377–401). New York: Social Science Research Council.

Richardson, M. W., & Kuder, F. (1939). The calculation of test reliability coefficients based upon the method of rational equivalence. *Journal of Educational Psychology*, *30*, 681–687.

Robinson, D. D. (1981). Content-oriented personnel selection in a small business setting. *Personnel Psychology, 34*, 77–87.

Roe, R. A. (2005). The design of selection systems: Context, principles, issues. In A. Evers, N. Anderson, & O. Voskuijl (Eds.), *The Blackwell handbook of personnel selection* (pp. 73–97). Malden, MA: Blackwell.

Roethlisberger, F. J., & Dickson, W. J. (1939). *Management and the worker.* Cambridge, MA: Harvard University Press.

Rogers, C. R., & Roethlisberger, F. J. (1952). Barriers and gateways to communication. *Harvard Business Review, 30*, 46–52.

Roose, J. E., & Doherty, M. E. (1976). Judgment theory applied to the selection of life insurance salesmen. *Organizational Behavior and Human Performance, 16*, 231–249.

Roth, P. L., Bobko, P., & Switzer, F. S. I. (2006). Modeling the behavior of the 4/5ths rule for determining adverse impact: Reasons for caution. *Journal of Applied Psychology, 91*, 507–522.

Roth, P. L., Huffcutt, A. I., & Bobko, P. (2003). Ethnic group differences in measures of job performance: A new meta-analysis. *Journal of Applied Psychology, 88*, 694–706.

Roth, P. L., Van Iddekinge, C. H., Huffcutt, A. I., Eidson, C. E., & Bobko, P. (2002). Corrections for range restriction in structured interview ethnic group differences: The values may be larger than researchers thought. *Journal of Applied Psychology, 87*, 369–376.

Roth, P. L., Van Iddekinge, C. H., Huffcutt, A. I., Eidson, C. E., & Schmit, M. J. (2005). Personality saturation in structured interviews. *International Journal of Selection and Assessment, 13*, 261–273.

Rothe, H. F. (1950). Use of an objectivity key on a short industrial personality questionnaire. *Journal of Applied Psychology, 34*, 98–101.

Rothstein, H. R. (2003). Progress is our most important product: Contributions of validity generalization and meta-analysis to the development and communication of knowledge in I/O psychology. In K. R. Murphy (Ed.), *Validity generalization: A critical review* (pp. 115–154). Mahwah, NJ: Lawrence Erlbaum Associates.

Rotundo, M., & Sackett, P. R. (2002). The relative importance of task, citizenship, and counterproductive performance to global ratings of job performance: A policy-capturing approach. *Journal of Applied Psychology, 87*, 66–80.

Rousseau, D. M. (1985). Issues of level in organizational research: Multi-level and cross-level perspectives. In L. L. Cummings & B. Staw (Eds.), *Research in organizational behavior*, (Vol. 7). Greenwich, CT: JAI Press.

Rubin, D. B. (2010). Reflections stimulated by the comments of Shadish (2010) and West and Thoemmes (2010). *Psychological Methods, 15*, 38–46.

Rucci, A. J. (2008). I–O psychology's "core purpose": Where science and practice meet. *Industrial–Organizational Psychologist, 46*(1), 17–24.

Ruch, F. L., & Ruch, W. W. (1967). The K factor as a (validity) suppressor variable in predicting success in selling. *Journal of Applied Psychology, 51*, 201–204.

Rulon, P. J. (1939). A simplified procedure for determining the reliability of a test by split halves. *Harvard Educational Review, 91*, 99–103.

Rupp, D. E., Gibbons, A. M., Runnels, T. A. L., & Thornton, G. C., III. (2003, August). *What should developmental assessment centers be assessing?* Presented at the 63rd annual meeting of the Academy of Management, Seattle.

Russell, C. J. (1994). Generation procedures for biodata items. In H. S. Stokes, M. D. Mumford, & W. A. Owens (Eds.), *Biodata handbook: Theory, research, and use of biographical information in selection and performance prediction* (pp. 17–38). Palo Alto, CA: CPP Books.

Russell, C. J. (2001). A longitudinal study of top-level executive performance. *Journal of Applied Psychology, 86,* 560–573.

Ryan, A. M., Daum, D., Bauman, T. G., Mattimore, M., Nalodka, T., & McCormick, S. (1995). Direct, indirect, and controlled observation and rating accuracy. *Journal of Applied Psychology, 80,* 664–670.

Ryan, A. M., & Kristof-Brown, A. (2003). Focusing on personality in person–organization fit research. In M. R. Barrick & A. M. Ryan (Eds.), *Personality and work: Reconsidering the role of personality in organizations* (pp. 262–288). San Francisco: Jossey-Bass.

Ryan, A. M., & Lasek, M. (1991). Negligent hiring and defamation: Areas of liability related to pre-employment inquiries. *Personnel Psychology, 44,* 293–319.

Ryan, A. M., Sacco, J. M., McFarland, L. A., & Kriska, S. D. (2000). Applicant self-selection: Correlates of withdrawal from a multiple hurdle process. *Journal of Applied Psychology, 85,* 163–179.

Ryan, A. M., & Sackett, P. R. (1987). A survey of individual assessment practices by I/O psychologists. *Personnel Psychology, 40,* 457–487.

Ryan, A. M., & Sackett, P. R. (1998). Individual assessment: The research base. In R. Jeanneret & R. Silzer (Eds.), *Individual psychological assessment: Predicting behavior in organizational settings* (pp. 54–87). San Francisco: Jossey-Bass.

Ryan, A. M., & Tippins, N. (2009). *Designing and implementing global selection systems.* Malden, MA: Wiley-Blackwell.

Rynes, S. L. (1991). Recruitment, job choice, and post-hire consequences: A call for new research directions. In M. D. Dunnette & L. M. Hough (Eds.), *Handbook of research methods in industrial and organizational psychology* (pp. 399–444). Palo Alto, CA: Consulting Psychologists Press.

Saad, S., & Sackett, P. R. (2002). Investigating differential prediction by gender in employment-oriented personality measures. *Journal of Applied Psychology, 87,* 667–674.

Sacco, J. M., & Schmitt, N. (2005). A dynamic multilevel model of demographic diversity and misfit effects. *Journal of Applied Psychology, 90,* 203–231.

Sackett, P. R. (2002). The structure of counterproductive work behaviors: Dimensionality and relationships with facets of job performance. *International Journal of Selection and Assessment, 10,* 5–11.

Sackett, P. R. (2007). Revisiting the origins of the typical–maximum performance distinction. *Human Performance, 20,* 179–185.

Sackett, P. R., Cornelius, E. T., III, & Carron, T. J. (1981). A comparison of global judgment vs. task-oriented approaches to job classification. *Personnel Psychology, 34,* 791–804.

Sackett, P. R., & DeVore, C. J. (2001). Counterproductive behaviors at work. In N. Anderson, D. S. Ones, H. K. Sinangil, & C. Viswesvaran (Eds.), *Handbook of industrial, work, and organizational psychology* (Vol. 1, pp. 145–164). London: Sage.

Sackett, P. R., & Dreher, G. F. (1982). Constructs and assessment center dimensions: Some troubling empirical findings. *Journal of Applied Psychology, 67,* 401–410.

Sackett, P. R., & DuBois, C. L. Z. (1991). Rater–ratee race effects on performance evaluation. *Journal of Applied Psychology, 76,* 873–877.

Sackett, P. R., DuBois, C. L. Z., & Noe, A. W. (1991). Tokenism in performance evaluation: The effects of work-group representation on male–female and white–black differences in performance ratings. *Journal of Applied Psychology, 76,* 263–267.

Sackett, P. R., Laczo, R. M., & Lippe, Z. P. (2003). Differential prediction and the use of multiple predictors. *Journal of Applied Psychology, 88,* 1046–1056.

Sackett, P. R., & Lievens, F. (2008). Personnel selection. *Annual Review of Psychology*, *59*, 419–450.

Sackett, P. R., & Ostgaard, D. J. (1994). Job-specific applicant pools and national norms for cognitive ability tests: Implications for range restriction corrections in validation research. *Journal of Applied Psychology*, *79*, 680–684.

Sackett, P. R., Shen, W., Myors, B., Lievens, F., Schollaert, E., Van Hoye, G., et al. (2010). Perspectives from twenty-two countries on the legal environment for selection. In J. L. Farr & N. T. Tippins (Eds.), *Handbook of employee selection.* New York: Routledge.

Sackett, P. R., & Tuzinski, K. A. (2001). The role of dimensions and exercised in assessment center judgments. In M. London (Ed.), *How people evaluate others in organizations* (pp. 111–129). Mahwah, NJ: Lawrence Erlbaum Associates.

Sackett, P. R., Zedeck, S., & Fogli, L. (1988). Relations between measures of typical and maximum job performance. *Journal of Applied Psychology*, *73*, 482–486.

Saks, A. M. (2005). The *I*mpracticality of recruitment research. In A. Evers, N. Anderson, & O. Voskuijl (Eds.), *The Blackwell handbook of personnel selection* (pp. 47–72). Malden, MA: Blackwell.

Salgado, J. F., Anderson, N., Moscoso, S., Bertua, C., de Fruyt, F., & Rolland, J. P. (2003). A meta-analytic study of general mental ability validity for different occupations in the European Community. *Journal of Applied Psychology*, *88*, 1068–1081.

Salgado, J. F., & Moscoso, S. (2002). Comprehensive meta-analysis of the construct validity of the employment interview. *European Journal of Work and Organizational Psychology*, *117*, 299–324.

Saucier, G., & Goldberg, L. R. (2003). The structure of personality attributes. In M. R. Barrick & A. M. Ryan (Eds.), *Personality and work: Reconsidering the role of personality in organizations* (pp. 1–29). San Francisco: Jossey-Bass.

Saunders, D. R. (1956). Moderator variables in prediction. *Educational and Psychological Measurement*, *16*, 209–222.

Schein, E. H. (1993). On dialogue, culture, and organizational learning. *Organizational Dynamics*, *22*(2), 40–51.

Scherbaum, C. A. (2005). Synthetic validity: Past, present, and future. *Personnel Psychology*, *58*, 481–515.

Scheuneman, J. D. (1979). A method of assessing bias in test items. *Journal of Educational Measurement*, *16*, 143–152.

Schippmann, J. S. (1999). *Strategic job modeling: Working at the core of integrated human resources.* Mahwah, NJ: Lawrence Erlbaum Associates.

Schmidt, F. L. (1996). Statistical significance testing and cumulative knowledge in psychology: Implications for training of researchers. *Psychological Methods*, *1*, 115–129.

Schmidt, F. L., & Hunter, J. E. (1977). Development of a general solution to the problem of validity generalization. *Journal of Applied Psychology*, *62*, 529–540.

Schmidt, F. L., & Hunter, J. E. (1981). Employment testing: Old theories and new research findings. *American Psychologist*, *36*, 1128–1137.

Schmidt, F. L., & Hunter, J. E. (1998). The validity and utility of selection methods in personnel psychology: Practical and theoretical implications of 85 years of research findings. *Psychological Bulletin*, *124*, 262–274.

Schmidt, F. L., & Hunter, J. E. (2003). History, development, evaluation, and impact of validity generalization and meta-analysis methods, 1975–2001. In K. R. Murphy (Ed.), *Validity generalization: A critical review* (pp. 31–65). Mahwah, NJ: Lawrence Erlbaum Associates.

Schmidt, F. L., Hunter, J. E., Croll, P. R., & McKenzie, R. C. (1983). Estimation of employment test validities by expert judgment. *Journal of Applied Psychology, 68,* 590–601.

Schmidt, F. L., Hunter, J. E., & Outerbridge, A. N. (1986). Impact of job experience and ability on job knowledge, work sample Impact of job experience and ability on job knowledge, work sample performance, and supervisory ratings of job performance. *Journal of Applied Psychology, 71,* 432–439.

Schmidt, F. L., & Kaplan, L. B. (1971). Composite vs. multiple criteria: A review and resolution of the controversy. *Personnel Psychology, 24,* 419–434.

Schmidt, F. L., Ones, D. S., & Hunter, J. E. (1992). Personnel selection. *Annual Review of Psychology, 43,* 627–670.

Schmidt, F. L., Pearlman, K., Hunter, J. E., & Hirsh, H. R. (1985). Forty questions about validity generalization and meta-analysis. *Personnel Psychology, 38,* 697–798.

Schmit, M. J., Kihm, J. A., & Robie, C. (2000). Development of a global measure of personality. *Personnel Psychology, 53,* 153–193.

Schmit, M. J., & Ryan, A. M. (1992). Test-taking dispositions: A missing link? *Journal of Applied Psychology, 77,* 629–637.

Schmitt, N. (1976). Social and situational determinants of interview decisions: Implications for the employment interview. *Personnel Psychology, 29,* 79–101.

Schmitt, N. (1996). Uses and abuses of coefficient alpha. *Psychological Assessment, 86,* 350–353.

Schmitt, N., & Chan, D. (1998). *Personnel selection: A theoretical approach.* Thousand Oaks, CA: Sage.

Schmitt, N., & Mills, A. E. (2001). Traditional tests and job simulations: Minority and majority performance and test validities. *Journal of Applied Psychology, 86,* 451–458.

Schneid, T. D. (1992). *The Americans with Disabilities Act: A practical guide for managers.* New York: Van Nostrand Reinhold.

Schneider, B. (1987). The people make the place. *Personnel Psychology, 40,* 437–453.

Schneider, B. (1996). When individual differences aren't. In K. R. Murphy (Ed.), *Individual differences and behavior in organizations* (pp. 548–571). San Francisco: Jossey-Bass.

Schneider, B., Goldstein, H. W., & Smith, D. B. (1995). The ASA framework: An update. *Personnel Psychology, 48,* 747–773.

Schneider, B., Kristof-Brown, A., Goldstein, H. W., & Smith, D. B. (1997). What is this thing called fit? In N. Anderson & P. Herriot (Eds.), *International handbook of selection and assessment* (pp. 393–412). Chichester, UK: Wiley.

Schneider, B., Smith, D. B., & Sipe, W. P. (2000). Personnel selection psychology: Multilevel considerations. In K. J. Klein & S. W. J. Kozlowski (Eds.), *Multilevel theory, research, and methods in organizations: Foundations, extensions, and new directions* (pp. 91–120). San Francisco: Jossey-Bass.

Schneider, R. J., Ferstl, K. L., Houston, J. S., Borman, W. C., Lords, A. O., & Bearden, R. M. (2006). *Revision and expansion of Navy Computer Adaptive Personality Scales (NCAPS).* Minneapolis, MN: Personnel Decisions Research Institutes.

Schneider, R. J., Goff, M., Anderson, S., & Borman, W. C. (2003). Computerized adaptive rating scales for measuring managerial performance. *International Journal of Selection and Assessment, 11,* 237–246.

Schneider, R. J., & Hough, L. M. (1995). Personality and industrial/organizational psychology. In C. L. Cooper & I. T. Robertson (Eds.), *International review of industrial and organizational psychology* (pp. 75–130). Chichester, UK: Wiley.

Schneier, C. E. (1977). Operational utility and psychometric characteristics of behavioral expectation scales. *Journal of Applied Psychology*, *62*, 541–548.

Schoenfeldt, L. F., & Mendoza, J. L. (1994). Developing and using factorially derived biographical scales. In H. S. Stokes, M. D. Mumford & W. A. Owens (Eds.), *Biodata handbook: Theory, research, and use of biographical information in selection and performance prediction* (pp. 147–169). Palo Alto, CA: CPP Books.

Shrout, P. E., & Fleiss, J. L. (1979). Intraclass correlations: Uses in assessing rater reliability. *Psychological Bulletin*, *86*, 420–428.

Schuler, H., Farr, J. L., & Smith, M. (1993). *Personnel selection and assessment: Individual and organizational perspectives.* Hillsdale, NJ: Lawrence Erlbaum Associates.

Scollay, R. W. (1956). Validation of personal history items against a salary increase criterion. *Personnel Psychology*, *9*, 325–336.

Sears, G. J., & Rowe, P. M. (2003). A personality-based similar-to-me effect in the employment interview: Conscientiousness, affect-versus competence-mediated interpretations, and the role of job relevance. *Canadian Journal of Behavioural Science*, *35*, 13–24.

Seigel, L. C., & Seigel, L. (1962). Item sorts versus graphic procedure for obtaining Thurstone scale judgments. *Journal of Applied Psychology*, *46*, 57–61.

Senge, P. M. (1990). *The fifth discipline: The art and practice of the learning organization.* New York: Doubleday.

Severin, D. (1952). The predictability of various kinds of criteria. *Personnel Psychology*, *5*, 93–104.

Shadish, W. R., & Cook, T. D. (2009). The renaissance of field experimention in evaluating interventions. *Annual Review of Psychology*, *60*, 607–629.

Shadish, W. R., Cook, T. D., & Campbell, D. T. (2002). *Experimental and quasi-experimental design for generalized causal inferences.* Boston: Houghton-Mifflin.

Shaffer, M. A., & Harrison, D. A. (2001). Forgotten partners of international assignments: Development and test of a model of spouse adjustment. *Journal of Applied Psychology*, *86*, 238–254.

Shaffer, M. A., Harrison, D. A., Gregersen, H., Black, J. S., & Ferzandi, L. A. (2006). You can take it with you: Individual differences and expatriot effectiveness. *Journal of Applied Psychology*, *91*, 109–125.

Shahani, C., Dipboye, R. L., & Gehrlein, T. M. (1991). *Educational and Psychological Measurement*, *51*, 1049–1061.

Sharma, S., & Kumar, A. (2006). Cluster analysis and factor analysis. In R. Grover & M. Vriens (Eds.), *The handbook of marketing research: Uses, misuses, and future advances* (pp. 365–393). Thousand Oaks, CA: Sage.

Shattuck, C. A. (1989). The tort of negligent hiring and the use of selection devices: The employee's right of privacy and the employer's need to know. *Industrial Relations Law Journal*, *11*, 2–17.

Shavelson, R. J., Webb, N. M., & Rowley, G. L. (1989). Generalizability theory. *American Psychologist*, *44*, 922–932.

Shepard, L. (1978). Setting standards [Special issue]. *Journal of Educational Measurement*, *15*(4), 237–327.

Shieh, G. (2006). Suppression situations in multiple linear regression. *Educational and Psychological Measurement*, *66*, 435–447.

Shields, J. (2007). *Managing employee performance and reward.* Cambridge, UK: Cambridge University Press.

Silzer, R., & Jeanneret, R. (1998). Anticipating the future: Assessment strategies for tomorrow. In R. Jeanneret & R. Silzer (Eds.), *Individual psychological assessment: Predicting behavior in organizational settings* (pp. 445–477). San Francisco: Jossey-Bass.

Simon, H. A. (1979). *Models of thought.* New Haven, CT: Yale University Press.

Sitzmann, T., Kraiger, K., Stewart, D., & Wisher, R. (2006). The comparative assessment of web-based and classroom instruction: A meta-analysis. *Personnel Psychology, 59,* 623–664.

Skaggs, G., & Lissitz, R. W. (1992). The consistency of detecting item bias across different test administrations: Implications of another failure. *Journal of Educational Measurement, 29,* 227–242.

Smith et al. v. City of Jackson, Mississippi, 95 FEP Cases (BNA) 641 (2005).

Smith, C. A., Organ, D. W., & Near, J. P. (1983). Organizational citizenship behavior: Its nature and antecedents. *Journal of Applied Psychology, 68,* 653–663.

Smith, D., & Robie, C. (2004). The implications of impression management for personality research in organizations. In B. Schneider & D. B. Smith (Eds.), *Personality and organizations* (pp. 111–138). Mahwah, NJ: Lawrence Erlbaum Associates.

Smith, J. E., & Hakel, M. D. (1979). Convergence among data sources, response bias, and reliability and validity of a structured job analysis questionnaire. *Personnel Psychology, 32,* 677–692.

Smith, P. C. (1985). *Global measures: Do we need them?* Division 14 Scientific Contribution Award Address, American Psychological Association, Los Angeles.

Smith, P. C., & Kendall, L. M. (1963). Retranslation of expectations: An approach to the construction of unambiguous anchors for rating scales. *Journal of Applied Psychology, 47,* 149–155.

Smither, J. W., & Reilly, R. R. (1987). True intercorrelation among job components, time delay in rating, and rater intelligence as determinants of accuracy in performance ratings. *Organizational Behavior and Human Decision Processes, 40,* 369–391.

Society for Industrial and Organizational Psychology. (1987). *Principles for the validation and use of personnel selection procedures* (3rd ed.). College Park, MD: Society for Industrial and Organizational Psychology.

Society for Industrial and Organizational Psychology. (2003). *Principles for the validation and use of personnel selection procedures* (4th ed.). Bowling Green, OH: Society for Industrial and Organizational Psychology.

South Africa, Department of Labour (2004, May 4). National Guidelines for EEO in South Africa. In *An information base on equal employment opportunities for women and men.* Geneva, Switzerland: International Labour Organization.

Spearman, C. (1927). *The abilities of man.* New York: Macmillan.

Spence, J. T., Helmreich, R. L., & Pred, R. S. (1987). Impatience versus achievement strivings in the Type A pattern: Differential effects on students' health and academic achievement. *Journal of Applied Psychology, 72,* 522–528.

Stang, S. W. (1985). *An interactive judgment analysis of job worth.* Unpublished doctoral dissertation, Bowling Green State University, Bowling Green, OH.

Stanley, J. C. (1971). Reliability. In R. L. Thorndike (Ed.), *Educational measurement* (2nd ed.). Washington, DC: American Council on Education.

Stanton, J. M., & Rogelberg, S. G. (2002). Beyond online surveys: Internet research opportunities for industrial–organizational psychology. In S. G. Rogelberg (Ed.), *Handbook of research methods in industrial and organizational psychology* (pp. 275–294). Oxford, UK: Blackwell.

Stark, S., Chernyshenko, O. S., & Drasgow, F. (2004). Examining the effects of differential item functioning and differential test functioning on selection decisions: When are statistically significant effects practically important? *Journal of Applied Psychology, 89,* 497–508.

Stark, S., Chernyshenko, O. S., Drasgow, F., & Williams, B. A. (2006). Detecting differential item functioning with confirmatory factor analysis and item response theory: Toward a unified strategy. *Journal of Applied Psychology, 91,* 1292–1306.

Stark, S., & Drasgow, F. (1998, April). *Application of an IRT ideal point model to computer adaptive assessment of job performance.* Presented at the Society for Industrial and Organizational Psychology, Dallas, TX.

Steel, P. D. G., Huffcutt, A. I., & Kammeyer-Mueller, J. (2006). From the work one knows the worker: A systematic review of the challenges, solutions, and steps to creating synthetic validity. *International Journal of Selection and Assessment, 14,* 16–36.

Steele, C. M., & Aronson, J. (1995). Stereotype threat and the intellectual performance of African-Americans. *Journal of Personality and Social Psychology, 69,* 797–811.

Steele-Johnson, D., Osburn, H. G., & Pieper, K. F. (2000). A review and extension of current models of dynamic criteria. *International Journal of Selection and Assessment, 8,* 110–136.

Stemler, S. E., & Sternberg, R. J. (2006). Using situational judgment tests to measure practical intelligence. In J. A. Weekley & R. E. Ployhart (Eds.), *Situational judgment tests: Theory, measurement, and application* (pp. 107–131). Mahwah, NJ: Lawrence Erlbaum Associates.

Sternberg, R. J. (1985). *Beyond IQ: A triarchic theory of human intelligence.* Cambridge, UK: Cambridge University Press.

Sternberg, R. J. (1990). *Wisdom: Its nature, origins, and development.* Cambridge, UK: Cambridge University Press.

Sternberg, R. J. (1991). Death, taxes, and bad intelligence tests. *Intelligence, 15,* 257–269.

Sternberg, R. J. (1997). Tacit knowledge and job success. In N. Anderson & P. Herriot (Eds.), *International handbook of selection and assessment* (pp. 201–213). Chichester, UK: Wiley.

Sternberg, R. J. (1999). The theory of successful intelligence. *Review of General Psychology, 3,* 292–316.

Sternberg, R. J., & Detterman, D. K. (1986). *What is intelligence?* Norwood, NJ: Ablex.

Sternberg, R. J., & Pretz, J. E. (Eds.). (2004). *Cognition and intelligence: Identifying the mechanisms of the mind.* Cambridge, UK: Cambridge University Press.

Sternberg, R. J., Wagner, R. K., Williams, W. M., & Horvath, J. A. (1995). Testing common sense. *American Psychologist, 50,* 912–927.

Stevens, S. S. (1946). On the theory of scales of measurement. *Science, 105,* 677–680.

Stevenson, M. K., Busemeyer, J. R., & Naylor, J. C. (1990). Judgment and decision making theory. In M. D. Dunnette & L. M. Hough (Eds.), *Handbook of industrial and organizational psychology* (2nd ed., Vol. 1, pp. 283–374). Palo Alto, CA: Consulting Psychologists Press.

Stewart, S. M., Bing, M. N., Davison, H. K., Woehr, D. J., & McIntyre, M. D. (2009). In the eyes of the beholder: A non-self report criterion measure of workplace deviance. *Journal of Applied Psychology, 94,* 207–215.

Stokes, G. S. (1994). Introduction and history. In G. S. Stokes, M. D. Mumford, & W. A. Owens (Eds.), *Biodata handbook: Theory, research, and use of biographical information in selection and performance prediction* (pp. xv–xix). Palo Alto, CA: CPP Books.

Sturman, M. C., Cheramie, R. A., & Cashen, L. H. (2005). The impact of job complexity and performance measurement on the temporal consistency, stability, and test–retest reliability of employee job performance ratings. *Journal of Applied Psychology, 90,* 269–283.

Sulsky, L. M., & Balzer, W. K. (1988). Meaning and measurement of performance rating accuracy: Some methodological and theoretical concerns. *Journal of Applied Psychology, 73,* 497–506.

Sutherland, S. (1996). *The international dictionary of psychology* (2nd ed.). New York: Crossroad.

Taggar, S., & Neubert, M. J. (2008). A cognitive (attributions)–emotion model of observer reactions to free-riding poor performers. *Journal of Business and Psychology, 22,* 167–177.

Taylor, E. K., & Hastman, R. (1956). Relation of format and administration to the characteristics of graphic rating scales. *Personnel Psychology, 9,* 181–206.

Taylor, E. K., & Manson, G. E. (1951). Supervised ratings: Making graphic rating scales work. *Personnel, 27,* 504–514.

Taylor, E. K., Parker, J. W., & Ford, G. L. (1959). Rating scale content: IV. Predictability of structured and unstructured scales. *Personnel Psychology, 12,* 247–266.

Taylor, H. C., & Russell, J. T. (1939). The relationship of validity coefficients to the practical effectiveness of tests in selection. *Journal of Applied Psychology, 23,* 565–578.

Taylor, P. J., Pajo, K., Cheung, G. W., & Stringfield, P. (2004). Dimensionality and validity of a structured telephone reference check procedure. *Personnel Psychology, 57,* 745–772.

Tenopyr, M. L. (1994, July). *Science, measurement, and social problems.* Presented at the American Psychological Society, Washington, DC.

Tett, R. P., & Burnett, D. D. (2003). A personality trait-based interactionist model of job performance. *Journal of Applied Psychology, 88,* 500–517.

Tett, R. P., & Guterman, H. A. (2000). Situation trait relevance, trait expression, and cross-situational consistency: Testing a principle of trait activation. *Journal of Research in Personality, 34,* 397–423.

Thayer, P. W. (1992). Construct validation: Do we understand our criteria? *Human Performance, 57,* 97–108.

Thissen, D., & Mislevy, R. J. (1990). Testing algorithms. In H. Wainer (Ed.), *Computerized adaptive testing: A primer* (pp. 103–135). Hillsdale, NJ: Lawrence Erlbaum Associates.

Thissen, D., Reeve, B. B., Bjorner, J. B., & Chang, C.-H. (2007). Methodological issues for building item banks and computerized adaptive scales. *Quality of Life Research, 16*(Suppl. 1), 109–119.

Thoresen, C. J., Bradley, J. C., Bliese, P. D., & Thoresen, J. D. (2004). The big five personality traits and individual job performance growth trajectories in maintenance and transitional job stages. *Journal of Applied Psychology, 89,* 835–853.

Thorndike, E. L. (1920). A constant error in psychological ratings. *Journal of Applied Psychology, 4,* 25–29.

Thorndike, R. L. (1949). *Personnel selection: Test and measurement techniques.* New York: Wiley.

Thorndike, R. L. (1971). Concepts of culture-fairness. *Journal of Educational Measurement, 8,* 63–70.

Thorndike, R. L., & Hagen, E. (1955). *Measurement and evaluation in psychology and education.* New York: Wiley.

Thornton, G. C., III, & Rupp, D. E. (2006). *Assessment centers in human resource management.* Mahwah, NJ: Lawrence Erlbaum Associates.

Thurstone, L. L. (1927). A law of comparative judgment. *Psychological Review, 34,* 273–286.

Thurstone, L. L. (1928). Attitudes can be measured. *American Journal of Sociology, 33,* 529–554.

Thurstone, L. L. (1931). *The reliablity and validity of tests.* Ann Arbor, MI: Edwards.

Thurstone, L. L. (1938). *Primary mental abilities.* Psychometric Monographs, No. 1. Iowa City, IA: The Psychometric Society.

Thurstone, L. L. (1947). *Multiple factor analysis.* Chicago: University of Chicago Press.

Thurstone, L. L., & Chave, E. J. (1929). *The measurement of attitude: A psychophysical method and some experiments with a scale for measuring attitude toward the church.* Chicago: University of Chicago Press.

Tiffin, J. (1942). *Industrial psychology.* New York: Prentice Hall.

Tinsley, H. E. A., & Weiss, D. J. (1975). Interrater reliability and agreement of subjective judgments. *Journal of Counseling Psychology, 22,* 358–376.

Tippins, N. T., Beaty, J., Drasgow, F., Gibson, W. M., Pearlman, K., Segall, D. O., et al. (2006). Unproctored internet testing in employment settings. *Personnel Psychology, 59,* 189–225.

Tippins, N. T., Papinchock, J. M., & Solberg, E. C. (2010). Decisions in developing and selecting assessment tools. In J. L. Farr & N. T. Tippins (Eds.), *Handbook of employee selection* (pp. 363–376). New York: Routledge.

Tisak, J., & Tisak, M. S. (2000). Permanency and ephemerality of psychological measures with application to organizational commitment. *Psychological Methods, 5,* 175–198.

Tombaugh, J. R. (1981). *The generalizability of job involvement scores.* Unpublished master's thesis, Bowling Green State University, Bowling Green, OH.

Toops, H. A. (1944). The criterion. *Educational and Psychological Measurement, 4,* 271–299.

Triandis, H. C. (1994). Cross-cultural industrial and organizational psychology. In M. D. Dunnette & L. M. Hough (Eds.), *Handbook of industrial and organizational psychology* (Vol. 4, 103–172). Palo Alto, CA: Consulting Psychologists Press.

Triandis, H. C. (1997). Raised in a collectivist culture, one may become an individualist. In M. H. Bond (Ed.), *Working at the interface of cultures: Eighteen lives in social science* (pp. 38–46). London: Routledge.

Truxillo, D. M., Bauer, T. N., Campion, M. A., & Paronto, M. E. (2002). Selection fairness information and applicant reactions: A longitudinal field study. *Journal of Applied Psychology, 87,* 1020–1031.

Tryon, R. C., & Bailey, D. E. (1970). *Cluster analysis.* New York: McGraw-Hill.

Tsacoumis, S. (2007). Assessment centers. In D. L. Whetzel & G. R. Wheaton (Eds.), *Applied Measurement: Industrial Psychology in Human Resources Management* (pp. 259–292). Mahwah, NJ: Lawrence Erlbaum Associates.

Tucker, L. R. (1964). A suggested alternative formulation in the development by Hursch, Hammond and Hursch, and by Hammond, Hursch and Todd. *Psychological Review, 71,* 528–530.

Tupes, E. C. (1964). A note on "Validity and nonlinear heteroscedastic models." *Personnel Psychology, 17,* 59–61.

Tye, M. G., & Chen, P. Y. (2005). Selection of expatriates: Decision-making models used by HR professionals. *Human Resource Planning, 28*(4), 15–20.

Tyler, L. E. (1978). *Individuality: Human possibilities and human choice in the psychological development of men and women.* San Francisco: Jossey-Bass.

Tzelgov, J., & Henik, A. (1991). Suppression situations in psychological research: Definitions, implications, and applications. *Psychological Bulletin, 109,* 524–536.

Tziner, A., Murphy, K. R., & Cleveland, J. N. (2005). Contextual and rater factors affecting rating behavior. *Group & Organization Management, 30*, 89–97.

Uggerslev, K. L., & Sulsky, L. M. (2008). Using frame-of-reference training to understand the implications of rater idiosyncracy for rating accuracy. *Journal of Applied Psychology, 93*, 711–719.

Uhlmann, E. L., & Cohen, G. L. (2007). "I think it, therefore it's true": Effects of self-perceived objectivity on hiring discrimination. *Organizational Behavior and Human Decision Processes, 104*, 207–223.

Uhrbrock, R. S. (1948). The personnel interview. *Personnel Psychology, 1*, 273–302.

Uhrbrock, R. S. (1950). Standardization of 724 rating scale statements. *Personnel Psychology, 3*, 285–316.

United States Civil Service Commission. (1972). Examining, testing standards, and employment practices. *Federal Register, 37*(198), 21552–21559.

United States v. New Orleans Public Service, 8 FEP Cases 1089 (1974).

Vacha-Haase, T. (2003). Reliability generalization: Exploring variance in measurement error affecting score reliability across studies. In B. Thompson (Ed.), *Score reliability: Contemporary thinking on reliability issues* (pp. 203–218). Thousand Oaks, CA: Sage.

van Dam, K. (2003). Trait perception in the employment interview: A five-factor model perspective. *International Journal of Selection and Assessment, 11*, 43–55.

Van de Ven, A. H., & Ferry, D. L. (1980). *Measuring and assessing organizations.* New York: Wiley.

Van de Vijver, F. J. R., van Hemert, D. A., & Poortinga, Y. H. (2008). *Multilevel analysis of individuals and cultures.* Mahwah, NJ: Lawrence Erlbaum Associates.

van der Linden, W. J., & Adema, J. J. (1998). Simultaneous assembly of multiple test forms. *Journal of Educational Measurement, 35*, 185–198.

Van Iddekinge, C. H., McFarland, L. A., & Raymark, P. H. (2007). Antecedents of impression management use and effectiveness in a structured interview. *Journal of Management, 33*, 752–773.

Van Iddekinge, C. H., & Ployhart, R. E. (2008). Developments in the criterion-related validation of selection procedures: A critical review and recommendations for practice. *Personnel Psychology, 61*, 871–925.

Van Iddekinge, C. H., Raymark, P. H., & Roth, P. L. (2005). Assessing personality with a structured employment interview: Construct-related validity and susceptibility to response inflation. *Journal of Applied Psychology, 90*, 536–552.

Van Iddekinge, C. H., Sager, C. E., Burnfield, J. L., & Heffner, T. S. (2006). The variability of criterion-related validity estimates among interviewers and interview panels. *International Journal of Selection and Assessment, 14*, 193–205.

Van Vianen, A. E. M., De Pater, I. E., & Caligiuri, P. M. (2005). Expatriate selection: A process approach. In A. Evers, N. Anderson & O. Voskuijl (Eds.), *The Blackwell handbook of personnel selection* (pp. 458–475). Malden, MA: Blackwell.

Van Vianen, A. E., & Willemsen, T. M. (1992). The employment interview: The role of sex stereotypes in the evaluation of male and female job applicants in the Netherlands. *Journal of Applied Social Psychology, 22*, 471–491.

Vardi, Y., & Weitz, E. (2004). *Misbehavior in organizations: Theory, research, and management.* Mahwah, NJ: Lawrence Erlbaum Associates.

Vicino, F. L., & Bass, B. M. (1978). Lifespace variables and managerial success. *Journal of Applied Psychology, 63*, 81–88.

Villanova, P. (1992). A customer-based model for developing job performance criteria. *Human Resources Management Review, 2*, 103–114.

Viswesvaran, C. (2002). Absenteeism and measures of job performance: A meta-analysis. *International Journal of Selection and Assessment, 10*, 12–17.

Viswesvaran, C. (2003). Introduction to special issue: Role of technology in shaping the future of staffing and assessment. *International Journal of Selection and Assessment, 11*, 107–112.

Viswesvaran, C., & Ones, D. S. (2005). Job performance: Assessment issues in personnel selection. In A. Evers, N. Anderson & O. Voskuijl (Eds.), *The Blackwell handbook of personnel selection* (pp. 354–375). Malden, MA: Blackwell.

Viswesvaran, C., Schmidt, F. L., & Ones, D. S. (2005). Is there a general factor in ratings of job performance? A meta-analysis framework for disentangling substantive and error influences. *Journal of Applied Psychology, 90*, 108–131.

Voskuijl, O. F. (2005). Job analysis: Current and future perspectives. In A. Evers, N. Anderson & O. Voskuijl (Eds.), *The Blackwell handbook of personnel selection* (pp. 27–46). Malden, MA: Blackwell.

Wagner, R. (1949). The employment interview: A critical summary. *Personnel Psychology, 2*, 17–46.

Wainer, H. (1976). Estimating coefficients in linear models: It don't make no nevermind. *Psychological Bulletin, 83*, 213–217.

Wainer, H. (2002). On the automatic generation of test items: Some whens, whys, and hows. In S. H. Irvine & P. C. Kyllonen (Eds.), *Item generation for test development* (pp. 287–305). Mahwah, NJ: Lawrence Erlbaum Associates.

Wainer, H. (2005). *Graphic discovery: A trout in the milk and other visual adventures.* Princeton, NJ: Princeton University Press.

Wainer, H. L., Dorans, N. J., Flaugher, R., Green, B. F., Mislevy, R. J., Steinberg, L., et al. (1990). *Computerized adaptive testing: A primer.* Hillsdale, NJ: Lawrence Erlbaum Associates.

Wainer, H., & Kiely, G. L. (1987). Item clusters and computerized adaptive testing: A case for testlets. *Journal of Educational Measurement, 24*, 185–201.

Wainer, H., & Thissen, D. (1996). How is reliability related to the quality of test scores? What is the effect of local dependence on reliability? *Educational Measurement: Issues and Practice, 15*(1), 22–29.

Wallace, S. R. (1965). Criteria for what? *American Psychologist, 20*, 411–417.

Wallace, S. R. (1974). How high the validity? *Personnel Psychology, 27*, 397–407.

Wallace, S. R., & Weitz, J. (1955). Industrial psychology. *Annual Review of Psychology, 6*, 217–250.

Walters, L. C., Miller, M. R., & Ree, M. J. (1993). Structured interviews for pilot selection: No incremental validity. *International Journal of Aviation Psychology, 3*, 25–38.

Wang, N. (2003). Use of the Rasch IRT model in standard setting: An item-mapping method. *Journal of Educational Measurement, 40*, 231–253.

Wang, W.-C., Chen, P.-H., & Cheng, Y.-Y. (2004). Improving measurement precision of test batteries using multidimensional item response models. *Psychological Methods, 9*, 116–136.

Wanous, J. P. (1980). *Organizational entry: Recruitment, selection, and socialization of newcomers.* Reading, MA: Addison-Wesley.

Wards Cove v. Antonio. (1989) (Vol. 490 U.S., p. 642).

Warr, P. (2007). *Work, happiness, and unhappiness.* Mahwah, NJ: Lawrence Erlbaum Associates.

Warren, D. E. (2003). Constructive and destructive deviance in organizations. *Academy of Management Review, 28,* 622–632.

Washington v. Davis. (1976) (Vol. 426 U.S. 229).

Watson v. Fort Worth Bank & Trust. (1988) (Vol. 487 U.S., p. 977).

Watson, G., & Glaser, E. M. (1980). *Watson-Glaser Critical Thinking Appraisal.* San Antonio, TX: The Psychological Corporation.

Weber v. Kaiser Aluminum & Chemical. (1977) (Vol. 563 F. 2d, p. 2126). CA5.

Weber v. Kaiser Aluminum & Chemical, 19 FEP (BNA) 1493 (1979).

Webster, E. C. (1964). *Decision making in the employment interview.* Montreal, Canada: Industrial Relations Centre, McGill University.

Weekley, J. A., & Ployhart, R. E. (Eds.). *Situational judgment tests: Theory, measurement, and application.* Mahwah, NJ: Lawrence Erlbaum Associates.

Weiner, A. S., & Ronch, J. L. (2003). *Culture change in long term care.* Binghamton, NY: Haworth Social Work Practice Press.

Weisbord, M. R. (1991). *Productive workplaces: Opening and managing for dignity, meaning, and community.* San Francisco: Jossey-Bass.

Weisskopf, T. E. (2004). *Affirmative action in the United States and India: A comparative perspective.* New York: Routledge.

Wenke, D., Frensch, P. A., & Funke, J. (2004). Complex problem solving and intelligence: Empirical relation and causal direction. In R. J. Sternberg & J. E. Pretz (Eds.), *Cognition & intelligence: Identifying the mechanisms of the mind* (pp. 160–187). Cambridge, UK: Cambridge University Press.

Wernimont, P. F., & Campbell, J. P. (1968). Signs, samples, and criteria. *Journal of Applied Psychology, 52,* 372–376.

Westerman, J. W., & Cyr, L. A. (2004). An integrative analysis of person–organization fit theories. *International Journal of Selection and Assessment, 12,* 252–261.

Wherry, R. J. (1931). A new formula for predicting the shrinkage of the coefficient of multiple correlation. *Annals of Mathematical Statistics, 20,* 446–457.

Wherry, R. J. (1957). The past and future of criterion evaluation. *Personnel Psychology, 10,* 1–5.

Wherry, R. J., Sr., & Bartlett, C. J. (1982). The control of bias in ratings: A theory of rating. *Personnel Psychology, 35,* 521–551.

White, T. H. (1982). *America in search of itself.* New York: Harper.

Whyte, W. H. J. (1957). *The organization man.* New York: Doubleday.

Wickens, T. D. (1989). *Multiway contingency table analysis for the social sciences.* Hillsdale, NJ: Lawrence Erlbaum Associates.

Wiesner, W. H., & Cronshaw, S. F. (1988). A meta-analytic investigation of the impact of interview format and degree of structure on the validity of the employment interview. *Journal of Occupational Psychology, 61,* 275–290.

Wilk, S. L., & Cappelli, P. (2003). Understanding the determinants of employer use of selection methods. *Personnel Psychology, 56,* 103–124.

Wilkinson, L., & the Task Force on Statistical Inference. (1999). Statistical methods in psychology journals: Guidelines and explanations. *American Psychologist, 54,* 594–604.

Williams, K. J., DeNisi, A. S., Blencoe, A. G., & Cafferty, T. P. (1985). The role of appraisal purpose: Effects of purpose on information acquisition and utilization. *Organizational Behavior and Human Decision Processes, 35,* 314–339.

Williams, L. J., Ford, L. R., & Nguyen, N. (2002). Basic and advanced measurement models for confirmatory factor analysis. In S. G. Rogelberg (Ed.), *Handbook of research methods in industrial and organizational psychology* (pp. 366–389). Malden, MA: Blackwell.

Williams, R. S. (1998). *Performance management: Perspectives on employee performance.* London: International Thomson Business Press.

Wise, L. L., Peterson, N. G., Hoffman, R. G., Campbell, J. P., & Arabian, J. N. (1991). *Army synthetic validity project: Report of Phase III results (Vols. 1 & 2)* (Tech. Rep. No. 922). Alexandria, VA: United States Army Research Institute for the Behavioral and Social Sciences.

Witt, L. A., Burke, L. A., Barrick, M. R., & Mount, M. K. (2002). The interactive effects of conscientiousness and agreeableness on job performance. *Journal of Applied Psychology, 87,* 164–169.

Woehr, D. J. (2008). On the relationship between job performance and ratings of job performance: What do we really know? *Industrial and Organizational Psychology, 1,* 161–166.

Woehr, D. J., & Arthur, W., Jr. (2003). The construct-related validity of assessment center ratings: A review and meta-analysis of the role of methodological factors. *Journal of Management, 29,* 231–258.

Woehr, D. J., Sheehan, M. K., & Bennett, W. J. (2005). Assessing measurement equivalence across rating sources: A multitrait–multirater approach. *Journal of Applied Psychology, 90,* 592–600.

Wood, J. L., Schmidtke, J. M., & Decker, D. L. (2007). Lying on job applications: The effects of job relevance, commission, and human resource management experience. *Journal of Business and Psychology, 22,* 1–9.

Wood, R. (1976). Trait measurement and item banks. In D. N. M. De Gruijter & L. J. T. van der Kamp (Eds.), *Advances in psychological and educational measurement* (pp. 247–263). London: Wiley.

Woodrow, H. (1938). The effects of practice on groups of different initial ability. *Journal of Educational Psychology, 29,* 268–278.

Wright, B. D. (1977). Solving measurement problems with the Rasch model. *Journal of Educational Measurement, 14,* 97–116.

Wright, O. R., Jr. (1969). Summary of research on the selection interview since 1964. *Personnel Psychology, 22,* 391–413.

Wygant v. Jackson Board of Education. (1986). U.S., 476, 267.

Yamaguchi, K. (1991). *Event history analysis (Applied social research methods,* Vol. 28, L. Bickman & D. J. Rog, Eds.). Newbury Park, CA: Sage.

Yoakum, C. S., & Yerkes, R. M. (1920). *Army mental tests.* New York: Holt.

Zedeck, S. (1986). A process analysis of the assessment center method. In B. M. Staw & L. L. Cummings (Eds.), *Research in organizational behavior* (Vol. 8, pp. 259–296). Greenwich, CT: JAI Press.

Zedeck, S., Tziner, A., & Middlestadt, S. E. (1983). Interviewer validity and reliability: An individual analysis approach. *Personnel Psychology, 36,* 355–370.

Zickar, M. J., & Broadfoot, A. A. (2009). The partial revival of a dead horse? Comparing classical test theory and item response theory. In C. E. Lance & R. J. Vandenberg (Eds.), *Statistical and methodological myths and urban legends: Doctrine, verity, and fable in the organizational and social sciences* (pp. 37–59). New York: Routledge.

Zickar, M. J., Cortina, J. M., & Carter, N. T. (2010). Evaluation of measures: Sources of error, sufficiency, and contamination. In J. L. Farr & N. T. Tippins (Eds.), *Handbook of employee selection* (pp. 400–415). New York: Routledge.

Author Index

Subject Index

Page numbers in *italic* indicate figures and tables.

Printed in the United States
By Bookmasters